D1526368

The Columbia Guide to
Religion in American History

COLUMBIA GUIDES TO AMERICAN HISTORY AND CULTURES

The Columbia Guide to Religion in American History

Edited by Paul Harvey and Edward J. Blum

Bibliography edited by Randall Stephens

COLUMBIA UNIVERSITY PRESS

NEW YORK

Columbia University Press
Publishers Since 1893
New York   Chichester, West Sussex
Copyright © 2012 Columbia University Press
All rights reserved

Library of Congress Cataloging-in-Publication Data
The Columbia guide to religion in American history / edited by Paul Harvey and
Edward J. Blum ; bibliography edited by Randall Stephens.
    p.   cm. — (Columbia guides to American history and cultures)
Includes bibliographical references and index.
ISBN 978-0-231-14020-1 (cloth : alk. paper)
1. United States—Religion—History. 2. United States—Church history.
I. Harvey, Paul, 1961–   II. Blum, Edward J. III. Title: Guide to religion in American history.
BL2525.C645   2012
200.973—dc23
                                                          2011024285

Columbia University Press books are printed on permanent and durable acid-free paper.
This book is printed on paper with recycled content.
Printed in the United States of America
c 10 9 8 7 6 5 4 3 2 1

References to Internet Web sites (URLs) were accurate at the time of writing.
Neither the editors nor Columbia University Press is responsible for URLs that may have
expired or changed since the manuscript was prepared.

To the memory of

William Gipson Harvey (1925–2008)

and

For the Young Scholars in American Religion,

Class of 2007–2009

CONTENTS

Religion is and has always been central in American society, politics, and culture. In the early twenty-first century, more than 90 percent of Americans claim to believe in some kind of god, a statistic that is baffling in light of the far lower percentages in other industrialized nations; millions in the United States attend religious services, oftentimes multiple times a week. Belief and religious institutions affect what people eat and how they dress, whom they vote for and what entertainment they enjoy (or don't enjoy). In 2004, Mel Gibson's film *The Passion of the Christ*—with no dialogue in English and with the vast majority of the attendees knowing how the story ended—was ranked first at the box office for almost a month and racked up more than $300 million in ticket sales. Religious iconography marks everything from bodies to buildings. Tattoos of saints adorn bulging biceps, and "What Would Jesus Do" bracelets are seen dangling from skinny-wrted teenagers (who, presumably, are unaware of the origins of this phrase in Charles Sheldon's ideas of Christian Socialism). In the art world, Andres Serrano's *Piss Christ* and Chris Ofili's *The Holy Virgin Mary* pushed visual limits, respectively, by soaking a cross in urine and by surrounding a darkened Madonna with snippets of pornography.

In politics as well, religion seems ubiquitous. The right and the left accuse each other of religious hypocrisy. While conservative media outlets lionized some Catholic priests for refusing to serve communion to John Kerry (a Catholic church member, Democratic senator, and challenger to President George W. Bush in

2004), Bush himself, a Methodist, avowed time and again that his politics were rooted in his faith. "I believe that God wants everybody to be free," he claimed in 2004. "That's what I believe. And that's one part of my foreign policy." Then in the election of 2008, the fiery words of a black preacher almost undid America's future first black president, Barack Obama.

The prominent, combative, and contested place of religion in the United States is nothing new. Although it has played a major role in the history and development of the United States, historians have been slow to recognize this. Certainly, there have long been "church historians" and students of theology who have discussed the place of religion in the nation, and a few of these early historians marvelously analyzed the intersection of religion and American history. These doyens of divinity schools often focused on specific denominations or theological controversies that many (if not most) everyday people had little interest in. Beginning in the 1960s, though, everything changed. With the rapid rise of new social history, the growing appreciation for African American studies, and the contributions of the feminist movement, scholars pulled apart the grand stories of American history. Finally, large numbers of historians were attending to the tales of everyday people, the politics of the seemingly powerless, the voices of the seemingly voiceless, and the faiths of the masses. In the wake of this academic revolution, all the old narratives came under scrutiny; all the old ideas had to be rethought. And religion had somehow become central in a history that seemed without centers.

Despite its late start and its tardy shedding of its Protestant bias, American religious history has emerged as a growth field in American history. Our basic understanding of American religious history has been transformed completely by the "social history revolution" of the 1960s, not to mention the indispensable contributions of scholars ranging over topics as diverse as the history of Asian religions in America and the development of "republican theology" in the nineteenth century. The result of all this "creative destruction," however, has been a fragmentation of narrative. The story lines holding those bytes of knowledge together have been broken. The burgeoning and, to some degree, fissiparous nature of the field have left many readers and scholars searching for reliable narratives as well as resource texts. This volume aims to fill that need. We seek to provide both a compendium of basic information and a synthetic and interpretive set of guides. Our goal is to assist general readers, students on research projects, scholars hoping to get a concise and broad overview of particular fields, and inquirers seeking specific information, media resources, and bibliographic suggestions (books, articles, films, musical CDs, and online resources) to navigate the various streams of religion in American history.

We begin with an introductory thematic exploration of American religious history from the colonial era to the present. By "America," we mean North America, and for a good deal of the book we focus more specifically on the United States. Where appropriate (as in the essays on Native Americans, colonial encounters, and religion and the environment), we include discussion of places—French and British Canada, the Caribbean, and parts of the Mexican Southwest—that eventually fell outside the United States proper or were later incorporated into the American nation-state through wars of conquest or diplomatic negotiation. Many of the essays, especially the first few, consider how religion (especially British Protestantism) became a part of how America—the United States—defined itself politically and socially, as well as how that definition restricted and excluded those who fell outside its conceptions. The religious "center" of the United States was in theory voluntary, but in actual practice legally and politically coercive. And the American Civil War proved that that center could not hold.

Previous scholarly generations focused on the Protestant "center," often to the exclusion of "others," who were not part of that conception of what America was. More recently, students of American religious history have focused on groups defined as outsiders, whether theologically, socially, or racially. These works have shown the extent to which American religious self-conceptions have drawn from—indeed, been dependent on—definitions drawn by implicit or explicit contrast. Thus, for example, just as definitions of "freedom" came to be dependent on defining what constituted slavery, conceptions of American Protestants depended on defining what they were *not*—Catholics.

Throughout this book, we have endeavored to place those scholarly traditions (of "Protestants" and "others") and those cultural realities in dialogue with one another. In the introduction, we approach this through consideration of a series of governing paradoxes of American religious history. The introduction outlines ten themes, each containing within it a paradox (such as "religious freedom and religiously sanctioned repression") to set in context the more specific information and interpretations provided in the individual essays. In this interpretive introduction, rather than attempting to summarize individual essays or provide some kind of broad historiographical introduction, we have chosen instead to outline a sort of interpretive synthesis through the lens of ten major themes that capture the diversity, dynamism, and dissension of religion *in* American history.

With this thematic and interpretive introduction in mind, readers can then survey the variety of shorter essays, as well as the bibliographic guides and statistical appendices. In the specific essays that follow, authors have been asked to

- Suggest a brief narrative overview of the topic
- Illuminate some of the major questions and lines of inquiry that have guided scholarship on that theme
- Articulate a thesis statement that summarizes the most up-to-date thinking on the topic
- Outline areas where more research is needed on a particular theme/topic, as well as areas of major scholarly argument between contending interpretations
- Provide a brief bibliography that points to the major scholarly resources on their topic

Reference and textbook volumes of the kind we provide here tend to be organized either by *traditions*, by *themes*, or by an *encyclopedic* attempt to cover the whole of a field (for a list of some of these volumes, see the bibliography at the end of this book). Various other textbook and reference volumes in the field of religion in America adopt those particular approaches, depending on their intent and the audience they seek to address. This volume, designed to serve as a substantial but not encyclopedic *guide* to further study in the field, takes in some elements of each of the above, without precisely replicating any of them. Some individual contributions take up individual traditions (such as "Catholicism in America," "American Judaism," "The Church of Jesus Christ of Latter-day Saints," and "Islam in America"). By design, these particular essays focus on providing information about these groups and basic guides to the scholarly literature about them. This is because these religious groups have developed particular scholarly niches and centers of study. Such is also the case with the chapter "Alternative Religious Movements in American History," which considers the congeries of groups that scholars have categorized with this label. In other cases, contributions consider groups historically defined by race—"Native American Religions," "Religion, Race, and African American Life," and "Asian American Religions." Each of these authors explores *how* and *why* these groups came to be racially defined and constructed, and the role that religion has played in *defining* what we refer to as "race" in American history.

In some cases, we asked contributors to consider themes that have developed in recent scholarly discussions, including "Civil Religion and National Identity," "Religion, War, and Peace," "Religion, Gender, and Sexuality," "Religion and the Environment," and "Religion and Popular Culture." These essays, by intent, are generally less explicitly historiographical or informational and more *interpretive*, appropriate to subjects that developed from interdisciplinary arguments, social movements, and political controversies. Some chapters consider important topics of American history through the lens of religion, including "Colonial Encounters," "Religion and Politics," "Religion and the Law in American History," and "Religion, Ethnicity, and the Immigrant Experience." Finally, we include individual topics that give due attention to the central importance of evangelical Protestantism in the history of the United States, including "Theology," "Evangelicals in American History," and "Religious Conservatism and Fundamentalism."

Following the individual essays with their accompanying specialized bibliographies, we have included an A–Z glossary, providing paragraph-length explanations of important people, events, movements, groups, and concepts in American religious history. Following the glossary are a bibliography, a filmography, a discography, and a list of electronic resources. The rapidly developing nature of the field of American religious history means that this bibliography will be dated just about from the moment it is printed, but we hope that these lists of major books, articles, films, musical CDs, and electronic resources will provide useful starting points for those seeking further resources.

American religious history has developed a large number of particular subspecialties, creating both an explosion of knowledge in the field and the problem of the fragmentation of the narrative, as noted earlier. Here, to conclude this preface, we want to suggest a few points of comparison, of cross-reading *between* the individual chapters; the lengthier thematic introduction that follows this preface develops some of these points at much greater length.

Taking the essays together suggests much about the varieties of approaches and ideological assumptions behind how historical narratives about religious history are created. For example, in this volume the authors Douglas Sweeney and Mark Noll tell a story about the rise of evangelical theology and how that theology became central to American religious expression in the nineteenth century. Reading these chapters alongside Ira Chernus's on religion, war, and peace, however, lends a different cast to that story, one in which evangelicalism and violence become related in the same story rather than separated into different historical and historiographical categories. The same might be said about the juxtaposition of Anthony Michael Petro's essay on religion and sexuality with Margaret Bendroth's piece on conservatism and fundamentalism. On the one hand, these two scholarly topics have very separate and different historiographies, and scholars of these topics ask different questions of their material. On the other hand, Bendroth's analysis makes it clear that particular conceptions of "religion, gender, and sexuality" are as central to "conservatism and fundamentalism" as are the theologies that underwrote the reaction to and attack on modernist religious thought in the twentieth century.

One final example comes from considering Frank Ravitch's chapter on religion and the law, in which the history of constitutional law provides a natural "grand narrative" against which to see how religious freedom has come to be interpreted, alongside Lynn Ross-Bryant's essay on religion and the environment, which suggests that scholarly approaches in this instance "focus on particularized—and necessarily fragmented—studies, rather than grand narratives." Moreover, while the contributions centering on theology, evangelicals, and politics necessarily place much emphasis on the word, on *texts*, as fundamental to the study of their topics, conceptualizing the study of religion and the environment necessarily leads us to contemplation of geography, of space, and thus outside of the written word. This contrast speaks to a broader development in the field, which is to consider religion not as belief but as practice, an approach developed especially by those who study Native American religions and students of "spirituality" outside the bounds of organized religious institutions.

We have made no attempt to impose an artificial uniformity on a field that features fruitfully contending approaches. Rather, we have let the differences be, and have in this short preface, and at greater length in the thematic introduction, suggested some ways to juxtapose and raise questions about the diverse and sometimes contradictory approaches taken in the chapters in this volume. Further, we have made no effort to force essays into one particular mold or style. Rather, we have let the contributors select the format most appropriate to their topics and fields. In cases where there is a well-developed literature, such as in Leslie Tentler's piece on Catholicism, the authors give much attention to the rich historiographies that have shaped understandings in their fields. In other cases, such as in Timothy Tseng's summary of the study of Asian American religions, the contributors endeavor foremost to provide basic information and resource guides for fields that are relatively in their infancy. Thus considering how the same material is treated (or left out of) various essays and contrasting scholarly approaches can yield much light on the various ways scholars have constructed American religious history.

We hope that this book provides a useful introduction and guide to studying American religious history in all its dynamism and diversity.

The Columbia Guide to
Religion in American History

INTRODUCTION

Major Themes in American Religious History

PAUL HARVEY AND EDWARD J. BLUM

This book highlights tension, conflict, and creativity in America's rich religious history. The twenty chapters, written by top scholars in their respective fields, follow particular religious traditions, movements, and time periods. In this broader interpretive overview, we will first explore ten themes, hoping to knit together particular threads of the diverse and ever-multiplying scholarship. Each individual essay in this volume will make reference to these themes as well, as they are intended to serve as a unifying center for the book:

- Religious freedom and religiously sanctioned repression
- (In)tolerance, diversity, and pluralism
- Racialized religion and the desire for a universal god
- Male hierarchy, female dominance, and gender codes in religion
- Communalist visions and their consequent commercial capitalist dreams (or, the Protestant ethic and the spirit of therapeutic consumerism)
- Proselytization: spiritual recruitment and the market economy of religion
- The folk origins of high theology, and the theological base of popular religious movements
- The sacralization of secular politics, and the politicization of the sacred
- Immigration, ethnicity, pluralism, and insularity
- Regional homogeneity amid national diversity

Each of the concepts highlights a central tension within the larger framework of American religious history. They can be taken as suggestive starting points for deeper inquiry. The remainder of this introduction explores each of these paradoxes of religion in American history in more detail, and suggests points where these themes may be found within the context of the individual topical essays in this book.

RELIGIOUS FREEDOM AND RELIGIOUSLY SANCTIONED REPRESSION

For generations, Americans passed down a national myth featuring intrepid settlers—Pilgrims and others—seeking refuge and finding religious freedom in the "New World." By now, even most schoolchildren learn a more complex story, and yet the stale cliché about America being founded by those seeking religious freedom still is reported back dutifully to professors on each opening day of undergraduate classes in American religious history. In recent years, skeptical scholars have highlighted the obverse of this myth. They have stressed how early colonists operated in a fury of conquest, colonialism, and enslavement of Native and African peoples. American religious idealism and greed propelled the expansion of American empire across the West and then abroad. This version of the tale foregrounds Euro-American repression as opposed to a universal human desire for freedom.

Both stories—that of religious freedom, and that of religious repression—can be true, all the more so when they are self-consciously juxtaposed against each other. For example, did the settlers come for religious freedom? That depends on what your definition of "freedom" is. Certainly the settlers sought freedom from religious persecution. At the same time, the Pilgrims, the Puritans, and the Anglicans all designed colonies to exclude or repress those outside their faith. They directed rhetorical blasts at Roman Catholicism, jailed and exiled Protestant dissenters, and executed Quakers. Moreover, they never made the slightest attempt to comprehend that black Africans or New World "sauvages" practiced anything that could be called "religion." More than anything, the persistence of the myth that early Anglo-Americans were proponents of "religious freedom" in the modern sense—that religion is a matter of individual conscience—enables the continuation of usable national mythologies. Linford D. Fisher explores these stories in "Colonial Encounters."

More accurately, one might say that many early Americans—English, Spanish, French, Dutch, and others—arrived seeking the right to cultivate purity for themselves and practice religious intolerance toward others within the bounds of their own habitations. With few exceptions, they believed in eliminating heretics, not encouraging them; they prized religious homogeneity, not pluralism. The Puritans, for example, despised the French Jesuits in Canada and furiously repressed Quakerism; this hardly left any room for sympathy toward Algonquian shamans or African Muslims. Europeans and others quite correctly saw a remarkably diverse world of peoples in North America, but British colonists closer to the scene recognized that de facto diversity was hardly a sufficient condition for tolerance. North America was far too large to support any sort of repressive action emanating from a strong centralized state, but individual localities frequently prohibited or disparaged religious practices that they either detested or misunderstood.

Many settlers came to enact their visions of holy societies. In the early colonial era, religious freedom for Anglo-American settlers as well as French and Spanish priests and colonists meant the ability to set up a religious commonwealth in which a particular set of beliefs would be normative. All other faiths and people were to be converted or else excluded, repressed, or punished. Ironically, it was the very proliferation of these visions that propelled a variety of intolerant early Americans toward the necessity of some religious tolerance. This, of course, did not entail any celebration of diversity for diversity's sake. The North American landmass was extensive enough geographically to separate Anglicans living out their idea of a "comfortable faith," Puritans ever-anxious about the fate of their city set upon a hill, Moravians practicing their love feasts and attracting a considerable following of slaves in North Carolina, Jesuits struggling to missionize in the land of the Iroquois, Franciscans introducing Natives in the Southwest to the Catholic gospel, and Quakers attempting the experiment of something more akin to a modern idea of religious freedom for all—even Indians—in Pennsylvania.

The Enlightenment in America was itself a religiously driven phenomenon in very good measure. It introduced more recognizably modern ideas about the heavy human costs of religious intolerance, and therefore the philosophical and social imperative of understanding religious faith as a compact between the individual and his or her God. When the state established or interfered with religious faith, James Madison and Thomas Jefferson vigorously argued, both religion and the state were harmed. "It does me no injury for my neighbor to say there are twenty gods or no God," Jefferson famously wrote in *Notes on the State of Virginia* (1781). "It neither picks my pocket nor breaks my leg." Jefferson and others had only to look to the recent (and ongoing) European religious wars to draw a bloodbath of evidence for their pleas for religious liberty. The views of the founding generation received classic expression in James Madison's "Memorial and Remonstrance" (a tract arguing against religious tax assessments in Virginia), in Jefferson's Virginia Statute of Religious Freedom, and finally, of course, in the Establishment Clause of the First Amendment: "Congress shall make no law respecting an establishment of religion, or prohibiting the free exercise thereof."

Still, individual states in the new United States could, and did, make laws "respecting an establishment of religion." New England, for example, was not about to disestablish Congregationalism (the institutional successor to Puritanism), even if Anglicans in Virginia were compelled to accept disestablishment and a name change as well, to "Episcopalians." The First Amendment was about what the federal Congress could and could not do. It did not circumscribe individual states. Nonetheless, the die was cast, and over the next thirty years even the "Standing Order" of Connecticut, the "land of steady habits," was felled by the ideological ax of religious freedom. The history of religious freedom in constitutional law through this era, and then the application of that history to the rest of American history, is explored further in Frank S. Ravitch's "Religion and the Law in American History."

One can find the dialectic of repression and freedom throughout the nineteenth and twentieth centuries. Irish Catholics fleeing dire poverty met anti-Irish mobs and nativist parties in mid-nineteenth-century America, as Leslie Woodcock Tentler details in "Catholicism in America." In an unceasing torrent of publications, Protestants excoriated Catholics as anti-democratic. Early Mormons found the freedom to establish their own commonwealth in the desert, but not before their first generation had experienced relentless persecution, and their founder, Joseph Smith, had been murdered. For more on that and on the early history of Mormonism, see D. Michael Quinn's chapter, "The Church of Jesus Christ of Latter-day Saints ('Mormons')." Later, in the 1920s, the Ku Klux Klan carried the American tradition of racist nativism and vigilante terrorism into the "jazz age." By winning political elections, lynching African Americans, enforcing Protestant customs of morality, and dispatching "poisoning squads of whispering women" to destroy the lives and reputations of those they attacked, Klansmen and -women guarded their vision of an Anglo-Protestant America. Through all this time, as well, millions of immigrants found their way into the United States, and many got what they came for: economic opportunity and personal freedom, including the ability to establish flourishing religious institutions.

African Americans, Mexican Americans, and Native Americans experienced the dialectic of repression and freedom in particularly sharp ways. Perhaps the most fundamental paradox and tension of American religious history is the fault line between religious freedom and democracy, on the one hand, and religiously sanctioned intolerance and repression, on the other. Both arose from American republican providentialism; that which is most honorable, and that which is most execrable, in the dominant story of American religion emerges from the same source. African Americans (and Native American writers and theologians such as William Apess) brought to light this deeply contradictory impulse in American religion, and in American life more generally. Thus the explosively providentialist and universalist rhetoric of the Second Great Awakening emerged alongside works forgotten or submerged or repressed, such as David Walker's *Appeal to the*

Colored Citizens of the World (1829), his *cri de couer* against the base hypocrisy of American Christianity.

Democratic politics and the rapid rise of populist Christian sects in the early nineteenth century created a new context for American ideas of religio-political freedom. The ebullient expressions of popular nationalism and the expansive and millennialist visions of religious groups such as the Methodists were part of a democratic culture that diverged radically from the more deferential and hierarchical cast of American thought and life in prior decades. From the underside of that millennium, however, American ideas of freedom promised universalist visions but delivered a republic that was, in practice, racially exclusivist and white supremacist. That paradox lay at the heart of African American religious thought and practice. Comparing Mark Noll's essay "Theology" with Edward J. Blum's contribution, "Religion, Race, and African American Life," and Suzanne Crawford O'Brien's chapter, "Native American Religions," makes painfully vivid this point about the racialized nature of American civil and religious freedom. The universalist language of democratic Christianity provided a base for alternative visions of American ideas of freedom. As expressed by James Forten, a free black man from Philadelphia who served in the colonial navy during the American Revolution, the truth that "god created all men equal" embraced the "Indian and the European, the Savage and the Saint, the Peruvian and the Laplander, the white Man and the African, and whatever measures are adopted subversive of the inestimable privilege, are in direct violation of the letter and spirit of our Constitution." Natives and African Americans alike seized on the universalist languages of Christianity and republicanism. With those two bodies of thought so directly paralleled and mutually reinforcing in American discourse, Natives and African Americans found a means to make race matter in exploiting the connection between religion and American ideas of freedom.

The United States guaranteed constitutionally protected religious freedoms, a legacy of the ideas of the Founding Fathers and Mothers and also the reality of religious diversity in early America. Anglo-Americans created the evangelical synthesis: the deep connection between Protestant belief, individual liberty, republican government, and human freedom. They also fostered a racially exclusivist and religiously restrictive culture that limited the freedom of those defined outside the ranks of the free and the citizen. This remained true during the era when America's God was a republican and providentialist one (as Mark Noll details further in his essay). American religious history fundamentally has been about this dialectic of religious freedom in the dominant nation-state, the racialization of peoples, and the resulting struggle to forge spaces of freedom and autonomy, often through the creation or preservation of religious customs and institutions. Religious freedom, democracy, and republicanism fostered religiously based repression, as well as the ideological power and universalist language of liberty that emboldened the fight against that repression.

FROM (IN)TOLERANCE TO DIVERSITY
TO PLURALISM

North America was one of the most diverse religious societies in the world in the colonial era, as Linford D. Fisher details in "Colonial Encounters." French Jesuits interacted with powerful Iroquois bands; Spanish Franciscans were more or less powerless to stop Puebloans in New Mexico, including Christianized as well as "heathen" Indians, from practicing kachina dances and other ceremonials of their heritage; Anglicans in Virginia and South Carolina sent out missionaries to preach the gospel to enslaved Africans who came from a diverse variety of religious backgrounds, ranging from Islam to Catholicism to tribal faiths; Protestants of all sorts in Pennsylvania interacted both peacefully and violently with Natives, who often used Christian intermediaries to try to protect their dwindling land base; Puritans in New England leveled charges against "popery" as Catholics in the originally Catholic colony of Maryland found themselves as minorities even in their own world; and Natives from hundreds of different tribes pursued richly diverse religious practices that differed from one another as much as from European forms. European observers, most famously the philosophe and wit Voltaire, saw in America, especially among the Quakers in Pennsylvania, a peaceable kingdom of diverse peoples and faiths living in harmony.

Voltaire's idea was not totally imaginary. Compared with many places, notably Europe, colonial North America appeared as a thriving ecosystem of religious profusions shooting up everywhere. Yet one must not date pluralism too early on American soil. Coexistence did not mean mutual understanding, and contact created conditions for *causus belli* more so than *pax Americana*. Whatever its primary economic and political motivations, the entire colonial project was shot through with religious justifications, including the conquering of Native peoples and the exponential growth of the trade in slaves.

Yet if homogeneity was the ideal, heterogeneity was the real. De facto diversity meant that tolerance existed simply because there was little other choice. Thus America's heritage of religious freedom became a reality on the ground before it arose as a philosophical or theological position. William Penn's vision for Pennsylvania—as a refuge for men to live peaceably, worship as they wished, and get along with the Natives who had been there for centuries already—was the first real expression of a diversity that was not just grudgingly tolerated but actively promoted. It worked better in theory than in practice, but even in its imperfect practice it appeared to some European intellectuals, such as Voltaire, as paradisiacal in contrast to the horrendous European religious wars of the seventeenth century.

As in so many other cases in American history, the very success of the experiment in Pennsylvania inevitably engineered its demise. As European settlers (especially Germans, with their variety of Anabaptist faiths, and Scots-Irish, with their revivalistic Presbyterianism) moved westward from Philadelphia into the backcountry, tensions grew. As early as 1737, the famous Delaware "Walking Purchase" presaged an era of treaty scams that invariably defrauded and therefore embittered the Natives. By the era of the American Revolution, Paxton's Boys and similar bands were terrorizing Natives in the countryside. This vigilantism culminated in the massacre at Gnadenhutten (in Ohio Territory) in March 1782. In a spasm of ethnic cleansing that set the stage for many more instances of the same to come, white backcountrymen slaughtered about ninety Delaware Indians who had been converted by the Moravians and moved to a "safe" town. The Delawares had already evacuated the village in the previous year, but had returned to harvest their crops when they were seized. Enraged by the massacre of two whites nearby earlier, the white band, led by Captain David Williamson, wielded their mallets and systematically crushed the skulls of their Indian victims, including thirty-nine children.

In the confusing world produced by the "Great War for the Empire" (1754–1763, formerly known as the French and Indian War, and sometimes now called the first world war), and then the American Revolution, religious and ethnic conflicts accompanied the territorial shifts toward Anglo-American dominance. Over time, the multicultural world of colonial America gave way to an Anglo-American state with various groups—French, Spanish, Indians, and others—adapting to its power. For the Anglo-Americans as well as other Europeans, "tolerance" meant the necessity of living on the same continent, and occasionally in the same neighborhood, with a proliferating variety of Protestant sects and with Anglicans and Catholics. In the minds of white settlers, this was a remarkable feat in and of itself. It was also a social reality that made the disestablishment of religion necessary, inevitable, and fruitful. What looks to us like Protestant homogeneity through much of the colonies, in other words, struck contemporaries as an amazing religious diversity. By the late eighteenth century, enlightened thinkers and even many plain-folk Americans were coming to see diversity among Christians as a strength rather than a violation of God's will that might implode on itself.

This was not "diversity" in our modern sense of the word, and certainly not pluralism. Diversity in a more contemporary sense was yet another accident of American history, deriving largely from homeland miseries and immigration opportunities that sucked in people from all over the world. Irish Catholics fleeing English oppression and the potato famine significantly "Catholicized" the American population beginning in the 1830s and 1840s, and their presence was augmented by a massive European Catholic and Jewish immigration from the 1870s to the 1920s—Poles, Italians, Catholic Germans, Hungarians, Czechs, Russian and eastern European Jews, and a multitude of other European nationalities. The waves of Catholic immigration in the nineteenth century were met with the usual strident attacks on their alleged inability to assimilate to republican ideals, their purported slavish obedience to the pope, their assumed inferior ethnic stock, and their supposed love of drink and hatred of work. Protestants developed their ideas of the "wall of separation" of church and state—a phrase originally coined by Jefferson in a letter to a Connecticut Baptist association in 1802, and promptly forgotten until revived by Protestant nationalists in the mid-nineteenth century— largely to combat what they perceived as a Catholic threat to the public school system. And still the Catholics came, permanently altering the religious and cultural landscape. And once again, Protestants acceded to reality.

In the twentieth century, far from being unassimilable, Catholics staunchly supported many of the most conservative forms of "Americanism," as seen especially by Catholic support for Father Charles Coughlin's nationalism in the 1930s and Joseph McCarthy's anti-Communist campaigns in the 1950s. By the late twentieth century, it was secular liberals rather than Protestant conservatives who most often expressed fears about Catholicism in the intellectual imagination, most notably in Paul Blanshard's *American Freedom and Catholic Power* (1949), which warned of the deleterious and pervasive Catholic influence over American institutions. Two years later, Blanshard, an editor at the liberal publication the *Nation*, extended his analysis in *Communism, Democracy, and Catholic Power* (1951), which argues that the Kremlin and the Catholic Church were organized on the same tyrannical principle.

Diversification of American religion was not limited to Irish Catholic immigration, of course. Later in the nineteenth century, eastern European Jews, southern and eastern European Catholics, Mexican and South American Catholics, Chinese men and women of various religious faiths, and Japanese Buddhists came to America in a mammoth wave of immigration (counting nearly 25 million people total) from 1870 to 1920. As usual, they were met with suspicion and considerable hostility for their exotic ways and strange (by American Protestant standards) faith practices; as usual, the reality of population shifts and migration trends eventually overwhelmed the increasingly defensive rhetoric about preserving a Protestant America. For the most part, immigrants set about constructing and preserving their own religious institutions regardless of the relentless assault on their foreign ways. Even in doing so, they nevertheless eventually wove themselves into the American fabric. By the early twentieth century, intellectuals such as Herbert Croly (author of *The Promise of American Life* [1909]) and literary critic Randolph Bourne celebrated an America beyond the melting pot that looked surprisingly like a modern understanding of pluralism, what Bourne famously called "Transnational America."

If tolerance came about fitfully and accidentally in the eighteenth century, and increasing diversity was a hallmark of the American religious landscape in the nineteenth century, then pluralism was the paradigm for the latter half of the twentieth century. Once again, the unceasing turmoil of population movements across the globe and onto American shores shattered long-cherished assumptions held by white Protestants about the necessary connection of Protestantism and

Americanism. While the National Origins Act of 1924 (which enforced a quota system on immigration allotments per country, with the vast majority going to the British islands and northern European countries) gave one last final push toward realizing an ideal of America as a white, northern European, largely Protestant republic, the Immigration Act of 1965 has spurred a dramatic pluralizing of the American population over the past forty years. In 1955, Will Herberg's *Protestant, Catholic, Jew: An Essay in American Religious Sociology* pointed out that the classic theological and sociological divisions between these major religious traditions had gradually been swallowed up by a larger tide of Americanism. Herberg himself could hardly have foreseen how limited and provincial the title of that work now appears, with the advent of large-scale immigration from South and Southeast Asia, China, Africa, the Caribbean, the Middle East, South America, and other parts of the world.

More recently, sociologist Robert Wuthnow has shown that religious divisions formerly based on animosities between Catholics and Protestants, and between contending versions of Protestantism, have transformed into cross-denominational "liberal" and "conservative" religious groupings. Conservative Protestants, Catholics, Jews, Mormons, and Muslims have more in common with one another, by this interpretation, than do, say, liberal and conservative Presbyterians. Religious groupings thus increasingly reflect a philosophical split between progressive and conservative ways of viewing the world. Nonetheless, the old sectarian divisions have little substantive meaning for most Americans, who accept the premises of religious pluralism and (inaccurately) read those backward into the American past. Nowhere is that anachronistic way of thinking more evident than in examining the painful legacy of racialized religion in American history.

RACIALIZED RELIGION AND THE DESIRE FOR A UNIVERSAL GOD

"God is a Negro," declared Bishop Henry McNeal Turner of the African Methodist Episcopal Church in 1898. Or, he suggested, at least African Americans should consider God to be black. People of color, Turner continued, had "as much right Biblically and otherwise" to believe that God was black, "as you buckra, or white, people have to believe that God is a fine looking, symmetrical, ornamented white man." With words that would echo decades later from Malcolm X, Turner denounced those who believed that God "is a white-skinned, blue-eyed, straight-haired, projecting-nose, compressed-lipped and finely-robed white gentleman, sitting upon a throne somewhere in heaven." Turner's anger was not directed at whites for creating God in their image. He fumed at blacks for believing in that white God, for failing to see God in their own likeness, and for generally buying into the tenets of white America.

By calling attention to the race of God and the importance of images of the sacred, Turner spoke to several pronounced and foundational questions in American religious history. Did ideas of the sacred transcend the racial ideas and structures in the United States? Was there a universal God, or did each ethnic, immigrant, and racial group have its own deity or deities? Did God legitimate, undermine, or determine race in the nation? In the twentieth century, the great black intellectual W. E. B. DuBois explored many of the same questions, and in the process pioneered the writing of the religious history of African Americans, a point that Edward J. Blum elaborates on in "Religion, Race, and African American Life."

Throughout much of American history, whites as the dominant group have tended to associate their race with the sacred. Rooted in a European heritage that not only whitened images of Christ, angels, and God, but also darkened characterizations of the devil, demons, and witches, America's European colonists seemed to assume, as the pithy phrase went, that "God was an Englishman," or at least European. Many British colonists also seemed assured that, if they were God's chosen ones, then Native Americans were "children of the devil." French Jesuits specifically used whitened depictions of Christ and the Madonna and darkened images of sinners in hell in efforts to evangelize Native Americans. Although New England Puritans largely disdained physical images of God (they considered such iconography to violate the Ten Commandments), many British colonists considered "black dogs" to be signs of the devil. Even those Indians who converted to Protestantism, such as the Mohegan Samson Occom, were objects of scorn. Occom's spiritual father and the founder of Dartmouth College, the Reverend Eleazer Wheelock (who would have never raised enough money for the college if it were not for Occom's preaching in England), routinely referred to Occom as his "black son."

From the mid-eighteenth to the mid-nineteenth century, in efforts to proselytize to enslaved and free African Americans, white Protestants solidified and symbolized racial hierarchy in their churches. Men and women of color were forced to sit in back pews or galleries, to accept physical abuse at the hands of white Christians, and to take communion after white congregants had done so. Then, in the early nineteenth century with technological and print production improvements, the American landscape was flooded with religious pamphlets, picture-book Bibles, Sunday School materials, and other religious ephemera that linked white superiority with God. Images of Jesus; his mother, Mary; Moses; and other biblical characters were made to look white. The Mormon Church, born in upstate New York at this time, took the whitening of the sacred to new levels. Its first leaders, Joseph Smith and Brigham Young, imagined that when Christ appeared in the New World after his crucifixion, he came as a bearded white man. It would not be until the 1970s, moreover, that the established Mormon hierarchy would ordain black ministers. In the twentieth century, the visual image of a white Christ became fixed in the artistic renderings of Warner Sallman, whose *Head of Christ* (1941) is probably the most well-known depiction of Jesus in the United States.

Especially in the South before the Civil War, slaveholding whites endeavored to indoctrinate African Americans with a specific and racialized brand of Christianity. Ministers to the slaves shied away from biblical stories that spoke of liberation and instead highlighted elements that lauded submissiveness. Catechisms developed distinctly for men and women of color pushed servility, passivity, and a subordinate work ethic. Black congregants were asked "How are they to try and please their Masters?" and were told to answer "With good will, doing service as unto the Lord and not unto men." Even if a slave suffers "*wrongfully*, at the hands of his Master, and to please God, takes it patiently, will God reward him for it?" Of course, the set answer was far less cumbersome than the question: "yes."

During the nineteenth century, moreover—especially as racial ideas took an even firmer hold—Americans looked to faith to explain the origins of races. The most common explanation for the creation of black men and women was with the biblical "curse of Ham" (or "curse of Canaan"), while one of the most vigorous scientific battles of the nineteenth century was a religious one. In the decades before the Civil War, a growing body of scientists began to claim that there was not one, single moment of human creation, but that somehow a divine figure created the various races of the earth at different moments and in different locations. The battle between the advocates of monogenesis and of polygenesis raged among scientists, ministers, theologians, and abolitionists. After the Civil War, "scientific racism" emerged from this theological cocoon and quickly morphed into numerous varieties of racist ideologies. In this way, the "son of Ham" thesis—derived originally from the mysterious and troubling story of Noah (Genesis 9:18–27), who, lying in a drunken stupor, was covered by his son, who was ashamed of his father's nakedness—had a long and viciously malignant career in Western thought and in American history. Even after being repudiated by theologians, it remained deeply imprinted in American folklore and was exacerbated by scientists who measured skulls and alleged "intelligence quotients" and, in the process, invariably and predictably reified the existing racial hierarchies.

After the Civil War, as African Americans acquired greater religious freedom, whites shifted their arguments from pro-slavery to pro-segregation. Now, instead of declaring slavery the heaven-ordained place for African Americans, white Protestants claimed that organized and legalized racial separation was God's mandate. By the end of the nineteenth century, the white Protestant linking of faith and whiteness was promoting violence. Extra-legal mob lynchings had all the trappings of religious rituals, while a host of northern and southern white Protestants suggested that they had been wrong all along to try to save the souls of black folk.

People of color had no souls, some white supremacists maintained; or, as other writers believed, they had souls but were forever cursed to be subordinate.

Religious arguments and leaders also played a role in immigrant exclusion. From the Know Nothings of the antebellum era to the second Ku Klux Klan of the twentieth century, the claim that Irish, Chinese, Japanese, Russian, Italian, and other non–western European immigrants were not Protestant Christians and therefore could not be true Americans resounded from anti-immigrant groups. Moreover, Protestant reform organizations such as the Woman's Christian Temperance Union (WCTU) singled out immigrants, especially immigrant men, as immoral drunkards who needed to be controlled or kept out.

Of course, African Americans, Native Americans, Asian Americans, Jewish Americans, Irish Americans, and the host of other groups that have been discriminated against never capitulated fully to white Christianity. In the colonial era, Native Americans often rejected the Christianity of the British settlers and turned with renewed vigor to their own traditions and visionaries. African Americans, who had largely adopted Protestantism by the middle of the nineteenth century, converted to the Christian God less than they converted the Christian God to themselves. In their own congregations in the North, formed in response to white church oppression and to the growing organizational needs of black communities, new "African" denominations became centers of spiritual nourishment and social uplift. In the South, enslaved men and women at times openly rebelled against pro-slavery Christianity. One white missionary recorded in his diary how slaves in South Carolina rejected a gospel of social control and oppression. After a preacher instructed them against fleeing, one slave responded: "That is not Gospel at all; it is all Runaway, Runaway, Runaway." Another retorted, "The doctrine is one-sided." Nat Turner went even further. Believing to see black spirits and white spirits fighting in the sky, he heard the Holy Spirit tell him to rise up, kill all the whites in Southampton County, Virginia, and lead local slaves to victory. Turner died for his failed revolution, but not before he and his crew killed more than fifty whites. More often, though, slaves crafted their own distinctive faith by fusing Christianity with West African traditions to create a vibrant, albeit underground, belief in their humanity, their chosen status with the divine, and their eventual liberation. Newly crafted black spirituals suggested a God who cared, with toil that would be recompensed someday, and with a future time of liberation and jubilee.

In ways akin to the practices of African Americans, other groups outside the American mainstream have used religious institutions to reinforce group bonding and protection. Irish Catholics, Russian Jews, Japanese Buddhists, Chinese Taoists, Pakistani Muslims, and Mexican Catholics created group enclaves (in part because of social, cultural, legal, and extra-legal disdain from established white communities) where they could carry on their faiths. Taoist temples became places for individual prayer and communal celebration for embattled Chinese men and women in California, while Catholic rituals established links to the Old

World for many new Italian Catholics. In the American context, beliefs and rituals were transformed. Jewish Americans in the nineteenth century, for instance, established places for women's activism to parallel the reform efforts of Christian women. At the same time, Jewish Americans invested Hanukah with new meaning, especially with a focus on gift-giving to mirror America's consumer-centered Christmas season. Some Buddhists, moreover, accepted Christ into their pantheon of role models.

During the second half of the twentieth century, especially following the civil rights movement, racial struggle continued to have decidedly religious overtones. Depictions of black Christ figures, first crafted during the Harlem Renaissance, found new life in the crusades of the 1950s and 1960s. The liberation theologies of African Americans like James Cone, Albert Cleage, and J. Deotis Roberts, of Peruvian Catholic priest Gustavo Gutiérrez, and of Indian scholar Vine Deloria Jr. associated the sacred with oppressed minority groups. From the streets of Detroit (where African Americans repainted white Christs and Madonnas with black paint) to the Catholic barrios of southern California, to the reservations of South Dakota, women and men of color stood against the whitening of the sacred with new strength and vitality. By the end of the twentieth century, even though other aspects of American society had integrated, churches and synagogues remained segregated by race far more than by any other factor.

Even amid such racialized religious diversity, however, religion at times served to undermine racism in the United States. Conversion from one faith to another was often an act of racial exchange and contact. In the seventeenth and eighteenth centuries, a sizable group of British settlers who had been captured by Indians chose to remain part of Native American society, becoming full members of Indian communities and faith. Then in the late nineteenth century, with growing numbers of Asian immigrants to the United States, spiritualist whites took up yoga, Buddhist meditations, and sometimes Japanese Buddhist paraphernalia. Hymns, spirituals, and gospel tunes were the creation of dynamic interplays between white and black Christians from the eighteenth to the twentieth century. Sometimes religion could serve as a binding tie against others. In the nineteenth century, many white and black Protestants, for all of their disagreements, found common ground in their distrust of Catholics, Jews, and Muslims. Finally, religious language and morals—especially those built on Jewish and Christian traditions— have served to challenge racial divisions and violence. From the eighteenth to the twentieth century, the biblical assertion that God made all men "of one blood" has been a key argument against slavery and racial discrimination. At the same time, the "Golden Rule" has been a rallying cry to oppose racism and the mistreatment of immigrant groups. Finally, the moral arguments of many in the civil rights movement, from the Reverend C. L. Franklin of Detroit to Ralph Abernathy of Alabama, were presented to all Americans as rooted in universal dreams for justice, fraternity, and love.

MALE HIERARCHY, FEMALE DOMINANCE, AND GENDER CODES IN RELIGION

Who runs church organizations? Who have been the pastors, rabbis, priests, and other kinds of ritual specialists? Who speaks for religious institutions? For most cases in the past, the answer to all these questions is the same: men. The exceptions to this rule have received much attention—as in Catherine Brekus's study (*Strangers and Pilgrims: Female Preaching in America, 1740–1845* [1998]) of female preachers in the United States in the eighteenth and nineteenth centuries, women who were erased from historical memory soon after their passing from the scene—but they have received such attention precisely because they were deliberately, ostentatiously countercultural. Throughout American history, religion has upheld male hierarchy, while at the same time providing spaces for women's authority and power. In America, as historian Anne Braude has explained, women go to church, as well as to synagogue and mosque. "Women's history," she has titled her notably bracing survey of the subject, "*is* religious history."

Probably beginning in the eighteenth century, and definitely a reality from the nineteenth century forward, women have made up the majority of the congregations of Christian churches, both Catholic and, even more so, Protestant. In African American churches, women historically have made up 60 percent or more of congregations, a percentage that has only increased in recent years as black churches have failed to attract younger generations of black men. In early-twentieth-century Italian Harlem, for example, women controlled the festival devoted to the celebration of the "Madonna of 115th Street." It was, on the one hand, a cult of female power, as Italians brought their everyday problems and sorrows to their long-suffering Virgin, who originally came to America with the immigrants in 1881 and took up residence in the basement of a Catholic church. On the other hand, it was a cult of female power celebrating female suffering. At its most extreme, it featured rituals of women dragging themselves on the hot mid-July New York pavement, their tongues licking the ground leading up to the Madonna. The act of extreme unction and obedience graphically symbolized the hold that the domus, the Italian conception of home and family rule, exerted over women in Italian Harlem. The domus was the center of women's power, and the place of their imprisonment as well. The celebration of the Madonna of 115th Street enshrined, symbolized, and reenacted the entire complex symbology of religion, gender, and power.

In New Mexico, a similarly complicated and multivalent set of rituals arose around Los Hermanos Penitentes, popularly known there as "the Penitentes." In this case, women were not in control; indeed, as the name "Los Hermanos" made clear, they could not participate at all in the secret brotherhoods, the male fraternities that organized the annual Penitente procession. Each year, the Penitentes slowly made their way up trails and roads in rural New Mexico. Members whipped themselves in acts of penance, mimicking the undeserved sufferings that the Lord Jesus Christ took on for the expiation of sin. At the same time, Latino Catholic men were famously anticlerical. They avidly, proudly, avoided Mass. "My son, there are three things which pertain to our religion," one Mexican American immigrant heard from his family: "Our Lord, Our Lady of Guadalupe, and the Church. You can trust in the first two, but not in the third." The Mexican immigrants interviewed by sociologist Manuel Gamio in the 1930s consistently distinguished between a deep, popular, family-based piety fundamentally based on veneration of the Virgen de Guadalupe, *la morenita*, the brown-skinned *Virgen* whose image materialized in front of the Indian Juan Diego on a hill in Mexico in 1531. Thus Latino religious traditions involved women who tended a home-based piety and anti-clerical men who organized religious processions blessed by the Virgin of Guadalupe, the approximate equivalent to the Madonna of 115th Street that New York Italians exalted in their own version of domus-based Catholicism.

Historians fascinated by the connection between women and religion in American history have written of the "feminization of religion," a controversial but long-lived thesis that grapples with major changes in American theology in the nineteenth century and the growing dominance of women in religious institutions. According to this thesis, the Calvinist patriarchy of the Puritan era eventually gave way to a "softer" nineteenth-century evangelicalism that, in turn, became a normative American religious style. The turning point was the Second Great Awakening, generally dated to about the first third of the nineteenth century, co-terminus with the "market revolution" in American life. Protestant women essentially engineered the Second Great Awakening, largely by converting first and then bringing along husbands, sons, and other family members to the "anxious seat" to mourn publicly over their sin and seek ultimate redemption. Historians who have studied the evangelical revolution in particular communities—specifically in upstate New York, where the evangelical fires scorched the "burned-over district"—have documented the transmission of religious ideas and sentiment from women to family members, from which it spread in a broader societal revolution. In this case, the "feminization of religion" has a real and empirical social correspondent.

The "feminization of religion" thesis also has a broader, if less empirically documentable, meaning. In Ann Douglas's well-known if controversial formulation, nineteenth-century evangelical women allied with Protestant clergy led the way in a "feminization" of religious style, away from doctrine and theological tracts and toward feeling and sentimental literature, especially heartrending tracts and popular novels. The novelist Nathaniel Hawthorne irritably complained about a generation of "scribbling women" who flooded the nation with a torrent of formulaically sentimental literature through the middle of the nineteenth century. Most of them are now forgotten, but a few, especially Harriet Beecher Stowe, created a revolution of their own when they harnessed the sentimental literary traditions to the hard struggle over slavery in America. *Uncle Tom's Cabin* (1852), the little book that Lincoln reputedly told its author, only half-jokingly, had started the great Civil War, masterfully employed the themes of sentimental literature, especially an angelic child whose necessary death forwards the denouement—the crucifixion of Uncle Tom. Stowe's conclusion—slavery is wrong because it is heartless and evil—climaxed in Tom's death; the old slave stands in for Jesus himself. In the book, Uncle Tom is no "uncle tom" of later caricature, but a Christian martyr who gives his life in expiation of the national sin. Stowe also effectively ridiculed the self-interested hypocrisy of pro-slavery theology. She showed that sentiment can be a devastating weapon of the weak.

Despite the "feminization of religion" thesis, the fact remains that religious hierarchies controlled by ritual specialists—preachers, priests, rabbis, shamans, seminarians, exhorters, bishops, congregational readers, deacons, and others—have been overwhelmingly male. They remain so today, even when now more than half of students in seminaries are female. The complete exclusion of women from posts of religious authority—even from being able to cast a vote in a church meeting—has gradually given way to women slowly entering the ranks of religious leadership. Even there, the glass ceiling blocking their rise upward has been documented time and again by recent surveys of women in church organizations. Moreover, many of the largest and fastest-growing religious organizations—the Mormons, the Assemblies of God (the largest Pentecostal denomination), the Southern Baptist Convention, and the Catholic priesthood, to name just a few—either tacitly discourage or actively exclude and prevent women from entering positions of religious leadership.

In the liberal/conservative divide, which a number of sociologists have depicted as the most clear-cut religious fracturing of contemporary America, gender remains a fundamental issue splitting progressive and conservative iterations of the same religious tradition. This applies not only to women (straight or gay) but to gay men as well. In 2003, Bishop Eugene Robinson's nomination and eventual election to the post of bishop in the Episcopalian Church split dioceses across the country in a bitter religious and philosophical war that centered squarely on sexuality. In this case, the globalization of Episcopalianism played a major role, as those from international dioceses, especially from Africa and South America, led the fight against Robinson's nomination, and threatened to split the church in two.

Gender in American religious history abounds in ironies and painful paradoxes. It was Protestant evangelicals in the nineteenth century, especially liberals of the day such as Horace Bushnell, who created what is now called the ideology of "separate spheres." That is, in an economic era in which home and workplace became increasingly separate and in which a competitive marketplace environment defined everyday working life, men were depicted as being prepared for the brutal jungle-like world of workaday competition, while women's naturally nurturing souls fitted them for domestic duties, especially the inculcation of morality in the next generation. A woman's gentle touch softened the moral calluses that the friction and pressure of the workaday world inevitably produced in its participants. As a concomitant of this view, women were naturally religious. This constituted a complete reversal from the early modern view, exemplified especially in the Salem witch trials of the 1690s, that women were congenitally more prone to penetration (in every sense of that word) by the devil, who craftily entered human souls through human orifices. By the nineteenth century, it was men whose harder souls left less leeway for the movement of the divine, in contrast to the close connection that women more fluidly maintained with holy influences.

At the same time, of course, this ideology broke down at the door of entrance into positions of religious leadership. The "feminization of religion" thesis cannot account for the astoundingly fierce defense of male privilege put up by religious educators and establishments over centuries of time. In the nineteenth century, women who felt the call of God faced a difficult road. At best, among the evangelical denominations (notably the Methodists), they could become exhorters, essentially traveling itinerants with no religious authority save for their own message, charisma, and guts. In a very few cases, women became the leaders of religious movements. The most famous example was Mother Ann Lee, founder of a small religious sect in England that in America became known as the Shakers. In another case, Mother Jemima Wilkinson, styling herself as "the Public Universal Friend," led an offshoot of Quakerism that preached the complete abolition of distinction between the sexes. The development of Spiritualism in the nineteenth century—the belief and practice of talking to the dead, usually deceased relatives, induced by séances and the like—encouraged women's active participation. Some women who went on to become abolitionists and women's rights speakers, for example, started as voices of a spirit come back to deliver a message through a particular vessel. In this way, women not otherwise allowed to speak in public at all gained a voice. In sometimes quite lengthy discourses, they channeled the voices of spirits.

Abolitionist and suffragist women moved quickly from purportedly inert channeling of a spirit voice to directly communicating their own radical thoughts and visions. Of course, in doing so they brought controversy and calumny on themselves and their male supporters. These "long-haired men and short-haired women" challenged the most fundamental verities of nineteenth-century American society, most especially including gendered religious conventions.

In the twentieth century, even as gender hierarchies in terms of religious leadership remained firmly in place for most religious organizations (save for new and marginalized ones, such as the early Pentecostal churches), women still made up the majority of church members, raised vast sums of money to fund home and foreign missions, served local churches in innumerable ways, and ran extensive national organizations that left a legacy of reform in public policy. Frances Willard's Woman's Christian Temperance Union, for example, not only influenced the passage of national Prohibition but also demonstrated how moral sentiment could be effectively channeled into political action, a lesson taken to heart by the suffrage movement. In addition, Progressive Era women's leaders organized massive campaigns for nearly every conceivable sort of social reform, ranging from the control of individual behavior (in Prohibition, strengthened prostitution laws, and the like) to reining in the behavior of government and corporations. Progressive Era women mixed evangelical sentiment with scientific rationality, at a time when church organizations themselves often adapted the language of "scientific management" and "efficiency."

While women inspired by Social Gospel sentiments of reforming the social order dominated religious activism in the Progressive Era, later in the twentieth century it was conservative women who led public discussions of religion and politics. In what is sometimes referred to as "the great reversal," the historic tendency of religiously based or religiously inspired activism to be concentrated on the left, toward movements of fundamental social reform, shifted rightward through the twentieth century, toward ideologies that stressed conserving "traditional values." In recent years, groups such as Concerned Women for America, Operation Rescue, the Eagle Forum, and the Christian Coalition inspired devout women from various religious traditions into organized political interest groups on behalf of conservative causes. Many expressed a devout opposition to feminism, despite the obvious fact that it was the women's movement that had afforded women such as conservative Phyllis Schlafly the opportunity to gain attention as nationally recognized sociopolitical voices. But, as Kristin Luker has shown in *Abortion and the Politics of Motherhood* (1984), hot-button "social issues" such as abortion have increasingly divided women along the lines of those who define themselves in secular terms, and those for whom religion is a primary locus of meaning. One cannot draw any such distinction too broadly, and certainly the Social Gospel faith of the Progressive Era accompanied any number of religiously inspired women in the feminist movement. Nonetheless, the rise of conservative evangelical women as a powerful social and political force is a significant development in American religious history.

It bears examination, too, insofar as gender itself is a religious construction, one that signifies an entire way of sacralizing the social arrangements of men and women—as explored in Anthony Michael Petro's "Religion, Gender, and Sexuality." In a previous era, the nexus between what the historian Jane Dailey has called "sex, segregation, and the sacred" had been a primary defense of southern apartheid. Dailey has explained that "it was through sex that racial segregation in the South moved from being a local social practice to a part of the divine plan for the world. It was thus through sex that segregation assumed, for the believing Christian, cosmological significance" ("Sex, Segregation, and the Sacred After *Brown*," *Journal of American History* 91 [2004]: 119–144). Gendered constructions of the social order, then, were fundamental to segregation.

In the post–civil rights era, conservative evangelicals recaptured and highlighted the biblical language about wifely "submission" from the biblical Pauline letters, while men's groups such as the Promisekeepers exalted men's roles as leaders of the family. In 1998, for example, delegates to the largest Protestant denomination in the country, the Southern Baptist Convention, voted overwhelmingly to proclaim a new faith and message statement. Originally adopted in 1963 as an informal but important statement of belief for Southern Baptists, the later adaptation added significant new sections addressing specific questions of gender relations. Dorothy Patterson, a noted conservative evangelical spokeswoman, wrote the statement:

> The marriage relationship models the way God relates to His people. A husband is to love his wife as Christ loved the church. He has the God-given responsibility to provide for, to protect, and to lead his family. A wife is to submit herself graciously to the servant leadership of her husband even as the church willingly submits to the headship of Christ. She, being in the image of God as is her husband and thus equal to him, has the God-given responsibility to respect her husband and to serve as his helper in managing the household and nurturing the next generation.

This resolution came five years after the SBC had issued an official apology for its complicity in and support of slavery and segregation. As white southern Christians belatedly acknowledged their historic support for slavery and racism in America, they moved explicitly into a definitive rejection of contemporary gender mores. In good measure, this move was engineered by women themselves, who felt that contemporary feminism violated norms of godly family structures. The terrain of battle in this culture war had shifted, in effect, from race to gender, but faith in a God-ordained hierarchy remained central.

COMMUNALIST VISIONS AND COMMERCIAL CAPITALIST CONSEQUENCES; OR, THE PROTESTANT ETHIC AND THE SPIRIT OF THERAPEUTIC CONSUMERISM

Alexis de Tocqueville's travels through the United States from 1829 to 1831 yielded penetrating insights defining how Americans have understood *Democracy in America* (1835, 1840), the title of the political classic resulting from his journeys. Tocqueville wondered about the exuberance of religion in the young democratic republic. One of Tocqueville's paradoxical nuggets involved the interplay between religion and the market. Americans, he observed, were at once spiritually devout and materially entrepreneurial, even avaricious. These two impulses, seemingly in contradiction, in fact have worked in tandem. Religion and materialism were like twin ventricles pumping blood through the American heart.

In *The Protestant Ethic and the Spirit of Capitalism* (1905), the German sociologist and intellectual Max Weber proffered perhaps the most famous thesis in the history of Western religion. He posited a direct connection between the Protestant Reformation and the economic revolution created by the rise of capitalist forms of economic organization. The link was theological and psychological: anxious about the state of their souls, Calvinist Christians accumulated wealth to reassure themselves of their place in the elect. This wealth ignited the explosion of commercial capitalism and, eventually, later developments such as the Industrial Revolution. Thus the anti-materialist Protestant ethic, born of biblically based critiques of Catholic priests who hocked "indulgences" and trinkets of salvation, fueled the greatest explosion of economic growth in human history.

Subsequent studies poked enough holes in Weber's trial balloon that it eventually plummeted. Italian bankers in the Renaissance, the famous families such as the Medicis, bankrolled much of the early capitalist ventures of entrepreneurial Italian Catholics; and the Portuguese and Spanish monarchs, fueled by the zeal of the Catholic Counter-Reformation, pumped huge sums into exploring the New World. Catholic explorers eagerly sought the Seven Cities of Cibola and the fabled lands of gold that the Natives in the New World kept telling the Spanish explorers were just a little way farther down the road. Perhaps they were located somewhere in the vicinity of the future Wichita, Kansas, some Indian pranksters told the humorless Francisco Vásquez de Coronado, who found no yellow brick road of gold in Kansas, or anywhere else for that matter. Weber's thesis, then, worked for places such as Calvin's Geneva, and for England during the tumultuous years of the Puritan revolution, but it could not explain Catholic entrepreneurialism.

Although Weber's argument collapsed, his impulse to seek connections between the theological and the material still animates much inquiry. Scholars have explored the paradox espied by Tocqueville and played out in myriad ways through American history: the tense yet inextricably intertwined relationship between spiritual purity and material gain. In the case of the early Puritans, the Weber thesis still appears to hold considerable explanatory value. Early New England Puritans came with visions of a city set upon a hill. But this was not to be a paradise modeled after some laissez-faire vision of economic freedom. It was quite the opposite—a communal utopian order in which individual economic behavior would be tightly controlled on behalf of the public good (a model also followed, brilliantly, by the early Mormon communities in Utah). What material wealth emerged from the experiment was to be devoted to God's glory, not to acts of conspicuous consumption—which, at any rate, would have violated the sumptuary laws tightly regulating how individuals could dress, what they could eat, and what household items they could own.

Both because of and in spite of their theology, Puritans accumulated wealth, which increased capital holdings, which fueled economic expansion, which created more wealth—and so "Puritans" evolved into "Yankees," and "Yankees" pioneered the market revolution of the nineteenth century that seemed to fit hand in glove with the evangelical explosion of that same era. Or did it? The evangelicals, of course, knew what the Bible had to say about Mammon, and evangelicals following the New Light stridently condemned wealth accumulation and conspicuous consumption. In their own minds, they were simply restoring the faith once known to their fathers, the faith constantly under assault by heretics and sinful commercial types alike. Early Methodists, for example, condemned the decline of piety in the older, more established denominations. They held class meetings to enforce communal norms of sin and repentance, and celebrated salvation in love feasts. They inculcated bonds of sharing between repentant sinners. Like most early evangelical and utopian groups, they valued communalism and distrusted capitalist innovation. Also like such groups, no matter what their intention, they contributed a remarkable range of innovations—theological, technological, and material—to the evolving commercial world. The Methodist emphasis on the free grace of God extended to all Americans in the expansive early republic; by later in the nineteenth century, Methodists were comfortably ensconced in the nation's cities, with impressive urban cathedrals belying their humbler beginnings. One may return to Weber and speculate on how much the ethic of discipline, self-sacrifice, and careful thrift contributed to the often close connection between evangelical zeal and personal success.

By the later nineteenth century, numerous public lecturers and self-promoting publicists made a good living by preaching, if not practicing, precisely that connection. The Philadelphia minister Russell Conwell grew wealthy preaching his famous sermon "Acres of Diamonds" thousands of times, with many in the audience returning repeatedly to hear his prosperity gospel even though his song remained the same. Like most self-help authors, Conwell first and foremost helped himself. The Gilded Age was full of what would later come to be called "Prosperity Theology," and more recently in its Pentecostal form, "Word of Faith Theology." This was not new in American history; one only need look to Benjamin Franklin's slyly sardonic witticisms to find the conflation of Protestant living and financial accumulation. The unapologetic crassness of the message in the Gilded Age, however, was the harbinger of the ubiquitous influence of the Norman Vincent Peale/Dale Carnegie school of thinking in the twentieth century. "Ask and ye shall receive" is a biblical maxim that Americans of all religious persuasions (or no persuasion at all) took literally and dispensed liberally, from Russell Conwell and Henry Ward Beecher to T. D. Jakes, John Hagee, Joel Osteen, and other contemporary prosperity gospelers.

Throughout American religious history, communalist groups, often born of profoundly conservative and anti-capitalist social visions, have fostered remarkable economic systems. Almost in spite of themselves, they have generated wealth and the social frictions that come with it. The Church of Jesus Christ of Latter-day Saints (the Mormons) have simultaneously fostered and controlled wealth creation and distribution probably better than any single communalist group in American history. Born of Joseph Smith's encounter with the Angel Moroni (detailed in D. Michael Quinn's "The Church of Jesus Christ of Latter-day Saints ['Mormons']"), the tiny, beleaguered, and relentlessly persecuted sect encouraged the most successful communalist experiment in American history—indeed, one of the relatively few that survived more than two generations. The Church of Jesus Christ of Latter-day Saints compelled believers to live and act within strict communal guidelines. It was their communalism, ultimately, that brought commercial life to the desert in Utah and made Salt Lake City the headquarters for a new religious empire. The Mormon Church emerged as one of the wealthiest non-profit entities in American history, with vast holdings in hotel chains, newspaper and electronic media, and other business enterprises. In the process church leaders, beginning especially with Brigham Young, adjusted to American economic norms, helping the Latter-day Saints become an economic powerhouse in the twentieth century. The model of tight control of church organization and doctrine combined with decentralized methods of spreading the gospel and a democratic message of salvation for all served the Mormons as well as, perhaps even better than, it did the Methodists. The Mormons present a striking picture of the intriguing paradox of communalist visions and capitalist triumphs.

The nineteenth century witnessed a veritable explosion of utopian and communalist movements, some of which are detailed by Stephen J. Stein in "Alternative Religious Movements in American History." The religious energies sparked by the Second Great Awakening exploded in the mid-nineteenth century, as Mormons, Shakers, Millerites, Spiritualists, Fullerites, Owenites, Transcendantalists at Brook Farm, and hundreds of other idealistic bands created societies generally featuring some mixture of experimental living. They became famous for unorthodox sexual arrangements, ranging from celibacy to what was termed "free love," meaning not so much sexual promiscuity as the drive to find one's "spiritual match" outside the conventional bounds of legally defined marriage. They also consistently proposed utopian theologies envisioning the creation of a perfect society on earth. Nearly all of these eventually died out; the very hyperindividualism of American society that spurred their creation also usually doomed them to dissolution. But if communalist utopias rarely survived beyond a generation or two, they frequently left long-lived products or economic arrangements. Thus such familiar consumer icons as Kellogg's Corn Flakes, Oneida flatware and silverware, and Tappan kitchen appliances can be traced back to the attempts of religious visionaries to promote health (as in the case of the corn flakes, considered a digestive cleanser) or to provide an economic means to support a utopian dream. Another example is the famous furniture produced by the Shakers. Putting their "hands to work" and their "hearts to God," Shaker craftsmanship today brings raised eyebrows of delight from the all-knowing appraisers on *Antiques Road Show*. Once again, the drive for communalist purity turned inward long enough to produce explosive economic energies that could not be contained and that helped to drive American economic expansion and consumerism. Religious communalism, in short, was part of the nuclear fusion that supercharged American commercial capitalism.

In his later work, Weber pondered the quandary of the "iron cage" of rationalist bureaucracy. In economic terms, historians such as Daniel Rogers have traced the gradual evolution of the "Protestant ethic" (which, as we have seen, was never all that Protestant to begin with) to the "work ethic." If, under the Protestant ethic, anxious souls worked to ensure their eternal fate, in the work ethic people labored long and hard mostly because it was by definition moral (hence the idle hands in the devil's workshop) or because (later in the twentieth century) upwardly mobile consumers desired ever-higher standards of living. Contemporary Americans work longer than Europeans, and even longer than the Japanese. That national work obsession has roots outside religion, but nonetheless Weber was on to something. The question that troubled Weber was whether there would be any human meaning within the wondrously efficient creation of the modern bureaucratic society. Everything would work, but not to serve any higher purpose; instead, rationality would become its own purpose, a gilded but soulless "iron cage." The machine would go of itself.

In short, the American religious ethic and the spirit of capitalism have worked in tandem, variously contradicting and undergirding each other. The city set upon a hill has grown into an economic empire producing and distributing a cascade of goods that moralists consistently fear will undermine the very virtue that was essential to its creation. Religious culture spurred market culture; religious culture consistently has responded and adapted to market culture; but market culture's imperatives of utilitarian profit- and pleasure-maximizing behavior always threaten to overwhelm religion's calls for self-restraint and obedience to a higher purpose.

PROSELYTIZATION: SPIRITUAL RECRUITMENT AND THE MARKET ECONOMY OF RELIGION

Bruce Barton's *The Man Nobody Knows* was a best seller in 1925 and 1926. It was a biography of Jesus, depicting Christ as the world's greatest businessman. "He picked up twelve men from the bottom ranks of business and forged them into an organization that conquered the world," wrote Barton, a minister's son and corporate public-relations specialist. The parables of Jesus were not only pearls of wisdom but also the "most powerful advertisements of all time." Barton crudely expressed common views about the selling of religion, converting people to the faith—proselytization. Certainly the minister in the 1920s who advertised his weekly sermon with a sign for "Three-in-One Oil" as the image for the Holy Trinity understood that marketing ploys might entice converts, or at least inquiries.

Such religious advertising and recruiting—whether they come from Protestant, Catholic, Mormon, Jewish, Islamic, Buddhist, Theosophist, Zoroastrian, or any other faith found (or founded) in the United States—were hardly new to the 1920s. Through much of American religious history, believers from diverse traditions have perfected techniques of aggressive salesmanship, active recruitment, niche marketing, and brand loyalty. To be sure, recruitment into religious groups does not amount simply to market competition. Religious conversion involves complicated human desires, not simply targeted pitches. Yet the market analogy provides one useful way to understand how faiths solicit, recruit, and hold members.

Proselytizing innovators have adapted religious traditions to the American free market of conversion. Obviously, this is true of evangelical groups, who are proselytizers by definition. To a remarkable extent, it is true also of Jews, Catholics, Asian religious groupings, and others. For one seeking to understand the spread of the evangelical model of proselytization in American history, a number of questions immediately arise. What are the motivations of the proselytizers and the proselytes—that is, the converts? Where does persuasion end and coercion begin? Does proselytization come down (in the cynical interpretation) to the creation and marketing of a brand name? Is the concept of proselytization itself based on a model of conversion that simply ill fits groups other than the self-consciously evangelical ones? To what extent, for example, can ethnically based religious groups (the German Lutherans, Pennsylvania Dutch, East Indian Sikhs, Acoma Pueblo, or African American Nation of Islam) be said to proselytize? What about Judaism and other religions into which adherents are normally born, rather than "born again"?

The free market of religion in America, protected by the Constitution and practiced in the daily spiritual quests of Americans, means that groups use persuasion to attract and hold converts. And the reality of the free market means that the winners (who for much of American history have been Protestants, especially of the evangelical variety) have written their own histories in triumphalist terms—as if those who have the most souls win. But proselytizers come in all shapes and sizes. They come with all sorts of motivations, too. Proselytizers generally see themselves as genuine and altruistic persuaders, as carriers of a message that may transform individual lives and perhaps even rectify injustices in the social order. Critics often see them as naïve cultural imperialists, as brainwashers, or as accomplices to one or another project of political or psychological coercion. Discerning the "true" motivation is difficult, perhaps impossible; altruistic persuasion and cultural imperialism, for example, may often be two sides of the same coin. The methods and effects of proselytization are easier to assess. The evangelical model has been adapted by various traditions to suit their own purposes, whether New York City Presbyterians, the League of the Iroquois, slave preachers, Reform Jews, or American Zen Buddhists.

Proselytizers are persuaders. Yet in terms of the spread of religious doctrine within the context of colonization, for example, and of white supremacy, persuasion and coercion can involve a fatal attraction. This may be seen most poignantly in the California missions from 1769 to the 1830s. Founded by Father Junípero Serra, the idea of the missions—Spanish-style compounds built from San Diego to San Francisco—was to take California Indians, the neophytes, and gradually civilize them, which necessarily meant Christianizing them. As with the Franciscans in New Mexico, the proselytizing padres used material enticement to attract Indians (especially younger men) into the fold, and then worked them and disciplined them harshly for their "barbarism." Serra readily admitted that the California padres whipped their Indian children, assuming this aided them spiritually. By the end of the missions period, the 1830s and 1840s, the padres had overseen the near-total extinction of the California Natives, through the breakdown of tribal ways, and the spread of disease, alcohol, and warfare. In this case, proselytization was the means to a "final solution" of the Indian question in California.

In New England, the Puritans, who began arriving in large numbers in the 1630s, also proselytized among Native populations, in fits and starts. John Eliot, the New England "Apostle to the Indians," translated the Bible into the language of the Massachusett Indians, intending to teach them the Word and train up their own ministers. "Some of them began to be seriously affected, and to understand the things of God," wrote Puritan leader John Winthrop in his journal, describing the effect of Eliot's preaching, "and they were generally ready to reform whatsoever they were told be against the word of God, as their sorcery (which they call powwowing,) their whoredomes, etc., idleness, etc." Eliot's well-intentioned endeavor could not prevent King Philip's War of the 1670s, an East Coast debacle of destruction that paralleled the contemporaneous Pueblo Revolt in northern New Mexico. During the war, Eliot's "Praying Indians" huddled on Deer Island, suffering desperately for lack of food, clothing, and fuel. But by that time, few New Englanders cared to distinguish any longer between Praying Indians and preying savages. The preeminent Puritan minister of the late seventeenth century, Cotton Mather, rejoiced at the victories of white New Englanders, convinced that God's plan called for less proselytization and more subjugation.

A more storied part of American religious history involves persuasive proselytization, seen most especially in the First and Second Great Awakenings. As a cultural force, American evangelicalism took off with a series of revivals in the American colonies in the eighteenth century, collectively known as the Great Awakening. Appearing sporadically from New England and the Middle Colonies in the 1740s to the Chesapeake and coastal lowland South in the 1760s, the Great

Awakening featured new styles of popular public evangelicalism. Challenging the authority of older established ministers, the so-called New Lights convicted the seemingly pious of sin and brought a new message of born-again Christianity. The theologian of the Awakening, Jonathan Edwards, provided a substantial intellectual framework for new modes of evangelization. He outlined a philosophy for and psychology of the conversion experience, in terms made familiar by John Locke and other leading philosophers of the time (for more explanations of this point, see Mark Noll, "Theology"). Revivalists during the Great Awakening attacked "dead" (unconverted) ministers and established churches. August divines such as the Bostonian Charles Chauncy fumed that preaching the Word could not be entrusted to roving packs of untested and theologically naïve proselytizers. "What is the Tendency of the Practice, but Confusion and Disorder," he asked. "If one Pastor may neglect his own People to take Care of others, who are already taken care of; . . . why not another, and another still, and so on, 'till there is no such Thing as Social Order in the Land." Despite fears of religious anarchy, there would be no turning back from the democratization of proselytization.

The eighteenth-century revivals were a transatlantic phenomenon, a fact exemplified in the life of George Whitefield. Born into a devout Anglican family, Whitefield attended Oxford as a servitor, a gopher boy for sons of the gentry. While there, he fell under the sway of John Wesley, who had begun an informal fellowship of pietists later pejoratively dubbed the "Methodists," referring to their emphasis on cultivating a method for spiritual practice. In 1740 and 1741, Whitefield preached in the northern colonies. Americans responded enthusiastically to his thunderous appeals. His journals were widely read in England and the colonies, turning him into one of America's first celebrities. Whitefield pleaded for reconciliation between the warring Old Lights and New Lights, aiming to make America safe for evangelical democracy. As the years progressed, Whitefield's public presence, adroit use of theatrical tactics, and unctuousness turned him into a kind of colonial Billy Graham, a unifying presence wholly unthreatening to authorities. He developed a friendship with Benjamin Franklin, whose sardonic as well as serious writings were, like Whitefield's sermons, classics of eighteenth-century American expression. In their own very different ways, the two famous Americans proposed that the wisdom of common men should form the basis of authority. These evangelists for common-sense enlightened rationalism (Franklin) and evangelical fire (Whitefield) both pointed to the coming revolutions in politics and religion.

Recently, scholars have even begun to speak of an "Indian Great Awakening" in the eighteenth century, a Native (and Nativist) pan-Indian response to the spread of the colonizing powers. Native American leaders used religious awakenings to revitalize their beleaguered communities. One Indian religious seer, an Iroquois from New York named Handsome Lake, went through a series of visionary journeys in the late eighteenth century, a time when the historical dominance of the Iroquois nations in the region fell prey to a rapidly advancing American civilization. Handsome Lake's original message melded Iroquois lore and Christian beliefs learned from Quaker missionaries. "Our lands are decaying because we do not think on the Great Spirit," Handsome Lake had written to President Thomas Jefferson, "but we are now going to renew our Minds and think on the great Being who made us all, that when we put our seeds in the Earth they may grow and increase like the leaves on our Trees." Originally consumed with apocalyptic visions of Iroquois destiny, in later years Handsome Lake turned to a gospel of sobriety and industry among Indians, peace with whites, and preservation of Iroquois lands. In the religion of Handsome Lake, salvation came through following the code of *Gaiwiio*, with a mixture of Iroquois practices (including a traditional ceremonial calendar and a mythology consonant with older beliefs) and Christian influences (temperance, confession, and a notion of conversion to a new religion). Handsome Lake presented himself originally as a messenger of the new code, a preacher, but later claimed special supernatural revelations and divine powers.

The religious ferment of the new republic came to a head in the early nineteenth century. One scholar has written that this era witnessed the "democratization of American Christianity." Other historians have referred to this time as the "Methodist century." In "Evangelicals in American History," Douglas A. Sweeney traces the explosive growth of evangelicals in this era. During the period from 1800 to 1850, church membership increased tenfold. In 1800, one out of every fifteen Americans was a Protestant church member; by 1850, that number was one in seven. The Methodists, a small sect in the late eighteenth century, numbered over 1 million by mid-century. With circuit-riding preachers combing the countryside on their horses, preaching to congregations throughout the newly settling areas, Methodists proved flexible enough to meet the need for religious organization on the frontier. Using their centralized church governance, Methodist leaders harnessed and controlled their expanding empire. Methodist theology, moreover, highlighted free will in accepting or rejecting God's grace, ideal for a society in which men seemed to control their own destinies. In short, Methodists were perfect for this new religious environment of westward expansion and permanent religious competition.

Later in the nineteenth century, while Protestants devised new ways of responding to corporate capitalist America, Catholics, Jews, and others formulated similar programs of proselytization. Fervent revivalism, for example, a practice normally associated with evangelical Protestants, had a close corollary in the missions and special services conducted by several generations of Catholic priests. From 1850 to 1920, Catholic congregants as a percentage of total church adherents in the United States doubled, from 14 to 28 percent; the percentage of Catholics in the total population also rose, from 5 to 16 percent (the huge growth of Catholicism in the nineteenth century may be explored further in

Leslie Woodcock Tentler's chapter "Catholicism in America"). This was no accident, nor was it a function only of Catholic immigration to the country from Ireland, Italy, eastern Europe, and Mexico. Certainly this immigration was part of the story, yet many of the immigrants were only nominally Catholics. Church leaders in America, recognizing the dangers to the "one true faith" from the myriad Protestant sects in the United States (as well as from indifference and traditional anticlerical attitudes), sponsored intense programs of parish missions, the Catholic counterparts to revivals. During one such revival in New York City in 1867, for example, a diarist reported that "one woman began to cry aloud; twenty others joined in as a chorus; and the whole congregation showed similar symptoms when the preacher said: 'Don't cry now but cry at your confession: then bewail your sins.'" Itinerant priests such as Francis Xavier Weninger served as the equivalent to the frontier exhorters of the Methodists, gathering in a harvest of souls to the faith. Weninger wrote, "I continually am giving Missions in the woods as well as in the metropolis going to every chapel, no matter how many families there are. In the course of the year I am preaching over 1,000 times." Parochial schools planted throughout the country in the nineteenth century and staffed by religious women institutionalized devotional Catholicism as the faith of the sons and daughters of immigrants, especially in urban America. For many Catholic children, parochial-school education became a rite of passage, and the nun teachers stereotypically infamous for their frighteningly disciplinary rulers thwacking errant pupils. The schools reinforced the growing ties between ethnic neighborhood enclaves and local parishes.

Jews likewise joined in adapting to the free market of American proselytization. Reform Jews were not seeking converts from outside Judaism, but they were attempting to attract disaffected Jews to a faith that responded to the realities of living in American society. Reform Judaism itself, as pioneered by Rabbi Isaac Mayer Wise in Cincinnati before the Civil War, was a recognition that Jews lived in an evangelical culture and would have to adapt accordingly. Reform Judaism thus jettisoned certain traditions viewed as archaic, modernized services, opened up seating to families (at about the same time that many conservative Protestants also did away with gender-segregated seating), and provided more open and inviting services. While Reform Jews in America (especially in areas of lesser Jewish concentration, such as the South and Midwest) did their best to become American, many Conservative Jews pressed the cause of Zionism, the religio-political platform that claimed that only a separate and independent Jewish homeland would save the race. In 1896, Theodor Herzl, a Hungarian Jewish intellectual, published *The Jewish State*, giving Zionism its manifesto for the next century. Conservative Judaism—whose members were not fully Orthodox but who objected to the complete set of innovations introduced by Reform Jews—were especially effective advocates for the Zionist program. Alan T. Levenson provides more in-depth discussion of these varieties in his piece, "American Judaism."

The gigantic foreign missionary enterprise conducted by American religious organizations during this era arose from a similar mixture of evangelical and socially progressive impulses. Today, American foreign mission efforts are dominated by conservative evangelical groups (the Southern Baptist Convention and the Assemblies of God being the two largest senders of career missionaries) and Mormons (by far the largest commissioner of non-career missionaries). In the Gilded Age and the Progressive Era, however, it was mainstream Protestant denominations that led the way, sending thousands of men and women to China, Africa, Japan, India, Burma, and South America. Some of these were explicitly "heathen" (meaning non-Christian) lands; others were Christian but considered so full of idolatrous Catholicism as to be equally pressing candidates for Christianization.

Foreign missions had begun in the early nineteenth century with the formation of the American Board of Commissioners for Foreign Missions. In the late nineteenth century, as the non-Christian world seemed to be opening (due largely to the Western powers' exercises in imperialism in Africa and Asia, where European nations wielded political authority), some American evangelicals and mainstream Protestants took up the mantle laid down by Robert Speer, a recruiter and publicist for the foreign missions effort, who spoke of the opportunity for the "evangelization of the world in this generation." Although Speer and his colleagues were part of the "muscular Christianity" of their era, it was in reality women's missionary societies that raised the bulk of the funds for the huge overseas proselytization effort. This "errand to the world" represented by the missionary enterprise showed Americans' great faith in proselytization itself. Americans actually took the imperious slogan "the evangelization of the world in this generation" as a serious goal. By the 1930s, many missionaries, less naïve for their experiences, began to argue that American-style emotional persuasion was not easily translatable to other cultures. They pressed for more money and manpower in educational enterprises. Conservative evangelicals, however, insisted on spreading the gospel in print and by word of mouth, just as they always had done, trusting that God would work results in men's hearts.

After World War II, Americans flocked to church in record numbers. More than 60 percent of Americans attended some religious service every week. Mainstream religious leaders eased Americans' transitions to corporate capitalism and a therapeutic culture of self-realization and autonomy. Liberal Protestants, post–Vatican II Catholics, and Reform Jews carried their religion into corporate boardrooms and neighborhood barbecues. Proselytization itself, among respectable Protestants at least, fell into disrepute. Christian evangelicals, Mormon missionaries, and other sectarian groups held no such compunction: recruitment remained their stock-in-trade. Their efforts paid off.

The Southern Baptist Convention provides a case in point. Emerging from the ashes of the Civil War, this denomination of small farmers and plain townsfolk had become the largest denomination in the South by 1900. As southerners migrated northward and westward in the twentieth century, the Southern Baptist Convention soon became the nation's largest Protestant denomination, numbering over 18 million adherents nationwide by the 1990s, with members spread all throughout the country. The First Baptist Church of Dallas, Texas, pastored by the irascible fundamentalist W. A. Criswell, was the nation's single largest congregation. Southern Baptists perfected professionalized proselytization. A large denominational apparatus sent out thousands of home and foreign missionaries. The denomination's Sunday School Board churned out millions of pages of edifying age-graded instructional material, hymnals, and worship aids. The convention's church-building program lent start-up money for congregations establishing outposts in new communities. Southern Baptists, in short, advertised and expanded in ways akin to successful retail chains.

The recent growth of megachurches also suggests that entertainment and theater remain central to religious persuasion, as they have since the days of George Whitefield. Surveys have demonstrated that contemporary Americans distrust an excess of moral earnestness in preaching, and desire anonymity as passionately as they ostensibly seek community. In response, interdenominational chapels and fellowships bring together congregants in mall-like structures, generally in suburbs, and present a generically Christian pitch in the format of an hourlong live television show. Indeed, many of them are specifically made for television, with the studio audience serving as a backdrop. These religious theaters provide a familiar setting for a predominantly white, middle-class consumer shopping experience.

As the megachurch example suggests, proselytization often has come in the form of, and been most effectively practiced by, conservative religious traditions. Recently, in fact, in books such as Dean Kelley's *Why Conservative Churches Are Growing: A Study in Sociology of Religion* (1972), some scholars as well as evangelical propagandists have suggested that more narrowly defined conservative religions give participants an effective incentive, a psychological wage of sorts, precisely because they define themselves as countercultural and because adherents must sacrifice in order to get the benefit. By contrast, "liberal" versions of religious traditions, according to this view, implicitly devalue their spiritual benefit by making it too broadly and easily available. There is much to dispute in this argument, but it does call attention to the close connection in American history between proselytization, the use of media, and commercialism. Consistently through the history of Christianity in America, at least, it has been the evangelicals who have been the quickest to adopt the mechanisms of modernity (especially through the use of the most advanced media forms of any given time, from George Whitefield's open-air theatrics to Pat Robertson's Christian Broadcasting Network) to advance their message warning against the perils of modernity and secularism. Evangelicals have brilliantly exploited popular culture, a point developed by Philip Goff in his chapter, "Religion and Popular Culture."

THE FOLK ORIGINS OF HIGH THEOLOGY
AND THE THEOLOGICAL BASE OF POPULAR
RELIGIOUS MOVEMENTS

The constantly interacting realms of the marketplace and religion represent one of the most fundamental relationships in American religious history. It may also be observed in arenas often (mistakenly) thought to be devoid of crass market or "popular" considerations: in high theology (that is, theological formulations defined by the writings of trained intellectuals). Conversely, groups thought to be opposed to, or perhaps just willfully ignorant of, "high" theology often have their roots (acknowledged or not) in deep theological traditions and innovations. Mark Noll's "Theology" and Douglas A. Sweeney's "Evangelicals in American History" illuminate the major patterns of Christian theology in America, particularly for evangelical Protestants. Here we wish to emphasize the interaction of theological traditions with the dynamic and innovative religious practices that have evolved in American religious history. The two Great Awakenings serve as an ideal example of this point, as does the twentieth-century "awakening" of Pentecostalism.

Unwittingly, Jonathan Edwards set the stage in the eighteenth century for the coming evangelical–republican alliance. Seeking to reinvigorate traditional Protestant piety, his innovative theology began a process of the "disruption of the historic colonial churches" and a merging of Protestant thought and republican intellectual/political culture. Along the way, the central intellectual concept of Puritanism—the covenant, by which God, individuals, and society were linked—was replaced with a Christian republicanism. The Great Awakening of the mid-eighteenth century was the turning point. It provided space for the ideas that spurred the American Revolution and then the democratic explosion of Christianity in the nineteenth century.

The Second Great Awakening of the nineteenth century encouraged a similar set of interchanges between high theology and popular expression. Popular evangelicalism as the characteristic style of American religious expression may be dated from the nineteenth-century awakening, beginning with the great camp meetings held at Cane Ridge, Kentucky, during the earliest years of the century, and extending to the expansion of evangelical dominance throughout much of the growing country during the first half of the nineteenth century. The staggering growth of evangelical churches impressed many at the time; a great number believed that they were entering the millennium of the book of Revelation. Some of them thought so literally; they dated the Second Coming precisely and retreated to their appointed locations to await the Messiah; some even did so repeatedly, after refiguring their end-time calculations and discovering that they had been slightly off the first time. They experienced "the great disappointment," but left behind a few of the new evangelical formations (including, in this case, the

Seventh-Day Adventist Church), which survived to become part of America's religious landscape. The evangelical awakening also spurred a host of moral reform movements, ranging from fad diets to prison reform to abolitionism.

Because the awakening in the early years of the republic is thought of as "popular," it is often not connected to formal theology. But it should be. Just as was the case in earlier centuries, popular movements compelled theological rethinking, just as theological innovation sometimes predated and often energized popular religious movements. Charles Finney—lawyer, president of Oberlin College, and the most famous of a generation of evangelical itinerants—provided a theological rationale for the movement of the spirit. This great Protestant preacher eased northern (especially New England) suspicions about the social turmoil that might be unleashed by potent plain-folk revivalism. Himself not exactly of the plain folk—he was a lawyer and college president as well as an evangelist—Finney articulated theological reasoning common to antebellum Christians. A revival, he explained, was simply "the *right* use of the appropriate means." Revival preachers sowed the seed. Ultimately, only God's blessing allowed the seed to blossom and the harvest to come. What was the result, Finney asked, of the older doctrine of divine sovereignty, that men had no agency in their own salvation? Finney's answer: while the church fiddled, America burned. Millions had "gone down to hell, while the church has been dreaming, and waiting for God to save them without the use of means. It has been the devil's most successful means of destroying souls." Just as political campaigning brought out the vote, revivalism produced sure results. Churches were "awakened and reformed," sinners saved, profligates reclaimed, "harlots, and drunkards, and infidels, and all sorts of abandoned characters, are awakened and converted. The worst part of human society are softened, and reclaimed, and made to appear as lovely specimens of the beauty of holiness" (Charles Finney, "What a Revival of Religion Is" [1835], available at http://www.concentric.net/~fires/revival.htm).

Initially uneasy about the plain-folk evangelicalism of the antebellum republic, American theologians gave it theological imprimatur. As demonstrated in Mark Noll's magisterial work, *America's God: From Jonathan Edwards to Abraham Lincoln* (2002 [a summary of which appears in his contribution to this book]), American theology was transformed in the period from the mid-eighteenth century to the Civil War. Noll suggests that American theology emerged from a synthesis of "evangelical Protestant religion, republican political ideology, and commonsense moral reasoning." The synthesis provided the theology, ethics, bases for action, and overarching intellectual framework for American thought from the 1790s to the Civil War. "The process by which evangelical Protestantism came to be aligned with republican convictions and commonsense moral reasoning," Noll concludes, "was also the process that gave a distinctively *American* shape to Christian theology by the time of the Civil War." The nexus between white evangelical Protestant thought, common-sense philosophy, and republicanism gave Americans their distinctive elaboration of the relationship between religion and freedom.

Nearly everywhere except in the United States, Christians held republican ideas in suspicion, precisely because they encouraged individual free thought and excoriated the organic institutions that European Christians had seen as anointed by God. What was regarded as the product of a "lunatic fringe" elsewhere took hold in America as a result of the absence of a strong church establishment and the alliance of classically trained elites and democratic evangelicals in the common cause of the Revolution and freedom of religion. White Americans created a powerful theological hermeneutic, one bolstering a democratic and individualist Reformed Protestantism. Indeed, even groups that might have been the foes of this synthesis in other places took hold of the same combination of evangelical and republican reasoning; it simply was omnipresent in the theology of the era. It was routine, Noll concludes, for "American believers of many types to speak of Christian and republican values with a single voice." Many were like the former Methodist turned Unitarian James Smith, who wrote to Thomas Jefferson that he had found "shelter under the mild and peaceable Gospel of Jesus Christ, the most perfect model of Republicanism in the Universe"; or the radical Christian Elias Smith, who exulted in "One God—one Mediator—one lawgiver—one perfect law of Liberty—one name for the children of God, to the exclusion of all sectarian names—A Republican government, free from religious establishments and state clergy—free enquiry— life and immortality brought to light through the Gospel." Over time, the high theological ideas of Jonathan Edwards and his disciples in subsequent generations (the neo-Edwardseans) wound their way into the common-sense thought of the nineteenth century. Most important, the notion that everyone could, and should, read the Bible for himself, and that the Bible spoke truth to ordinary people, defined American evangelicalism through the mid-nineteenth century. Of course, southerners and northerners employed this same theological reasoning and arrived at diametrically opposed understandings of slavery. And then, by Appomattox, this evangelical synthesis lay in ruins.

A twentieth-century example of the interaction of high theology and popular religious movements may be seen in the birth of Pentecostalism and fundamentalism. Both grew from roots in high theology; both became major social and political movements in the twentieth century; and both drew most of their adherents from common folk disaffected by mainstream churches. Margaret Bendroth considers this history in "Religious Conservatism and Fundamentalism."

Pentecostalism was a twentieth-century extension of the nineteenth-century holiness movement, a set of doctrines that embraced eighteenth-century Methodist ideas of the soul's quest for perfection. Holiness believers looked for a work of God following conversion—what believers referred to as a "second blessing" or "sanctification"—when the Holy Spirit infused and completely purified the soul. In the antebellum era, the informal Bible studies of the New York Meth-odist Phoebe Palmer, who revived John Wesley's musings about achieving an ideal state of spiritual purity, popularized the holiness movement for an urban, northern audience influenced by the pervasive ideas of perfectionism. Palmer and her followers retooled *sanctification* into a distinct and discrete event follow-ing conversion, one wholly cleansing the believer of sin. Holiness drew few fol-lowers in the South until after the Civil War, largely because of the movement's connection with social radicalism, especially abolitionism. By the late nineteenth century, however, holiness had been denuded of some of its earlier theological and political implications. It then spread quickly, especially among Methodists in the Southeast.

Twentieth-century Pentecostal doctrine added speaking in tongues as evidence of the movement of God's spirit. The significance of tongues speech was heat-edly disputed among the faithful. Some assumed that it was a required "initial evidence" of sanctification. Others called it a "third blessing" following conver-sion and sanctification. Still others interpreted tongues speech as just one of many gifts that God bestowed differentially on individuals. Holiness teacher Charles Parham's revivals at his Bible school in Topeka, Kansas, in 1901 set a theologi-cal precedent for the emergence of the new Pentecostal doctrines. The second baptism of sanctification—the ultimate cleansing from sin explained by holiness theologians—was necessary but not sufficient, he preached. Only the final Holy Spirit baptism could complete the initiate's spiritual quest. When God's power suffused the human vessel, the believer spoke in tongues, a practice that was evidence of the "latter rain" of the Holy Spirit. The early Pentecostals anxiously anticipated the imminent and catastrophic coming of the "end times" (in contrast to the more optimistic postmillennialism common to many in the nineteenth-century northern holiness movement) and espoused a literalist biblicism that very nearly merged into fundamentalism. Like the fundamentalists, too, the Pentecos-tals shunned the consumption of tobacco and alcohol and what they perceived as adornment in dress (jewelry for women and neckties for men being the most vili-fied worldly baubles). However, Pentecostals remained distinct from fundamen-talists because of the doctrine of tongues speech as evidence of the baptism of the Spirit, an innovation too closely akin to antinomian anarchy for the guardians of a literalist evangelical orthodoxy.

The history of fundamentalism, as Margaret Bendroth shows in her chapter, suggests a similar evolution from high theology to mass cultural movement. Fun-damentalism—defined by one historian as militant and angry anti-modernism in theology—emerged originally as an intellectual movement in nineteenth-century northern seminaries, Bible institutes, summer camp meetings, and interdenomi-national schools. The early theological fundamentalists kept alive the Scottish common-sense realist tradition once pervasive in American thought. God's will, went their reasoning, was manifest in the world; his workings were abundantly evident for anyone who would examine them using the principles of Baconian inductive science. The order of the natural world, for example, glorified the workings of the Creator, and the movement of God's spirit in the individual soul left a sensory impression that only the willfully stubborn (meaning most of mankind) could ignore.

Premillennialism, another key tenet of fundamentalist doctrine, originated in the nineteenth century among conservative English theologians who schematized the world's history into seven "dispensations," or discrete periods leading to the millennium. They prognosticated that the return of Jesus to gather up his disciples would precede a time of tribulation and Armageddon, speeding human history to a catastrophic end. Human history, they imagined, already had entered the concluding era of the seventh dispensation. Fundamentalists also objected to the higher textual criticism of the Bible imported from German universities, which increasingly shaped American seminary education, as well as modern modes of scientific thought such as Darwinism. Fundamentalism was not synonymous with anti-intellectualism, at least in its origins. More accurately, early fundamentalism defended an intellectual tradition drawn from eighteenth- and nineteenth-century schools of theology and philosophy against the assaults of modern theology, science, and psychology.

But "fundamentalism" as a social movement emerged in the twentieth century with the publication of *The Fundamentals*, a series of pamphlets in the 1910s that attempted to set in concrete those biblical doctrines that were not negotiable. In the 1920s, fundamentalists increasingly created fights within, and withdrew completely from, the mainstream Protestant churches. They suffered through the media debacle of the Scopes Trial in 1925, when their hero William Jennings Bryan (himself a progressive Social Gospeler in politics, even while a conservative in theology—a common combination in his era) was humiliated on the stand by the agnostic and iconoclastic defense lawyer Clarence Darrow. From the 1920s through the 1960s, fundamentalists created an entire set of institutions—nondenominational megachurches, radio stations, schools, colleges and universities, newspapers, publishing houses, and the like—and nurtured a generation of evangelical activists. Then, from the 1970s forward, they experienced their own Second Coming, first in anti-abortion activism and then through political organizations such as the Moral Majority and the Christian Coalition. Along the way, they cultivated an intellectually coherent worldview on which this conservative religious social movement could be built. Far more than the conservatives, it was the liberals who experienced a "high–low" split, as the intellectual ideas flourishing in mainstream church seminaries and religious studies programs grew increasingly disconnected from the concerns of everyday church folk.

A final example of the popularization of profound theological traditions may be seen in the spread of Asian religious ideas on American soil. American dabbling in Asian religions dates from the nineteenth century, when Henry Steel

Olcott became America's "first [white] Buddhist," and when the World's Parliament of Religions, meeting at Chicago's mammoth World's Columbian Exposition in 1893, introduced many Americans to Asian religious ideas (despite the liberal Protestant cast of the parliament itself). But it was only after World War II that Asian religions came to attract followers other than intellectuals and eccentrics. In a reverse missionary motion, figures such as the British Episcopalian intellectual Alan Watts and the Japanese priest Shunryu Suzuki instructed a growing American audience in Japanese Buddhism and Taoism. "What I saw in Zen," Watts told his listeners in the 1950s, "was an intuitive way of understanding the sense of life by getting rid of silly quests and questions." Watts delivered more than a thousand lectures and published twenty-six books through the 1950s and 1960s, teaching countercultural luminaries such as the poets Allen Ginsberg (himself interested primarily in Tibetan Buddhism) and Gary Snyder. Watts remained at some distance from Asian religious practitioners in San Francisco, where he taught, having heard too many assimilated Japanese Buddhists chanting lines such as "Buddha loves me this I know/For the sutra tells me so." Under the guidance of Shunryu Suzuki, however, Japanese Buddhism established a strong presence on the West Coast. Suzuki touted the total meditative practice of *zazen*. "The state of mind that exists when you sit in the right posture is itself enlightenment," he explained to his mostly white audience. "In this posture there is no need to talk about the right state of mind. You already have it. This is the conclusion of Buddhism."

The most recent Asian immigrants—Thais, Cambodians, and others—have brought their own Buddhist traditions (especially Theravada Buddhism) to this country. In 1999, the Dalai Lama, the exiled religious leader of Tibetan Buddhism, explained his philosophy to 40,000 interested listeners in New York's Central Park. He specifically rejected the role of proselytizer, but his celebrity presence served to make known his hopes for ecumenical peace and harmony. The scholar Timothy Tseng explores the broader story in "Asian American Religions." Spreading from intellectuals on the coasts, Asian Buddhism as expressed through its acolytes has slowly found its way into the heartland. For example, growing up in Montana, future basketball guru Phil Jackson, son of a Pentecostal minister, sought religious enlightenment beyond his narrow upbringing. He eventually found it in the practice of *zazen*, and it did not hurt his basketball game either. "The more skilled I became at watching my thoughts in zazen practice, the more focused I became as a player," he explained. Sitting *zazen* taught him to "*trust the moment*—to immerse myself in action as mindfully as possible, so that I could react spontaneously to whatever was taking place." Baseball player Yogi Berra's dictum—"You can't think and hit at the same time"—illustrates in a folk koan the same principles that Jackson brought to his championship basketball teams. His players might have been more interested in television endorsements than Eastern ways, but their disciplined yet creative playing symbolized the very virtues Jackson sought to teach. In this case, an ancient theology meshed perfectly with the triangle offense and a disciplined but gentle guru. It was a striking yet familiar combination of high theology and everyday practice. It was also an example of the intertwining of religion and popular culture of the kind Philip Goff explores in "Religion and Popular Culture."

THE SACRALIZATION OF SECULAR POLITICS AND THE POLITICIZATION OF THE SACRED

During the 1950s, as the Cold War pulled Americans into a whirlwind of fear over the possibility of nuclear devastation and the reality of ideological competition with Communists at home and abroad, the government of the United States turned to religion, a point elaborated on further by Ira R. Chernus in "Religion, War, and Peace" and Andrew M. Manis in "Civil Religion and National Identity." With a national faith, it hoped to find protection and victory. In 1954, Congress added the phrase "under God" to the Pledge of Allegiance and then in 1956 replaced the national motto "E Pluribus Unum" ("one from many") with "In God We Trust." The actions of Congress seemed to defy openly the foundations of American government. The original Constitution makes no reference to God and only one mention of religion. Article VI expressly outlaws "religious tests" for federal office-holding. For those in the 1950s who feared that the United States was fast becoming some form of Judeo-Christian theocracy, President Dwight D. Eisenhower had an answer. He sought to clarify the relationship between religion and politics with definitive ambiguity: "Our government makes no sense unless it is founded on a deeply religious faith," he boasted. "[A]nd I don't care what it is."

Attempts to place religion somehow in the middle of American politics in the 1950s without offending the diversity of faith in the nation reflected a long pattern and problem in the nation's religious history. How could religious ideas and institutions play a role in the government without jeopardizing religious and political liberty? In the realm of politics, American religion is built on a paradoxical answer to this question. The nation has sought to uphold a "wall of separation" (a phrase from Thomas Jefferson in 1802) between organized religion and the machinations of the state, while advancing itself as a moral, God-ordained country—a point explored further by Jason C. Bivins in "Religion and Politics" and Frank S. Ravitch in "Religion and the Law in American History." Perhaps even more paradoxically, the inclusion of religion in the political sphere has done as much to challenge the political status quo of racial, gender, and immigrant exclusion and discrimination as it has done to uphold these structures.

Early British settlers of the colonial era ventured to the "New World" with financial and moral concerns. The plan across the Eastern Seaboard was to create small Christian commonwealths that would stand as beacons of light to the world, convert or kill the Indians, and allow the settlers to practice their brand of Protestantism with freedom and liberty. Of course, sometimes the missionary rhetoric clearly masked outright financial greed, and "Christian" settlers showed about as much regard for the souls of Indians as they did their bodies. "Reducing" the Indians to civility often meant either Christianizing or murdering them. In colonial America, the church and state were anything but separate. Church leaders and civil leaders worked hand-in-hand to administer law, judge the innocent and the guilty, and shape the government. One could be banished from a community or executed as easily for theft as for religious dissent, a fact that many Quakers, Baptists, and any women who wanted to interpret faith publicly on their own learned the hard way. Moreover, in New England, efforts to convert local Indians to Christianity often entailed the formation of "Praying Towns" where Indian men, women, and children would be segregated into their own communities and governed by laws allegedly based on the Bible.

The American Revolution ushered in a new era in American, if not world, religion. Led by a diverse group of Deists, Quakers, and both orthodox and lukewarm Protestants, the Founders endeavored to create a nation that would somehow separate religion and politics for the benefit of both politics and religion. The Founders seemed to envision a nation in which the voice of "the people" (considered to be white men of substantial property) would rule, and not the voices of clerics or gods. While the Declaration of Independence invokes a universal "Creator," the Constitution fails to mention such a being. The Constitution makes certain, though, that "no religious test shall ever be required as a qualification to any office or public trust under the United States." But the founding generation left an ambiguous legacy. Article VI says nothing of the use of religious tests by individual states. Moreover, while the Founders avoided mention of God or even a "Creator" in the Constitution, they nonetheless imagined their liberation from Great Britain as akin to the exodus of the biblical Israelites. On July 4, 1776, John Adams, Benjamin Franklin, and Thomas Jefferson were appointed to devise a seal for the newborn United States. Franklin suggested a design featuring Moses with a background of drowning Egyptian soldiers, while Jefferson offered one with children led by "a cloud by day and a pillar of fire by night." These Founders seemed to want their religion and politics separated and linked, and Americans have remained similarly conflicted for much of the history of the United States, as Jason C. Bivins explains in his contribution.

As hard as the Founders sought to separate religion and politics, they could not stop individuals from voting their moral consciences or ministers from using their public power for political purposes. Thomas Paine and Thomas Jefferson became the bêtes noires of devout Christians. During the election of 1800, for instance, Thomas Jefferson found himself assailed by New Englanders as a "French infidel" and a "howling atheist." Then in the years before the Civil War, religion seemed to be everywhere in political life. Fueled by the Second Great Awakening, which generated mass movements throughout the United States to bring religion to bear on all of society, American politics was overhauled. Leading politicians like Henry Clay and John C. Calhoun lamented that the denominational splits of the Methodists, Baptists, and Presbyterians, which tended to be sectional divisions over slavery, would hurt national political unity. Historian Richard Carwardine has detailed how American politicians and political parties from the age of Jackson to the age of Lincoln were compelled to represent themselves as authentically religious and their opponents as immoral. Some in the new and fragile Republican Party of the 1850s boasted that they were "the evangelical party in politics."

The deep connection built between religion and politics led those without full citizenship and political rights to use moral arguments for their inclusion. Churches and Christian rhetoric were central to the proto-feminist movement of the antebellum era. Female reformers like Angelina and Sarah Grimké, Lucretia Mott, Elizabeth Cady Stanton, Lydia Maria Child, and Sojourner Truth routinely relied on religious arguments to advocate for women's political inclusion. By the end of the nineteenth century, Stanton had become so convinced that the Bible was at the root of women's political oppression that late in life she dedicated herself to revising and reinterpreting it.

This was equally true for oppressed African Americans. According to the abolitionist Frederick Douglass, the fiction of liberty contrasted with the reality of slavery constituted a political and religious problem. To the slave, Douglass contended, Fourth of July celebrations—where white Americans commemorated their national independence and existence as the handiwork of God— were a sham: "Your boasted liberty, an unholy license; your national greatness, swelling vanity; . . . your prayers and hymns, your sermons and thanksgivings, with all your religious parade and solemnity, are, to him, mere bombast, fraud, deception, impiety, and hypocrisy—a thin veil to cover up crimes which would disgrace a nation of savages." For many African Americans like Douglass, religious motivations became central to their political imaginations, especially in the light of the biblical story of Exodus. The story of the subjugation and liberation of the ancient Israelites supplied a political meta-narrative for northern and southern blacks who put their faith in God to liberate them from slavery and discrimination.

During the Civil War, religion merged with politics as never before. In his second inaugural address, President Abraham Lincoln claimed that both the North and the South "read the same Bible and pray[ed] to the same God," but did so in very different ways. Southern Confederates built their defense of secession, in part, on the pro-slavery theological consensus that God had ordained the American slave system. Several Confederate states, in addition, rhetorically inserted "Christ" and "God" into their state constitutions in an effort to improve on the original federal Constitution. In the North, Lincoln—although himself of unorthodox Christian faith—called for numerous prayer and fast days so that northerners could have God on their side. He also, as part of the Union crackdown on political and military dissent, squelched the voices of Protestant Democrats by imprisoning or threatening them. By the war's end, even Lincoln was speaking of slavery as a religious wrong that could be righted only through political and military action.

In the decades after the war, religion continued to play a powerful role in American politics. Jurists used religious ideas and concepts to decide court cases, and presidents prayed to God to determine whether to initiate wars. Oftentimes, political imperialist efforts around the globe followed missionary activities. By the time of the Spanish-American War of 1898, American Protestant missionaries were all over the world and routinely calling for the federal government to intervene in foreign lands. President William McKinley spent a night in prayer to decide whether to invade the Philippines. On the home front, a growing number of Protestant, Catholic, and Jewish religious leaders felt a deep concern with the transformation of the United States into an industrial and urban nation. Through politics, this new breed of "Social Gospelers" looked to state and federal legislation to curb child labor, to purify the nation's food, to limit the amount of alcohol consumed, and to root out vote buying, boodle, and corruption. This group of Progressive reformers sought to clean up the nation by, as Theodore Roosevelt said, battling "for the Lord."

There were limits to religion's power over politics during the nineteenth century, though. Following a congressional law in 1810 that mail in the United States would travel every day of the week and that all post offices that received mail must be open each day, some evangelicals swamped the federal government with petitions for the termination of Sunday mail delivery. To them, this was a clear violation of the biblical injunction to rest on the Sabbath. But Congress refused to bow, and it was not until 1912 that Congress determined to close all post offices on Sunday. This change, however, had much more to do with labor laws and technological changes than religious pressure. Also, in the years following the Civil War, the federal government time and again resisted petitions to amend the Constitution to include recognition of God or Jesus Christ or to proclaim that the United States was a "Christian government."

At the middle of the twentieth century, a politicized black Protestantism took to the streets in the civil rights movement. Through the efforts of the churches and religious culture of African Americans throughout the United States in the 1950s and 1960s, American politics at the local, state, and national level were transformed. Black churches served as organizational locations for marches, petitions, and civil rights planning. Black preachers became the moral voices of the nation and took an active role in challenging white supremacy in American law and government. While the doctrines of nonviolence and civil disobedience may have been based in Gandhi's teachings or those of Henry David Thoreau, biblical archetypes like Jesus, Moses, and Daniel seemed more pervasive in the hearts and minds of many civil rights activists. Perhaps the greatest political speech in American history, Martin Luther King Jr.'s "I Have a Dream" at the March on Washington for Jobs and Freedom in 1963, was not only delivered by a minister, but also based on the prayers of a black civil rights worker in Georgia.

The lessons of the civil rights movement—the use of church organizations and religious language to wield political leverage—were learned by politically conservative white evangelicals, fundamentalists, and Catholics. In the 1970s and 1980s, as part of a general backlash to the various civil rights crusades of the mid-century and to new cultural forces in popular entertainment, a new so-called moral majority of Protestants—predominantly although not exclusively white—empowered what some called the "conservative resurgence." Led by Pat Robertson, Ralph Reed, Jerry Falwell, and Tim and Beverly LaHaye, moral majoritarians used the tactics first created by civil rights activists. With grassroots organizing, marches, rallies, and political speeches in the guise of sermons, they sought to outlaw abortion, stop the teaching of evolution in public schools, reinstitute prayer in schools, and drive liberals from politics. For the most part, the moral majority supported a distinct brand of Christian politics, despising political liberals like President Jimmy Carter, an avowed evangelical Baptist, and supporting political conservatives who seemed to hold lukewarm personal faith, such as Ronald Reagan.

If there has ever been any semblance of a "wall" separating church and state in the United States, it has been either very low or moveable or porous. More often than not, it has been nonexistent. The contentious and intimate relationship of religion and American politics has continued to play a vital role in the culture wars of the twenty-first century. Should nativity scenes of Christ's birth be placed in civic spaces? Must public schools teach both evolution and intelligent design, a thinly veiled version of creationism? Should granite tablets symbolizing the Ten Commandments be placed in courthouses or outside state legislatures? Did President George W. Bush violate the Constitution when he claimed in 2002 that he would appoint only federal judges "who understand that our rights were derived from God." It may be impossible to imagine American religious history without the constant interaction and struggle of religion and politics.

IMMIGRATION, ETHNICITY, PLURALISM, AND INSULARITY

The national myth expressed in Emma Lazarus's poem "The Great Colossus"— "Bring me your tired, your poor, your huddled masses"—speaks to America's historic symbolic role as a receiver of oppressed peoples. In part, the myth reflects reality. Compared with living through the Irish potato famine or the Cossacks' pogroms in Russia, compared with hopeless poverty in rural Italy or ethnic repression in Poland, America appeared as a beacon of economic opportunity and peaceably coexisting religions. By contemporary standards, though, one constant theme of American religious history is the distrust and hatred expressed toward one group of immigrants after another: from Benjamin Franklin's distaste for "boorish" Germans in the eighteenth century, to the relentless flow of anti-Catholic propaganda in the nineteenth century, to Father Charles Coughlin's anti-Semitic screeds on the radio in the 1930s, to the attacks on Indian Sikhs mistaken as Middle Eastern Muslims in the days following the attacks of September 11, 2001. America's embrace of migrants has always been less than total. Frequently it has engendered ethno-racial nativist political movements in defense of the country's supposed Anglo-Saxon heritage. From the Know-Nothings of the 1850s to the self-styled Minutemen of the early twenty-first century, America's immigrant heritage has consistently been confronted by a grassroots nativist heritage that perceives a threat to American Protestantism and white democracy.

Taken as a whole, immigration to the United States has produced an incredibly open, dynamic, and diverse society, a pluralist wonderland that certainly compares favorably with the difficulties that European societies have experienced in assimilating much smaller numbers of immigrants. Looked at with a more focused lens, however, American immigration has produced intensely bonded and bounded ethnic communities that have worked precisely because they were not dynamic and diverse, but insular and self-protecting, as Roberto R. Treviño points out in "Religion, Ethnicity, and the Immigrant Experience." Furthermore, European immigrants have assimilated into, and contributed to, American notions and practices of "whiteness." Scholars have disagreed on whether particular immigrant groups were "whitened" over time—described by scholarly books with titles such as *How the Irish Became White* (2009)—or were, as one scholar has described Italians coming to Chicago, "white on arrival." No matter how one times the process by which European immigrants achieved the status of full-fledged "white persons," the key is that they were not black, or illegal, or permanently foreign; that is to say, they were not of African, Mexican, or Asian descent. As the historian Mae Ngai has expressed it,

> [W]hile Euro-Americans' ethnic and racial identities became uncoupled, non-European immigrants—among them Japanese, Chinese, Mexicans, and Filipinos—acquired ethnic and racial identities that were one and the same. The racialization of the latter groups' national origins rendered them unalterably foreign and unassimilable to the nation. The Immigration Act of 1924 thus established legal foundations for social processes that would unfold over the next several decades, processes that historians have called, for European immigrants, "becoming American" (or, more precisely, white Americans), while casting Mexicans as illegal aliens and foredooming Asians to permanent foreign-

ness. ("The Architecture of Race in American Immigration Law: A Reexamination of the Immigration Act of 1924," *Journal of American History* 86 [1999]: 70)

The United States was a white republic in more than just a cultural sense; it was a white republic in a strict legal sense as well. According to the Naturalization Act of 1790, citizen status was to be confined to white migrants. Complications arose in the nineteenth century with the advent of the huge Irish Catholic migration. The immigrants were indisputably phenotypically white, but they were Catholic as well, accused of being in a state of slavish subservience to Rome. Could Catholics be Americans? They *were* Americans, in ever-increasing percentages, but this did not stop the ideological ground war from raging. Protestant intellectuals and propagandists inveighed against "papism" and trumpeted the historic connection between Protestantism (in which one read the Bible for one's self) and democracy—a connection that also had racial roots when connected to the glorious heritage of Anglo-Saxons from the Magna Carta forward. Catholics, by contrast, were purportedly inherently monarchist; their very religious belief structure abrogated against democratic ideals. Besides this kind of intellectual connection of Protestantism to American democracy, both ideologically and racially, a generation of imaginative writers produced novels, imaginary "memoirs," tracts, pamphlets, and newspaper accounts of the unspeakable practices of priests, nuns, and their duped parishioners. Most famous of all was Maria Monk's grotesquely lurid *Awful Disclosures of Maria Monk; or, The Hidden Secrets of a Nun's Life in a Convent Exposed* (1836). This ludicrous fantasy, masquerading as a memoir, was allegedly produced by an escaped nun. It unforgettably set in place the classic formulation: priests secretly visited convents and impregnated nuns, whose children were then consumed in gruesome Catholic parodies of the rite of Eucharist. Such antebellum-era Protestant porn rose above its fraudulent origins precisely because it encapsulated the darkest fears of the still-present, if already declining, Protestant majority. More serious than such Protestant fantasy fulfillment were anti-Irish and anti-Catholic riots that rocked urban life in the antebellum North.

The end result, as was often the case with numerous ethnic-immigrant groups in American history, was to create ethnic and communal-national bonds even when those might have been weak, or even nonexistent, in the past. The consistent pattern was that European immigrants who identified by region or some sub-ethnicity increasingly assumed nationalized identities within the context of a diversifying America. "Italians" often became "Italians" in America, where an appellation such as "Bolognese" or "Milanese" would not have registered, and where workers of Italian ancestry banded together in search of economic opportunity and to build institutions (including churches) that could serve their community. The same held true for Germans in Pennsylvania in the eighteenth century, who recognized their "Germanness" far more in America than in their more provincialized home identities. The same held true even for involuntary immigrants, for that matter, as Africans of diverse backgrounds learned to recognize themselves as "Africans" rather than as hailing from some particularized locale or ethnicity. The same, arguably, is under way today with Middle Eastern migrants, who can more easily transcend intra-Islamic divisions (Sunni, Shi'ite, Sufi, and others) when faced with the reality of attacks on mosques in American cities, or with the humiliations of trying to make it through airport security or answer periodic evangelical outbursts at their "evil religion," as detailed further in Jane Smith's "Islam in America."

The same immigration patterns that have internationalized the populace of the United States, then, have also fostered ties of communal ethnic identification. Nowhere is this more the case than with religious expressions. Through much of American history, believers from diverse religious traditions and of various ethnic and national backgrounds defined their religious expressions within, or against, or outside the implicit white Protestant norm. Sometimes this has meant hiding or denying particular religious practices or belief in order to protect them, a response familiar to Native Americans. This has also been a common practice of African Americans, whose religious expressions elicited fear among white slavecowners and others who sometimes perceived their elusively subversive messages.

At other times, this communal ethno-religion has meant cultivating a religious form drawn from the homeland but given a special place of prominence that had never been the case originally. One may look, for example, at the celebration of the Madonna of 115th Street, which drew on Italian roots but took on a meaning for New York Italians that it could never possibly have in a more provincial, less alien setting. The adoration of Our Lady of Charity in Miami, the Virgin who tends to the suffering of Cuban Catholic exiles from Castro's regime, speaks to how religious practices become tied to political struggles. In this case, Cubans looked to "our lady of the exile" for a spiritual home even as they created a network of successful institutions in the United States. One also thinks of Old World religious systems, such as Buddhism, whose practitioners sometimes devoted themselves to the oldest and most venerated of Buddhist schools, and others who created new Buddhist organizations unknown before American immigration. The advent of Reform Judaism in the United States also illustrates the adaptation of immigrant religious mores to American realities. Strict Sabbath laws had to accommodate urban lives in an industrial society.

Immigration is at once the source of American religious diversity, dynamism, and insularity. Further, because the relation between ethnic identity and religious practice is often so close, and because religions tie people to regional and national self-identities, immigrant religions have reinforced communal bonds, even as they have expanded ideas of what it means to be American.

REGIONAL HOMOGENEITY AMID
NATIONAL DIVERSITY

While diversity and even pluralism are the hallmarks of the contemporary religious landscape viewed nationally, local and regional realities often appear very differently. That is to say, if the national story of American religion is diverse and pluralistic, local communities often look much more homogeneous. In American religious geography, locale and region matter. Environment matters too, perhaps most especially in the American West, where the sheer grandeur of the natural geography has always invited a religious language to describe it, as Lynn Ross-Bryant details in "Religion and the Environment."

Atlases of American religion document this historic pattern of local and regional homogeneity set amid national diversity. We emphasize the point about localism and regionalism in American religious geography precisely because it is too often forgotten in discussions of pluralism. America is a pluralist society, and yet historically most Americans have not lived in pluralist regions or towns, or even neighborhoods. There are plenty of exceptions, of course, but the exceptions highlight the rule. Not surprisingly, religious folk typically tend to overestimate the size and influence of their own particular religious group, precisely because that's mostly who they encounter in religious settings. Even earlier historians of American religion, largely trained in New England colleges and universities, focused almost exclusively on New England Protestantism.

Regional homogeneity amid national diversity is a direct heritage from the patterns of colonial settlement, the practices of overland migration, and the recent trends of immigration. In other words, immigration and migration patterns through American history often have reinforced the predominance of one religious group or another on a street or in a neighborhood, in a particular city, in a state, or throughout a region. It is no accident that Utah in general and Salt Lake City and its environs in particular are called "Zion" by many Latter-day Saints, no more so than Garrison Keillor's fictional Lake Wobegon is chock full of Lutherans and that "Southie" in Boston is as synonymous with Irish Catholicism as the North End of Boston is with Italian Catholicism; suburban Colorado Springs with conservative white evangelicals; Dearborn, Michigan, with Muslims; Amite County, Mississippi, with black Baptists; or blocks and blocks of Chicago with Polish Catholics. The list could go on indefinitely, but the point is clear: most Americans historically have not experienced religious pluralism in their everyday lives. Instead, they have tended mostly to live and worship with those who look, live, and worship like them.

In terms of regional patterns of religious identification, the South may serve as the best example. According to the American Religious Identification Survey

(ARIS), the South stands as having the highest percentage of churchgoers within the region who affiliate themselves with Baptists (23.5 percent), Presbyterian (3 percent), and black Protestant (14 percent, well over half of whom are Baptists). No other region comes close in terms of Baptist affiliation statistics. The Evangelical Belt of the South is, in very many counties, effectively a Baptist Belt as well. One may compare the presence of Baptists in the region with the figure of 5.7 percent of Baptists in the region of New England and a national low of 3.8 percent in the Coastal Northwest. Moreover, in the ARIS data, the South has the lowest count of those who responded "no religion" when asked generally about their religious beliefs and affiliations (10 percent in the region), and nearly the lowest count for white Catholics (9.7 percent of churchgoers in the region).

This is not to suggest that evangelical Protestantism has a uniform dominance across the South. On the contrary, evangelical Protestant adherents as a percentage of the population are heavily concentrated in particular regions and counties, numbering especially heavily in a broad swath that cuts directly through the historic cotton country and some upcountry regions of the Old South. This is why the term "Evangelical Belt" is apt, for Evangelical Protestant dominance measured by county does look very much like a belt when mapped on a county-by-county basis (albeit with a considerable belly overhang in regions of the Upper South).

A contrast of two southern states in 2000 makes this point clearly. In Mississippi that year, Baptist adherents (excluding historically African American Protestants) numbered 34 percent of the total population, and historically African American Protestants accounted for another 29 percent of residents of the Magnolia State. Just over 16 percent of Mississippians were "unaffiliated" or "uncounted." Jews existed in too small a number to form even a 1 percent slice on the pie chart. Some counties of Mississippi actually registered 0 percent reporting "unaffiliated" or "uncounted." In Amite County, Mississippi, for example, 44 percent of the population described itself as Baptist, and 42 percent were adherents to historically black churches. With Methodists at 5 percent and Mormons racking up a surprisingly high 4 percent of the county's population, Amite County stood as one of the most religious counties in the entire country, with virtually every individual recorded as being an adherent of some religious tradition.

In Virginia, by distinct contrast, almost 50 percent of the population surveyed in 2000 went into the "unaffiliated or uncounted" category—a larger percentage than the country as a whole. Baptist adherents, excluding historically African American churches, counted for 12 percent of the state, a figure approximating the national average (in contrast to much of the rest of the South). The religiosity of Amite County, Mississippi, stood off against the relative indifference of Albermarle County, Virginia. The county that includes Charlottesville and the University of Virginia as its centerpiece ranked unusually high, by either regional or national standards, in the category of "unaffiliated or uncounted," almost 64 percent of its population. Baptist adherents made up only 8 percent of the population, and black Protestants just 3 percent. On the whole, Albermarle County looked in 2000 more like the Pacific Northwest or other regions of high levels of indifference than it did most counties in the South.

In short, the South's religiosity is relatively high, but varies considerably by region. There is a clear "historically black Protestant belt," and one equally clear for an Evangelical Belt. Mapping the two together, one finds an almost exact parallel in the Deep South states to the historic region of southern staples: cotton and tobacco. The Evangelical and Black Protestant belts cut a wide swath through the Deep South and then, nearing the coastlines and reaching into the northern half of Virginia or the lower half of Florida, fade from view almost entirely.

Recent trends in immigration (explored further in Roberto R. Treviño's "Religion, Ethnicity, and the Immigrant Experience") may spell a gradual diminishing of these historically homogeneous locales and neighborhoods. The flood of Latino migration to historically white and black Protestant towns in the South serves as one example. Tens of thousands of Vietnamese refugees just north of the capitol in Oklahoma City, the influx of Middle Easterners seeking opportunity in Michigan towns, Hmong migrants fishing in the lakes of Minnesota, Cambodian refugees shucking oysters on the Gulf Coast, and Latino laborers staffing the carpet factories in Dalton, Georgia, serve as examples.

The challenge for the American religious future is whether heightened diversity within particular communities, as opposed to pluralism when averaged out over a national scale, will lead to a peaceable kingdom or increase suspicion. The historic repression of minorities, and minority faiths, would not seem to augur well in that regard, nor does the racial profiling of Arabic- or Middle Eastern–looking peoples after September 11, 2001. For much of American history, though, de facto diversity has been corrosive of the most extreme forms of intolerance. In this sense, perhaps America yet can live up to its pluralist promise. The final essay in this volume, Jane Smith's "Islam in America," provides reason for hope that the pluralist promise is capacious enough to extend even to the most recent immigrant groups, who practice a religious faith reviled and slandered by many Americans.

We hope this brief exploration focusing on the paradoxes and contradictions of the American religious experience will serve to introduce readers to the richness of study in this field. Americans historically have been, and remain today, among the most religious people of the Western world. Certainly, the religiosity of Americans stands in striking contrast to the relatively low rates of religious adherence (and interest) in the United Kingdom, Sweden, and most of Europe. But the point goes beyond measuring rates of religious adherence or church membership, for Americans use religious language in a casual way and live in a culture suffused with religious themes. The free market of religion in the United States, protected by the Constitution and practiced in the daily spiritual quests of Americans, means that groups use persuasion to attract and hold converts. Religious traditions in America coexist in an environment of toleration and competition, of entrepreneurial drive and theological innovation, of diversity and multiplicity.

We hope this book may be successful in introducing the reader to the broad contours of religion in American history, in providing resources and guides for students and others, and in paving the way for further inquiry.

1. COLONIAL ENCOUNTERS

In 1528, three Spanish Catholics and an African wandered through the American Southwest, visiting Native American villages and performing religious healing rituals that astonished their Indian hosts. The three Spaniards—Álvar Núñez Cabeza de Vaca, Alonso del Castillo, and Andrés Dorantes—along with Dorantes's Moroccan slave, Estebanico (who was possibly a Muslim convert to Christianity), had been part of a failed 1528 Spanish attempt to permanently settle La Florida. After being captured and enslaved by the Apalachee Indians, a small group of Spanish soldiers escaped and, in a precariously rigged raft, sailed their way across the Gulf of Mexico, where they shipwrecked on the coast of present-day Texas, near Galveston. The only survivors of the shipwreck, this foursome meandered their way for eight years through Indian territory, hoping to be rescued by Spanish explorers. At the mercy of the Natives, who saw them as powerful shamans, or holy men, Cabeza de Vaca and his companions were thrust into the position of religious healers. Cabeza de Vaca later described how, at the Indians' insistence and instruction, the foursome performed their healings by "making the sign of the cross on the sick persons, breathing on them, saying the Lord's Prayer and a Hail Mary over them, and asking God our Lord, as best we could, to heal them and inspire them to treat us well." Their prayers were reportedly so effective that grateful Natives brought baskets of prickly pears, pieces of meat, and bows and arrows to the men.

This unexpectedly early collision of people, cultures, and religious practices from three continents brings to the fore myriad questions about the traditional narratives of religious encounter in colonial America. Building on a Protestant historiography dating back to at least the nineteenth century, historians for most of the twentieth century gave Protestantism—particularly reformed Protestantism—center stage in the story of early American religious history. Starting in the mid-twentieth century, however, emerging trends in historical writing that borrowed from ethnohistory, anthropology, and the new social history opened up new kinds of questions that, while not completely de-centering reformed Protestantism, made it difficult to responsibly narrate the history of religion in America without recognizing the incredible diversity of religious experiences, beliefs, and practices in the colonial period.

In more recent years, with the growth of the wider Atlantic world as a serious field of inquiry, historians of race, economics, empires, and commerce have forced historians of religion in America to widen the scope of their field of vision and ask different kinds of questions. To adequately account for the religious diversity present in colonial America, scholars have broadened their traditional geographical boundaries to include New France, New Spain, the Caribbean, and even Africa, and have enlarged their chronological scope to include the traditions of pre-Columbian Native Americans and the vibrant and diverse religious worldviews that Africans brought to the New World in the holds of slave ships, which included a fascinating blend of African traditional religions, Islam, and (in some cases) loosely adopted Catholic rituals. This enlarged geographical and chronological focus has coincided with other interests in religious rituals, religious healing, slavery (African and Indian), conversion, and the persistence of culturally integrated, co-created "borderlands," or culturally mixed areas of settlement, all across the Americas.

Scholars following this vein of thought have identified an intensely diverse tri-racial society that emerged in the opening decades of European colonization on the North American continent (Africans were in Virginia before the Pilgrims landed in Plymouth, for example) and grew exponentially in the decades leading up to the Revolutionary War as Swedish, Dutch, French Huguenot, Scots-Irish, German, African, and, of course, English men and women of the more traditional variety swarmed through the port cities of British North America and poured into the colonial backcountry—areas, that is, largely occupied and claimed by Native Americans—taking with them their diverse and distinctive religious idioms and practices.

One of the most salient features of the religious encounters in the colonial period is the seemingly incessant friction between and within specific religious groups. These disagreements, often originating in social, cultural, and theological circumstances, resulted in ongoing cycles of schism and the creation of new subgroups and denominations. Although the question of just how religious colonists were (and how that religiosity should be measured) continues as a point of contention among historians, scholars have often noted the striking contrast between the rise in church affiliation from the eighteenth into the nineteenth century in the colonies and the decline in membership experienced by European churches at precisely the same time. Historians have often cited various possible explanations, including the lack of a state church in the colonies, the ongoing attraction of European religious dissenters to the region, and the general voluntary and grassroots nature of religious associations. It was this populist, voluntary, and endlessly dissenting and dividing character of religious adherence in America that made the colonies a uniquely religiously diverse place.

Historians of religion in early America have often utilized differing strategies for understanding the various kinds of religious encounters that took place. Successful strategies include looking at a particular region, such as New England; a specific denomination, like the Baptists or Anglicans; certain immigrant groups, like the Scottish Presbyterians or German Moravians; an outstanding individual, such as the German Lutheran leader Henry Melchior Muhlenberg; or the co-created worlds of the borderlands that might have involved diverse groups of Indians and Europeans. Each of these approaches has much to offer and has led to important contributions on the issue of religious encounter in the colonial period. Over the past decade, another helpful lens has been that of "lived religion," which takes as its overall point of departure the premise that the religious lives of people are far more complex than might be represented by affiliation (or not) with more "official" organizations, denominations, or systems of thought. Shying away from an overly cerebral definition of religion as simply an intellectual assent to particular theological doctrines, lived religion tends to look at the ways farmers and housewives, ministers and magistrates, sailors and slaves, lived out their religious ideas in ways that reflected, in the words of David D. Hall in his introduction to *Lived Religion in America: Toward a History of Practice*, "the tensions, the ongoing struggle of definition, which are constituted within every religious tradition and that are always present in how people choose to act" (xi). In this model, change is constant and any synthesis is provisional. A lived religion approach also cautions against isolating something called "the religious" from the rest of ordinary life for colonial men and women. All "Americans"—newcomers and original inhabitants alike—felt a certain affinity with practices, idioms, and ideas that were simultaneously cultural and religious. "Religious encounters" in the colonial period, then, should be seen as ongoing processes that tugged at an intricate package of values, beliefs, and practices that encompassed the totality of individuals' lives and experiences.

From the perspective of the hundreds of distinct sociolinguistic groups of Natives that were spread over the full expanse of the North American continent prior to 1492, the encounter with Europeans was full of religious meaning. Many, like the Natives who lived along the Hudson River in 1609, were astonished by the sight of massive European ships, which they took to be floating islands, and Europeans themselves, whom they often viewed as "Mannittoo," or supreme beings. Dozens of such "first encounter" stories were recorded by Europeans and disseminated around Europe. Within Native communities, too, first encounter stories were passed down through the generations and occasionally recounted to European missionaries centuries later, as when the Moravian missionary John Heckewelder was told by a Delaware a detailed version of the first Dutch and Lenni Lenape meetings in the 1610s.

Similarly, Europeans brought with them heavily Eurocentric frameworks of religious orientation informed by specific branches within Western Christianity, and often—especially prior to the Protestant Reformation in the sixteenth century—defined specifically with oppositional reference to Jews and Muslims, who seemed dangerously close to controlling parts of Europe. Narratives of the religious history of North America have begun to recognize the multiple religious voices that colonization in North America—taken in a wider perspective—brought. The first permanent European colony on the North American continent was St. Augustine in La Florida, established by the Spanish in 1565, a full forty-two years before the founding of the first permanent English settlement in North America at Jamestown (Virginia) in 1607. And even as English adventurers and indentured servants were weathering disease and starvation and warring with the local Powhatan in Jamestown, two other major and permanent sites of settlement were being established in 1608, one by the French on the banks of the Saint Lawrence River in present-day Canada, called Quebec City, and the other by the Spanish just off the banks of the Rio Grande in present-day New Mexico, named Santa Fe. From this continental perspective, the origins of permanent European settlement in North America were overwhelmingly Catholic, with settlements by European Catholic empires outnumbering Protestant England's Jamestown three to one. From the perspective of the Atlantic world as a whole, however, the Spanish settlements in St. Augustine and Santa Fe were the northernmost points of a massive, wealthy, and politically aggressive Spanish empire in the Americas (Cabeza de Vaca and his crew, for example, to return to the opening vignette, started their journey in Spanish Cuba and after their rescue were taken to one of the hubs of the Spanish empire in the Americas, Mexico City). This geopolitical reality of Catholic European empires in North America, in fact, animated English concerns through much of the colonial period as England worked hard not just to defend claims on the North American mainland, but also to stake out claims in parts of the Caribbean. The role of the Caribbean wing of the English empire was not limited to merely the lucrative sugar islands like Barbados (founded in 1627); Puritans—who historians often assume were uninterested in questions of empire—were heavily involved in a daring Caribbean colonization attempt in the heart of the Spanish Caribbean, as Karen Kupperman has demonstrated in *Providence Island, 1630–1641: The Other Puritan Colony.*

As a result of this early Catholic colonial dominance, religious encounters between Europeans and American Indians for the first century of European colonial exploration and settlement in North America were almost exclusively between indigenous communities in particular geographical regions of North America and Catholics of all stripes—lay Catholic men and women of varying degrees of religious fervency, conquistadores and servants, commanders and merchants, regular priests and members of Catholic religious orders, and recent converts to Catholicism, including Jews and Africans. From the early *entradas* of Spanish conquistadores like Hernando de Soto, Francisco Vásquez de Coronado, and Cabeza de Vaca in the American Southeast and Southwest to the Franciscan mission towns in the panhandle of La Florida to the Recollect and (later) Jesuit missionary efforts on both sides of the Saint Lawrence River in New France, cultural and religious encounters between Old World Catholics and the regionally specific religious orientations of Indian communities figured prominently in the early colonization of the New World.

Such religious encounters often ended in either death or disappointment. One of the more tragic encounters has been poetically retold by Emma Anderson in *The Betrayal of Faith: The Tragic Journey of a Colonial Native Convert*, in which the Innu youth Pierre-Anthoine Pastedechouan was befriended by Catholic missionaries in New France, sent to Paris for intensive study, returned to his own people, and subsequently rebelled against his increasingly invasive and confrontational mentor, the Jesuit Paul LeJeune, a rebellion that ultimately ended in Pastedechouan's untimely death. Similarly, on the other side of the Saint Lawrence River, the Jesuit missionary Jean de Brébeuf lived among and sought to evangelize the Huron in New France in the 1630s and 1640s. Refusing to leave his catechumens during a period of sustained Iroquois raids, Brébeuf was captured, tortured, and executed by the Iroquois, who were so impressed with his bravery that they ate his heart and drank his blood in hopes of receiving some of his power and strength.

Not all religious and cultural encounters involved the more "official" religious showdowns mediated by missionaries, however. Indians on the coasts of North America and along the waterways winding their way into the interior of the continent encountered a constant trickle of explorers, fishermen, merchants, traders, and slavers who made regular visits for purposes of trade and exploration. Such chance meetings usually met with varied economic success but had a catastrophic demographic impact, as "virgin soil" diseases ravaged coastal and inland Indian communities in the wake of first contact, no matter how brief or sustained.

By the time the first permanent nodes of English New World settlement were established in Virginia in 1607 and Plymouth in New England in 1620, Indians and Europeans alike had had more than a century of sporadic contact and plenty of experiences with which to fashion both practical and cosmological opinions of each other. Although English and Dutch traders and fishermen had occasionally hunted and traded up and down the East Coast of North America in the sixteenth and early seventeenth centuries, in terms of permanent settlements, Protestants were latecomers to the colonial world. Nonetheless, despite this fact, and despite the presence of Spain and France on the North American continent until mid-eighteenth century (and beyond, for Spain), most historians continue to be dispro-portionately drawn to the regions dominated by English settlement, largely on the Eastern Seaboard of the present-day United States.

Even assuming for the moment that the eventual thirteen colonies should be the primary focus, in this region, too, religious diversity abounded. The English inden-tured servants and planters who first peopled Jamestown in 1607 and beyond were largely Anglican. Within a decade of the founding of Jamestown, however, Dutch traders and merchants (Protestants, too, but of a Dutch Reformed confession) laid claim to North American territory with the establishment of Fort Nassau (present-day Albany, New York) in 1614. The Pilgrims (separating Puritans, really) arrived in Plymouth, Massachusetts, in 1620, having fled first to Holland. But even as English fishing villages like Salem (1626) began to dot the American seacoast north of Plym-outh, the Dutch had already established their trading dominance among the vari-ous Indian communities along the Hudson and Connecticut rivers and around the perimeter of Long Island Sound. In 1626, four years prior to the founding of Boston, the Dutch had officially established New Amsterdam on the southern tip of present-day Manhattan, which quickly became the center of the Dutch empire in North America. By the time John Winthrop and the vanguard of the nonseparating Puri-tans established Boston in New England, much of present-day New York and parts of Connecticut were demonstrably under Dutch influence, while the French domi-nated the fur trade farther north along the Saint Lawrence. As political and religious circumstances in Old England grew undesirable, the ensuing "Great Migration" in the 1630s of 20,000 Puritan refugees flooding into New England quickly altered the demographics in favor of the English over local Indian communities, the Dutch, and the French. Despite their shared Protestant faith, the Dutch were bitter com-mercial rivals of the English, as numerous clashes revealed.

In recent years, historians have begun to recover the religious diversity even in the most seemingly homogeneous regions, like Puritan New England. Often available sources are typically not self-reflective with regard to the experiences of Puritan life among Natives and servants from Africa and/or the Caribbean. But glimpses of the daily rhythms of religious encounter can be seen in the texts, whether in the passing references of the General Court in Boston, which note the arrival of French Huguenots, or in the anguished writings of the Deerfield minis-ter John Williams, whose daughter Eunice chose to stay with her Indian captors and convert to Catholicism in the months following the 1704 French and Indian raid on Deerfield, Massachusetts.

Upon closer inspection, however, beneath the thin veneer of Puritan consen-sus a wide variety becomes evident with regard to visions for society, church, and the marketplace. Historians are perennially drawn to moments of conflict that played out in print, in courtrooms, or before church councils and involved individuals like Roger Williams, who directly challenged the church–government synthesis in the early 1630s by questioning (among other things) whether colonial governments could and should enforce religious practices, which he considered to be a matter of conscience; Anne Hutchinson, who challenged Puritan gender norms by holding weekly discussions in which she accused Boston's Puritan ministers of preaching a "covenant of works" (versus a covenant of grace); and Robert Keayne, who in 1639 was charged with "oppression," or overcharging on basic colonial imports like thread, buttons, and nails. Colonial governments had their ways of dealing with such dissidents, and Puritan New England was particularly efficient in punishing the most unrepentant in their midst: Hutchinson was excommunicated and banished, and Williams, facing deportation, fled south to the Narragansett, while Keayne was slapped with an outrageously high fine of £200 (later reduced to £100, which he grudgingly paid but never forgave). Williams remained a thorn in the side of the Puritan leadership of the Massachusetts Bay Colony by founding a new colony around his small settlement of Providence at the head of Narragansett Bay on land he purchased from the Narragansett Indians (another thing he criticized the Massachusetts Bay Colony Puritans for failing to do). Rhode Island, as Williams's colony was later called, quickly became known as a place of religious toleration and refuge, attracting the perceived religious riffraff of New England, including banished Puritans, Baptists, Jews, and Quakers. Religious freedom had its limits, however, even in Rhode Island, as later heated disputes between an aging Williams and the Quaker leader George Fox attest.

Even aside from these obvious examples of Puritan diversity, the more numerous and convincing examples of differences in religious opinion emerge in less dramatic ways, in the rhythms of everyday life and practice, as David D. Hall has described in *Worlds of Wonder, Days of Judgment: Popular Religious Belief in Early New England*. The church and court records of the Massachusetts Bay Colony are bursting with examples of individuals who—against their ministers' wishes—relied on charms and quasi-magical remedies for daily problems, practiced defensive magic, and otherwise sought to both control and shape their enchanted world. Similarly, colonial diaries are filled with all manner of Puritan orthodoxies and heterodoxies that continued undetected in the lives of ordinary men and women. At a more basic level, deviant New Englanders stole cattle from their neighbors; sold guns and ammunition to local Natives; abandoned their spouses or fathered children with consorts, Indians, or slaves; and sold corn, lumber, and their own labor for higher than the deemed market value.

All of this serves as a reminder that New England was not simply a "Puritan" colony. Throughout the seventeenth century, English Quakers, Anglicans, Baptists, Anabaptists, Huguenots, and, of course, a wide variety of "horseshed Christians" (to borrow another term from *Worlds of Wonder*) who cared little for the rigors of Puritanism trickled into the Northeast, at times provoking direct confrontation with New England authorities. Legislation in Puritan colonies was designed to forcibly encourage these religious outsiders to conform. Quakers often fared the worst, suffering imprisonment, confiscation of property, brandings, whippings, and—for especially unrepentant repeat offenders like Mary Dyer—hanging on Boston Common.

New England Puritans—like other New World settlers—had to also decide how to deal with the numerically reduced but militarily and politically significant Indian nations in close proximity to their towns and farms. Although early letters, diaries, and reports from Pilgrims and Puritans alike demonstrate the potentially amicable relationship many colonists had with local Natives, evangelization of these perceived heathens in their midst received no sustained attention for several decades. Instead, within six years of the founding of Boston, the Puritans had decimated one of the most powerful chiefdoms in the region, the Pequot, killing 700 Pequot women, children, and old people in one particularly brutal attack. The bloody Pequot War, as this conflict has often been termed, shocked sponsors in Old England and other neighboring Indian nations alike. Not all colonists agreed with this policy, and, as Richard Cogley has argued in *John Eliot's Mission to the Indians Before King Philip's War*, most Puritans practiced an "affective" evangelism in which they hoped that their own good examples and beliefs might attract the few surrounding Natives who actually got close enough to observe the rhythms of Puritan religious life. Intentional evangelism eventually got under way in the 1640s and quickly mushroomed into a well-funded enterprise, led by Roxbury minister John Eliot and the Society for the Propagation of the Gospel in New England and Parts Adjacent (often called the New England Company), which was founded as a Puritan and Independent missionary society in London in 1649. Between 1644 and 1675, Eliot produced dozens of Indian-language books and tracts (including the entire Bible in 1663), founded fourteen Indian "Praying Towns," and boasted well over a thousand "Praying Indians" in Massachusetts. Thomas Mayhew Jr. had even greater success on Martha's Vineyard, and others labored on Cape Cod. In 1674, the New England Indian missionary enterprise was by far the largest and most successful anywhere in the English colonies, with as many as 4,500 Christianized Indians between Massachusetts and Plymouth Colony combined.

Such sustained cultural contact often provoked indigenous revolts that included varying levels of explicit religious motivation. Virginia experienced the deadly Powhatan Uprising in 1622; in New England, an intertribal Indian uprising known as King Philip's War (1675–1676) ravaged the New England colonies and temporarily set back the evangelization project (fourteen Praying Towns in Massachusetts were reduced to four, for example). The ambiguous place of Christianized Indians in larger colonial society was tragically demonstrated in the way in which Praying Indians around New England were mistrusted by Indians and colonists

alike and targeted for violence. At the height of the war, 500 of these Christianized Indians were rounded up and placed on Deer Island in Boston Harbor to
weather a long New England winter with insufficient housing, food, and clothing. In the American Southwest, a century of Spanish occupation and oppressive Franciscan mission towns triggered the Pueblo Revolt in 1680. Despite these
tangible evidences of Indian resistance, neither missionaries nor empires gave up.
Franciscans eventually returned to Santa Fe, and the New England Company
continued to fund book translations and missionaries for northeastern Algonqui-
ans in the decades following King Philip's War. Although many individual Indians
joined Anglo-American churches in the Great Awakening of the 1740s, in many
cases these same Indians later abandoned English churches for the more informal
Indian-run churches on reserved lands and adapted Christian practices for their
own purposes.

Outside Puritan New England, new and existing colonies greatly increased the
religious diversity of the seventeenth century as well as the potential for religious
conflict. New Amsterdam (present-day New York City) was quickly becoming one
of the most diverse nodes of colonial settlement, in part because of relatively tolerant
Dutch religious policies and New Amsterdam's connection to its Old World urban
namesake, Amsterdam. With Amsterdam the trading center of the Atlantic world in
the early seventeenth century—having eclipsed the English, Spanish, Portuguese,
and French in terms of its international empire of trade—people from almost every
portion of Europe and beyond passed through Old World Dutch cities, often en
route to other destinations in the far-flung Dutch empire. The Dutch, in fact, completely dominated the colonization of the Mid-Atlantic region in the early decades
of the seventeenth century, including present-day Delaware, New Jersey, and New
York. Thousands of Dutch immigrants poured into these regions, particularly the
area surrounding New Amsterdam and the lands along the Hudson River extending
northward to present-day Albany. Dutch settlement extended eastward onto Long
Island as Dutch merchants, families, and ministers bought land from local Natives
and set up towns, churches, and trading houses. By 1655, at the same time Boston
was enforcing its New England Way and flogging Quakers and other dissenters,
New Amsterdam was, in the words of the Dutch minister Johannes Megapolensis,
teeming with "Papists, Mennonites and Lutherans among the Dutch; also many
Puritans and Independents, and many Atheists and various other servants of Baal
among the English." Added to this blend was a group of recently arrived Jews, who
came to New Amsterdam from Dutch-controlled Brazil in 1654 (having fled first
from Spain to the Netherlands and then to Brazil) and quickly set up a congregation of worship; Megapolensis feared that the Jews had "no other aim than to
get possession of Christian property." Omitted from Megapolensis's description, of
course, were the regional Indians who came to the city to trade and barter, and free
and enslaved Africans who arrived in Dutch trading ships from the Caribbean and
the coasts of West Africa.

A little farther south along the Eastern Seaboard, the founding of Maryland exemplifies precisely the ways religious differences intertwined with issues of religious affiliation and class. Maryland was settled in 1634 on land purchased from local Indian tribes by descendents of the English Catholic George Calvert and approximately 150 immigrants, who included several dozen Catholic gentlemen, two Jesuit priests, and dozens of Protestant servants. Although it was founded as a place of Catholic refuge (as Pennsylvania was to become later in the century for Quakers), from the beginning the Catholics could not agree on how "Catholic" the colony should become (and, indeed, it was the only English Catholic colony). The Calverts and many of the gentlemen preferred private, household Catholic worship, while some of the gentry and the Jesuit priests preferred a more public and exclusive organization. Despite the trickle of settlers into Maryland, Catholics never constituted a demographic majority, and in 1649 the Protestant planters, farmers, and servants forced the Calverts to make concessions to the clearly Protestant majority.

Meanwhile, in smaller enclaves along the Delaware River in present-day southwestern New Jersey, some Swedish colonists—largely Lutheran—settled a few towns on Lenape Indian land. New Sweden, as it was called, officially founded in 1638, proved to be a relatively short-lived experiment, and in 1655 the neighboring Dutch subsumed the colony into its own expanding North American holdings.

The classic model for colonial diversity, however, is Pennsylvania. It serves as something of a case study for one major theme of this book: (in)tolerance, diversity, and pluralism. Founded in 1682 by the ardent Quaker William Penn as an intentional "holy experiment" and a place of refuge for ethnic and religious communities from Europe, Penn's commonwealth quickly exceeded the diversity even he envisioned. Penn early advertised his colony in England and throughout Europe and labored tirelessly to ensure that well-oiled mechanisms of governance were in place to deal with what eventually became a tidal swell of immigrants drawn to the religious freedom and fertile lands of eastern Pennsylvania. In the first few decades, English Quakers and a variety of German immigrants flooded into Penn's new colony. Lutherans, German Reformed, Moravians, German Baptists, Mennonites, Amish, Schwenkfelders, and Catholics each entered through Philadelphia and set up smaller ethnic communities in the rich farmland on the outskirts of what was quickly becoming a major East Coast metropolis. The tenor of the commonwealth was captured by Peter Kalm, a Swedish naturalist, who reported in 1748 that Philadelphia was a place "quite filled with inhabitants, which in regard to their country, religion, and trade, are very different from each other." Furthermore, anyone who acknowledged God was "at liberty to settle, stay, and carry on his trade" in Philadelphia, "be his religious principles ever so strange." Pennsylvania's relative freedom and diversity attracted the religiously fervent and indifferent alike, producing in the mid-eighteenth century the unlikely mutual admiration and friendship of the Anglican revivalist George Whitefield and the Philadelphia printer, inventor, public intellectual, and humanist Benjamin Franklin. Penn's fabled good dealings with Indian nations also attracted Native refugees from surrounding colonies who saw in Penn's "holy experiment" a possible escape from ongoing land encroachment and mistreatment.

Historians have long neglected religion in seventeenth-century Virginia. And compared with the religious flourishes of the Puritans in New England, or the devotionalism of Pennsylvania's Quakers, the rough, materialistic workaday world of tobacco-obsessed Virginia seemed unconcerned with religion. The Anglican Church agreed and tried with little success in the first hundred years to change it. The lack of well-organized towns and the spatial separation of tobacco plantations strung out over hundreds of acres made for difficult regulation on all fronts, and ministers found it equally hard to maintain workable parishes for much of the seventeenth century (a fact that was exacerbated in part by the lack of effective Anglican organizational leadership—like bishops—in the colonies). In the eighteenth century, however, as Lauren Winner has shown in *A Cheerful and Comfortable Faith: Anglican Religious Practice in the Elite Households of Eighteenth-Century Virginia*, planters and their families practiced Anglican rituals at home, following a calendar of domestic life that implanted a lived religion in the homes of people who may or may not have spent much time in church pews.

Very quickly in the seventeenth century, Virginia became the most intensely tri-racial of the early colonies, and perhaps the most ripe for religious encounters of all kinds, as historians have only recently begun to uncover. Virginia might have lacked missionaries, but tens of thousands of Indians around Jamestown called the region home. Similarly, African slaves first arrived in 1619 on a Dutch merchant ship, and by mid-century the African population began growing exponentially as indentured labor became increasingly scarce. No discernible attempt was made to evangelize the tribes of the Powhatan confederacy around Jamestown, although—like in New England—over the course of the seventeenth century colonists waged several wars against the Natives and provoked a devastating Indian uprising in 1622. Planter patience for the more measured Indian policy pursued by royal governors after 1624 ran out in 1676 as Nathaniel Bacon led a revolt against Virginia's governor William Berkeley.

Although many Euro-American observers in this time period believed blacks to profess no discernible religion (in part because, as had been true in the case of American Indians, colonists were rather impatient interpreters of "inferior" cultures), in fact Africans brought with them a wide variety of religious backgrounds, including African tribal religions, Islam, and varying versions of Christianity. Particularly after the 1650s in Virginia, when legislation began to more explicitly define and constrict the freedom and rights of blacks (through mid-century, some Africans owned land and even slaves on Virginia's Eastern Shore), Virginia planters were increasingly hesitant to encourage or even allow blacks any forms of religious expression for fear that they might encourage unity and rebellion. The

Anglican priest Morgan Goodwin lamented this trend in a dismal report on the state of religion in Virginia in 1684, when he noted that ministers failed to inform the planters and masters in their congregations "of the Indespensable Necessity of Instructing and Baptizing, even those, Negroes or Indians." Quakers readily took Virginians to task for this omission and—later—faced resistance when they and other missionaries sought to evangelize the growing masses of slaves in the southern colonies.

One of the most influential sources of religious and cultural change in the late seventeenth and early eighteenth centuries was the orchestrated attempt by the Church of England to "Anglicize" what it perceived to be widespread irreligion in the colonies. The primary arm for this was the Society for the Propagation of the Gospel in Foreign Parts (SPG), founded in 1701 by Thomas Bray. Although the ostensible purpose of this ardently Anglican institution was to convert Africans, Indians, and backslidden colonists to the Church of England, it also was founded to curb the growth of boisterous independent and dissenting congregations—for which the colonies were infamous in England. Up and down the colonies, evangelistically oriented SPG missionaries and other colonial leaders seeking to strengthen Anglicanism in their jurisdictions encountered resistance to their attempts to bring people into the Anglican fold. In 1707, the Anglican New York governor Edward Cornbury had the Presbyterian itinerant minister Francis Makemie arrested for preaching without a license. From prison, Makemie contested—and won—what he perceived to be a violation of the English Declaration of Toleration of 1698. Similarly, when the SPG began sending its missionaries and educators to New England in the 1710s, Congregationalist ministers immediately resented and protested what they viewed as an intentional invasion of their parishes.

Anglican presence in New England dated back to the founding of King's Chapel in Boston in 1686, when the hated royal governor Edmund Andros created an Anglican congregation by royal fiat. The SPG's actions, however, represented a more aggressive policy. In 1763, Jonathan Mayhew, minister of Boston's West Congregational Church, protested in print the intentional strategy of the SPG ministers who would target New England urban centers where Congregational churches were in abundance and "encourage and increase small disaffected parties" in each town to attend the new Anglican church instead. So great was the perceived menace posed by Anglicanism in New England that a vocalized threat to "turn Anglican" at times prompted disciplinary actions by Congregationalist and Presbyterian ministerial associations, as the disgruntled Mohegan Indian minister Samson Occom found in the 1760s when he publicly contemplated turning to the Church of England.

SPG missionaries also faced fierce resistance within the Anglican fold when, in the early eighteenth century, they began intentionally targeting the ever-increasing slave population in Virginia and the Carolinas. Francis Le Jau, for example, who served in South Carolina's Goose Creek Parish in 1709, grew frustrated with his parishioners who refused to send their slaves to his weekly religious educational services and classes. In Virginia, many planters believed that conversion to Christianity made slaves "proud and undutiful" and encouraged "thoughts of freedom." Missionaries and ministers sought to placate planters and masters with assurances to the contrary, as did laws passed by colonial legislatures beginning in 1664 that stated clearly that conversion to Christianity did not change a slave's status. Nonetheless, Le Jau required slaves in his classes to swear two oaths declaring that, first, they were not seeking Christian instruction and baptism in order to secure their own freedom, and second, that they would abandon their polygamous practices.

Planter fears were confirmed in occasional slave revolts and rumors of riots, particularly in the 1739 Stono Rebellion in South Carolina, which had at its core hundreds of discontented Catholic Africans from the kingdom of Kongo in modern-day Angola. Furthermore, Le Jau himself recorded instances of slave converts who spoke of disturbingly vivid visions that seemed to presage a world turned upside down; these were visions very much akin to those recorded in the nineteenth century by the slave rebel and messianist Nat Turner, who saw a sign from God that led him to spark a bloody uprising in Southampton County, Virginia (discussed further in Blum, chap. 10, this volume).

Slave converts, moreover, retained an older, more radical view of Christian conversion wherein their religious status gave them rights to freedom and respect, for which they were in turn willing to fight—in courtrooms, in letters to imperial officials, and, as a last resort, in rebellions. Our language of Christian Englishmen and non-Christian Africans interacting in the Chesapeake here fails completely, for what we see instead are Christianized Afro-Virginians utilizing the levers of power to try to transform Christianity into freedom. They knew the language of power, and they spoke it eloquently and at great risk to themselves. This is clear from a recently rediscovered letter from 1723 in which a group of mixed-race slaves wrote to the newly appointed Anglican bishop, asking for their freedom based on their grounding in the Christian faith. They were, they wrote, "Baptised and brouaht up in a way of the Christian faith and followes the wayes and Rulles of the chrch of England." They complained about the law "which keeps and makes them and there seed Slaves forever." The hardness of their masters, they said, kept them from following the Sabbath: "wee doo hardly know when [Sabbath] comes," they wrote, "for our task mastrs are as hard with us as the Egyptians was with the Chilldann of Issarall." Their letter concludes with an explanation of why they did not sign their names, "for freare of our masters for if they knew that wee have Sent home to your honour wee Should goo neare to Swing upon the Gallass tree" (quoted in Thomas N. Ingersoll, "Releese Us Out of This Cruell Bondegg: An Appeal from Virginia in 1723," *William and Mary Quarterly*, 3rd ser., 51 [1994]: 776–782).

Perhaps one of the greatest areas of neglect in writing the history of religion in America concerns the great masses of immigrants who poured into the American backcountry in the eighteenth century, and the ways in which the arrivals of these immigrants altered colonial demographics and reshaped religious practices over the course of that century. Several important studies have shed some light on these groups. Leigh Eric Schmidt, in *Holy Fairs: Scottish Communions and American Revivals in the Early Modern Period*, traces the ways Scottish Presbyterian practices of a prolonged, multiday "holy fair" were brought to the New World and contributed to an emerging American revivalism in surprising ways. Similarly, recent studies of the Moravians such as *Jesus Is Female: Moravians and Radical Religion in Early America* by Aaron Spencer Fogleman reveal that distinctive Moravian ideas about Christ's blood and death and their more egalitarian views of women and society challenged established cultural and religious norms in the colonies.

Examples abound of the friction created between these newcomers and the established colonial groups. When Louis XIV revoked the Edict of Nantes in 1685 (which provided legal protection for Protestants in France), French Huguenots fled their motherland in droves, often making the arduous journey to the American colonies. As Anglicans exerted increasing authority in places like South Carolina, Huguenots (and later, rabble-rousing revivalists) became the target of protective ministers and bishops wary of "foreign" ministers operating in their parishes. Such conflicts often took on transatlantic importance, as when the Huguenot pastor John Lapierre in 1726 complained directly to the bishop of London of the ill treatment received at the hands of the Anglican minister Alexander Garden.

Similarly, when the Presbyterian Scots-Irish immigrants began flooding the Pennsylvania backcountry in the 1740s and 1750s, they quickly grew impatient with the unwillingness of the Pennsylvania Assembly (largely Quaker and pacifist) to deal forcibly with the Delaware, Nanticoke, and Shawnee Indian communities that were resisting the westward encroachment of the colonists. After the French and Indian War (1754–1763) and the expulsion of the French empire from North America failed to bring about the reduced restrictions on expansion these immigrants desired, a rowdy group of frontiersmen from Paxton County, Pennsylvania, took matters into their own hands, massacring more than a dozen friendly Conestoga Indians and marching to Philadelphia to have their demands heard.

The larger imperial context of the colonial period often framed—and shaped—religious colonial encounters. Within the colonies there might have been endless confrontations and squabbles about theology and religious practices, but when it came to colonists dealing with England's longtime Catholic rivals France and Spain, scholars have increasingly recognized an ardent anti-Catholic and—by the 1750s—an anti-Indian consensus that served to galvanize and unify the colonists. In times of crisis what Thomas Kidd terms a "Protestant Interest" eclipsed inter- and intra-colony rivalries in pursuit of a common Catholic enemy. Similarly, in the eighteenth century, when many of the Indian nations just beyond the periphery of English settlement often sided with the French and Spanish during times of ongoing imperial warfare, little justification was given or apparently needed for total warfare being waged against these Indian nations. Particularly for those colonies situated on the fringes of the British empire—Maine (an exclave of Massachusetts), New York, Pennsylvania, South Carolina, and (later) Georgia—the concern was both practical and ideological. Colonial leaders detested the ongoing French and Spanish presence, in part because these Catholic merchants, traders, and missionaries provided constant (and effective) competition for Indian furs, souls, and allegiance. More than just economic or imperial rivalry, however, at stake for many Protestants was nothing less than the triumph (or defeat) of "true" Christianity. In 1700, for example, the New York Assembly passed an act that ordered "every Jesuit and Seminary Priest missionary or other Spirituall or Ecclesiasticall person" who received their authority from Rome to leave the colony. Persons who defied this law would "suffer perpetuall Imprisonm't"; repeat offenders (should they escape from prison) would be executed.

Such threats were not mere saber-rattling. France and England were officially at war at least four times in the sixty years preceding the onset of the French and Indian War in 1763, both in Europe and in the colonies. Even in times of peace, individual colonies took decisive action against perceived Catholic threats. When the Jesuit priest Sebastian Rale set up a successful mission town among the Wabanaki in southern Maine in the early eighteenth century, Massachusetts magistrates and ministers collaborated to outperform him by sending their own rival Protestant missionaries. When these Puritan evangelists failed to draw the Indians away from Catholicism, and when Rale began encouraging the Wabanaki to assert their land rights against English settlers, Massachusetts governor William Dummer sent 208 soldiers to Norridgewock in 1724, where they razed the Catholic missionary village and killed Father Rale.

Similarly, when English and German Moravians with their mystifying blend of pre-Reformation and Protestant religious sensibilities showed up in New York and western Connecticut just a decade and a half later in the 1740s and began preaching to the Housatonic and Pachgatgoch Indians, local colonial officials, settlers, and ministers feared that these rather mysterious individuals might be Catholics in disguise, seeking to turn the Indians' allegiances away from England and toward its rival and geographical neighbor in the New World, France. In part because of the increased religious tensions caused by the Great Awakening and the heightened political sensitivity caused by preparations for King George's War (fought against France), in May 1743 two Moravians were arrested and marched fifty-two miles from Kent to Milford, Connecticut, and placed on trial for a week as the Connecticut governor and local ministers tried to figure out who in fact these people were. The trial itself illuminates the religiously contested region New England had become. Over the course of their weeklong detention in Milford, these pacifistic Moravians received inquiring visits from Anglicans, Presbyterians, Congregationalists, New Light ministers, and Indians, who alternately accused them of being Catholic, New Light, Anglican, and Quaker. The options for religious affiliation in the Awakening and post-Awakening years were proliferating; gone were the days when Puritan churches fairly effectively exerted a modicum of control over the events in their towns.

One of the greatest periods of intensified religious encounters and transformations in the colonial era, in fact, was triggered by the loosely connected and ongoing series of revivals in the 1730s and 1740s often referred to as the First Great Awakening. These revivals were part of a larger, transatlantic Protestant Awakening that involved the full spectrum of religious and ethnic groups in the colonies, including Puritan ministers of all stripes, Anglicans on both sides of the Atlantic, Quakers, Baptists, Seventh-Day Adventists, Rogerenes, Scots-Irish Presbyterians, German and English Moravians, Native Americans, and free and enslaved blacks, who came from all strata of society—farmhands as well as ministers, housewives and sailors, merchants and lawyers. At the core of the revivals were a series of questions regarding religious experience of a particular sort, mostly related to individual regeneration, or salvation. Although the most publicized revivals originated under the Puritan minister Jonathan Edwards in Northampton, Massachusetts, in 1735/1736 (building on the prior "seasons of grace" there under his grandfather and previous minister, Solomon Stoddard), historians have often highlighted the involvement of other ministers and laypeople, such as the Dutch Reformed minister Theodore Frelinghuysen in the Raritan Valley of New Jersey, who led a series of revivals in the 1720s; the Presbyterian minister Gilbert Tennent, also in New Jersey; and the Anglican minister George Whitefield, based in Old England. Whitefield's regular evangelistic preaching tours throughout the colonies from 1739 until his death in 1770 thrust a particular kind of revivalistic Protestantism not only into the colonial spotlight, but into immediate friction with ministers of established churches up and down the colonial seaboard.

Largely following Whitefield's emphasis on personal regeneration and Gilbert Tennent's call to reject unconverted ministers, lay men and women throughout the colonies began to challenge the authority of ministers and magistrates in ways that deeply unsettled colonial leaders, who believed that social order was essential for societal stability. The result was innumerable showdowns in dozens, if not hundreds, of Congregational, Presbyterian, and Anglican churches along the East Coast. Ministers who could not (or would not) produce narratives of their conversion experiences were ousted if possible; when parishioners concerned with such tests of spiritual authority failed to constitute a majority (and the power to depose the minister), collections of members separated and formed their own churches or joined other Separate or Baptist associations. Radical pro-revivalist ministers like James Davenport and Daniel Rogers forced the issue more than most revivalists, often staging public showdowns between themselves and local ministers, many of whom were moderately supportive of the revivals. In just one such public encounter, on July 26, 1741, Davenport preached outdoors to a large crowd in Stonington, Connecticut, and very pointedly suggested that one of the local ministers, Nathaniel Ells—who was present—might not be converted. The disgusted and offended Ells retreated into the nearby meetinghouse with his own less-radical supporters in tow while Davenport and his followers continued the lengthy New Light service.

The more radical aspects of the Awakening similarly drew in large numbers of Native Americans and enslaved and free Africans, who were, historians have argued, attracted to the more participatory and emotional elements of revival services, such as boisterous singing, praying, preaching, exhorting, and an emphasis on individual religious experiences (often with an anti-authoritarian tinge). Itinerants and self-proclaimed exhorters emerged from the woodwork, preaching indoors and out to any who would listen. Although some Indians and blacks eventually ceased formal affiliations with white colonial churches as the Awakening fervor subsided, for many this encounter with Christianity had long-term effects. Scholars of religion among Indians have recently focused more on the emergence of an indigenous Christianity that was deeply inflected by regional, personal, and tribal factors, and became central for some Indians' self-understanding and identity.

Although the Awakening fervor lessened in the colonies over time, the tensions between religious communities continued in waves and cycles, often sparked by the growth of certain denominations, like the Baptists and (later) the Methodists in the South, along with the ongoing immigration of Scots-Irish Presbyterians into the backcountry of Anglican-dominated Virginia and North and South Carolina. As in New England during the 1740s, such conflicts between the Scots-Irish pro-revivalists and the Anglican parish priests resulted in public showdowns, as when an Anglican minister in Culpepper County, Virginia, sat in the front row of a Baptist minister's church and after the sermon ended proceeded to pronounce the Baptist minister "a schismatick, a broacher of false doctrines," and someone who "held up the damnable errors that day" (quoted in Keith Harper and C. Martin Jacumin, eds., *Esteemed Reproach: The Lives of Rev. James Ireland and Rev. Joseph Craig* [Macon, Ga.: Mercer University Press, 2005], 10). Far from just being limited to the 1740s, the controversies raised during the Awakening resurfaced throughout the colonies over the ensuing hundred years.

The point in all of this is simply that no comparable proliferation of faiths existed in the Old World, particularly when one considers the North American mixture of European immigrant religions alongside long-standing, emergent, and diverse African and Indian religious traditions and practices. On the eve of the Revolutionary War, the colonies and the Mid-Atlantic region in particular—Pennsylvania, New York, New Jersey, Delaware, and northern Maryland—had become, in the words of historian Peter Silver, "perhaps the most racially, ethnically, and religiously mixed place in the world." The religious diversity of the American colonies was in large part a by-product of external forces (immigration) and internal factors (lack of state–church consensus and enforcement). As scholars have pointed out, the American Revolution only increased the growing traditions of individualism and anti-authoritarianism in American religions, a pattern that intensified during the early decades of the nineteenth century.

Despite all of this fresh and invigorating scholarship, many avenues of research need further attention. The first, mentioned earlier, is with regard to specific immigrant groups like the Scots-Irish, Huguenots, and myriad German ethnic groups that flooded into the colonial backcountry in the eighteenth century, particularly in the middle and southern colonies. Second, and more generally, historians of religion in America have often struggled to adequately describe and account for the masses of men and women from all walks of life who had little desire to affiliate with the more lively religious traditions in the colonies (or any religious movement at all, for that matter). Similarly, scholars are often unattuned to what might be termed the "everydayness" of religious encounter: a Dutch Reformed farmer bantering with his Anglican neighbor; a Congregational master and head of household disagreeing with his New Light Baptist African slave; French Huguenot parents pleading with their daughter to not marry her Lutheran suitor. Third, historians of religion in the colonial period continue to have difficulty giving adequate attention to the experiences of women in society and in the churches. This is especially curious considering that colonial women constituted a clear numerical majority in churches across denominations, even as they were largely excluded from leadership positions. Finally, historians have yet to satisfactorily account for the role of religion in the countless wars and armed conflicts—official or not—during the colonial period.

As a whole, however, historians of religion in America continue to ask new and interesting questions that illuminate in ever-greater detail the contentious religious landscape of colonial America. Slowly but surely, narratives of religion in the colonial period are being enlarged to include the full geographical and chronological spread of religious diversity in North America, which was present from the first attempts at colonization, as the circuitous wanderings of Álvar Núñez Cabeza de Vaca, Alonso del Castillo, Andrés Dorantes, and Estebanico among southwestern Indians remind us.

REFERENCES

Anderson, Emma. *The Betrayal of Faith: The Tragic Journey of a Colonial Native Convert*. Cambridge, Mass.: Harvard University Press, 2007.

Balmer, Randall. *A Perfect Babel of Confusion: Dutch Religion and English Culture in the Middle Colonies*. New York: Oxford University Press, 1989.

Brekus, Catherine A., ed. *The Religious History of American Women: Reimagining the Past*. Chapel Hill: University of North Carolina Press, 2007.

Butler, Jon. *Awash in a Sea of Faith: Christianizing the American People*. Cambridge, Mass.: Harvard University Press, 1990.

Clark, Emily. *Masterless Mistresses: The New Orleans Ursulines and the Development of a New World Society, 1727–1834*. Chapel Hill: University of North Carolina Press, 2007.

Cogley, Richard. *John Eliot's Mission to the Indians Before King Philip's War*. Cambridge, Mass.: Harvard University Press, 1999.

Engel, Katherine Carte. *Religion and Profit: Moravians in Early America*. Philadelphia: University of Pennsylvania Press, 2009.

Fisher, Linford D. "'I believe they are Papists!': Natives, Moravians, and the Politics of Conversion in Eighteenth-Century Connecticut." *New England Quarterly* 81, no. 3 (2008): 410–437.

Fogleman, Aaron Spencer. *Jesus Is Female: Moravians and Radical Religion in Early America*. Philadelphia: University of Pennsylvania Press, 2007.

Frey, Sylvia R., and Betty Wood. *Come Shouting to Zion: African American Protestantism in the American South and British Caribbean to 1830*. Chapel Hill: University of North Carolina Press, 1998.

Greer, Allen. *Mohawk Saint: Catherine Tekakwitha and the Jesuits*. New York: Oxford University Press, 2004.

Hall, David D. *Lived Religion in America: Toward a History of Practice*. Princeton, N.J.: Princeton University Press, 1997.

——. *Worlds of Wonder, Days of Judgment: Popular Religious Belief in Early New England*. New York: Knopf, 1989.

Hatch, Nathan. *The Democratization of American Christianity*. New Haven, Conn.: Yale University Press, 1989.

Hoffman, Ronald, and Peter J. Albert, eds. *Religion in a Revolutionary Age*. Charlottesville: University Press of Virginia, 1994.

Kidd, Thomas. *The Great Awakening: The Roots of Evangelical Christianity in Colonial America*. New Haven, Conn.: Yale University Press, 2007.

Kupperman, Karen. *Providence Island, 1630–1641: The Other Puritan Colony*. New York: Cambridge University Press, 1993.

Merritt, Jane T. *At the Crossroads: Indians and Empires on a Mid-Atlantic Frontier, 1700–1763*. Chapel Hill: University of North Carolina Press, 2003.

Pestana, Carla. *Protestant Empire: Religion and the Making of the British Atlantic World*. Philadelphia: University of Pennsylvania Press, 2009.

Pointer, Richard W. *Encounters of the Spirit: Native Americans and European Colonial Religion*. Bloomington: Indiana University Press, 2007.

Riley, Carroll L. *The Kachina and the Cross: Indians and Spaniards in the Early Southwest*. Salt Lake City: University of Utah Press, 1999.

Schmidt, Leigh Eric. *Holy Fairs: Scottish Communions and American Revivals in the Early Modern Period*. Princeton, N.J.: Princeton University Press, 1989.

Silver, Peter. *Our Savage Neighbors: How Indian Warfare Transformed America*. New York: Norton, 2008.

Thornton, John K. "African Dimensions of the Stono Rebellion." *American Historical Review* 96, no. 4 (1991): 1101–1113.

Wheeler, Rachel. *To Live upon Hope: Mohicans and Missionaries in the Eighteenth-Century Northeast*. Ithaca, N.Y.: Cornell University Press, 2008.

Winner, Lauren F. *A Cheerful and Comfortable Faith: Anglican Religious Practice in the Elite Households of Eighteenth-Century Virginia*. New Haven, Conn.: Yale University Press, 2010.

Young, Jason. *Rituals of Resistance: African Atlantic Religion in Kongo and the Lowcountry South in the Era of Slavery*. Baton Rouge: Louisiana State University Press, 2007.

2. NATIVE AMERICAN RELIGIONS

SUZANNE CRAWFORD O'BRIEN

Native North America is incredibly diverse, comprising nearly 800 distinct tribal groups, each with its own sense of history and its own cultural and linguistic traditions. Each tribe's experience of colonialism and history of religious practice has been different, deserving individual attention. And certainly such attention should not be limited to the years since colonization began—for Native people lived and thrived on this continent for millennia before the arrival of Euro-Americans. Of course, in an essay this brief, such a detailed survey is not possible. Rather, in the pages that follow I attempt to give a sense of the general shape of religious history for Native Americans since they first came into contact with Euro-American people. I focus on those events, policies, and historical trends with regional, national, or ongoing influences.

If scholarship in this area expresses a common theme, it is this: the assimilationist colonial agenda of Euro-Americans wrought havoc on Native communities, devastating their land, their languages, and their physical, spiritual, and social well-being. However, Native communities drew on their own religious traditions and worldviews in creative ways that enabled them to survive centuries of oppression and empowered them (particularly in the late twentieth and early twenty-first centuries) to revive their cultures and religious practices in ways both contemporary and traditional, engaging with Christianity and modernity while retaining central features of their indigenous worldviews.

IMPACTS OF COLONIALISM ON
NATIVE AMERICAN RELIGIOUS LIFE

The earliest Euro-American influences on Native American religious life were indirect and often preceded the arrival of white settlers. Illness spread across the continent faster than Euro-Americans did, devastating indigenous communities. By the time settlers arrived, often the communities they encountered had already been weakened by disease. Violence also often preceded settlers: as new colonies in the East pushed Native communities west, those tribes often engaged in warfare with the tribes they in turn sought to displace. The arrival of the newcomers from Europe had disrupted the political equilibrium of the continent. Native communities in the early centuries became strategic allies for the various European interests as they vied for control of the New World, and as a result fought with one another. In many instances, missions had a crucial role in such encounters.

The earliest missionaries on the continent were Roman Catholic: Franciscan missions in the Spanish Southwest began as early as the 1590s, and Jesuit efforts in New France as early as 1608. Protestant Anglo-American missionaries did not follow until considerably later, well into the seventeenth century. Particularly during these early years, missionaries served political as well as religious purposes, sent out by their colonial governments to secure the friendship and cooperation of Native peoples, and at times their alliance against other tribes or nations. French, British, Spanish, and American colonial governments employed missionaries to "subdue the savages" and to help open up land for settlement.

These early missions varied in style and method: Jesuits generally preferred venturing individually or in small groups into Native territories, where they lived among the people, learning their language and lifeways, with an eye toward building a mission in their midst, converting them to Christianity, and gradually reforming their moral lives to fit European expectations—including their approaches to family, marriage, and gender roles. Franciscan missions were large, inclusive of a church, agricultural and commercial endeavors, dormitories for single men and women, schools, and orphanages. They were generally established adjacent to a military compound, and served to pacify the Native population, with an eye toward creating docile subjects for the Spanish crown. Franciscans were extremely harsh in their tactics, punishing people who resisted them by public beatings and lock-downs, or refusing to allow them to see their families. In California, missions reduced the Native population to a near-slave status as they worked on Franciscan plantations. Early Protestant missions in New England followed yet another model. In general, the ideal was to construct "Praying Towns," ideal utopian communities, isolated from Euro-Americans, wherein Native people could be converted to Anglo-American cultural practices and values (including farming, animal husbandry, textile manufacturing, and marketing of these goods), as well as cultural norms such as the nuclear family, private property, monogamy, and sexual chastity. These early Protestant missions emphasized cultural as well as religious conversion.

Particularly outside California, the success of missions varied widely. While many converted in the early years of missionary efforts, most Native people rejected conversion, seeing little inducement to change their entire ways of life, and unable to reconcile major conflicts between Christianity and their own worldviews. There were fundamental issues that complicated the conversion of many Native people to Christianity. Perhaps most important was the fact that Native religious culture and traditions were intricately bound to the entirety of Native life. Religious life was not segregated to a particular day in the week or a particular set of rituals. Rather, indigenous religious practices were interwoven throughout every aspect of life: religious activities and symbols imbued seemingly mundane activities with meaning and empowered individuals for success in their society; this included hunting, fishing, gathering, cooking, raising children, maintaining families, governing communities, planting and harvesting crops, treating illness, or traveling. And most missionaries considered traditional modes of leadership, of family structures, of gender roles, of economy, of language or worship to be hindrances to the full assimilation and conversion of Native people. To convert to Christianity often meant severing ties with sacred societies or traditions that governed politics, healing, social organization, hunting, warfare, agriculture, and political leadership.

In addition to this, the tenets of Christianity stood in stark contrast to many indigenous worldviews and theological positions. For instance, the notion of original sin was foreign to Native people. While Native communities clearly had highly complex ethical systems, they did not weigh ethical decisions against a notion of original sin that saw human beings as intrinsically depraved. Native cultures, in fact, tended to view human beings as inherently good, inclined toward right action and balance, though certainly capable of great wrong. Likewise, the notion of a nonnegotiable eternal list of rules decreed by an otherworldly being often did not sit well with Native congregants, who regarded ethics as being dictated by the needs and well-being of the community. Monotheism also posed a challenge to Native people, who saw the natural world as being filled with powerful spiritual beings. For there to be one powerful God or Creator among many was not difficult to accept—but to reject the possibility of any other spiritual power in the cosmos was much more of a challenge, and carried with it enormous social and material repercussions.

The political position of Native tribes declined dramatically after the War of 1812. The new U.S. government adopted a policy of securing a unified nation with a single homogeneous culture. Native people were to blend into the melting pot, or be removed to make room for white settlers. Within this context, two options were available: removal or assimilation. Many government officials shared missionaries' view that assimilation into Anglo-American culture was a necessary part of this process, and in 1819 passed the Indian Civilization Fund Act, setting aside funds to assist missionaries in their efforts to "civilize" the Natives, establishing missions and boarding schools to teach Native people English, Christianity, and Anglo methods of farming and commerce. Native assimilation into Euro-American culture brought the added bonus of freeing up land for white settlement—since farming required much less land than hunting and gathering.

Assimilationist policy makers and missionaries had to contend with lawmakers who preferred the outright removal or extermination of Native people, a policy that also held sway in the federal government throughout much of the nineteenth century, particularly from the 1830s to the 1880s. Rather than emphasizing assimilation, this policy pushed for the elimination of "the Indian Problem" by simply removing the people from the land. In some places, officials tacitly condoned the genocide of local populations or even offered a $5 bounty for the heads of Native Americans, as happened during the Gold Rush era—from 1850 to 1880—in southern Oregon and northern California. Atrocities such as the Sand Creek Massacre exemplify such policies of removal. In 1864 John M. Chivington, an ordained Methodist minister and a major in the U.S. Army, took up the call of a Denver newspaper to "exterminate the red devils." At Sand Creek, Chivington attacked the village of the Cheyenne chief Black Kettle, who was in favor of peace with whites and was flying an American flag at the time. Chivington and his men murdered between 200 and 400 Cheyenne, mostly women and children, and afterward scalped and sexually mutilated many of their bodies, displaying them before cheering crowds in the Denver streets. A handful of soldiers who had refused to participate later publicized the atrocity, and Chivington was placed under investigation. He was never punished, although the government and army later condemned his actions.

The government rarely condoned such violence, preferring legislative means to remove Native people and to curtail their religious and cultural freedoms. During the nineteenth century, the government passed a series of laws supporting the forcible removal of Native people from lands deemed worthy of Euro-American settlement. The Cherokee, Navajo (Diné), and Lakota provide striking examples of this historical trend. Early in the nineteenth century, the Cherokee Nation had become known for its remarkable commitment to assimilating to Euro-American society. The Cherokee built wood-frame houses that mirrored those of their white neighbors; they adopted agriculture, owned African American slaves, a printing press, and a newspaper (the *Cherokee Phoenix*, established in 1829), translated the Bible into Cherokee, modeled their governance after U.S. structures (with Supreme Court and legislature), and abandoned their traditional gender equity for Euro-American patriarchy. The Cherokee likewise welcomed Protestant missions, mission schools, and churches. However, they also established themselves as an independent republic with claims to their traditional homeland, refusing to become citizens of the United States. After Euro-Americans discovered gold in Georgia, President Andrew Jackson signed the 1830 Indian Removal Bill into law. By 1838, the Cherokee, Choctaws, Chickasaws, Creeks, and Seminoles had all been forcibly removed from the Southeast, and relocated to Indian Territory (what would later become Oklahoma). Over a quarter of the Cherokee population died en route, a tragic moment in history known as the Trail of Tears.

By contrast, the Diné (Navajo) avoided cultural assimilation and conversion until relatively late in their history. While their Pueblo neighbors complied to some degree with Spanish authorities and tolerated the presence of Franciscan fathers, the Diné avoided contact with them, protected by their semi-nomadic lifestyle until the mid-nineteenth century, when the Diné, along with the rest of Native America, came up against the U.S. policy of establishing reservations. The Diné fiercely resisted efforts to reduce their land, until 1863, when they were forced to capitulate to the brutal military incursions led by Kit Carson. Exiled to the Bosque Redondo Reservation, the people were compelled by Carson and his troops to walk 300 miles across the desert from their home in Arizona to Fort Sumner, New Mexico. In their five years of exile, approximately one-quarter of their population died from hunger, poor sanitation, and disease, despite the army's promises to care for them. Agriculture was impossible in the arid land, and disease and hunger skyrocketed. Four years later, in 1868, the U.S. government realized its mistake, and the Diné returned home.

The Lakota provide another example of the impact of removal policies on Native life. The Lakota signed the Fort Laramie Treaty of 1868. It established the Great Sioux Reservation, which stretches across all of present-day South Dakota west of the Missouri River, and a vast unceded territory encompassing much of Wyoming, Nebraska, and Montana. When Euro-Americans broke the treaties, continuing to trespass on Lakota lands, the Lakota responded with military action, and a fierce war with the U.S. Army began. The commander of the U.S. forces, General William Tecumseh Sherman, argued before Congress for an intentional effort to exterminate the bison, the central source of the Lakota economy and a central symbol in Lakota religious life. He insisted: "Kill the bison, and you kill the Indians." The Lakota would lose much of their treatied land after Euro-Americans discovered gold in the Black Hills in 1874, and thousands of white settlers and prospectors poured into the region. Despite their illegal status, the federal government protected these prospectors, reducing the size of the Lakota reservation and forcibly confining the Lakota to new reservation boundaries. By 1880, the Lakota were living in poverty, their reservation reduced to a fraction of its original size. While they retained a small piece of their original homeland, the Lakota nonetheless suffered under the same federal policies of removal, as they lost access to the great majority of their homeland, and as a result could not participate in the subsistence practices that had defined them for centuries.

The reservation system, established between 1850 and 1880, served to meet federal agendas of both removal and assimilation. The U.S. government and its military forcibly removed Native people to reservations, and then assigned missionaries as "Indian agents," tasking them with the responsibility of teaching Native people the tools for assimilating to Anglo-American life. Separated from their traditional land bases, Native people lost access to the sacred sites and resources necessary for performing ceremonies and conducting vision quests. They lost access to subsistence resources, which had for millennia supplied their food, clothing, shelter, and medicines. Entire economies, sacred societies, and social structures were upended, even as knowledgeable elders and leaders were lost to disease, violence, and hunger. Despite federal treaties that guaranteed that Native people would have access to food, shelter, clothing, education, and medical care, such supplies often did not arrive—or arrived only to be misappropriated by dishonest reservation officials. Poverty skyrocketed on many reservations, and as a result Native religions and cultures were under severe stress: they could not continue as they had, since the traditional social, political, and economic structures and subsistence practices that had been intrinsically intertwined with religious life were now gone.

It was during the reservation era that missionaries saw the most success in their efforts to convert Native people. Indeed, many missionaries were moved by the crises of poverty, illness, and despair that were evident in these early years of reservation life. Such individuals and their backers in the federal government were reform-minded people who insisted that the best and only recourse for Native people was to assimilate to Euro-American society. They saw reservations as a temporary phenomenon, a stepping-stone on the path to assimilation. They set out to provide Native people with the tools to become American citizens: English, Christianity, agriculture, commerce, and the moral virtues of Euro-Americans. A change in governmental policies, inspired by President Ulysses S. Grant's Peace Policy of 1869, supported these missionaries. The policy sought to replace corrupt Bureau of Indian Affairs Indian agents with missionaries who would, it was hoped, be more ethical in their dealings. Grant established the Board of Indian Commissioners, composed of Christian laymen, to monitor reservation officials.

Under Grant's Peace Policy, missionaries now possessed a cadre of legal and military resources, and could enforce the elimination of traditional practices. And, importantly, Native cultures and communities were profoundly vulnerable during these early reservation years. Euro-Americans had brought epidemic diseases that decimated their communities. Many had fought unsuccessful and bloody conflicts with the American military. Confined to reservations, they had lost access to most of their traditional subsistence activities and sacred places. Poverty, hunger, and despair were rampant. Many turned to alcohol—the other tool of acculturation that Euro-America offered them. In this context, missions offered many

Native people hope, and they seized on the possibility of renewal, and of gaining the means to cope with the new world that they faced.

The Peace Policy also established a system of boarding schools, with the intention of removing Native children from their homes and confining them to mission schools that would teach them English, Christianity, and Euro-American culture. Mission schools, most of which had their tenure from the 1870s to the 1930s, had an enormous impact on Native life. Entire generations were lost, as some children, sent away from their families and communities for years at a time, returned speaking only English, in some instances no longer able to communicate with their parents. For some, the experience was positive: they valued the education they received and the opportunity to enter the white world. For most, however, it was devastating, leaving scars that Native communities are still working to heal today.

However, even under such conditions, Native people persisted in practicing their traditional faith, continually frustrating missionaries' attempts. The federal government responded with a series of laws and ordinances that gave missionaries the power to curtail Native religious freedom. For instance, the Rules for Indian Courts (1882) directed Indian agents and missionaries to actively suppress any ritual activity on the reservations, with punishments ranging from withholding of rations, to imprisonment (thirty days for participation, six months for officiating). The Indian Religious Crimes Code of 1883 reiterated these rules, mandating prison sentences and suspension of rations for Native people participating in or leading traditional ceremonies. In 1922, government officials issued Circular 1665, again encouraging agents to prohibit any traditional religious gatherings or practices.

As part of this ongoing assimilation effort, reformers envisioned transitioning Native communities from tribal communities that held land collectively to loose groupings of nuclear families, each with its own privately owned plot of farmland. As one Indian agent noted, the best thing for "the Indian" was to "give him his portion and turn him lose to work out his own salvation." This perspective led to the establishment of the Dawes, or Allotment, Act of 1887. The act divided reservation land into allotments, assigned to individuals and their families. The remainder of the land was declared "surplus" and opened for white settlement. As a result, between 1887 and 1934, Native people lost 60 percent of reservation lands to white settlers. The act thus struck another blow at the cultural cohesion on which Native religions depended.

Federal policies toward Native religious traditions would not change until 1933, when President Franklin Delano Roosevelt appointed John Collier as Commissioner of Indian Affairs. Collier established policies that sought to protect and preserve Native cultures, languages, and religions. Collier abolished the Board of Indian Commissioners, and worked to return self-governance to Native communities, through the Indian Reorganization Act (or Wheeler-Howard Act) of 1934. Collier's leadership made an end to mandatory boarding schools for Native children, terminated the allotment system, and sought to restore unallotted lands to tribes. Collier funded Native higher education and reformed the school system. Importantly, he ended the official governmental suppression of Native religious practice.

The termination and removal polices of the 1950s and 1960s interrupted Collier's reforms, however. These new policies sought to terminate tribal status and remove Native people (particularly young men) to urban centers throughout the country. Government officials saw this new policy as the solution to "the Indian Problem," which would effectively free up reservation land for white settlement and assimilate Native people into mainstream society. However, the promised jobs, training, and housing rarely appeared, and many Native people found themselves homeless in unfamiliar cities. These policies had an enormous impact on the spiritual well-being of communities, as family members suffered the damaging effects of poverty and alcoholism.

Sweeping legislation of the 1970s would resurrect the spirit of Collier's reforms. Such legislation affirmed Native nations' right to self-rule and religious protections under the constitution. The Indian Self-Determination and Education Assistance Act (1974) granted local tribes control over their health care and education. The Indian Child Welfare Act (1978) formally ended a federal policy of out-adoption of Indian children. It was not until the American Indian Religious Freedom Act of 1978, however, that the federal government formally confirmed the rights of Native people to practice their traditional faiths. After nearly two centuries of coerced assimilation and missionization, the act affirmed Native peoples' "inherent right of freedom to believe, express, and exercise the traditional religions of the American Indian, Eskimo, Aleut, and Native Hawaiians, including but not limited to access to sites, use and possession of sacred objects, and the freedom to worship through ceremonials and traditional rites." Federal policies still curtailed Native religious freedoms in many respects, however, particularly those relating to religious practice in prison or the use of controlled substances such as peyote. The Native American Free Exercise of Religion Act (1994) later ensured the right of card-carrying members of the Native American Church to participate in peyote ceremonies, and Native prisoners the right to practice traditional religions while in prison.

As this brief description of Euro-American policies toward Native peoples and religious practices illustrates, goals of assimilation and removal guided federal Indian policies between the eighteenth century and the mid-twentieth century. It was not until the 1930s that the federal government introduced a new approach: one that recognized Native sovereignty and the intrinsic value of Native cultures and religions. The late twentieth century saw a series of legal reforms that would dramatically change Native life in the twenty-first century. In contrast to this legacy of pain and struggle, this more recent history is marked by an emphasis on sovereignty, increasing economic prosperity (in some communities), and a remarkable renaissance of Native cultures, arts, and religious practices.

INDIGENOUS RESPONSES TO EURO-AMERICAN CULTURAL AND RELIGIOUS ASSIMILATION

Native communities responded in a variety of ways to Euro-American incursions on their sovereignty and spirituality. Such responses ranged from violent revolt to creative cultural accommodation, to religious revival. Violent resistance to religious conversion was relatively rare, but did occasionally occur. One example, and one of the most remarkable military revolts against a European presence in North America, was the Pueblo Revolt of 1680.

By the early seventeenth century, Franciscan fathers had begun missions in what would become the American Southwest. The Franciscans, accompanied by the Spanish army, sought to secure Pueblo territory for Spain. Seeking to "civilize" the Natives, Franciscans worked to transform Pueblo political, cultural, and religious life. In a context such as the pueblo, where religious, social, and political life are intricately interwoven, conversion to Christianity did not entail merely a shift in belief, but a radical transformation of one's approach to community, family, agriculture, politics, and social organization—and a loss of one's place within that whole. For this reason, among others, most Pueblo people declined conversion to Franciscan Christianity. Franciscan fathers, with the support of the military, took a hard line, outlawing traditional religious practice, desecrating kivas, destroying sacred masks and regalia, making daily mass attendance mandatory, and punishing those who resisted with public beatings. In 1680, after the fathers arrested sixty-seven political and religious leaders and executed three of them, the Pueblo communities revolted. The revolt was overwhelmingly successful, and drove the Spanish from the region for over a decade.

While infrequent, violent resistance did occasionally occur, such as when local tribal communities drove out missionaries they perceived as being responsible for the arrival of devastating illnesses, or who had simply imposed on the community too greatly. One such instance was the infamous "Whitman massacre" in Washington Territory. In 1847, Cayuse and Umatilla warriors killed the Whitman family and twelve others, partly in retaliation for what was seen as their responsibility for the arrival of a measles epidemic. The Indian Wars of the mid-nineteenth century are perhaps the most significant example of this resistance, as Native communities throughout the West resisted their confinement to reservations. While violent resistance did occur at times, more common by far were modes of subtle resistance to conversion. Rather than wholeheartedly assimilating to Euro-American expectations and undergoing religious conversion, communities tended to responded in two ways: by following prophetic movements that sought to revive traditional religious life, or by seeking out a creative middle ground that incorporated elements of Christianity, but did so on Native people's own terms.

Revitalistic prophetic movements powerfully shaped Native religious life in the nineteenth and twentieth centuries. They occurred throughout the country, in many tribal communities, and are far too numerous to list here. One of the earliest and best known of these prophets was Handsome Lake, or Ganiodaoi. During an era of political crisis (the Iroquois had lost their political influence with the British in the Revolutionary War), Handsome Lake called for a revival of traditional Iroquois cultural and religious practices, founding the Longhouse Religion, or *Gaiwiio*, which integrated some aspects of Christian culture but emphasized traditional Iroquois beliefs and practices.

Such movements would be found in other parts of the country as well. Around 1870, a Paiute named Tavibo experienced a series of visions and went on to form the revitalistic movement known as the Ghost Dance. Nearly twenty years later, his son Wovoka (also known as Jack Wilson) revived the movement. This Ghost Dance began in 1889, when Wovoka was near death and experienced a number of visions that directed him to instruct his people to dance a traditional circle dance. According to his vision, if the people would be faithful to dance (typically in five-night sequences), the world would be renewed, the Europeans would be sent back where they had come from, and the dead would return, along with the animals and natural resources that had been destroyed in the wake of Euro-American conquest. To hasten this day, Wovoka instructed dancers to return to a traditional mode of living, adopting traditional dress, values, and lifestyles. During Ghost Dances, individuals would enter into a trance in which they would visit with the spirits of departed relatives. These ancestors would teach visionary songs, prayers, powerful symbols, and rituals. This movement spread rapidly from Nevada, as far west as northern California, and east across the Rocky Mountains and throughout the Northern and Southern Plains. It was among the Lakota that the Ghost Dance took on a slightly militarized tone. The Lakota, still struggling against the U.S. Army, found a new hope for resistance in the movement. Lakota spiritual leaders Kicking Bear and Black Elk both had visions of sacred shirts, Ghost Dance shirts, which, when painted with the symbols from their visions, would become bullet proof, protecting them from violence. The spiritual comfort and encouragement provided by the ceremony of the Ghost Dance and the symbol of the Ghost Dance shirts enabled the movement to spread quickly among the Lakota, and throughout much of the western United States. The movement was an affirmation of the power and legitimacy of Native traditions and worldviews. Even when, ultimately, the visions did not literally come to pass, the movement succeeded in reviving Native cultures and traditions that were under attack. In this moment of extreme cultural crisis, when Native people were suffering in new reservations and struggling to recover a meaningful sense of self, the act of coming together in prayer and dance, of pooling their collective memory in visions, songs, and storytelling, worked to ensure that Native culture was preserved.

The movement experienced an abrupt end, or at least a hiatus, with the bloody aftermath of the massacre at Wounded Knee. As the Ghost Dance spread throughout the Pine Ridge Reservation, the Indian agent P. F. Wells became convinced that it would inspire the Lakota to violence. On October 19, 1890, he warned the Indian agent at Standing Rock, James McLaughlin, of this, telling him: "If you can nab him [Kicking Bear] before he can get them started you will save yourself no end of trouble. I say this because you or anyone else can have no idea how bad it takes hold of the Indians as some of our best Indians are nearly crazy over it" (quoted in Vestal, *New Sources of Indian History, 1850–1891*, 9). Fearful of potential violence, agents sought to arrest any Ghost Dance leaders, including Sitting Bull, who was killed during the attempt. Shortly after Sitting Bull's death, another leader, Big Foot, determined to turn himself in at Pine Ridge. It was winter, and his people were in desperate need of supplies. Along the way, they encountered the Seventh Cavalry, which surrounded Big Foot and his 350 followers at Wounded Knee Creek. The army instructed Big Foot and his community to make camp for the night, but the next morning, for reasons that remain obscure, the Seventh Cavalry opened fire on the community, killing more than 300 people, most of whom were women and children. The incident was originally referred to as a "battle," and its soldiers were awarded medals. After being covered in the press, however, the incident became known as a massacre and became emblematic of the violence that Native people suffered at the hands of the U.S. government during this era.

It was during this period that the famous Lakota spiritual leader Black Elk came of age. He was only five when the Fort Laramie Treaty was signed in 1868, participated in the Ghost Dance, and witnessed the aftermath of the massacre at Wounded Knee. Black Elk experienced a series of visions in his early life that prepared him to become a powerful spiritual leader, ceremonialist, and healer. He remains a significant figure not only because he was the subject of a bestselling epic narrative (*Black Elk Speaks* [1932]), but because he embodied the creative and painful process of spiritual survival that Native cultures faced in the nineteenth century. Black Elk's visions provided blueprints for powerful ceremonies that helped his people survive devastating years of poverty and cultural displacement. And yet, later in his life Black Elk would also convert to Catholicism, becoming a catechist in his local community. His life story exemplifies the way in which historical circumstance forced many Native people, particularly between the 1870s and 1930s, to live parallel lives, keeping indigenous traditions, but only privately, lest they evoke the ire of Agency officials and missionaries. At the same time, he genuinely found meaning and comfort in the Christian faith—seeing the two as complementary practices that spoke to different aspects of life. When he collaborated with John G. Neihardt in the 1930s to record his visions and life story, he remained optimistic that their work together would produce good, as quoted by Raymond DeMallie:

> At that time I could see that the hoop was broken and all scattered out and I thought, "I am going to try my best to get my people back into the hoop again," I am just telling you this, Mr. Neihardt. You know how I felt and what I really wanted to do is for us to make the tree bloom. On this tree we shall prosper . . . we shall go back into the hoop and here we'll cooperate and stand as one . . . our families will multiply and prosper after we get this tree to blooming. (*Sixth Grandfather*, 294)

The Ghost Dance did not spread to the Pacific Northwest, and many scholars attribute this to the vibrant prophetic tradition that already existed in the region. Early explorers recorded various accounts of regional and local prophets, who spoke to their people regarding the dramatic changes that they all experienced during this time. Many called for a return to traditional ways of life, and some called for new religious practices that incorporated elements of Euro-American culture, such as meeting for weekly worship on Sundays and collective prayer. In the late nineteenth century, a movement emerged known variously as the Seven Drum Religion, Longhouse Religion, Washat, or Washani tradition. Prophets such as Smohalla (Wanapum), Jake Hunt, and the more contemporary Puck Hyat Toot were instrumental in bringing this tradition to its present form. The Washat tradition is perhaps the dominant mode of traditional religious practice on the Columbia Plateau today. The tradition blends elements of older indigenous practices—such as "first foods" ceremonies that honor the first roots, berries, salmon, or hunt of the year, with traditional songs, prayers, and oratory—alongside relatively new elements, such as meeting weekly on the sabbath, an emphasis on cultural revival in the face of colonialism, and an emphasis on sobriety.

While many Native prophets responded to the threat posed by colonial Euro-America by calling for a return to traditional practice and a rejection of Christianity, some prophets called for the formation of new religious movements that drew on traditional culture, while also incorporating a belief in the Christian God and adopting certain elements of Christian ritual and ceremony. Consider, for instance, the Indian Shaker Church, which emerged in the Puget Sound region of the Pacific Northwest. By 1880, Native cultural and religious life in the Northwest had been severely disrupted. Communities had been relocated to reservations, had lost access to many of their traditional subsistence practices, and in turn had become dependent on poorly paying wage labor. Communities struggled with poverty, high rates of disease, and increasing rates of alcoholism. It is estimated that between 1805 and 1855, Native populations in the region dropped by 88 percent. Faith in traditional healers waned, as their efforts to address the physical, spiritual, and social ailments of their communities were unavailing. Native religious gatherings had been outlawed, and missionaries, whose efforts had not met with much success prior to the 1870s, began to see converts during this new reservation era.

In 1882, John "Squisachtun" Slocum died. He was a member of the Squaxin Island Nation, and three days after his death, the community had prepared his funeral. Slocum shocked the attended crowd by waking up and telling his guests that he had visited heaven, communicated with God, and been instructed to return to earth and found a new church. This new church would be for Native people alone, and would become a source of healing for them. God would send them a new medicine, he told them. Slocum instructed the people to build a church and to worship every Sunday. They were to abstain from drinking, smoking, violence, and gambling, and lead industrious lives of kindness and generosity. He also instructed the people to worship the Christian God, but in a distinctly Native fashion. The next year, Slocum became ill again, and while his wife, Mary, was praying over him, she received what would be known as the "shake," a powerful spirit that gifted her with a song, and gave her healing power. Slocum was miraculously cured. Soon after, other church members received this gift of the "shake," and the movement spread widely as followers began to offer healing services for the ill. Between 1885 and 1933, the movement expanded as far north as British Columbia, as far south as northern California, and as far east as the Columbia Plateau. The church adopted many Christian elements, such as the use of crosses, the invocation of the trinity, prayer on one's knees, and a reverence for the Holy Spirit. It also retained indigenous elements: a healing tradition and view of illness very similar to that of their ancestors, as well as a focus on hospitality, care for community, and collective well-being. Despite its Christian elements, many missionaries saw the church as a threat to their own efforts, describing it as Native religion with a thin veneer of Christianity. They exerted pressure on Shaker leaders, imprisoning them, and putting them to forced labor. Perhaps inspired by such opposition, the Shaker Church flourished. It continues today as one of the most important aspects of religious life on reservation communities throughout the Northwest.

Another important contemporary religious movement, the Native American Church, or Peyote Movement, has its roots in this historical era as well. Traditional use of peyote originated among the Huichol of Mexico, who have made use of the cactus for ceremonial purposes for approximately 10,000 years. The Lipan Apache learned about the use of the plant from the Huichol and Carrizo of northern Mexico in the early nineteenth century, and it soon became an important part of their cultural life. With the arrival of the reservation system, and the increased communication afforded by rail travel, the movement would spread rapidly throughout much of North America, particularly throughout the Northern and Southern Plains. By 1920, the movement had become firmly entrenched among the tribes of Indian Territory in Oklahoma, where the ritual structure associated with the contemporary Native American Church took shape.

The movement had two prominent prophetic leaders during its early years: Quanah Parker (Comanche) and John Wilson (Caddo). Parker taught his style of worship, the "half-moon" style (so-called because an altar of earth shaped like a half-moon is formed at the center of the ceremonial tipi), to the Osage, Pawnee, Ponca, Arapaho, Caddo, and Cheyenne nations. Wilson created a similar all-night ceremony, with significant differences—the altar at the center is different, and the ritual has more Christian elements. Despite their differences, these styles of worship share key characteristics: individuals gather in the ceremonial tipi, partake of the sacrament of peyote, and sing and pray through the night. Worship is led by a Roadman, who guides people through the service. The Roadman holds a staff and a gourd rattle, sings a series of four songs, and then leads the group in prayer. Everyone is invited to pray in turn, as the staff and gourd are passed around the circle. When the circle is concluded, attendants partake of the peyote, and the rest of the night is spent in prayer, singing, and contemplation. At dawn, a young woman arrives carrying water, which she distributes to the assembled guests. The event is followed by a celebratory breakfast. The success of the movement can be attributed, in part, to its inclusivity. One can engage fully in worship regardless of whether one is praying to Jesus, the Virgin Mary, the saints, a more abstract notion of God, or more traditionally indigenous objects of prayer such as ancestors, powerful spiritual beings, or the Great Mystery. Adherents established the first peyote church in Redrock, Oklahoma, in 1914, calling it the First Born Church of Christ. By 1918, the Native American Church was formally registered with the federal government, with a membership of 12,000. Today, the church has at least 80 chapters in 70 nations across the country. Estimates at membership vary widely, from 10,000 to 250,000.

Earlier scholarship tended to see conversion in stark terms: one either "really" converted to Christianity, or one did not. Contemporary studies of Native Christian communities have demonstrated the diverse and complex ways in which Christianity has been interwoven into Native life. For instance, as studies among the Ojibwe, Kiowa, and Tlingit have shown, conversion to Christianity did not necessarily mean abandoning one's culture. Michael McNally's study of Ojibwe hymn singers illustrates how Ojibwe elders incorporated Christian hymns into community life. Such hymns had been translated into Ojibwe in the nineteenth century, and in the late twentieth century they became a central feature of mourning on the reservation. Ojibwe elders sing the hymns in a distinctly Ojibwe way and to accomplish distinctly Ojibwe ends: to comfort the community, to affirm a connection to previous generations, and to remind the assembly of the importance of collective well-being and salvation.

Sergei Kan's work with the Tlingit provides yet another compelling case study. Russian fur traders, trappers, and early missionaries introduced Orthodoxy to Tlingit communities in the early nineteenth century. Orthodoxy's openness to traditional culture and language, and its willingness to engage in dialogue with religious leaders, earned Orthodox missionaries a cordial welcome, although Tlingit did not convert in large numbers. However, Kan argues, with the arrival of Protestant missionaries in the late nineteenth century who sought to transform Native culture and impose Euro-American ways of life, the Tlingit turned to the Orthodox Church in record numbers. Kan discusses in particular the ways in which the Tlingit transformed the traditional memorial potlatch to become part of Orthodox funeral rites, and how Tlingit parishioners integrated Orthodox traditions into previously existing Tlingit ceremonialism and celebration. The end result was that the Eastern Orthodox Church here came to be referred to as not *Russian* Orthodoxy, but *Tlingit* Orthodoxy.

CONTEMPORARY CULTURAL AND SPIRITUAL REVIVAL

Since the 1970s, Native American religious life has been increasingly defined by a revival of traditional practice, often alongside Christianity. Indigenous traditions that early-twentieth-century anthropologists thought were on the road to extinction made a remarkable revival since 1969. One excellent example of this can be found in Coast Salish spirit dancing. Traditional Coast Salish territory extends from Puget Sound in Washington State north to Vancouver in present-day British Columbia. The tradition of winter spirit dancing at longhouses was a central part of religious life for the Coast Salish until the nineteenth century, but had all but vanished by the 1950s. By contrast, when anthropologist Pamela Amoss visited the communities in the 1970s, she was surprised at the increasing number of dancers returning to the fold, a development that has continued to the present. From perhaps twenty families, the movement had grown until nearly two-thirds of the community had some form of participation in winter spirit dances. Throughout the continent, a national trend toward returning to indigenous practices—exemplified in traditions such as the Longhouse in the Northwest, the Jump Dance of the Columbia Plateau, the World Renewal dances of northern California, the Iroquois Longhouse traditions, and the Sun Dance and sweat-lodge ceremonies of the Northern Plains—has continued unabated. The Native American Church has become increasingly prominent among contemporary Native people, and a key element of the broader Wellbriety movement, which draws on traditional Native American spiritualities to enable Native people to heal from the soul wounds of colonialism and the impact of generational alcoholism. Today, many Native people practice modified forms of their religious traditions, often alongside participation in Christian churches and communities. Many see little contradiction in being both a practitioner of traditional religions and a Christian.

Of course, great challenges remain for Native cultures and religions. Native languages are disappearing at a rapid rate, despite tribal efforts to preserve languages and teach them to their children. Likewise, Native communities are struggling in the face of some of the highest rates of poverty, suicide, infant mortality, and violent death in the country. Native communities have some of the highest per capita rates of diabetes and heart disease. Many traditions are also at risk. As elders pass away, their knowledge goes with them. Sacred places, which function as memory, text, and living presence of spiritual traditions, are threatened by development, mining, water depletion, and other resource extraction. In the midst of this, many ceremonies that *had* been lost are being revived based on the secondary accounts and ethnographic descriptions recorded by anthropologists and ethnographers in previous generations. Such religious revival is intricately intertwined with the twentieth-century political movements that encouraged pride in traditional culture, and affirmed Native rights to sovereignty, protection of sacred sites, and subsistence resources.

The wisdom and spiritual guidance of traditionalist elders have profoundly influenced Native political movements, such as the American Indian Movement (AIM). The American Indian Movement first gained attention in 1969 with the occupation of Alcatraz Island in San Francisco Bay by a group of young Native demonstrators. The occupation lasted for nineteen months. Indigenous activists from all over the country converged at the event, sharing stories and inspiring one another to continue the movement. The Trail of Broken Treaties, which followed soon after, led to the occupation of the Bureau of Indian Affairs building in Washington, D.C. And, perhaps most famously, in 1973 the group led the occupation of Wounded Knee. Religion remained central to that protest. AIM leaders were deliberate about welcoming Lakota elders and spiritual leaders into their work and sought their advice. Ceremonies were held throughout the siege, including a peyote ceremony and a sweatlodge. AIM's spiritual leader, Leonard Crow Dog, led the group in a Ghost Dance—the first time a Ghost Dance had occurred on the reservation since the original massacre at Wounded Knee.

Political mobilization of Native communities has continued unabated throughout the country, as local communities have fought to secure treaty rights to subsistence resources and protect sacred places. Consider, for example, "fish-ins" of the Pacific Northwest. During the 1960s and 1970s, Native individuals gathered to fish (illegally) in traditional areas, arguing that treaties had guaranteed them the right to do so. Protesters were arrested, and on at least one occasion brutally beaten. Fish-ins garnered national attention and inspired legal challenges, eventually resulting in the Boldt Decision (1974), which transformed the fishing industry and granted half the legal catch to Native communities. Protests have also continued over the desecration of sacred sites, resulting in the protection of some, such as Mount Shasta in northern California, which narrowly avoided being destroyed by a proposed ski resort.

Native groups likewise continue to lobby to protect burial sites and to advocate for the return of human remains and sacred objects that are held in private and public collections throughout the country and internationally. As early as 1868, the federal government and various private institutions were voraciously collecting the remains and cultural artifacts of Native communities. Euro-American scholars and politicians believed that Native Americans were destined for extinction, and institutions sought to secure their remains for future study. Many such remains and cultural objects were stolen, purchased without proper permission, or taken from battlefields. The Archaeological Resources Protection Act of 1979 made some steps toward redressing this issue, creating new regulations that required archaeologists to consult with local tribes regarding human remains. The Native American Graves Protection and Repatriation Act of 1990 made major strides toward ensuring that such remains and cultural patrimony would be returned from publicly funded institutions, but no such law mandates the return of these items (whether obtained scrupulously or not) from private collections.

A new generation of archaeologists is committed to building mutually respectful relationships with tribal communities and their cultural resource managers. Larry Zimmerman describes this as "indigenous archaeology," an approach that partners with tribal communities and incorporates their oral histories and tribal researchers. An early example of this can be cited in the case of the Zuni War Gods, returned by the Denver Art Museum to the Zuni Nation in 1977. The museum also provided the Zuni with a $10,000 donation to help in the construction of facilities to house the deities. Tribally directed archaeology programs are also proliferating, as Native communities take more control over telling their own stories.

MAJOR ISSUES AND QUESTIONS IN THE STUDY OF NATIVE AMERICAN RELIGIOUS HISTORY

As the preceding discussion illustrates, historical inquiry regarding Native Americans has been informed by a number of recurring questions. Some of the most prominent of these consider the impact of missionization on Native people's lives and cultures. Native scholars such as George Tinker have asked how the origins of contemporary social problems might be found within the cultural genocide wrought, intentionally or not, by missions. Others have looked at the ways in which Christianity has been remade when shaped by Native people. Contemporary studies also ask questions about how Native communities have been reviving their traditions since the late twentieth century, and how this reconstruction of identity, or identities, occurs. Still other students of Native traditions investigate how religious life helped communities live sustainably prior to colonialism, or how religious traditions helped them cope with the violence that colonialism wrought on Native spirits, bodies, and communities. Finally, some scholars have explored the ways in which non-Natives have historically sought to appropriate Native traditions, taking them for their own, and the distortions of those traditions that occurred in the process.

Other more theoretical concerns are also in need of further consideration. When considering the ways in which Native traditions were challenged by colonialism, the ways in which communities responded creatively to Christianity and strategically accommodated elements of Euro-American practice and worldview, one must consider the very tricky question of "tradition." What does "traditional" mean? Early scholarship had a tendency to see "traditional" culture as static and unchanging, in which case change was a sign that "tradition" had been contaminated or lost altogether. Yet the nature of tradition itself is to be continually changing. This nuanced perspective has allowed scholars to consider the ways in which Christianity may be functioning as a "traditional" element of culture and the ways in which contemporary cultures have revived older religious practices in new forms.

Related to the fluid and adaptive nature of "tradition" is the issue of identity. In a similar way, identity had been seen by scholars for many years as a static, monolithic, and unquestioned phenomenon. Contemporary theorists, however, have focused on the notion of the cultural construction of identity—that the very nature of selfhood and how the self and community are defined is the product of one's particular cultural and historical context. As such, the very notion of "Indian" (or Lakota, or Cheyenne) is a malleable one, which can be deconstructed and reflected on critically. Such ideas have inspired scholarship emphasizing the complex heterogeneous nature of Native identity and the ways in which Native people have managed to craft a sense of a self that might be, for instance, Tewa *and* Pueblo, *and* part of a network of Southwest Natives, and yet *also* identifying as part of a national pan-Indian identity. This same person may be simultaneously Catholic *and* traditionalist, *and* a herbalist, *and* a mother, *and* a botanist, and so on. However, such postmodern theorizing on identity is also profoundly problematic in an era of postcolonial concerns. While scholars must be wary of creating homogeneous essentialist categories of identity, the people whom they study *need* identifying categories for political mobilization and for recovery. Much of the work of Native spirituality today is about re-creating a strong and healthy sense of indigenous identity.

To suggest that such identities now must be deconstructed in scholarship has enormous implications and must be explored with care and sensitivity to indigenous concerns. Jace Weaver has engaged this question, reminding scholars that deconstructing identities becomes problematic and destructive within communities, where identities are both fragile and vitally necessary for survival. Both Weaver and Dale Stover have called instead for a "postcolonial hermeneutic." Such an interpretive mode would first affirm the legitimacy and vitality of traditional religious expressions. Such a mode would also be spatially oriented, recognizing the importance of place and the sacrality of Creation. And, finally, it would emphasize the primary importance of community cohesion and communal consensus in the process of cultural interpretation and meaning making: that religious traditions exist for and are interpreted by local communities.

REFERENCES

Axtell, James. *The Invasion Within: The Conquest of Cultures in Colonial North America*. New York: Oxford University Press, 1986.

Bierwert, Crisca. *Brushed by Cedar, Living by the River: Coast Salish Figures of Power*. Tucson: University of Arizona Press, 1999.

Biolisi, Thomas, and Larry Zimmerman. *Indians and Anthropologists: Vine Deloria Jr. and the Critique of Anthropology*. Tucson: University of Arizona Press, 1997.

Buckley, Thomas. *Standing Ground: Yurok Indian Spirituality, 1850–1990*. Berkeley: University of California Press, 2002.

Bucko, Raymond. *The Lakota Ritual of the Sweatlodge: History and Contemporary Practice*. Winnipeg: Bison Books, 1997.

Crawford, Suzanne. *Native American Religious Traditions*. Upper Saddle River, N.J.: Prentice Hall, 2007.

Crow Dog, Mary. *Lakota Woman*. New York: HarperPerennial, 1991.

Deloria, Vine. *God Is Red: A Native View of Religion*. Boulder, Colo.: Fulcrum Press, 1973.

DeMallie, Raymond. *The Sixth Grandfather: Black Elk's Teachings to John G. Neihardt*. Lincoln: University of Nebraska Press, 1985.

DuBois, Cora. *The 1870 Ghost Dance*. Reprint, Lincoln: University of Nebraska Press, 2007.

Fienup-Riordan, Ann. *Eskimo Essays: Yup'ik Lives and How We See Them*. New Brunswick, N.J.: Rutgers University Press, 1999.

Frey, Rodney. *Landscape Traveled by Coyote and Crane: The World of the Sch'itsu'umsh (Coeur d'Alene Indians)*. Seattle: University of Washington Press, 2001.

Goulet, Jean-Guy. *Ways of Knowing: Experience, Knowledge, and Power Among the Dene Tha*. Lincoln: University of Nebraska Press, 1998.

Harrod, Howard. *Becoming and Remaining a People: Native American Religions on the Northern Plains*. Tucson: University of Arizona Press, 1995.

Hoxie, Frederick. *A Final Promise: The Campaign to Assimilate the Indians, 1880–1920*. Lincoln: University of Nebraska Press, 2002.

Irwin, Lee, ed. *Native American Spirituality: A Critical Reader*. Lincoln: University of Nebraska Press, 2000.

Kan, Sergei. *Memory Eternal: Tlingit Culture and Russian Orthodox Christianity Through Two Centuries*. Seattle: University of Washington Press, 1999.

Kidwell, Clara Sue. *Choctaws and Missionaries in Mississippi, 1818–1918*. Norman: University of Oklahoma Press, 1997.

Kluckhohn, Clyde, and Dorothea Leighton. *The Navajo*. Reprint, Cambridge, Mass.: Harvard University Press, 1991.

Lassiter, Luke, Clyde Ellis, and Ralph Kotay. *The Jesus Road: Kiowas, Christianity, and Indian Hymns*. Winnipeg: Bison Books, 2002.

Martin, Joel. *The Land Looks After Us: A History of Native American Religion*. New York: Oxford University Press, 2001.

——. *Sacred Revolt: The Muskogees' Struggle for a New World*. Boston: Beacon Press, 1988.

McNally, Michael. *Ojibwe Singers: Hymns, Grief, and a Native Culture in Motion*. New York: Oxford University Press, 2000.

Mihesuah, Devon, ed. *Repatriation Reader: Who Owns Native American Remains?* Lincoln: University of Nebraska Press, 2000.

Mooney, James. *The Ghost Dance Religion and Wounded Knee*. Reprint, New York: Dover, 1991.

Nelson, Richard. *Make Prayers to the Raven: A Koyukon View of the Northern Forest*. Chicago: University of Chicago Press, 1986.

Noley, Homer. *First White Frost: Native Americans and United Methodism*. Nashville, Tenn.: Abingdon Press, 1991.

Perdue, Theda, and Michael D. Green, eds. *The Cherokee Removal: A Brief History with Documents*. New York: St. Martin's Press, 1995.

Pesantubbee, Michelene. *Choctaw Women in a Chaotic World: The Clash of Cultures in the Colonial Southeast*. Albuquerque: University of New Mexico Press, 2005.

Schwarz, Maureen Trudelle. *Navajo Lifeways: Contemporary Issues, Ancient Knowledge*. Norman: University of Oklahoma Press, 2001.

Stover, Dale. "Post Colonial Sundancing at Wakpamni Laike." *Journal of the American Academy of Religion* 6, no. 4 (2001): 817–836.

St. Pierre, Mark, and Tilda Long Soldier. *Walking in the Sacred Manner: Healers, Dreamers, and Pipe Carriers—Medicine Women of the Plains*. New York: Simon and Schuster, 1995.

Sullivan, Lawrence. *Native Religions and Cultures of North America: Anthropology of the Sacred*. London: Continuum, 2003.

Tinker, George. *Missionary Conquest: The Gospel and Native American Cultural Genocide*. Minneapolis: Augsburg Fortress, 1993.

Vestal, Stanley. *New Sources of Indian History, 1850–1891: The Ghost Dance, The Prairie Sioux—A Miscellany*. Norman: University of Oklahoma Press, 1934.

Watt, Eva Tulene, and Keith Basso. *Don't Let the Sun Step Over You: A White Mountain Apache Family Life, 1860–1976*. Tucson: University of Arizona Press, 2004.

Weaver, Jace. *Native American Religious Identity: Unforgotten Gods*. New York: Orbis Books, 1998.

Wenger, Tisa. *We Have a Religion: The 1920s Pueblo Indian Dance Controversy and American Religious Freedom*. Chapel Hill: University of North Carolina Press, 2009.

3. CIVIL RELIGION AND NATIONAL IDENTITY

ANDREW M. MANIS

The study of civil religion requires a tolerance for a certain amount of asceticism. Ever since 1967, when Robert N. Bellah borrowed the term from Rousseau, sociologists and historians of religion in the United States have meditated on America's religious meaning and sought to find it in a religious dimension of American culture called civil religion. Much of the navel-gazing has been eye-crossingly metaphysical in nature, focused largely on whether this phenomenon actually exists and whether it exists in the same way that the traditional religions do. In the past four decades, many novitiates have joined that monkish company and have spent a great deal of time contorting mind and body in search of enlightenment regarding these matters. Absent the promise of any complete Buddhahood on the subject, perhaps we can identify an Eightfold Path to wisdom (or as close as one can get to it) regarding the analysis of American civil religion.

RIGHT DEFINITION

We begin, as one might expect, with *right definition*. However one may define it, the phenomenon has many names. "Civil religion" is the most common, but some scholars prefer "civic faith," "public religion," "public piety," "public theology," "public philosophy," or any number of others. Some of these are distinctions without a difference, but some are not. The path of *right definition*, however, is a path of simplicity whereby all these names become essentially synonyms. Rousseau conceived of it as a religion focused on the meaning of the society that consciously constructed it. Bellah argued that this "religious dimension" was properly to be considered to be well institutionalized in American life but clearly differentiated from the organized churches.

Outside the sociological sandbox, even before Bellah's more famous formulation, the historian Sidney Mead seemed to be talking about the same phenomenon but calling it the "religion of the Republic." This "religion of democracy," Mead argued, unified Americans who were otherwise divided by the more sectarian theologies of the churches. In a number of writings, John F. Wilson indicated his preference for the name "public religion," which exists but fails to meet the criteria of a religion socially differentiated from America's religious or political institutions. It has no clearly identifiable offices of leadership, no binding membership requirements, no life cycle of rituals to meet members' needs, and no fully coherent theology (including affirmation about existence). Gradually, as the debate unfolded over the last third of the twentieth century, a consensus among historians (and a number of sociologists) came to agree with Wilson that while it does not meet the definition of full-fledged, full-orbed, differentiated religion, civil religion does exist as a "cluster of meanings" central to American culture and attached to the nation.

This cluster of meanings is expressed in ideological themes that symbolize what Americans have historically articulated as the ultimate meaning of their society. To a great extent, these themes derive from the Puritan experiments in the colonies of Plymouth and Massachusetts—that is, Puritan self-conceptions of being God's "Chosen People" entrusted with an "errand in the wilderness" to build a "city on a hill." This Christian society, or "Bible commonwealth," would in turn become an exemplar for corrupt Old England and eventually the rest of the world.

Partly because of New England's leadership in the American Revolution, the Puritans' deuteronomic theology ("Success is a sign of God's blessing; failure betokens a divine curse") increasingly interpreted military victories against the heavily favored British army as miraculous interventions proving divine favor on the fledgling United States. By the successful end of the war, the status of New Israel—complete with George Washington as the new Moses—had been transferred from one region to the entire nation. The *new* New Israel's appointed task was also changing. Increasingly derived from "Providence" instead of God or Jesus, America's role was increasingly expressed in less religious language. The United States was also becoming less an exemplar of a pure Christian society than a passive example—and still later an active guardian—of liberty and an asylum for the world's oppressed. After the revolution, as argued by Paul C. Nagel, from the end of the Washington presidency to the Spanish-American War, Americans viewed their nation as a "sacred trust" and themselves as stewards.

Carlton J. H. Hayes's classic perception of nationalism as a religion preceded the civil religion debate but, without using the term, grapples with the same phenomenon as Bellah. In this vein, historian of religion Catherine Albanese suggests "religious nationalism" as a useful shorthand for civil religion. Keeping all such conceptions in mind, it appears that any ideological construction that relates the nation in some special way to the sacred would fit under the wide umbrella of civil religion. Thus the path of *right definition* leads to more simplicity than Bellah's original conception. Whatever name one chooses to give it, civil religion can best be understood as a cultural blending of religion and patriotism that interprets the nation as unique by virtue of its special relationship with that society's conception of the sacred. As such, in the American context civil religion could be accurately conceived as American exceptionalism in a religious mode. Civil religion is the system of mythic meanings, embedded and diffused throughout their culture, by which Americans interpret the ultimate meaning of their nation. A general definition like this makes it possible to find the themes of civil religion sprinkled rather liberally in the nation's political and religious institutions, rather than clearly differentiated from either. One can thus find creedal or ritual expressions of civil religion in both church services and political rallies.

RIGHT FUNCTIONALITY

The second path to wisdom might be called *right functionality*. Sociologists typically offer two kinds of definitions of religion. Substantive definitions, such as the one arrived at via the previous path, focus on what religion is. Functional definitions emphasize what religion does or how religions function in society. For historians, however, the questions answered by the former lead logically to those raised by the latter. The simpler the substantive definition, the more possibilities exist for a multiple functionality. This path leads (rightly, of course) to a simple truth: civil religion performs many functions within the society it deems sacred. Borrowing from the sociological tradition of Émile Durkheim, Bellah emphasizes the role of social integration. For him, civil religion functions similarly to Mead's "religion of the Republic," binding together citizens who are otherwise divided by more sectarian faiths. In this manner, generalized civil religions integrate or unify citizens in much the same ways that more sectarian forms of religion did in Catholic medieval Europe or Anglican England—premodern societies before the rise of church–state separation.

Civil religion accomplishes this integration by providing a sense of ultimate meaning for the society. Even if the traditional religions or denominations divide the loyalties of citizens, the civil or national religion can provide a belief system about the nation around which all or most citizens can rally. This creed of civil religion expresses Americans' conviction of their nation's exceptionalism by embodying what they believe to be America's divine purpose. These beliefs are called to mind by the sacred symbols (the flag), sacred rituals (pledging allegiance), sacred objects (the Liberty Bell), sacred holidays (the Fourth of July), sacred spaces (the Lincoln Memorial), and sacred personages (Washington, Jefferson, Lincoln). By reference to these components, Americans celebrate their country's unique status and recommit themselves to its values and its task in the world.

Legitimation, or sanction, for the national polity is another function of civil religion. This use arises, argues sociologist Marcella Cristi, from the traditions of Rousseau. Unlike Durkheim, who saw an integrative religion arising naturally and inevitably from the structure of society, Rousseau viewed civil religion as the conscious creation of political leaders seeking to exert influence or even control over the citizenry. In such a context, a nation's leaders may deliberately put civil religion to use for the purpose of legitimating their particular political order. Cristi appropriately criticizes American scholars for overemphasizing civil religion's integrative function, with little analysis of it as a "consciously 'designed' religion that leaders have to create and encourage."

RIGHT VARIETY

Too much attention to civil religion's integrative function tends to minimize the historical pluralism of the American religious context. Hence a third path to civil religious wisdom is *right variety*. Critics of the civil religion thesis have rightly argued that it largely fails to integrate heterogeneous societies with high levels of religious and cultural pluralism. That is another reason why working definitions must define civil religion in such a way as to account for America's history of religious pluralism.

While America has been religiously plural from its colonial era onward, non-Christian and non-Protestant religions or subcultures remained invisible enough to allow a Protestant dominance over American life. While any religious establishment at the federal level was outlawed by the First Amendment, and gradually died out in the states by 1833, Protestantism could remain an unofficial national religion until sometime in the twentieth century. Exactly *when* is, of course, a matter of debate among historians of American religious history. Nonetheless, as minority religious groups established and enlarged their presence in the United

States, they also gained and amplified their respective voices in public life. Their treatment at the hands of the Protestant majority shaped the notes they sounded in addressing the larger American religious and political cultures. The result was the development of alternative versions of the American civil religion. As Martin E. Marty observed, there are subspecies of civil religion analogous to Christianity and its denominations.

Although in many ways regionalism has been an important and often over-looked factor in understanding religion in American history, it has been anything but ignored by historians of the South. Charles Reagan Wilson was the first to take regional varieties into account in an analysis of civil religion, producing the classic interpretation of the "religion of the Lost Cause" as the *southern* civil religion. His book *Baptized in Blood: The Religion of the Lost Cause, 1865–1920*, analyzes a different form of the American civil religion, one that healed and unified the white South in the aftermath of the Civil War. Through its theology, rituals, sacred days, and sacred spaces, this civil religion became the South's theodicy, explaining God's mysterious ways of bringing the South to triumph despite the defeat of the Confederacy.

The most historically significant expression of regionalism was, of course, the Civil War. Given the importance of evangelicalism to both North and South, to both the abolition of slavery and its defense, it is surprising that it took until 2006 for someone explicitly to interpret the Civil War as a conflict of civil religions. Harry S. Stout's *Upon the Altar of the Nation: A Moral History of the Civil War* advances a larger moral interpretation of the Civil War, but one that claims that by 1863 the language of martyrdom and "political preaching in the North and South had virtually completed the apotheosis of 'patriotism' into a full-blown civil religion" (248). A stronger argument could perhaps be made that as the South's defense of slavery gradually transformed southern sectionalism into Confederate nationalism, its version of evangelicalism helped create a distinctive version of civil religion that, in fact, preceded and propelled the South into the Civil War, rather than emerging from that conflict.

RIGHT RACE CONSCIOUSNESS

Inadequate attention to the varieties of civil religion in America creates the most glaring weakness in the literature—the ways in which civil religion deals with the intertwined roles of race and African American religion. Thus the fourth path to understanding is *right race consciousness*. The encounter between Euro- and African Americans, as David W. Wills has often pointed out, must be understood as a central theme of the subfields of American and African American religious history.

(One could also add American history in general.) Despite occasional claims that civil religion is a Eurocentric concept that renders the black presence invisible, there is strong evidence that African Americans have addressed questions of national chosenness, both for themselves and for the larger American nation.

Throughout the nineteenth century, black leaders expressed nationalistic sentiments both about their color and capabilities *and* about the superiority of American ideals. During the Civil War, the *Christian Recorder*, the official organ of the African Methodist Episcopal Church, held that America's providential role was to "be the great field of training for the development of the human mind, the display of genius, and solving the great problem of a universal brotherhood, the unity of the race of mankind, and the eternal principles of intellectual, moral, and spiritual development" (quoted in Walker, *Rock in a Weary Land*). Within this task, many black leaders argued, African Americans were also called to test out America's fidelity to its central values.

Two recent studies bear this out. David Howard-Pitney's study *The African American Jeremiad: Appeals for Justice in America* focuses on black appeals to the white American conscience for racial justice from Frederick Douglass to Jesse Jackson and Alan Keyes. The very category of the jeremiad—a sermon calling on a people to change their ways or else face divine judgment—presupposes a chosen people's covenant with God and their failure to keep it. Similarly, Eddie S. Glaude Jr.'s *Exodus! Religion, Race, and Nation in Early Nineteenth-Century Black America* argues that the idea of chosenness provided a religious base for America's political ideology and its national identity. While noting whites' and blacks' contrasting uses of the Exodus motif, nation language among African Americans expressed their ambivalence toward America. It emerged from the "collective humiliation caused by a violently racist nation." This tradition chose America as its own, despite black America's parallel focus on racial solidarity. From what might be called a prophetic civil religion, African Americans chose America not as it was, but as they hoped it might become.

Of course, the respective Euro- and African American ideas of chosenness and destiny clash rather directly in the civil rights movement, which certainly can be understood as a conflict of civil religions. The role of testing whether America would "live out the true meaning of its creed" carried over from Douglass and other nineteenth-century spokespersons to the twentieth-century prophetic legacy of Martin Luther King Jr. and other black minister–civil rights leaders. The South became a battlefield of civil faiths, the one racially inclusive and the other racially exclusive, each violating the sacred values of the other. Mid-twentieth-century civil rights battles blend into civil religious conflict, both of which eventually meld into the larger "culture wars" of the past twenty years or so. Through them all, race consciousness remains central to the American story.

Two recent studies draw out the role of race in the shaping of late-nineteenth-century American nationalism. Edward J. Blum's *Reforging the White Republic:*

Race, Religion, and American Nationalism, 1865–1898, critiques northern Protestants for using whiteness and nationalism to repair sectional discord at the expense of racial justice. By accepting racial separation in intrasectional denominational agencies, in the revivals of Dwight L. Moody, and in the reforms of the Woman's Christian Temperance Union, the North sold out the post–Civil War possibilities for racial justice in exchange for reconciliation with the white South. Reconciling with former Confederates in support of the Spanish-American War, northern white Protestants nourished segregation and supported imperialism, linking race, religion, and nationalism in the process.

This path underscores the reality that the task of interpreting America's rise to the status of world power requires some reference to race consciousness. The racial context of the Spanish-American War should be recalled. Launched just two years after the Supreme Court's ruling in *Plessy v. Ferguson* (1896), which upheld Jim Crow in the South, the war had a racial edge to it. Teddy Roosevelt judged President William McKinley to have the backbone of a chocolate éclair for his reluctance in declaring war on Spain. Roosevelt believed that fighting "savages" (Indians) on the American frontier had welded disparate European colonists into Americans. Fighting "savages" in Cuba, and especially in the Philippines, would do the same for northerners and southerners still in the process of reconciliation. Later, while the U.S. Senate debated American policy toward the Philippines, Senator Albert Beveridge of Indiana touted "the mission of our race: trustee, under God, of the civilization of the world." Senator Orville Platt, from Connecticut, hailed every American ship in the Philippines as "a new *Mayflower* . . . the harbinger and agent of a new civilization."

In this connection, Daniel B. Lee discusses the war as part of "a great racial commission," whereby white Americans used religion to help create an Anglo-Saxon America. He argues that "from the Jews . . . white Americans inherited the status of a chosen people living in a New Israel. As Christians, they accepted a great commission to 'enlighten the world.' From the Anglo-Saxons . . . white Americans purportedly inherited the manifest destiny of civilizing the world by planting the seeds of democracy" ("Great Racial Commission," 107). The "Chosen Nation"'s late-nineteenth-century departure from isolationism to begin the process of becoming the leader of the family of nations is certainly a pivotal moment in American civil religion and a moment directly related to race.

RIGHT ETHNICITY

The latter half of the twentieth century, however, saw significant racial and cultural change in the United States. What early in the century had been variously labeled the "Negro problem" and the "immigrant problem" became for many Americans the interrelated problems of multiculturalism and political correctness. Dealing with civil religion in contemporary America will thus require a new path, which is *right ethnicity*. America's dominant civil religion has not done well by the nation's minority religious groups, particularly those combining theological deviation with significant racial and cultural difference. From the point of view of Native Americans, James G. Moseley has quipped, "manifest destiny has been neither civil nor religious." This shadow side of civil religion makes it mandatory for the concept to be analyzed with a proper appreciation for not only race consciousness, but also America's widening ethnicity. Amanda Porterfield registers important caveats about unified religious visions of America that tend to overlook the great variety of those visions.

Since the 1960s, minority groups have articulated their self-understandings and their visions of America much more boldly than in previous generations. Joseph Tilden Rhea narrates these developments in his book *Race Pride and the American Identity*. As a spinoff of the civil rights movement, advocates of Black Power began to celebrate the accomplishments of black (later "African American") culture. On college campuses, black students complained of their absence from the canons of American higher education and black studies departments were born.

Within a generation colleges were won over to a "multicultural" perspective on American life, evidenced by the rise of Native American studies, women's studies, and Asian American studies departments. Outside academe, these groups fought traditionalists for inclusion within American museums and historic sites. Examples include African American efforts to support a national holiday honoring Martin Luther King Jr., concessions to Lakota Sioux perspectives at the Little Bighorn Battlefield National Monument, and Japanese American agitation for reparations for their internment during World War II. Black Power thus spawned what Rhea calls the "race pride movement," an umbrella under which various racial and cultural minorities (African Americans, Native Americans, Asian Americans, and, to a lesser extent, gay and lesbian Americans) sought cultural inclusion in schools and public history venues throughout America. Such change developed not from any general drift toward a more multicultural nation based on the good will of the majority. Rather, progress toward a more inclusive America derived, notes Rhea, from self-conscious political actions by minority groups themselves.

The process of amplifying the voices of America's ethnic and racial minorities has presented a growing challenge to a nation whose self-image during its first 125 years was overwhelmingly white, Anglo-Saxon, and Protestant. Part of the challenge has been America's task of redefining itself in the face of rapid, large-scale cultural and religious change. When Americans articulate the themes of civil religion, they are in effect offering a definition of the United States. Defining America is precisely what civil religions do. Thus the conflict of civil religions during the civil rights movement opened a Pandora's box that more recently has broadened into the "culture wars," the widely known phrase by which sociologist James Davison Hunter refers to "the struggle to define America." Debating whether to call these developments a clash of civil religions or "culture wars" is much less important than understanding that they raise the crucial issue of American identity.

RIGHT IDENTITY

The sixth path to wisdom then is that of *right identity*. The civil rights movement opened the door a crack to blacks wanting a place at the American table. In response to the movement, Congress finally became more sensitive to implications of racism and nativism and in 1965 passed the Immigration Act, which lifted earlier quotas on newcomers to the United States. The result has been a level of religious and cultural diversity unprecedented in earlier stages of American history. It is indeed a radical pluralism, including both greater raw numbers of newcomers, higher levels of diversity, and more significant theological and ideological deviations from what had historically been viewed as the Protestant "norms." Skyrocketing immigration and the multicultural impulse have conspired to create concerns, even among erstwhile liberals like Arthur Schlesinger Jr., about "the disuniting of America." Concerns about diversity of race, culture, religion, and language began to swirl, leading many began to ask, "In the face of growing diversity, what will American identity become?" A more foreboding version of the question was, "Who are the *real* Americans?"

Bill Ong Hing, an attorney specializing in immigration law, notes that the nation's immigration policy is the realm where Americans wrestle with ethnicity and the limits of tolerable pluralism. This policy has reflected tensions in the American psyche regarding the place of "foreigners" in the country. Not at all a recent problem, this issue split even the nation's Founders. Whereas Benjamin Franklin had raised alarms about incorporating German immigrants (whom he regarded as stupid) into the "holy experiment" in Pennsylvania, George Washington took a more welcoming view: "The bosom of America is open to receive not only the opulent and respectable stranger, but the oppressed and persecuted of all nations and religions; and they shall be welcomed to a participation of all our rights and privileges, if by decency and propriety of conduct as they appear to merit the enjoyment."

As many have pointed out, these conflicting mind-sets can both be found on the base of the Statue of Liberty, in the famous verses of Emma Lazarus: "Give me your tired, your poor, your huddled masses" has the Washingtonian sound of welcome; "the wretched refuse of your teeming shore" reflects Franklin's concern about unassimilable newcomers. Hing argues that the nation consistently has been of two minds regarding the immigrant, and the issue of "who is an American?" has been defined and redefined throughout its history. In periods of open immigration policy, the restrictionist mind-set narrows the definition of what traits constitute true Americanness. Such concerns about immigration's threat to American identity bring us back to the realm where civil religions do their work. If civil religions really do exist in twenty-first-century America, they will be obligated to speak usefully to the issue of immigration and the questions of American identity that it raises.

Similarly, the rise of radical pluralism also raises important questions regarding civil religion. Can civil religion survive radical pluralism? Is the United States condemned to fighting culture wars where opposing civil religions compete for adherents like political parties or candidates vie for voters? Is civility among Americans forever to be replaced by polarization? Or might it be possible for a consensus to develop around a more inclusive vision of America?

Answers to these questions remain to be developed. What is certain at present is that the polarization is real and continuing. In a real sense, the civil religious conflict of the civil rights era has remained a part of the American landscape and broadened into more than an argument about white America's acceptance of African American equality. Other issues like abortion, capital punishment, stem cell research, immigration, the role of religion in public life, and the "war on terrorism" have divided Americans into opposing camps. Many scholars have described and attempted to name these competing perspectives. Perhaps the most celebrated of these attempts was by sociologist James Davison Hunter. In his original argument regarding the culture wars, Hunter sketched two moral worldviews, which he named progressivism and traditionalism. Robert Wuthnow judged these to be liberal and conservative civil religions.

Social commentator Michael Lind, nervous about what he considers the over-involvement of religion in American public life, avoids attaching the label "civil religion" to the two perspectives he sees clashing in contemporary America. The two kinds of nationalism he describes nonetheless function the way civil religions do. His nativist nationalism corresponds to Wuthnow's conservative civil religion, imposing racial and religious tests for membership in the national community. Lind prefers what he calls liberal nationalism, which rejects such qualifications for being an American. Liberal nationalism advocates a colorblind racial integration in the Frederick Douglass–Martin Luther King Jr. tradition. Regarding immigration, this perspective accepts the image of the melting pot, updated to fuse together not only white immigrants but Americans of all races. The almost-millennial result envisioned by this brand of nationalism would be a "transracial nation." Most provocatively, Lind describes a nationalism (or civil religion) that rejects American exceptionalism. For liberal nationalists, "patriotism does not depend on overblown claims about American uniqueness or superiority. One should cherish one's nation as one should cherish one's family, not because it is the best in the world, but because, with all of its faults, it is one's own."

Historian Gary Gerstle's important *American Crucible: Race and Nation in the Twentieth Century* examines the intertwined careers of race and nation in contemporary America. He describes a "racial nationalism" with "ethnoracial" images of an America unified by "common blood and skin color and by an inherited fitness for self-government." His alternative is a "civic nationalism" that defines Americanism as a commitment to the core political ideals of the United States. Here Gerstle's formulation matches the concept of a "cosmopolitan patriotism" that Jonathan M. Hansen views as the "lost promise of patriotism" in a book by the same name.

These studies, as well as Lind's, make little or no reference to religion, but their formulations would not preclude their insights in conceiving of a civil religion that pointed toward the civic-mindedness or cosmopolitanism they advocate. Bellah himself held out hope for a kind of world civil religion that would avoid exclusivism or jingoism. A civil religion shorn of the more arrogant aspects of American exceptionalism, which focused on loyalty to the core American values of freedom, equality, and democracy, and which eschewed racial or religious qualifications for being an American, could yield an armistice in the ongoing culture wars.

RIGHT *KAIROS*

The penultimate path to wisdom in considering the relationship of civil religion and national identity is *right kairos*. The Greek word *kairos* refers to an opportune moment in time. It is used here as a reminder that national and international crises have almost always elicited important developments in the nation's civil faith. Robert N. Bellah himself followed up his initial article on civil religion with the book-length essay *The Broken Covenant: American Civil Religion in Time of Trial*. A powerful jeremiad in its own right, Bellah's book describes how civil religion responded to the crises of the American Revolution and the Civil War, and he calls for a renewed covenant in the wake of the Vietnam debacle. In reality, many periods of American history have raised questions of American identity and spawned new ways of articulating Americans' sense of national destiny. The outcomes of these developments have not always been pretty, although some have been among the nation's finest moments.

The period of American mythic origins, the colonial era, saw the Puritan ethos generate civil religion's basic ideas of chosenness and covenant. In the revivals of the Great Awakening, divines like Jonathan Edwards interpreted the mass conversions as recoveries from early religious declension, but more importantly as signs that the millennium would begin in America.

The Revolutionary era nationalized the covenant that had originally been struck with New England and solidified Americans' conviction that Providence had watched over their doings ("Annuit coeptis") and blessed a "new order for the ages" ("Novus ordo seclorum"). In the process, a rather deistic god had become involved enough with the world to create a New Israel with a New Exodus made possible by a New Moses. The national covenant was rechartered in the writing of one of that period's civil religion's sacred documents, the Constitution. Many thought of that summer of 1787 as "the miracle in Philadelphia."

The eras of Indian Removal and the Mexican War saw the nation act on its conviction of a "manifest destiny" to gain dominion over the entire North American continent. The Civil War marked what Bellah views as America's second major *kairos*, when Abraham Lincoln would become one of the most profound interpreters of American destiny. His handling of the war saved the nation, and his prophetic reinterpretation of America's status as an "almost Chosen people" created a new covenant that would include persons of color—or at least move in that direction.

During the two world wars, the nation heard a call to "make the world safe for democracy," which it also sought to do throughout the anti-Communist days of the Korean War and McCarthy. Like Bellah, many have understood the 1960s— the civil rights and anti–Vietnam War eras—as another time of crisis that not only tried men's souls, but also provided a broader civil religion where the racially oppressed began to find a place at the table. In that era, the creative tension of nonviolent protest and Martin Luther King Jr.'s planting the dream of African Americans deep in the soil of the American Dream helped the nation reap a small but as yet incomplete harvest of justice. Now in the midst of culture wars at home and a war on terrorism abroad, the American civil religions face new challenges and the nation faces another critical time of trial.

Factors at home and abroad make the current era another *kairos* for the United States. The clearest of these is the nation's post–September 11 efforts to combat terrorism. The role of Islamist fervor and anti-Americanism in the Arab and Muslim world make this era a particularly challenging crisis for America and its civil religion. Despite efforts to portray this effort as focused exclusively on al-Qaida and its terrorist activities, millions of Americans still view Islam itself as the enemy and expect American military strength to take care of the problem "in the name of God and the American way of life." A key question is whether this crisis will serve to revitalize the triumphalistic, militaristic side of the American public religion, or whether it will help the world's only superpower rise above chauvinistic impulses and renew its more inclusivist traditions.

At least two interpreters fear that to date the momentum is in the direction of chauvinism. Biblical scholar Robert Jewett has written of this style of civil religion in a classic study, *The Captain America Complex: The Dilemma of Zealous Nationalism*. More recently, he has collaborated with historian John Shelton Lawrence in revising his earlier argument in light of the war on terrorism and its theaters in Afghanistan and Iraq. Jewett and Lawrence note that in this time of crisis, as in earlier times, the theme of "peacemaking through holy war" has reappeared. They also perceptively note ways in which Captain America's "zealous nationalism" has come to parallel the ethic of jihad. First, both sides justify their anger toward the enemy as blessed by the deity. This increases the zeal of both combatants and "eliminates normal restraint." Both sides attribute the opponents' tendencies to absolute evil, making compromise immoral and unlikely. Third, both sides stereotype the opponents as suffering from an absolute deformity of the spirit, leaving only the alternatives of killing the enemy or converting him. Fourth, each side believes that its own violence is necessary and redemptive, while that of the enemy is senseless and unjust. Fifth, defeat by this enemy is considered absolutely unacceptable. Finally, all of the enemy's actions are believed to desecrate the other's sense of the holy and that overcoming such a foe is both a religious *and* a political duty.

Other important questions arise regarding civil religion in the age of terrorism. Will reformulations of our religious nationalism make it easier or more difficult for American political and military leaders to justify torture of prisoners? Under legislation like the USA Patriot Act (2001), will the civil liberties of citizens be violated or their privacy invaded? With terrorist cells established in upward of forty nations worldwide, how long will our leaders commit the country to military solutions to terrorism? Will the American people tolerate the level of militarization necessary to keep fighting the "good" fight long enough to root out all terrorists and their allies throughout the world? Will peoples around the world deepen their hatred for the world's remaining superpower?

A second issue relates to the revival of nativism spawned by the fervor of our war on terrorism. American history has shown that in times of war, America's leaders and citizens have succumbed to the temptation to dehumanize their enemies. From the rejection of Spanish Catholicism in the Mexican War to the demonization of the Filipinos; to the "Huns" of the "war to make the world safe for democracy"; to the "Japs," "Krauts," and Japanese Americans in the war after that; to the "gooks" in Vietnam; and now the "towel-heads" among our current enemy, the question remains: Will our civic piety encourage or discourage such reactions?

Such exclusivist, even racist, reactions will only alienate America's allies around the world and make victory in the war on terrorism less likely. Worse still, these reactions will exacerbate America's growing unease with its own deepening cultural diversity. While America's political system has been stable throughout its history, its racial, ethnic, religious, and cultural makeup has radically changed since the nation's inception. Concepts of chosenness forged when a majority of Americans were homogeneously white and Protestant can be maintained only with great difficulty in a time when Caucasians are gradually losing their majority status and non-Protestant, non-Christian, and non-religious Americans are growing at a rapid pace.

Both of America's current crises—dealing with terrorism and dealing with a rapidly developing religious and cultural diversity—address the pressing issue of national identity. The same is true of civil religions. Despite predictions regarding secularization, religion has grown in importance at the beginning of the postmodern twenty-first century. Positivism notwithstanding, religion is not going away as a factor in societies around the world. Still less likely is it to wither away in the United States, which is by all accounts the most institutionally religious nation among all modern Western democracies. Religion in general, and civil religion in particular, is unlikely to disappear from American politics, American international relations, or American efforts to define who and what we are as a people.

In the 1830s, Alexis de Tocqueville's paean to *Democracy in America* had but one area of concern regarding the future of the American experiment—the presence of blacks and the unwillingness of the white majority to accept them on the basis of equality. The Frenchman further predicted: "If there ever are great revolutions there [in America], they will be caused by the presence of blacks upon American soil. . . . It will not be the equality of social conditions but rather their inequality which may give rise thereto." While the problem of race, understood narrowly in terms of black–white relations, is still a piece of unfinished business for the United States and its civil religion(s), the problem raised by Tocqueville has melded into the larger problem of religious and cultural diversity. To proceed with discussions of civil religion without taking into account these two contemporary crises would be unwise, indeed. If, as has often been the case, times of crisis engender creative revitalizations of our civil religion, it is to be hoped that such a renewal will transcend conflicting visions of America and culture wars and develop a new American identity that no longer battles over the presence of foreigners or asks who the real Americans are.

RIGHT SERIOUSNESS

Thus the final path of wisdom is *right seriousness*. Metaphysical as the discussion of civil religion has been in the forty years since Bellah brought the term into American parlance, the subject still requires serious attention. The issues raised in this discussion are far from academic exercises equivalent to pinheaded medieval debates about angels and dancing: questions of identity are crucial for nations as well as individuals. More important, as long as there are political leaders who continue to talk about America's unique role in the world, civil religion will be a relevant discussion. And it is more than mere talk. Given America's propensity to express that unique role through military engagements, civil religion is more than just serious. It can be a matter of life and death.

REFERENCES

Albanese, Catherine. *America: Religions and Religion*. 3rd ed. Belmont, Calif.: Wadsworth, 2006.

——. *Sons of the Fathers: The Civil Religion of the American Revolution*. Philadelphia: Temple University Press, 1977.

Bellah, Robert N. *The Broken Covenant: American Civil Religion in Time of Trial*. New York: Seabury Press, 1975.

——. "Civil Religion in America." *Daedalus* 96 (1967): 1–21.

Beneke, Chris. *Beyond Toleration: The Religious Origins of American Pluralism*. New York: Oxford University Press, 2008.

Blum, Edward J. *Reforging the White Republic: Race, Religion, and American Nationalism, 1865–1898*. Baton Rouge: Louisiana State University Press, 2003.

Bowden, Henry Warner. "A Historian's Response to the Concept of American Civil Religion." In *Modern American Protestantism and Its World: Historical Articles on Protestantism in American Religious Life*, edited by Martin E. Marty, PAGES. Munich: Saur, 1992.

Corrigan, John, and Lynn Neal, eds. *Religious Intolerance in America: A Documentary History*. Chapel Hill: University of North Carolina Press, 2009.

Cristi, Marcella. *From Civil to Political Religion: The Intersection of Culture, Religion, and Politics*. Waterloo, Ont.: Wilfrid Laurier University Press, 2001.

Gerstle, Gary. *American Crucible: Race and Nation in the Twentieth Century*. Princeton, N.J.: Princeton University Press, 2002.

Glaude, Eddie S., Jr. *Exodus! Religion, Race, and Nation in Early Nineteenth-Century Black America*. Chicago: University of Chicago Press, 2000.

Guyatt, Nicholas. *Providence and the Invention of the United States, 1607–1865*. Cambridge: Cambridge University Press, 2007.

Hammond, Phillip E., Amanda Porterfield, James G. Moseley, and Jonathan Sarna. "Forum: Civil Religion Revisited." *Religion and American Culture* 4 (1994): 1–23.

Hansen, Jonathan M. *The Lost Promise of Patriotism: Debating American Identity, 1890–1920*. Chicago: University of Chicago Press, 2003.

Hayes, Carlton J. H. *Nationalism: A Religion*. New York: Macmillan, 1960.

Hing, Bill Ong. *Defining America Through Immigration Policy*. Philadelphia: Temple University Press, 2004.

Howard-Pitney, David. *The African American Jeremiad: Appeals for Justice in America*. Rev. ed. Philadelphia: Temple University Press, 2005.

Jewett, Robert. *The Captain America Complex: The Dilemma of Zealous Nationalism*. Philadelphia: Westminster Press, 1973.

Jewett, Robert, and John Shelton Lawrence. *Captain America and the Crusade Against Evil: The Dilemma of Zealous Nationalism*. Grand Rapids, Mich.: Eerdmans, 2003.

Lee, Daniel B. "A Great Racial Commission: Religion and Construction of White America." In *Race, Nation, and Religion in the Americas*, edited by Henry Goldschmidt and Elizabeth McAlister, 85–110. New York: Oxford University Press, 2004.

Lind, Michael. "Are We a Nation? An Argument for 'Trans-America.'" *Dissent*, Summer 1995, 355–362.

Manis, Andrew M. "The Civil Religions of the South." In *Religion and Public Life in the South: In the Evangelical Mode*, edited by Charles Reagan Wilson and Mark Silk, 165–194. Religion by Region, no. 6. Walnut Creek, Calif.: AltaMira Press, 2005.

——. *Southern Civil Religions in Conflict: Civil Rights and the Culture Wars*. Macon, Ga.: Mercer University Press, 2002.

Marty, Martin E. "Two Kinds of Civil Religion." In *American Civil Religion*, edited by Russell E. Richey and Donald G. Jones, 139–157. New York: Harper & Row, 1974.

Mead, Sidney E. *The Nation with the Soul of a Church*. New York: Harper & Row, 1975.

Nagel, Paul C. *This Sacred Trust: American Nationality, 1778–1798*. New York: Oxford University Press, 1971.

Porterfield, Amanda. *The Transformation of American Religion: The Story of a Late Twentieth-Century Awakening*. New York: Oxford University Press, 2001.

Rhea, Joseph Tilden. *Race Pride and the American Identity*. Cambridge, Mass.: Harvard University Press, 1997.

Richey, Russell E., and Donald G. Jones, eds. *American Civil Religion*. New York: Harper & Row, 1974.

Schultz, Kevin. *Tri-Faith America: How Postwar Catholics and Jews Helped America Realize Its Pluralist Promise*. New York: Oxford University Press, 2010.

Scott-Childress, Reynolds J., ed. *Race and the Production of Modern American Nationalism*. New York: Garland, 1999.

Stout, Harry S. *Upon the Altar of the Nation: A Moral History of the Civil War*. New York: Penguin, 2007.

Walker, Clarence E. *A Rock in a Weary Land: The African Methodist Episcopal Church During the Civil War and Reconstruction*. Baton Rouge: Louisiana State University Press, 1982.

Wills, David W. "Beyond Commonality and Pluralism: Persistent Racial Polarity in American Religion and Politics." In *Religion and American Politics: From the Colonial Period to the 1980s*, edited by Mark A. Noll, 199–224. New York: Oxford University Press, 1990.

Wilson, Charles Reagan. *Baptized in Blood: The Religion of the Lost Cause, 1865–1920*. Athens: University of Georgia Press, 1980.

Wilson, John F. *Public Religion in American Culture*. Philadelphia: Temple University Press, 1979.

Wuthnow, Robert. *The Restructuring of American Religion: Society and Faith Since World War II*. Princeton, N.J.: Princeton University Press, 1988.

4. THEOLOGY

MARK NOLL

Americans have changed the world much more by action than by thought. In the religious realm, it is the same. The activity of religious believers has been constantly transformative within American culture and, since the late nineteenth century, for the world, but the impact of what Americans have thought about God has been less obvious and less extensive. Nonetheless, the history of American theology shows how both inherited traditions and popular innovations have interacted with pressing circumstances to produce theological reflection of surprising breadth and unexpected depth.

Three characteristics have been most important in the history of American theology. First in time was the colonial debt to Europe. To the present day, "American theology" has often simply meant religious reflection carried out in the United States on sources, authorities, guidelines, and agendas coming from Europe. From the time of the American Revolution or slightly before, two more characteristics became prominent. A populist democratization of theology occurred as creative individuals took advantage of a free environment without established churches to disseminate their own religious ideas. In addition, a widespread deference to the authority of science gained special strength in a society that repudiated many of the traditions that had been so important for all religious groups in the Old World. A capsule history of theology in America keyed to these three characteristics cannot be structured neatly, for the most visible theologians have reflected these characteristics with great variety. But it can highlight some of the exemplary figures, the conceptual challenges, and the dominant issues that have defined theology in the American experience and that have made it a surprisingly fruitful arena for reflecting on the more general dynamics of religion in American history.

THE COLONIAL ERA

The colonial character of American religious experience was already evident in the theological achievements of the New England Puritans, the early European settlers who were most self-conscious about theological issues. In setting out to establish a "godly commonwealth" during the middle decades of the seventeenth century, they adapted for the new American environment what British Puritans had been proposing in their effort to reform the Church of England. Prominent in that thinking was devotion to the Holy Scriptures, concentration on the "new birth," an assumption about the unity of society under God, and commitment to the church as the key bond between personal religion and national righteousness.

The biblical theme of covenant provided the grand device for binding Puritan theology together. The many meanings of the covenant began with God's choice of Old Testament Israel and his work in Jesus Christ, but went on to provide a framework for forming churches and a device for reforming society. The genius of covenantal theology was the provision of a single concept for personal religion, formal theology, church formation, and social order. Capable first-generation ministers like John Cotton of Boston and Thomas Hooker of Connecticut, along with conscientious laymen like the governor of Massachusetts Bay, John Winthrop, articulated this unified theology with considerable success. Later, leading pastors like Increase Mather and his prolific son, Cotton Mather, were forced to patch up the covenantal system in adjusting to changing circumstances at the end of the seventeenth century.

In what would become a common American pattern, strong theological positions generated strong theological dissent. In the first Puritan generation, Roger Williams of Rhode Island challenged the theology used by leaders of Massachusetts to justify their appropriation of Indian lands and their insistence on religious uniformity. The Bible-savvy Anne Hutchinson was expelled from Massachusetts for daring to suggest that the Puritan system of covenants undercut the strong emphasis on grace that had sparked the original Puritan movement. By the third generation, significant criticism of "the New England Way" came from Solomon Stoddard of Northampton, Massachusetts, who argued that the Lord's Supper should be used to seek converts rather than to ratify covenant privileges for church members. John Wise of Ipswich, Massachusetts, challenged church leaders like the Mathers by urging more independence for local congregations. Such criticism joined with the pluralization of New England society—which by the eighteenth century included Baptists, Anglicans, Scots dissenters, and even a few Catholics and Jews—to render full-orbed Puritan theology defunct. But even as it declined as a total system, elements of Puritan theology continued to shape later American history, especially the Puritan pattern of reasoning directly from the Bible to contemporary issues and Puritan ideas about the possibility that nations could be in covenant with God.

Perhaps the high point in American theological history occurred right at the end of the Puritan era, and just as the colonies were beginning to feel new effects from populist and scientific movements. Jonathan Edwards (1703–1758), a grandson of Solomon Stoddard and successor in his pulpit, has increasingly been recognized as America's most compelling theologian. The remarkable recovery of interest in Edwards was spurred first by secular historians during the 1930s, especially Perry Miller, who was responsible for propelling a sharp renewal of interest in the Puritans. Since Miller's death in 1963, fascination with Edwards has continued to expand in a flood of scholarship. That scholarship pays tribute to the subtlety of his thought, which was marked by creative fidelity to traditional orthodox Calvinism and immersion in the Scriptures, but also by unusually perceptive engagement with his era's foremost intellectual problems.

Edwards's writings on the colonial revival known as the Great Awakening kept his name alive during the nineteenth century, but his more demanding studies in metaphysical theology and religious psychology came to be largely dismissed by thinkers who favored faculty psychology as an explanation for human action and evolutionary naturalism as the best rendering of the physical world. At the end of the nineteenth century and the start of the twentieth, Edwards's reputation suffered another setback among theological modernists who found his view of God too demanding and his view of human nature too pessimistic. For their part, fundamentalists neglected Edwards because of his consistent intellectual rigor, despite the fact that they maintained at least a shadow of some of Edwards's own convictions. The striking renaissance in Edwards scholarship took place in the 1930s, with the rise of neo-orthodox theology, the use made of Edwards by major figures like H. Richard Niebuhr, and the growing realization that Edwards had engaged the thought of his age with rare prescience.

Edwards's writings ranged broadly over theology proper, theological metaphysics, ethics, religious psychology, and the person. His vision penetrated as deep as his reach was broad. In constant engagement with both scriptural sources and modern learning, he proposed a God-centered conception of the universe that incorporated many findings of modern thinkers. Thus he read with appreciation Sir Isaac Newton on gravity and the natural world, John Locke on perception, and "the new moral philosophers" (Francis Hutcheson and the Earl of Shaftesbury) on the affections as basic for moral reasoning. Yet in all cases, Edwards also offered criticisms that tried to pull modern thinking toward classical Calvinism. Specifically, he postulated God's will as an ongoing cause of the physical universe in order to counteract materialist implications drawn from Newton. He undermined Locke's empiricism with a counterargument asserting a theocentric idealism centered on the mind of God . And while accepting a voluntaristic ethics, he reversed Hutcheson and Shaftesbury by insisting that God's grace was an essential foundation for genuine virtue.

Edwards's writings, which aimed at differentiating genuine religion from the spurious, have never been out of print, but his metaphysical theology and his theocentric ethics have found only a few adherents. If, however, the recent recovery of interest in Edwards is marked more by respect than imitation, that respect is wide and deep, and it continues to grow.

THEOLOGY IN THE NEW UNITED STATES, 1776–1865

By the era of the American Revolution, populist theological activity and a growing concern for scientific plausibility were assuming new importance. Both emphases reflected adjustment to the swiftly changing circumstances that created the new United States and then led to the construction of a democratic social order. Without a national state church, with few widely revered theological traditions, with no centralized scheme of national education, with all of the denominations compelled to enter into vigorous popular competition for adherents, with new modes of communication implemented by ordinary people, and with at least some wealth available for establishing colleges, publishing houses, and newspapers—the religious landscape was open for innovation but also desperate for intellectual stability.

In the realms of intellectual discourse, what E. Brooks Holifield, the foremost historian of American theology, has called "reasonableness: the evidential temper" came everywhere into view. Principles of the moderate Scottish Enlightenment associated with the ethics of Francis Hutcheson and the epistemology and metaphysics of Thomas Reid provided American thinkers with intellectual foundations for reconstructing theology without relying on tradition. Enlightenment principles also included a strong appeal to empiricism defined by reference to Francis Bacon; a belief that the human mind could be studied objectively as natural philosophers (i.e., scientists) studied the material world; a great respect for the labor of Sir Isaac Newton as the best model for knowledge in general; and a great confidence in reasoned discourse for establishing intellectual first-principles.

Armed with these weapons, a generation of American Christian thinkers diligently employed rational apologetics, natural theology, and common-sense interpretation of the Bible to advance Christianity and construct a national culture. For them, the products of scientific reasoning replaced Europe's traditions as main props for the churches. Their number included college leaders like Congregationalist Timothy Dwight of Yale (president, 1795–1817), Unitarian Henry Ware Sr. of Harvard (professor of divinity, 1805–1845), Presbyterian Samuel Stanhope Smith at Princeton (president, 1794–1812), and somewhat later Baptist Francis Wayland of Brown University (president, 1827–1855). Energetic frontier organizers like Alexander Campbell of the Churches of Christ may have been even more influential in promoting common-sense reasoning as a substitute for church tradition. One of the most important reasons for the success of Protestantism in the period between 1790 and 1865 was the ability of these leaders to convince other Americans that Christianity met the highest standards of modern scientific discourse. Church traditions, inherited ecclesiastical practices, and the dictates of bishops who had never faced a popular election might lead the church astray, but the sanctified voice of scientific reason would not.

Populists also became skilled users of evidentialist reason, but their importance rested more on the new energy they brought to religious thought as they worked to form churches and create voluntary societies. In the early decades of U.S. history, the growing influence of Methodist theology arose directly from the ability of Francis Asbury and his fellow itinerants to establish Methodist cells, circuits, and publishing networks in the open spaces of a rapidly expanding country. The dominant theology of the colonial period had been Calvinistic, with a strong emphasis on God's control over the path that sinners took from the self to God. The popular colonial revivalist George Whitefield innovated in many things, but in his theology he held firmly to Calvinism. For Whitefield, humans responded to God's initiatives, rather than originating the move to God in themselves. The Methodists, as Arminians, shared many convictions with the Calvinists—belief in the holy Trinity, belief in the Bible as a revelation from God, belief that God redeemed sinners by his grace. They differed in maintaining a stronger sense of human capability. Methodists believed that people had been given freedom by God to chose for or against the offer of salvation. With their founder John Wesley they also held that faithful exercise of the will could move a person toward Christian "perfection" (or an end to willful sin after conversion). These beliefs about human capability and the possibility of a higher form of Christian life after conversion fueled—and were fueled by—the rapid expansion of the Methodists. They became more important in the United States than anywhere else in the Western world.

Several other significant theologians and theological movements of the nineteenth and twentieth century also developed "from below"—that is, from the circles of ordinary people who, if usually not beneficiaries of formal education, nonetheless mastered popular means of communication, understood popular religious psychology, and were themselves gripped by a powerful religious vision. As one prominent example, Phoebe Palmer effectively used prayer meetings in her New York City home to promote "holiness unto the Lord." Palmer was not fortified by formal intellectual resources, but her theology, which she eventually spread through effective public speaking, prepared the way for Holiness movements that emphasized physical healing and led on to Pentecostalism.

The same broad effects were exerted by the popular revivalist Charles Finney, who was the best-known preacher of the mid-nineteenth century. Finney's scholarly aspirations rose higher than Palmer's, as indicated by the publication of his formidable *Lectures on Systematic Theology* in 1846. Yet the considerable influence exerted by the common-sense Arminianism of this work, and the much greater influence of his *Lectures on Revivals of Religion* (1835), lay in their power to shape the thinking of the ordinary laity.

The early nineteenth century also witnessed the emergence of influential African American religious leaders. More than any other Christian group in American history, blacks have lived under the cross. The result—from the early nineteenth century to the present—has been a series of significant theologians who saw more clearly than most of their white contemporaries the contradictions to Christianity that, along with the openings for Christianity, characterized American society. The founder of the African Methodist Episcopal Church, Richard Allen, expertly exploited the Methodism of John Wesley and Francis Asbury in preaching a message attuned to the status of slaves and freed blacks. One of his successors as guiding bishop of that church, Daniel Alexander Payne, put the traumas of enslavement, emancipation, and Reconstruction to excellent theological use through his sermons and writings in the middle decades of the nineteenth century. In the era of the Civil War, the abolitionist Frederick Douglass adeptly contrasted the Christianity of the whip with the Christianity of Christ, as did numerous other black theologians (discussed further in Blum, chap. 10, this volume).

A similar combination of open intellectual space and energetic religious advocacy also empowered a host of more sectarian movements. The Church of Jesus Christ of Latter-day Saints (Mormons), Seventh-Day Adventism, Christian Science, and the Jehovah's Witnesses are among the main religious movements that sprang to life in this fertile period of religious innovation. These movements all possessed clarity of theological vision, often elaborated in surprising detail to treat questions of epistemology, metaphysics, and ethical casuistry as well as central religious concerns. Their claims of special revelation—usually to the group's founder—made them unacceptable to the broad range of Christian churches. But their dynamism in promoting those claims have preserved these groups as powerful religious forces. Sometimes, as with the Mormons in Utah and Idaho, they have become the dominant religion in a single region. Sometimes, as with the Mormons, Jehovah's Witnesses, and Seventh-Day Adventists, missionary commitment has led to dramatic expansion of the group's teachings overseas. Over time, the Seventh-Day Adventists have moved much closer to more common evangelical beliefs, and the Mormons have made preliminary moves in the same direction. But in the nineteenth century, their broader significance was to show the power of ordinary Americans to formulate and disseminate accounts of God that proved convincing to many of their contemporaries.

Even as populist theology became prominent in the early United States, the earlier pattern of interacting with European influences went on. In the early decades of the nineteenth century, works by the Scottish minister-scholar Thomas Chalmers guided some Americans in thinking about astronomy, natural theology, and the reform of urban blight. German and French scholarship on the life of Jesus, books growing out of England's High Church Anglican Oxford Movement, and volumes introducing European controversies on the nature of sacred Scripture also had an effect on this side of the Atlantic.

Much of the best formal theology in this period combined attention to these European trends with skillful adaptation to American contexts. Throughout this and later periods, a style that might be called elite popularization has flourished in the United States. Characteristically, it has embodied high academic standards, has been written in dialogue with major theological voices in Europe, and has been read with appreciation by significant ecclesiastical communities. Although theology of this sort has not gained widespread attention from secular intellectuals and remains important mostly to those who share the theologian's religious perspectives, this academic, mediated theology has provided effective anchorage for many religious communities.

The nineteenth century was the great period for such work. Trinitarian New England Congregationalists during the Revolutionary period, led by Joseph Bellamy and Samuel Hopkins, showed how historic Calvinism could be broadened to accommodate Revolutionary notions of law and moral responsibility. In the next theological generation, a broader range of New England theologians made further adjustments to the Puritan tradition in the effort to offer their communities theological self-understanding in an era of rapid cultural change. The most important of these theologians was Nathaniel William Taylor of the Yale Divinity School, who adjusted Calvinist tradition to meet the need for a theology of revivalism. The Unitarian William Ellery Channing made even more changes in Calvinism's historic views of human nature and of Christ as divine, but also communicated his views very effectively to the increasingly wealthy upper classes of New England. In the middle decades of the nineteenth century, several theologians propounded other versions of Calvinism and so contributed to the general sway of a Reformed perspective as the dominant religious discourse in the nation's formal intellectual life. From Princeton Theological Seminary, Charles Hodge gained a reputation for thorough, often polemical, exposition of historic Calvinist theology. The Christo-centric New York Presbyterian Henry Boynton Smith drew more directly on European mediating theologies, but shared many of Hodge's concerns. R. H.

Dabney and James Henley Thornwell were southern Presbyterians whose defense of slavery damaged their later reputations; but in their day they provided a wide range of southerners with expert tutelage in traditional Reformed thought.

Before the Civil War, a few theologians began to question the standard forms of Christian rationalism that prevailed so strongly from the late eighteenth century. In Hartford, Connecticut, Horace Bushnell made inherited New England Calvinism more Romantic by heeding insights from Germany's Friedrich Schleiermacher and, even more, from England's Samuel Taylor Coleridge. Bushnell's proposal that religious language should be construed symbolically rather than literally sparked intense controversy that, in altered form, continues to this day. Other theologians who also drew afresh on Europe to challenge standard American positions included John W. Nevin, a German Reformed minister who stressed the importance of the historic church and the sacraments. He was moved in his work by opposition to the standard practices of American revivalism and by reading the German neo-pietists of his day. Nevin taught at the German Reformed Seminary in Mercersburg, Pennsylvania, where he was joined by the Swiss-born, German-educated Philip Schaff, who wrote about the modern churches in positive relationship to historic forms of Christianity (including Roman Catholicism). Nevin enjoyed scant influence during his own lifetime, and Schaff became a widely noticed figure only after he moved to Union Theological Seminary in New York and oversaw prodigious scholarship on the text of the New Testament and in general church history. But because Nevin and Schaff made greater use of European organic theology, featured the sacraments prominently, and explored the development of theology over the centuries, they have enjoyed increased attention from modern scholars who share an interest in their main themes.

As an indication of America's relatively modest place in the world, it is noteworthy that the only one of these nineteenth-century theologians with overseas influence was Charles Hodge, who was read in Canada, Scotland, and Northern Ireland, but mostly among his fellow conservative Presbyterians. Otherwise, the influence of these worthy theologians was usually restricted to their individual ecclesiastical communities in the United States.

For American Catholics, the nineteenth century was mostly a period of adjusting inherited theological positions to the needs of immigrant churches and for defense against the nation's overwhelming majority of often hostile Protestants. That defense was carried out with skill in several public debates undertaken by knowledgeable bishops like John Baptist Purcell of Cincinnati and John Ireland of Savannah. Francis Patrick Kenrick, archbishop of Baltimore, pioneered in the production of formal theology, with a widely read textbook in dogmatic and moral theology; he also produced a translation of the Bible in order to provide the Catholic faithful with an alternative to the Protestants' King James Version.

The most widely noticed Catholic thinker of the era was the lay convert Orestes Brownson, who published many books and hundreds of articles offering a self-consciously Catholic assessment of all things American. Brownson's public positions included the contention that American republican government required the historical stability of Roman Catholicism if it was to succeed. What Brownson had to say about political and social matters, as well as Catholic theology, was important in itself, but even more for showing that a distinctly Catholic voice could be heard in an American culture otherwise dominated by strong Protestant interests.

THE THEOLOGICAL LANDSCAPE SHIFTS,
1865–1945

A defining era in theological history emerged in the last third of the nineteenth century as political trauma was compounded by intellectual innovation. The Civil War itself posed severe theological problems, especially the realization that Americans who were using the same methods of interpreting the Bible differed violently on the momentous question of whether Scripture permitted slavery. Even with the victory of Union armies, the inability to find peaceful resolution on this issue—and then on related questions concerning the civil rights of African Americans—left traditional Protestantism shaken, divided, and uncertain.

Equally shaking was the conviction that came to be expressed by more and more Americans that science should be viewed not as the handmaiden of theology, but as an autonomous power in itself. The publication in 1859 of Charles Darwin's *On the Origin of Species* had been an omen. Darwin seemed to embody rigorous, critical thought of the sort highly esteemed by American church leaders. But Darwin's science did not celebrate God's design of the natural world, as these leaders had done. Rather, he proposed that randomness, rather than God, provided the best explanation for natural development.

The problem was not evolution as such, since many traditionalists felt that God may have used evolutionary processes to fill the realms of creation. Benjamin B. Warfield, from his post at Princeton Theological Seminary, enjoyed a reputation as one of the country's most conservative theologians. Yet Warfield also felt that the Bible could be read to sanction theories of evolution that accounted for the development of life, including human beings. The problem was rather that evolution as a grand scientific scheme was being used increasingly to undermine traditional views of God and his design of the world. In prominent universities, leaders like the educational theorist and public philosopher John Dewey simply dropped the earlier American effort to demonstrate the harmony of science and Scripture. Others in the last third of the century acted even more aggressively. Andrew Dickinson White, the founding president of Cornell University, vowed that his institution would "afford an asylum for Science—where truth shall be sought for truth's sake, where it shall not be the main purpose of the Faculty to stretch or cut sciences exactly to fit 'Revealed Religion.'" It was not so much that university intellectuals were giving up the idea of a universal controlling intelligence, but that for at least some influential voices the controlling intelligence was now defined as science itself.

The new learning disrupted the settled relationship between Protestantism and the nation's intellectual life. It began the process that eventually ended Protestant control of higher education. And it opened up a possibility that had barely existed in America before the last third of the century, which was a willingness of some intellectuals to publicly question the existence of God.

A parallel challenge in the same era concerned the Scriptures. Much of the new scholarship from the European Continent seemed to undermine the confidence most Christians had placed in the truthfulness of the Bible. A rapid increase in knowledge about the ancient world was one of the factors that led some scholars to look on Christianity as merely one of the many similar religions of the ancient Near East. An increased willingness to view ancient writings as simply products of the authors' worldview led other academics to question some or all of the miracle stories in the Bible. Advances in the study of ancient texts convinced still more scholars that much of the Bible was actually composed, or at least collected, many centuries after traditional views had held.

While these innovations were pushing public intellectuals away from former positions, other voices offered their respective ecclesiastical communities more traditional guidance in negotiating between historical convictions and contemporary American challenges. Among Presbyterians, the moderately liberal Charles A. Briggs joined the conservative Warfield in marshaling vast quantities of exegetical and historical materials for constructive theological purposes. Baptist churches, which were expanding rapidly in this period, enjoyed the services of several distinguished theologians. The northerner A. H. Strong adapted a cautious account of evolution to his moderately Calvinist views. E. Y. Mullins, a distinguished educator and leader of the Southern Baptist Convention, combined a romantic sense of human dependence on God with an effective restatement of conservative Protestant principles.

A substantial number of important theologians made more extensive adjustments of the inherited faith to what were seen as the new scientific realities. Usually, these theologians viewed God as imminent in creation and saw human nature as progressing amelioratively through time. Romantic conceptions of humanity advanced by famed preachers like Henry Ward Beecher paved the way for this move. It was carried forward more vigorously by figures like Lyman Abbott, who as an influential New York editor combined liberal theology with a progressive appeal to social reform. For American liberal theology, European sources were once again unusually important. Especially from German scholars like Albrecht Ritschl, Adolf Harnack, and Ernst Troeltsch, Americans found examples of deep learning that used theories of social cohesion, philosophical idealism, and human brotherhood to replace the harder-edged doctrines of earlier orthodox Christianity. Such views received particularly sharp expression at the University of Chicago, where the Baptist ecumenicist Shailer Mathews promoted a scientifically informed and socially progressive version of liberal Christianity. Mathews's *The Faith of Modernism* (1924) was a much-noticed statement of these views.

Progressive theology and progressive reform also lay behind the loosely organized movement known as the Social Gospel. Early proponents included Washington Gladden, who used his Columbus, Ohio, pulpit to chastise tycoons for their callousness and encourage an "applied Christianity" in response to the traumas of large-scale industrialization. The most effective Social Gospel theologian was Walter Rauschenbusch, a German-trained pastor who had experienced the realities of a New York City slum before becoming an influential teacher and author. Rauschenbusch's perspective was forthrightly biblical in its echo of Old Testament prophets and straightforwardly reformist in its challenge to American commercial capitalism.

Even as this period witnessed the development of the modern research university, where questions of traditional religious thought were gradually marginalized, a significant number of academics still worked on problems that had been shaped by Christian concerns. An outstanding early example was the Harvard psychologist and philosopher William James, who, though far from orthodox, nonetheless wrote so well about subjects like conversion that his works have affected religious psychology abroad as well as in the United States.

One of the most notable American theologians of the twentieth century was directly influenced by Rauschenbusch's determination to effect social change and indirectly by James's effort to recast traditional theology in contemporary terms. Reinhold Niebuhr (1892–1971) worked as a pastor in industrial Detroit before moving to Union Theological Seminary in New York, where, amid the tumults of Depression and World War II, he provided an unusual degree of sober theological reflection for both the mainline Protestant churches and some of the nation's premier intellectuals. The key to Niebuhr's thought was his dialectical reasoning about the human situation: humankind was sinful and capable of sainthood, subject to history and social forces but also shaper of history and society, egotistical but capable of living for others. In the Bible, and especially the example of Christ, Niebuhr found his key leitmotif of power growing out of powerlessness. As a testimony to influence that reached beyond American borders, the South African novelist Alan Paton once wrote that Niebuhr was the most "enthralling" speaker he had ever heard.

Unlike those who were willing to use contemporary ideas and problems as a guide for rethinking traditional faith, several substantial American constituencies remained skeptical about the new authority of secular science and nervous about the stress on Christian social reform. Holiness and conservative Methodist theology, as promoted by John Miley at Drew Seminary and the Nazarene leader H. Orton Wiley, brought traditional Wesleyan insights to bear on the challenges of the recent past.

From its emergence in 1906 at Los Angeles's Azusa Street Mission, Pentecostalism has been much more a movement of dynamic spiritual renewal than of formal theology. Yet from its earliest days, Pentecostal emphasis on the special gifts of the Holy Spirit has provided a pneumatic focus in American popular theology. That focus, and the theology it has stimulated, evidently became important for the whole world, with the twentieth century's explosion of charismatic Christianity around the globe (discussed further in Sweeney, chap. 5, this volume).

The broadest negative reaction to religious and intellectual innovation of the late nineteenth century came from those who have been described as fundamentalists. If "modernists" were prepared to adjust theology to what they took to be modern life, so "fundamentalists" held on to what they considered the fundamentals of inherited Christianity: the truthfulness of the Bible, the supernatural activity of God, and the unique saving work of Christ. Fundamentalism always represented a diverse confluence of forces. One prominent emphasis was biblical prophecy linked to a literal exegesis of Scripture. This view was promoted most effectively by C. I. Scofield in an influential study Bible first published in 1909. That kind of prophetic emphasis has remained a mainstay of American populist theology.

Among fundamentalists, deliberately anti-intellectual loyalty to the King James Version of Scripture was balanced by the intellectually precise theology of J. Gresham Machen of Princeton Theological Seminary. Machen's *Christianity and Liberalism* (1924), with its denial that progressive theology deserved the name Christian, represented a forceful alternative to the modernism advocated by Shailer Mathews.

During the decades between the Civil War and World War II, Catholic theologians were mostly content to follow the guidance of the Vatican. When in the late nineteenth century Pope Leo XIII promoted the teaching of Thomas Aquinas, the American faithful responded with a wide-ranging neo-Thomist program that came to invigorate ethics, psychology, and political thought as well as theology. American Catholics were kept on course (or hemmed in, depending on perspective) by papal encyclicals that mandated fidelity to Vatican teaching. Pope Leo XIII condemned "Americanism" in 1899 as an excessive embrace of democracy; his immediate successor, Pius X, spoke out more strongly in 1907 against "modernism" in an effort to insulate Catholics from opinions that devalued the Church's historic positions. Within these boundaries, notable theologians of society, especially John A. Ryan, would later develop perceptive analyses of modern economic life, while leading moral theologians, especially John C. Ford, provided equally serious wrestling with contemporary ethical concerns.

THE RECENT PAST

Since World War II, American theology has moved in many directions. Most obviously, the long monopoly that Christians of various sorts exercised in the public sphere gave way as theologians of all world religions and many home-grown varieties competed for attention. Likewise, since the reopening of immigration in the mid-1960s, Christian theology has also become manifestly more international. Influences from abroad, especially from Korea, have strengthened concerns for migration, social marginality, and the supernatural among Protestants. Such influences are even stronger among Catholics, especially as themes from Latin American liberation theologians have become a mainstay of Catholic theological concern.

Throughout the twentieth century, American Catholics continued to be influenced by the work of Europeans, especially the French theologians Jacques Maritain, Étienne Gilson, and Henri de Lubac, and the Germans Karl Rahner and Hans Urs von Balthasar. But American Catholicism produced creative theological voices as well, with Dorothy Day and John Courtney Murray as prominent examples. Day took the integral theology of Thomas Aquinas that she learned from European mentors and transformed it into the powerful basis for her Catholic Worker Movement. That movement, in turn, offered an unusually powerful combination of social critique (ministry to the poor, advocacy for peace, and challenge to nominal religion) alongside liturgical and theological renewal. Murray's training in neo-Thomism took him in a different direction. By arguing carefully, over a period of decades, for the essential compatibility between Catholic theology and American practices of religious liberty, Murray convinced Americans that the Catholic Church could enhance citizenship while at the same time convincing Catholics around the world to promote religious liberty. Murray's mature thinking became a critical factor when the Second Vatican Council's "Declaration on Religious Freedom" (*Dignitatis Humanae*, 1965) unambiguously defined religious freedom as an essential right for all humanity.

European influence has been even stronger among the American Orthodox churches than it has for Roman Catholics. For the Orthodox, Europe has often meant the physical presence of refugees who continued in this country what they had begun to do overseas. The Communist revolution in Russia was responsible for bringing a distinguished line of Russian theologians to America—Alexander Schmemann, Georges Florovsky, and John Meyendorff. They have been crucial in providing strong theological direction to American Orthodox churches in the recent past.

At university levels, the influence of European neo-orthodoxy has probably sustained greater attention than the work of any American. The teachings of Emil Brunner on creation and of Karl Barth on revelation have formed dominant themes. One exception that, however, supports the generalization about European influence was provided by the American career of Paul Tillich, who gained wide notice for his analysis of *kairos* moments defined as the in-breaking of the divine into temporal spheres. Tillich's American reputation rested in part on his status as an immigrant fleeing the depredations of Nazi Germany.

The European impress on American theology extends deep into the middle levels of popular writing as well. The pattern of significant influence from overseas was well established by England's G. K. Chesterton earlier in the twentieth century. It has been carried on among the church-going population as well as among interested nonbelievers in the great popularity of figures like the Oxford don C. S. Lewis; the German Lutheran killed by the Nazis, Dietrich Bonhoeffer; the Anglican evangelicals John R. W. Stott and J. I. Packer; and the German Roman Catholic Hans Küng.

As before, however, recent decades have also witnessed strong American contributions, especially from individuals who sustain the earlier practice of mediating between elite religious thinking and specific Christian communities. One of the first women to participate in what had been an almost exclusively male activity was Georgia Harkness, who effectively blended philosophical personalism and neo-orthodox elements into her own Methodist tradition. Her fellow Methodist Albert Outler enlisted intensive study of early church fathers and of John Wesley to serve the same purposes. For the neo-evangelicals who arose out of northern fundamentalism in the 1930s and 1940s, Carl F. H. Henry provided an able exposition of moderately rational Reformed perspectives in his wide-ranging work as editor and author.

The emergence of Anabaptist churches from linguistic and sectarian isolation allowed several theologians from Mennonite, Church of the Brethren, or Brethren in Christ backgrounds to engage with circumstances of American public life with especially creative reasoning from the Anabaptist tradition. Among these were John Howard Yoder, who argued forcefully for Jesus as a model of the nonresistance that all believers should follow, and Ronald Sider, who has appealed for Western Christians to make a biblical identification with the poor.

In the end, the most notable recent American contribution to theology must certainly be the religious thinking that inspired the civil rights movement of the 1950s and 1960s. Although many things made this movement the most significant moral event of the last half-century, one indispensable factor was the multiform African American theology that inspired its leaders and sustained its foot soldiers. As articulated by Martin Luther King Jr. (1929–1968), the theology of the civil rights movement has already exerted an impact around the world by inspiring many other movements of social liberation.

King's own thinking was a singular blend of formal influences learned academically and visceral influences absorbed from his black Baptist heritage. King's theology took in the legacy of Social Gospel teachings from Walter Rauschenbusch, the Christian realism of Reinhold Niebuhr, and philosophical personalism from King's doctoral study at Boston University. It also included a strong dose of nonviolence, which was compounded from Christian sources (mostly mediated by Quakers) and Hindu sources (particularly from Mahatma Gandhi). But what brought King's theology alive for a wide spectrum of Americans was what it reflected from the long tradition of African American biblical preaching, especially as that preaching stressed the Scripture's prophetic denunciation of oppression and its comforting solace for the oppressed.

While these elements of King's theology have already become subjects of serious investigation, less attention has been paid to the long line of forceful black theologians that led up to King. These began with the first African American Christians to embrace the Christian faith. In the late nineteenth century, the African Methodist Episcopal bishop Henry McNeal Turner made a telling contribution to that tradition when, in an effort to connect traditional Christian theology with the plight of oppressed people, he proclaimed that "God is a Negro." A few decades later, in 1938, Benjamin Mays published *The Negro's God, as Reflected in His Literature*, which singled out Jesus as a model of servant leadership, exalted brotherhood as the key perspective on humanity, and defined racial pride as sin. May's contemporary Howard Thurman experienced sharp confrontations with non-Christians on the Indian subcontinent who rebuked him for upholding a religion that had been used to subjugate "dark-skinned" people. Thurman's response was to depict Jesus as preeminently God's reaching out to the poor, the outcast, and the despised of the whole world. Also in the 1940s, George Kelsey of Morehouse College invoked God as creator, judge, and redeemer in ways that anticipated some of King's most famous public pronouncements.

Together, this line of stalwart theologians prepared the way for King. They anticipated what he would say so effectively about the "beloved community" as God's intended pattern for human interaction, and they also set the pattern for using the biblical themes that he employed to demand justice for the marginalized. King was a great theologian for what he did himself, but also for how effectively he communicated the fruits of a classic theological tradition.

Like Jonathan Edwards, who developed his theology to probe the effects of revival, and Reinhold Niebuhr, whose theology sought perspective on the conflicts of modernity, Martin Luther King Jr. proclaimed a theology for action—in his case, for overcoming entrenched discrimination. The ongoing creativity of ordinary men and women continues to play a central role in American theology, as does continued attention to what Europeans say. Yet it fits neatly with the main themes of American religious history that America's most impressive theologians have also been the theologians who most creatively applied Christian traditions to the urgent issues of their own day. This survey of theology also provides many examples of one major theme of this work: the folk origins of high theology and the theological base of popular religious movements. Jonathan Edwards's high theology paved the way for the popular movement of the Great Awakening, while the "folk" tradition of preaching in the black church vitally influenced Martin Luther King Jr.'s formal theological statements. In both cases, ideas and action were in dialogue.

REFERENCES

Bozeman, Theodore Dwight. *Protestants in an Age of Science: The Baconian Ideal and Antebellum American Religious Thought*. Chapel Hill: University of North Carolina Press, 1977.

Branch, Taylor. *At Canaan's Edge: America in the King Years, 1963–68*. New York: Simon and Schuster, 2006.

——. *Parting the Waters: America in the King Years, 1954–63*. New York: Simon and Schuster, 1988.

——. *Pillar of Fire: America in the King Years, 1963–65*. New York: Simon and Schuster, 1998.

Dickerson, Dennis. "African American Religious Intellectuals and the Theological Foundations of the Civil Rights Movement, 1930–55." *Church History* 74 (2005): 217–235.

Dorrien, Gary. *The Making of American Liberal Theology: Crisis, Irony, and Postmodernity, 1950–2005*. Louisville, Ky.: Westminster John Knox Press, 2006.

——. *The Making of American Liberal Theology: Idealism, Realism, and Modernity, 1900–1950*. Louisville, Ky.: Westminster John Knox Press, 2003.

——. *The Making of American Liberal Theology: Imagining Progressive Religion, 1805–1900*. Louisville, Ky.: Westminster John Knox Press, 2001.

Finstuen, Andrew S. *Original Sin and Everyday Protestants: The Theology of Reinhold Niebuhr, Billy Graham, and Paul Tillich in an Age of Anxiety*. Chapel Hill: University of North Carolina Press, 2009.

Holifield, E. Brooks. *Theology in America: Christian Thought from the Age of the Puritans to the Civil War*. New Haven, Conn.: Yale University Press, 2003.

Hughes, Richard T., and C. Leonard Allen. *Illusions of Innocence: Protestant Primitivism in America, 1630–1875*. Chicago: University of Chicago Press, 1988.

Hutchison, William R. *The Modernist Impulse in American Protestantism*. Cambridge, Mass.: Harvard University Press, 1976.

Kuklick, Bruce. *Churchmen and Philosophers: From Jonathan Edwards to John Dewey*. New Haven, Conn.: Yale University Press, 1985.

Lacey, Michael J., ed. *Religion and Twentieth-Century American Intellectual Life*. New York: Cambridge University Press, 1989.

Lee, Sang Hung, ed. *The Princeton Companion to Jonathan Edwards*. Princeton, N.J.: Princeton University Press, 2005.

Lesser, M. X. *Reading Jonathan Edwards: An Annotated Bibliography in Three Parts, 1729–2005*. Grand Rapids, Mich.: Eerdmans, 2008.

Marsden, George M. *Fundamentalism and American Culture*. 2nd ed. New York: Oxford University Press, 2006.

———. *Jonathan Edwards: A Life*. New Haven, Conn.: Yale University Press, 2003.

May, Henry F. *The Enlightenment in America*. New York: Oxford University Press, 1976.

Miller, Perry G. *The New England Mind*. Vol. 1, *The Seventeenth Century*. New York: Macmillan, 1939.

———. *The New England Mind*. Vol. 2, *From Colony to Province*. Cambridge, Mass.: Harvard University Press, 1953.

Noll, Mark A. *America's God: From Jonathan Edwards to Abraham Lincoln*. New York: Oxford University Press, 2002.

Roberts, Jon H. *Darwin and the Divine in America: Protestant Intellectuals and Organic Evolution, 1859–1900*. Madison: University of Wisconsin Press, 1988.

Shea, William M., and Peter A. Huff, eds. *Knowledge and Belief in America: Enlightenment Traditions and Modern Religious Thought*. New York: Cambridge University Press, 1995.

Toulouse, Mark G., and James O. Duke, eds. *Makers of Christian Theology in America*. Nashville, Tenn.: Abingdon Press, 1997.

Turner, James. *Without God, Without Creed: The Origins of Unbelief in America*. Baltimore: Johns Hopkins University Press, 1985.

Weber, Timothy P. *Living in the Shadow of the Second Coming: American Premillennialism, 1875–1982*. Chicago: University of Chicago Press, 1987.

5. EVANGELICALS IN AMERICAN HISTORY

DOUGLAS A. SWEENEY

About one out of every ten people in the world is an evangelical—so say the number crunchers who keep the closest tabs on global religion. By the first year of the twenty-first century, the world population had topped 6 billion. More than 2 billion people identified themselves with Christianity. Of these, well over 500 million were "evangelical" Christians.

A century ago, the number of Christians of any kind was smaller than this, and the vast majority of the world's Christians lived in Europe and North America. But the twentieth century witnessed a virtual explosion of evangelicalism, a blast that rocked the two-thirds world more powerfully than the West. By the early 1970s, most Christians lived outside the West, a result of evangelical growth that has shifted their churches' center of gravity. Global evangelicalism is now an enormous movement of which American evangelicals comprise a small minority. But Americans have played a larger role than anyone else in spreading evangelical faith around the world.

DEFINITIONS

Defining evangelicalism is difficult to do. In fact, the most contested issue facing scholars of evangelicalism pertains to its definition. Evangelicals are diverse—

unusually diverse for a modern Christian movement. Men and women on every continent count themselves as evangelicals. Some of them are rich, but even more of them are poor. Some are highly educated; others, self-taught. In America alone, evangelicals belong to dozens of different denominations—some of which were founded in opposition to some of the others. Most of them are Protestant, but even among the Protestants there are Lutheran, Reformed, and Anabaptist evangelicals. There are Anglicans, Methodists, Holiness people, and Pentecostals. There are untold millions of "independent" evangelicals, some of whom worship in extremely large churches (usually called megachurches). There has never been a *comprehensive* evangelical church. Evangelicals do not have a formal constitution. There are plenty of famous leaders and institutions they rally around (Billy Graham, *Christianity Today* magazine, the World Evangelical Alliance), but none of these has final authority to govern the whole movement.

Among historians, David Bebbington's definition is best known. In his widely used book entitled *Evangelicalism in Modern Britain: A History from the 1730s to the 1980s* (1989), Bebbington writes:

> There are . . . four qualities that have been the special marks of Evangelical religion: *conversionism*, the belief that lives need to be changed; *activism*, the expression of the gospel in effort; *biblicism*, a particular regard for the Bible; and what may be called *crucicentrism*, a stress on the sacrifice of Christ on the cross. Together they form a quadrilateral of priorities that is the basis of Evangelicalism. (2–3)

Some scholars complain, however, that Bebbington fails to distinguish evangelicalism from Protestantism, or even from Christianity. They argue that *most* Christians define their faith and practice in these terms, whether or not they think of themselves as evangelicals. Others contend more strongly that self-professing "evangelicals" have commandeered this label, ignoring its use by groups that predate their movement by centuries. Still others have decided to *cease* defining evangelicals. They claim that the movement defies neat and tidy definitions.

As I have discussed elsewhere, I believe that evangelicals do comprise a common movement, one that can be defined. They are certainly diverse. Most resist attempts to pigeonhole them firmly. Still, for the purpose of analysis, we can define evangelicals in terms of their common history: modern evangelicals comprise a religious movement rooted in ancient Christianity, shaped by a largely Protestant understanding of the Christian faith, and distinguished from other such movements by an eighteenth-century twist. Or put more simply (though less precisely), evangelicals are a movement of orthodox Protestants with an eighteenth-century twist. They are certainly not the only authentic Christians in the world. Nor are they the only ones to whom the term "evangelical" applies. But they are unique in their commitment to spreading the Christian gospel message. And their uniqueness is best defined by adherence to (1) beliefs most clearly stated during the Protestant Reformation, and (2) practices shaped by the revivals of the so-called Great Awakening (more on this later).

A brief word is in order here about a few of the key terms in this definition of evangelicalism: "movement," "orthodox Protestants," and "eighteenth-century twist." First, evangelicals comprise a *movement*, not a church or denomination. They are a coalition of Christians from all sorts of different backgrounds working together in pursuit of a vibrant, ecumenical witness. Second, evangelicals are descendants of the *Protestant* Reformation with a commitment to the *orthodoxy* (that is, right doctrine and right worship) expressed in the ancient Christian creeds and repackaged by reformers like Martin Luther and John Calvin. Some people disparage commitments to "orthodoxy" as repressive and intolerant—but evangelicals rarely do. Although not always socially, culturally, and politically conservative, most evangelicals prove conservative theologically. Finally, modern evangelicals differ from other Christian groups in that their movement emerged from a definite, *eighteenth-century* cultural context that yielded a *twist* on Protestant orthodoxy. Modern evangelicals, as distinguished from others who use the word or share their view of the gospel message, stand as heirs of the Great Awakening—a Christian renewal movement that reconfigured the Protestant world over the course of the eighteenth century.

ORIGINS

Modern evangelicalism emerged three centuries ago out of a spiritual movement the likes of which the world had never seen. Known then and since as a "Great Awakening" of Protestant Europe's state churches, this movement began in the middle of Europe, quickly spread to the British Isles and Britain's North American colonies, and impressed the entire West with the spiritual power of what evangelicals term the born-again experience.

Before the Great Awakening, the Protestant world had been divided in both its worship and its witness by various ethnic and cultural boundaries. The heirs of the Reformation (which began in the 1510s) had long been fighting among themselves over matters of biblical interpretation and control of their churches' resources. As a result of this infighting, the Protestant world was broken apart, and its state churches were not the only signs of division. Its theologians developed competing doctrinal statements, called confessions, that buttressed their rulers' tendencies toward intramural partisanship. They granted religious support to the rise of European nation-states, fracturing the superficial unity of Christendom.

During and after the Great Awakening, much of this would change for good—not overnight, and never completely, but considerably and noticeably. Hundreds of Protestant leaders began to join hands across the boundaries that had long divided their churches and collaborate in the work of gospel ministry. The reasons they did so are complex; they involve factors of theology (described in Noll, chap. 4, this volume), popular culture (discussed further in Goff, chap. 15, this volume), encounters with racial "others" such as blacks and Indians (elaborated on in Fisher, chap. 1, this volume), and a growing democracy of communication technologies such as newspapers. The Awakeners did not establish a new church. Rather, they labored ecumenically—*inter*-denominationally and *pan*-geographically—co-sponsoring revivals, "concerts of prayer," and other spiritual exercises. They traded pulpits with one another, promoting itinerant gospel preaching and thereby undermining the zoning system that had long divided their churches.

They accomplished these things with the help of a new communications network, which linked all kinds of evangelicals living in Europe and North America. Historians refer to the eighteenth century as the great age of letter writing. Evangelicals, for their part, traded tens of thousands of letters. This was also the time of the rise of British magazines and newspapers, media used by Christians to promote the cause of revival. Further, spiritual books outsold all other titles in this period of colonial American history, uniting evangelicals and helping those who struggled to make sense of the revivals. These communications offered a new sense of religious identity that transcended their readers' national and denominational ties. Many now felt that they were part of a new *international* movement of God. Their horizons expanded dramatically. They often grew more excited about reaching out together for Jesus than about propping up much older and more parochial Protestant projects. Consequently, many thousands of Americans would date their spiritual births to the time of the Great Awakening.

In short, the Great Awakening engendered a new sense of gospel urgency and spirit of partnership. Of course, its evangelical leaders would never experience perfect peace. And the new movement that they founded would know its fair share of sibling rivalry. During and after these revivals, however, a host of evangelicals pushed their differences aside and worked together for the gospel. Led by the Anglican George Whitefield (said by many to be the greatest preacher in all of Christian history), the Congregationalist Jonathan Edwards (known as "America's theologian"), and the Methodist John Wesley (the revivals' organizational genius), they transgressed their state–church boundaries, said that the *world* was now their parish, and labored diligently to promote what they considered "true religion." Many made new friends with Protestant leaders in other places. They learned to trust one another's judgments. They came to see that their numerous differences need not keep them from working together.

MODERN HISTORY

No sooner did the Great Awakening hit America's shores than it led to some major realignments in its people's religious lives. In the colonies of New York, Pennsylvania, and New Jersey it split the Presbyterian Church into rival "New Side" and "Old Side" synods, the former led by Gilbert Tennent, pushing revival and renewal, and largely responsible for the founding of the College of New Jersey (in 1746; later Princeton University). In the South, it revolutionized the liturgical, hierarchical, heavily Anglican way of life as evangelical insurgents battled against what they considered social and spiritual oppression. (The Anglican Church was established by law in the South, and its leaders usually resisted evangelical encroachments.) It yielded a harvest of Indian Christians, as hundreds of Native Americans joined the ranks of the born again and a surge of Indian missions paved the way for political partnerships that bolstered the English against the French and their own Native American allies. It also made deep inroads among America's African slaves, contributing powerfully to the formation of the historic black churches; conversely, African styles of outward spiritual expression (the holy dance, the shout, and the extemporaneous sermon) vitally influenced white evangelical expression.

Nowhere did the Awakening produce more spiritual institutions than in New England, the regional center of early American evangelicalism. For several decades after the rise of the transatlantic Great Awakening, New England led in constructing new evangelical organizations—new churches, schools, missions, and a host of outreach agencies—dividing and even destroying older structures in the process. Beginning as early as 1740, this region's "standing order" churches, the Congregationalists—state-supported scions of the Puritans—divided into "New Light" and "Old Light" factions, initiating the multiplication of ministry organizations. Fighting most forcefully over the "enthusiasm" attending the revival and the itinerant preaching ministries of its New Light organizers, their struggle eventually sundered more than 100 congregations and led to a movement of "Separates," who started sectarian ministries.

It is no coincidence that the rise of the modern evangelical movement took place at roughly the same time as the last gasp of Christendom. Throughout much of Christian history, the faith was extended most powerfully by the territorial expansion of Christian nations—nations with legally "established" churches, the will to colonize foreign lands, and the audacity to Christianize their populations by force. But in the eighteenth and nineteenth centuries, most state churches in the West began to weaken, as did their goal of imposing religious unity. Modern thinkers began to defend the right to freedom of religion, the official leaders of state churches lost much of their secular authority, and the kind of toleration most Americans now expect began to find its champions in the halls of power.

Early on, most evangelicals were nervous about these trends. They feared the loss of Christian influence on America's cultural life. They also opposed the "infidelity" (unfaithfulness, or unbelief) of the more open, liberal champions of religious toleration. Eventually, however, evangelicals would embrace the social order these trends produced—and exploit it to promote their *transdenominational* movement. They came to see that "disestablishment" could unleash a spirit of voluntarism that boosted the work of evangelism and spiritual renewal. On the one hand, it would yield an exponential increase in religious institutions, none of which was able to claim a legally sanctioned authority. On the other, however, it deregulated the marketplace, enabling new religious groups to flourish like never before. Evangelicals have always excelled at "marketing" their faith. Disestablishment created a "free market" for religion in which their entrepreneurs enjoyed tremendous success, exemplifying the theme of this volume of proselytization, spiritual recruitment, and the market economy of religion.

On the eve of the Revolution (that is, in 1776), more than half of the nation's churchgoers went to Congregational, Presbyterian, or Anglican worship services— and supported the legal establishment of their churches. By 1850, though, these denominations boasted fewer than 20 percent of churchgoers, while evangelical Protestants predominated the landscape. Baptists and Methodists alone composed over half of the nation's attenders. Scores of other denominations seemed to be sprouting up overnight. A democratization of religion accompanied American independence. All kinds of previously marginal groups—evangelicals, Roman Catholics, people of color, many women—began to enjoy the new opportunities for ministry.

Most prodigious by far was the growth of Baptists and Methodists. Historians estimate that at the outbreak of the American Revolution, there were 494 Baptist congregations in the colonies. By 1795, however, this number had more than doubled (to 1,152), and Baptists were poised to exert an enormous effect on the church of the next century. They proved most powerful in the South and on the ever-expanding frontier, largely due to their flexibility in forming rural churches. The Southern Baptist Convention, which has now become the largest Protestant body in the land, coalesced in 1845 to facilitate this growth. German and Swedish Baptist groups emerged at roughly the same time (in 1843 and 1852, respectively). By 1850, Baptists trailed only Roman Catholics and Methodists in size among America's Christian churches.

America's Methodist Church did not exist until 1784, when it was founded at the historic Christmas Conference in Baltimore under the leadership of Thomas Coke and Francis Asbury. In 1770, fewer than 1,000 Americans had identified with Methodism. By 1844, however, the first year that Methodists topped the denominational charts, they claimed 1,068,525 members; 3,988 itinerant preachers; and 7,730 local ministers. Needless to say, their impact was great. Much like the Baptists, they enjoyed their greatest numerical successes in the Mid-Atlantic states, in the Southeast, and on the frontier, serving people often neglected by the older denominations. In an era when the United States grew faster than ever before or since—and when most of the growth took place to the west of the Appalachian Mountains—the Methodists' rough-and-ready approach to ministry proved essential. Thousands of "circuit riders" took up the cause of preaching out in the country. Their work was grueling. They were poorly paid. They often lived out of saddlebags, slept outdoors, and died young (from exhaustion and frequent exposure to the elements). But they evangelized the country like no other Christian group. As a result, the nineteenth century is often called "the age of Methodism."

Despite the gains of the Great Awakening and religious deregulation, by the end of the eighteenth century many evangelical leaders had grown concerned about the spiritual life of the new United States. They felt that the churches had grown lethargic, they feared that the Revolution had bred an unhealthy interest in the most secular forms of Enlightenment rationality (which were often hostile to Christianity), and they knew that westward migration demanded a doubling of their efforts in home missions and church planting. A revival was needed, they thought, to fuel the growth of the new nation. Thanks to the efforts of various evangelical leaders across the country, a long season of revival, called the Second Great Awakening, is exactly what they got.

The Second Great Awakening had at least three regional centers—New England, upstate New York, and the Cumberland River Valley—during the first three decades of the nineteenth century. New Englanders provided its early theological leadership. Revivalists in New York, especially Charles Grandison Finney, garnered the lion's share of attention for their controversial methods (such as the use of the "anxious bench," placed at the front of the auditorium, where anxious sinners received attention during services). And Cumberland Valley clergy like Barton Stone and Peter Cartwright played the greatest role in spreading Christianity on the frontier.

The greatest revival of all during the Second Great Awakening happened in Cane Ridge, Kentucky (1801), near the city of Lexington. Known as "America's Pentecost" for the amazing effervescence of spirituality it produced, the Cane Ridge revival also attracted huge crowds—estimates range from 10,000 to 25,000 people altogether—at a time when Lexington, the largest town in all of Kentucky, had only 1,795 inhabitants. "Signs and wonders" appeared all around, as hundreds of worshipers, slain in the Spirit, barked liked dogs, jerked uncontrollably, fell into trances, danced, and shouted. Some compare its emotional ambiance to that of a rock concert.

As a result of the revivals, and in the wake of disestablishment, evangelical institutions moved to the center of American culture, rendering the nation what some have called a "righteous empire." During the early nineteenth century, evangelical groups provided most of the country's social services, prefiguring the nationalization of U.S. public culture. They founded special needs asylums for the disabled and mentally ill. Some of them worked for temperance reform, abolition, and Indian outreach. They raised millions of dollars in support of education. They printed tens of millions of books, tracts, and periodicals. They organized on a grand scale at a time when the Bank of the United States was this country's only truly national corporation and the Post Office its only national government agency.

As evangelicals sidled to the center of the Protestant "mainline," however, critics complained that they had sold out to secular, "worldly" values. Beginning in roughly the 1830s, Christians in several denominations raised an alarm about the domestication of evangelicalism. They claimed that power had corrupted America's evangelical leaders, many of whom grew fat and happy at the top of their righteous empire. Evangelicals showed signs of conformity and spiritual apathy. They needed revival again to reignite their passion for holiness.

By the late 1860s, such concerns led to the launching of a massive "Holiness movement," which would eventually revolutionize American evangelicalism. A number of major revivalists—from Finney to Phoebe Palmer, a leading Methodist female preacher—had promoted the message of holiness ever since the 1830s. But not until 1867 was a revival held that focused first and foremost on this theme. It boasted 10,000 participants, most of them evangelicals, and led to the institutional rise of the Holiness movement.

In July 1867, near the town of Vineland, New Jersey, a group by the name of the National Camp Meeting Association for the Promotion of Holiness organized this revival. At its conclusion they incorporated, elected a Methodist president, and decided to sponsor a *series* of Holiness meetings. Riding a wave of spiritual passion, its leaders attracted more than 20,000 to each of their next two meetings—first in Manheim, Pennsylvania (1868), and then in Round Lake, New York (1869). Soon they founded a publishing house, started a Holiness periodical (*Christian Witness and Advocate of Bible Holiness* [1870–1959]), formed a missions organization, and changed their name to the simpler National Holiness Association (later the Christian Holiness Association).

The Holiness movement flourished during the late nineteenth century, reshaping evangelicalism all around the world. Its most important contribution to the evangelical cause (and to global Christianity), though, transcended its founders' vision for personal righteousness. Indeed, by the late nineteenth century, the most radical Holiness leaders were calling for more than holy living. They were seeking divine power—supernatural ability to spread the gospel message, live a higher Christian life, and hasten the second coming of Christ. By the early twentieth century, they found what they were looking for in modern Pentecostalism.

Although Pentecostal practices predate the twentieth century, the place to begin the story of the Pentecostal movement is with the ministry of Charles Fox Parham. In 1895, Parham left the Methodist Church to itinerate as a Holiness evangelist. Like many Holiness leaders, Parham practiced faith healing. In fact, in 1898 he took his ministry to Topeka, Kansas, and founded the Bethel Healing Home, welcoming people seeking divine cures to stay and receive prayer. He engaged in outreach to the homeless. He founded a Holiness periodical (*Apostolic Faith*). Most important, however, he started the Bethel Bible School (1900), to which he attracted thirty-four students for Bible study and Holiness training. He taught his students to anticipate an awesome outpouring of the Holy Spirit's power in a monumental revival that would precede the return of Christ. Before long, the Bethel community was hoping, praying, and longing for a mighty work of God.

By December 1900, Parham had concluded that what he called the "Bible evidence" that one had received a complete "infilling" of the Holy Spirit's power was the gift of speaking in tongues, technically known as "glossolalia," the defining feature of early Pentecostalism. He said that this gift was part of the "latter rain" foretold in the book of Joel, to be released in preparation for the final Day of the Lord. Its recipients could be sent abroad to witness to the gospel—instantaneous missionaries who needed no language training at all—much as the first apostles did on the day of Pentecost: "tongues of fire" descended upon them, they "were filled with the Holy Spirit," and, miraculously, the foreigners in Jerusalem "hear[d] them declaring the wonders of God in [their] own tongues" (Acts 2). Soon the earth would be full of the knowledge of God and Jesus would return. Parham's teaching aroused excitement in Topeka.

On New Year's Day 1901, one of Parham's students at Bethel, Agnes Ozman, started to write in an unknown language (Chinese, as it was thought). Soon she was speaking in tongues as well. So were half of the others at Bethel. Revival ensued. Parham became a sensation virtually overnight. Before he knew it, several thousand people had flocked to his ministry. He preached another major revival toward the end of 1903—this time in small-town Galena, Kansas, near the state's southeastern corner. Then in early 1905, Parham moved to Houston, Texas, where he preached and planted churches in its rapidly growing suburbs.

In December 1905, Parham opened another Bible school, where he offered a ten-week training course in Pentecostal doctrine. Among the students he drew to Houston was an unassuming, thirty-five-year-old son of former slaves, a humble waiter turned Holiness preacher named William Seymour. Seymour was blind in one eye. He was a poor public speaker. Because he was black, moreover, and segregation ruled the day in Texas, he was forced to sit outside Parham's classroom (near the door, which was left ajar for him). Seymour quickly became convinced of Parham's Pentecostal teaching and soon surpassed Parham himself in Pentecostal leadership. No one ever would have guessed it. But less than a year after Seymour had enrolled in Parham's training course, he became the world's most famous Pentecostal. He soaked up everything he could before he left the school in Houston. Then in early 1906, he headed west to work as a pastor in Los Angeles.

On April 9, 1906, glossolalia broke out in one of Seymour's worship services. Word of this spread like wildfire, eliciting so much interest that Seymour had to move his meetings to an old, abandoned warehouse, 2,400 square feet in size, on Azusa Street, the former home of the First African Methodist Episcopal Church of Los Angeles. A major revival erupted. Large crowds thronged Azusa Street. Seymour held three services a day for over three years. The "Azusa Street Revival" proved to be so influential that insiders still refer to it as "the cradle of Pentecostalism." During the twentieth century, Pentecostalism would grow to become a major religious force, attracting hundreds of millions of people. With the help of "charismatics," who imported Pentecostalism to other Christian churches, its leaders have ensured that every major Christian tradition—in every sector of the globe—has now come under the sway of Pentecostal piety. (Charismatics are evangelicals who have taken Pentecostal doctrine and practice into non-Pentecostal churches, inspiring spiritual enthusiasm and lively corporate worship to a degree unprecedented in history.)

But just as Pentecostalism was starting to stoke the fires of the evangelical furnace, the intellectual ground began to shift beneath the movement, placing it closer than ever before to the forces of naturalism and modernism. Doubt, and even fear, began to spread within the churches, as traditional, supernaturalistic views of God and the world gave way to modern, naturalistic criticism. Evangelicals, of course, had dealt with modern "infidelities" since the early days of their movement. But now the stakes were raised. For the first time ever, *accommodation* to such views, even to anti-Christian carping, had begun to carry the day among denominational activists. Some began to wonder about the future of the faith. "Fundamentalists" resisted adaptation to these trends, bearing the brunt of the heaviest blows to Christianity.

In addition to the blows received from intellectual trends, evangelicals in this era were disoriented by their nation's massive social changes, especially the rapid growth of America's cities. In 1790, shortly after the nation's independence from England, only 5.1 percent of its citizens lived in urban areas. In 1870, 25.7 percent did. By 1920, 51.4 percent, half its people, dwelled in cities. Another way of depicting the growth of America's urban landscapes is to say that in the years from 1800 to 1890, the nation's general population grew by twelve-fold, while its urban population grew by eighty-seven-fold—more than seven times as fast as the nation at large. Chicago, for example, which had been a tiny hamlet only half a century earlier, was the fifth-largest city in the world by 1890.

In response to urban growth, progressive Protestant reformers like Washington Gladden and Walter Rauschenbusch promoted what later came to be called the Social Gospel. Their work was rooted in a critique of evangelical revivals—for their allegedly excessive concern with the souls of individuals and their ignorance of larger, more organic, social problems. But the Social Gospel *arose* with nineteenth-century socialism, as well as the birth of sociology as an academic discipline that emphasized analysis of modern social structures. It applied gospel principles to the practice of urban ministry, especially to the needs of the urban poor. By the late nineteenth century, it had inspired hundreds of pastors and other urban social workers to establish settlement houses and charter "institutional churches," congregations offering a wide range of social ministries—including bathing facilities, job training, and educational services—to America's working class.

Evangelicals fretted about the Social Gospel's secularity. They worried that Social Gospelers were substituting social work for evangelism. So evangelical ministry leaders—Dwight L. Moody, J. Wilbur Chapman, Billy Sunday, and many others—mounted their own urban campaigns, holding *revivals* for the common man on America's city streets. They also continued to show concern for the physical needs of the poor. In fact, evangelicals founded several hundred soup kitchens, "rescue missions," during this very period, ladling "soup, soap, and salvation" to the nation's down-and-outers. But their efforts usually focused on the individual sinner, placing the gospel message first and frequently forcing people to listen to an evangelistic sermon before they received physical care.

By the early 1910s, in response to the rise of naturalism, modernism, and secularism, a massive group of conservative evangelicals converged to protect the old-time gospel and its "fundamental" doctrines. Sharing an evangelical pedigree, they worked together to guard "the faith that was once for all entrusted to the saints" (Jude 3, a favorite fundamentalist verse). By the late 1910s, they had won several battles for control of leading mainline Protestant ministry organizations. Finally, in 1920, the Reverend Curtis Lee Laws, a Baptist minister and the editor of the weekly *Watchman-Examiner*, coined the word "fundamentalist." Today, many attach this word to people they dislike. Most associate it with bigotry and religious zealotry. But Laws himself was a fundamentalist. He deemed it a badge of honor. As he defined them in his paper, fundamentalists were those "who still cling to the great fundamentals and who mean to do battle royal for the faith." During the early 1920s, "battle royal" bludgeoned nearly every mainline Protestant body. Few of them met with amputations (ecclesiastical schisms), but most hemorrhaged profusely. In almost every case, moreover, fundamentalists met with overwhelming opposition, losing control of mainline Protestantism for good.

Nothing symbolized the defeat of mainline Protestant fundamentalists like their "victory" at the Scopes trial in Dayton, Tennessee (1925). John T. Scopes, a junior teacher at the local public high school, was solicited by the fledgling American Civil Liberties Union (ACLU) to test his state's new law against the teaching of evolution. Clarence Darrow, a celebrity lawyer (and obstreperous agnostic), was retained for his defense; the prosecution was led by William Jennings Bryan. A famous Presbyterian populist and fundamentalist spokesman, Bryan had served as a federal congressman, a presidential candidate (three times), and the secretary of state under President Woodrow Wilson. But he had not tried a case in court for twenty-eight years. Darrow made him look foolish. The eastern news media made him look even worse. The Scopes case, in fact, turned into a raucous "Monkey Trial." A total of twenty-two telegraphers sent 168,000 words per day from Dayton's courtroom to media posts around the world. Dayton's local chamber of commerce, which had helped the ACLU bring the trial to Dayton's doors, capitalized on its publicity. Peddlers hawked souvenirs. A regional Baptist fundamentalist pitched a tent and preached to the crowds. By the time the trial had ended, few cared, or even noticed, that Scopes had lost. Fined $100 for teaching evolution against the law, he never paid the state a dime. His conviction was later overturned on a technicality. Bryan died soon after the trial, literally exhausted by the fiasco. Fundamentalists, who were always strongest in northern, urban areas, have been ridiculed ever since as country bumpkins.

During the 1930s and 1940s, fundamentalists licked their wounds. Some withdrew into a hostile state of Christian separatism, giving up on the larger culture and defining themselves in opposition to mainline Protestantism. But many others got back up and reinvested in the culture, repairing their ministries and reaching out to others. In fact, fundamentalism *grew* throughout this period of recovery—and has continued to grow apace, though usually out of the range of vision of our cultural connoisseurs. Fundamentalists lost their place at the helm of mainline Protestant churches. They were sidelined at the nation's elite educational institutions. But they survived, and even thrived, within America's "heartland," which had never embraced the modernists or cared much for elitists.

Those who worked the most assiduously to reengage the culture eventually called themselves the *new* (or neo-) evangelicals—both to signify their youthful passion for social and cultural relevance and to distance themselves from antisocial forms of fundamentalism. They sported a new style of fundamentalist performance, projecting less concern to master the Christian martial arts. While retaining a firm grasp on older forms of Protestant orthodoxy, they reached out again in the mode of its eighteenth-century twist.

Evangelicals such as J. Elwin Wright and Harold John Ockenga had scurried to build support for this new venture during the 1930s. However, its first major foray into American public life came through the National Association of Evangelicals (1942). In the 1940s and 1950s, dozens of other neo-evangelical institutions emerged, some of them dwarfing their competitors in the mainline Protestant world. Important to their success was their leaders' use of the media—especially Christian radio, but television, magazines, and best-selling books as well. Beginning in 1956, for example, neo-evangelicals launched their own periodical, *Christianity Today*, which soon became the mouthpiece of the evangelical movement. And no one played a greater role in leading evangelicals into the second half of the century than the magazine's founder, evangelist Billy Graham, a master of the media who became the best-known Protestant in the world for his "crusades" (massive revivals), attended by millions over more than half a century.

Despite their losses during the early years of the twentieth century, then, evangelicals were thriving by the late twentieth century. Pentecostalism continued to grow. The charismatic movement spawned a host of new, self-described charismatic churches, revolutionizing Christian worship everywhere else as well. The neo-evangelicals attracted new supporters, building colleges and seminaries to train their future leaders. Black evangelicals organized like never before, reconciling with white Christians (who had often been their oppressors), contributing significantly to evangelical ministries (especially through the media), and founding self-consciously evangelical institutions, such as the Voice of Calvary Ministries (1960) and the National Black Evangelical Association (1963). Since 1965, moreover, the "new immigration" has added color to evangelicalism, enriching it with contributions from Asia and Latin America. The benchmark Immigration Act of 1965, in fact, has netted several million new American evangelicals. Theirs will likely be the next chapter in the story of evangelicals in America, which has always been a multicultural nation of immigrants.

American evangelicalism has grown so large and diverse that its membership is difficult to quantify—and nearly impossible to analyze coherently. No one speaks for them all. Their leaders struggle to keep them together. Thus the fears of secular critics regarding their cultural, political, and environmental potential are most certainly exaggerated. Nevertheless, evangelicals comprise a common movement—a potent *religious* movement—one of the most important movements of our time.

The study of American evangelicals has become a major industry in the past generation, although far more work has been done on Anglo- and African American evangelicals than on Hispanic and Asian American evangelicals. Since the landmark Immigration Act of 1965, Hispanic and Asian American immigrants have quietly contributed several million new adherents to the evangelical movement. In the next generation, then, scholars would do well to continue working on the history of "mainstream" evangelicals while devoting the bulk of their energy to these previously understudied minority groups. Other contributions to this volume, including those by Roberto Treviño (chap. 11) and Timothy Tseng (chap. 12), provide some guides for doing so.

REFERENCES

Balmer, Randall. *Blessed Assurance: A History of Evangelicalism in America*. Boston: Beacon Press, 1999.
Boles, John. *The Great Revival, 1787–1805: The Origins of the Southern Evangelical Mind*. Lexington: University Press of Kentucky, 1972.
Butler, Jon. *Awash in a Sea of Faith: The Christianization of the American People*. Cambridge, Mass.: Harvard University Press, 1992.
Carpenter, Joel. *Revive Us Again: The Reawakening of American Fundamentalism*. New York: Oxford University Press, 1997.

Dayton, Donald W., and Robert K. Johnston, eds. *The Variety of American Evangelicalism*. Knoxville: University of Tennessee Press, 1991.

Evensen, Bruce. *God's Man for the Gilded Age: D. L. Moody and the Rise of Modern Mass Evangelism*. Oxford: Oxford University Press, 2003.

Hankins, Barry, ed. *Evangelicalism and Fundamentalism: A Documentary Reader*. New York: New York University Press, 2008.

Hatch, Nathan. *The Democratization of American Christianity*. New Haven, Conn.: Yale University Press, 1989.

Heyrman, Christine. *Southern Cross: The Origins of the Bible Belt*. New York: Knopf, 1996.

Kidd, Thomas. *The Great Awakening: The Roots of Evangelical Christianity in Early America*. New Haven, Conn.: Yale University Press, 2007.

Lee, Shayne, and Philip Luke Sinitiere. *Holy Mavericks: Evangelical Innovators and the Spiritual Marketplace*. New York: New York University Press, 2009.

Lindman, Janet. *Bodies of Belief: Baptist Community in Early America*. Philadelphia: University of Pennsylvania Press, 2009.

Lippy, Charles H., and Robert H. Krapohl. *The Evangelicals: A Historical, Thematic, and Biographical Guide*. Westport, Conn.: Greenwood Press, 1999.

Long, Kathryn. *The Revival of 1857–58: Interpreting an American Religious Awakening*. Oxford: Oxford University Press, 1998.

Marsden, George M. *Understanding Fundamentalism and Evangelicalism*. Grand Rapids, Mich.: Eerdmans, 1991.

McLoughlin, William L. *Revivals, Awakenings, and Reform: An Essay on Religion and Social Change in America, 1607–1977*. Chicago: University of Chicago Press, 1978.

Miller, Perry, and Alan Heimert, eds. *The Great Awakening: Documents Illustrating the Crisis and Its Consequences*. Indianapolis: Bobbs-Merrill, 1967.

Noll, Mark A. *American Evangelical Christianity: An Introduction*. Oxford: Blackwell, 2001.

Noll, Mark A., David W. Bebbington, and George A. Rawlyk, eds. *Evangelicalism: Comparative Studies of Popular Protestantism in North America, the British Isles, and Beyond, 1700–1900*. New York: Oxford University Press, 1994.

Sobel, Mechal. *Trabelin' On: The Slave Journey to an Afro-Baptist Faith*. Princeton, N.J.: Princeton University Press, 1988.

Stephens, Randall J. *The Fire Spreads: Holiness and Pentecostalism in the American South*. Cambridge, Mass.: Harvard University Press, 2008.

Sutton, Matthew Avery. *Aimee Semple McPherson and the Resurrection of Christian America*. Cambridge, Mass.: Harvard University Press, 2007.

Sweeney, Douglas A. *The American Evangelical Story: A History of the Movement*. Grand Rapids, Mich.: Baker Academic, 2005.

Synan, Vinson. *The Holiness-Pentecostal Tradition: Charismatic Movements in the Twentieth Century*. Grand Rapids, Mich.: Eerdmans, 1997.

Wacker, Grant. *Heaven Below: Early Pentecostals and American Culture*. Cambridge, Mass.: Harvard University Press, 2001.

Wigger, John. *Taking Heaven by Storm: Methodism and the Rise of Popular Christianity in America*. Oxford: Oxford University Press, 1998.

6. RELIGION AND POLITICS

JASON C. BIVINS

It is a truism that one should not talk about religion and politics in "polite company." Yet Americans have always—for reasons good and bad, sensible and sensationalist—been drawn to the subject. Aside from the social awkwardness the topic can create, it presents analytical and historical challenges that are equally daunting to students of American religion. Conversations about such issues can be unclear even as to exactly what constitutes their subject or where it is found; a lack of precision dims the perception not only of "religion" and "politics" but also of the "and" conjoining them. While it is common in religious studies to wring hands about the impossibility of defining religion, similar scrutiny is rarely extended to considerations of what constitutes politics. Those studies that have engaged this area of inquiry—and these are few, since no distinct subdiscipline yet exists in religious studies—have frequently been limited in one of three ways: they equate politics with government; they rely anachronistically on themes specific to early periods of American life or earlier scholarly moments in order to explain contemporary phenomena; and they are reluctant to interrogate what Russell McCutcheon identifies as the "religion and" problem, the assumption that both "religion" and "politics" are fixed entities that become conjoined, rather than emerging in some combinative experience captured better by terms like "political religion" or "religious politics."

Flowing from such presumptions, the religious experiences of public life—or motivations for engaging matters of political concern—have tended to be grouped by scholars into a few well-worn analytical frames. Perhaps the most prominent of these is the "church–state" framework. While illustrious texts like Edwin Scott Gaustad's *Dissent in American Religion* have emerged from this paradigm, this association tends to reduce the complexity of political religion to a single relationship, seems to privilege Christian traditions, and suggests that analysis should be focused simply on two discrete institutions, "church" and "state" (apparently self-evident in their meanings). A second familiar scholarly path focuses on "civil religion," usually a meditation on the relationship between civic and religious obligation or on the reverence paid to civic institutions and customs. While such studies like Robert N. Bellah and Phillip E. Hammond's *Varieties of Civil Religion* help capture some enduring tensions in political religions, they too frequently render political life as an abstract decision about consent. Other writings—including textbooks like Robert Booth Fowler's *Religion and Politics in America: Faith, Culture, and Strategic Choices* and Kenneth Wald's *Religion and Politics in the United States*—tend to accept such matters, often including analyses of voting patterns, religious petitions for legislation, and a smattering of social movements (usually the civil rights movement and the Christian right). Theoretical interventions—in the work of Robert Audi and Michael J. Perry, for example—often interrogate the permissibility of religious arguments in public discourse.

Historically both "religion" and "politics" have been intertwined in American public life, mutually defining and at times placing checks on each other, each upholding critical principles against the perceived dangers of the other. Indeed, for a number of reasons, American religions are de facto political (or at least politicized); because of the high degree of controversy surrounding religions' involvement in public matters, and due to the engagement with such issues during the constitutional period, the two are clearly bound to each other. This is obscured by the assumption that politics is simply government (and thereby something in which religion has had no place—either in the historical record or for normative reasons). This is clouded in vague accounts of the admixture of "the sacred" and "the political," positing that religions become involved in or concerned with politics by invoking "prophetic" themes or by fashioning religious "arguments," claims that either are tautological or point out the obvious. These odd locutions are quite commonplace, having circulated in scholarly literature for many decades, and have yielded an important literature, as embodied by texts like Michael J. Perry's *Under God? Religious Faith and Liberal Democracy* and Richard John Neuhaus's *The Naked Public Square: Religion and Democracy in America*. These texts, however, often act more as criticism or theory than as guides to the lived culture of political religions. Religion obviously involves far more than language, symbols, narratives, and suasion. While these inspire and motivate in interesting ways, American religio-political history is equally (or perhaps more significantly) about what specific people and communities have done and produced.

In many ways, these prevalent orientations take their cues from studies of seventeenth- to eighteenth-century American religious culture; works by scholars like Perry Miller and Bellah, for example, focused on themes like religious nationalism, prophetic religion and the jeremiad, or civil religion, concepts that continue to circulate beyond their initial formulations. Elsewhere, work has focused often on constitutional debates (as with Catharine Cookson's *Regulating Religion: The Courts and the Free Exercise Clause*), accommodation and pluralism (in the work of Martin Marty and William Hutchison), and religious dissent (such as Robert Craig's *Religion and Radical Politics: An Alternative Christian Tradition in the United States*), applying these lenses to various groups (whether Catholic pacifists or post-1960s new religious movements) and time periods (first-wave modernism or the 2004 presidential election). As fine as many of these studies are, they have not adequately captured the breadth or the significance of American political religions.

American religions have been expressed or represented in political spaces in multiple ways. If by "politics" we mean simply "government," we must look to a particular constellation of legal, juridical, administrative, and institutional arrangements. Such an examination might include the theocratic rule of the early commonwealths, debates surrounding the scope of the First Amendment, the expression of religion in public education, or the continuing saga of Supreme Court jurisprudence. American religious traditions have lined up on all sides of these debates, which have continued since the constitutional era.

Yet if by "politics" we mean a larger arena of public life, power, and communication, then religions could be seen to have been even more ubiquitous in American political history. This broadened understanding of politics would take in not only familiar institutions and debates but also manifestations like riots, alternative communities, interreligious conflicts, debates, and ideologies. Is politics, then, everywhere? Certainly it is in many more spaces than those customarily acknowledged, but it is not found simply in any public space or whenever conflict occurs. However, when such matters relate to the organization of social life (especially in matters of law, resources, recognition, power and discrepancies thereof, and pluralism, in addition to conventional areas), then politics emerges. For the purposes of this essay, I use the terms "religio-political" and "political religion" not to suggest that these religious expressions differ essentially from others but in the hope of capturing the cultural politics of American religions and their encounter with political powers. Political religions are shaped and expressed in specific conflicts (between competing forms of authority, for instance), in particular places (including, or perhaps especially, that which is not typically seen as religious space), and focused on issues that (like feminism or the war in Iraq) provoke American religions to become political.

How, then, should these expressions best be traced throughout American history, and what kinds of narratives are best suited to this expanded understanding of political religions? A chronological narrative is only partly revealing. Such an account might begin with a survey of the colonial era commonwealths and move through the Great Awakenings; the emergence of a purported "civil religion" during the Revolutionary period; the nascent pluralism, new religions, and reform movements that arose during the nineteenth century's expansion and consolidation of state power; the combined transitions, accomplished largely in the decades following the Civil War, to political centralization, industrialization, and urbanism, coextensive with dramatic increases in immigration (which itself inspired considerable backlash); the subsequent emergence of fractious protest and agitation, much of it religious in inspiration, challenging the legitimacy of political bureaucracy and the equality of economic arrangements; the emergence of religious socialism and strengthening of religious pacifism between the world wars; the diversification of religious protest in the civil rights movements, the Catholic Worker Movement, and 1960s feminism; and the legitimation crisis developing since the late 1960s and early 1970s, accompanied by the flourishing of identity politics, a new upsurge in new religious movements, and the rise of the "New Christian Right."

Yet while it is possible to tell a story about American political cultures and the expressions of religions in and around political developments, such a narrative is too teleological, excluding too much in the name of linearity. Instead, I single out several themes and orientations that have surfaced regularly throughout American history and that capture something about American political religions:

- The embattled legacies, both practical and theoretical, of the constitutional period
- The dynamics of allegiance and dissent (as these are understood by specific traditions, community, or practitioners), or the relation between religious obligations and those required by good citizenship (overlap generally yields sociopolitical harmony, while divergence may yield dissent)
- The embodied experience of political religions, as felt in areas like gender, race, identity, and will-formation
- The texture of public discourse and argumentation

Within each of these broad areas of questioning and self-fashioning, specific areas of American religio-political history emerge. These categories recur throughout each period of transition in American religio-political culture. They demonstrate the cyclical nature of political consent and dissent, engagement and apathy, as these affinities cycle through institutional changes and changes in media and organizing. There is overlap between these themes, their boundaries are porous, and the examples I give within each are neither exhaustive nor exclusive (in a different telling, they might reasonably migrate elsewhere). But I hope that by foregrounding an expanded set of categories, I might give readers a sense of both chronology and comparison.

CONSTITUTIONS AND LEGACIES

By what means is a political order constituted, and what legitimate role do religions have therein? This is a question that has resurfaced regularly during American history, particularly during periods of transition and crisis. It is also an area of considerable scholarly inquiry. Instead of focusing merely on institutional or juridical issues, though, I see this trajectory as one of contestation and polyvocality, where American political religions situate themselves in an ongoing argument about political fundamentals.

Studies of Puritan New England's attempts to institutionalize righteousness in religiously grounded commonwealths constitute some of the earliest efforts to chart the intermingling of the political and the religious in American culture. Perry Miller and Edmund Morgan described how the settlers in Massachusetts and elsewhere would shape not only American public culture (in ways both admirable, as with the town hall meeting, and lamentable, as in the lingering ambivalence about religious "outsiders" that reared up in the Salem witch trials) but also themes and self-understandings long part of the way in which Americans have thought about themselves and their political legitimacy. John Winthrop's seventeenth-century "A Model of Christian Charity" provided perhaps the richest source for thinking about the link between religion and national identity. Because of Winthrop's assertions that the Puritan flight from Europe recalled that of Moses from Pharaoh, that theirs was a sacred journey ending in the establishment of a new covenant between a providential God and a "New Israel," his belief that this new country would serve as an example to the nations, a place privileged in the eyes of God, would preoccupy Americans well into the Cold War.

This institutionalization of righteousness demanded that government and education be guided by religious precepts. With religion "established" by the state, it was thought that not only civil magistrates but the citizenry as a whole should submit to the will of God. Yet despite the fact that religious authorities of the day generally insisted that only they knew the divine will, and despite efforts to condemn heretics (not simply those perceived to be "witches" but political heretics like the Baptist Roger Williams, who criticized the admixture of religion and government), there was religious pluralism of the sort that thrived as political and economic independence loosened the constraints of the Puritan theocracies beginning in the late seventeenth century.

The religious energy and creativity that began to bubble up more steadily in the eighteenth century—through immigration, revivalism, and mobility—seemed to demand the development of legal norms to address the reality of religious pluralism before conflict erupted. Economic interest was behind early sponsorship of religious pluralism, as the Lords of Trade in London—seeking to ensure the stability of profitable colonies—asserted to the magistrates of Virginia that religious liberty was important to the economic vitality of the colonies (sentiments echoed by mid-eighteenth-century Christians like Isaac Backus). During and after the Revolutionary period, the opportunity to consider such matters arose amid the efforts of "the Founders" to constitute a new political order. As David Holmes and Frank Lambert have written, the degree of conventional piety practiced by the Founders varied (and often entailed radicalism that would surprise many today). Thomas Jefferson believed that religion did not need the support of government and that, based on their dubious history in Europe, the two were probably best left separated. James Madison and others contended that the state and civil policy should not be guided by religious precepts; they did not want religion to disappear, and indeed believed it important to the development of personal and communal morality, but sought to disentangle it from government to the mutual benefit of both religion and the state.

In the Constitution there eventually appeared, after much vicious argumentation, a more refined presentation of these ideas. Most colonies had abolished the establishment of religion by 1789, when Article VI, clause 3 of the Constitution insisted that "no religious test shall ever be required as a qualification to any office or public trust under the United States." Some delegates to the Constitutional Convention believed that more needed to be said about religion, with some believing that the scope of religious liberty had to be clarified while others sought more of an official governmental position with regard to "right religion." As Isaac Kramnick and R. Laurence Moore show in *The Godless Constitution: A Moral Defense of the Secular State*, aborted House and Senate versions of the First Amendment reveal the contested nature of these ideas, whose formulation eventually was settled: "Congress shall make no laws respecting an establishment of religion, or prohibiting the free exercise thereof."

These clauses still shape and control legal discourse not only about religion in political life (though the distinction between politics and government is elided in the actual text) but about appropriate modes of religious action, about the disposition of the state toward religions, and about the duties that religious practitioners may or may not owe to the state (about which more later). Specific political assertions—particularly in the conceptual space between Winthrop's redeemer nation and Jefferson's moral commonwealth (protected by the infamous "wall of separation" he once described in his correspondence)—have generated protracted debates and differences that continue to shape American life. Americans continue to disagree in particular about whether ours is a secular polity or a religious one (usually, a "Christian nation"). Historically, this disagreement has surfaced in controversy over Sunday mail delivery, over the use of McGuffey's *Readers* in nineteenth-century public schools, and, most recently in the Ninth Circuit, over the constitutionality of the Pledge of Allegiance modified in 1954 to include the phrase "under God."

Americans have also disagreed about the relation between "public" and "private" realms. This reveals a deep and long-standing ambivalence about the liberal constitutionalism of the Founders (some of whom favored a more participatory, civic republican model of governance). American liberalism has generally privileged individual over collective rights, favored negative liberty (freedom from coercion) over positive liberty (freedom to participate in politics in active, constructive ways), and sought to protect moral and religious pluralism by separating public from private realms of society, keeping the public free from contentious moral or religious beliefs that are regarded as threats to political stability.

Vigorous religious critiques of this political order have been staples of American public life. While Alexis de Tocqueville wrote approvingly (in *Democracy in America* [1835–1840]) of the ways in which Americans' religious sentiments (and "habits of the heart") underwrote democratic institutions, evangelicals like Lyman Beecher and Charles Finney cautioned that believers could not expect too much from government and ought to save the social order themselves; some citizens worried about the loyalties of the growing number of Catholic immigrants, fearing that "true Americanism" might become dissolute should pluralism grow; and the waves of reformism spanning the mid-nineteenth to early twentieth centuries (including, among other religious engagements with political matters, first-wave feminism, abolitionism, populism, the Social Gospel, and Christian socialism) show that American religious practitioners—for all their disagreements and against the protestations of figures like nineteenth-century secular figurehead Robert Ingersoll—were alike in seeking to crash the boundaries that liberalism had erected. These contests over constitutional legacies have deepened since the mid-twentieth century, a period of renewed judicial engagement with religious matters and increased political discontent among American citizens. Following a time of apparent quiescence in the aftermath of World War II, profound reservations about the moral direction of an increasingly bureaucratic state, about the risks incurred by the Cold War, and about racial inequality ushered in an era of intense and often creative religious protest that revealed how deeply Americans are divided about constitutional essentials.

Perhaps nowhere are these issues presented more clearly than in the courts. Despite the prominence of the First Amendment, and of the continued proliferation of new religions throughout the nineteenth century, it was not until the mid-twentieth century that the "religion clauses" of the First Amendment were applied at the state level as well as the federal. After the passage of the Fourteenth Amendment, which restricted the power of states to abridge the liberties of its citizens, a new kind of jurisprudential engagement with the questions about the relation between public and private and the extent to which liberal regimes should accommodate religious liberty was likely. While the court did not see fit to acknowledge the free exercise of Latter-day Saints in *Reynolds v. United States* (1878), beginning in the 1940s a number of establishment cases (from *Everson v. Board of Education* [1947], to the *Engel v. Vitale* [1962] ruling that mandatory school prayer is unconstitutional, to the *Lemon v. Kurtzmann* [1971] decision establishing judicial neutrality and secular legislative purposes as desiderata, to the *Zelman v. Simmons-Harris* [2002] decision upholding a Cleveland school voucher program using public funds to help students transfer to religious schools) and free exercise cases (from the *Cantwell v. Connecticut* [1940] ruling that excessive burdens be removed from Jehovah's Witness proselytizers, to the *Wisconsin v. Yoder* [1971] decision that the Old Order Amish should be granted an exception to a state law requiring mandatory public schooling until age sixteen, to the controversial decision in *Employment Division v. Smith* [1990], which held that Native American substance-abuse counselors who had been fired and denied unemployment compensation owing to their sacramental ingestion of peyote were not protected under the Free Exercise Clause) have both answered and raised these questions for American practitioners.

Stephen L. Carter suggests, in *Dissent of the Governed: A Meditation on Law, Religion, and Loyalty*, that this judicial lineage reveals not only liberalism's contested nature but the ways in which courts are detached from the citizenry. Eric Michael Mazur's *The Americanization of Religious Minorities: Confronting the Constitutional Order* and Cookson's *Regulating Religion* explore the ways in which religious "others" have often been disadvantaged in this lineage. Winnifred Fallers Sullivan claims, in *The Impossibility of Religious Freedom*, that no coherent standard of religion jurisprudence exists that can be meaningfully applied to the complicated and ever-changing terrain of American religions. However, attending to the incoherence and fractiousness surrounding these norms and documents is a productive way of narrating American political religions (further discussion on the incoherence of the Supreme Court's decisions on many of these issues is in Ravitch, chap. 7, this volume).

HOLY DISOBEDIENCE, FAITHFUL ALLEGIANCE

Attending to the legacies of the constitutional moment reveals one of the most important dynamics in any account of American political religions. Related to ambivalences about religious freedom and secularism are mixed messages about disobedience and protest, combining a deep reverence for order (one sometimes at odds with democracy) with a tradition of (often religious) dissent. This tension tells a different story about political religions than is customarily told in the literature of civil religion. The liberal constitutional project, which aims to secure a set of legal and political principles that can unite a diverse citizenry, has often been judged insensitive to the things that are crucial to character and identity, whether culture, religion, or biology. While a certain kind of religious patriotism runs deep in American culture, religions have served often as a critical principle against which political order is judged. When the obligations and directions of political order overlap or harmonize with those of religions, allegiance usually follows. But when there is no such harmony or overlap, dissent frequently issues forth from American religions.

These questions vary considerably, across time and place, and within each tradition. While grumblings about "politics as usual" or "big government" are familiar to all Americans, there is perhaps no political impulse more recognizably American than a religious denunciation of political power, for its perceived intrusiveness or immorality. When allegiance is not understood as a mark of piety, holy disobedience may at times seem obligatory, in the form of: ritual protest, the establishment of separatist communities, or organizing and mobilizing around specific issues or interests. As Craig shows in *Religion and Radical Politics* and Robert H. Abzug in *Cosmos Crumbling: American Reform and the Religious Imagination*, since the founding era religious outsiders and dissidents—including the abolitionists, the populists, and the early waves of Christian fundamentalists, to name only some widely recognized examples—have often challenged the moral legitimacy of the state or of particular policies. The historical range of such dissent is quite broad, as evident in Roger Williams's denunciation of the Massachusetts magistracy in 1636, the religious exhortations contributing to Bacon's and Shays's rebellions, William Lloyd Garrison's burning of a copy of the Constitution in 1854, Christian suffragist or trade union activism, Catholic pacifists between and following the world wars, the Nation of Islam's intentional communalism, and the elusive subculture of post-Vietnam Christian militias, among many others.

As I write in *The Fracture of Good Order: Christian Antiliberalism and the Challenge to American Politics*, underlying these varied forms of religious dissent from political authority are three general criteria: an aversion to centralized power, a concern about the inability of citizens to shape the decisions affecting them, and a contention that the state is not tethered to sound morality. Some pursue these concerns with the hope of reforming the state, as did Martin Luther King Jr., and as the Christian Coalition continues to do; such practitioners generally still see value in electoral participation (as increasing numbers of conservative evangelicals have since the 1970s) and in seeking recognition from the state (often in the form of legislation). Others, however, contend that political order cannot be salvaged and that piety requires demonstrating signs of difference; examples of this separatist impulse range from Gerald L. K. Smith's Depression-era screeds denouncing pluralism and industrialism to Daniel and Philip Berrigan's iconoclastic and highly suggestive protests against U.S. militarism.

These religio-political sentiments, which turn on the relationship between sovereign allegiances, have often taken shape not just as part of arguments about public life but in response to specific concerns or cultural changes thought to demand a choice between separate authorities or to increase tensions along the boundaries. The rise of pluralism and urbanism between the Jacksonian era and the Gilded Age, for example, provoked numerous religious challenges to political order (in, for example, abolitionist campaigns or in nativist attempts to counteract state tolerance of pluralism) or attempts to engage sociopolitical matters through means independent of this authority (as in Jane Addams's Hull House). Concerns about industrial and postindustrial capitalism have prompted Americans to fashion from their religious traditions a moral language either denouncing economic inequalities (in the Social Gospel, the Catholic Worker Movement, or the social justice activism of Buddhist Karma Lekshe Tsomo) or defending free market economies (in writings by Reconstructionists like R. J. Rushdoony). American wars have perhaps been the sharpest test cases for religious allegiances, provoking fervent patriotism (Billy Graham's longtime Cold War anti-Communism) and fierce dissent, in addition to rich theological traditions reflecting on the difficulties such matters present (such as public intellectuals from Reinhold Niebuhr to Stanley Hauerwas).

Still another fruitful way of thinking through the historical relation between religious allegiance and dissent is to focus on the spatialization of political religions. In recent decades in particular, American religions have shaped their political sensibilities through a concern with physical space and limits: in ecology (discussed further in Ross-Bryant, chap. 14, this volume), in the extent of governmental authority in the educational sphere in particular, and in the establishment of alternative communities (detailed in Stein, chap. 13, this volume). While each of these concerns has historic roots that predate the contemporary period, since World War II there has been a sharpening of concerns about boundaries in American political religions. The rise of ecological consciousness has prompted many practitioners—such as the Coalition on the Environment and Jewish Life— to investigate their traditions for intellectual resources that might help promote environmental responsibility.

It has become more common also to express concern about religious autonomy by focusing on the relation between governmental and educational space. Ubiquitous curricular battles over sex education and evolutionary theory point to larger debates about parental responsibility, scientific rationalism, and religious liberty that have focused frequently on schooling. While these debates have yielded reforms both legal and curricular, another response—most notably from conservative Christians like Michael Farris, a longtime home-schooling advocate—has been to challenge or even withdraw from public educational space and establish alternatives more clearly under citizens' control. This last impulse has often been pursued by religious practitioners, as the establishment of intentional communities (whether they explicitly aim to resist or simply to evade the scope of political authority) has regularly been an occasion for creative ways of establishing religiopolitical identity or will. Some examples include Catholic Worker houses, the

Sojourners Fellowship in Washington, D.C., Philadelphia's MOVE, or even new religious movements like the People's Temple. As Donald E. Pitzer's anthology *America's Communal Utopias* shows, by their willingly adopting the status of marginalization or opposition, a clear sense emerges that for these practitioners the features of their religious tradition constitute signs against political order. Whether rhetorical device or material change, this position crystalizes some of the broader questions about allegiance for American religions—whether and how to profess it—while also shaping the specific textures of religious dissent.

THE BODY

At the heart of many political religions is an acute sense of boundaries, both permeable and inviolable. In American religious history, we see such a preoccupation not only with the widely remarked boundary between public and private but also between self and other, body and culture. The body has of course been the subject of considerable religious work—both the bodies of religious selves and the bodies of others thought to require healing or coercion—and an orientation to this work contributes to a broadened understanding of political religions.

American religious history is filled with bodies that have been vehicles for the expression of political religions: through religious dissent, through being "out of place," through disruptions or professions of allegiance. Yet additionally, the bodies of religious Americans have often been marked or designated as political either through their own volition or by the actions of others. In some ways, debates about embodiment tend to focus on the debates over identity politics and multiculturalism that have emerged since the 1960s. This is sensible, given how many contemporary new social movements—in which American religions have participated—have either demanded specific forms of recognition (of homosexual rights, for example) or have politicized specific modes of identity associated with embodiment (race and gender, most obviously; further elaboration in Petro, chap. 9, this volume). Yet concerns about the religious body have been quite long-standing in the United States, not just in terms of gender, race, and sexuality, but also in debates about the "appropriate" manner of bodily comportment and expression in public life.

As is widely known, the anatomical body (its genitalia, skin pigmentation, and sexual activity) is continually interpreted through cultural categories, paramount among which are religious understandings of embodiment. American politics has historically privileged individual over collective rights, so these features of bodily identity and will have often been seen as vehicles through which to define, for example, women's rights, African American rights, or gay rights. These questions have at times turned on understandings of the "essential" differences between males and females, between races, between people with different sexual orientations; elsewhere they have been resolved through challenges to such "essences" in the name of radical egalitarianism. In all such cases, religions have actively shaped political understandings of the body.

We see this in, for example, the history of religious feminism (and its critics) in the United States. Elizabeth Cady Stanton and Lucretia Mott helped to organize the first international women's rights convention in 1848, extending the rights-based struggles of the abolitionist movement—along with activists like Sojourner Truth—to a concern for the rights of women. As scholars like Catherine Brekus show, Lydia Sexton and other activists helped use evangelicalism's egalitarian emphasis to challenge its traditionalist strand, seeking to uncover the ways in which justification for male privilege had been harvested from texts and traditions that pointed in other directions. Economic and pacifist critics like Mother Jones and Dorothy Day helped the long process of reshaping "traditional" women's identities (in the form of participation, suffrage, or preaching), processes that continue on the ground in everyday devotional contexts. One could even regard the establishment of feminist theologies (such as those articulated by Mary Daly) or the establishment of alternative communities (under the leadership of figures like Starhawk) as political acts.

In changing social and political contexts, the female body has become a site of struggle over the meanings of particular religions. Scholars like Margaret Bendroth and Betty DeBerg show how assertions of "traditional" gender roles have frequently followed efforts to expand the rights and recognition afforded to women. One such example includes the Muscular Christianity of the late nineteenth and early twentieth centuries. Clifford Putney describes two strands of this impulse, one of which valorized manly virtue and physical discipline, while the other (in some ways embodied by star preacher Billy Sunday) directly confronted feminism. A more recent, and widely known example, is Promise Keepers, the Christian men's movement founded by former college football coach Bill McCartney in the early 1990s. Initially making its name by opposing a Colorado gay rights bill, Promise Keepers achieved huge and visible success during the Clinton years by filling sports stadiums for highly emotional rallies emphasizing not only what it claimed were biblical teachings about male headship but also elements of therapeutic culture, confessionalism, and sports rhetoric.

Sexuality, too, has become a key battleground on which American political religions have met, as Kathleen M. Sands's anthology *God Forbid: Religion and Sex in American Public Life* documents. This has most obviously been the case in struggles over reproductive rights, especially abortion. Following decades of legal reform, the *Roe v. Wade* (1973) decision seemed single-handedly to spur conservative evangelicals into political action. And, indeed, during the 1970s and 1980s—from Jerry Falwell's "I Love America" rallies to the inception of many powerful New Christian Right organizations beginning in 1979—groups like the Moral Majority and the American Coalition for Traditional Values sought to block the passage of an equal rights amendment and to create anti-*Roe* sentiment. Yet concerns about sexuality had been developing for decades, in efforts to monitor purportedly licentious entertainments like rock music and comic books but perhaps more evidently in curricular efforts to restrict sex education classes in public schools. Indeed, notable political figures Tim LaHaye and Michael Farris fashioned some of their larger anti-liberal critiques in curricular struggles like these. Homosexuality and gay rights have, since the late 1960s, assumed an important position in American religio-political discourse. This issue has generated not only specific religious voices (as with Mel White's theology) and controversies (debates in many communities about gay ordination, for example), but also vigorous backlash (seen in Fred Phelps's bilious "God Hates Fags" campaigns).

One of the most intense areas of religio-political struggle over the body has been in the contentious domain of race. "Race" in American discourse is generally thought to refer solely to the complicated history between African and European Americans. This discourse has been, from the importation of the first slaves in 1619, one of both political and cultural control, and religions have contributed energetically to it. From the seventeenth through the nineteenth century, American religions legitimated a number of initiatives—from the slave trade and plantation system to sanctions against specific Native American practices like the Ghost Dance, for example—that established or maintained racial distinctions and discrepancies of power. During this same period, of course, American religions also challenged such initiatives, most notably in the abolitionist movement that encompassed Quaker relief stations and the preaching of Sarah and Angelina Grimké, the Underground Railroad, the "free produce" movement, plantation revolts, and even John Brown's raid on Harper's Ferry. Michael O. Emerson and Christian Smith's *Divided by Faith: Evangelical Religion and the Problem of Race in America* shows that, as with gender, different interpretations of sacred texts were used to justify and advance multiple positions on politicized race. Toward the end of the nineteenth century, an era of African American new religions opened as many practitioners became dissatisfied with the ways in which conventional Christianity had failed to undo racial inequality. Pan-Africanism and the worship of a black God emerged—in a lineage stretching from Martin Delany to Henry McNeal Turner to W. E. B. DuBois and Marcus Garvey—as symbolic and material challenges to a political order characterized by Jim Crow laws and the purportedly "separate but equal" treatment of different races.

Nativism and white supremacist cultures continued to exist during this time period, and racism seemed in some sense to flourish in the crowded, pluralist, industrial North. As new legal initiatives were passed limiting (or even eliminating) immigration from Asia, some religious practitioners sought to craft alternative communities wherein they could fashion their own understandings of race and public life. These efforts ranged from interracial communities like Father Divine's peace mission and Clarence Jordan's Koinonia Partners to the Nation of Islam's explicitly racialized separatism, one focused on political and economic autonomy. Religious engagements with race became more pointedly activist during the 1950s, a time when the Nation of Islam became more visible (and to some extent confrontational, especially in the public activism of Malcolm X prior to his 1964 break with the group) and when the civil rights movement erupted in the wake of the *Brown v. Board of Education* (1954) decision (reversing the *Plessy v. Ferguson* [1896] "separate but equal" ruling). The well-known story of this movement, along with Martin Luther King Jr.'s ministry, is one of the most important in twentieth-century political religion (as documented impressively in Taylor Branch's work). In addition to its obvious role in generating support for the Civil Rights Act (one component of which, the Immigration Act of 1965, ended previous quotas restricting immigration from Asia and Latin America), King's theological bricolage (combining Niebuhr, Marx, and Gandhi) and use of direct action protest provided a template for much of the religious activism that has occurred since the 1960s.

Since the 1980s in particular, conventional wisdom has suggested that the "problem" of "race" was solved by the Civil Rights Act. Many religious communities—including the Nation of Islam under the leadership of Louis Farrakhan, resistance groups like MOVE, or even paramilitary groups linked to the white supremacist theology known as Identity Christianity—remind Americans in various ways that this is not so. Along with gender and sexuality, race remains an important area where religions and politics become integrated, yielding new sensibilities that emerge from the registers of identity rather than from external affiliations like political party, union, or even denomination.

DISCOURSE

A final angle of vision onto American political religions involves religious discourse and criticism. Rather than focusing—as much scholarship does—on the proper mode of religious reason and argumentation in public life, I invoke this category to highlight the historically enduring ways in which the self-understandings and motivations of those active in political religions, as well as citizens concerned by such activism, have been shaped by and articulated in public speech, argumentation, symbolism, and narrative. Religious exhortations and social criticism have framed many of the engagements discussed in this chapter, justifying resistance or informing demands for recognition and redress. Declarations to remake or reform the social order were heard as early as the Puritan jeremiads and continued to take shape during the reformist urgings of Lyman Beecher and Charles Finney. Later,

Christian exhorters like Billy Sunday and Samuel P. "The Sledgehammer" Jones excoriated the polis for its moral backsliding, intellectual fuzziness, and openness to immigrants; while, on a different part of the religio-political spectrum, King's address to the 1963 March on Washington continues to reverberate in public life. Religious writing, too, has constituted an enduring means by which practitioners have expressed their political will, in documents both obscure (angry open letters to sitting presidents) and familiar (the impassioned anti-war courtroom testimony of Daniel Berrigan, or the anti-liberal screeds of Tim LaHaye). It is not only in moral exhortation and calls to adhere to religious truth, however, that political will has historically been articulated. Apocalypticism and religious demonology have long constituted rich discourses by which practitioners have crafted socio-political sensibilities ("Judge" Joseph Rutherford of the Jehovah's Witnesses denouncing the social order as the devil's handiwork), identified threats to the polity (Jim Jones's declarations that America stood on the brink of a racial apocalypse), and sought to commend a vision of public life (eschatological imagery in the foreign policy speeches of Presidents Ronald Reagan and George W. Bush).

This category also captures the way in which Americans continually debate not only the merits of political religion but also the legitimacy of the categories that generally structure thinking about public matters. We see such protracted argumentation everywhere, from perennial vexation by strict secularists that the mere whiff of religions in public life threatens constitutional order to claims by certain evangelical conservatives that liberal democracy often masks "anti-Christian bigotry." The vitality and longevity of such conversations suggest that a narrative focused on the discourse of political religions helps to frame long-standing debates about the relation between public and private, the ability of the judiciary to regulate religious practice, or the role of religions in electoral politics. Plotting a course through the complicated texture of American history in this way enables us to avoid the idea that a simple sequence of events has unfolded—from Puritans to the First Amendment to the civil rights movement—that encompasses the history of "religion and politics." An awareness of the recurrence of debates and conflicts, and the differing ways in which religious Americans fashion their political will, is a productive orientation to this topic.

In many ways, then, the categories proposed here constitute different modes of organizing similar materials; for example, each mode of narration provides a different angle of vision onto, say, the meanings of founding debates about religious liberty, the influence of the civil rights movement, or links between the New Christian Right and electoral politics. The scope of this essay does not afford a fuller discussion of these matters, and there is clearly much more not included here than otherwise. Taken together, these orientations to—and ways of narrating—American political religions suggest that it is misleading to think that religion and politics have only intermittently been entangled in American history (declining, for example, with the Puritan magistracies and rising like a phoenix in the "culture wars" since the 1970s) or that political matters are merely those of elections or state power rather than the broader range of contests I have described herein. Historically, Americans have imagined many relationships between religions and the political, each of which has revealed something important about the imaginers.

Scholars have most consistently been guided by the approaches noted at the outset. And while sound work continues to be done in the areas of civil religion, church–state studies, and the like, this is a conversation in need of expansion. I hope to have proposed some alternative orientations to American political religions, ones not intended as radical rethinkings but as supplementary paths for scholars and interested readers, ones that may help both to orient historically and to provoke theoretically. The future's work will exist at this intersection of history and theory.

REFERENCES

Abzug, Robert H. *Cosmos Crumbling: American Reform and the Religious Imagination.* New York: Oxford University Press, 1994.

Audi, Robert. *Religious Commitment and Secular Reason.* Cambridge: Cambridge University Press, 2000.

Bellah, Robert N., and Phillip E. Hammond. *Varieties of Civil Religion.* San Francisco: Harper & Row, 1982.

Bendroth, Margaret Lamberts. *Fundamentalism and Gender, 1875 to the Present.* New Haven, Conn.: Yale University Press, 1996.

Bivins, Jason C. *The Fracture of Good Order: Christian Antiliberalism and the Challenge to American Politics.* Chapel Hill: University of North Carolina Press, 2003.

——. *Religion of Fear: The Politics of Horror in Conservative Evangelicalism.* New York: Oxford University Press, 2008.

Branch, Taylor. *Parting the Waters: America in the King Years, 1954–63.* New York: Simon and Schuster, 1988.

Carter, Stephen L. *The Dissent of the Governed: A Meditation on Law, Religion, and Loyalty.* Cambridge, Mass.: Harvard University Press, 1998.

Casanova, José. *Public Religions and the Modern World.* Chicago: University of Chicago Press, 1994.

Chappell, David. *Stone of Hope: Prophetic Religion and the Death of Jim Crow.* Chapel Hill: University of North Carolina Press, 2004.

Cookson, Catharine. *Regulating Religion: The Courts and the Free Exercise Clause.* New York: Oxford University Press, 2001.

Craig, Robert H. *Religion and Radical Politics: An Alternative Christian Tradition in the United States.* Philadelphia: Temple University Press, 1992.

DeBerg, Betty A. *Ungodly Women: Gender and the First Wave of American Fundamentalism*. Macon, Ga.: Mercer University Press, 2000.

Emerson, Michael O., and Christian Smith. *Divided by Faith: Evangelical Religion and the Problem of Race in America*. New York: Oxford University Press, 2001.

Fowler, Robert Booth, Allen D. Hertzke, Laura R. Olson, and Kevin R. den Dulk. *Religion and Politics in America: Faith, Culture, and Strategic Choices*. 3rd ed. Boulder, Colo.: Westview Press, 2004.

Gaustad, Edwin Scott. *Dissent in American Religion*. Rev. ed. Chicago: University of Chicago Press, 2006.

Holmes, David L. *The Faiths of the Founding Fathers*. New York: Oxford University Press, 2006.

Hulsether, Mark. *Religion, Culture, and Politics in the Twentieth-Century United States*. New York: Columbia University Press, 2007.

Hutchison, William R. *Religious Pluralism in America: The Contentious History of a Founding Ideal*. New Haven, Conn.: Yale University Press, 2003.

Kramnick, Isaac, and R. Laurence Moore. *The Godless Constitution: A Moral Defense of the Secular State*. New York: Norton, 2005.

Lambert, Frank. *The Founding Fathers and the Place of Religion in America*. Princeton, N.J.: Princeton University Press, 2006.

Lienesch, Michael. *Redeeming America: Piety and Politics in the New Christian Right*. Chapel Hill: University of North Carolina Press, 1993.

Marty, Martin. *Politics, Religion, and the Common Good*. New York: Jossey-Bass, 2000.

Mazur, Eric Michael *The Americanization of Religious Minorities: Confronting the Constitutional Order*. Baltimore: Johns Hopkins University Press, 1999.

McCutcheon, Russell. *Manufacturing Religion: The Discourse on Sui Generis Religion and the Politics of Nostalgia*. New York: Oxford University Press, 1997.

Miller, Steven P. *Billy Graham and the Rise of the Republican South*. Philadelphia: University of Pennsylvania Press, 2009.

Morgan, Edmund S. *Visible Saints: The History of a Puritan Idea*. Ithaca, N.Y.: Cornell University Press, 1965.

Morone, James. *Hellfire Nation: The Politics of Sin in American History*. New Haven, Conn.: Yale University Press, 2003.

Neuhaus, Richard John. *The Naked Public Square: Religion and Democracy in America*. 2nd ed. Grand Rapids, Mich.: Eerdmans, 1986.

Noll, Mark A., and Luke E. Harlow, eds. *Religion and American Politics: From the Colonial Period to the Present*. 2nd ed. New York: Oxford University Press, 2007.

Perry, Michael J. *Under God? Religious Faith and Liberal Democracy*. Cambridge: Cambridge University Press, 2003.

Pitzer, Donald E., ed. *America's Communal Utopias*. Chapel Hill: University of North Carolina Press, 1997.

Putney, Clifford. *Muscular Christianity: Manhood and Sports in Protestant America, 1880–1920*. Cambridge, Mass.: Harvard University Press, 2003.

Sands, Kathleen M., ed. *God Forbid: Religion and Sex in American Public Life*. New York: Oxford University Press, 2000.

Shields, Jon A. *The Democratic Virtues of the Christian Right*. Princeton, N.J.: Princeton University Press, 2008.

Sullivan, Winnifred Fallers. *The Impossibility of Religious Freedom*. Princeton, N.J.: Princeton University Press, 2005.

Wald, Kenneth. *Religion and Politics in the United States*. 4th ed. Lanham, Md.: Rowman & Littlefield, 2003.

Wolterstorff, Nicholas, and Robert Audi, eds. *Religion in the Public Square: The Place of Religious Convictions in Political Debate*. Lanham, Md.: Rowman & Littlefield, 1996.

7. RELIGION AND THE LAW IN AMERICAN HISTORY

FRANK S. RAVITCH

Numerous volumes have been written about the history of law and religion in the United States. This history has been used to argue both for and against the separation of church and state. Numerous decisions by the United States Supreme Court reflect this use of history. Yet frequently the interaction between law and religion in American history is far more complicated and textured than it is portrayed by those who wish to use it to effect legal norms. There is no one story of law and religion in U.S. history, and thus no one side in the broader church–state debate can rely on this history without first choosing which "history" it will rely on. This essay attempts to address the broad topic of law and religion in American history in an accessible way. Given space limitations, the text will necessarily be an overview of selected historical and legal events. I will try to focus both on early history and on what has occurred more recently. An important caveat is that the history of law and religion is addressed only in the context of U.S. constitutional law. Therefore, the cultural history of law and religion and issues of religious law are beyond the scope of this chapter.

LAW AND RELIGION IN THE COLONIES AND THE UNITED STATES, 1750–1870

There are many misconceptions about the history of law and religion in the late colonial and early United States eras. These misconceptions have been perpetuated by those on all sides of the broader church–state debate, who wish to use the history to support a particular political or legal outcome. One frequently hears statements like "The Ten Commandments are the basis for American law" or "The Framers intended strict separation between church and state." Neither of these statements is true, although the second statement may be accurate in regard to several of the Framers. The point is that for their time period, the Framers held relatively diverse views on the place of religion within government and society. This hodgepodge of viewpoints on religion and law heavily reflected the various positions held by individuals in the late colonial period.

Major influences on late colonial and early American law were the English common law system, the emerging concepts of social contract and constitutionalism, and colonial charters. In the Massachusetts Bay Colony, earlier experiments with enacting biblical law as government law had failed, and even Massachusetts moved away from attempting this. Many of those who ultimately became Framers were familiar with the writings of Locke, Montesquieu, and Rousseau. Certainly, some of the Framers were familiar with Locke's statements on separating religion from civil government, and others were aware of the religious argument for separation (that is, to protect religion from civil society and government). Still, many Framers would not have been major supporters of the separation concept. Some Framers, such as Thomas Jefferson, James Madison, and Benjamin Rush, seemed to support separation at some level. Yet other Framers, such as Patrick Henry and John Adams, were not major supporters of the concept. Some, such as Benjamin Franklin, can be considered at best ambivalent, when all their writings are considered. This brief listing does not include many Framers who may have held a variety of views or the many ratifiers at the state conventions. In terms of religious affiliation, many of the Framers were devoutly religious and many were not. Some were Deists, Baptists, Congregationalists, Quakers, and Seekers, and many were Anglican. There was simply no one view regarding religion or its role in law.

Yet most of the current debates over the role of religion in law in the late colonial and early United States periods are over the role of separation. As will be seen, however, until the ratification of the Fourteenth Amendment—a century after the framing—much of the discussion over law and religion in the United States was at the level of state laws and state constitutions. These documents were remarkably diverse in their content and in their interpretation by courts and other government actors. Interestingly, a number of state constitutions did contain elements that would today be regarded as separationist, but the application of these elements in the early United States period varied. Some states provided strong religious protection for all religions and kept government and religion somewhat at arm's length apart. Others required religious tests and oaths for officeholders and directly funded religious institutions, sometimes only those of the majority faith and sometimes those of all faiths or a select group of faiths.

An essential component of the history of law and religion in the United States is the story of the Virginia Statute of Religious Freedom (1786), which mandated that the state government could not interfere with religious freedom or assess money from citizens to support any church. The statute involved an important confrontation between those, such as James Madison and Thomas Jefferson, who supported greater religious freedom and those, such as Patrick Henry, who were supporters of the religious orthodoxy prevailing in Virginia at that time (the Anglican Church); the history of the statute has been relied on repeatedly by courts and commentators. Ultimately, the statute arose in response to the state (and prior to that, the colonial) government's practice of assessing money from citizens in Virginia to support churches. Jefferson and Madison, along with others, objected to the assessment of money by the government for any religious institution, whether the established church or otherwise.

In 1785, Madison wrote his famous "Memorial and Remonstrance Against Religious Assessments" in response to a proposal by Patrick Henry to impose a state tax to support religious "teachers." The "Memorial and Remonstrance" clearly stated that requiring citizens to give any money to a religious institution constituted an overstepping of state authority. This sentiment was also reflected in the Virginia Statute of Religious Freedom, which was written by Jefferson but was passed primarily through Madison's efforts. Following post-Enlightenment teachings—in which Madison was well versed—decisions he viewed as personal, such as to which religious institutions one wished to give his or her money, were outside the purview of the state. Madison viewed state attempts to impose religious assessments as a fundamental interference with this personal choice and as an assault on freedom of conscience and religion—an assault of a type he had seen all too often. In one letter, he wrote that men had often been imprisoned over theological disagreements, and he had no sympathy for such intolerance. Ultimately, Madison's "Memorial and Remonstrance" and the Virginia Statute of Religious Freedom stand as major examples of the "natural rights" concepts of religious freedom that influenced some of the Framers. They also suggest how these key Framers addressed one underlying theme of religion in early American history: the paradox of religious freedom and religious repression (as outlined in the introduction to this volume).

The legacy of Jefferson's and Madison's ideas may be seen in the First Amendment to the Constitution: "Congress shall make no law respecting an establishment of religion, or prohibiting the free exercise thereof." The religion clauses in the First Amendment to the Constitution were rarely an issue in the courts during the early history of the nation. Major writings on the religion clauses in this period came not from the courts, but from political figures, historians, those interested in politics and society in the United States (including Alexis de Tocqueville), and on occasion from those who wrote about constitutional law. Thus we will leave discussion of the federal religion clauses until later in this essay.

During this early era, religion did play a role in law. Unfortunately, this role was often based in anti-Catholicism. Colonies sometimes passed laws that punished citizens for being Catholic or teaching Catholicism. Most colonies precluded Catholics, and often non-Christian religious groups, from holding office. Soon after the founding of the nation, many parts of the United States experienced the Second Great Awakening at the very time that Irish Catholic immigration was reaching new heights (especially between 1820 and 1850). This led to laws and practices that were generally aimed at Catholics, or at least Catholic immigrants. Most of these laws did not directly attack Catholics, and most did not mention religion, but the impact of the laws fell, as intended, most heavily on Catholic and other non-Protestant immigrants. These early laws had parallels in later laws aimed at Catholics and Mormons in the latter part of the nineteenth and early twentieth centuries (discussed in the next section, and in Tentler, chap. 17, and Quinn, chap. 19, this volume).

Outside this one relatively common legal phenomenon, there was a great deal of diversity in the role of religion and law during this era. Some states kept religion separate from the law, while others did not do so. The last state to disestablish its state church was Massachusetts, in 1833. Most of the southern and Mid-Atlantic states either had had no established churches or had disestablished their churches before or shortly after the United States came into being. New England was the last region to disestablish, with Maine, New Hampshire, Vermont, and Connecticut all doing so later than most other states. Maine, for example, disestablished its state church in 1820. Rhode Island was the exception in this entire matter, however, as Roger Williams had founded the colony on religious freedom, and it never had an established church.

States also utilized common law, and in some cases statutes, that at least reflected common religious views of earlier eras. There were numerous laws against adultery and fornication in communities and states. Whether these were simply a reflection of the legal system that was in place before the founding, a reflection of then-dominant social norms, or religiously based is not clear, but some have used these laws to suggest that law in the United States was based in biblical law. Given the earlier experience with attempts to enact biblical law directly, however, this claim is not likely. Laws against murder and robbery could be argued to be biblically based as well, but like much law these prohibitions generally reflect social norms that happen to also be reflected in a variety of religious texts. The same would appear to be true of adultery and fornication laws. After all, those who carved patriotic and/or artistic statues were not prohibited from carving graven images under most colonial or early United States law. Nor were Deists prosecuted for not believing in the God of the Bible.

THE MIDDLE AGES OF LAW AND RELIGION IN THE UNITED STATES, 1870–1940

Religion played a bigger role in law during the era from 1870 to 1940. First, anti-Catholicism and anti-Mormonism were rampant. A number of federal laws were passed to try to disenfranchise or otherwise negatively affect Mormons. To do this, many of these laws targeted the practice of polygamy. Thus various penalties were enforced against any member of an organization that tolerated or promoted polygamy. These ranged from criminal prosecution and disenfranchisement to tax penalties and, of course, the famous requirement that polygamy be renounced for Utah to gain statehood. Ironically, few Mormons actually practiced polygamy, but the Mormon Church did allow it at that time.

During this time frame, the U.S. Supreme Court heard several cases that dealt with religion. *Reynolds v. United States* (1878) and *Davis v. Beason* (1890) are well-known cases in which the Court upheld federal laws against challenges under the Free Exercise Clause of the First Amendment that were aimed at polygamy and Mormonism. These cases were later relied on by Justice Antonin Scalia in the famous free exercise case *Employment Division v. Smith* (1990) (see next section). Moreover, the Court decided *Pierce v. Society of Sisters* (1925), which dealt with state laws mandating public school attendance. These laws were generally aimed at Catholic schools (although *Pierce* also involved a military academy) and attempted to destroy those schools through compulsory public school attendance. In these cases, however, the Court struck down the state laws and held that such laws violated the Fourteenth Amendment by interfering with parental liberty to raise children and make related (including educational) choices for their children.

A lesser-known but quite important case, *Watson v. Jones* (1871), was also decided during this era. *Watson* dealt with church property disputes and supported the doctrine that civil courts are precluded from interfering with ecclesiastical decisions. The Court looked to the nature of the church—that is, whether it was hierarchical or congregational—and set forth criteria based on the nature of the church for determining property disputes, without deciding ecclesiastical questions.

Moreover, state courts were active on issues that we see today in many federal cases. For example, in the late nineteenth and early twentieth centuries a number of state courts held that public school prayer violated state constitutional provisions protecting religious freedom. The reasoning of a number of these opinions was later reflected in the 1962/1963 school prayer decisions by the Supreme Court. Examples of such decisions can be seen in Louisiana, Illinois, Indiana, and Ohio.

Still, for all the progress made in decisions like *Pierce*, *Watson*, and the state school prayer rulings, the legacy of *Reynolds*, anti-Mormonism, and anti-Catholicism lived on. There were numerous attempts to deny funding to Catholic schools because they were Catholic, even in states where the supposedly public schools were heavily dominated by Protestant practices, and, as noted earlier, there were numerous federal laws aimed at Mormons. The most famous example of an anti-funding law was the attempt by Congressman James G. Blaine to pass a federal constitutional amendment prohibiting funding to parochial schools. Several states already had such laws, and the federal amendment failed by only four votes in the Senate. Many other states, however, soon passed what are today called "baby-Blaines," which prohibited funding to Catholic schools. Much of the funding prohibited by these amendments would have been unconstitutional under modern First Amendment doctrine anyway, at least until recently, but it was the motivation for the "baby-Blaine" amendments that is most relevant here.

Interestingly, this era also saw an increase in the language of separationism. Some of this was motivated by anti-Catholicism, but some of it was based in separationist theology and political theory, as well as a growing anti-organized religion movement. Separationist values and rhetoric had been around from the beginning of the United States, but it was in this era that it found a strong public voice for the first time. Unfortunately, some of this was the result of nativist anti-Catholicism. It is important to note, however, that not all of the separationist thought and rhetoric in this era was so based.

Moreover, during this era religious diversity continued to grow as a variety of new Christian sects sprang up, Catholic immigration continued, and Jewish immigration grew exponentially. This increase in religious diversity and the move toward pluralism, as explained in the theme of "intolerance, diversity, and pluralism" in the introduction, was likely, at least in part, a catalyst for the incorporation of and decisions under the First Amendment during the years that followed. While the era from 1870 to 1940 was heavily marked by the assertion of mainstream Protestant domination, this would soon change as both that domination and the law shifted toward a more pluralistic model.

THE POST-INCORPORATION ERA: 1940/1947–PRESENT

In 1940, the U.S. Supreme Court decided *Cantwell v. Connecticut*, which incorporated the Free Exercise Clause through the Fourteenth Amendment. Seven years later, the Court decided *Everson v. Board of Education* (1947), which incorporated the Establishment Clause. Incorporation was key to the current era of law and religion. "Incorporation" means that the relevant constitutional provision (in these cases, the religion clauses) are made binding on the states through the Due Process Clause of the Fourteenth Amendment. Thus for the first time in United

States history, all the states were bound by the First Amendment to the United States Constitution.

Significantly, the incorporation doctrine was more than simply a legal mechanism for applying parts of the Bill of Rights to the states. It reflected a fundamental shift in the perception of rights and power that began with the passage of the Thirteenth, Fourteenth, and Fifteenth Amendments. No longer were the states viewed as the primary guardians of civil rights and civil liberties. State and local governments were now (and in many cases correctly) seen as the government entities most likely to interfere with civil liberties and civil rights. The federal government, and increasingly the federal courts, came to be regarded as the guardians of civil rights and civil liberties.

The nation was also in the midst of coming to terms with racial, ethnic, and religious pluralism, a process still going on today. As some have noted, this led to a shift in perceptions of the role of government in protecting various groups and in modern notions of equal protection. At the nexus between law and religion, these notions of group equality merged with notions of religious liberty to spur new doctrines. These emerging doctrines first became evident in cases that involved freedom of expression as well as free exercise. The most famous of these cases was *West Virginia State Board of Education v. Barnette* (1943), which held that a student who was a Jehovah's Witness could not be made to say the Pledge of Allegiance or salute the flag (this was before the words "under God" were added to the pledge). The case was focused primarily on freedom of expression, but also raised free exercise concerns. In a famous passage from the case, Justice Robert Jackson eloquently summed up the emerging doctrine during this era of increased recognition of pluralism:

> The very purpose of a Bill of Rights was to withdraw certain subjects from the vicissitudes of political controversy, to place them beyond the reach of majorities and officials and to establish them as legal principles to be applied by the courts. One's right to life, liberty, and property, to free speech, a free press, freedom of worship and assembly, and other fundamental rights may not be submitted to vote; they depend on the outcome of no elections. (*Barnette*, 319 U.S. 624, 638)

This sentiment has resonated in Establishment Clause cases as well. In fact, as will be seen, today its primary vitality is in the Establishment Clause area.

It seems clear that by the mid-1940s there was a sentiment growing on the Supreme Court that favored tolerance of diverse values and freedom of expression, including non-mainstream religious expression and practices. Yet it remained unclear whether government could fund, endorse, or favor any particular set of religious values, even if it could not interfere with less mainstream practices. In 1947, the Court decided *Everson v. Board of Education*, which involved a New Jersey law that enabled local districts to arrange for transportation of schoolchildren and the decision by Ewing Township to reimburse parents of parochial school students for the students' bus fares on public buses to get to and from school. The Court's solution seemed to be that government could not support religion or a particular religion, but could also not inhibit religion: while the Framers intended a "high and impregnable" "wall between church and state," at the same time government must be "neutral" in its dealings with religion. This meant that government could not support the parochial schools, but at the same time Ewing Township did not have to deny the reimbursement for transportation, because it also provided transportation for those students attending public, and ostensibly nonparochial, schools. As a practical matter this latter point was highly questionable, as Justice Jackson pointed out in dissent. Moreover, the dissenting opinions explained that there was a certain amount of tension between the strong statements on separation in the majority opinion and the majority's holding allowing for the bus fare reimbursement. The beginnings of modern Establishment Clause jurisprudence had arrived.

Over the next thirty-five years, the tensions apparent in *Everson* reasserted themselves. In cases involving released time (allowing students out of public school classes to attend religious school classes), incompatible cases were decided by the Supreme Court less than five years apart. It may be that the specter of McCarthyism influenced the latter of these two decisions, but the released-time cases were not the only incongruent decisions. Various types of aid to religious institutions were either allowed or found to be unconstitutional. At the same time, Sunday-closing laws were upheld under both religion clauses, but soon after that the failure of a state to give unemployment benefits to someone who could not work on Saturday was struck down under the Free Exercise Clause. Likewise, school prayer and Bible reading were struck down under the Establishment Clause. By 1970, the one area where consistency seemed to reign was where government sought to speak religiously in the schools through school prayer and Bible reading or through curricular decisions, such as banning the teaching of evolution. In government aid and free exercise cases, consistency was not as easily found—if at all.

Then, in 1971 and 1972, respectively, a legendary Establishment Clause case, *Lemon v. Kurtzman*, and a legendary Free Exercise Clause case, *Wisconsin v. Yoder*, were decided. Both had antecedents in earlier cases, but both gave clearer voice to doctrines that had been developing over the years. Both would, however, lose much of their force over time: *Lemon* because of the supposed inconsistencies it created and *Yoder* because of the Court's inability or unwillingness to consistently apply its core holding.

Lemon combined requirements from the school prayer case *Abington School District v. Schempp* (1963), that government must have a secular purpose for its laws/actions and that the primary effect of any government law/action must neither advance nor inhibit religion, with the prohibition on government entanglement with religion that had been most recently set forth in a case involving property-tax exemptions for religious institutions, *Walz v. Tax Commission of the City of New York* (1970). This gave rise to the famous three-pronged *Lemon* test, requiring that government action (1) have a secular purpose, (2) have primary effects that neither advance nor inhibit religion, (3) and not excessively entangle government with religion (institutionally or through political divisiveness). This test remains in effect in some contexts, along with other tests, but its ultimate fate remains up in the air. *Lemon* itself was a case about state support for teachers in parochial schools, but ironically today it is in the school aid area that *Lemon* seems to have the least relevance. In areas like school prayer and religious symbolism, it seems to retain some vitality, but is often secondary to, or analyzed through the lens of, other tests, such as the endorsement and coercion tests discussed later.

Meanwhile, when *Yoder* was decided it was widely viewed as the realization of the doctrine set forth in the earlier free exercise case *Sherbert v. Verner* (1963), which had substantially expanded the protection available to religious minorities and others whose religious practices were interfered with by generally applicable laws. Yet as cases in the 1980s and 1990s would soon demonstrate, the victory was either short lived, pyrrhic, or both. In a string of cases, the Court either failed to apply the approach reflected in *Yoder*, applied it in a way that minimized its impact, or applied it only in the limited context of unemployment compensation cases, which was the issue in *Sherbert* itself.

This has been the modern history of religion clause cases. Doctrines and approaches are born and seem to thrive (for better or worse, depending on one's viewpoint) for a while, only to be altered or abandoned as different issues and justices become involved. What makes this area of constitutional law so different from many other areas is how rapidly the law seems to shift and the fact that it seems to remain the same in some contexts even as it shifts in others. Moreover, at least since the late 1980s, these shifts have rarely been openly acknowledged by the Court so that it is frequently hard to determine what the relevant principles or doctrines are. So what trends can be seen in law and religion since the 1980s? Under the Establishment Clause, it is worth exploring four major types of problems that arise:

- Government aid to religious entities
- Government speech in schools such as school prayer and curricular decisions
- Equal access for religious groups to government facilities open to nonreligious groups
- Religious symbolism

Finally, a unique group of cases involving what some might call ceremonial deism or traditional religious expression must be mentioned; although this category has little coherence in its application outside of the justices who tend to favor it (that is, it could be applied in any number of the other cases if an adequate number of justices supported it in those contexts).

In the aid context, two major trends have emerged from the 1940s until the present. The first is a focus on separation of government and religion that takes on a realist approach; that is, most (although not all) advocates of this approach are concerned about whether and how government aid actually flows to religious entities. The second, which we may now call formal neutrality, is less concerned with the actual effect of the government aid, but focuses on the mechanism through which the government allocates aid. Those cases that most closely use the *Lemon* approach are representative of the separationist or realist conceptions. A recent case involving school vouchers, *Zelman v. Simmons-Harris* (2002), is the most reminiscent of the formalist approach. There were, of course, also cases that attempted to meld these approaches.

The separationist cases based in *Lemon* led to some odd results. For example, parochial schools could be lent secular textbooks but not equipment because the equipment might be diverted for use in religious classes (even though the giving of this aid in the first place provides financial benefit to the schools, which as a result of it need not purchase the books or equipment). At the same time, the formal neutrality approach currently in use leads to an acontextual view of government aid, wherein—as long as a law is neutral on its face (what aid program would not be?) and the cash or amount of aid is based on the number of students or participants who have "chosen" a given religious program—the government could virtually underwrite religious schools. The latter line of cases is mostly inconsistent with the earlier, although there are a few cases where the two methods work together. These cases have two things in common. First, they remain concerned about the real-world effects of aid; and second, they demonstrate concern that government not exclude religious entities from truly broad aid programs where the aid indeed does go through individual aid recipients.

Perhaps the best example of this type of case is *Witters v. Washington Department of Services for the Blind* (1986), which involved a blind student who requested aid under a generally available aid program for disabled individuals so that he could attend college, which in this case happened to be a religious university and involved a religious course of study. The Court allowed the student to receive the aid because he could have used it at any number of secular or religious institutions and in the scope of the program only a small percentage of aid was likely to flow to religious institutions for religious courses of study. Thus the primary focus of the program was aid to disabled students, who had a truly wide range of options at which to use the aid. This case, of course, was still concerned about the real-world effects of the program.

Over time, however, the Court began to apply the formal neutrality approach outside of the middle-ground cases (the Court had already done so in a case or two, but those were seen as the exception, not the rule), and the tension between the two approaches continued. Today, formal neutrality has won out in the aid context—see *Zelman v. Simmons-Harris* (2002) (tuition voucher case)—

but dissenting justices regularly argue that this is inconsistent with *Lemon*, its underlying principles, its predecessors, and its progeny.

One area where the results, if not the doctrine, have been consistent involves school prayer and attempts to insert a religiously based curriculum in science courses. Altogether, including the 1962 and 1963 cases, the U.S. Supreme Court has heard five cases involving school prayer (one of these involved a moment-of-silence law designed to promote prayer). In all these cases, the Court struck down the prayer. In some cases, the Court used the *Lemon* test or its predecessor. In other cases, the Court used the more recent endorsement or coercion tests. In one case, it used all three. The endorsement test, originally created by Justice Sandra Day O'Connor, looks at whether an objective observer would find that government action has the purpose or effect of endorsing religion by fostering a perception that some members of the community are religious insiders and that others are religious outsiders. It is often applied as a gloss on the first two elements of the *Lemon* test.

The coercion test looks at whether the government has engaged in a formal religious exercise and directly or indirectly coerces objectors to participate in that religious exercise. Regardless of the test used, school prayer has never been upheld by the U.S. Supreme Court. The same is true for attempts to insert creationist teaching into public school curricula or to disparage evolution as a result of religious views on human origins. A majority of the Court has, however, noted that an appropriately drafted moment-of-silence law would be constitutional.

Another area where the Court has been reasonably consistent is the issue of equal access. This involves requests by student religious clubs or outside groups such as churches to access government buildings, usually schools, on the same terms as other non-curriculum-related groups. These cases generally involve significant free speech concerns because the Court has determined that when a school or another government building opens its facilities to non-government-related groups it has created a limited public forum for private speech and cannot discriminate based on viewpoint or content (including religious viewpoint or content) in allocating use of the forum. This doctrine has also been applied in cases involving private religious displays on public property that is generally open to private displays. There have also been attempts to use this doctrine to allow "student-initiated" prayer at school events, but since these events are rarely public fora for speech, the argument is much weaker in the school prayer context; see *Santa Fe Independent School District v. Doe* (2000).

Finally, religious symbolism cases may be among the most controversial in recent years. This is especially true of displays of the Ten Commandments. The Court has been inconsistent in its approach to these issues. It seems that the majority of the Court would apply the endorsement test and maybe the *Lemon* test, unless a case presents unique circumstances. Yet a number of justices would apply a "tradition" test that views such displays as part of the religious and historical traditions of the United States or a given locale. Both positions have prevailed in recent cases, but at least for now it appears that the endorsement approach would be applied in most of these cases, barring unusual facts. Both historically and recently, however, this is an area of law and religion that is intensely context-reliant and subject to doctrinal change and/or incoherence.

There are other contexts in which the "tradition approach" has been applied by a majority or plurality of the Court. For example, in two religious symbolism cases (one involving a Ten Commandments display and the other a crèche) the tradition approach was applied. Aside from these two cases, however, it has been applied by a majority of the Court only in a case involving legislative prayer and the unique history of that practice, *Marsh v. Chambers* (1983). That decision has been questioned, but remains good law. Any number of justices have argued for broader reliance on the "tradition approach," which would allow government to be much more involved in endorsing and perhaps supporting religion. Yet it has not generally commanded a majority of the Court.

In the Free Exercise Clause context, there appears to be a clearer trend since 1972. From the 1972 decision in *Yoder* until 1990, the Court rarely followed the approach set forth in *Sherbert* and *Yoder*. In some cases, the Court used the context of a dispute (the military or prisons) to fail to apply the earlier approach. In others, the Court did not apply it because the claim was considered to be one requesting government to reorder its own activities. In still others the test was applied, but the government was held to meet the standard. Finally, in *Employment Division v. Smith* (1990), the Court effectively overturned *Sherbert* and *Yoder*. Of course, the Court did not acknowledge that it was doing so, but it significantly limited the reach of the earlier decisions and went back to the rule from the latter part of the nineteenth century that the Free Exercise Clause does not mandate religious exemptions to generally applicable laws. Thus if a law applies to people or entities regardless of religion, then there is no constitutional duty to create exemptions even to prevent significant hardship on religious practices. Such exemptions may be provided, but whether they are or not is left to the political process. Thus by 1990 in the Free Exercise Clause context and 2002 in the Establishment Clause context, the focus on religious pluralism and legal realism that had taken hold in the 1940s had shifted to a focus on formalism and the democratic, yet frequently majoritarian, political process.

Significantly, since the late 1980s at least there has been a tendency to pretend that decisions that are wholly inconsistent with earlier decisions are not *really* inconsistent. Additionally, sometimes the earlier decisions are argued to be limited to contexts to which they did not initially appear limited. It is not that this does not happen in other areas of law, or that it had not happened before in law and religion, but rather the rate of such decisions since the late 1980s and their inconsistency is rather remarkable by any standard. For example, whether or not *Zelman v. Simmons-Harris* (2002) (school voucher case) or *Employment*

Division v. Smith (1990) (free exercise exemption case) are good or bad law, they are certainly not consistent with earlier precedent that each opinion claims not to overturn.

The Constitution has not been the only locus for law and religion issues over the past seven decades. State constitutions, while taking a bit of a back seat to the United States Constitution on law and religion issues, have continued to be relevant. In many instances, the state courts simply apply the federal courts' interpretations of the Constitution to state law issues. However, this is not always the case and in some cases state constitutions have provided stronger free exercise or establishment protections than the Constitution has been interpreted to apply. Several states—for, example, Michigan—have constitutional provisions that prohibit any funding to nonpublic schools, whether parochial or not. This would prohibit much aid that would be allowed under the Constitution. Some states have similar provisions that apply only to parochial schools. Some of these are the descendants of the "baby-Blaine" amendments mentioned earlier. If these state constitutional provisions are constitutional under the U.S. Constitution (currently an open question), the state provisions would provide more robust protection against state endorsement of religion.

States have perhaps been most active in promoting greater free exercise rights than those allowed under the Constitution after *Employment Division v. Smith*. A number of states interpret their state free exercise clauses to provide wider protection than that under the Constitution. Moreover, a number of states have passed state Religious Freedom Restoration Acts (RFRAs), which are designed to require state and local governments to provide religious exemptions unless the state can meet the compelling interest and narrow tailoring requirements set forth in *Sherbert v. Verner*. Interestingly, these state RFRAs are modeled on the federal RFRA, which today applies only to the federal government. Congress also recently passed the Religious Land Use and Institutionalized Persons Act, which is designed to apply nationally to situations where government action interferes with religious land use or the religious beliefs or practices of institutionalized persons. Thus, regardless of what is going on in federal constitutional cases, Congress and the states are providing alternative means for addressing law and religion issues.

Today, as in years past, law and religion play a part in everyday political affairs as religious groups, and groups seeking to minimize government endorsement of religion, are regular participants in political discourse. Issues such as the display of Ten Commandments monuments and government aid to religious entities are direct examples of this. Additionally, religious actors lobby on both sides regarding many controversial issues, such as reproductive rights, gay marriage, stem cell research, and civil rights.

This essay has provided a brief overview of some of the major eras and events involving law and religion in American history. The material is certainly not comprehensive; the references list a number of sources that treat in much greater depth both the various issues raised here and other issues relating to the history of law and religion in the United States. The history of law and religion in the United States obviously reflects the various eras in our nation's history. It also reflects the contradictory and paradoxical impulses outlined in the introduction to this volume—between communalist visions and diverse realities, between the religious freedom to proselytize and the religious freedom to be free from proselytization, and between the sacred and secular impulses of politics. Thus post-Enlightenment philosophy, increasing religious pluralism, immigration, and the shift in the perception of the states from protectors of individual freedoms to potential inhibitors of religious freedom have all played a role in this history. The history of the interplay of law and religion is rich and diverse, and presents a rich field for analysis of the paradoxes and tensions of religion in American history.

REFERENCES

Adams, Arlin, and Charles J. Emmerich. *A Nation Dedicated to Religious Liberty: The Constitutional Heritage of the Religion Clauses.* Philadelphia: University of Pennsylvania Press, 1990.

Alley, Robert S., ed. *The Supreme Court on Church and State.* New York: Oxford University Press, 1988.

Berg, Thomas C. *The First Amendment: The Free Exercise of Religion Clause: Its Constitutional History and the Contemporary Debate.* Amherst, N.Y.: Prometheus Books, 2007.

Davis, Derek H. *Religion and the Continental Congress, 1774–1789: Contributions to Original Intent.* New York: Oxford University Press, 2000.

DelFattore, Joan. *The Fourth R: Conflicts over Religion in America's Public Schools.* New Haven, Conn.: Yale University Press, 2004.

Feldman, Noah. *Divided by God: America's Church–State Problem—and What We Should Do About It.* New York: Farrar, Straus and Giroux, 2005.

Feldman, Stephen M. *Law and Religion: A Critical Anthology.* New York: New York University Press, 2000.

——. *Please Don't Wish Me a Merry Christmas: A Critical History of the Separation of Church and State.* New York: New York University Press, 1997.

Finkelman, Paul, ed. *Religion and American Law: An Encyclopedia.* New York: Garland, 2000.

Gaustad, Edwin S. *Proclaim Liberty Throughout All the Land: A History of Church and State in America.* Oxford: Oxford University Press, 2003.

——. *Sworn on the Altar of God: A Religious Biography of Thomas Jefferson.* Grand Rapids, Mich.: Eerdmans, 1996.

Gordon, Sarah Barringer. *The Mormon Question: Polygamy and Constitutional Conflict in Nineteenth-Century America*. Chapel Hill: University of North Carolina Press, 2002.

Hall, Timothy. *Separating Church and State: Roger Williams and Religious Liberty*. Urbana: University of Illinois Press, 1998.

Hamburger, Philip. *Separation of Church and State*. Cambridge, Mass.: Harvard University Press, 2002.

Hamilton, Marci A. *God Versus the Gavel: Religion and the Rule of Law*. New York: Cambridge University Press, 2005.

Hitchcock, James. *The Supreme Court and Religion in American Life*. Vol. 1, *The Odyssey of the Religion Clauses*. Princeton, N.J.: Princeton University Press, 2004.

——. *The Supreme Court and Religion in American Life*. Vol. 2, *From "Higher Law" to "Sectarian Scruples."* Princeton, N.J.: Princeton University Press, 2004.

Israel, Charles A. *Before Scopes: Evangelicalism, Education, and Evolution in Tennessee, 1870–1925*. Athens: University of Georgia Press, 2004.

Levy, Leonard W. *The Establishment Clause: Religion and the First Amendment*. Chapel Hill: University of North Carolina Press, 1994.

McConnell, Michael W. *Religion and the Constitution*. New York: Aspen Law and Business, 2002.

McGarvie, Mark D. *One Nation Under Law: America's Early National Struggles to Separate Church and State*. Dekalb: Northern Illinois University Press, 2004.

Muñoz, Vincent Phillip. *God and the Founders: Madison, Washington, and Jefferson*. Cambridge: Cambridge University Press, 2009.

Pfeffer, Leo. *God, Caesar, and the Constitution: The Court as Referee of Church–State Confrontation*. Boston: Beacon Press, 1975

Ravitch, Frank S. *Masters of Illusion: The Supreme Court and the Religion Clauses*. New York: New York University Press, 2007.

——. *School Prayer and Discrimination: The Civil Rights of Religious Minorities and Dissenters*. Boston: Northeastern University Press, 1999.

Witte, John. *Religion and the American Constitutional Experiment*. Boulder, Colo.: Westview Press, 2005.

8. RELIGION, WAR, AND PEACE

IRA R. CHERNUS

Issues of war and peace have been intertwined with religious concerns throughout American history in a wide variety of ways, too many to survey comprehensively in one brief chapter. Contemporary discussions of the subject usually circle around one central question: What role has religion played in leading the nation into war? But every view of war implies a corresponding view of peace, and vice versa. So the question may be put more precisely: How, and to what extent, has religion motivated Americans to consider, pursue, and practice both war and peace?

Unfortunately, motivations always remain obscure at best. We can never read other people's minds. We can know only what people say and do. So we can only ask: When Americans have explained their motives in pursuing war and peace — when they have justified their policies and practices — what role has religion played? For that question, we have a mine of evidence so rich that scholars have scarcely begun to dig into it. The evidence that scholars have studied is still overwhelmingly from "the dominant mainstream which controls public language [and] becomes internalized in structures of consciousness" (Albanese, *Sons of the Fathers*, 15). The mainstream has always been predominantly created by, and thus skewed toward the interests of, white men (especially more powerful and wealthy white men). A scholarship on war and peace incorporating the diverse voices of women and communities of color is still to come. This essay focuses on some of the most important and interesting interpretations of mainstream discourse that scholars have already offered and some hypotheses they might explore in the future.

Mainstream American discourse about war and peace has always drawn most heavily on four distinct narratives, each of them rooted in an ancient Christian tradition:

1. The "holy war" tradition says that all humanity is divided into two groups: the good, who are on God's side, and the evil, who are on the devil's side. The evil people will not stop doing evil until they dominate the whole world. So the good must fight against the evil until they are totally eliminated. Every battle is an apocalyptic battle; it prefigures the final apocalypse, when the world will be permanently cleansed of all evil. Only when evil is wholly gone will the world and its people live in peace. Since the stakes are absolute, the good can use any means to win their victory. In American religious history, this tradition provides the link between religious freedom and religious repression, a theme outlined in the introduction to this volume.

2. The "just war" tradition says that all humanity is divided into two groups: the civilized, who live in an ordered society administered by a legitimate government, and the barbarians, who live chaotically in the wilderness. The state's government is sanctioned by God, who wants everyone to enjoy the benefits of safe order. But the state's rulers (and most of its people) are sinners. So God gives them strict rules to make sure that they fight wars not for personal gain, but only to prevent the barbarians from destroying civilized order. And God gives strict rules to make sure that they fight in a just and civilized way, doing only the minimum harm necessary to keep the borders of civilization firmly defended. When those borders—and thus society's orderly structures—are secure, that is the condition of peace.

3. The "Christian humanist" tradition says that all humanity is divided into two groups: those who live rationally and those who live irrationally. The rational understand that all people need one another's help to live the best lives they can. People have to trade with one another, learn from one another, and help one another. When they do that, they are living in peace. The wider the network of peaceful mutuality extends, the better off everyone is. Ideally, it should include everyone in the world. That is the goal of God's plan for history. The rational, who know all this, recognize that war is always irrational because it deprives everyone of the benefits of peace, the winners as well as the losers. So the rational do everything they can to compromise on differences reasonably in order to avoid war.

4. The "nonviolence" tradition does not see humanity divided into two groups. It says that God wants everyone to follow the words ascribed to Jesus in the New Testament: "Do not resist violently against one who is evil. . . . Turn the other cheek. . . . Love your enemies" (Matthew 5:39, 44). War, the ultimate form of violence, not only goes against God's will but also inevitably creates more violence. The only way to attain peace is to renounce all violence and treat even the most

immoral people with love, recognizing that they, too, are our brothers and sisters in the human family. However, it is permissible, or even obligatory (some say), to resist their immoral actions nonviolently.

In Christian thought, these four traditions are quite distinct. It is hard to reconcile them logically. But in American history, the first three, which have dominated the culture, have been woven together in a wide variety of ways. Nonviolence, always the position of a small minority, has tended to stand alone or to be combined with Christian humanism. Christian humanism fits well with nonviolence because both traditions view all people as actual or potential partners in an ever-widening social network that benefits everyone.

But nonviolence cannot be adapted to just war or holy war, because both of those traditions assume that every human group must define some other group as a threatening enemy that stands outside the network of mutual benefit. Just war and holy war thus require what David Campbell calls a discourse of danger: a pattern of language that defines a group's identity by defining a threat that the group faces and responds to, either (in just war) holding the threat at bay or (in holy war) exterminating it. Throughout the history of American discourse about war and peace, Christian humanism has typically been blended with just war and holy war. Thus Christian humanism, which in itself avoids a discourse of danger, has been made to legitimate and reinforce discourses of danger.

That pattern was already evident in the 1630s, when the first sizable immigration of Puritans came to the region they called New England. Like all Calvinists, they were deeply influenced by the Christian humanist tradition, claiming always to use reason to understand the revealed word of God. Their first leader, John Winthrop, captured the essence of the humanist vision in a famous sermon aboard the ship *Arbella*: "Wee must be knitt together, in this worke, as one man. . . . Wee must uphold a familiar commerce together." Anglican Thomas Morton extended this vision to the Indians by establishing a trading post where Indians were welcome to develop a peaceful "familiar commerce" of every kind. Morton viewed his experience through the symbolic frame of the Bible, likening Puritans to Israelites and Native peoples to Canaanites. In his book *New English Canaan*, he offered a very positive portrait of these "Canaanites," detailing (as his title page put it) "their manners and customes, together with the[ir] tractable nature and love towards the English."

Morton was not explicitly committed to nonviolence. The New Englanders first heard that ideal preached by Quaker missionaries, whom they banished in 1656 and hanged a few years later. The Quakers soon found a haven in Pennsylvania, where founder William Penn enjoined his colonists to "live together as neighbors and friends" with the Native people. But the vast majority of English colonists were unable or unwilling to treat the Indians consistently as neighbors and friends (discussed further in Fisher, chap. 1, this volume).

In 1636, when Puritans went to war against the Pequot Indians, they drew on all three dominant traditions to explain it. Many viewed the New World in apocalyptic terms, as "a spiritual battleground between the Elect and the Forces of Darkness." Casting the Pequots (and, indeed, all Indians) as worshipers and agents of the devil, they sanctified their violence as a holy war that would regenerate both individuals and the whole world and thus advance God's plan for human salvation. Many (often the same people) legitimated the war in "just war" language too, as a defense of Christ's church against a satanic plot to destroy it. For the Puritans, the church was the voice of reason and order in the wilderness. So they justified their war (and their persecution of Thomas Morton) as a defense of Christian humanist values.

The tension between just war and holy war discourse reflected a more basic tension within Calvinist spirituality—one that would run throughout American history—between the impulse to transform the world and the more conservative impulse to protect a fragile civic order against chaotic forces that were believed to threaten all around. But both modes of war talk made the categories of Christian humanism serve the discourse of danger by which Puritans forged their distinctive identity.

In 1675, another war erupted in New England, much larger than the Pequot War, pitting the colonists against a coalition of Indian tribes led by the sachem known to the British as King Philip. Even the apostle of Christian humanism, Roger Williams, justified his people's violence, using both just war and holy war language. "Having lost the true and living God their maker," he wrote, the Indians "had forgotten they were Mankind, and ran about the Countrie like Wolves tearing and Devouring the Innocent and peaceable. . . . God would help us to Consume them." From King Philip's War onward, unlimited destruction became the norm on both sides. The idea that Indian violence was God's way of punishing the British for their own sins, once a staple of Puritan ministers, was gradually replaced by the message that God approved the colonists' violence and extermination of Indians because it glorified him.

Jill Lepore argues that "New England colonists waged war to gain Indian lands, to erase Indians from the landscape, and to free themselves of doubts about their own Englishness" (Name of War, 8). The Puritans were plagued by fears that they might be degenerating into savagery: "Against their constructed and idealized notion of civility and decency, the alleged paganism and barbarity of the indigenous people was a constant reminder of what colonists would become if differences inside and out were not confined, contained, and controlled." To assuage their fears, the Puritans—and (perhaps less obviously) other colonists—used religiously legitimated wars, which made the distinction between self and other vivid, absolute, and painfully clear. By focusing on the conflict between themselves and the Indians, they resolved—or evaded—the conflicts and tensions within their own community. But they sought this security through a discourse of danger that heightened their sense of insecurity.

From 1754 until 1763, when the British colonists fought against an alliance of French and Indians, they again insisted that their war was just because they were defending themselves and their true religion against evils that threatened their growing domain. But those evils now included "popery" (since they were fighting the Catholic French, as well as the Indians' "savagery") and political "slavery." Many colonists were coming to embrace a new political vision, deeply influenced by the rationalist philosophies of the Enlightenment, the secularizing heirs of Christian humanism. The new vision "made liberty synonymous with the absence of state intervention and defined political allegiance as an act of voluntary association" (*Dominion of War*, 14), as Fred Anderson and Andrew Cayton explain. Liberty was depicted as fragile, always needing to be defended against enemies who would impose the slavery of forced allegiance to the state.

Most colonists saw their new notion of liberty as a direct reflection of their Protestant faith. To defend one was to defend both: "The civil and religious liberty of British Protestants became the divine standard against the antichristian foe of French popery and slavery." Ernest Tuveson traces to this era the birth of "a conception of the colonies as a separate chosen people, destined to complete the Reformation and to inaugurate world regeneration" (*Redeemer Nation*, 102). Most colonists were likely to say that God was on their side—the side of liberty—while the enemy served the devil and slavery. So the French and Indian War fostered an apocalyptic goal: not merely to prevent the encroachment of slavery and popery, but to wipe out these evils by expanding the colonists' godly civilization into the wilderness and eventually usher in the millennium, when Christ would reign in a perfect world. Apocalyptic goals and fears seemed to justify any and all means of warfare.

Even many Quakers broke with the ideal of nonviolence at least far enough to pay war taxes to fight the French and Indians. Others, incensed at this deviation, rallied a reform movement to uphold more fervently the traditional ideal. That reform movement helped to spur most Quakers (along with Mennonites and other peace churches) to refuse to fight when the colonies erupted in revolution in 1776. Quakers were also influenced by their political conservatism, as were many other Protestant colonists who doubted that revolution could make life better for anyone. They often cited pacifist sources in the Bible and Christian tradition to justify their refusal to fight.

Most colonists who supported the Revolution were also quick to invoke religious legitimations. The covenant with God was fused with and transmuted into the political covenant binding the citizenry, Catherine Albanese argues, creating a foundational myth for the new nation: "The reason the cause succeeded was bound up with the essential *power* of the myth" (*Sons of the Fathers*, 14). As Albanese shows, the myth was so powerful largely because, like the Bible, it turned political life into a cosmic drama that could be enacted both in historical events and in ritual celebrations.

This myth depicted the British government as a satanic conspiracy of power-hungry elites scheming to extinguish the rights of Englishmen. In 1776, the Continental Congress proclaimed a fast day in response to the "impending calamity and distress when the liberties of America are immediately endangered." In 1779, the Congress proclaimed another fast and suggested that the "just and necessary" war was dragging on because too few Americans had learned "to amend their lives and turn from their sins." But most justifications of the Revolutionary War tended to focus on the sins of the enemy. The common dualistic apocalyptic view of the war was typified by minister Abraham Keteltas, who preached that the Americans were fighting on God's side in "the cause of pure and undefiled religion against bigotry, of liberty against arbitrary power . . . the cause of heaven against hell." The Americans' victory would bring "universal love and liberty, peace and righteousness . . . a paradise of God." As always, a holy war view prompted many to drop all restraints on their mode of fighting. Christian-based protest against excessive violence was sometimes voiced, but not often heeded.

Revolution and apocalypse were easily conjoined because both evoked images of total transformation, destroying the sinful old reality to usher in a new and perfect reality. In his pamphlet *Common Sense* (1776), Thomas Paine wrote: "We have it in our power to begin the world over again." The same apocalyptic frame encouraged the colonists to interpret the deaths among them as imitations of Christ, preludes to resurrection. In this respect as in many others, the myth of the Revolution, based on biblical prototypes, became itself a prototype: "The theme of regenerative sacrifice is a persistent one in American life, and we will meet it in each war period."

The political life of the new nation was dominated by Hamiltonian Federalists and Jeffersonian Democratic-Republicans. Both championed the principles of Christian humanism that were reflected in liberal democratic capitalism; both sought peaceful order, though in different ways. Hamiltonians assumed that a nation having mutually beneficial trade relationships with all others would remain at peace with all and grow in prosperity, thus preserving its domestic order. They also wanted a military strong enough to secure the peace by winning wars, if necessary. Jeffersonians expected the nation to prosper, and remain peaceful and orderly, by acquiring new lands for its burgeoning population. The United States would be something never seen before: an ever-expanding yet peaceable "empire for liberty" that would avoid foreign entanglements and thus have little need for military power. But Jefferson also valued international trade as a necessary complement to domestic expansion. Both sides agreed that dynamic growth was the route to stability.

As the young nation increased its wealth through international trade, it ran into conflict with the preeminent sea power of the day, Great Britain. A movement of southern and western War Hawks wanted to secure U.S. trade routes and expand west by going to war with Britain. In 1812, they got their wish. The War of 1812 was legitimated more by the language of honor and manly virtue than by religion. But the War Hawks proclaimed their war just, and most Americans agreed. The values they felt they were justly defending were deeply rooted in Christian humanism. Yet to historian Ralph Beebe it appears in retrospect that "the War of 1812 in some ways approaches the medieval church's definition of a holy war. . . . The patriotic zeal carried a quasi-religious quality" (quoted in Wells, *War of America*, 54), because war supporters drew on the political-religious millennialism preached by New England ministers (who, ironically, tended to oppose the war and cited Scripture for their antiwar purpose). This fusion of millennialism and religious nationalism remained as an influential discursive legacy for the whole nation (developed further in Manis, chap. 3, this volume).

The year the war ended, 1815, saw the first American peace movements (as distinct from religious groups that were theologically pacifist) emerge. They did not advocate strict nonviolence and sectarian withdrawal from political life. Rather, they acted in the political arena to try to eliminate war as a way of solving disputes. They carried on the old tradition of Christian humanism while joining in the new, rapidly growing movement to reform society through an evangelical Protestant crusade to combat (and, some hoped, eliminate) sin. The reform impulse also gave a powerful boost to the movement to abolish slavery.

One wing of the abolitionists, led by William Lloyd Garrison, argued that it was not merely slavery but all forms of violence that were illegitimate rebellions against God's rule. Garrisonians championed nonviolence in language that often mirrored the apocalyptic fervor of the holy war tradition; Garrison urged his followers to "put on the whole armor of God," including perfect nonviolence, "that we may be able to stand against the wiles of the devil" and achieve "universal emancipation . . . from the government of brute force, from the bondage of sin."

Many more Americans embraced the martial spirit symbolized by war hero turned president Andrew Jackson. A Romantic vision of national greatness was emerging—spurred, some say, by the wave of evangelical religious revivals sweeping the nation, with their emphasis on emotion as a basis for truth. The classical liberal concept of liberty, which the Founding Fathers had reasoned out so carefully, now became more of a slogan to justify nationalistic pride, territorial expansion, and violence. Ignoring a sizable public protest, Jackson approved an all-out assault on Indians and confiscation of all their lands east of the Mississippi.

In 1846, the same martial nationalism and desire for land led to war with Mexico. Some historians suggest that the rapid changes of the era (including new technologies, the newly dominant market economy, and the breakdown of traditional social hierarchies) led to internal tensions that were resolved—or evaded—by focusing on an external enemy. But war supporters supplied plentiful arguments that their war was just. It was easier than ever to place blame on the enemy because now, for the first time, the enemy was a foreign nation of darker-skinned people.

The most common pro-war arguments were based on the claim that it was the manifest (that is, obvious and irrefutable) destiny of the United States to expand to the Pacific, annexing Mexican lands (notably California and Texas) in the process. John O'Sullivan, the journalist who popularized the term "manifest destiny," affirmed that Americans were destined "to manifest to mankind the excellence of divine principles," especially democracy, which was simply "Christianity made effective among the political relations of men." American democracy would be "the noblest temple ever dedicated to the worship of the Most High—the Sacred and the True. For this blessed mission to the nations of the world, which are shut out from the life-giving light of truth, has America been chosen."

Exponents of manifest destiny argued in a wide variety of ways that the laws of nature, created by God, dictated that their nation must expand and rise to world supremacy. They insisted that it was only natural, and thus moral, that civilized (that is, white Protestant) people should conquer (darker-skinned non-Protestant) "savages" and teach them how to be rational and civilized. Thus while they gave new expression to the old millennialism, with its apocalyptic overtones, they also drew heavily on the tradition of Christian humanism, though in a way that Christian humanists would never have approved. Still, "the clergy and the constituencies of most [Protestant] denominations were generally prowar," says Ronald Wells. "Evangelical priorities caused them to approve of Manifest Destiny's 'mission of civilization'" (*Wars of America*, 78).

The discourse of manifest destiny expressed what Anders Stephanson calls a widespread sense of "social, economic, and spatial *openness*," a new way to express the old idea that the United States was unfinished, "a sacred-secular *project*, a mission of world-historical significance" (*Manifest Destiny*, 28). This "project" entailed endless change and constant conflict, most visibly at the frontier, where godly civilization was always said to be imposing itself on the heathen wilderness. Yet if the American "project" was the cutting edge of God's plan for history, it embodied values that were eternal. So it encouraged Americans to feel that they, alone among all peoples, were using the process of history to transcend history and thus escape from the conflicts that time and history inevitably bring. To achieve this escape, though, they would have to define their national identity through a discourse of danger and face the dangers that the discourse prescribed.

There was significant opposition to the Mexican War, especially from the Christian reform movements centered in New England. Most of the antiwar voices agreed with the principle of manifest destiny. They merely denied that the principle could justify, or needed, war and violence to implement it. Even O'Sullivan himself at one point wrote: "Democracies must make their conquests by moral agencies." He was advocating "pacific penetration *by commercial means*, which would 'beget a community of interest'" between expanding America and the nations it conquered. After the Mexican War, this theme took on increasing importance in the pursuit of American destiny and interests.

The main result of the Mexican War was to sharpen the question of whether slavery would be extended to new territories, which heightened the growing tension between North and South that engulfed every sphere of life, including the religious. Many national denominations split into two irreconcilable organizations. When the Civil War erupted, most clergymen on both sides cited the Bible to justify and sacralize their side's cause. In the Union, the cause was identified at first as the preservation of the Union; gradually the theme of liberty for all, including slaves, came to the fore. Ministers preached that God had brought war to test the nation's faith or (less commonly) to punish it for its own sins. Abraham Lincoln also attributed the war to, and advised acceptance of, God's will: "The purposes of the Almighty are perfect and must prevail." But in his second inaugural address he expressed a broad-minded view that very few on either side achieved: "Both [sides] read the same Bible and pray to the same God. . . . With malice toward none, with charity for all . . . let us strive on to . . . achieve and cherish a just and lasting peace among ourselves and with all nations."

The Civil War's massive scale of death combined with the prevalent sense of absolute righteousness to foster an apocalyptic mood on both sides, which helped to fuel a major wave of religious revivals, especially among soldiers. In the North, apocalypticism was expressed most famously in "The Battle Hymn of the Republic," heralding "the glory of the coming of the Lord." Theologian Phillip Schaff called the war "a very baptism of blood [entitling] us also to hope for a glorious regeneration." The regeneration would be universal, most northerners believed; prominent minister Henry Ward Beecher proclaimed: "We are fighting not merely for our liberty, but for those ideals that are the seeds and strength of liberty throughout the earth." After the war was over, most northerners interpreted it as a blood sacrifice that had baptized the United States, cemented its unity, and made it seem more than ever God's agent to advance transcendent spiritual values—especially freedom—for all humankind.

Yet the Civil War also cemented the idea that Americans need abide no limits on the violence and destruction they inflict in war, because their cause is always just. General Ulysses S. Grant was famed for the success he had achieved by waging total war against civilians as well as soldiers. As president, though, Grant opposed unlimited violence against the Indians in the West. Instead he championed a program of peacefully "civilizing" the Native peoples and bringing them under the sway of Christian humanist values. But the continuing Indian wars made the frontier the principal focus of holy war as well as just war discourse.

By the late 1890s, with the domestic frontier gone, fears of rapid change and disorder at home evoked a new vision: domestic tranquility required a stable global order upheld by American values. A progressive ideological consensus emerged that combined the impulse to "civilize the [non-white] savages" with a call for a just political order, the expansion of U.S. commercial interests abroad, masculine self-discipline, and a "muscular Christianity" to be spread by missionaries around the world. All of this should be protected by a stronger U.S. military, many argued, to ensure that America fulfilled its manifest destiny. The frontier, and all that it had symbolized, was now (actually or potentially) everywhere. And the frontier still embodied a basic paradox: It was the prime site of constant movement, change, and conflict; yet that dynamism was supposed to be the prime guarantor of stability.

In 1898, this ideological mélange served to legitimate a war against Spain, purportedly to liberate its colonies in Cuba and the Philippines. Although the United States was not defending itself against any attack, war supporters argued that the war was just because it was fought on behalf of the Christian values at the heart of "civilization." Senator Albert J. Beveridge spoke for the new imperialists, who saw their cause as a sacred mission: "We are a conquering race and must obey our blood and occupy new markets and, if necessary, new lands . . . as a part of the Almighty's infinite plan." American "lords of civilization . . . [would] establish system where chaos reigns. . . . Nations shall war no more without the consent of the American Republic." President William McKinley explained that after long nights of prayer, asking God for guidance, he discovered that the United States had to rule over the Filipinos, to "uplift and civilize and Christianize them . . . as our fellow-men for whom Christ also died." All of this religious language reinforced the widespread belief that all of the United States' actions were morally justified because its aims were always morally pure.

Not all Americans agreed. The same values used to promote war and imperialism could also promote peace. Theodore Roosevelt was the most famous champion of "muscular Christianity" and a stronger U.S. military force. But he also promoted the Progressives' ideal of world order secured by treaties and negotiations among the nations that were the most rational and, as it happened, the most powerful. A new peace movement emerged to advance that ideal, believing in "the violent irrationality of the masses and in the necessity for Great Power harmony and control of the underdeveloped world."

These peace advocates did not eschew all violence. (The U.S. nonviolence movement had long been in eclipse, since the Civil War, when William Lloyd Garrison and most of his followers had dropped their commitment to nonviolence in order to support the Union cause.) But they did argue that both Christian values and common sense were opposed to imperialism; the U.S.–led world order could be secured more morally and efficiently by peaceful, especially commercial, means; the global expansion of commerce and Christianity would lead to a mutually beneficial order of reason, democracy, and capitalism that would secure peace for all—even, many hoped, to a kingdom of God on earth.

Woodrow Wilson shared this outlook. His outstanding traits were "his fixation on order and his stubborn belief that humankind was essentially reasonable." But Wilson believed that Christianity was the prerequisite for an orderly rational life and the path to universal salvation, "the process by which the world itself is regenerated." As president, despite his and the nation's professed desire for peace, he dispatched troops to combat political forces he deemed irrational and sinful, first in Mexico and then, on a much larger scale, in Europe during World War I.

Knowing that most Americans had wanted to avoid fighting in Europe, Wilson initiated an unprecedented propaganda campaign that legitimated World War I as a just war, using a stark apocalyptic dualism: German victory would destroy civilization and all the rational liberal values that America stood for, while Allied victory would bring a virtual kingdom of God on earth. Thus Wilson framed the war in classical Christian terms: the prerequisite for ultimate redemption was to defeat absolute evil in a totalizing war that threatened to destroy the world. Such language quickly turned public opinion around. Not surprisingly, "the churches fell into line" too, as Martin E. Marty comments, quoting a prominent minister: "This conflict is indeed a Crusade . . . in the profoundest and truest sense a holy war." Marty summarizes the millennialist war aims preached by the clergy: "to bring wholeness to the world. . . . [T]o reclaim the purity and innocence that came with [America's] founding. . . . The world would be safe for democracy, peace would come, and religious America would take its place at last as the conscience and example and unifier of the world" (*Modern American Religion*, 1:40).

Wilson continued to use apocalyptic language after the war as he campaigned for U.S. membership in the League of Nations. Although the United States failed to join the league, a popular reaction against war boosted the fortunes of the peace movement. More than any other era in American history, the 1920s and 1930s were marked by an energetic and well-organized resistance to U.S. military involvement and armament. As always, religious leaders played a central role, blending the Social Gospel, socialist influences, and pragmatic concerns with what would work in social life. A minority among them hoped to go further and eliminate all violence; the American nonviolence movement had been spurred into much greater activity in response to the violence of World War I, defying the Wilson administration's intense effort to repress opposition to the war.

In the 1930s, the peace movement turned inward and helped feed the growing opposition to any intervention abroad. In his 1939 State of the Union address, President Franklin D. Roosevelt urged Americans to resist the rise of fascism and "prepare to defend, not their homes alone, but the tenets of faith and humanity on which their churches, their governments and their very civilization are founded." But only after the Japanese bombed Pearl Harbor in December 1941 did virtually all Americans agree that the United States had to fight (though a small number of conscientious objectors, nearly all religious, clung to their commitment to nonviolence).

As war weakened the other great powers, the Roosevelt administration planned for the United States to take control of the postwar world in order to stave off another depression and preserve democratic capitalism. Their liberal internationalism carried on the secularized version of Christian humanism that had begun in the era of Jefferson and Hamilton, with its premise that stability depended on dynamic economic growth. It also carried on the age-old millennialist dream of global peace and prosperity.

Neither FDR nor most other liberal internationalists acknowledged that they were reviving a traditional perfectionist impulse. They, like the leading opinion-makers in the Christian community, were deeply influenced by the resurgence of the old doctrine of original sin, expounded most influentially by Reinhold Niebuhr. "The selfishness of human communities must be regarded as an inevi-tability," Niebuhr wrote. "Thus society is in a perpetual state of war. . . . Its peace is secured by strife. That is a very realistic interpretation of the realities of social life." Roosevelt and his foreign policy elite agreed that this was "realism." However they also spoke as if the United States were an exception—a wholly innocent and altruistic nation, no matter how much violence it wreaked in war, because it was fighting to safeguard liberal internationalism for the whole world.

Thus FDR could use the holy war language of good against evil to justify the war. Most Christians agreed that "the democratic way of the West was engaged in a battle to the death against the forces of totalitarianism," Gerald Sittser finds. But the churches generally eschewed fanatic patriotism and holy war language in favor of a "cautious patriotism" that made "biblical principles more absolute than America's interests" and "called for a resurgence of religion." Roosevelt was cau-tious, too. Rather than offer hopes for universal redemption, he generally depicted the war as a way to protect Americans in the sanctity of their homes by keeping savage criminals away from their doorsteps. As a means to this end, he called on all nations to treat one another as good neighbors and create an orderly global neighborhood (through the United Nations and international economic organiza-tions)—not to bring the kingdom of God on earth, but merely to prevent chaos and evil from overwhelming civilization.

This typified a fundamental shift in American public discourse during the Roosevelt era. Previously, when Americans had fought wars and pursued peace, they had drawn on both sides of the Calvinist heritage. They claimed that were trying not only to deter evil and prevent life from getting worse, but also to make life better or even perfect for themselves and (sometimes, at least) for the whole world. Liberal internationalism implied a similar optimism, drawing on human-ist values and the utopian impulse of apocalypticism. But precisely because it embodied those traditions' aspiration to perfection, it demanded that every nation in the world be integrated into a global system based on what pundit Wal-ter Lippmann called "the evangel of Americanism." So it had to see America standing guard on the frontier everywhere, all the time. Any recalcitrant nation or faction became an apocalyptic threat to the entire system. The international-ists' "realism" told them that there would always be such a threat somewhere to stave off. They took it for granted "that there would be no end to the perils the nation now faced. . . . The nation was slipping into a twilight world of neither-war-nor-peace." So there was no way to dislodge millennialist and humanistic language from an enveloping discourse of apocalyptic danger. The axiom of permanent insecurity, now outweighing the hope for improvement, became the all-pervading foundation of American life.

The first clear evidence of this change came after the United States and its allies achieved total victory in 1945. Although the war had been framed in apocalyptic terms, victory did not elicit expressions of absolute salvation. The celebrations were dampened by widespread anxieties about economic depression, social chaos, Communism, and nuclear war. The nation's main project, it seemed, was now to stave off these threats. The rapid transformation of the Soviet Union and the Communist bloc from wartime ally to postwar foe gave a concrete form and focus to the broader range of inchoate anxieties. All of the nation's resources would now be coordinated to serve the highest goal: meeting the Communist threat. War became "the paradigm in which Americans defined themselves." But that paradigm required a permanent enemy threat. So though it is often said that the United States became a "national security state," it would be more accurate to say that the United States became a "national insecurity state."

In the earliest years of the Cold War, a sizable body of American opinion called for the United States to inflict a nuclear apocalyptic defeat on the Soviet Union. But the Truman administration opted for a policy of containment. As long as Communism was contained, it was hoped, the United States could implement the Rooseveltian program of liberal internationalism throughout the "free world." In the spirit of the just war tradition, the goal of containment was to keep the "free world" (now equated with civilization itself) free and secure by preventing attacks from the savage "Red menace." Containment was confirmed as the operative goal during the Korean War, when Truman refused to use nuclear weapons. When the war ended in a negotiated stalemate, the new president, Dwight D. Eisenhower, declared that containment (preventing North Korea from conquering South Korea) constituted victory. His Cold War discourse consistently reaffirmed this notion of containment as victory—and as the key to world peace.

For eight years, Eisenhower pursued this kind of peace. In his discourse, and in mainstream American public discourse, the threat of nuclear war and the threat of Communist aggression merged into a single menace to "civilization" with no foreseeable end. Talk of apocalypse no longer suggested hope for a renewed world, but only fear of total obliteration. Now it seemed the best to hope for was to fend off this apocalyptic threat forever. So the Cold War the nation waged and the peace it sought defined a new sense of the American project: an endless process of managing apocalyptic crises, a permanent state of apocalypse management. Although the threat was defined in apocalyptic language, the solution was framed in terms of the just war tradition: a static state that would preserve the status quo and thus keep the enemy forever outside of the boundaries of the civilized world. That became the goal of American policy and the foundation of American discourse about the nation's identity; it became fundamental to American conceptions of civil religion and national identity.

Many Americans found the most threatening aspect of Communism in its official stance of atheism. The idea of a nuclear-armed America as bearer of religious faith and truth was a major weapon in the Cold War crusade. "Spiritual Armageddon Is Here—Now," the *Reader's Digest* declared. America's hydrogen bomb could be "the saving Star of Bethlehem." In the 1950s, the Cold War did spark a wave of pro-religion sentiment and a significant growth of religious institutions across the country. Those institutions, and the faith they nurtured, offered a sense of a secure dwelling place to protect against a world that seemed threatening on every side. In religious as in political discourse, there was an overriding sense that any fundamental change would be potentially apocalyptic and thus had to be avoided.

Yet the goal of achieving security through apocalypse management was inherently self-defeating. Because public discourse assumed that the Communist threat, the nuclear arms race, and the twilight world of neither-war-nor-peace were all permanent, they entrenched the nation even more firmly in a discourse of danger and a deepening state of national insecurity. When religious discourse was used to cope with this insecurity, it only legitimated the threats further and sacralized the national insecurity state, one of many examples in this essay of this book's theme, articulated in the introduction, of the sacralization of secular politics.

The first challenges to this Cold War consensus came in the late 1950s in the movement for nuclear disarmament and in the nonviolence preached by leaders of the civil rights movement, most notably Dr. Martin Luther King Jr. After President John F. Kennedy, who largely continued the discourse of apocalypse management, signed the Limited Nuclear Test Ban Treaty in 1963, concerns about nuclear disarmament quickly faded from public view. But the Vietnam War soon sparked the largest peace movement in American history. Both Lyndon B. Johnson and Richard Nixon drew on all the resources of Cold War discourse to legitimate the U.S. military project in Vietnam. Yet massive and nearly always peaceful peace demonstrations made the peace movement a significant voice in the public arena.

Prominent religious leaders often played major roles in antiwar activities. One of the best-known antiwar groups was Clergy and Laity Concerned About Vietnam, which "pushed various denominations to debate and formulate positions that advocated a quicker end to the war . . . [and] reinforced the idea that clerics could appropriately address social action as part of their ministry." Working to end the war in such a multifaith coalition was itself "a profoundly important religious experience for many people," theologian Harvey Cox recalled. Peace activists were moved by ideals drawn from the Christian humanist and nonviolence traditions; the latter especially received unprecedented attention. The many peace activists affiliated with religious institutions were often well aware of this religious heritage. Secular peace activists were often unaware of it, but they generally allied quite comfortably with religious activists in pursuit of their common goal.

The more radical wing of the peace movement called into question not merely the Vietnam War but the validity of apocalypse management, the holy war, and sometimes even the just war traditions. In the early 1970s, it seemed that the nation might be ready to debate and reevaluate its fundamental principles and narratives in relation to war and peace. But that was not to be. In the late 1970s, a resurgent conservative mood, spearheaded by Ronald Reagan, ensured that the traditional modes of discourse would remain the basis of national identity. As president, Reagan often used apocalyptic rhetoric, as when he labeled the Communist bloc "an evil empire" and called the nation to wage a relentless struggle between good and evil. But he said (in the same speech) that "the real crisis we face today is a spiritual one," a test of faith, adding that it was better to die in a nuclear war, still believing in God, than to live under atheistic Communism. Reagan was acknowledging the political right's debt to the growing strength of conservative religiosity, which linked traditional forms of faith with militant patriotism. ("A political leader, as a minister of God, is a revenger to execute wrath upon those who do evil," declared religious right leader Jerry Falwell.) Although Communism was ostensibly the great evil that threatened America, the political-religious right aimed to use renewed Cold War fervor to reverse the liberalizing cultural trends of the 1960s and 1970s.

Reagan's nuclear buildup provoked an antinuclear protest, the "freeze" movement, which received substantial support from liberal religious groups that championed more humanist values. The Catholic Conference of Bishops also weighed in with a pastoral letter that questioned the legitimacy of nuclear weaponry from a just war perspective. Faced with widespread support for the "freeze," the Reagan administration backed away from its apocalyptic Cold War rhetoric and turned to the discourse as well as the policies of containment and arms control—though public discourse often depicted even arms negotiations as apocalyptic showdowns.

By the end of the 1980s, the Cold War was over. Liberal internationalists, who still dominated discourse and policymaking, could aspire to their original goal of an all-encompassing global order. But they warned that the world was now more dangerous than ever, because the neatly bifurcated world was gone. There was no well-defined border to defend; chaos might threaten anywhere. And if chaos won anywhere, the argument went, it would spell apocalyptic disaster for the whole world-system (now called "the international community"). So apocalypse management was still necessary.

The first major test of this new situation came with the Persian Gulf War of 1991. Saddam Hussein was depicted as a Hitler-like symbol of apocalyptic evil. But the war was legitimated mainly in just war terms, and the defeated Saddam was allowed to remain in power behind a reaffirmed border, suggesting that the war had aimed only to keep evil from encroaching on civilization. Perhaps the main result of the war in the United States was to help revive the power of the traditional narratives used to legitimate war. As President George H. W. Bush put it: "We have kicked the Vietnam syndrome."

When the Clinton administration attacked and quickly defeated Serbia in 1998, it offered a new rationale for war: humanitarian interventions to rescue imperiled people, even in situations where the United States purportedly had no national interest to protect. This rationale was rooted in the Christian humanist demand for acts of moral conscience and in just war thinking: gross acts of injustice are barbaric and threaten the order of civilization, the argument went, so all civilized people have a duty to restore order. However, some critics argued that this was an illegitimate extension of the just war tradition, one that could too easily be used as a moralistic cover for violence aiming to serve the liberal internationalist project.

That whole debate became rather secondary on September 11, 2001, when airliners crashed into the World Trade Center towers and the Pentagon. In response, the George W. Bush administration declared a war on terrorism. The president often used millennialist language: "This will be a monumental struggle between good and evil. But good will prevail . . . [and] rid the world of evil." Bush's war discourse closely paralleled his evangelical Christian discourse about the need to fight sin. He and his neoconservative advisers, along with many evangelical Christians, identified the cultural changes of the 1960s as the root of most of the nation's current problems. They saw the peace movement's protest against the Vietnam War as a part of a broader challenge to all forms of authority. They viewed the willingness to fight an external enemy as a way to revive respect for the authority of traditional institutions, including religious institutions.

Yet their discourse was based on a Niebuhrian premise that evil stemmed from original sin, so the battle against it would have to go on forever. Indeed, several top administration officials drew parallels between the war on terrorism and the Cold War, suggesting that the goal was only to contain an evil that would never be extirpated. As the war went on with no end in sight, Bush confessed: "I don't think you can win it. . . . I don't have any . . . definite end." The best to hope for might be endless apocalypse management.

Most of the public, knowing only the more widely touted apocalyptic rhetoric, supported the war on terrorism at first. That support began to slide after the Bush administration decided (over the objections of many citizens and national church organizations) to oust Saddam Hussein and occupy Iraq with a large number of U.S. troops. The administration's shifting rationales for the Iraq war drew on all the familiar traditions, adding the claim that Iraq had become the "front line" in the war on terrorism. The rationale that garnered some continuing support from the public and the liberal internationalist establishment (at least through 2007) was the old just war theme that the United States had an obligation to bring order out of chaos, using only as much force as necessary.

The battle between order and chaos, cast in both holy war and just war terms, is an enduring narrative theme that has brought a religious dimension to issues of war and peace in every era of American history. The co-opting of the Christian humanist tradition to serve a discourse of danger is another enduring theme. However, historians have fleshed out many other important themes only for specific eras. Since most of the research has focused on war, most of these themes have been found in particular times of war. This chapter has noted, for example, instances of

- Belief in American innocence and superiority
- Universalizing American ideals (what is good for the United States is good for the world, and vice versa)
- Viewing America as a spiritual project and Americans as God's chosen people, leading the world to the millennium
- Promoting dynamic growth as a means to stability
- Using political ideology to express romantic nationalism
- Belief in original sin
- A sense of American values being permanently threatened
- Tension between impulses to intervene and to avoid intervention in foreign lands
- Americans being reluctant to fight, but when they do fight wanting a quick apocalyptic victory
- Using violence against the "other" to resolve or evade tensions and anxieties within one's own community
- The fusion of just war and holy war ideals
- A tendency to ignore just war's limitations on violence

In every era, there has been strenuous debate about war and peace. The narratives developed by advocates of peace drew surprisingly often on elements of the same narratives that legitimated war. This chapter has noted, for example, instances of peace advocates

- Wanting to use the process of history to experience and express timeless values beyond history
- Viewing religion as an inherently positive value
- Fusing religion and politics in a unified worldview and value system, typically equating religious virtue with political freedom
- Expecting mutually beneficial (especially economic) interactions to be a means to peace
- Invoking natural law to legitimate cultural values
- Using the Bible as a prototype
- Hoping for regeneration or total transformation of self and world, often through sacrifice

- Interpreting war as punishment for the sins of one's own community
- Using religious emotion as a spur to both war and peace

Each of these themes was evident in at least one era. It is plausible to speculate that they may have been evident in other eras. The themes that are found to be important in all (or most) eras could provide a broad interpretive framework for understanding issues of religion, war, and peace in American history. Historians would do well to explore these hypotheses.

Beyond the specific content of narratives about religion, war, and peace, there is a broader hypothesis to explore. Many, perhaps most, Americans have looked to the narratives with which they talked about war and peace to get a sense of clarity, certainty, stability, and thus security in life. But the dominant narratives usually undermined themselves because they assumed either endless progress, which implies constant change and thus no stability, or a stability that was actually a state of confrontation with an enemy—a discourse of danger that precludes the possibility of security. Often the narratives embodied both assumptions, reflecting an enduring tension between a desire for and a fear of change. Since World War II, the desire for stability and security has predominated, making its self-defeating quality ever more evident.

However, in every era there have been peace advocates who rejected the discourse of danger and its premises. Thus they were less likely to make stability and security the highest goals. The nonviolence tradition and the Christian humanist tradition—if it is disentangled from a discourse of danger—can offer rich resources for moving beyond the national insecurity state.

REFERENCES

Albanese, Catherine. *Sons of the Fathers: The Civil Religion of the American Revolution.* Philadelphia: Temple University Press, 1976.

Anderson, Fred, and Andrew Cayton. *Dominion of War: Empire and Liberty in North America, 1500–2000.* New York: Viking, 2005.

Applebaum, Patricia. *Kingdom to Commune: Protestant Pacifist Culture Between World War I and the Vietnam Era.* Chapel Hill: University of North Carolina Press, 2008.

Bennett, Scott. *Radical Pacifism: The War Resisters League and Gandhian Nonviolence in America, 1915–1963.* Syracuse, N.Y.: Syracuse University Press, 2003.

Blum, Edward J. *Reforging the White Republic: Race, Religion, and American Nationalism, 1865–1898.* Baton Rouge: Louisiana State University Press, 2005.

Brock, Peter. *Pacifism in the United States: From the Colonial Era to the First World War.* Princeton, N.J.: Princeton University Press, 1968.

Campbell, David. *Writing Security: United States Foreign Policy and the Politics of Identity*. Minneapolis: University of Minnesota Press, 1998.

Cave, Alfred. *The Pequot War*. Amherst: University of Massachusetts Press, 1996.

Chernus, Ira. *American Nonviolence: The History of an Idea*. Maryknoll, N.Y.: Orbis Books, 2004.

——. *Monsters to Destroy: The Neoconservative War on Terror and Sin*. Boulder, Colo.: Paradigm, 2006.

Chernus, Ira, and Edward T. Linenthal, eds. *A Shuddering Dawn: Religious Studies and the Nuclear Age*. Albany: State University of New York Press, 1986.

DeBenedetti, Charles. *The Peace Reform in American History*. Bloomington: Indiana University Press, 1980.

Ebel, Jonathan H. *Faith in the Fight: Religion and the American Soldier in the Great War*. Princeton, N.J.: Princeton University Press, 2010.

Faust, Drew Gilpin. *This Republic of Suffering: Death and the American Civil War*. New York: Knopf, 2008.

Hall, Mitchell K. *Because of Their Faith: CALCAV and Religious Opposition to the Vietnam War*. New York: Columbia University Press, 1990.

Hatch, Nathan. *The Sacred Cause of Liberty: Republican Thought and the Millennium in Revolutionary New England*. New Haven, Conn.: Yale University Press, 1977.

Hudson, Winthrop. *Nationalism and Religion in America: Concepts of American Identity and Mission*. New York: Harper & Row, 1970.

Kosek, Kip. *Acts of Conscience: Christian Nonviolence and Modern American Democracy*. New York: Columbia University Press, 2008.

Lepore, Jill. *The Name of War: King Philip's War and the Origins of American Identity*. New York: Knopf, 1998.

Linenthal, Edward T. *Changing Images of the Warrior Hero in America: A History of Popular Symbolism*. New York: Mellen, 1982.

Marty, Martin E. *Modern American Religion*. Vol. 1, *The Irony of It All, 1893–1919*. Chicago: University of Chicago Press, 1987.

Mollin, Marian. *Radical Pacifism in Modern America: Egalitarianism and Protest*. Philadelphia: University of Pennsylvania Press, 2006.

Pahl, Jon. *Empire of Sacrifice: The Religious Origins of American Violence*. New York: New York University Press, 2010.

Sherry, Michael. *In the Shadow of War: The United States Since the 1930s*. New Haven, Conn.: Yale University Press, 1995.

Sittser, Gerald. *A Cautious Patriotism: The American Churches and the Second World War*. Chapel Hill: University of North Carolina Press, 1997.

Stephanson, Anders. *Manifest Destiny: American Expansionism and the Empire of Right*. New York: Hill and Wang, 1995.

Stout, Harry S. *Upon the Altar of the Nation: A Moral History of the American Civil War*. New York: Viking, 2006.

Tuveson, Ernest. *Redeemer Nation: The Idea of America's Millennial Role*. Chicago: University of Chicago Press, 1968.

Wells, Ronald A. *The Wars of America: Christian Views*. Grand Rapids, Mich.: Eerdmans, 1981.

9. RELIGION, GENDER, AND SEXUALITY

ANTHONY MICHAEL PETRO

The academic study of gender and sexuality in American religious history has grown rapidly in the past three decades as scholars have built on important gains first pioneered in the field of women's history. In the 1980s, Rosemary Radford Ruether and Rosemary Skinner Keller brought the devotional lives of American women into focus with the publication of *Women and Religion in America*, a three-volume collection of documentary history. Women's religious history found its first comprehensive narrative coverage with the publication in 1996 of Susan Hill Lindley's *"You have Stept out of your Place": A History of Women and Religion in America*. Today, our portrait of American religion includes important leaders such as black preacher Jarena Lee and Pentecostal media mogul Aimee Semple McPherson, as well as the religious experiences of ordinary women within Protestant, Catholic, and Jewish communities. More recently, the lives of Muslim, Hindu, and Buddhist women living in the United States have also come into view. The consideration of religious women has not only increased the number and diversity of voices in our narratives; it has also reshaped how we study American religious history.

Growing out of church history, the study of American religion through the 1970s largely focused on the intellectual history of Protestantism. Scholars examined theological writings authored almost exclusively by men, while they often overlooked how women not only shaped this religious thought, but also participated in devotional activities of their own. As a result of this oversight, the intellectual history of religion largely left women out of the picture and consequently skewed our understanding of America's religious past. By attending to the experiences of women, scholars have revised pervasive themes in American religious history. In "Women's History Is American Religious History," Ann Braude, for instance, challenged the unacknowledged bias of historians preoccupied with the absence of men in America's churches, an assumption undergirding the classic narrative of religious declension. The story of the decline of a churchgoing America cannot be sustained, she claimed, if we admit women to the picture—the same women who have constituted a steady majority of religious participants for virtually all of America's past. By underscoring the presence of women, historians have pushed scholarly accounts that could once get by with meager attention to exceptional women leaders like Anne Hutchinson and Catharine Beecher to reexamine the participants and locations of religious practice: considering women's activities, from public preaching to domestic devotion, necessarily led scholars to redefine the boundaries of what they took to be religious life in America.

Since the 1980s, new studies devoted to analyzing the construction of gender and the history of sexuality in American religion have supplemented, extended, and even challenged the history of religious women. Historians have interrogated the gendered discourse of Puritan piety in the seventeenth century and the sexualized rhetoric of Protestant anti-Catholicism in the nineteenth. They have pushed women's historians to ask: What, exactly, has constituted "woman" in different historical contexts, and how have differences of religion, race, class, age, and sexuality delineated who counts as a woman? Attention to sexuality, meanwhile, has complemented religious histories of women and gender while at the same time it has introduced new questions about religion and sexual identity in modern America. These three areas of analytic focus—women, gender, and sexuality—have substantially revised how we think about religion in America. This essay traces the development of these categories out of women's history and surveys key themes from the history of colonial America to our contemporary context.

THINKING WOMAN'S SPHERE

Women's historians writing in the 1960s and 1970s first challenged the traditional study of American history, which up to that point had privileged political institutions and the state, spheres historically reserved for men. Women's historians refocused scholarly attention onto places more likely to be inhabited by women, including the house, the family, the school, and the church. They shifted not only the sites of historical investigation, but also the types of questions scholars asked, by developing new analytical models that have been essential for the study of women and religion. In "The Cult of True Womanhood: 1820–1860," Barbara Welter emphasized the development of separate, gendered spheres after the Revolutionary War, pejoratively dubbing the domestic sphere the "cult of true womanhood." Throughout the nineteenth century, the ideology of separate spheres, she contended, increasingly associated women with domesticity, purity, piety, and submissiveness. Qualifying Welter's analysis in "The Lady and the Mill Girl: Changes in the Status of Women in the Age of Jackson," Gerda Lerner suggested the potential for separate spheres to raise women's status within their society, while Carroll Smith-Rosenberg, in "The Female World of Love and Ritual: Relations Between Women in Nineteenth-Century America" and *Disorderly Conduct: Visions of Gender in Victorian America*, discerned the unique cultural and class effects that separate spheres held for women. Within the domestic sphere, women cultivated intimate homosocial relationships that laid the groundwork for the development of a unique women's culture.

Building on these studies, Nancy Cott's *Bonds of Womanhood: "Woman's Sphere" in New England, 1780–1835* depicts the daily context of this "woman's sphere" and emphasizes the significant place that religion held for women across the turn of the nineteenth century. As private and public life became ever more divided—and women's work more firmly associated with the domestic sphere—evangelical Christians began to regard women as more naturally pious than men. The church became one of the few venues available for women to express themselves and to develop a supportive community. Indeed, women challenged pressures to contain their activities within the household through their participation in Christian voluntary associations and other activities. The rhetoric of moral reform and woman's sphere ideology also served, however, to subordinate women's roles to male clerical leadership. Women may have been empowered, Cott claimed, but only within roles delimited by male ministers.

Published in 1977, the same year as Cott's study, literary scholar Ann Douglas's *Feminization of American Culture* popularized the notion first introduced by Barbara Welter that Protestant Christianity became feminized over the course of the nineteenth century. Echoing Perry Miller's classic theme of religious declension, Douglas claimed that the sentimentalized writings of liberal male pastors and middle-class women watered down the Calvinist rigor of previous generations. Douglas bemoaned the failure of women in Victorian America, such as Sarah Josepha Hale and Harriet Beecher Stowe, to move beyond a model of feminine influence and found in their sentimental publications the seeds of modern America's mass-consumer culture. The feminization of American Christianity has proved a pervasive, if contentious, theme, and an important critique of it can be found in Karin Gedge's *Without Benefit of Clergy: Women and the Pastoral Relationship in Nineteenth-Century American Clergy*. Since the 1970s, scholars have drawn on, expanded, and critiqued each of these themes—the ideology of separate spheres, the development of a definable women's culture, the simultaneous

subordination and empowerment of women through religion, and the feminization (and masculinization) of religion—in their analyses of women and gender in
American religious history.

WOMEN AND RELIGION IN COLONIAL AMERICA

Historians have made great strides in accounting for the lives of women in the
American colonies and their participation in colonial religion. Laurel Thatcher
Ulrich's *Good Wives: Image and Reality in the Lives of Women in Northern New
England* paints a vivid portrait of the daily lives of New England women from
1650 to 1750 and stresses the importance that church membership status held for
them. According to Ulrich, women led efforts to establish Christian faith among
people living at the outskirts of arborous colonial towns, they used their private influence to weigh in on ministerial matters, and, though formally powerless within
the churches, women served as intermediaries between the natural and supernatural realms through their ecstatic utterances. More concerned with religion specifically, Marilyn J. Westerkamp's *Women and Religion in Early America, 1600–1850:
The Puritan and Evangelical Traditions* provides a valuable starting point for the
history of Puritan and evangelical women. Westerkamp extended the discussion
over the empowerment and disempowerment of women through their religious
involvement while also attending to the distinct experiences of white and black
women in early America. Broadening our portrait of colonial religion, Rebecca
Larson's *Daughters of Light: Quaker Women Preaching and Prophesying in the Colonies and Abroad, 1700–1775* recovers the lives of eighteenth-century Quaker wom-
en—while Puritans strictly limited women's ability to speak in church, the Society
of Friends supported women's participation in public preaching by regarding the
"inner lights" of women as much as those of men. And the lives of colonial Jewish
women find attention in Hasia R Diner and Beryl Lieff Benderly's *Her Works Praise
Her: A History of Jewish Women in America from Colonial Times to the Present.*

Scholars are only beginning to understand the place of women in African
American and Native American religions before the Civil War. While women's
historians provided important correctives to historical narratives populated almost
exclusively by men, early studies in women's history often assumed a static definition of "woman," allowing the experience of white, middle-class Christian women
living in New England to stand as "woman's experience" writ large. In the late
1980s, historians of color and feminist theorists criticized the universalized category of "women" for failing to encompass significant lines of difference, including
dissimilarity of race, class, and gender, but also region, sexuality, age, and religion.
Two pioneering studies, Deborah Gray White's *Ar'n't I a Woman? Female Slaves*

in the Plantation South and Hazel Carby's *Reconstructing Womanhood: The Emergence of the Afro-American Woman Novelist*, examine the intersections of race and gender in the ideology of womanhood among enslaved and free black women. Their contributions paved the way for recent work that has begun to expand scholarship on the religious lives of women of color. Jon R. Sensbach's *Rebecca's Revival: Creating Black Christianity in the Atlantic World* recovers the fascinating role that freed slave Rebecca Protten, a convert to Moravian Christianity, played in sparking religious conversions among slave populations throughout the Atlantic world. Yvonne P. Chireau's *Black Magic: Religion and the African American Conjuring Tradition* and Sharla M. Fett's *Working Cures: Healing, Health, and Power on Southern Slave Plantations* note that black women often gained social influence through their knowledge of conjuring and healing tactics. Although focused largely on later periods of American history, they offer models for future research on the religious lives of slave women, which have yet to be fully illuminated.

American religious historians are also just beginning to narrate the religious experiences of American Indian women, though Allan Greer and Michelene Pesantubbee have made advances in this direction. Greer's *Mohawk Saint: Catherine Tekakwitha and the Jesuits* provides an important model for studying the encounter between Native Americans and Europeans in his account of the seventeenth-century journey of Catherine Tekakwitha from her Mohawk background to Catholic sainthood. Pesantubbee's *Choctaw Women in a Chaotic World: The Clash of Cultures in the Colonial Southeast* reconstructs the history of Choctaw women living in the colonial Southeast and the changes they endured over the course of the eighteenth century. The arrival of Europeans led to increased warfare and violence that circumscribed the public role of women, while the presence of French Jesuits effected more subtle changes in women's religious consciousness. Pesantubbee underscored the continued relevance that religious ceremonies held for Choctaw women and the survival of traditional methods for dealing with birth, family responsibilities, and death.

THINKING GENDER IN COLONIAL AND REVOLUTIONARY AMERICA

In addition to recovering the lives of colonial women, religious historians have also examined constructions of gender in this period. Historians increasingly employed the category of gender in the 1980s and 1990s. While European historians Natalie Zemon Davis and Caroline Walker Bynum drew from cultural anthropology and ritual studies to analyze the symbolic work of gender, Joan Scott drew on poststructuralist theories of language to argue that gender was a discursive construction. Together, they made a strong case for analyzing how gender has been symbolically and socially constructed and for expanding historical coverage to include men. As these historians made clear, "man" was just as constructed as "woman," and histories of gender needed to examine both. Taking up this important trend, American religious historians Amanda Porterfield, Elizabeth Reis, and Susan Juster shifted scholarly attention to the gendered language employed in colonial and revolutionary America in the construction of religious experience.

In *Female Piety in Puritan New England: The Emergence of Religious Humanism*, Porterfield foregrounded the feminine piety of seventeenth-century Puritans who employed nuptial metaphors to describe grace and the church and located their proper expression within the domestic sphere. Conflating the metaphor of divine marriage with earthly wedlock, Puritan ministers imbued husband–wife relations with religious meaning; significantly, this move elevated the status of domestic life and of women in general, since the well-ordered family stood as the model for church and state organization. But the discourse of female piety held different meanings for Puritan men and women, as women's restricted social lives fit more accurately with the metaphor of wifely submission. Women such as Anne Hutchinson and Anne Bradstreet obtained authority by accenting their humility and maintained belief in the value of redemptive suffering. As churches began to grow in the mid-seventeenth century, women outnumbered men, and the metaphorical language that coded the church and New England as "female" acquired literal significance. Puritans employed the language of female piety to negotiate the material changes they experienced in the modernizing world: adulteresses and whores represented unchecked lust and greed, while wifely devotion signified self-control, the veneration of authority, and a sense of social responsibility. As burgeoning colonial towns became geographically and socially fractured, the power of feminine religious devotion to maintain social order began to wane. The Salem witch trials of 1692 marked the breaking point for this feminine piety and the ascent of a more masculine form.

While Porterfield located the shift away from feminine piety and the ensuing witchcraft trials in the social disorder brought on by a budding capitalist order, Elizabeth Reis offered a fuller account of the religious impetus for colonial witchcraft. In *Damned Women: Sinners and Witches in Puritan New England*, Reis revised the social, economic, and psychological explanations of colonial witchcraft popularized by historians Paul Boyer and Stephen Nissenbaum, John Demos, and Carol F. Karlsen. Karlsen's The *Devil in the Shape of a Woman: Witchcraft in Colonial New England*, for instance, asks, importantly, why women were most often accused of witchcraft, a question she only partially answered through attention to economic conflicts. Amending these studies, Reis placed religious belief and the construction of women's subjectivity at the heart of seventeenth-century witchcraft. Puritan men and women, she argued, lived out their Christian faith differently. Women, more so than men, thought of themselves as depraved, bound to Satan, and destined for hell.

Convinced of their own depravity—and held to a greater burden of proof—women found it harder than men to disprove accusations of witchcraft, and both sexes began to assume that women were more likely to become witches.

While colonial women suffered significant backlash at the close of the seventeenth century, the rise of evangelical "awakenings" in the decades following increased their religious standing once again. In *Disorderly Women: Sexual Politics and Evangelicalism in Revolutionary New England*, Susan Juster analyzed the gendered discourse of evangelical Christians in the eighteenth century. As waves of revival rippled across New England during the First Great Awakening, increased religious emotionalism contributed to a feminized piety; within this context, marginalized Baptists authorized greater religious freedom and leadership for women participants. In the late eighteenth century, Baptist churches began to organize into a denomination and to move away from the margins of American religious culture. After 1780, for Baptist leaders who preferred a more patriarchal structure, the feminine nature of the church proved a liability. Denominational language began to restrict women's participation in church politics, and church authorities largely ignored their voices in religious matters, accusing those who spoke up of being "disorderly." By looking at the lives of women alongside constructions of gender, Juster highlighted a shifting model of religious authority that curtailed women's religious freedom as Baptists became more organized and piety more masculine—an observation that tempers the triumphalist account of "the democratization of American Christianity" made famous by Nathan Hatch and other historians who have neglected the experience of women in evangelical Christianity (discussed further in Sweeney, chap. 5, this volume).

Historians like Westerkamp and Juster have made great strides in writing women back into the history of colonial and revolutionary America, and they have highlighted the shifting gendered dimensions of evangelical piety. But many questions still remain: How did Puritan and evangelical women imagine the relationship between their devotional activities and their daily toils? What roles did enslaved African women play in the perpetuation of African religions in the New World? Further attention to women's roles outside the home, including participation in healing practices and less orthodox religious activities, would further advance our portrait of colonial and revolutionary America.

LEADING WOMEN: GENDER AND RACE IN THE NINETEENTH CENTURY

Historians of the nineteenth century have focused on documenting women's roles as leaders and preachers. In *Strangers and Pilgrims: Female Preaching in America,*

1740–1845, Catherine Brekus recovered the history of female preaching from the mid-eighteenth to the mid-nineteenth century. Long overlooked in the historical memory of women's rights activists and evangelical Christians alike, preaching women existed along the margins of religious life and often came from the lower and lower-middling classes. From these margins, however, they vehemently defended their right to preach long before the battles for female ordination that would arise in the twentieth century. Moving beyond a static definition of womanhood, Brekus asked how definitions of "woman" changed during the period she investigated. She found a shift from a one-sex model in the eighteenth century that figured women as incomplete men toward a two-sex model in the nineteenth that depicted men and women as demonstrating distinct sexual natures. This shift, in turn, influenced how women preachers defended their vocation. In the eighteenth century, preaching women attempted to transcend their gendered status, to appear not as "women" but as instruments of God, whereas nineteenth-century women employed the language of female difference to assert their right to preach as women.

Brekus also discerned the differences between white and black women preachers, thereby joining William Andrew's earlier recovery of black women preachers' autobiographical writings in *Sisters of the Spirit: Three Black Women's Autobiographies of the Nineteenth Century* and Jualynne Dodson's later research in *Engendering Church: Women, Power, and the AME Church*. More often than white women, black women such as Julia Foote closely identified themselves with biblical prophets by insisting on the authority of their ecstatic experiences to illustrate that their power to preach issued directly from the Holy Spirit. Published in 1998, the same year as *Strangers and Pilgrims*, Bettye Collier-Thomas's *Daughters of Thunder: Black Women Preachers and Their Sermons, 1850–1979* extends the history of black women preachers from the second half of the nineteenth century into the late twentieth. Collier-Thomas's more recent *Jesus, Jobs, and Justice: African American Women and Religion* highlights the central place of African American women in the black freedom struggle.

While women preachers operated in the religious margins, evangelical women in the Christian mainstream steered their efforts toward reforming the new nation. Linda Kerber made famous the trope of "republican motherhood" to describe a new ideology that arose in post-Revolutionary America as an earlier ideology of separate spheres merged with a new national politics that privileged autonomy and individualism. Woman's sphere was redefined to validate women's moral influence and maternal nature, and republican mothers were credited with the formation of benevolent societies in the early nineteenth century. Several excellent biographies have narrated women's leadership in reform efforts. Gerda Lerner's classic *The Grimké Sisters from South Carolina: Rebels Against Slavery* tells of the exceptional lives of abolitionist leaders Angelina and Sarah Grimké, while Kathryn Sklar depicted the life of Catherine Beecher in *Catherine Beecher: A Study in American Domesticity*. Nell Irvin Painter's *Sojourner Truth: A Life, a Symbol* recounts the journey of this itinerant Pentecostal preacher from the bonds of slavery to the leading ranks of abolitionism and women's suffrage. Treating reform efforts more broadly, Barbara Leslie Epstein's *Politics of Domesticity: Women, Evangelism, and Temperance in Nineteenth-Century America* covers the emergence of women's popular consciousness through the revivals of the First and Second Great Awakenings and leading up to the formation of the Women's Christian Temperance Union, while Lori Ginzberg's *Women and the Work of Benevolence: Morality, Politics, and Class in the Nineteenth-Century United States* traces the role of antebellum women in temperance, suffrage, and abolition movements and underscores the changing class dynamics of this period. Anne M. Boylan's *The Origins of Women's Activism: New York and Boston, 1797–1840* narrates women's work in New York and Boston during the first half of the nineteenth century and revises historical narratives that track a linear development from women's missionary efforts in the late eighteenth century to antislavery and women's rights campaigns by the mid-nineteenth century. And Maureen Fitzgerald further enriched the history of women's reform efforts with her study of the activism of Irish Catholics nuns, *Habits of Compassion: Irish Catholic Nuns and the Origins of New York's Welfare System, 1830–1920*.

Building on this history of women's reform, Bruce Dorsey's *Reforming Men and Women: Gender in the Antebellum City* challenges the notion of "republican motherhood" that centered on mostly middle-class white women. Dorsey pushed scholars to include a broader range of women participants in early reform activities. In Philadelphia, he found, formerly enslaved black women organized the first independent women's association, the Female Benevolent Society of St. Thomas, in 1793—two years before white women formed a similar organization. Far from being republican mothers, moreover, it was young, single Quaker women who started the first white women's societies. Adopting the interpretative lens of poststructuralist gender history, Dorsey also illustrated how reformers in antebellum Philadelphia constructed notions of femininity and masculinity against the backdrop of differences in religion, ethnicity, race, class, and age. In this regard, Dorsey's separate chapters on urban poverty, prohibition, abolition, and immigration also demonstrate the differently constructed forms of manhood that operated among working-class nativists, black leaders supporting African colonization, and Irish immigrants settling in Philadelphia, while explaining how each in turn affected cultural definitions of womanhood.

Historians have also documented the power of normative gender ideologies in the American experiences of Jews and Catholics in the nineteenth century. The place of women in American Judaism found eloquent coverage in Karla Goldman's *Beyond the Synagogue Gallery: Finding a Place for Women in American Judaism*. To gain respectability in the United States, Jewish leaders adopted mixed-sex or family seating patterns more similar to those of their Protestant neighbors, who looked suspiciously on the separation of men and women in the synagogue. Pamela S. Nadell followed the history of women's struggles for ordination into the twentieth century in *Women Who Would Be Rabbis: A History of Women's Ordination.* Carol K. Coburn and Martha Smith outlined the significant role that white Catholic nuns played in the formation of American Catholicism in the nineteenth and early twentieth centuries in *Spirited Lives: How Nuns Shaped Catholic Culture and American Life, 1836–1920,* while Diane Batts Morrow made significant progress in recovering the history of black nuns in *Persons of Color and Religious at the Same Time: The Oblate Sisters of Providence, 1828–1860,* her study of the Oblate Sisters of Providence in Baltimore. Also recovering the place of Catholic women, Emily Clark's *Masterless Mistresses: The New Orleans Ursulines and the Development of a New World Society, 1727–1834* traces the history of the earliest Catholic women's order from the eighteenth into the early nineteenth centuries. The New Orleans Ursulines were masterless in the sense of operating relatively autonomously, and mistresses because they were slaveowners.

Throughout the nineteenth century, religious women fought not only for greater recognition within their churches but also for gender equality at the national level. Writing against the tendency of women's historians to neglect religious activists, Ann Braude asserted in *Radical Spirits: Spiritualism and Women's Rights in Nineteenth-Century America* that women's participation in the mid-nineteenth-century Spiritualist movement bolstered the development of the women's rights movement. Spiritualism allowed women to achieve a relatively high degree of religious authority, and nearly all Spiritualists advocated women's rights. Kathi Kern's *Mrs. Stanton's Bible* also treats the religious history of the women's suffrage movement, covering the controversial campaign launched by Elizabeth Cady Stanton to produce the Woman's Bible. Braude and Kern have begun to narrate the important role that religious women played in the movement for women's rights, but still more attention needs to be given to the participation of religious women from liberal and conservative Christian backgrounds in the rise of feminism toward the close of the nineteenth century. The religious lives of lower- and working-class women also have yet to receive significant attention: To what extent did evangelical piety pervade the worlds of working-class women in the nineteenth century, and did they find it empowering or restrictive? And how did immigrant women envision their religious duties as they settled in America?

MODERNIZING WOMEN AND MASCULINE RELIGION AT THE TURN OF THE TWENTIETH CENTURY

Around the turn of the twentieth century, Protestants, Catholics, and Jews alike wrestled with a rapidly modernizing world. Anxious fears rooted in the purported

feminization of Protestant Christianity in the mid-nineteenth century climaxed
with the announcement of a crisis of masculinity by the turn of the twentieth. Per-
plexed church leaders asked why men had fled the fold—often for the homosocial
environs of fraternal lodges, as Mark Carnes has aptly illustrated in *Secret Ritual
and Manhood in Victorian America*—while they overlooked the women populating the pews before them. Confronting this perceived crisis, as Gail Bederman has
noted in "'The Women Have Had Charge of the Church Work Long Enough':
The Men and Religion Forward Movement of 1911–1912 and the Masculinization
of Middle-Class Protestantism," they developed a new strategy intended to make
church piety and polity alike more manly. For starters, a more powerful and vir-
ile America—an imperialist America, no less—needed a new Jesus: sentimental
representations of a loving, caring Christ popular in Victorian America gave way
to depictions of Jesus as a manly carpenter and shrewd businessman. Jesus still
cared, but he wasn't going to put up with any nonsense. This masculinization of
American Christianity, depicted in Clifford Putney's *Muscular Christianity: Manhood and Sports in Protestant America, 1880–1920*, had palpable consequences for
women.

Historians have effectively demonstrated that the ethos of masculine religion
and the growth of evangelical Christianity did not signal women's flight from
religious participation. Beryl Satter's *Each Mind a Kingdom: American Women,
Sexual Purity, and the New Thought Movement, 1875–1920* and Evelyn A. Kirkley's
*Rational Mothers and Infidel Gentlemen: Gender and American Atheism, 1865–
1915* have importantly documented women's attraction to the New Thought and
Freethought movements, respectively. But scholarship on this period has focused
most effectively on women in more conservative faiths. Questions of women's
empowerment and subordination running throughout much of the historiography
of women's religious history reached a climax in discussions of women in conservative religious traditions in the twentieth century. Evangelical historians and
scholars of African American religious history have recovered the participation of
women in conservative Christian movements while also writing against depictions
of religious women as voiceless or wholly oppressed within these traditions.

Betty DeBerg and Margaret Lamberts Bendroth analyzed the gendered theological dimensions and differing roles of women and men in American fundamentalism. In *Ungodly Women: Gender and the First Wave of American Fundamentalism*, DeBerg unsettled foundational theological and social analyses of
fundamentalism written by Ernest Sandeen and George Marsden that focused
reductively on dispensational premillennialism, biblical inerrancy, evolution, and
modernism. She argued, in contrast, that fundamentalist theology arose as a popular reaction against the disruptions of Victorian gender norms. Put more directly,
the New Woman sapped men's manhood and raised the "apocalyptic alarm" of
many conservative evangelicals. Middle-class men depended on the nineteenth-
century ideology of separate spheres to construct their own sense of manliness, and

the disintegration of these gendered spheres threatened this identity. Bendroth's *Fundamentalism and Gender, 1875 to the Present* extends this analysis through the twentieth century and explains why so many women found fundamentalism attractive in the first place—the movement, for instance, upheld many women's sense of the importance of family life. Bendroth trained her analysis on theological debates concerning the traditional roles of women, as many fundamentalists increasingly defined themselves against evangelical feminists, and she outlined important changes in fundamentalist approaches to gender during the first half of the twentieth century. By the 1920s, for instance, conflicts between male leaders and laywomen led to a reversal of women's metaphorical role as the guardians of religion, as men began to define themselves as both morally and psychologically superior. The history of white Pentecostal women in the early twentieth century remains understudied, though several biographies cover Pentecostal media magnate Aimee Semple McPherson—Matthew Avery Sutton's *Aimee Semple McPherson and the Resurrection of Christian America* is a recent example. Black women's participation in Pentecostalism in the early twentieth century received attention in theologian Cheryl J. Sanders's study of the Sanctified Church, *Saints in Exile: The Holiness-Pentecostal Experience in African American Religion and Culture*, while Anthea Butler's *Women in the Church of God in Christ: Making a Sanctified World* focuses more specifically on black women's roles in the Church of God in Christ, chronicling the role of the "Women's Department" in providing the context for women's work in the denomination between 1911 and 1964. Religious belief supported women's activism in the church, argued Butler, as sanctification—far from redirecting women to otherworldly concerns—actually encouraged the religious activities of church mothers.

Attention to black Pentecostal women built on earlier efforts to recover the religious experiences of African American women more generally spearheaded in the 1980s and 1990s by scholars such as Cheryl Townsend Gilkes and Evelyn Brooks Higginbotham. A sociologist by training, Gilkes wrote several important essays in the mid-1980s devoted to the study of black women in Pentecostal and Holiness traditions that were collected in *If It Wasn't for the Women: Black Women's Experience and Womanist Culture in Church and Community*. She explored the essential role black women held in their churches and the effect that religious belief wielded in their efforts to promote social change within their communities. In *Righteous Discontent: The Women's Movement in the Black Baptist Church, 1880–1920*, Higginbotham examined the women's movement within the black Baptist church in the decades following Reconstruction. She employed a gender perspective for studying the black church—one that looked at the role of the black female laity in the Baptist movement. The National Baptist Convention and the Woman's Convention, which was founded in 1900, allowed black men and women social spaces within which to critique the prevailing legal and cultural racism they witnessed in America. The women's movement, moreover, simultaneously fostered a separate community in which women could discuss issues of sexism and racism specific to their experiences. Higginbotham also addressed class issues: the push for respectability among middle-class Baptist women led them to esteem white middle-class values of temperance, industriousness, refined manners, and Victorian sexual mores and to rally poor, working-class blacks to the cause of racial self-help. While white and black women reformers often united through a common dedication to this "politics of respectability," such reform efforts led black women's organizations to disavow the expressive folk culture of many poor blacks in the rural South—one that provided its own means for resisting white racism. Enlarging this historical portrait, Judith Weisenfeld's *African American Women and Christian Activism: New York's Black YWCA, 1905–1945* covers the history of the black YWCA in New York in the first half of the twentieth century. Weisenfeld illustrated how black women leaders in this movement also were committed to the doctrine of racial uplift and self-help and actively sought to maintain their reputations as virtuous women.

These histories of women's religious participation in white and African American evangelical traditions in the early twentieth century suggested the complexity of women's agency. More recently, historians have also begun to recover the activist work of Catholic religious women during this period. Suellen Hoy's *Good Hearts: Catholic Sisters in Chicago's Past* traces the ministry work of Catholic nuns in Chicago from the early to the mid-twentieth century, while Amy L. Koehlinger's *The New Nuns: Racial Justice and Religious Reform in the 1960s* details Catholic sisters' quest for racial and religious reform in the turbulent 1960s. Religious women, far from the assumptions of many feminists and women's historians, were not simply denied agency in conservative churches. Nor were they fully silenced by the often sexist attitudes of male religious authorities. But neither were religious women wholly empowered, as Higginbotham and Weisenfeld have suggested. Scholars of lived religion writing since the late 1990s have further developed accounts of women's agency that have complicated simple depictions of religion as either empowering or oppressive.

LIVING GENDER AND RELIGION IN MODERN AMERICA

Scholars working within the paradigm of "lived religion" since the 1990s have made important gains in the study of women and gender in the twentieth century. Drawing from cultural anthropology and French theorists of practice, scholars of lived religion have been especially attentive to gender and the daily experiences of women. In *Thank You, St. Jude: Women's Devotion to the Patron Saint of Hopeless Causes*, Robert A. Orsi portrayed the complicated ways that Catholic women negotiated their religious lives in the second half of the twentieth century through devotion to Saint Jude, the patron saint of hopeless causes. And R. Marie Griffith redirected the scholarly analysis of evangelical women in her ethnography of the Women's Aglow Fellowship, an international charismatic women's organization. In *God's Daughters: Evangelical Women and the Power of Submission*, she critiqued liberal feminist characterizations of conservative women as duped or wholly oppressed, while simultaneously eschewing both the impulse to romanticize the resistance of women living under oppressive conditions and the tendency to view women as free agents who willfully embraced their submission. Shifting the terms of the debate, Griffith described how these religious actors were able to "make room" for themselves in a world already marked by social relations of power and religious ideologies.

Scholars have also depicted negotiations of agency among Mexican American, Muslim, and black Baptist women in modern America. Jeanette Rodriguez's *Our Lady of Guadalupe: Faith and Empowerment Among Mexican-American Women* recognizes the empowerment of Mexican American women through their devotion to the Virgin of Guadalupe, while Carolyn Moxley Rouse's *Engaged Surrender: African American Women and Islam* centers on African American Sunni Muslim women in two mosques in southern California. She illustrated how they developed a "resistance consciousness" that opposed the hegemonic power of racism, sexism, and classism. Complementing Rouse's ethnography, Yvonne Yazbeck Haddad, Jane I. Smith, and Kathleen M. Moore's anthology *Muslim Women in America: The Challenge of Islamic Identity Today* extends the scholarly coverage to include Muslim women of Middle Eastern descent whose families immigrated to the United States in the twentieth century. Finally, Marla Faye Frederick's *Between Sundays: Black Women and Everyday Struggles of Faith* demonstrates both the significance of "spirituality" (which her informants opposed to the more stagnant concept of "religion") for reconfiguring Baptist women's notions of self and the way these transformations of self informed black women's mode of creative agency and social protest in a small town in North Carolina.

The study of religious practice leads directly to questions about the site at which that practice occurs—the human body. Scholars of lived religion have been especially attentive to this concern, asking: Should we take the sexed body, male or female, as a biological given, and does religious discourse influence the formation of the body? Feminist philosopher Judith Butler famously argued, in *Gender Trouble: Feminism and the Subversion of Identity*, that we have no recourse to a prediscursive body; rather, the natural "givenness" of the sexed body can be given only in the already socially constructed terms of gender. Scholars of lived religion have recently taken up questions of corporeality by reflecting on the significance of religious discourse and practice in the construction of gendered and sexed bodies. R. Marie Griffith's *Born Again Bodies: Flesh and Spirit in American Christianity* traces religious discourses on embodiment, ranging from traditions of phrenology and New Thought to the dieting and fitness programs of contemporary evangelicals, to examine the construction of American body ideals—standards, she argued, often marked as well by race and gender. Pamela E. Klassen's *Blessed Events: Religion and Home Birth in America* also investigates the construction of the body through religious discourse. Klassen surveyed women from a variety of religious backgrounds who chose to give birth at home. Their religious views, she claimed, contributed to how they understood their bodies and often provided the grounds for women to challenge biomedical authority over the process of reproduction. These studies illustrate the significant gains to be made from examining the body in religious practice. Future research might continue to observe how religious discourses have contributed to constructions of the body in other historical contexts, and what role the body plays in negotiations of agency. Martha L. Finch's *Dissenting Bodies: Corporealities in Early New England*, which examines theological and cultural notions of corporeality among Puritan separatists in seventeenth-century New England, offers one useful model for how such studies could be undertaken. In addition, further attention should be paid more generally to the lives of women throughout the twentieth century. For instance, what role did women play in modernizing mainline religions across the turn of the century and through World War II? And how did the lives of Catholic sisters change in the first half of the twentieth century?

THINKING SEX IN AMERICAN RELIGION

While historians of women and gender have often addressed the sexual dimensions of American religion, they have tended to subsume the analysis of sexuality within the paradigm of gender, rather than taking sexuality itself as a starting point. Historians of religion and gender have fruitfully linked Puritan anxieties about women's sexuality to the witch trials of the seventeenth century, but they have offered less discussion of Puritan sexual norms and their religious justifications. Likewise, historians of fundamentalism have framed this movement within the cultural formation of norms surrounding masculinity and femininity in the early twentieth century, but they have stopped short of considering how the construction of gender was connected to the rise of the new medical category of homosexuality in the late nineteenth century. Following feminist and queer theoretical writing of the 1980s and 1990s—especially Gayle Rubin's important essay "Thinking Sex: Notes for a Radical Theory of the Politics of Sexuality"—there is good reason to question whether sexuality should be subsumed within the study of women and gender. At different historical moments, for instance, sexuality has had as much to do with race and imperialism, class and geography, age and religion, as it has with women and gender. Although scholars have only begun to recount America's religious past from the standpoint of sexuality, two promising themes have emerged: the representation of sexual otherness in the construction of a Christian nation and the relationship between religion and sexual identity.

Ann Taves provided one of the first (though very few) attempts to rethink religious history through the lens of sexuality in her essay "Sexuality in American Religious History." She focused on the role of religion and the state in the delineation of legitimate and illegitimate religious and erotic practices—a theme central for ascertaining how representations of sexual and religious otherness have contributed to constructions of "civilization," race, sexual identity, and Christian practice. The Puritans, in particular, have offered a continuing source of fascination for understanding contemporary American sexual mores and attitudes. In *The Puritan Origins of American Sex: Religion, Sexuality, and National Identity in American Literature*, for instance, the literary scholars Tracy Fessenden, Nicholas F. Radel, and Magdalena J. Zaborowska provocatively traced the Puritan roots of American sexual culture, while sex among the Puritans themselves has found attention since Edmund S. Morgan's essay "The Puritans and Sex." Morgan sought to dispel pervasive rumors that Puritans were anti-sex. Within the confines of marriage, the only restriction they placed on sex was that it must not interfere with religion. Despite a high rate of fornication and adultery in the colonies, such offenses were actually punished quite moderately, usually through fines, whippings, and public humiliation. Richard Godbeer's *Sexual Revolution in Early America* extended Morgan's effort and found a general tolerance among lay settlers for informal marriages and premarital sex between committed partners. Sexual relations with nonwhites often proved more troublesome for colonists than fornication, adultery, and sodomy among whites—so much so that as a preventative measure Virginia passed a law against interracial marriage in 1691. But attitudes toward interracial coupling also varied among the early colonies.

The significance of sexuality in the religious and colonial endeavors of Spanish Catholics in the sixteenth century found coverage in Ramón Gutiérrez's *When Jesus Came, the Corn Mothers Went Away: Marriage, Sexuality, and Power in New Mexico, 1500–1846*. Arriving in New Mexico in 1540, Spanish colonizers and Franciscan priests encountered the advanced societies of the Pueblo Indians, which were marked, they found, by a fairly free expression of sexuality. Serial monogamy was the most common form of sexual practice, though some elite men took more than one wife, and same-sex sexual relations were not forbidden. Spanish priests associated these sexual mores with a lack of civilization that they used to justify their efforts to bring Indian culture under their religious control. This link between civilization and Christianity was repeated on the Eastern Seaboard, where initial prejudices against blacks and Native Americans in the early years of colonization issued not from biological racism (which would come in the nineteenth century) but from the association of black and Native sexual practices with a lack of civilization. As Susan Juster, in "The Spirit and the Flesh: Gender, Language, and Sexuality in American Protestantism," and Ann Taves have separately observed, colonial Christians commonly associated sexual deviance with the status of non-Christians, so that blacks, Native Americans, and unconverted whites alike drew the ire of the converted. Anthropologist Sally Engle Merry told a similar story in *Colonizing Hawai'i: The Cultural Power of Law*, about the efforts of New England missionaries after 1820 to impose a new legal system steeped in Protestant values on native Hawaiians. Civilizing Hawaiians meant bringing women, traditionally free to engage in serial monogamy and flexible unions, under the strict control of their husbands. Scholars have only started to comprehend how Mormons, Catholics, Jews, and others departing from Protestant norms also drew the ire of nineteenth-century middle-class evangelical Americans, as definitions of civilization continued to bear religious and sexual overtones. In this direction, Lawrence Foster detailed the lives of celibate Shakers, polygamous Mormons, and Oneida Perfectionists in *Religion and Sexuality: The Shakers, the Mormons, and the Oneida Community*, while Sarah Barringer Gordon illustrated in *The Mormon Question: Polygamy and Constitutional Conflict in Nineteenth-Century America* how Protestants linked Mormon plural marriage with slavery to decry "the twin relics of barbarism."

While Protestants employed sexual rhetoric to mark the marginal status of religious outsiders, they questioned as well the religious status of racial and sexual minorities in America and often restricted their access to full citizenship. Across the turn of the twentieth century, as Hazel Carby, in "On the Threshold of 'Woman's Era': Lynching, Empire, and Sexuality in Black Feminist Theory, "and others have argued, representations of black women's sexuality as excessive fueled arguments for their racial and religious inferiority, blocking their access to achieving "true womanhood." Religious and racial fears undergirding Virginia's 1691 law against interracial marriage survived on the books until the Supreme Court decision in *Loving v. Virginia* (1967). And until the twenty-first century, homosexual Americans were criminalized for committing sex acts that failed to conform to normative "Christian" standards. In the famous Supreme Court case *Bowers v. Hardwick* (1986), the majority opinion upheld Georgia's law prohibiting sodomy on the grounds that sodomy overran the boundaries of legitimate sex (meaning marital, heterosexual, monogamous) circumscribed by the Judeo-Christian tradition. Janet R. Jakobsen and Ann Pellegrini further examined this regulation of sexuality through legal means in *Love the Sin: Sexual Regulation and the Limits of Religious Tolerance*. Future scholarship should continue to interrogate how notions of "mainstream" and "legitimate" sexual practices have been constructed through religious and legal means, and how religious thought about sexuality has, in turn, informed the ways in which people have constructed categories of race and gender since the discovery of the New World.

The construction of religious and sexual identities is a second theme raised through the study of religion and sexuality, particularly as scholars have recently become aware of the religious lives of lesbian, gay, bisexual, and transgender people. Sociologist Gary David Comstock's *Unrepentant, Self-Affirming, Practicing: Lesbian/Bisexual/Gay People Within Organized Religion* recounts the participation of lesbians, gay men, and bisexuals within organized religion, but the longer history of lesbian and gay religious life and of the "ecclesial wing" of the gay rights movement has yet to be covered. Through the 1960s, as Heather White has shown in "Homosexuality, Gay Communities, and American Churches: A History of a Changing Religious Ethic, 1946–1977," mainline denominations supported anti-discrimination laws, although most reaffirmed the sinfulness of homosexual behavior. By the 1970s, though, nearly every mainline denomination developed caucuses that supported the inclusion of lesbians and gays in their denominations. Defrocked Pentecostal minister Troy Perry launched the gay church movement when he organized the first Metropolitan Community Church (MCC) in Los Angeles in 1968, and the independent Catholic Church movement soon followed. Horace L. Griffin's *Their Own Receive Them Not: African American Lesbians and Gays in Black Churches* began recounting the history of African American lesbians and gays, including the formation of Unity Fellowship Church in Los Angeles by Carl Bean and of Faith Temple in Washington, D.C., by James Tilley in the early 1980s.

Recent studies by sociologists and anthropologists have centered on the negotiation of seemingly incompatible religious and sexual identities among homosexuals. Melissa M. Wilcox's *Coming Out in Christianity: Religion, Identity, and Community* examines the sexual and religious narratives of members of two MCC congregations in California, while Dawne Moon's *God, Sex, and Politics: Homosexuality and Everyday Theologies* analyzes debates about homosexuality among the members of two Methodist congregations in the Chicago area. Mark D. Jordan's *The Silence of Sodom: Homosexuality in Modern Catholicism* discusses the controversial role of male homosexuality within contemporary Catholicism, while Moshe Shokeid's *A Gay Synagogue in New York* expands beyond a Christian focus to include movements within Judaism to establish gay congregations, focusing on the Congregation Beth Simchat Torah in New York City. In *Queering Creole Spiritual Traditions: Lesbian, Gay, Bisexual, and Transgender Participation in African-Inspired Traditions in the Americas*, Randy P. Conner and David Hatfield Sparks illuminated the participation of people with alternative sexual and gender identities practicing within African-inspired traditions, including Vodou, Santería, and Candomblé. While many of these studies provided new ways for understanding how lesbians and gay men negotiated their religious identities, Tanya Erzen's *Straight to Jesus: Sexual and Christian Conversions in the Ex-Gay Movement* details how religious discourse produced a new form of sexual identity. Erzen drew from poststructuralist models of identification to illustrate how conversion tropes within evangelical Christianity set the groundwork for ex-gay conversions. Men living in the ex-gay residential center Erzen studied constructed new identities, seeing themselves not as gay or straight, but as "ex-gay."

New themes arise if we consider American religious history from the standpoint of sexuality, including questions about the religious regulation of sexual bodies, the place of religion in national debates over which forms of sexual practice are legitimate, and the proliferation of new sexual and religious identities. Scholars will also continue to develop the history of lesbian and gay Americans and the influence of the gay church movement on American religious practice. Suggestive, recent queries into the curious erotics of seventeenth-century Quakerism by Anne Miles ("Border Crossings: The Queer Erotics of Quakerism in Seventeenth-Century New England"), the transgressive associations of American Spiritualists by Molly McGarry (*Ghosts of Futures Past: Spiritualism and the Culture Politics of Nineteenth-Century America*), the queer roots of American fundamentalism by Kathryn Lofton ("Queering Fundamentalism: John Balcom Shaw and the Sexuality of a Protestant Orthodoxy"), and the religious constructions of the AIDS epidemic by Anthony Petro ("After the Wrath of God: AIDS, Sexuality, and American Religion") might also prompt scholars to consider the prospects of "queering" American religious history—a project that would entail writing against the normative assumptions of heterosexuality that undergird most histories of American religion as well as the secular assumptions that govern most histories of sexuality.

Scholars of women, gender, and sexuality in American religion have made considerable gains since the 1970s. They have expanded scholarly attention from male-dominated theology, intellectual history, and the public sphere to incorporate the daily lives of religious women working both at home and in the mediating spaces of religious organizations. They have revised narratives of declension and feminization that overlooked the nearly constant majority of women in the churches. Historians have underscored, as well, the gendered dimensions of Christian piety while locating the workings of gender and religious ideologies in the body. They have pushed historians to analyze the category of "woman" (and "man") while scholars of sexuality have pressed for better understandings of the religious regulation and construction of sexual practices and identities. Future efforts will surely continue to illustrate how the experiences of women, constructions of gender, and analyses of sexuality necessarily revise well-established narratives of the religious history of the United States. Scholars will likely continue to elaborate women's negotiations of agency—hopefully in ways that continue to advance beyond too-simple dichotomies of subordination and empowerment—as they assess the leadership and participation of women in America's religious past. Further attention to the lives of women and men in more diverse religious traditions may well lead to the development of new paradigms for assessing women, gender, and sexuality in American religion and will without doubt push scholars to continue to interrogate the very categories of sex, gender, religion, and the body central to this endeavor.

REFERENCES

Andrew, William. *Sisters of the Spirit: Three Black Women's Autobiographies of the Nineteenth Century*. Bloomington: Indiana University Press, 1986.
Bederman, Gail. "'The Women Have Had Charge of the Church Work Long Enough': The Men and Religion Forward Movement of 1911–1912 and the Masculinization of Middle-Class Protestantism." In *A Mighty Baptism: Race, Gender, and the Creation of American Protestantism*, edited by Susan Juster and Lisa McFarlane, 107–140. Ithaca, N.Y.: Cornell University Press, 1996.
Bendroth, Margaret Lamberts. *Fundamentalism and Gender, 1875 to the Present*. New Haven, Conn.: Yale University Press, 1993.
Bendroth, Margaret Lamberts, and Virginia Lieson Brereton, eds. *Women and Twentieth-Century Protestantism*. Urbana: University of Illinois Press, 2002.
Botham, Fay. *Almighty God Created the Races: Christianity, Interracial Marriage, and American Law*. Chapel Hill: University of North Carolina Press, 2009.
Boylan, Anne M. *The Origins of Women's Activism: New York and Boston, 1797–1840*. Chapel Hill: University of North Carolina Press, 2002.
Braude, Ann. *Radical Spirits: Spiritualism and Women's Rights in Nineteenth-Century America*. Bloomington: Indiana University Press, 2001.
——. "Women's History Is American Religious History." In *Retelling U.S. Religious History*, edited by Thomas A. Tweed, 87–107. Berkeley: University of California Press, 1997.
Brekus, Catherine, ed. *The Religious History of American Women: Reimagining the Past*. Chapel Hill: University of North Carolina Press, 2007.
——. *Strangers and Pilgrims: Female Preaching in America, 1740–1845*. Chapel Hill: University of North Carolina Press, 1998.
Butler, Anthea. *Women in the Church of God in Christ: Making a Sanctified World*. Chapel Hill: University of North Carolina Press, 2007.
Butler, Judith. *Gender Trouble: Feminism and the Subversion of Identity*. New York: Routledge, 1990.
Bynum, Caroline Walker. *Fragmentation and Redemption: Essays on Gender and the Human Body in Medieval Religion*. New York: Zone Books, 1991.
Carby, Hazel. "On the Threshold of 'Woman's Era': Lynching, Empire, and Sexuality in Black Feminist Theory." *Critical Inquiry* 12 (1985): 262–277.
——. *Reconstructing Womanhood: The Emergence of the Afro-American Woman Novelist*. New York: Oxford University Press, 1987.
Carnes, Mark C. *Secret Ritual and Manhood in Victorian America*. New Haven, Conn.: Yale University Press, 1989.

Chireau, Yvonne P. *Black Magic: Religion and the African American Conjuring Tradition.* Berkeley: University of California Press, 2003.

Clark, Emily. *Masterless Mistresses: The New Orleans Ursulines and the Development of a New World Society, 1727–1834.* Chapel Hill: University of North Carolina Press, 2007.

Coburn, Carol K., and Martha Smith. *Spirited Lives: How Nuns Shaped Catholic Culture and American Life, 1836–1920.* Chapel Hill: University of North Carolina Press, 1999.

Collier-Thompson, Bettye. *Daughters of Thunder: Black Women Preachers and Their Sermons, 1850–1979.* San Francisco: Jossey-Bass, 1998.

——. *Jesus, Jobs, and Justice: African American Women and Religion.* New York: Knopf, 2010.

Comstock, Gary David. *Unrepentant, Self-Affirming, Practicing: Lesbian/Bisexual/Gay People Within Organized Religion.* New York: Continuum, 1996.

Conner, Randy P., with David Hatfield Sparks. *Queering Creole Spiritual Traditions: Lesbian, Gay, Bisexual, and Transgender Participation in African-Inspired Traditions in the Americas.* New York: Harrington Park Press, 2004.

Cott, Nancy F. *The Bonds of Womanhood: "Woman's Sphere" in New England, 1780–1835.* New Haven, Conn.: Yale University Press, 1977.

Curtis, Heather. *Faith in the Great Physician: Suffering and Divine Healing in American Culture, 1860–1900.* Baltimore: Johns Hopkins University Press, 2008.

Davis, Natalie Zemon. *Society and Culture in Early Modern France.* Stanford, Calif.: Stanford University Press, 1975.

DeBerg, Betty A. *Ungodly Women: Gender and the First Wave of American Fundamentalism.* Minneapolis: Fortress Press, 1990.

Diner, Hasia R., and Beryl Lieff Benderly. *Her Works Praise Her: A History of Jewish Women in America from Colonial Times to the Present.* New York: Basic Books, 2002.

Dodson, Jualynne E. *Engendering Church: Women, Power, and the AME Church.* Lanham, Md.: Rowman & Littlefield, 2002.

Dorsey, Bruce. *Reforming Men and Women: Gender in the Antebellum City.* Ithaca, N.Y.: Cornell University Press, 2002.

Douglas, Ann. *The Feminization of American Culture.* New York: Knopf, 1977.

Epstein, Barbara Leslie. *Politics of Domesticity: Women, Evangelism, and Temperance in Nineteenth-Century America.* Middletown, Conn.: Wesleyan University Press, 1981.

Erzen, Tanya. *Straight to Jesus: Sexual and Christian Conversions in the Ex-Gay Movement.* Berkeley: University of California Press, 2006.

Fessenden, Tracy, Nicholas F. Radel, and Magdalena J. Zaborowska. *The Puritan Origins of American Sex: Religion, Sexuality, and National Identity in American Literature.* New York: Routledge, 2001.

Fett, Sharla M. *Working Cures: Healing, Health, and Power on Southern Slave Plantations.* Chapel Hill: University of North Carolina Press, 2007.

Finch, Martha L. *Dissenting Bodies: Corporealities in Early New England.* New York: Columbia University Press, 2009.

Fitzgerald, Maureen. *Habits of Compassion: Irish Catholic Nuns and the Origins of New York's Welfare System, 1830–1920.* Urbana: University of Illinois Press, 2006.

Foster, Lawrence. *Religion and Sexuality: The Shakers, the Mormons, and the Oneida Community*. Urbana: University of Illinois Press, 1981.

Frederick, Marla Faye. *Between Sundays: Black Women and Everyday Struggles of Faith*. Berkeley: University of California Press, 2003.

Gedge, Karin E. *Without Benefit of Clergy: Women and the Pastoral Relationship in Nineteenth-Century American Clergy*. New York: Oxford University Press, 2003.

Gilkes, Cheryl. *If It Wasn't for the Women: Black Women's Experience and Womanist Culture in Church and Community*. Maryknoll, N.Y.: Orbis Books, 2000.

Ginzberg, Lori. *Women and the Work of Benevolence: Morality, Politics, and Class in the Nineteenth-Century United States*. New Haven, Conn.: Yale University Press, 1990.

Godbeer, Richard. *Sexual Revolution in Early America*. Baltimore: Johns Hopkins University Press, 2002.

Goldman, Karla. *Beyond the Synagogue Gallery: Finding a Place for Women in American Judaism*. Cambridge, Mass.: Harvard University Press, 2000.

Gordon, Sarah Barringer. *The Mormon Question: Polygamy and Constitutional Conflict in Nineteenth-Century America*. Chapel Hill: University of North Carolina Press, 2002.

Greer, Allan. *Mohawk Saint: Catherine Tekakwitha and the Jesuits*. Oxford: Oxford University Press, 2005.

Griffin, Horace L. *Their Own Receive Them Not: African American Lesbians and Gays in Black Churches*. Cleveland: Pilgrim Press, 2006.

Griffith, R. Marie. *Born Again Bodies: Flesh and Spirit in American Christianity*. Berkeley: University of California Press, 2003.

——. *God's Daughters: Evangelical Women and the Power of Submission*. Berkeley: University of California Press, 1997.

Gutiérrez, Ramón A. *When Jesus Came, the Corn Mothers Went Away: Marriage, Sexuality, and Power in New Mexico, 1500–1846*. Stanford, Calif.: Stanford University Press, 1991.

Haddad, Yvonne Yazbeck, Jane I. Smith, and Kathleen M. Moore, eds. *Muslim Women in America: The Challenge of Islamic Identity Today*. New York: Oxford University Press, 2006.

Higginbotham, Evelyn Brooks. *Righteous Discontent: The Women's Movement in the Black Baptist Church, 1880–1920*. Cambridge, Mass.: Harvard University Press, 1993.

Hoy, Suellen. *Good Hearts: Catholic Sisters in Chicago's Past*. Urbana: University of Illinois Press, 2006.

Jakobsen, Janet R., and Ann Pellegrini. *Love the Sin: Sexual Regulation and the Limits of Religious Tolerance*. New York: New York University Press, 2003.

Jordan, Mark D. *The Silence of Sodom: Homosexuality in Modern Catholicism*. Chicago: University of Chicago Press, 2000.

Juster, Susan. *Disorderly Women: Sexual Politics and Evangelicalism in Revolutionary New England*. Ithaca, N.Y.: Cornell University Press, 1994.

——. "The Spirit and the Flesh: Gender, Language, and Sexuality in American Protestantism." In *New Directions in American Religious History*, edited by Harry S. Stout and D. G. Hart, 334–361. New York: Oxford University Press, 1997.

Juster, Susan, and Lisa McFarlane, eds. *A Mighty Baptism: Race, Gender, and the Creation of American Protestantism*. Ithaca, N.Y.: Cornell University Press, 1996.

Karlsen, Carol F. *The Devil in the Shape of a Woman: Witchcraft in Colonial New England*. New York: Norton, 1987.

Kern, Kathi. *Mrs. Stanton's Bible*. Ithaca, N.Y.: Cornell University Press, 2001.

Kirkley, Evelyn A. *Rational Mothers and Infidel Gentlemen: Gender and American Atheism, 1865–1915*. Syracuse, N.Y.: Syracuse University Press, 2000.

Klassen, Pamela E. *Blessed Events: Religion and Home Birth in America*. Princeton, N.J.: Princeton University Press, 2001.

Koehlinger, Amy L. *The New Nuns: Racial Justice and Religious Reform in the 1960s*. Cambridge, Mass.: Harvard University Press, 2007.

Larson, Rebecca. *Daughters of Light: Quaker Women Preaching and Prophesying in the Colonies and Abroad, 1700–1775*. New York: Knopf, 1999.

Lerner, Gerda. *The Grimké Sisters from South Carolina: Rebels Against Slavery*. Boston: Houghton Mifflin, 1967.

——. "The Lady and the Mill Girl: Changes in the Status of Women in the Age of Jackson." *Midcontinent American Studies Journal* 10 (1969): 5–15.

Lindley, Susan Hill. *"You have Stept out of your Place": A History of Women and Religion in America*. Louisville, Ky.: Westminster John Knox Press, 1996.

Lofton, Kathryn. "Queering Fundamentalism: John Balcom Shaw and the Sexuality of a Protestant Orthodoxy." *Journal of the History of Sexuality* 17, no. 3 (2008): 439–468.

McGarry, Molly. *Ghosts of Futures Past: Spiritualism and the Culture Politics of Nineteenth-Century America*. Berkeley: University of California Press, 2008.

Merry, Sally Engle. *Colonizing Hawai'i: The Cultural Power of Law*. Princeton, N.J.: Princeton University Press, 2000.

Miles, Anne G. "Border Crossings: The Queer Erotics of Quakerism in Seventeenth-Century New England." In *Long Before Stonewall: Histories of Same-Sex Sexuality in Early America*, edited by Thomas A. Foster, 114–143. New York: New York University Press, 2007.

Moon, Dawne. *God, Sex, and Politics: Homosexuality and Everyday Theologies*. Chicago: University of Chicago Press, 2004.

Morgan, Edmund S. "The Puritans and Sex." *New England Quarterly*, December 1942, 591–607.

Morrow, Diane Batts. *Persons of Color and Religious at the Same Time: The Oblate Sisters of Providence, 1828–1860*. Chapel Hill: University of North Carolina Press, 2002.

Nadell, Pamela S. *Women Who Would Be Rabbis: A History of Women's Ordination*. Boston: Beacon Press, 1998.

Orsi, Robert A. *Thank You, St. Jude: Women's Devotion to the Patron Saint of Hopeless Causes*. New Haven, Conn.: Yale University Press, 1996.

Painter, Nell Irvin. *Sojourner Truth: A Life, a Symbol*. New York: Norton, 1996.

Pesantubbee, Michelene. *Choctaw Women in a Chaotic World: The Clash of Cultures in the Colonial Southeast*. Albuquerque: University of New Mexico Press, 2005.

Petro, Anthony M. "After the Wrath of God: AIDS, Sexuality, and American Religion." Ph.D. diss., Princeton University, 2011.

Porterfield, Amanda. *Female Piety in Puritan New England: The Emergence of Religious Humanism*. New York: Oxford University Press, 1992.

Putney, Clifford. *Muscular Christianity: Manhood and Sports in Protestant America, 1880–1920*. Cambridge, Mass.: Harvard University Press, 2001.

Reis, Elizabeth. *Damned Women: Sinners and Witches in Puritan New England*. Ithaca, N.Y.: Cornell University Press, 1997.

Rodriguez, Jeanette. *Our Lady of Guadalupe: Faith and Empowerment Among Mexican-American Women*. Austin: University of Texas Press, 1994.

Rouse, Carolyn Moxley. *Engaged Surrender: African American Women and Islam*. Berkeley: University of California Press, 2004.

Rubin, Gayle. "Thinking Sex: Notes for a Radical Theory of the Politics of Sexuality." In *Pleasure and Danger: Exploring Female Sexuality*, edited by Carole Vance, 267–293. Boston: Routledge, 1984.

Ruether, Rosemary Radford, and Rosemary Skinner Keller, eds. *Women and Religion in America*. Vol. 1, *The Nineteenth Century, a Documentary History*. San Francisco: Harper & Row, 1981.

——. *Women and Religion in America*. Vol. 2, *The Colonial and Revolutionary Periods, a Documentary History*. San Francisco: Harper & Row, 1983.

——. *Women and Religion in America*. Vol. 3, *1900–1965, a Documentary History*. San Francisco: Harper & Row, 1986.

Sanders, Cheryl J. *Saints in Exile: The Holiness-Pentecostal Experience in African American Religion and Culture*. New York: Oxford University Press, 1996.

Satter, Beryl. *Each Mind a Kingdom: American Women, Sexual Purity, and the New Thought Movement, 1875–1920*. Berkeley: University of California Press, 1999.

Scott, Joan W. "Gender: A Useful Category of Historical Analysis." *American Historical Review* 91, no. 5 (1986): 1053–1073.

Sensbach, Jon F. *Rebecca's Revival: Creating Black Christianity in the Atlantic World*. Cambridge, Mass.: Harvard University Press, 2005.

Shokeid, Moshe. *A Gay Synagogue in New York*. New York: Columbia University Press, 1995.

Sklar, Kathryn. *Catherine Beecher: A Study in American Domesticity*. New Haven, Conn.: Yale University Press, 1973.

Smith-Rosenberg, Carroll. *Disorderly Conduct: Visions of Gender in Victorian America*. New York: Oxford University Press, 1986.

——. "The Female World of Love and Ritual: Relations Between Women in Nineteenth-Century America." *Signs* 1 (1975): 1–29.

Sutton, Matthew Avery. *Aimee Semple McPherson and the Resurrection of Christian America*. Cambridge, Mass.: Harvard University Press, 2007.

Taves, Ann. "Sexuality in American Religious History." In *Retelling U.S. Religious History*, edited by Thomas A. Tweed, 27–56. Berkeley: University of California Press, 1997.

Ulrich, Laurel Thatcher. *Good Wives: Image and Reality in the Lives of Women in Northern New England*. New York: Knopf, 1982.

Weisenfeld, Judith. *African American Women and Christian Activism: New York's Black YWCA, 1905–1945*. Cambridge, Mass.: Harvard University Press, 1997.

Welter, Barbara. "The Cult of True Womanhood: 1820–1860." *American Quarterly* 18 (1966): 151–174.

Westerkamp, Marilyn J. *Women and Religion in Early America, 1600–1850: The Puritan and Evangelical Traditions.* London: Routledge, 1999.

White, Deborah Gray. *Ar'n't I a Woman? Female Slaves in the Plantation South.* New York: Norton, 1985.

White, Heather. "Homosexuality, Gay Communities, and American Churches: A History of a Changing Religious Ethic, 1946–1977." Ph.D. diss., Princeton University, 2007.

Wilcox, Melissa M. 's *Coming Out in Christianity: Religion, Identity, and Community.* Bloomington: Indiana University Press, 2003.

10. RELIGION, RACE, AND AFRICAN AMERICAN LIFE

EDWARD J. BLUM

The modern academic study of African American religion was born in 1903. In that year, two works by W. E. B. Du Bois, the foremost African American intellectual of the first half of the twentieth century, laid the foundation for the evaluation of religion, race, and African American life. The better-known work, both then and now, was *The Souls of Black Folk: Essays and Sketches*. Mixing history, autobiography, musicology, and biography with poetry, short stories, and personal anecdotes, Du Bois endeavored to display the spiritual lives of African Americans to American readers. He focused on how American systems of slavery, racism, and economic exploitation had almost crushed their souls, on how African Americans valiantly fought back, on how they linked political rights with faith in God, on how black religious leaders experienced racial discrimination as religious challenges, and on how southern slaves created sacred songs to articulate their deepest feelings. Then, with his co-edited sociological volume *The Negro Church*, Du Bois established a variety of ways to study black religious life. It was a work of epic proportion. Beginning with a historical account of the transition from West Africa to the New World and the process of African American religious institution–building, *The Negro Church* then analyzed the role of black religion and the church in the formation of African American religious, racial, class, and regional identities. With field operatives reporting from southern towns and northern cities, Du Bois included interviews and examinations of the young and the old, the clergy and the laity, and the rich and the poor.

These two studies set the path for a century of scholarship. Du Bois's interdisciplinary approach and his expansive vision of religion as central to African American life have dominated the academic discipline. With *The Souls of Black Folk* and *The Negro Church*, Du Bois established themes and parameters that future historians have tested, expanded, explored, and exploded. His focus on the forging of Africans into African Americans, the creation and vitality of slave religion, the importance of churches as pioneering black institutions, the effects of emancipation on the minds and psyches of African Americans, and the devastating consequences of racism, lynching, and discrimination have long served as overarching themes in African American history. Du Bois continually stressed the creative powers of everyday black folk (although he bemoaned their "emotionalism" at times), the institutional bulwarks created by courageous black church leaders, and the interconnections of religion, society, culture, and politics for people of color.

As the twentieth century progressed, other social and historical forces revolutionized black life and the study of African American religion. The Great Migration of African Americans from the rural South to the urban North, the Great Depression, and the modern civil rights movement have been particularly transformative. Scholars since Du Bois have found greater diversity within black religious history and expressions, and they have shown the vital roles played by women in these traditions. Although African American religious history in the first half of the twentieth century focused primarily on whether black religion resisted or accommodated to structures of racial oppression, research in the past thirty-five years has shown greater insight and appreciation for diversity and debate. It has revealed the hidden conflicts amid supposed consensus. Through all the historical twists and turns, historians have discovered rich tapestries of religious life among African Americans.

EARLY HISTORY

Most historians of African American religion in the first half of the twentieth century focused on three main issues: slave religion, the conversion of a significant number of African Americans to Protestantism, and black religious institution-building. These scholars debated whether black religious beliefs and practices accommodated to racial discrimination or resisted it. Most of these studies downplayed religious diversity among African Americans and the roles of black women. The most heated debate was between anthropologist Melville Herskovits and sociologist E. Franklin Frazier over the transmission of African traditions among the enslaved. In *The Myth of the Negro Past* (1941), Herskovits asserted that a significant number of "Africanisms" persisted among the enslaved. These Africanisms, he continued, served as the basis for African American culture even after large-scale conversions to Christianity. Herskovits claimed that through ecstatic, emotional, and raucous church services; holy dances; and the association of water with the sacred, early African Americans retained much of their African culture. Frazier disagreed. In several studies, he asserted that the horrors of transportation to the New World, coupled with the fact that most of the enslaved from West Africa were young men (and young men, Frazier suggested, do not carry culture or cultural traditions well), destroyed the deep meanings of these practices. Enslavement, Frazier claimed, created a vacuum of black culture, one that was filled by Protestant Christianity. Conversion to Protestantism bound African Americans together and made then ostensibly more American than African. Early churches, moreover, played a vital role in black uplift and resistance to discrimination. Following the Civil War, though, black Protestant churches lost their radical edge and began accommodating to the racial status quo.

The Herskovits–Frazier disagreement mirrored the resistance–accommodation debate and cut to the heart of questions about African American identity in the United States: Were African Americans, in culture and religion, African or American? In the second half of the twentieth century, scholars continued to discuss vigorously the effects of enslavement on African American religious life and how African Americans created new traditions in the Americas.

Focusing on religious institution–building, Carter Woodson followed Du Bois with *The History of the Negro Church* (1922). Woodson looked at the establishment and rise of black denominations, especially the Colored Methodist Episcopal Church, the African Methodist Episcopal Church, and the African Methodist Episcopal Zion Church. So doing, he detailed the vital importance of black churches to black social life. As the social center of the community, African American churches offered the most important venue for black leadership. This institution-building solidified the power of Protestantism in black culture and life, since the vast majority of independent black churches were Protestant based, and they served as focal points of resistance and autonomy for African Americans.

Perhaps the most innovative work of the first half of the twentieth century was Arthur Huff Fauset's *Black Gods of the Metropolis: Negro Religious Cults of the Urban North* (1944). The Great Migration of African Americans from the rural South to the urban North in the late 1910s and the 1920s led to the emergence of several new black religious traditions in northern cities. As migrants endeavored to make sense of their new environments, and especially as the Great Depression shattered the economy, many turned to new religious teachings and expressions. Fauset focused on five "cults" in Philadelphia: Mount Sinai Holy Church of America, Inc.; the United House of Prayer for All People; the Church of God; the Moorish Science Temple of America; and the Peace Mission Movement of Father Divine. Fauset approached his study with an eye for diversity and with interdisciplinary genius. He analyzed their histories and written works; he took part in and observed their ceremonies and rituals; and he conducted a series of interviews with participants.

Amazingly diverse in ritual and theology, all these groups broke in some significant way with their black Protestant heritage. Mount Sinai was not only established by a woman, Bishop Ida Robinson, but also led by female elders. The United House of Prayer praised Bishop Charles Emmanuel Grace—"Sweet Daddy Grace" to his followers—as God in human form. Similarly, Father Divine at his Peace Mission Movement preached a new message of his own seeming divinity. The Church of God, known more commonly as the Black Jews, and the Moorish Science Temple looked to Judaism and Islam, rather than Christianity, for their sacred teachings.

Before the 1950s, the vast majority of work on African American religion focused on church institution–building, the continuity or discontinuity of African traditions in the New World, and the rise of black "cults." All of this changed, however, following World War II. The modern civil rights movement drastically altered the terrain of African American religious history. The 1960s, 1970s, and 1980s witnessed an explosion of works seeking to locate the power and force of black life within religious faith. This emerged from a variety of forces. In part, the civil rights leadership of ministers like Martin Luther King Jr. led scholars to reappraise the place of religion in black culture. Also, the opening of the American academy that resulted from the civil rights movement led to increased attention to minority and oppressed groups. Finally, the rise of Black Power movements led historians to look with new vigor for historical traditions of black religious resistance. For historians, the outcomes were nothing short of revolutionary. Liberation and womanist theologians—such as James Cone, James Deotis Roberts, Delores Williams, and Jacquelyn Grant—propelled historians to rethink the entire trajectory of African American religion. Drawing attention to the liberating force of Christ's teachings and then linking God's work with the black freedom struggle, these theologians sent historians back to African American sources with renewed attention to the beliefs and ingenuity of black folk. Many of these themes can be witnessed in the primary documents collected and edited by Milton C. Sernett in *African American Religious History: A Documentary Witness* and by Cornel West and Eddie S. Glaude Jr. in *African American Religious Thought: An Anthology*. Approaches to the making of Africans into African Americans, to slavery, to the impact of emancipation, to black life during the Gilded Age, to the Great Migration, and to the origins and meanings of the civil rights movement would never be the same.

ENSLAVEMENT AND MAKING AFRICANS INTO AFRICAN AMERICANS

The resistance–accommodation dichotomy took a serious blow in 1972 with *Black Religion and Black Radicalism*. In it, theologian-historian Gayraud Wilmore re-centered African American religious studies in a decidedly resistance model. He suggested that African American religion has been defined by its radicalism, by its drive for human liberation, and by its refusal to accept second-class status for people of color. The Black Power movements, which seemed to many as rejections of African American religion, were in fact a natural part of the stream of black religion. From slave rebellions to the rise of Marcus Garvey, from the birth of the African Methodist Episcopal Church to the calls for militancy from David Walker, from storefront churches to the emergence of black liberation theology, black religion consistently challenged the white status quo. Even when black churches "de-radicalized" in the late nineteenth and early twentieth centuries (focusing more on institution-building than on social rights), other African American leaders and groups, such as the National Association for the Advancement of Colored People, drew on religious arguments for social activism. Wilmore exploded the accommodation–resistance dichotomy by showing that even in moments of seeming accommodation or times of church de-radicalization, African American found ways to rebel. His work, in many ways, was a call for church leaders of the early 1970s to join the Black Power crusades in the quest for liberation.

Following the civil rights movement and the opening of the American academy to greater numbers of minorities, scholars reapproached the issue of the importance of religion in the transformation of Africans into African Americans in the context of enslavement. Building on the earlier Herskovits–Frazier debate, Sterling Stuckey and Albert Raboteau examined the role of religion in the process of cultural transmission to the New World and of the formation of an African American nationalist identity. Rallying to further Herskovits's focus on the vital importance of Africanisms in the New World, Sterling Stuckey in *Slave Culture: Nationalist Theory and the Foundations of Black America* suggested that two West African traditions clearly and powerfully marked early African American religion and culture: burial rituals and the ring shout. Of the ring shout, a religious and cultural ritual in which participants danced counterclockwise singing and praising, Stuckey maintained that it provided a place for all Africans in America. Amid the dance and during elaborate burial rites, slaves of varied ethnic and tribal backgrounds created new identities and new senses of peoplehood. In *Slave Religion: The "Invisible Institution" in the Antebellum South*, Raboteau offered a more nuanced appraisal. He found that both Frazier and Herskovits were right. Herskovits was correct to point out the influence of African cultural practices in the New World, that the cultural practices and beliefs of enslaved Africans were neither destroyed in the Middle Passage nor obliterated in the New World. But Frazier was right that the meanings of these rituals—the burials, the shouts, the theologies, the cosmologies—changed, especially in the United States. Catholicism in Latin America was more conducive to mapping West African faiths onto Christianity, Raboteau claimed, while new gods in Protestant America, particularly the Christian God and Jesus, replaced the older gods and ancestors of Africa.

All in all, Raboteau found a great deal of syncretism in the New World—where West Africans mixed and blended religious rituals among one another and with the Protestant and Catholic Europeans they encountered. By the middle of the nineteenth century, African American Protestants had created and sustained a religious "invisible institution," apart from their white masters and mistresses, where they taught and lived this hybridized faith.

Raboteau, Stuckey, and a host of other scholars were quick to point out that within slavery, black Christianity became a central focus of life, experience, and community cohesion. In an expansive study of the ideologies and realities of slavery, *Roll, Jordan, Roll: The World the Slaves Made*, Eugene Genovese considered religion the basis of slave community. He did not find radicalism everywhere, as Wilmore had, though. Genovese maintained that although Christianity inhibited slaves' desires to rebel violently against their masters, it did provide them with an idea of humanity and spirituality that was necessary to endure enslavement. Christianity supplied a moral weapon of judgment, whereby slaves could evaluate their masters. Looking closely at the folklore, songs, rumors, stories, and gossip of African Americans, Lawrence Levine asserted in *Black Culture and Black Consciousness: Afro-American Folk Thought from Slavery to Freedom* (1977) that enslaved black men and women created their own cosmology and culture that allowed them to speak to one another and interact. Their songs and community rituals bound them together across time and space to their African ancestors and sacred heritages.

Building on this work, in the 1980s and 1990s numerous scholars demonstrated how blacks and whites in the colonial and antebellum eras influenced one another religiously. This model of scholarship found significant amounts of interracial religious contact amid the conflict endemic to enslavement. These works—including Mechal Sobel's *Trabelin' On: The Slave Journey to an Afro-Baptist Faith* (1979) and *The World They Made Together: Black and White Values in Eighteenth-Century Virginia* (1987), Jon Sensbach's *A Separate Canaan: The Making of an Afro-Moravian World in North Carolina* (1998), Erskine Clarke's *Dwelling Place: A Plantation Epic*, and Charles F. Irons's *The Origins of Proslavery Christianity: White and Black Evangelicals in Colonial and Antebellum Virginia*—focused on the dynamic cultural and religious exchange in which whites and blacks shared and swapped approaches to the sacred, rituals of faith, and spiritual behavior. This was especially apparent during times of revivals and in the context of integrated churches. At camp meetings, in church services, during prayer meetings, through songs and poems, and with dream and conversion narratives, African Americans and whites learned from and taught one another how to connect with the sacred and with one another.

The most current research has found even more depth and religious complexity within early black communities. Scholars have done so primarily by giving greater attention to issues of gender, by examining the presence of Muslim slaves, and by reading closely early African American written texts. In *Come Shouting to Zion: African American Protestantism in the American South and the British Caribbean to 1830*, Sylvia Frey and Betty Wood asserted that the conversion of African Americans to evangelical Protestantism was the most important factor in transforming Africans into African Americans and that black women were central to this process. Beginning their study in West and West Central Africa and analyzing religious and cultural change in the American South and the British Caribbean, Frey and Wood explored the roles of women and gender conceptions in cultural transmissions, religious rituals, and the formation of black Protestantism. Frey and Wood first demonstrated that religion in West Africa had never been static or unchanging. In the centuries before the Atlantic slave trade, tribal faiths, Catholicism, and Islam had battled one another and interacted. Thus the Herskovits–Frazier debate becomes irrelevant, since West Africans had always been in the process of reshaping their faiths amid cultural interchange and conflict. The cultural mixing in the New World, then, was not so dissimilar from that in the Old World. Frey and Wood showed how the formation of African American Protestantism, although the central bulwark of African American culture and resistance, entailed the circumscribing of black women and their roles as religious leaders. In the process of resisting white supremacy and slavery, African American men created religious traditions that privileged black men over black women. Michael Gomez told a similar story in *Exchanging Our Country Marks: The Transformation of African Identities in the Colonial and Antebellum South* (1998), except that in this account the conversion to Protestantism was built as well around the silencing of Muslim voices and the acceptance of class differentiation among African Americans. With innovative interpretations of slave advertisements, slave runaway notices, and oral histories from the 1930s, Gomez found a vibrant and embattled community of African Muslims in the colonial and antebellum periods. In the process of converting to Protestantism and claiming a place in the United States, African American leaders distanced themselves from Muslim slaves.

Even more recently, textual analysis of written works from enslaved and free African Americans in the late eighteenth and early nineteenth centuries has led to new focus on literate blacks in the north and their manipulations of Christian traditions and ideas. Katherine Clay Bassard's *Spiritual Interrogations* (1999) centers on black women's writing from the end of the eighteenth century to the Civil War. Looking at Phillis Wheatley, Ann Plato, Jarena Lee, and Rebecca Cox Jackson, Bassard found that in their appropriation of Protestant religious rhetoric and idioms, these women claimed profound personal subjectivity. Religious ideas were central to their understanding of self, other, and community. Black women's challenges to enslavement and discrimination, Bassard concluded, were built with reframed Christian rhetoric. In *Exodus! Religion, Race, and Nation in Early Nineteenth-Century Black America*, Eddie S. Glaude Jr. claimed that the biblical narrative of Exodus became the principal political text and metaphor for African American group formation, especially in the North. Black religion, especially its focus on the Exodus narrative, provided the basis for black politics and black nationalism. Examining the formation of independent black churches, freedom celebrations, the black convention movement, and the writings of David Walker, Samuel Cornish, and Henry Highland Garnet, Glaude demonstrated that black nationalism was not built on notions of inherent racial difference, but rather on the experiences of bondage, discrimination, and liberation (all tropes that could be articulated with reference to the Exodus saga).

Literary critic Joanna Brooks provided a different biblical metaphor to understand the work of early African American writers in *American Lazarus: Religion and the Rise of African-American and Native American Literatures*. Through close readings of Native American and African American texts by Samsom Occom, Prince Hall, Richard Allen, and John Marrant, Brooks contended that Native American and African American writers redirected the democratizing, charismatic, and separatist energies of American evangelicalism into the formation of new religious communities, theologies, and literatures. In the process, these communities came to believe that Christ had raised them proverbially from the dead just as he had the biblical Lazarus.

Many of the primary documents analyzed by Brooks, Glaude, and Bassard can be found in *Pamphlets of Protest: An Anthology of Early African-American Protest Literature, 1790–1860* (2000), edited by historians Richard Newman, Patrick Rael, and Phillip Lapansky. In works by Richard Allen, Daniel Coker, James Forten, Maria Stewart, David Ruggles, Mary Ann Shadd, and numerous others, scholars can witness the vibrant and diverse use of biblical rhetoric among free African Americans in the north from the 1790s to the 1860s.

Most recently, through an intensive reading of African American "race histories" from the late eighteenth and nineteenth centuries, Laurie Maffly-Kipp in *Setting Down the Sacred Past: African-American Race Histories* found that African Americans in the North and the South wrote and rewrote, imagined and reimagined their pasts in order to find places in their contemporary worlds. She finds that African American preachers, missionaries, and writers showed an intense interest in biblical history, classical history, African history, and their own stories to comprehend what God intended for them in the United States. She found significant diversity within and among these histories; while "Africans" certainly became "African Americans," they did so on varied and various paths.

Of the period before the Civil War, African American religious historians have done amazing work on the religious impact of the Middle Passage and enslavement, on the importance of religion in the slave communities, on the rise of separate black denominations, and on the roles of women and Muslims in these communities. More work needs to be done to connect the experiences and faiths of African Americans in the northern United States with those in the South. Did enslaved southerners conceptualize the Exodus story in the same way that the northern black writers in Glaude's *Exodus!* did? What role did the narrative of Lazarus play in the sacred cosmologies of the ring shouters, if any? Did religious beliefs and institutions bind or divide northern and southern African Americans? Events and interactions following the Civil War suggest that perhaps northern and southern blacks created distinct approaches to Christianity and that their differences sometimes troubled their alliances. The uniting and dividing power of religion among early African Americans is a topic still in need of much labor.

IMPACT OF EMANCIPATION AND THE NADIR

Although slavery has been the focus of most scholarship on African American religion, the impact of the Civil War, emancipation, and the descent to the "nadir" have been also critical in the course of black history in the United States. With the collapse of the Confederacy and the emancipation of 4 million southern blacks during the Civil War, the entire world seemed to change. As W. E. B. Du Bois described it in *Black Reconstruction in America* (1935), emancipation could not be separated from faith: "The mass of slaves, even the more intelligent ones, and certainly the great group of field hands, were in religious and hysterical fervor. This was the coming of the Lord. This was the fulfillment of prophecy and legend. It was the Golden Dawn, after chains of a thousand years. It was everything miraculous and perfect and promising." The "invisible" institution of the antebellum era could now become visible, and the black denominations that had grown in the North now had the opportunity to travel south. Within only a few years of emancipation, a great denominational "exodus" had occurred in which the vast majority of southern blacks left white-dominated denominations and formed their own.

The process of emancipation, the many meanings of freedom, and the denominational "exodus" have been the focus of several important books. In *A Rock in a Weary Land* (1982), Clarence Walker analyzed the missions of the African Methodist Episcopal Church into the Civil War and Reconstruction South. Walker showed how the war opened the South as new religious terrain for denominational battles and how northern black missionaries experienced cultural tensions with their southern brethren. New black churches in the South became hotbeds of political activism, producing a high number of black politicians. Moreover, Walker suggested that Methodism offered a common belief system of individualism, self-control, and thrift for a budding black middle class that emerged in the decades following the war. Katharine Dvorak, in *An African-American Exodus: The Segregation of the Southern Churches* (1991), maintained that religion lay at the center of why the vast majority of African Americans left white denominations after the Civil War. She suggested that black religion, especially its focus on the wholeness of salvation for the entire self and not just the soul, led to mass dissatisfaction with white churches and denominations. The church exodus, she concluded, was rooted far more in religious differences than in political or social discrimination by whites. Reginald Hildebrand explored the dynamic interactions among various Methodists—white and black, northern and southern—in the era of emancipation in *The Times Were Strange and Stirring: Methodist Preachers and the Crisis of Emancipation*. He claimed that in the process of making religious decisions, former slaves took political steps to redefine themselves as free people. Hildebrand showed, moreover, how a gospel of freedom, as taught by African American missionaries, ultimately triumphed among people of color in the postwar South. New churches, denominations, and theologies, these historians maintained, were crucial to the transition from slavery to freedom.

While these studies focused on the rise of racial separation in churches, other scholars have paid attention to continued interracial religious interaction following the Civil War. Works by Daniel Stowell, Paul Harvey, James Bennett, and Edward J. Blum found persistent and dynamic religious contacts among whites and blacks, northerners and southerners, in the era of Reconstruction and the Gilded Age. In *Rebuilding Zion: The Religious Reconstruction of the South, 1863–1877*, Stowell examined the roles of northern whites, southern blacks, and southern whites in rebuilding the spiritual life of the South following the war. He claimed that each group held particular visions of what freedom would mean (and their ideas of freedom were connected to their religious backgrounds). Ultimately, northern whites retreated from the field and left southern whites to reestablish white supremacy anew. Harvey, in *Redeeming the South: Religious Cultures and Racial Identities Among Southern Baptists, 1865–1925*, analyzed the persistent interactions of white and black Baptists in the postwar South and how their paths diverged by the end of the century. Harvey showed how religious parallels and divergences among white and black Baptists revealed continued processes of racial contact, conflict, and sharing. Examining Methodists and Catholics in New Orleans, James Bennett found that racial segregation in the churches did not develop there until the very end of the nineteenth century—and specific local and denominational factors led racial segregation to develop quite distinctly. While Catholic churches remained integrated because of neglect (the church hierarchy was uninterested in African Americans and so did not consider building them their own church until the turn of the century), Methodists vigorously debated the importance of racial integration in their church leadership. People of color, Catholic and Methodist, experienced the rise of Jim Crow as a distinctly religious problem and attacked it as such. And in *Reforging the White Republic: Race, Religion, and American Nationalism, 1865–1898*, Blum contended that religious ideals were at the core of the radical Reconstruction experiment to unite northern whites and African Americans after the Civil War. In locales throughout the war-torn South, white women and black communities forged unprecedented political, social, and communal bonds. This interracial fraternity, however, was undermined and then overwhelmed by the moral imperative of national reunion taught by northern white religious leaders, including Henry Ward Beecher, Dwight Lyman Moody, and Frances Willard, from the 1870s to the turn of the century.

Curtis Evans, in his thoughtful *The Burden of Black Religion*, found that whites' conceptions of black religion (and sometimes how African American leaders reinforced these stereotypes) constituted a burden for African Americans that hamstrung them spiritually and politically. Evans claimed, especially in opposition to Blum's *Reforging the White Republic*, that white–black interaction was marked by whites' "romantic racialism" wherein whites' evaluations of black religion focused on the savagery, backwardness, and emotionalism of African Americans. Stereotypes of black religion hampered blacks' progress and compelled African American leaders into complicated rebuttals of these stereotypes or (more likely) denunciations of everyday blacks.

Beginning with Rayford Logan in the 1950s, historians have routinely referred to the end of the nineteenth century and the beginning of the twentieth as "the nadir" in black life. This was an era of lynchings, of hardening segregation laws, of debt peonage and convict-labor systems, and of political imperialism against peoples of color throughout the world. It looked and felt like neo-slavery. Scholars of African American religion have found that even within such trying circumstances, men and women of color continued to persevere. Faith and religious institutions stood at the base of their resolve. The nadir became a time of fruitful institution-building and spiritual innovation. James Melvin Washington demonstrated how desires for freedom and autonomy marked the black Baptist struggle in slavery and freedom. During and after Reconstruction, Washington suggested in *Frustrated Fellowship: The Black Baptist Quest for Social Power* (1986), antebellum black abolitionists were transformed into black religious separatists. By the end of the nineteenth century, the all-black National Baptist Convention had become a bulwark of political and social autonomy amid an atmosphere of racial violence and discrimination. Evelyn Brooks Higginbotham revised Washington's work and all other studies on black church life with her *Righteous Discontent: The Women's Movement in the Black Baptist Church*. In it, she demonstrated how African American churches stood as social spaces of unifying and conflicting discourses. Black Baptist women, Higginbotham showed, transformed their churches into arms for both African American and women's rights, successfully creating a feminist theology amid a broader culture of patriarchy and racism. Using what Higginbotham referred to as the "politics of respectability," these women employed middle-class ideologies and subversive readings of the Bible to drive for civil rights and for women's empowerment.

Women were also crucial to the emerging Pentecostal and holiness traditions of the late nineteenth and twentieth centuries. While the Baptist and Methodist churches became associated with middle-class black life and seem to have had

more urban than rural proclivities, holiness, Pentecostal, and storefront churches were viewed as catering to working-class and rural African Americans. With
particular attention to sanctification (a second conversion experience where the
believer is freed to live without sin), to emotional worship services that included
intense bodily movements, and to speaking in tongues, holiness and Pentecostal
churches sprang up in the early twentieth century and appealed to thousands of
African Americans. While previous scholars focused on the lack of civil rights
activism within these congregations and bemoaned their seeming otherworldly
nature, newer scholarship has focused on the cultural vitality and power offered
by them. What Wilmore viewed as de-radicalization may have very well been a
powerful cultural shift of which he was unaware. As part of the "cultural turn" in
American history, scholars now view Pentecostal and holiness churches as locations where African Americans could celebrate themselves and find wholeness.
Hence, whether or not they preached against lynching or joined marches becomes
irrelevant. Faith and their faith communities became overarching cultures of resistance that allowed them to survive and thrive in the American context.

Both theologian Cheryl J. Sanders, in *Saints in Exile: The Holiness-Pentecostal
Experience in Religion and Culture*, and sociologist Cheryl Gilkes, in *If It Wasn't
for the Women . . . : Black Women's Experience and Womanist Culture in Church
and Community*, chronicled the vibrancy and importance of holiness-Pentecostal
churches among African Americans. Both scholars celebrated how Pentecostalism, amid the culture of white supremacy and the racial uplift ideology of middle-
class African Americans, recovered previous traditions of black religious autonomy, spiritual vigor, and folk life. In a wide-ranging study of music, worship rituals,
body movements, and theologies, Sanders showed how black Pentecostalism
developed from the defense of African-derived rituals. The totality of Pentecostalism—its attention to the body, to actions, to emotions, to song, to identity, and to
community—appealed to embattled African Americans. Their every action may
have been judged harshly by whites and aspiring blacks, but within the sanctified churches, their actions were part of holy performances. Gilkes revealed how
women constituted the backbone of these sanctified churches. Building on Sanders's study, Gilkes demonstrated that women led by example, by numerical participation, and often with great autonomy and authority. In a series of oral history
interviews, Gilkes found that women were cognizant of their central roles in the
churches, their families, and their communities and that they developed dynamic,
interactive, and innovative approaches to social problems within these communities. Black Pentecostal and holiness women, Gilkes concluded, lived the teachings of womanist theology—the theological celebration of black womanhood and
its multivalent approach to black community honor and uplift—in their everyday
and spiritual lives.

In the twenty-first century, the focus on African American women and religion has been advanced by many works. Two of the finest are Marla Frederick's

Between Sundays: Black Women and Everyday Struggles of Faith and Bettye Collier-Thomas's *Jesus, Jobs, and Justice: African American Women and Religion*. In these studies, Frederick and Collier-Thomas show how religion influenced every aspect of black women's lives. Whether fighting for jobs, battling racism, watching television, or raising their families, black women continually look to faith as the animating aspect of their lives.

The religious jubilee of emancipation was followed by the spiritual frustration of the nadir. Methodist and Baptist churches became powerful political and social bodies, while sanctified and holiness churches grew in the late nineteenth and early twentieth centuries. Historical questions remain as to which African Americans were more likely to flock to new holiness traditions and why others remained in the traditional churches. Moreover, more scholarship is needed to examine the loss of traditional faiths during the late nineteenth century because of racial discrimination, of those who turned against organized religion completely.

FROM GREAT MIGRATION TO
GREAT DEPRESSION

For the early twentieth century, the Great Migration of southern, and predominately rural, African Americans to northern cities and the devastating impact of the Great Depression have generated significant scholarly work. How did the movement of millions of individuals and families influence the course of black religion? How did migrants experience their transitions religiously? What new religious cultures emerged? How did established African American traditions respond to the migration? And how did African Americans in these new urban arenas adapt to the economic catastrophe and social dislocation of the Great Depression?

From the perspective of established traditions, Milton Sernett and Wallace Best have provided fine studies of how black denominations in the North responded to the migration. Sernett's *Bound for the Promised Land: African American Religion and the Great Migration* examines the reasons for the "second Exodus." Sernett first found that push factors—primarily racial violence, political disfranchisement, and social attacks in the early-twentieth-century South—drove African Americans to the North. Then Sernett looked to the North. With thousands of new migrants, northern urban churches had to respond. They turned to social services and practical needs, joining the broader Social Gospel movement wherein American Protestant, Catholic, and Jewish congregations focused more on bettering life in this world and less on saving souls for the next. In *Passionately Human, No Less Divine: Religion and Culture in Black Chicago, 1915–1952* (2005), Wallace Best demonstrated how migrating southern African Americans transformed the religious landscape of Chicago. The Great Migration propelled northern and southern blacks to adjust their faiths—such as bringing together spirituals, gospel, and jazz. In the process a new sacred order emerged in which older traditions and newer ones mixed and in which women came to dominate black church life.

Amid the migration, a host of new African American religious traditions blossomed, including the Nation of Islam and Father Divine's Peace Mission Movement. Historians have looked to these movements and their leaders to further understand the migration and its effects on black religion. In *God, Harlem U.S.A.: The Father Divine Story*, Jill Watts set the life of George Baker Jr., known to friend and foe as Father Divine, in this context. Watts demonstrated how Father Divine, originally from Maryland but rising to prominence in New York, created his new theology with a rich blend of African American Protestantism, Catholicism, and New Thought beliefs. His insistence that race did not exist, that it was merely a sickness and delusion of the mind, constituted a unique religious approach. Just as New Thought and Christian Science believers considered material existence an illusion and physical ailments to be products of wrong thinking, Divine maintained that racism was merely an illness of the mind that could be cured through proper religious thought. Moreover, with a focus on economic advancement and social welfare that included rehabilitation centers for the sick and occupational therapy for the jobless, Divine appealed to whites and blacks alike who were in need of social help. And of course, as a black man, his claim to be God in the flesh made headlines in a culture that largely associated God with the white race.

The Nation of Islam, which grew up in 1930s Detroit under the direction of W. D. Fard and his successor Elijah Muhammad, also focused on economic development. The first and still informative study of the movement was C. Eric Lincoln's *The Black Muslims in America* (1961). Claiming that African Americans were Asiatic peoples (the "Lost-Found Nation of Islam"), Fard and Muhammad created a new religion, with a temple, written and oral catechisms, ministers, and schools. They claimed that Allah, their God, was black and that the first humans were black. White people, in fact, were created by a diabolical scientist thousands of years ago and were literally devils incarnate. Their religious centers served as social and economic hubs where Nation of Islam followers pooled their financial and social resources. Although its most famous devotee, Malcolm X, has received the lion's share of popular and scholarly attention, his mentor Elijah Muhammad was probably more vital in creating and sustaining the Nation of Islam. As Claude Andrew Clegg maintained in *An Original Man: The Life and Times of Elijah Muhammad* (1997), Elijah Muhammad was primarily responsible for the rise of the Nation of Islam and for its becoming a viable alternative to African American Christianity. According to Clegg, Muhammad's quest for economic power played a foundational role in the ideas and public image of the Nation of Islam. The Great Migration and Great Depression had a clear influence on the rise of the Nation of Islam. As a separatist and economic-based organization, it appealed principally to recent migrants and the economically dislocated. Recently, Edward Curtis IV's *Black Muslim Religion in the Nation of Islam, 1960–1975* (2006) examines the rituals, theologies, narratives, and ethics of the Nation of Islam when it was in the national spotlight.

Because of his prominence as a civil rights advocate, Malcolm X has received substantial scholarly notice. Before the work of Louis DeCaro, however, most historians focused on Malcolm X's political and social work, just as they focused mostly on the politics and economics of the Nation of Islam in general. With two books, *On the Side of My People: A Religious Life of Malcolm X* and *Malcolm and the Cross: The Nation of Islam, Malcolm X, and Christianity* (2000), DeCaro portrayed Malcolm X as a religious leader and thinker. DeCaro highlighted the religious elements of the Nation of Islam and the deep spirituality of Malcolm X. His parents exposed him to a variety of religious and black nationalist traditions—including Garveyism, Baptism, Pentecostalism, and Adventism—and from this mix Malcolm X was always interested in the power of spirituality. DeCaro read Malcolm X's life as a series of conversions—from gangster to Elijah Muhammad acolyte, from Nation of Islam minister to Islamic and civil rights activist. When Malcolm X rose to prominence in the 1950s and 1960s, moreover, it was because he offered a compelling prophetic call for social justice.

Well before the terrorist attacks of September 11, 2001, on New York City and the subsequent American wars in Afghanistan and Iraq, which generated increased awareness of Muslims in the United States, historians of African American religion had been examining the influence of Islam in black life and culture. In large part, this was due to the notoriety of the Nation of Islam. Scholars of antebellum America, for instance, have claimed that 10 to 20 percent of slaves were Muslim. With short biographies of enslaved West African Muslims in the United States, several of whom wrote autobiographies or other materials, Allan D. Austin displayed the rich Islamic heritage among black Americans in *African Muslims in Antebellum America: Transatlantic Stories and Spiritual Struggles* (1997). Other scholars, including Aminah McCloud and Richard Brent Turner, have pushed the narrative into the late nineteenth and twentieth centuries. In perhaps the most ambitious work on Islam among Africans and their descendants in the New World, Michael Gomez traced the experiences of African Muslims throughout the Americas from the fifteenth century to the end of the twentieth. In *Black Crescent: The Experience and Legacy of African Muslims in the Americas*, Gomez showed how on some occasions African Muslims were crucial players in revolts, including the impressive uprising in Brazil in 1835. He also demonstrated the perseverance of Islamic beliefs among African Americans that eventually emerged in the teachings of Noble Drew Ali, Elijah Muhammad, and Malcolm X. More than any scholar before him, Gomez rooted the emergence of the Nation of Islam in a long trajectory of African American interactions and connections to Islam.

Together, the Great Migration and the Great Depression wrought a revolution in black religion. Mass migration was conceived in religious terms; established black denominations in the North had to adjust, first to the newcomers and second to the economic dislocation of the Great Depression. Mobility, urbanization, economic hardship, and the continued presence of racial segregation and violence led men and women of color to search for new spiritual answers to their everyday problems. Out of this mix, new traditions emerged, including Pentecostalism, the ministry of Father Divine, and the Nation of Islam. New work will be needed to discern more accurately what within these traditions was new and what was old. Was the Nation of Islam connected to the prior Islamic tradition within African American communities, or was it a new religious invention? How did women and gender affect these traditions? What roles did interaction among various racial groups have in defining and redefining these groups?

THE CIVIL RIGHTS MOVEMENT AND BEYOND

Although historians debate when to date the beginning of the twentieth-century civil rights movement, and while most focus on laws, social organizing, education, and tactics, all at least agree that religion played a role in the movement. Led by ministers, organized in churches, replete with sacred rhetoric and song, the widespread drive by African Americans and their supporters for civil rights was a religious crusade. In their efforts to overturn racial segregation and violence, to end voter disenfranchisement, to rectify economic disparities, and to stop the cultural abuse of black folk, reformers and activists turned to their churches and their faiths to make social change. How exactly religion influenced the civil rights movement has become a ripe field for historical inquiry, one that will produce even more volumes in subsequent years.

The influence of religion on the civil rights movement has been tackled from various disciplinary and methodological angles. Both sociologist Aldon Morris, in *The Origins of the Civil Rights Movement: Black Communities Organizing for Change*, and political scientist Dennis Chong, in *Collective Action and the Civil Rights Movement* (1991), showcased the roles of churches in the movement. They focused on how churches offered facilities, money, communication networks, membership, and leadership to create and sustain the movement. They concluded that the black church, through its leaders, resources, and culture, was vital in developing and sustaining the movement.

Theologian Charles Marsh has suggested that the civil rights movement stood as a moment when differing conceptions of God intersected and clashed. Looking at the summer of 1964 in Mississippi, referred to by civil rights activists as

"Freedom Summer," Marsh followed the lives of five personalities in *God's Long Summer: Stories of Faith and Civil Rights* (1997). Each individual looked to God for his or her cause. Fannie Lou Hamer, southern black activist and voice of the Mississippi Freedom Democratic Party, embodied a liberating, reconciling faith that was created by a mix of spirituality, prophetic religion, and an indefatigable belief in Jesus as deliverer of the poor; Sam Bowers Jr., the Imperial Wizard of the White Knights of the Ku Klux Klan in Mississippi, felt called to be a priest of white supremacy and protect his nation from the sins of interracialism; William Douglas Hudgins, the state's leading Baptist minister, tried to maintain an emphasis on personal spirituality while the walls separating the personal and the political were clearly crumbling; Edwin King, a white chaplain in a black college, lent his name to the civil rights crusade because he felt God's call to do so; and Cleveland Sellers, a leader in the Black Power movement, had his early Christian faith radically altered during the summer. Out of it, Sellers developed a new racial spirituality and nationalistic consciousness, one concerned more with tearing down the old order than building up a new one.

Broader and more provocative studies of religion in the civil rights movement have been offered by David Chappell and Paul Harvey. In *A Stone of Hope: Prophetic Religion and the Death of Jim Crow*, Chappell presented four main questions to attempt to redirect scholarship on the civil rights movement:

1. Why did liberalism, the dominant voice in American politics, fail to achieve substantial rights for African Americans in the 1930s?
2. Where did black southerners discover a philosophical inspiration for their rebellion?
3. How did African Americans sustain confidence, solidarity, and discipline throughout the hard years?
4. And finally, why were the opponents of the civil rights movements so weak during the late 1950s and early 1960s?

Better at presenting new questions than at producing definitive answers, Chappell suggested that prophetic religion stood as the philosophical heart and soul of the civil rights crusade. In opposition to liberalism's optimism, black reformers approached the world in ways similar to those of the Hebrew prophets of the Bible. They saw injustice everywhere and relied on godly intervention, more than state reform, to make change. Chappell also contended that the movement could be considered a great religious awakening. Civil rights meetings had an air of religious revival surrounding them, as numerous African Americans discussed the presence of God, Christ, and angels among them. Chappell asserted that the enemies of civil rights were so weak because they failed to pull religion into their defense of segregation. Southern white ministers seemed confused and uncertain. Their lack of support for segregation, Chappell concluded, left the bulwark of white supremacy undefended and able to be destroyed.

Jane Dailey has complicated Chappell's argument in "Sex, Segregation, and the Sacred After *Brown*" (*Journal of American History* 91 [2004]: 119–144). She demonstrated how a wide array of southern white Protestants associated interracial sexuality with sinfulness and considered segregation necessary to uphold sexual separation. The conflation of social integration, sexual interaction, and Christian theology created a framework by which some white Protestants rallied to protect Jim Crow. Ultimately, Dailey found that religious arguments were central to both civil rights activists and their opponents, for both struggled to claim the mantle of Christian orthodoxy.

Paul Harvey offered a more comprehensive view of religious culture and the emergence of the civil rights movement in *Freedom's Coming: Religious Culture and the Shaping of the South from the Civil War Through the Civil Rights Era.* Harvey positioned the civil rights movement in a century-old tradition of struggles over race and religion in the South. Finding both widespread antagonism and cultural exchange between white and black southerners, Harvey contended that the civil rights movement emerged from the beliefs of everyday individual African Americans who never stopped trusting in the power of faith and God to make social change. Examining the songs of the movement, Harvey found that it was a religious crusade sustained by Protestant imagery, fervor, and a vision of Christian interracialism. All the religious mass meetings, revival preaching, and sacred songs of the nineteenth century coalesced into a struggle for social, political, and human rights. Of the years following the civil rights movement, moreover, Harvey maintained that southern white churches turned their attention from restricting the lives of African Americans to infringing on those of women. Resigned that they had essentially lost the war over black inclusion, white Protestantism (particularly Baptists) turned to controlling white women within their organizations.

Barbara Dianne Savage, in *Your Spirits Walk Beside Us: The Politics of Black Religion*, claimed that the civil rights movement drastically altered how scholars thought about black religion. Before that, she claims, historians interested in black religion—especially W. E. B. Du Bois, Carter Woodson, and Benjamin Mays—created the notion of a unified "Negro church" that had little power to effect political change. These scholars wanted black churches to do so and called on them to reform themselves (become more modern) and join the battle for political and legal rights, but they did not. The civil rights movement shattered this approach to the black church and was itself a religious rebellion. Through a new genre of writing, the civil rights memoir, participants discussed their conversion to political and social radicalism. In so doing, they created a new vision of the relationship of black religion and black politics. This new vision saw the two as connected, rather than divided.

Understandably, significant focus on religion in the civil rights movement has centered on the figure of Martin Luther King Jr. His presence looms so large in studies of the movement that for his Pulitzer Prize–winning *Parting the Waters*,

Taylor Branch gave the subtitle *America in the King Years, 1954–63* (1988). Historians debate where to most accurately situate King's theological and religious roots. Did he follow in the footsteps of previous black religious leaders, or did he break from them? If he was different, what made King distinct? Was his blend of religion and social activism new, borrowed, refined, or old? Branch set the terms for the modern debate on King by suggesting that Reinhold Niebuhr's theology was the most influential factor in King's theological and social approach. According to Branch, reading Niebuhr's groundbreaking *Moral Man and Immoral Society* changed King's "fundamental outlook on religion." It destroyed his confidence in the Social Gospel and in natural progress, and it compelled King to focus on the evil in social institutions. From then on, King preached from the basis of tension: between love and evil, heaven and hell, justice and oppression. Noel Leo Erskine, in *King Among the Theologians* (1995), disagreed with Branch. He claimed that King's African American religious heritage—his experiences as the son of a prominent black minister, as a regular at a black church, and as a student at Morehouse College under Benjamin Elijah Mays—led to his appeal and his social outlook. Richard Lischer provided perhaps the finest study of King as a preacher and theologian in *The Preacher King: Martin Luther King Jr. and the Word That Moved America*. As the voice of the civil rights movement, King appealed to white and black listeners. He somehow developed a way to spiritually and socially move women and men from various walks of life. Lischer located this ability in King's dual heritage: his nurturing in the Afro-Baptist tradition and in the liberal theological tradition of Reinhold Niebuhr and other white northerners. In short, King blended his academic training with his cultural background to become the mouthpiece of the movement for whites and blacks.

The central historical debate of the post–civil rights era is over continuity or discontinuity. Did the broad conservative political turn of the 1970s and 1980s fundamentally alter the religious terrain for African Americans, or did their pursuits continue in the same manner? While Harvey suggested that the focus of conservative whites turned from controlling and confining African Americans to confining white women, Andrew Billingsley, in *Mighty Like a River: The Black Church and Social Reform* (2003), claimed that very little has changed in the everyday activities of black churches. They continue to serve as a social and racial uplift center for the black community, just as they had before the civil rights movement and during it. Sociologists C. Eric Lincoln and Lawrence H. Mamiya found black church history defined by continuous tension before, during, and after the movement. In *The Black Church in the African American Experience* (1990), Lincoln and Mamiya situated almost 2,000 interviews of Protestant clergy in rural and urban areas within more than 200 years of black church history, following in the footsteps of E. Franklin Frazier, Carter Woodson, and W. E. B. Du Bois. They found black churches and particularly male church leaders—of the past and the present—involved in an unending series of conflicts between survival and liberation, between an otherworldly focus and a worldly social orientation, between the universality of Christianity and the particularity of African American faith, and between accommodation to the American mainstream and independence from it.

New scholarship has moved the focus away from church leaders and the church to broader African American cultural communities. Michael Eric Dyson's *Between God and Gangsta Rap: Bearing Witness to Black Culture* (1996) and Anthony Pinn's *Why, Lord? Suffering and Evil in Black Theology* (1995), for example, look to rap music for spiritual insight into black America in the post–civil rights years. Pinn claimed to have found a nitty-gritty theology in blues and rap music, wherein rappers offer a religious challenge to the destructiveness of material-driven goals. In the early 1980s, for instance, Grandmaster Flash and the Furious Five juxtaposed the bleakness of urban street life with the recognition of divine presence, care, and judgment. "God is smiling but he's frowning too," they rapped in "The Message" (1982): "cause only god knows what you go through." Rappers—just as preachers, social activists, and bluesmen—have sought to speak to the religious conditions of black folk. In the twenty-first century, Melissa Harris-Lacewell's *Barbershops, Bibles, and BET: Everyday Talk and Black Political Thought* and Jonathan Walton's *Watch This! The Ethics and Aesthetics of Black Televangelism* reveal diversity amid contemporary black political and spiritual life. Whether debating sports, the Bible, or clothing styles, African Americans refuse any single approach to economics, politics, or religion.

There is still much work to be done on religion and the civil rights movement and beyond. Oftentimes, historians of the civil rights movement exaggerate the extent of change wrought by the struggle. For instance, David Chappell subtitled his work *Prophetic Religion and the Death of Jim Crow*. But racial segregation, at least within religious organizations, did not die. Studies of segregation in religious organizations, especially those done by sociologist Michael Emerson, have shown that churches, synagogues, and Muslim temples remain more segregated at the beginning of the twenty-first century than does the broader society. Even the rappers and entertainers discussed by Pinn and Dyson recognized the failings of the civil rights era. What we need are more studies of the religious impact of the conservative rise following the 1960s. How did white flight and suburbanization affect black religion and religious communities? Has religion played a vital role in the rise of a new black middle class? Do black mega-churches resist racism and economic exploitation in the same ways that black churches have done so traditionally?

Much has changed and much has remained the same in the century since W. E. B. Du Bois published *The Souls of Black Folk* and *The Negro Church* in 1903. Historians, sociologists, literary critics, theologians, and anthropologists have looked to religion to understand the shape and heart of African American lives and experiences. They have discovered and looked to new resources and novel sources. Scholars have found, as Du Bois did, that black churches are vital social centers, places of leadership training, spaces for public discourse, and locations for political organizing. They have found, as Du Bois did, that music and sacred songs have been avenues for expressing the hopes and dreams, sorrows and frustrations, of people of color in slavery and freedom. Especially since the 1970s, scholars have demonstrated rich religious variety among African Americans and have shown that women often constituted the backbones of their cultural traditions. Future work will most likely address the role played by this diversity in binding and dividing African Americans; it will look beyond categories we traditionally think of as religious, to issues such as business practices, consumerism, material production, mobility and movement, sexuality, and political ideologies. New work will search for broader conceptual models, paradigms that move beyond Protestantism, Christianity, and Islam, to express the religious problem and possibility of being "African" and "American," issues that in 1903 Du Bois approached so thoughtfully and eloquently.

REFERENCES

Blum, Edward J. *Reforging the White Republic: Race, Religion, and American Nationalism, 1865–1898*. Baton Rouge: Louisiana State University Press, 2005.

——. *W. E. B. Du Bois, American Prophet*. Philadelphia: University of Pennsylvania Press, 2007.

Brooks, Joanna. *American Lazarus: Religion and the Rise of African-American and Native American Literature*. New York: Oxford University Press, 2003.

Carter, J. Kameron. *Race: A Theological Account*. New York: Oxford University Press, 2008.

Chappell, David. *A Stone of Hope: Prophetic Religion and the Death of Jim Crow*. Chapel Hill: University of North Carolina Press, 2004.

Clarke, Erskine. *Dwelling Place: A Plantation Epic*. New Haven, Conn.: Yale University Press, 2005.

Collier-Thomas, Bettye. *Jesus, Jobs, and Justice: African American Women and Religion*. New York: Knopf, 2010.

Cone, James H. *The Spirituals and the Blues: An Interpretation*. New York: Seabury Press, 1972.

DeCaro, Louis A., Jr. *On the Side of My People: A Religious Life of Malcolm X*. New York: New York University Press, 1996.

Douglas, Kelly Brown. *The Black Christ*. Maryknoll, N.Y.: Orbis Books, 1994.

Evans, Curtis J. *The Burden of Black Religion*. New York: Oxford University Press, 2008.

Frederick, Marla Faye. *Between Sundays: Black Women and Everyday Struggles of Faith*. Berkeley: University of California Press, 2003.

Frey, Sylvia, and Betty Wood. *Come Shouting to Zion: African American Protestantism in the American South and the British Caribbean to 1830*. Chapel Hill: University of North Carolina Press, 1998.

Genovese, Eugene D. *Roll, Jordan, Roll: The World the Slaves Made*. New York: Vintage, 1974.

Gilkes, Cheryl Townsend. *If It Wasn't for the Women . . . : Black Women's Experience and Womanist Culture in Church and Community*. Maryknoll, N.Y.: Orbis Books, 2000.

Glaude, Eddie S., Jr. *Exodus! Religion, Race, and Nation in Early Nineteenth-Century Black America*. Chicago: University of Chicago Press, 2000.

Gomez, Michael. *Black Crescent: The Experience and Legacy of African Muslims in the Americas*. Cambridge: Cambridge University Press, 2005.

Griffith, R. Marie, and Barbara Dianne Savage, eds. *Women and Religion in the African Diaspora: Knowledge, Power, and Performance*. Baltimore: Johns Hopkins University Press, 2006.

Harris-Lacewell, Melissa. *Barbershops, Bibles, and BET: Everyday Talk and Black Political Thought*. Princeton, N.J.: Princeton University Press, 2004.

Harvey, Paul. *Freedom's Coming: Religious Culture and the Shaping of the South from the Civil War Through the Civil Rights Era*. Chapel Hill: University of North Carolina Press, 2005.

——. *Redeeming the South: Religious Cultures and Racial Identities Among Southern Baptists, 1865–1925*. Chapel Hill: University of North Carolina Press, 1997.

Higginbotham, Evelyn Brooks. *Righteous Discontent: The Women's Movement in the Black Baptist Church*. Cambridge, Mass.: Harvard University Press, 1993.

Hildebrand, Reginald F. *The Times Were Strange and Stirring: Methodist Preachers and the Crisis of Emancipation*. Durham, N.C.: Duke University Press, 1995.

Irons, Charles F. *The Origins of Proslavery Christianity: White and Black Christianity in Colonial and Antebellum Virginia*. Chapel Hill: University of North Carolina Press, 2008.

Lischer, Richard. *The Preacher King: Martin Luther King Jr. and the Word That Moved America*. New York: Oxford University Press, 1995.

Maffly-Kipp, Laurie. *Setting Down the Sacred Past: African-American Race Histories*. Cambridge, Mass.: Harvard University Press, 2010.

Morris, Aldon D. The *Origins of the Civil Rights Movement: Black Communities Organizing for Change*. New York: Free Press, 1984.

Raboteau, Albert. *Slave Religion: The "Invisible Institution" in the Antebellum South*. New York: Oxford University Press, 1978.

Sanders, Cheryl J. *Saints in Exile: The Holiness-Pentecostal Experience in African American Religion and Culture*. New York: Oxford University Press, 1999.

Savage, Barbara Dianne. *Your Spirits Walk Beside Us: The Politics of Black Religion*. Cambridge, Mass.: Harvard University Press, 2008.

Sernett, Milton C., ed. *African American Religious History: A Documentary Witness*. Durham, N.C.: Duke University Press, 1999.

——. *Bound for the Promised Land: African American Religion and the Great Migration*. Durham, N.C.: Duke University Press, 1997.

Stowell, Daniel. *Rebuilding Zion: The Religious Reconstruction of the South, 1863–1877*. New York: Oxford University Press, 1998.

Stuckey, Sterling. *Slave Culture: Nationalist Theory and the Foundations of Black America*. New York: Oxford University Press, 1987.

Turner, Richard Brent. *Islam in the African-American Experience*. Bloomington: Indiana University Press, 2003.

Walton, Jonathan L. *Watch This! The Ethics and Aesthetics of Black Televangelism*. New York: New York University Press, 2009.

Watts, Jill. *God, Harlem U.S.A.: The Father Divine Story*. Berkeley: University of California Press, 1995.

West, Cornel, and Eddie S. Glaude Jr., eds. *African American Religious Thought: An Anthology*. Louisville: Westminster John Knox Press, 2003.

Wilmore, Gayraud. *Black Religion and Black Radicalism: An Interpretation of the Religious History of African Americans*. New York: Doubleday, 1972.

11. RELIGION, ETHNICITY, AND
THE IMMIGRANT EXPERIENCE

ROBERTO R. TREVIÑO

In my former professional life in the early 1980s, I worked in a migrant education program based in an inner-city elementary school whose enrollment was overwhelmingly Mexican American and included a large number of Mexican immigrants. Since my office was a classroom in the building I would hear the Pledge of Allegiance crackle over the public address system every day, earnestly blurted out by young Spanish-accented voices issuing from the principal's office and echoing in the rooms around me. Inevitably during this morning ritual, a smile would spread across my face when the chorus reached the part—". . . under God, indivisible [*often mangled*], *for* liberty, *for* justice, *for* all!" The staff members whom I supervised were all Spanish-speaking Mexican Americans, except for one young man, who was a South Vietnamese immigrant. One day during lunch, I strolled into his office and found him sitting in the dark with his eyes closed. Ignorant about his Buddhist faith and its practice of meditation, I quietly stole out of the room and walked straight to a colleague's office to ask what I should do about employees who napped at work!

Now, as a social historian who studies ethnicity and religion in U.S. history, I wonder what the future held for those immigrants. How did those Mexican immigrant children fare as they sought to fit in to their new homeland, poignantly struggling to get the Pledge of Allegiance right? How did their ethnicity and their religious traditions affect their dreams *for* liberty, *for* justice? And what about the meditating staffer? How did his ethnic and religious background—so "foreign" to many of us some thirty years ago—influence his quest for a new life? Did his Buddhist traditions blunt the trauma that he and other "boat people" experienced in coming to the United States?

In recent years, historians of religion have pondered similar questions and sought to unravel the complex and often interrelated nature of religion, ethnicity, and immigration. However, until fairly recently their task had been hindered because they worked in isolation—traditionally, study of U.S. religion and of immigration were separate fields of historical scholarship. Generally speaking, historians who wrote about religion did not consult the work of those who wrote about immigration, and vice versa, because they represented two distinct approaches to the study of history—one divinely inspired, the other secular. On the one hand, virtually all historians who wrote about U.S. religion from colonial times through the nineteenth century—meaning essentially Christianity and especially Protestantism—were men formally trained in, loyal to, and vocationally affiliated with their faith traditions. These "church historians" were theologians, pastors, priests, or other educated representatives who were charged with and fervently accepted the defense and promotion of their religions. For them, God directed history. Their writings presented history as the unfolding of a divine plan, with an interpretive twist that highlighted their religion's role in facilitating divine intervention in human affairs. On the other hand, historians who began writing about immigration—a field of study that originated only in the middle decades of the twentieth century—were scholars trained in a secular scientific methodology that rejected the notion of using divine intervention to understand the workings of history. Rather than explaining history as something directed by a supernatural force, they based their interpretations on human factors and institutions. These were "social" historians who studied "the history of the people and their culture," as historian Jay Dolan put it; for them, human beings made history, not God.

In the early twentieth century, church history entered a prolonged transformation from its sectarian isolation—which, as one historian described it, "was divisive, narrow, and unappealing except to the zealot"—into what today is called history of religion, the study of religion from a secular social history perspective. Throughout the early and middle decades of the twentieth century, church historians gradually abandoned the notion of divine causation and began to adopt the perspectives and methodologies that secular academic historians were using to write about the role of religion in the nation's history. At roughly the same time, an important shift occurred among social historians, who began expressing more interest in the history of immigration to the United States. These two historiographical trends—the secularization of church history and the rise of immigration studies among social historians—began to converge in the 1960s and 1970s. They came together at a time when racial unrest among minorities and increasing immigration from Latin American and Asia were stirring the public's interest in ethnic identity and the nation's immigrant past, coinciding, as the noted religious historian Sidney E. Ahlstrom aptly noted in 1970, with the United States becoming "a post-Puritan, post-Protestant, post-Christian, post-WASP America."

The upshot of all these developments has been a reshaping and cross-fertilization of once-separate historical fields and a better understanding of the interrelatedness of religion, ethnicity, and immigration, and of their role in the larger story of U.S. history. Thus this chapter focuses especially on the ninth theme outlined in the introduction: immigration, the globalization of American religious communities, and the history of insularity and homogeneity emanating both from nativists and from within embattled immigrant communities. Further, this contribution provides a case study of this book's second major theme: (in) tolerance, diversity, and pluralism. As we will see, the long history of intolerance of immigrant ethnicities and religions could not forestall the eventual development of a national identity defined by diversity and pluralism.

Seeking to understand some fundamental aspects of the immigrant experience, historians of religion have probed the range of U.S. faith traditions—with their sometimes contradictory claims and myriad institutional forms and movements—and asked such questions as: How have religion and ethnicity helped immigrants endure the hostilities they encounter as outsiders in a new land? How have religion and ethnicity functioned in reconstituting a sense of identity and community among immigrants? And how have religion and ethnicity steeled immigrants against oppression? These overlapping questions about nativism, identity, and resistance represent, of course, but one way to understand the historical role of religion and ethnicity in the immigrant experience; in an overview such as this, many other questions could be posed and still not exhaust the range of historians' concerns and findings. Obviously, such a survey cannot include or even touch on the experiences of all ethnic groups because there are simply too many.

But why these particular themes here? For one thing, nativism, identity, and resistance stand out as major aspects of immigration that historians have studied for some time now; because of the insights they have yielded, these topics have endured and continue to attract the attention of historians and other scholars. Also, these particular topics speak to our concerns today. We need to examine them in order to gain historical perspective on their deeply rooted and intertwined nature and thus be better equipped to understand the current debates swirling around such hot-button issues as the role of religion in our society, immigration, and the nature of race and ethnic relations. This chapter, then, is meant to provide a starting point for those interested in examining the historical relationships between religion, ethnicity, and the American immigrant experience. It will review how historians have treated these themes and, along the way, suggest new angles of research aimed at advancing our understanding of this central feature of U.S. history.

Questions about religion, ethnicity, and immigration go straight to the heart of the American experience and reveal much about the nature of our society as it has evolved over time. In particular, it is patently clear that religion and ethnicity have played crucial roles in the lives of generations of immigrants and their descendents. It is also apparent, however, that religion and ethnicity functioned as a double-edged sword for those immigrants. Closely associated and at times inseparable, religion and ethnicity formed the basis for social divisions, discrimination, and even violence among and between native-born and immigrant Americans throughout much of U.S. history, while at the same time they served as a buffer and a refuge that helped newcomers survive the hardships associated with migration so that they could establish themselves and prosper in their adopted land.

RELIGION, ETHNICITY, AND NATIVISM

How has the United States received its immigrants? History provides a number of answers: some groups were certainly welcomed; some probably went largely unnoticed; others were grudgingly accepted; and still others faced fierce rejection. In early-twentieth-century Houston, for example, a priest remarked that the Mexican immigrants in his parish had come "hopeful of finding respect and love" but found instead "only contempt and hatred. 'Greasers' they are called and looked down upon and considered pariahs" (quoted in Treviño, *Church in the Barrio*, 86). The patterns of immigrant reception have varied, but two things are clear: religion and ethnicity historically have been integral factors in shaping those receptions, and nativist sentiment has been an enduring aspect of the immigrant experience.

The nativist—"someone who fears and resents immigrants and their impact on the United States, and who wants to take some action against them, be it through violence, immigration restriction, or placing limits on the rights of newcomers already in the United States" (Anbinder, "Nativism," 177)—is a familiar figure in American history. Long before the founding of the United States, Europeans competing for dominance in the New World had established a pattern of varying degrees of inhospitability toward one another based on their religious and ethnic differences. For example, even before the arrival of British colonists in North America, Spanish Catholics who claimed what is now the state of Florida provided a less than neighborly reception for French Protestants (Huguenots) who established a colony near present-day Jacksonville in 1564. In the spirit and practice of the deadly religious wars then raging between Protestants and Catholics in Europe, Spanish soldiers laid waste to the new Huguenot colony in 1565, killing nearly 300 of the so-called Protestant devils. With time, British, Dutch, and other European settlers would reflect similar attitudes toward one another in North America, albeit with varying degrees of severity.

As more European settlers came to North America throughout the seventeenth and eighteenth centuries, they brought with them a natural affinity for their own kind but also a clear propensity toward intolerance of other peoples and religious traditions. As a result, they found ways to try to keep one another at more than arm's length. For instance, Britain's first colony, Virginia, clearly expressed its Protestant-Anglican preferences by passing a law in 1641 barring Catholics from public office and warning Catholic priests to stay out of the territory altogether. It also tried to keep out Quakers. A law passed in 1680 made it illegal for ship captains to bring them in, and colonial authorities also tried to induce them to leave by occasionally branding them, lopping off their ears, punching holes in their tongues, and even hanging a handful. In a similar spirit, Dutch Reformed Protestants wanted nothing to do with other Christians—be they Puritans, Mennonites, Lutherans, or other sects that made up the polyglot colony of New Amsterdam (later, New York) in the mid-seventeenth century. As for Jews in New Amsterdam, Governor Peter Stuyvesant and Reformed minister Johannes Megapolensis tried hard to run them off. Invoking the age-old slur of the moneygrubber proved useful for painting Jews as an economic threat and for creating obstacles when they tried to buy homes and burial sites. Examples such as these are too numerous to recount, but no one revealed the underlying ethno-religious tensions that vexed early America more clearly than Benjamin Franklin when he asked in 1755 why German immigrants should be allowed "to swarm into our Settlements, and by herding together establish their Language and Manners to the Exclusion of ours? Why should Pennsylvania, founded by the English, become a Colony of *Aliens*, who will shortly be so numerous as to Germanize us instead of our Anglifying them, and will never adopt our Language or Customs, any more than they can acquire our Complexion?"

Anglo-Saxon Protestant dominance in the early years of the republic—coupled with the optimistic afterglow of independence and, more importantly, the relatively low immigration of ethnic and religious "others"—prevented sentiments like Franklin's from metastasizing into virulent widespread nativism. However, that changed over the course of the nineteenth century as new patterns of immigration and American westward expansion into Mexican territories made Protestants neighbors and co-citizens of ever-increasing numbers of Catholics and even non-Christians.

The first signs of change began in the 1820s with an upswing of immigration. That shift quickly became a veritable flood that brought more than 4 million newcomers to the United States during the 1840s and 1850s, three-quarters of whom were from Ireland and the German provinces, with the majority being Catholics. Fearing their own political and cultural demise, nativists attacked Catholic immigrants through word and deed, claiming that the newcomers threatened the nation's identity and its security. The middle decades of the nineteenth century saw widespread verbal and physical assaults in eastern and midwestern cities where recently arrived Germans and Irish congregated. Newspaper editorials succeeded in inciting bloody violence against Irish and German voters during elections; sensationalistic novels such as Maria Monk's *Awful Disclosures of Maria Monk; or, The Hidden Secrets of a Nun's Life in a Convent Exposed* (1836) fabricated tales of rampant sex and violence among Catholic priests and nuns; mobs attacked Catholic individuals, neighborhoods, and at times even schools and convents; and the nativist Know Nothing Party won an a remarkable number of elections at least partly by harnessing the anti-immigrant hysteria of the time.

Meanwhile, ethno-religious tensions flared as native-born Americans began settling in the area stretching from present-day Texas to California, where they encountered Mexican Catholics and eventually non-Christian Asians. In the first arena of contact, Mexican Texas of the 1820s, Anglo-Americans soon reneged on promises they had made to respect the rule of Mexican law—including state-sanctioned Catholicism—and broke free of Mexico through armed insurrection in 1836. Granted, religious conflict was not the major cause of the Texas Revolt. Nonetheless, ethnic and religious differences between Anglo-American Protestants and Mexican Catholics in Texas were indeed a source of tensions and, more importantly, Americans' air of superiority—based on an assumed sense of ethnic and religious superiority—is palpably evident in the historical record. Thus the Texas episode again reflects how many native-born American Protestants of the time saw "outsiders." Ironically, of course, in the case of westward expansion it was they who were the outsiders as they entered a long-established Spanish-Mexican Catholic region; in Americans' eyes, it was the Spanish-speaking Catholics who were the "foreigners." Those attitudes and frictions surfaced again throughout the Southwest after the United States took control of the territory through the Mexican War (1846–1848). After 1850, California presented nativists with even more targets. There, in addition to denigrating Mexican Catholics, nativists often treated Chinese and other Asian immigrants in more degrading ways than they did any other newcomers. For Americans desperately trying to keep the United States a white Protestant nation, non-Christian Asians and their religions—Confucianism, Taoism, Buddhism, Hinduism, and a host of others that began appearing on the West Coast in the later nineteenth century—elicited the most brutal responses in the history of voluntary immigration to the United States.

While the ethnic and religious diversity of the American West kept nativists occupied there, a flood of "new" immigrants stirred the wrath of nativists in Eastern Seaboard cities in the late nineteenth and early twentieth centuries. Most of these newcomers were eastern and southern Europeans, quite different in language and religion from old-stock Americans. Between 1880 and 1910, 8.4 million Russians, Poles, Slovaks, Greeks, Hungarians, Lithuanians, Italians, and many other groups came from the Mediterranean and Slavic regions. Among the waves of new "others," the southern Italian Catholics and Orthodox Jews drew the most attention from nativists. The emotional fervor of southern Italian Catholicism put off more conservative Catholics and Protestants alike, especially such rituals as *lingua strascinuni*, the practice of women honoring a patron saint by crawling or being carried toward a saint statue while dragging their tongue along the church floor. Similarly, the poverty-stricken, Yiddish-speaking, easy-to-spot Orthodox Jews seemed the very embodiment of Europe's "wretched refuse" and "huddled masses" immortalized by poet Emma Lazarus. Holding fast to their ancient ways, Orthodox Jewish immigrants resented and fought efforts to Americanize them; in turn, they often felt the sting of rabid anti-Semitism, especially at the hands of a revived Ku Klux Klan in the early twentieth century.

Toward the middle of the twentieth century, historians Ray Allen Billington, Oscar Handlin, and John Higham broke new ground by focusing attention on the less-than-friendly receptions that European immigrants received upon arriving in the United States. Although not the first to deal with nativism, historian Ray Allen Billington's study *The Protestant Crusade, 1800–1860: A Study of the Origins of American Nativism* (1938) initially set the standard for examining anti-immigrant sentiment in U.S. history. Billington's masterful detailing and documentation of the fervency of nineteenth-century anti-Catholicism and its horrors—the convent burnings, rioting, and other anti-immigrant violence—won him enduring stature. However, in 1955 historian John Higham overshadowed Billington's influential book with his own classic, *Strangers in the Land: Patterns of American Nativism, 1860–1925*. Higham's more sophisticated analysis of nativism as an ideology not only rooted in anti-Catholicism (as Billington had argued) but also interwoven with nationalism, anti-radicalism, and racism make it the unsurpassed study of U.S. nativism. Other historians during the middle decades of the twentieth century wrote about the prejudice immigrants faced, chief among them Oscar Handlin. Handlin's community study, *Boston's Immigrants, 1790–1865: A Study in Acculturation* (1941), threw light on American nativism by revealing the fierce conflict that marked the Irish Catholic experience in that city. Ten years later, in 1951, Handlin published his Pulitzer Prize–winning work on immigration, *The Uprooted: The Epic Story of the Great Migrations That Made the American People*, in which he poignantly recounted the human toll extracted by migration, including the immigrant's sense of alienation brought on by encounters with nativist antipathy.

While these early studies established nativism as a central part of the U.S. immigrant experience, the flowering of the "new" social and religious history in the 1960s and 1970s brought significant advances to the study of the theme by greatly expanding the variety of ethnic groups studied and making religion the framework of analysis. The prolific church historian Martin Marty described Protestant reactions to immigrants in *Righteous Crusade: The Protestant Experience in America* (1970). Jay P. Dolan's treatment of the implications of nativism against Catholic immigrants in nineteenth-century New York was but one of the contributions of his seminal study, *The Immigrant Church: New York's Irish and German Catholics, 1815–1865*. In *Catholic Immigrants in America* (1987), James S. Olson surveyed the nation's often less than neighborly reception of the host of "new" Catholic immigrants who crowded onto its shores in the late nineteenth and early twentieth centuries. Leonard Dinnerstein's *Anti-Semitism in America* synthesized a small body of literature on anti-Jewish discrimination, arguing that its persistence sprang from deeply rooted antipathy embedded in Christian teachings. These studies rounded out a growing body of historical literature that provided new perspectives on various expressions of nativism aimed at European immigrants.

Since the 1980s, a new generation of historians and other scholars of religion interested in non-European ethnic and immigrant groups have further illuminated U.S. nativist sentiment in wide-ranging works. Similarly, historians and other religious studies scholars who have been recovering Asian American religious history since the closing decades of the twentieth century revealed yet another side of American nativism. Granted, historians of the American West had earlier documented the persecution of Asian immigrants (especially the Chinese) who came to the United States in the nineteenth century. However, by uncovering the history of lesser-known Asian immigrants in the West, these recent studies have provided new contexts in which to examine anti-immigrant sentiment and have extended the theme from the nineteenth century well into the twentieth.

In summary, the historical study of nativism as a central feature of the American immigrant experience has benefited significantly from the convergence of social and religious history in the years since the 1960s and 1970s. What remains to be done? One obvious need is to fill some gaps. For instance, we know much more about the history of nativism that was directed against the "new" immigrants from Europe than we do about anti-Asian or anti-Latino sentiment. Take the important chapter in Chicano history where nativism was clearly operating, the deportations of the 1930s. While many historians have studied this episode, none have explored it in any meaningful way through the perspective of religion. What might we learn from a close examination of how religious institutions, individuals, and ideas were related to the nativism of the time, as well as to responses to it?

Historians should also pursue more comparative studies. Was nativism the same in all places? How did the religious context of the South affect the reception of late-nineteenth- and early-twentieth-century southern Italian immigrants there, as opposed to their experiences in the Far West or on the East Coast? The myriad religious traditions and ethno-racial distinctions among Asian immigrants would seem fertile ground for comparing the nature of their reception in various American settings. Did Asian Christians find a more welcoming society than their non-Christian companions from the same homelands? Was nativism against Asians generalized, or were there significant differences among the various groups along ethnic and religious lines?

Another area that has lacked attention is nativist sentiment among and between immigrant communities themselves. One topic that has never really been studied is the degree and nature of anti-immigrant feeling within Latino communities. For example, historians should move beyond anecdotal references about historical conflict between Mexican-origin Catholics and Protestants. Similar questions, of course, could be posed with regard to Asian immigrant groups. To what extent has nativism in America been more than a majority–minority issue, and how have immigrant ethnicity and religion been related to it? Ignoring this arena skews our understanding of the history of both nativism and the immigrant experience.

RELIGION, ETHNICITY, AND IDENTITY

The migration process can be disorienting, forcing immigrants to deal with basic existential questions of identity. As the immigrant Sang Hyun Lee eloquently stated in 1980, "We find ourselves in a wilderness, living as aliens and strangers. And the inescapable question arises from the depth of our being: What is the real meaning of our immigrant existence in America? What is the spiritual meaning of our alien status?" For some time, historians and other scholars of religion have grappled with the complicated question of how religion and ethnicity function in immigrant identity and community-building.

In 1977, historian Randall M. Miller neatly summarized what many scholars have concluded about this theme: immigrant religion, "the very bone and sinew of ethnicity" as he described it, "was intertwined and imbedded in the psyche, the folklife, the very identity of each immigrant." It was what "gave meaning, a system of moral values, self-definition, and community to the immigrants." Miller was not the first to capture the importance of religion in immigrant life, for indeed others before him had underscored its centrality, including Oscar Handlin in *The Uprooted* and Will Herberg in *Protestant, Catholic, Jew: An Essay in American Sociology* (1955), to name but two.

But while Handlin emphasized the inability of immigrants to reconstitute and find empowering solace in Old World faiths, historians of more recent times have argued the opposite. Catholic historian Jay P. Dolan led the way with his study *The Immigrant Church*, which showed that immigrants leaned heavily on their religious traditions and institutions in ways that powerfully benefited their lives. In the same vein, *Immigrants and Religion in Urban America* (1977), a volume of essays edited by Randall M. Miller and Thomas D. Marzik, found that religion played an important role in the daily lives of Poles, Czechs, Armenians, eastern European Jews, and other "new" immigrants of the late nineteenth and early twentieth centuries as they built their communities by propagating the ethnic and religious traditions of their homelands. With the publication of Timothy L. Smith's provocative article "Religion and Ethnicity in America" (*American Historical Review* 83 [1978]: 1155–1185), the validation of the role of religion and ethnicity as a unifying "theologizing experience" among European immigrants seemed assured, despite its failure to resonate among Latinos and Asians. Robert Anthony Orsi significantly advanced our understanding of the intertwined nature of religion and ethnicity in his influential book, *The Madonna of 115th Street: Faith and Community in Italian Harlem, 1880–1950.* The study's intricate analysis vividly revealed how a Catholic devotion sustained family- and community-centered identity as southern Italian immigrants carved a place for themselves in New York City.

Historians who turned their attention in the 1990s and early 2000s to non-European immigrants and non-Christian religions in the United States have produced a growing body of literature that sheds light on how religion and ethnicity affected identity and community formation among a wide variety of Latino, Asian, and Middle Eastern immigrants. An early effort to bring attention to Latino religions in the United States was made by Jay P. Dolan and Jaime R. Vidal in their anthology *Puerto Rican and Cuban Catholics in the U.S., 1900–1965* (1994). Contributing authors Jaime R. Vidal and Lisandro Pérez surveyed the relationship between the U.S. Catholic Church and Puerto Ricans and Cuban Americans, respectively, including issues about ethnic identity and assimilation. Among the slowly growing number of scholars who studied Latino religions, Thomas A. Tweed's *Our Lady of the Exile: Diasporic Religion at a Cuban Catholic Shrine in Miami* stood out for its theoretical innovation and incisive analysis. In this, the first book-length history of Cuban American Catholicism, Tweed revealed the power of religion to shape and reconstitute a sense of individual and community identity among people living in exile.

Two other community studies advanced the recovery of Mexican American religion and added further insights about its relation to identity formation. In *Guadalupe and Her Faithful: Latino Catholics in San Antonio, from Colonial Origins to the Present*, Timothy Matovina revealed how fervent devotion to the central figure in Mexican Catholicism, Our Lady of Guadalupe, historically had contradictory effects in the lives of her devotees—preserving ethnic identity and community yet maintaining social cleavages and hierarchies at the same time. In a different setting, Roberto R. Treviño's *The Church in the Barrio* argued that urban Mexican and Mexican American Catholics responded to social marginality by finding a strong sense of self and community in the interlocked nature of their religious and ethnic traditions. In 2006, David A. Badillo's *Latinos and the New Immigrant Church* provided a much-needed survey of the three major Latino ethnic groups—Mexican Americans, Cuban Americans, and Puerto Ricans—that skillfully laid out patterns of Catholic leadership and institutions as well as immigrant community-building in urban settings.

As for the multiplicity of religions and ethnicities represented in the wave of Asian immigration since the 1970s and the more recent arrival of Middle Eastern peoples, historical studies are few. Nonetheless, the few historical articles and monographs that have appeared testify to the importance religious traditions and ethnoracial identity have played in immigrant community-building. For example, Brian Hayashi's *"For the Sake of Our Japanese Brethren": Assimilation, Nationalism, and*

Protestantism Among the Japanese of Los Angeles, 1895–1942 argued that Japanese Protestants held strong racial and nationalist sentiments that seemed to fly in the face of the assumption about the ability of Christian churches to inculcate American values and promote assimilation. David Yoo's *Growing Up Nisei: Race, Generation, and Culture Among Japanese Americans of California, 1924–49* examined unexplored territory with a cogent analysis of the complexities involved in formulating individual and group identity among Buddhist and Christian Japanese. Historically grounded monographs such as these, however, have been the exception. More common are anthologies that bring together one or two historical articles and contemporary theological reflections or social scientific findings—for example, the volume of essays edited by Pyong Gap Min and Jung Ha Kim, *Religions in Asian America: Building Faith Communities* and *Religion and Immigration: Christian, Jewish, and Muslim Experiences in the United States*, edited by Yvonne Yazbeck Haddad, Jane I. Smith, and John L. Esposito.

The recent spate of mainly sociological and anthropological studies has, of course, contributed important insights into the nature of religion, ethnicity, and identity, among other themes. Much of this social scientific data about post-1965 immigrants can inform today's volatile debates about immigration. In particular, these studies are timely in that they address globalization and transnationalism and how the advent of such concepts complicates traditional understandings and patterns of immigrant incorporation and the meaning of citizenship. They include *Gatherings in Diaspora: Religious Communities and the New Immigration* (1998), edited by R. Stephen Warner and Judith G. Wittner; *Religion and the New Immigrants: Continuities and Adaptations in Immigrant Congregations* (2000) and *Religion Across Borders: Transnational Immigrant Networks*, both edited by Helen Rose Ebaugh and Janet Saltzman Chafetz; *Globalizing the Sacred: Religion Across the Americas* (2003), edited by Manuel A. Vásquez and Marie Friedmann Marquardt; and *Immigrant Faiths: Transforming Religious Life in America* (2005), edited by Karen I. Leonard, Alex Stepick, Manuel A. Vásquez, and Jennifer Holdaway.

Clearly, other disciplines have far outpaced the production of historical studies about Latino and Asian religions. As emergent fields, the need for basic spadework in many areas is obvious and the relationship between religious life and immigrant identity and community-building is but one theme that requires historians' attention. That particular theme, it could be argued, should have a high priority for at least two reasons. First, tracing how religion and ethnicity have affected Asian and Latino identities over time will allow historians to connect these lesser-known but equally American stories to the larger and better-known history of American immigration. Historians involved in the recovery of Asian and Latino religious history should pursue themes such as this one to influence the ongoing construction of larger narratives about the American immigrant experience. What might comparative studies of Latino or Asian groups reveal about the relative importance of religion, ethnicity, and religious institutions in community-building? As a comparison between Asians and Latinos, or with the European immigrant experience, what might these kinds of studies further illuminate about how religion and ethnicity inform the basic notion of community itself as understood by different Americans?

The second rationale for giving priority to the theme of religion, ethnicity, and identity among Latinos and Asians is similar but arguably more pressing, given the current need for a better historical understanding of the latest "new" immigration—the post-1965 wave from Latin America, Asia, and the Middle East. In a time when fears abound about the so-called fraying fabric of American culture brought on by the supposed failure of the Americanization of immigrants and exacerbated by rising chants of protests among documented and undocumented immigrants, historians must do their part to complement the efforts of social scientists actively studying these immigration phenomena. What can historians of religion contribute in this regard? One thing to consider is the idea of transnationalism, or the practice among international migrants of maintaining social, economic, political, and religious lives in both their lands of origin and in their migration destinations. Social scientists in recent years have provided rich descriptions about how religious institutions and practices facilitate transnationalism, especially among Latino immigrants. But, how new is transnationalism? How different might the diasporic Mexican community in the Southwest during the years of the Mexican Revolution of 1910—the community known as *México de afuera* (Mexicans living outside Mexico)—look when reexamined from the perspective of religious life? Contemporary scholarship about Latino transnationalism could benefit from in-depth historical studies of religion among groups that have a long history of contact with the United States, including the Mexican and the Puerto Rican communities.

RELIGION, ETHNICITY, AND RESISTANCE

Throughout the nation's history, immigrants and their children have turned to their faith traditions to find strength and strategies to confront forces that would deny them human dignity and equality. In 1938, for example, a young second-generation Japanese American explained, "Faith is a necessity in our everyday Christian living. For with faith, we, as Christians, are able to face the huge obstacles of our chaotic life with an optimistic attitude. It gives us the strength, the power, and the hope in the face of un-Christian forces at work in the world today" (quoted in Yoo, *Growing Up Nisei*, 65).

The historical literature that began focusing squarely on the interrelatedness of religion and ethnicity in the 1960s and 1970s offered some of the earliest insights into this theme. Thus the studies that broke new ground in immigration, ethnic, and religious history in the 1970s—Dolan's *The Immigrant Church* and Miller and Marzik's *Immigrants and Religion in Urban America*—brought attention in varying depth to how religion helped immigrants resist different kinds of social subordination. A volume of historical documents edited by Antonio M. Stevens-Arroyo, *Prophets Denied Honor: An Anthology on the Hispano Church of the United States*, added to this effort by recovering important statements of resistance by Mexican American and Puerto Rican religious activists.

Historians and other religious scholars returned to the topic in the 1990s and have since greatly expanded the theme. Here, again, the publication of historical monographs has lagged behind that of the social sciences and other religious studies. An early anthology edited by historian Jonathan D. Sarna, *Minority Faiths and the American Mainstream*, offered a number of essays that presented a variety of views on strategies of survival and resistance to domination that were used at various times in history by Jewish, Catholic, and even "minority" Protestant immigrant communities (Mennonite, Christian Reformed, and Missouri Synod Lutheran). Among the few historical monographs that devote significant attention to the intertwining of resistance, religion, and ethnicity are Yoo's *Growing Up Nisei*; Lara Medina's *Las Hermanas: Chicana/Latina Religious-Political Activism in the U.S. Catholic Church*; Rudy V. Busto's *King Tiger: The Religious Vision of Reies López Tijerina*; and Treviño's *The Church in the Barrio*. Yoo revealed that survival strategies in California's Japanese immigrant communities included the formation of ethnic-religious organizations among both Christian and Buddhist Japanese. In tracing the history of the Mexican American activist sisters' organization, Medina added much to our understanding of the Chicano movement and the civil rights era, as did Busto's biography in bringing to light the Pentecostal roots of the politics of one of the Chicano movement's main leaders.

Another developing body of historical literature related to the theme of religion, ethnicity, and resistance began to appear in the 1990s—the study of religious and lay women, particularly Catholic sisters (developed further in Tentler, chap. 17, this volume), their lay counterparts, and women who served as Protestant missionaries. While some may cast these evangelizers as oppressors, historians have mostly studied them in their opposite role as defenders of immigrant and ethnic communities. In any case, the history of religious women of various Christian traditions has begun to replace the amateur hagiographies that for many generations characterized this aspect of traditional church history. These analytical histories highlighted the social ministry of pioneering teachers, nurses, social workers, and other advocates of downtrodden immigrants in different eras and places.

Recent years have also seen the publication of edited volumes that bring together essays primarily from the perspectives of history, sociology, anthropology, and theology, a number of which examine the theme of immigrant-ethnic religion and resistance to oppression. *Recognizing the Latino Resurgence in U.S. Religion: The Emmaus Paradigm*, by Ana María Díaz-Stevens and Antonio M. Stevens-Arroyo, incorporates a rare historical perspective in its sociological analysis of religion among Latinos, which includes the theme of ethnic- and religion-based social activism. Two other book-length treatments of the topic of religion and resistance are *PADRES: The National Chicano Priest Movement*, by Richard Edward Martínez, and *The Virgin of El Barrio: Marian Apparitions, Catholic Evangelizing, and Mexican American Activism*, by Kristy Nabhan-Warren.

Intense media coverage of immigration—especially the rise of protests and demands among immigrants themselves—has undoubtedly helped spur the recent scholarly interest in the role of religion and ethnicity in immigrant resistance to subordination. While social scientists and other religion scholars have produced thoughtful analyses of these contemporary events, most of these works retain a "snapshot" quality of current issues. Even though historians have treated aspects of this theme, there is a need to expand research into arenas such as modes of resistance in today's immigrant and ethnic communities. The recent resurgence of unionized labor activism among Mexican and other Latino immigrants raises questions about historical antecedents. Aside from the support many churches gave César Chávez and the farm workers movement of the 1960s and 1970s, we know very little about how Catholic parish societies or other church-sponsored organizations might have been involved in labor organizing in the more distant past. For that matter, do we even know the whole story regarding religion and the farm workers' struggles? What about other settings and more recently arrived immigrant groups?

Of course, labor struggles alone do not tell the whole story about the immigrant quest for social justice. Equally important to recover are the experiences on many fronts in which immigrants struggled to attain fair treatment—particularly in schools, hospitals, and other public institutions. How did religion enter into the daily struggles for human dignity that many immigrant groups confronted in these settings, where nuns and other religious women often formed the front line of immigrant defense in hostile environments? We are beginning to understand more about the social ministry of these advocates of fairness for immigrant and ethnic minorities, but the work in this field—and its corollaries in other religious traditions—has barely begun. With its potential for bringing greater gender balance and new perspectives, this area of research holds great potential for eventually revising numerous aspects of religious, ethnic, immigrant, and other fields of American history.

Millions of immigrants throughout American history were affected by their ethnicity and religion as they sought to find their place in this society. Through migration, immigrants learned life's lessons about the double-edged nature of their ethnic and religious identities and traditions. They came to understand that while ethno-religious solidarity with their compatriots and coreligionists could be a balm and bring them other kinds of succor, those same ethnic and religious traits set them apart and often formed the basis for conflict with others—while at the same time arming them to defend their rights and communities.

The scholarly literature sampled in this chapter serves as a starting point for studying the paradoxical and entwined nature of religion and ethnicity in the immigrant experience. Clearly, focusing on nativism, identity, and resistance can reveal only *parts* of how religion and ethnicity affected immigrant lives—but these are important parts of the immigrant experience, past *and* present. Given the need for historically informed dialogue on the pressing issue of immigration today, it is incumbent on historians to redouble their efforts in this area of study. On the one hand, the fact that nativism has been an integral and fairly constant part of the immigrant experience and, consequently, the building of the nation, is an important lesson of history; the idea that it remains very much a part of migrant life today justifies its further study. On the other hand, ethno-religious identity formation and resistance to oppression historically have accompanied and at least partially blunted nativism, and thus these themes also merit further historical analysis. Religion and ethnicity combined in positive ways in the lives of immigrants in the past, providing them protection, giving them dignity and hope, and eventually helping them carve a place for themselves as Americans. In the process, those dynamic elements of immigrant life helped to move our society, however slowly and unevenly, closer toward fulfillment of its democratic promise. Historical studies of how this happened could contribute to the process of moving this ideal further along for yet another generation of new Americans.

REFERENCES

Alba, Richard, Albert Raboteau, and Josh DeWind, eds. *Immigration and Religion in America: Historical and Comparative Perspectives.* New York: New York University Press, 2009.

Anbinder, Tyler. "Nativism and Prejudice Against Immigrants." In *A Companion to American Immigration,* edited by Reed Ueda, 177–201. Malden, Mass.: Blackwell, 2006.

Badillo, David A. *Latinos and the New Immigrant Church.* Baltimore: Johns Hopkins University Press, 2006.

Barton, Paul. *Hispanic Methodists, Presbyterians, and Baptists in Texas.* Austin: University of Texas Press, 2006.

Botham, Fay, and Sara M. Patterson, eds. *Race, Religion, Region: Landscapes of Encounter in the American West.* Tucson: University of Arizona Press, 2006.

Busto, Rudy V. *King Tiger: The Religious Vision of Reies López Tijerina.* Albuquerque: University of New Mexico Press, 2005.

Coburn, Carol K., and Martha Smith, eds. *Spirited Lives: How Nuns Shaped Catholic Culture and American Life, 1836–1920*. Chapel Hill: University of North Carolina Press, 1999.

Díaz-Stevens, Ana María, and Anthony M. Stevens-Arroyo. *Recognizing the Latino Resurgence in U.S. Religion: The Emmaus Paradigm*. Boulder, Colo.: Westview Press, 1998.

Dinnerstein, Leonard. *Anti-Semitism in America*. New York: Oxford University Press, 1994.

Dolan, Jay P. *The Immigrant Church: New York's Irish and German Catholics, 1815–1865*. Baltimore: Johns Hopkins University Press, 1975.

Ebaugh, Helen Rose, and Janet Saltzman Chafetz, eds. *Religion Across Borders: Transnational Immigrant Networks*. Walnut Creek, Calif.: AltaMira Press, 2002.

Espinosa, Gastón, Virgilio Elizondo, and Jesse Miranda, eds. *Latino Religions and Civic Activism in the United States*. New York: Oxford University Press, 2005.

Haddad, Yvonne Yazbeck, Jane I. Smith, and John L. Esposito, eds. *Religion and Immigration: Christian, Jewish, and Muslim Experiences in the United States*. Walnut Creek, Calif.: AltaMira Press, 2003.

Hayashi, Brian Masaru. *"For the Sake of Our Japanese Brethren": Assimilation, Nationalism, and Protestantism Among the Japanese of Los Angeles, 1895–1942*. Stanford, Calif.: Stanford University Press, 1995.

Hondagneu-Sotelo, Pierrette, ed. *Religion and Social Justice for Immigrants*. New Brunswick, N.J.: Rutgers University Press, 2007.

Leonard, Karen Isaksen. *Making Ethnic Choices: California's Punjabi Mexican Americans*. Philadelphia: Temple University Press, 1992.

Martínez, Juan Francisco. *Sea la Luz: The Making of Mexican Protestantism in the American Southwest, 1829–1900*. Denton: University of North Texas Press, 2006.

Martínez, Richard Edward. *PADRES: The National Chicano Priest Movement*. Austin: University of Texas Press, 2005.

Matovina, Timothy. *Guadalupe and Her Faithful: Latino Catholics in San Antonio, from Colonial Origins to the Present*. Baltimore: Johns Hopkins University Press, 2005.

——. *Tejano Religion and Ethnicity: San Antonio, 1821–1860*. Austin: University of Texas Press, 1995.

Matovina, Timothy, and Gary Riebe-Estrella, SVD, eds. *Horizons of the Sacred: Mexican Traditions in U.S. Catholicism*. Ithaca, N.Y.: Cornell University Press, 2002.

Medina, Lara. *Las Hermanas: Chicana/Latina Religious-Political Activism in the U.S. Catholic Church*. Philadelphia: Temple University Press, 2004.

Min, Pyong Gap, and Jung Ha Kim, eds. *Religions in Asian America: Building Faith Communities*. Walnut Creek, Calif.: AltaMira Press, 2002.

Nabhan-Warren, Kristy. *The Virgin of El Barrio: Marian Apparitions, Catholic Evangelizing, and Mexican American Activism*. New York: New York University Press, 2005.

Orsi, Robert Anthony. *The Madonna of 115th Street: Faith and Community in Italian Harlem, 1880–1950*. New Haven, Conn.: Yale University Press, 1985.

Sarna, Jonathan D., ed. *Minority Faiths and the American Protestant Mainstream*. Urbana: University of Illinois Press, 1998.

Stevens-Arroyo, Antonio M., ed. *Prophets Denied Honor: An Anthology on the Hispano Church of the United States*. Maryknoll, N.Y.: Orbis Books, 1980.

Treviño, Roberto R. *The Church in the Barrio: Mexican American Ethno-Catholicism in Houston*. Chapel Hill: University of North Carolina Press, 2006.

Tweed, Thomas A. *Our Lady of the Exile: Diasporic Religion at a Cuban Catholic Shrine in Miami*. New York: Oxford University Press, 1997.

Tweed, Thomas A., and Stephen Prothero, eds. *Asian Religions in America: A Documentary History*. New York: Oxford University Press, 1999.

Walker, Randi Jones. *Protestantism in the Sangre de Cristos, 1850–1920*. Albuquerque: University of New Mexico Press, 1991.

Yoo, David K. *Growing Up Nisei: Race, Generation, and Culture Among Japanese Americans of California, 1924–49*. Urbana: University of Illinois Press, 2000.

12. ASIAN AMERICAN RELIGIONS

TIMOTHY TSENG

The study of Asian American religions centers on the religious expressions of *Asian Americans* themselves. Transplanted Asian religious traditions with non-Asian adherents can be included, but the primary focus must be on Asian Americans and their religions. In this way, race, ethnicity, and Christianity (which is not traditionally considered Asian) become key sites for scholarly investigation. From this perspective, Asian American religion creates a set of issues and themes that have been overlooked until recently in historical studies of religion in the United States.

The neglect of Asian American religions throughout much of the twentieth century was in part the result of the concentration of Asian Americans in the American West, a region that has only recently engaged the attention of American historians. But a major factor was the dominance of *assimilation* and *secularization* motifs in social scientific literature. As sociologists weaned sociology from its theological roots and established it as an independent scientific discipline in the early twentieth century, they often portrayed religious and ethnic communities as residuals of premodern society. Asian American communities were therefore destined to cast off their "Old World" ethnic traits and assimilate into a modern society. Furthermore, Asian Americans, especially the American-born, were expected to convert into a modernized Protestant–Catholic–Jew "triple melting pot." These powerful sociological perspectives rendered the Asian American religious population virtually invisible in historical, religious, and theological studies.

The emergence of Asian American studies in the 1970s gave rise to significant studies by Ron Takaki, Sucheng Chen, Gary Okihiro, and others that have started to restore Asian Americans to U.S. history. Nevertheless, these studies remain rooted in social theories that view religion epiphenomenally. But although religious and theological studies have broadened beyond Christian boundaries, until fairly recently more attention has been given to Asian religions than to the ethnic and racial dimensions of Asian American religions. Similarly, American religious historians have also enlarged their scope of research, but have tended to shape their narratives within either a biracial (i.e., black and white) or an immigration history framework. It was not until the mid-1980s that scholars of American religion came to view Asian American religion as a significant area in its own right.

Over the past twenty years, a number of publications and scholarly activities have fostered the growth of Asian American religious studies. Sociology of religion studies by Donald Tuck, John Fenton, and Fenggang Yang have not only advanced Asian American religious scholarship, but also challenged assimilation and secularization theories. Works such as Jung Young Lee's *Marginality* (1995), Fumitaka Matsuoka's *Out of Silence: Emerging Themes in Asian American Churches*, and Peter Phan's *Christianity with an Asian Face: Asian American Theology in the Making* (2003) have carved out space in the Christian theological landscape to engage in contextualized religious reflection. The sections on Asian American religions in *Religion and American Cultures: An Encyclopedia of Traditions, Diversity, and Popular Expressions*, edited by Gary Laderman and Luis León, are perhaps the most helpful overview of the current state of research in this field.

Despite the new energies around the study of Asian American religions, historical research remains sparse. Brian Hayashi's *"For the Sake of Our Japanese Brethren": Assimilation, Nationalism, and Protestantism Among the Japanese of Los Angeles, 1895–1942* and David K. Yoo's *Contentious Spirits: Religion in Korean American History, 1903–1945* remain two of the few published historical studies of an Asian American religious community. This lack of historical attention can be attributed, in part, to the difficulty of locating and translating records of pre-1965 Asian American religious communities. But the fact of the matter is that Asian American religious history is still in its infancy.

ASIAN AMERICAN RELIGIOUS HISTORY: AN OVERVIEW

The terms "Asian American" and "Asian and Pacific Islander American" are used to identify the 18 million people in the United States who trace their roots to Asia and Oceania. East Asian Americans (Chinese, Japanese, Korean) and Vietnamese are strongly influenced by Mahayana Buddhism, Taoism, Confucianism, and Christianity. Southeast Asian Americans (Cambodian, Laotian, Thai, and Burmese) identify more with Theravada Buddhism. While South Asian Americans are largely Hindu, among this group are many Jains, Zoroastrians, Muslims, Sikhs, and Orthodox Christians. Pakistanis and Afghans are predominantly Muslim. Pacific Islanders and Filipinos have very high Christian affiliation, the latter predominantly Roman Catholic. According to the American Religious Identification Survey conducted by the City University of New York in 2001, 43 percent of the Asian Americans surveyed profess to be Christians, while 28 percent identified as practitioners of "Asian" religions (it is likely that the latter have been undercounted). The tremendous growth and diversity of Asian Americans today is largely a result of the Hart-Celler Act (or the 1965 Immigration Act), which liberalized U.S. immigration policy. Historians usually consider 1965 as the dividing line between two waves of Asian American immigration.

THE FIRST WAVE

First-wave Asian immigration history is usually placed within the context of the increasing economic and geopolitical presence of nineteenth-century America. Although European traders had thrust Hawaii into the world economy prior to the arrival of American missionaries in 1820, the missionaries accelerated the pace of social transformation by promoting wage labor, capitalist markets, and Western manufactured goods. American commercial ventures in China and Japan opened the channels for migration. Dramatic social change and internal unrest in China and Japan coupled with demand for labor in the American West to create "push–pull" forces for Asian migration. Finally, when the United States annexed Hawaii, Guam, and the Philippines in 1898, doors opened for additional migration.

Although the earliest Chinese immigrants were independent merchants and miners, American entrepreneurs started recruiting large teams of Chinese laborers to the Hawaiian sugar plantations in the 1850s and to the American West in the 1860s. This followed the postabolition British practice of importing contract Asian Indian and Chinese laborers for sugar plantations in the Caribbean islands. The earliest Asian immigrants were overwhelmingly male as a result of these labor practices. In Hawaii, the descendents of the first missionaries introduced landownership and sugar plantations in the mid-nineteenth century, which was resisted by the native Hawaiians, to no avail. In fact, diseases introduced by contact with Europeans decimated the native population from a high of 800,000 to about 40,000 in 1878. Encouraged by the success of the Caribbean sugar industry, Hawaiian plantation owners recruited Chinese labor between 1851 and 1864. Later they imported Japanese, Portuguese, Korean, and Filipino laborers in hopes of creating a workforce too diverse to organize. In the United States, after Chinese immigration was banned, industrialists imported Japanese and Korean laborers— many of whom were recruited from the Hawaiian plantations. The 1907 Gentlemen's Agreement between Japan and the United States ended Japanese and Korean labor immigration, although a "picture bride" system that allowed wives of laborers to migrate was permitted. Consequently, the Japanese and Korean American groups were the only Asian communities to develop nuclear families during the first wave. Asian Indian and Filipino workers were subsequently recruited to fill the labor demand in the 1920s and 1930s.

American public sentiment grew increasingly hostile toward Asian immigrants, leading to numerous incidents of anti-Asian violence and the passage of discriminatory laws. The Chinese Exclusion Act (1882), the proscription of Japanese, Indian Asian, and all Asian immigration (1924), and the banning of Filipinos (1934)—despite their status as American nationals—effectively closed the door to Asian migration. In 1870, Asian immigrants were deemed ineligible for American citizenship. The Cable Act of 1922 revoked the citizenship of any American woman who married an alien ineligible for citizenship. The following year, the U.S. Supreme Court upheld the constitutionality of the alien land laws of several Western states that denied aliens ineligible for citizenship the right to own property. Anti-Asian sentiment reached a new apex with the relocation of 120,000 Japanese Americans into internment camps during World War II. Although Chinese exclusion was repealed in 1943, many discriminatory laws remained in effect during the middle decades of the twentieth century.

Discriminatory laws and anti-Asian hostility had major impacts on the first-wave Asian American population. The accompanying table illustrates the decline of the Chinese population after the passage of the 1902 anti-Chinese immigration act. It is not until the 1920s and 1930s, as the number of nuclear families increased, that we witness growth in the Chinese American community. Legislation directed toward Filipinos and Asian Indians in the 1930s led to the decline of their population. Only the Japanese populations witnessed sustained growth before World War II. The increased birthrate was a result of the normalization of sex ratios that occurred shortly after "picture brides" were admitted to the United States.

There is no doubt that the history of Asian Americans has been shaped by geopolitical and economic forces. But lost in many studies that focus on these alone are the stories of Asian Americans as historical actors. Recent studies have demonstrated that first-wave Asian Americans often struggled for better work conditions, protested racial discrimination, and supported nationalist efforts in their home counties. But few studies reveal how Asian Americans thought and acted outside the economic and political spheres. Religious history is a part of scholarly efforts to broaden our understanding of the arenas of Asian American historical agency. Because religion touches community, family, individual, and almost every

Asian American Population Table, 1860–2000

Year	Chinese	Japanese	Filipino	Korean	Indian
1860	34,933	—	—	—	—
1870	64,199	—	—	—	—
1880	105,465	—	—	—	—
1890	107,488	—	—	—	—
1900	118,746	85,716	—	—	—
1910	94,414	152,745	2,767	5,008	5,424
1920	85,202	220,596	26,634	6,181	—
1930	102,159	278,743	108,424	8,332	3,130
1940	106,334	285,115	98,535	8,568	2,405
1950	150,005	326,379	122,707	7.030	—
1960	237,292	464,332	176,310	11,000	12,296
1970	436,062	591,290	343,060	69,150	72,500
1980	812,178	716,331	781,894	357,393	387,223
1990	1,645,472	847,562	1,406,770	798,849	815,4447
2000	2,858,291	1,152,324	2,385,216	1,226,825	1,899,590

Sources: Bill Ong Hing, *Making and Remaking Asian America Through Immigration Policy, 1850–1990* (Stanford, Calif.: Stanford University Press, 1993); Terrance J. Reeves and Claudette E. Bennett, *We the People: Asians in the United States,* Census 2000 Special Report 17 (Washington, D.C.: U.S. Census Bureau, 2004).

sphere of life, the study of religious history may be one of the most important keys to unlocking the lived experiences of first-wave Asian Americans.

The religions of first-wave Asian Americans are complex medleys of human aspirations for survival and dignity amid a hostile, racialized, and predominantly Protestant American society. This is illustrated by the high degree of cultural blending among their religious organizations. For example, most Hawaiians embraced the Christianity introduced by Congregationalist missionaries to Hawaii in the mid-nineteenth century, but many integrated their indigenous religious worldviews into their new faith. Protestant missions (Presbyterian, Baptist, Methodist, and Congregationalist) among Chinese, Japanese, and Korean immigrants, the earliest Asian American religious organizations in the United States and Hawaii, also incorporated a strong sense of homeland nationalism despite the perception that they were the most assimilated Asian Americans. The Buddhist Church of America—the predominant religion among Japanese Americans with roots to Jodo Shinshu (Pure Land) Buddhism in Japan—traces its North American origins to the Hawaiian plantations in the 1880s. During this time, Chinese Americans were reported to have built 62 temples and 141 shrines in twelve states. Although Filipinos participated in mainstream Catholic parishes, they also created informal social organizations that perpetuated and transformed indigenous cultural and religious practices within the community.

The religions of Hawaiians and other Pacific Islanders underwent the most dramatic transformation in the face of intense missionary efforts. The indigenous religions of this diverse group share "an intimate connectedness with the land, the sea, and their creatures." But as mission schools and presses taught literacy and Westernization, Protestantism came to be the dominant religion of Hawaiians by the end of the nineteenth century. Hawaiian and Pacific Islander Christianity, however, creatively blended indigenous traditions with Christianity even while professing orthodox Christian commitments.

The first Asian American Protestant congregation, the Presbyterian Church in Chinatown, was organized in San Francisco in 1852 by a small group of Chinese Christians who had studied at the Morrison School in Macao. By the 1870s, Methodist, Congregational, and Baptist missions had been formed in the San Francisco Bay area, Sacramento, and other urban centers with significant Chinese presence. In 1931, there were forty-four Chinese congregations. These grew to sixty-six in number by 1952. Until the mid-twentieth century, the Chinese missions served an overwhelmingly male population. Family-oriented Chinese congregations would not appear until the 1940s, when women and American-born children became a significant presence in the Chinese American community. White missionary women in the congregations, schools, and rescue missions provided role models for Chinese Protestant women. Many of these American-born women would eventually assume public leadership roles.

The first Japanese Christian congregation was established in 1877 by a group of students who met in the basement of the Chinese Methodist Church in San Francisco. In Hawaii, the Evangelical Association recruited Shinichi Aoiki to work among the Japanese in 1885. Later, Kanichi Miyama and Takie Okumura (1865–1952) became prominent evangelists and pastors among the Japanese in Hawaii and the United States. By World War II, there were close to eighty Japanese American Christian congregations in the United States and in Hawaii. Because Japanese migrants were allowed to bring "picture brides" from overseas, the Japanese congregations in the early twentieth century were composed of more stable nuclear families than the Chinese missions.

The presence of missionaries among the first Asian American Protestant congregations encouraged identification with denominations. Nevertheless, Chinese and Japanese Protestants organized interdenominational ethnic organizations such as the Chinese and Japanese YMCAs, the Northern and Southern California Japanese Christian Church Federations, and the North American Chinese Church Convention.

Korean American Protestantism had its origins in Hawaii, when 7,300 laborers were recruited for the sugar plantations, beginning in 1903, to offset growing Japanese power. Protestant communities were quickly established on these plantations. Many of the immigrants also came to the United States. With the help of white missionaries such as Florence Sherman, leaders such as the Reverend Hugh Heung-wo Cynn (1883–1959), Chang Ho Anh (1878–1938), and Dae-wi Lee (1879–1928) formed Korean missions in Los Angeles and San Francisco in the early twentieth century. Japan's annexation of Korea in 1910 precipitated a movement for national independence that, while largely led by Korean Christians, also created tensions within the church community. The March 1, 1919, uprising in Korea and brutal Japanese reprisals led to the formation of the Korean Church Council of North America, which called for prayers for independence and world peace. Nevertheless, fissures among Korean American Christians emerged when Syngman Rhee (1875–1965) started churches and organizations that severed ties to Presbyterian and Methodist denominations. Despite these struggles, their small numbers, and the sense of denominational neglect, Korean American church-es persevered and developed programs for their second generation in the 1930s. Unlike the Chinese and Japanese churches, which never won very many converts, 40 percent of Korean Americans were Protestant.

First-wave Chinese, Japanese, and Korean Protestants exhibited strong nation-alistic tendencies. As much, if not more, attention was given to East Asian as to American affairs. Furthermore, their leaders were as interested in Asian politics as they were in the Asian evangelization. Indeed, nationalism was one of the stron-gest motives for Chinese, Japanese, and Korean identification with Protestantism during this period. Many believed that Protestantism provided an effective cri-tique of premodern societies and could be used to rebuild these nations into pow-erful, modern Christian democracies.

Although the Roman Catholic presence among East Asians predates the Prot-estant missionary movement, Catholics' work among East Asians in the United States started later. After failed efforts in the late nineteenth century, Chinese American Catholicism gained a foothold in San Francisco in 1904 as a result of the efforts of the Paulists and the Society of Helpers (a women's society). The Maryknoll Catholic Foreign Mission Society established Japanese schools and orphanages among the Japanese as early as 1915. The steady growth of Catholicism among East Asians and the Chinese, in particular, in the first half of the twentieth century overshadowed the Protestant efforts. But this effort could not compare with the deeply rooted Catholicism among Filipinos.

Like other Asian immigrants, Filipino Americans brought a rich spiritual heri-tage with them. Like Hawaiians and other Pacific Islanders, Filipinos have had a long history of affiliation with Christianity—Roman Catholicism, in particular. The conversion process to Christianity experienced by Filipinos ensured that indigenous religiosity would continue to interact with the predominant faith and create local-ized expressions of folk Christianity and popular religions. Furthermore, the 1896 revolution created conditions for the establishment of the Iglesia Filipina Independ-iente (Philippine Independent Church) in 1902, a nationalist movement that broke from the Roman Catholic Church. Finally, after the United States annexed the Philippines, American missionaries introduced Protestantism. Therefore, the reli-gious history of first-wave Filipino immigrants is a complex story. They were not only Catholic and Protestant, but also practitioners of nativist religion and char-ismatic leaders of popular religious movements. Between 1909 and 1930, 112,800 Filipinos settled in Hawaii. In the 1920s, over 100,000 migrated to the United States.

The white American encounter with Buddhism predated the arrival of Asian American Buddhism. Both Buddhism and Hinduism were topics of great interest among New England Victorians and in Protestant seminaries in the mid-nineteenth century. Theravada Buddhism was introduced to the United States in 1893, when Anagarika Dharmapala, a Buddhist layman from Ceylon, delivered a speech at the World's Parliament of Religions in Chicago. Asian American practitioners of Mahayana Buddhism likely arrived with Chinese immigrants. But no membership statistics are available, and Chinese Buddhists did not send missionaries to the United States or Hawaii. Furthermore, the Chinese were rather syncretistic regarding religions and preferred to blend Buddhism, Taoism, Confucianism, and folk religion than to claim one tradition exclusively.

Japanese American Buddhism, in contrast, quickly developed into an important institution in the immigrant community. In response to rumors about successful Japanese Protestant efforts in Hawaii and the United States, the Reverend Soryu Kagahi was sent by the Jodo Shinshu to Honolulu in 1889. After inspecting the spiritual conditions of the immigrants and observing the malaise among the plantation workers, he concluded that a Buddhist mission needed to be established. He helped organize the first Hawaiian Buddhist Temple, the Hilo Honpa Hongwanji, on the Big Island. Upon his return to Japan, his appeal to develop the Buddhist mission in Hawaii fell on deaf ears, since the Japanese laborers were considered merely transient. Subsequently, however, as Protestants gained ground in the Japanese community, concern was raised about helping their children to maintain their culture and language. In 1898, Honpa Hongwanji in Japan sent Eryu Honda and Ejun Miyamoto to San Francisco to study the spiritual condition of immigrants to the United States. As a result, the Young Men's Buddhist Association was organized, and the first Buddhist Temple in America was established in San Francisco. The following year, the Reverends Shuye Sonoda and Kakuryo Nishijima were dispatched to San Francisco to minister to the growing Japanese population on the mainland United States. By 1906, nine Jodo Shinshu temples were established in California, two in Washington, and one in Chicago. Some 3,165 members were reported, but that appears to be an undercount. In 1944, the Jodo Shinshu was renamed the Buddhist Churches of America.

The explicitly religious institutions (temples and congregations) and less explicitly religious organizations (such as mutual aid societies, fraternities, and hometown or surname associations) of first-wave Asian American immigrants made at least three important contributions to their communities: spiritual comfort and cultural continuity, cultural adaptation, and support for political and social activism. First-wave Asian American religions provided a safe haven where the members of their community could participate in cultural symbols and rituals from the homeland. Religion also provided pathways of cultural adaptation to life in modern America. Japanese Buddhist adaptations included using pews in the temples, establishing Sunday schools, and singing Christian-sounding hymns such as "Onward, Buddhist Soldiers." Finally, first-wave Asian American religions, in varying degrees, became centers for political activism and social amelioration. Chinese Protestant churches in the United States and the Chinese diaspora were the source of a revolutionary nationalism that toppled the Qing dynasty in China in 1911.

The story of first-wave Asian American religions raises a number of questions for historical investigation. The first set relates to the characteristics of religious practice in male-dominated immigrant and racialized communities. How did male kinship patterns influence religious behavior and beliefs among the Chinese, Filipino, and South Asian populations? Another set of questions looks to intercultural and interracial relationships. For example, given the multicultural reality of Hawaiian sugar plantation life, what role did religion play in interethnic and owner–labor relationships? What role did it play among the diverse Asian communities in the United States? A third set of questions concerns the transnational or diasporic religious connections between Asian Americans and Asians in their homelands. Recent studies have emphasized the material and ideological exchanges between Asia and Asian America, but transnational religious exchange has not been fully explored. Fourth, is it possible to construct an intellectual history of Asian American religions? What did religious leaders whose primary context was the Asian American communities believe and teach? Fifth, as American-born Asians came of age in the 1930s, how did religion affect intergenerational transitions and tensions?

The 1940s and 1950s were pivotal decades in the religious history of first-wave Asian Americans. The perception that immigration had ceased and that the assimilated second-generation Asian Americans were loyal to the United States resulted in the misplaced belief that ethnic institutions and ghettos would vanish. Religion in America also underwent dramatic changes during this period. On the surface, it appeared that the reconfigured Protestant–Catholic–Jewish "melting pot" had positioned itself as the new religious establishment. Beneath the surface, however, were signs of changes that would manifest themselves more fully during the second wave of Asian American immigration.

First, led by intellectuals and foreign policy experts, the American mainstream became more tolerant of and informed about Asian culture and religions in the middle decades of the twentieth century. Although Japanese Zen teachers such as Nyogen Senzaki and Shigetsu Sakaki had taught and established centers in San Francisco, Los Angeles, and New York in the early twentieth century, it would not be until the 1950s that Jack Kerouac and other Beat writers as well as Alan Watts "discovered" and popularized Buddhism. Second, immigration from Asia never stopped. The repeal of the Chinese Immigration Act in 1943 allowed 105 immigrants from China annually (this was also extended to other Asians). Furthermore, other exceptions for war brides, refugees, scholars, and students slowly opened the gates for Asians in the 1950s and 1960s. Ironically, the new immigration revitalized a demand for ethnic-specific religious organizations. Most of the founders of existing Asian American religious organizations arrived in the United States during this period. Third, many of the "assimilated second-generation" Protestant Asian Americans during this period repudiated the assimilationist policies of mainline denominations during this period. In the late 1960s and early 1970s, Asian American Protestants, inspired by the civil rights movement, advocated for greater representation in and resources from their denominations. Caucuses were formed amid a growing Asian American consciousness. Even as they noted the impact of a rapidly growing "second wave" of Asian immigration population, neither the caucus leaders nor the mainline Protestant denominations were prepared for the explosion of ethnic and religious diversity in the 1980s and 1990s.

THE SECOND WAVE

The growth and diversity of Asian American religions since 1965 have paralleled overall changes in the Asian American population. Asian American Christians have become much more visible during the past three decades. While an overwhelming majority of Filipino Americans and a large minority of Vietnamese Americans identify as Roman Catholic, these communities have a small Protestant presence. But the more than 3,000 Korean, more than 1,000 Chinese, and hundreds of other second-wave Asian and Pacific American congregations today are predominantly evangelical and/or Pentecostal-charismatic in orientation. Unlike the first-wave Asian American Protestants, who maintained close ties to mainline Protestant denominations, those of the second wave exhibit stronger independent and "separatist" tendencies. The "separatist" evangelical-Pentecostal characteristics of most second-wave Asian American Protestants can be traced to a number of sources. The continuing presence of fundamentalist and evangelical missionary work that continued throughout mid-twentieth century influenced at least one generation of immigrants. Also, the "separatist" evangelical and Pentecostal identity provided stronger popular religious resources to weather the dramatic transformations in twentieth-century Asia. Finally, many of the second-wave Asian immigrants easily incorporated their indigenous expressions of faith into the evangelical revivalism that they were exposed to.

Sociological studies of second-wave Asian American religions have increased markedly in the past twenty years. These are influenced by racialization, postcolonial, diasporic, and transnational theories. A number of studies of intergenerational transition or second-generation Asian American religions have also been published very recently, but very few historical studies of the second-wave communities. Historians can contribute to the study of second-wave Asian American religions by emphasizing continuity and change in religious communities and organizations as well as developing biographical studies of significant individuals. They can also highlight the interactions of these communities with broader American, Asian, and, indeed, global historic movements and contexts. Finally, they can offer comparative frameworks to help track the similarities and differences among second-wave Asian American religious communities. The future of the history of Asian American religions holds great promise.

REFERENCES

Burns, Jeffrey, Ellen Skerrett, and Joseph M. White, eds. *Keeping Faith: European and Asian Catholic Immigrants.* Maryknoll, N.Y.: Orbis Books, 2000.

Cadge, Wendy. *Heartwood: The First Generation of Theravada Buddhism in America.* Chicago: University of Chicago Press, 2005.

Carnes, Tony, and Fenggeng Yang. *Asian American Religions: The Making and Remaking of Borders and Boundaries.* New York: New York University Press, 2004.

Chan, Sucheng. *Asian Americans: An Interpretive History.* Boston: Twayne, 1991.

——. *This Bittersweet Soil: The Chinese in California Agriculture, 1860–1910.* Berkeley: University of California Press, 1987.

Chang, Derek. *Citizens of a Christian Nation: Evangelical Missions and the Problem of Race in the Nineteenth Century.* Philadelphia: University of Pennsylvania Press, 2010.

Ecklund, Elaine Howard. *Korean American Evangelicals: New Models for Civic Life.* New York: Oxford University Press, 2006.

Fenton, John Y. *South Asian Religions in the Americas: An Annotated Bibliography of Immigrant Religious Traditions.* Westport, Conn.: Greenwood Press, 1995.

——. *Transplanting Religious Traditions: Asian Indians in America.* Westport, Conn.: Praeger, 1988.

Guillermo, Artermio R., ed. *Churches Aflame: Asian Americans and United Methodism.* Nashville, Tenn.: Abingdon, 1991.

Hawley, John Stratton, and Gurinder Singh Mann, eds. *Studying the Sikhs: Issues for North America.* Albany: State University of New York Press, 1993.

Hayashi, Brian. *"For the Sake of Our Japanese Brethren": Assimilation, Nationalism, and Protestantism Among the Japanese of Los Angeles, 1895–1942.* Stanford, Calif.: Stanford University Press, 1995.

Iwamura, Jane, and Paul Spickard. *Revealing the Sacred in Asian and Pacific America.* New York: Routledge, 2003.

Jeung, Russell. *Faithful Generations: Race and New Asian American Churches.* New Brunswick, N.J.: Rutgers University Press, 2005.

Joshi, Khyati Y. *New Roots in America's Sacred Ground: Religion, Race, and Ethnicity in Indian America.* New Brunswick, N.J.: Rutgers University Press, 2006.

Kim, Rebecca Y. *God's New Whiz Kids? Korean American Evangelicals on Campus.* New York: New York University Press, 2006.

Kurien, Prema A. *A Place at the Multicultural Table: The Development of an American Hinduism*. New Brunswick, N.J.: Rutgers University Press, 2007.

Laderman, Gary, and León, Luis, eds. *Religion and American Cultures: An Encyclopedia of Traditions, Diversity, and Popular Expressions*. Santa Barbara, Calif.: ABC-CLIO, 2003.

Mann, Gurinder Singh, Paul David Numrich, and Raymond B. Williams. *Buddhists, Hindus, and Sikhs in America: A Short History*. New York: Oxford University Press, 2007.

Mark, Diane Mai Lin. *Seasons of Light: The History of Chinese Christian Churches in Hawaii*. Honolulu: Chinese Christian Association of Hawaii, 1989.

Matsuoka, Fumitaka. *Out of Silence: Emerging Themes in Asian American Churches*. Cleveland: United Church Press, 1995.

Min, Pyong Gap, and Jung Ha Kim, eds. *Religions in Asian America: Building Faith Communities*. Walnut Creek, Calif.: AltaMira Press, 2002.

Okihiro, Gary Y. *Cane Fires: The Anti-Japanese Movement in Hawaii, 1865–1945*. Philadelphia: Temple University Press, 1991.

——. *Margins and Mainstreams: Asians in American History and Culture*. Seattle: University of Washington Press, 1994.

Pascoe, Peggy. *Relations of Rescue: The Search for Female Moral Authority in the American West, 1874–1939*. New York: Oxford University Press, 1990.

Phan, Peter. *Vietnamese-American Catholics*. Mahwah, N.J.: Paulist Press, 2005.

Prebish, Charles, and Kenneth Tanaka, eds. *The Faces of Buddhism in America*. Berkeley: University of California Press, 1998.

Takaki, Ronald. *Strangers from a Different Shore*. Boston: Little, Brown, 1989.

Tuck, Donald R. *Buddhist Churches of America: J do Shinsh* . Studies in American Religion 28. Lewiston, N.Y.: Mellen, 1987.

Tweed, Thomas A., and Stephen Prothero, eds. *Asian Religions in America: A Documentary History*. New York: Oxford University Press, 1999.

Williams, Duncan, and Christopher Queen, eds. *American Buddhism: Methods and Findings in Recent Scholarship*. London: Curzon Press, 1998.

Williams, Raymond Brady. *Christian Pluralism in the United States: The Indian Immigrant Experience*. New York: Cambridge University Press, 1996.

——. *Religions of Immigrants from India and Pakistan: New Threads in the American Tapestry*. New York: Cambridge University Press, 1988.

Yoo, David K. *Contentious Spirits: Religion in Korean American History, 1903–1945*. Stanford, Calif.: Stanford University Press, 2010.

——. *Growing Up Nisei: Race, Generation, and Culture Among Japanese Americans of California, 1924–49*. Urbana: University of Illinois Press, 2000.

——, ed. *New Spiritual Homes: Religion and Asian Americans*. Honolulu: University of Hawai'i Press, 1999.

13. ALTERNATIVE RELIGIOUS MOVEMENTS IN AMERICAN HISTORY

STEPHEN J. STEIN

Any account of the manifold alternative religious movements in American history must begin with a series of reflections on the diverse terms used to identify such movements over the course of several centuries. Among the variety of terms employed, perhaps the clearest is "sect," which derives from the Latin verb *sequor*, meaning "to follow or attend to." Religious sects traditionally have been defined as persons or groups following an individual leader or adhering to a set of distinctive principles. Often the term has been employed for groups breaking away from prevailing religious patterns and following alternative leaders or doctrines. The term "sect" can also be used outside the framework of religion.

Historians and sociologists who have studied sects or alternative religious movements in American history have attempted to identify the principal elements that set such groups apart from other religious communities. That attempt has resulted in the use of several adjectives that have taken on a substantive quality and have resulted in new terminology applied to such movements. Among the common adjectives employed are "dissenting," "outsider," "emergent," "fringe," "marginal," and "alternative." Each of these words conveys the sense of a contrasting relationship between the religious groups so designated and the dominant, mainstream, or majority religious groups in a particular locale, region, or nation. With the passage of time, these adjectives have become substantive categories conveying diverse implications with respect to the religious movements under discussion.

Two other terms commonly employed for such religious movements require additional commentary. One word with a long history is "cult," a designation derived from the Latin verb *colere*, meaning "to till" or "to cultivate." The same agricultural verb was also used when implying "to care for," "to honor," or "to respect." Employed as a noun in a religious context, "cult" designated a system of worship or ritual, such as the "cult" of Apollo in ancient Greece. In more recent times, the term has taken on a sense of extreme or undue attachment to a person or a principle. When employed in a religious context, it has been interpreted commonly in a negative fashion, declaring such attachment excessive or potentially abusive. Because "cult" was used widely as a very negative term in the closing decades of the twentieth century, scholars working in the field of alternative religions have created another category for groups that might be designated sects, cults, or one of the other terms. The new category is "New Religious Movements" (NRMs). This term, first used by sociologists, conveys some of the qualities linked to the other terminology, but it does so without a pejorative ring. Interestingly, NRMs can be quite "old," some having existed for decades or longer. The category implies something "new" or different about the religious movements in question, but it does so without precision, prejudice, or negativity. The phrase "New Religious Movements" has a kind of scientific cachet and intentional neutrality. It is important to be aware of the diverse terminology used to reference alternative religious movements.

The academic study of alternative religious movements has evolved over the past several decades. Once it was the province of only a few scholars, many of whom were intent on condemning particular religious groups by contrasting them with mainstream Christian beliefs. Now it has become a fully developed subdiscipline in the larger field of religious studies. Today most of those working in this area are historians or sociologists, and they often utilize theoretical insights from those disciplines in their judgments.

In this expanding context, a number of issues have occupied scholars dealing with these movements. Attention to the character and role of founders and charismatic leaders has been a consistent scholarly concern. In the anti-cult literature, that focus has been a near-preoccupation. The processes of joining and leaving such movements, whether construed as voluntary or compulsory decisions, have encouraged consideration of both conversion and deconversion in NRMs. Description of the membership in such communities is standard fare. At times, the rise and fall of such movements has been linked to violence studies—violence within the communities, violence directed against them, and violence perpetuated by them. Violence, of course, can be physical or psychological. Another area of study sometimes linked to violence involves issues related to sexuality: What rules control sexual relations? Who determines that aspect of life? Are abusive relationships present in the movement? The status of women and children in these movements is another standard research topic, arising because these religious movements often are led by men. There are, of course, notable exceptions to that gender pattern.

America has been a rich seedbed for the growth of alternative religious movements from earliest times to the present. The historical account that follows will examine representative examples of such groups in three time periods: colonial America, the national period (extending from 1790 to 1940), and an international era (from World War II to the present). In all these periods, alternative religious movements prospered but were also controversial. Often creative and contested religious developments were linked to these movements.

COLONIAL ERA

The colonial period of American history begins the story of alternative religious movements formed in response to or dissent against powerful religious forces in both the Old World and the New World. Roman Catholicism exercised religious hegemony in both Spanish and French colonies in America, reflective of the ecclesiastical situations in those two European nations. That dominance was conditioned in modest ways both by the diverse theological and devotional emphases of particular religious orders in scattered missionary locations and by the presence of Native American tribal religious traditions. The Church of England played an equally powerful role in America, where Anglicanism became the established religion in many of the English colonies, including Virginia, the Carolinas, Georgia, and parts of Maryland and New York beginning in the 1690s. The other English colonies were established and dominated by individuals and groups that had left the Church of England.

In New England, the Pilgrims who settled Plymouth in 1620 and the Puritans who founded Massachusetts Bay in 1630 dissented against the Anglican community. The issues over which they disagreed with the Church of England included patterns of worship, matters of authority, the role of tradition, and the need for continuing reform. In New England's first colonies, dissenters therefore occupied the dominant or majority religious position and exercised political sovereignty. But that situation did not prevent new alternative religious movements from developing. Powerful personalities became the foci of new dissenting groups in New England.

In Massachusetts Bay, two dissenters who broke ranks with the colony's Puritan leadership were Roger Williams (1604–1683/1684) and Anne Hutchinson (1591–1643). Williams came to Massachusetts, himself enjoying a reputation as a powerful Puritan preacher in England. Within a short time, however, he took issue with both the religious and the political patterns in Massachusetts.

He rejected the practice of using force to obtain religious compliance. He also believed that religion and politics should remain separate. When Williams was banned from Massachusetts, he left and founded the town of Providence, which became the center of the colony of Rhode Island, the first location in America where religious freedom, or "soul liberty," was a right and where the separation of church and state was maintained. Anne Hutchinson came to Massachusetts as a devout follower of the Puritan preacher John Cotton. She began the practice of presiding over private gatherings where religious issues were discussed by both women and men. Religious and political leaders feared such unsupervised conversations. Hutchinson also accented the role of the Holy Spirit in the life of the believer, downplaying the place of legal traditions in the Christian life. She exercised growing influence on those who shared her views, even claiming at one point that she received direct communications from the Holy Spirit. The authorities in Massachusetts moved against her and her followers, banishing her. The cases of both Williams and Hutchinson confirm the fact that even religious communities founded for reasons of dissent often fear dissent within their own ranks. Dissenting religious communities sometimes give rise to other alternative religious movements.

But New England was not the only region in colonial America where religious dissent took root and prospered. The colony of Pennsylvania was founded in 1681 by William Penn (1644–1718), who—despite a privileged background— was attracted to the dissenting religious views of the Society of Friends, or the Quakers, founded in England by George Fox. Fox, who criticized many of the external trappings of the Christian tradition and who underscored the centrality of an inner spirituality, experienced hostility and persecution. Penn, after receiving a land grant from the king for a debt owed his family, established Pennsylvania as a refuge for English Quakers and for other religious groups being persecuted in Europe. Pennsylvania became a haven for persons seeking religious toleration and freedom, no matter what their particular beliefs or practices. In this case, again, what had begun as a refuge for those experiencing religious persecution became a stimulant for alternative spiritualities that grew up under the tolerant climate of the colony. Religious groups from the European continent that found Pennsylvania a safe haven included Mennonites, Schwenkfelders, Moravians, and the Church of the Brethren. Each of these groups had arisen as a dissenting alternative religious movement.

Evangelicalism is another religious movement that originated in the colonial period. From within the Congregational, Presbyterian, and other Protestant churches in the English colonies, in the 1740s an alternative Protestant spirituality arose that elevated an identifiable conversion experience to primacy within the Christian life. The focus on this spiritual experience, which according to evangelicals became the ultimate measure of a true Christian, brought conflict within the ranks of Protestant Christians. Several new evangelical organizations emerged with distinguishing beliefs and practices. The Separate Baptists, for example, were a product of the evangelical revivals that swept the colonies in the 1740s and 1750s. Baptists distinguished themselves from other evangelical Protestants by their views regarding baptism—who should be baptized, how they should be baptized, and by whom should they be baptized.

One other cluster of outsider religious movements in the colonial era resists exact description. Many of the slaves who were imported from Africa to the English colonies beginning in 1619 brought with them tribal religions and/or Islamic traditions. The adversity they experienced as slaves destroyed the social and religious contexts for continuing those religious traditions. Very little information is available regarding slaves who were successful in retaining and practicing their traditional African religions. It is difficult to know how far any of the slaves succeeded in that retention—whether tribal or Islamic—for the greater their success in this, the more they became an invisible part of the world of alternative religious movements.

The colonial period of American history is rich with groups formed in dissent against powerful religious forces in both the Old World and the New. Dissent gave rise to an expanding variety of alternative religious options available to colonial residents.

FROM THE AMERICAN REVOLUTION
TO WORLD WAR II

The formation of the United States following the War for Independence and the adoption of the Constitution and the Bill of Rights played a major role in the history of alternative religious movements in American history. The two clauses of the First Amendment ended the privileging of any particular religious group or denomination on the national scene and created an open competitive context for all religious communities. In short order, religious groups that were already present in the nation took advantage of the changed circumstances, and other new religious communities also sprang up and prospered.

One alternative religious movement in its infancy in America in 1790 was the United Society of Believers in Christ's Second Coming—the Shakers. Followers of an English immigrant, Ann Lee (1736–1784), who had come to America with a handful of followers in 1774, the Shakers survived the Revolutionary years, which had been difficult because they were pacifists. In the decades following, they drew new members from the ranks of evangelical Protestants, challenging them to pursue a higher form of Christianity. Shakers were celibate and communal, and they regarded males and females as equals. They established villages apart from the rest of American society, and for much of the nineteenth century prospered, even though they experienced hostility because they rejected traditional family patterns and the principle of private property.

The early decades of the nineteenth century witnessed the rise of other new dissenting religious movements, some imported with the waves of immigrants coming to America, others homegrown. Another example of an imported alternative religious movement is the Harmony Society, which was composed of the followers of George Rapp (1757–1847), a German who had left the Lutheran state church over a series of theological judgments. Rapp, a millennialist who emigrated to the United States in 1805, asked his followers to accept a disciplined, celibate lifestyle as well as a communal economy. During his lifetime, the society occupied different sites in Pennsylvania and Indiana. The Rappites never became large in number because of their ethnicity and distinctive lifestyle, but they added substantially to the diversity of the religious options in the new nation.

Among the homegrown alternative religious movements that achieved success in the first half of the nineteenth century were two led by very controversial founders. The first of these is the most successful dissenting religious community to arise out of the American circumstances. The Church of Jesus Christ of Latter-day Saints, founded in 1830 by the prophet Joseph Smith (1805–1844), arose on the strength of his unique claims to divine revelation. (A fuller history of the LDS may be found in Quinn, chap. 19, this volume.) Vaulted into the public eye by the publication of the Book of Mormon, Smith attracted both converts and violent opposition. From its origins in western New York, the Mormon community under Smith's leadership moved successively to Ohio, Missouri, and Illinois. Missionary successes in America as well as in Europe resulted in a rapidly expanding movement. Smith's new revelations, violent encounters with non-Mormon neighbors, and controversies evoked by rumored social experiments led to open conflict and to the ultimate martyrdom of Smith and his brother. Following Smith's assassination, beginning in 1846, a majority of the LDS community under the leadership of Brigham Young (1801–1877) journeyed to the Salt Lake basin. In that location, despite experiencing recurrent and vigorous opposition—including open conflict with the U.S. Army—to the polygamous social arrangements publicly acknowledged in 1852, Mormonism became the most successful homegrown alternative religious movement in American history. Even in that case, however, a dissenting note was sounded. Smith's own family split with the Mormons who trekked westward, rejecting claims about his acceptance of plural marriage. The result was the founding of the Reorganized Church of Jesus Christ of Latter-day Saints, today renamed the Community of Christ.

The second homegrown alternative religious movement with a very controversial founder was the Oneida community of "perfectionists" founded by John Humphrey Noyes (1811–1886). Noyes, a well-educated college graduate, mounted arguments that the path to sinlessness led to Christian communalism or holding all things in common. His hope was that this version of socialism might bring the heavenly kingdom to earth. Most controversial among his ideas was Noyes's extension of the communal principle to wives, a practice identified as "complex marriage." In 1848 the society moved to Oneida, New York, where it enjoyed relative economic success for a time. But the social and sexual side of community life brought unending controversy despite claims by Noyes that they were following the path of perfectionism laid down by Christ. When the controversy over marriage patterns led to legal action, Noyes took flight to Canada in 1879. Two years later, Oneida was transformed into a joint stock company.

In the pre–Civil War period, other alternative religious movements arose as by-products of the Protestant evangelical movement, which was the dynamic engine powering Presbyterian, Congregational, Methodist, and Baptist growth. Energized by revivals that historians have called the Second Great Awakening, many evangelicals immersed themselves in the study of the Bible and especially its prophetic texts. William Miller (1782–1849) was one evangelical who converted to the Baptist tradition and then became preoccupied with the question of Christ's return. Miller's close study of biblical prophecy led him to conclude that Christ would return physically around 1843. He lectured widely and convinced others, who spread the word across the country by preaching and publications. Thousands were persuaded to prepare for Christ's appearance. When a precise dating scheme was established, excitement rose; but then the announced time passed, and disappointment resulted. A recalculation occurred with a new burst of popular attention, but then that date too passed, and the "Great Disappointment" was a reality. At that point, only true believers were able to cope with the situation, but some did. Among the disappointed was a young woman, Ellen G. Harmon (1827–1915), a resident of Portland, Maine. Despite the disappointment, she began receiving visions that reaffirmed the adventist message. After marrying James White, Ellen White spent a lifetime teaching and writing on behalf of the adventist cause. She was the founder of Seventh-day Adventism, a religious movement that focused on the eschatological hope. But White was also committed to a variety of reform causes relating to the present order, including lifestyle changes, healthful practices, and educational issues as well as sabbatarianism, or the observance of the seventh day as the holy day.

Often alternative religious movements in America have reflected a genetic relationship to earlier movements. As the Seventh-Day Adventists were linked to the Millerites, so the eschatological movement renamed the Jehovah's Witnesses in 1931 was connected with adventism. Begun by Charles Taze Russell (1852–1916) as a group committed to the study of biblical prophecy, the community known for a time as the Watchtower Bible and Tract Society examined adventist teachings, including questions regarding the eternal damnation of sinners. Millennialism became another preoccupation of the group, and Russell taught that 1914 would be the year of Christ's return to earth. When that return did not materialize, Russell declared that Christ had indeed returned, but "in spirit" only. The visible return was therefore still impending, but it would occur soon, he affirmed. Subsequent leaders, including Joseph Rutherford (1869–1942), built on the apocalyptic message and organized the Witnesses' visitation and publication activities. With the passage of time, the movement sharpened its critique of American society, declaring many of the religious, political, and economic institutions of the land to be evil. At Christ's return, they declared, those forces of evil will be destroyed in the battle of Armageddon. Then will follow the millennial reign of the saints with Christ. The Jehovah's Witnesses are explicit in their outsiderhood. They do not salute the flag, serve in the military, vote in elections, or accept blood transfusions. They rest their confidence in these matters on the apocalyptic texts in the Bible.

Another alternative religious movement that emerged in the post–Civil War years, the Church of Christ, Scientist, was founded by Mary Baker Eddy (1821–1910). Through much of her childhood and adult years, Eddy suffered mental and physical distress and illness. After years of searching for relief and after trying a variety of nine-teenth-century cures, she found a spiritual answer to her problems in the metaphysical discovery that God is the source of all reality, that God is good, that matter does not exist, and that sin, sickness, and death are illusions caused by erroneous thinking. As both a teacher and an author, Eddy struggled to articulate her insights. In 1875, she published the first edition of her textbook, *Science and Health with Key to the Scriptures*, which became the authoritative statement of her theology and practice. She also built the structures and established the rules that governed Christian Science during her lifetime and in the century following her death. Christian Science, with its focus on spiritual healing and an alternative view of reality, represents one of the more philosophical outsider religious options on the American scene.

Another way in which religious outsiderhood was expressed in the post–Civil War context was through the formation or expansion of religious communities and movements that were largely defined along racial lines. In the world of Protestant evangelicalism, for example, the two black Methodist denominations established in the North before the war, the African Methodist Episcopal Church and the African Methodist Episcopal Zion Church, spread throughout the South. The National Baptist Convention, U.S.A., Inc., was also organized. Many black Baptists also built independent local congregations. Pentecostalism emerged as an identifiable movement around the close of the nineteenth century, often taking biracial form. For example, the black Holiness preacher William Seymour (d. 1923), nurtured in the Midwest on the notion of promoting an apostolic faith, carried that teaching to Los Angeles in 1906, where for three years he presided over a charismatic revival in which gifts of the Spirit were abundantly evident. This outpouring of Spirit, including the gifts of speaking in tongues, healing, and other miracles at the African American congregation on Azusa Street, marked the beginning of a surge of religious enthusiasm and ecstatic gifts that became characteristic of Pentecostalism. Pentecostalism, however, though it attracted widespread participation by African Americans, was not racially defined.

Over the course of the following decades, a number of alternative religious movements that did emerge on the American scene spoke directly to dilemmas faced by persons of color. The economic problems of the 1920s and 1930s formed the immediate context for the emergence of Father Divine (1877?–1965), an African American born George Baker in the South. The founder of the Peace Mission Movement, he presided over a community that attracted both blacks and whites with a gospel of positive prospects and better times accompanied by a series of unique claims regarding his own divinity. Divine declared the nonexistence of racial differences, but his movement drew its primary support and membership from African Americans in need. Another movement that provided similar assistance was the United House of Prayer for All People, founded by Charles Emmanuel Grace (1881–1960), known affectionately as Sweet Daddy Grace. Both Divine and Grace offered material and psychological assistance through their religious centers. Both also drew black and white members into their organizations.

Another group of racially oriented alternative religious movements in the first half of the twentieth century were "outside" in yet another way: they linked their African American constituencies with Islam. Timothy Drew (1886–1927), who founded the Moorish American Science Temple in New Jersey in 1913, preached that blacks were Moors, or Muslims. His movement had several distinctive views, including that Jesus was black. It also had its own sacred text, which was not the Qur'an of Islam. Another African American prophet who emerged in an urban context during the Depression era was W. D. Fard, who circulated in the ghettos of Detroit. When he disappeared in 1934, Elijah Poole (1897–1975) emerged as his successor to lead what became known as the Nation of Islam, a religious and social organization that rested on an explicit anti-white polemic. Poole, as "Elijah Muhammad," led this movement, which challenged the prevailing religious and racial patterns in America. This movement provided a unique forum for the gifted Malcolm Little (1925–1965), who as Malcolm X became the leading public spokesperson for this racially defined fringe movement in the 1950s and 1960s. The Black Muslims, as this group was also called, consciously identified with the "fringe" because of both its religious and its racial positions.

The years between 1790 and 1940 give testimony to the strength and vitality of alternative religious movements in the young and maturing United States. The First Amendment established a context congenial to the inauguration and growth of highly diverse religious groups, many of which have become established and continuing organizations and denominations.

WORLD WAR II TO THE PRESENT

The years since 1940 have witnessed increasing proliferation and growth of new religious movements in America. Several factors have contributed to this acceleration.

World War II opened the United States to the Pacific Ocean and the continent of Asia. Subsequent military conflicts in Korea, Vietnam, and Iraq have intensified the Asian and Middle Eastern orientation. There has also been a massive surge in immigration from countries outside western Europe, a surge that was in part a product of legislation in 1965 that changed the laws governing immigration. In addition, millions of Spanish-speaking immigrants—legal and illegal—have come into the United States during these same decades. These changing demographics have contributed to the expanding growth of new religious movements in the nation.

A long tradition of fascination with Eastern religious thought and religious movements has existed in America, extending back to Ralph Waldo Emerson (1803–1882) and the New England Transcendentalists in the 1830s. But that was at best a limited engagement, with its own ups and downs. One moment of public attention to Eastern religious traditions occurred in 1893 at the World's Parliament of Religions in Chicago. There, for example, Swami Vivekananda (d. 1902) spoke about the Hindu tradition and subsequently played a role in founding the Vedanta Society. Vedanta drew on the Upanishads and stressed the role of meditation. Although the society never became large or widespread, Vedanta has managed to maintain a presence in America through contemporary times. Another Hindu organization, the Self-Realization Fellowship, founded by Swami Yogananda in the 1930s, continued to espouse a universalism that maintains a harmony between all religions, Christianity included. In the 1960s, Maharishi Mahesh Yogi imported yet another Hindu-related movement, Transcendental Meditation (TM), to the United States; its meditative practices profess to offer both religious and psychological advantages. Each of these imported movements had periods of high visibility and intense public interest, often as a result of well-known converts drawn to them or outstanding representatives speaking for them. Prominent figures from the entertainment world and other well-known individuals have often advertised their fascination with such groups. Perhaps the most respected contemporary spokesperson for Asian religions, for example, is the Dalai Lama, who has generated interest in Tibetan Buddhism and support for the cause of Tibetan freedom.

Some imported Eastern religious groups, by contrast, have attracted controversy from the outset. The International Society of Krishna Consciousness (ISKCON), begun in the United States by Swami Prabhupada in 1965, is a striking example of this. He set out to spread the worship of Krishna and by that means to assist devotees in realizing their true identity. To that end, Prabhupada taught the chanting of a simple mantra, "Hare Krishna, Hare Krishna, Krishna, Krishna, Hare Hare / Hare Rama, Hare Rama, Rama, Rama, Hare Hare." This movement went through periods of public and hostile attention, triggered by its own distinctive patterns of dress and behavior and by lawsuits and litigation brought by former members. It has been a sustained object of attention by the anti-cult movement. Other Eastern teachers have also generated attention and controversy. Bhagwan Shree Rajneesh (d. 1990), an Indian spiritual teacher who came to America in

1981, moved across religious traditions in his teachings. Often he was sharply critical of both Eastern and Western religions. He favored the pursuit of truth and
self-realization through a variety of unorthodox meditative practices. Eventually,
Rajneesh purchased land in Oregon and established an ashram where individual
seekers gathered and pursued self-discovery. That community, however, aroused
local opposition and eventually governmental attention. In 1985 Rajneesh was
deported, and he returned to India.

One Eastern alternative religious movement that has provoked little controversy is the Soka Gakkai/Nichiren Buddhist organization, imported into the
United States in the 1950s from Japan. It offers the prospect of self-transformation
based on teachings from the Lotus Sutra. It affirms that each person has the ability to achieve Buddhahood and happiness and to realize a powerful and dynamic
life. One part of the ritual and discipline of Soka Gakkai involves chanting an
invocation that brings harmony with the universe—*Nam-myoho-renge-kyo*, which
means, "I devote myself to the Mystic Law of the Lotus Sutra." Members have
also consciously worked to promote world peace. Ultimately, they hope for a new
world order.

The second major path of immigration since World War II is from the Caribbean and from Mexico and Central and South America. Millions of Spanish-speaking
immigrants—both legal and illegal—have flooded into the United States, bringing
with them a variety of alternative religious movements. From the Caribbean have
come religious traditions linked to the African heritage of the former slaves resident on those islands. Santeria, for example, draws on religious practices from the
Yoruba peoples in West Africa and from Cuban Spanish Catholicism. The world
of Santeria is filled with diverse *orishas*, deities representing all dimensions of the
universe. Priests, or *santeros*, play a critical role in the ritual life of Santeria, which
involves divination, animal sacrifice, and various initiation rites. Family values also
play a critical role for participants in this new religious movement. Members view
participation in this movement as a step toward a better life. Vodou, a combination
of West African religion with elements of Roman Catholicism in Haiti, features
rituals through which sacred power is accessed for purposes of magic, both good
and bad, and healing. Song and dance accompany ritual work by the priests and
priestesses. From similar historical circumstances in Jamaica has come Rastafari,
a tradition that draws selectively on African, Jewish, and Christian narratives and
symbols and is informed by modern political developments. The ideological and
religious mix in this alternative movement includes hatred and hostility toward the
white race as well as preparation and hope for a return to Africa. "Dreadlocks," or
long, matted hair, serve as a symbol of conflict and opposition to white society; reg-
gae music is an expression of the political and cultural message of this movement,
which calls for a new global black religious society.

The 1960s witnessed a burst of new religious movements in America, some
imported from abroad, and others homegrown products. Many of these groups

gained public attention and became the focus of a growing anti-cult movement in the United States. The Unification Church, for example, founded by Sun Myung Moon in Korea, arrived in the United States in the early 1960s. Moon, a visionary who thought that he had been chosen to complete the messianic task of Jesus and who had suffered at the hands of the North Korean Communists, published the *Divine Principle* (1966), a scriptural text for the movement. In 1971 he moved to the United States and took direct control of his church, which attracted intense opposition from the anti-cult movement, especially for its recruitment tactics, denounced as "brainwashing." The formal title of the movement is the Holy Spirit Association for the Unification of World Christianity. That title and the community's accent on marriage and the family, including its public ceremonies for multiple arranged marriages, have aroused intense opposition from Christian anti-cult groups.

But the American "cult problem" gained national and international attention in November 1978 with the mass "suicide/murder" of more than 900 followers of the Reverend Jim Jones, leader of the People's Temple, a new religious movement that had relocated from Indiana to California, and then to Guyana in South America. The social/political odyssey of this community began with participation in the civil rights movement; it ended with a nearly uncritical acceptance of the complete authority of Jones over the life and destiny of the community. The tragedy at Jonestown left an indelible stain on alternative religious movements from that time forward, perhaps even to the present. That negative cast was also the prevailing construction placed on the outcome of the attempted forced entry in 1993 by the Bureau of Alcohol, Tobacco, and Firearms at the communal site owned by the Branch Davidians outside Waco, Texas. The fifty-one-day standoff that followed ended with the death of eighty-six members, including many children as well as the leader of the community, David Koresh. Koresh was driven in his resistance to the federal forces by an explicit adventist and millennialist outlook. This tragic episode reinforced the strongest anti-cult judgments throughout the land, even though the government's handling of the crisis was inept and grossly misinformed. And although the anti-cult movement seemed to need no further proof for its negative opinion—that all alternative religious movements falling outside the bounds of traditional Judeo-Christian lines are dangerous and should be suppressed—in fact it received further confirmation in March 1997 when a new religious movement led by Marshall Herff Applewhite, composed of thirty-nine individuals, took part in a group suicide. This community, known subsequently as Heaven's Gate, aspired to ascend to the "Evolutionary Level Above Human." The appearance of the Hale-Bopp comet became the trigger for implementation of their effort to enter a better world through group suicide. These three tragic outcomes seemingly confirmed the truth of the anti-cult movement's viewpoint, namely, that alternative religious movements were dangerous and should be carefully controlled.

CLASSIFYING CONTEMPORARY
ALTERNATIVE RELIGIOUS MOVEMENTS

The complexity of the category "New Religious Movements" is a final and necessary observation here. No single essay on the topic can catalogue or even point to the full range of such groups. These communities defy systematic observation, as the expanding and sophisticated scholarly literature on the topic documents. This chapter makes no attempt to be systematic; nor is there evidence from the existing scholarly literature that any prior such efforts have been successful. Some authors use geographical points of origin for cataloguing these groups; others employ major religious traditions or groupings to do the same; still others arrange their inventory of alternative religious movements using diverse disciplinary approaches. Almost every systematic effort to chart the world of alternative religious movements closes with some kind of catchall category with no single identifiable feature. There is no canonical system of classification.

Therefore, it may be fitting that this survey closes by pointing to a few additional alternative religious movements that attest the astonishing diversity among such groups and demonstrate how easily they defy categorization. Various expressions of the pagan outlook—a view that reaches back to the prehistoric past—have been given new life in the new religious movements classified as neo-pagan, Wicca being perhaps the most prominent contemporary expression of this in America. Another category that encompasses numerous individual groups is the New Age movement; each of these groups also defies generalization. Perhaps it is the belief in communication with entities of another order that is the most definitive feature of New Age religions, whether those entities are extraterrestrial beings or spiritual beings of another nature. Communication with UFOs, "Ascended Masters," or aliens—as propounded by groups such as the Raelians—is established through channeling, or Spiritualism, as employed by figures such as JZ Knight. The world of Marian apparitions among contemporary Roman Catholics can be considered a somewhat parallel phenomenon. The Internet has become a major tool for recruiting and persuading converts to these diverse perspectives. For some, perhaps the most problematic new religious movement within the field is Satanism, a term lacking clarity of definition that has multiple uses among groups committed to the anti-cult movement. Satanism often evokes the specter of an underground world of criminality and violence.

Alternative religious movements have played a major role in the development of American religious history. These religious groups have been abundant in every stage of American history. They are, however, perhaps more numerous today than ever before. As the population of the United States becomes more and more diverse, there is every reason to believe the religious diversity in the nation will also increase. Therefore, it seems very likely that alternative religious movements will play an ever-expanding role in America's religious future. At the same time, the very fact that we have a catchall term such as "alternative religious movements" suggests the power of mainstream theologies and traditions to define what constitutes the "center" and what is an "alternative."

This chapter has highlighted the irony that what nowadays constitutes the "mainstream" is itself a series of offshoots of what once would have been considered "alternative religious movements," such as the Baptists in colonial-era Virginia, black churches in the nineteenth century, or practitioners of Asian religions. Thus sometimes "alternative" simply means "dissenting," which places NRMs squarely within American religious history. Scholars in the future may ask further how, when, and why groups become "alternative." How do we decide, and who gets to decide, what is the mainstream and what is the margins? Groups such as the Mormons, for example, now place themselves squarely in the "center," but are considered by some conservative evangelicals to be in the "margins." As NRMs become increasingly central to American religious expression, the very question of what constitutes "alternative," and how narratives of religious groups are constructed, will centrally shape scholarship in the field.

REFERENCES

Albanese, Catherine. *Nature Religion in America: From the Algonkian Indians to the New Age*. Chicago: University of Chicago Press, 1990.

Andryszewski, Tricia. *Communities of the Faithful: American Religious Movements Outside the Mainstream*. Brookfield, Conn.: Millbrook Press, 1997.

Bednarowski, Mary. *New Religions and the Theological Imagination in America*. Bloomington: Indiana University Press, 1989.

Bender, Courtney. *The New Metaphysicals: Spirituality and the American Religious Imagination*. New York: Columbia University Press, 2010.

Carroll, Bret. *Spiritualism in Antebellum America*. Bloomington: Indiana University Press, 1997.

Chmielewski, Wendy E., Louis J. Kern, and Marlyn Klee-Hartzell, eds. *Women in Spiritual and Communitarian Societies in the United States*. Syracuse, N.Y.: Syracuse University Press, 2003.

Clifton, Charles. *Her Hidden Children: The Rise of Wicca and Paganism in America*. Lanham, Md.: AltaMira Press, 2007.

Dawson, Lorne L. *Comprehending Cults: The Sociology of New Religious Movements*. Toronto: Oxford University Press, 1998.

Ellwood, Robert. *Alternative Altars: Unconventional and Eastern Spirituality in America*. Chicago: University of Chicago Press, 1979.

Enroth, Ronald, ed. *A Guide to New Religious Movements*. Downers Grove, Ill.: Inter-Varsity Press, 2005.

Fogarty, Robert S. *All Things New: American Communes and Utopian Movements, 1860–1914*. Lanham, Md.: Lexington Books, 2003.

Foster, Lawrence. *Women, Family, and Utopia: Communal Experiments of the Shakers, the Oneida Community, and the Mormons*. Syracuse, N.Y.: Syracuse University Press, 1991.

Gallagher, Eugene V. *The New Religious Movements Experience in America*. Westport, Conn.: Greenwood Press, 2004.

Gallagher, Eugene V., and Stephen W. Ashcraft, eds. *Introduction to New and Alternative Religions in America*. 5 vols. Westport, Conn.: Greenwood Press, 2007.

Hunt, Stephen J. *Alternative Religions: A Sociological Introduction*. Burlington, Vt.: Ashgate, 2003.

Jenkins, Philip. *Mystics and Messiahs: Cults and New Religions in American History*. New York: Oxford University Press, 2000.

Lewis, James R., ed. *Odd Gods: New Religions and the Cult Controversy*. Amherst, N.Y.: Prometheus Books, 2001.

Lewis, James R., and Jesper Aagaard Petersen, eds. *Controversial New Religions*. New York: Oxford University Press, 2005.

McGarry, Molly. *Ghosts of Futures Past: Spiritualism and the Cultural Politics of Nineteenth-Century America*. Berkeley: University of California Press, 2008.

Melton, J. Gordon. *Encyclopedic Handbook of Cults in America*. Rev. ed. New York: Garland, 1992.

Miller, Timothy, ed. *America's Alternative Religions*. Albany: State University of New York Press, 1995.

——. *The Quest for Utopia in Twentieth-Century America*. Vol. 1, 1900–1960. Syracuse, N.Y.: Syracuse University Press, 1998.

Partridge, Christopher H. *New Religions: A Guide: New Religious Movements, Sects, and Alternative Spiritualities*. New York: Oxford University Press, 2004.

Pike, Sarah M. *New Age and Neopagan Religions in America*. New York: Columbia University Press, 2004.

Pitzer, Donald E., ed. *America's Communal Utopias*. Chapel Hill: University of North Carolina Press, 1997.

Saliba, John A. *Understanding New Religious Movements*. 2nd ed. Walnut Creek, Calif.: AltaMira Press, 2003.

Satter, Beryl. *Each Mind a Kingdom: American Women, Sexual Purity, and the New Thought Movement in America, 1875–1920*. Berkeley: University of California Press, 1999.

Stein, Stephen J. *Communities of Dissent: A History of Alternative Religions in America*. New York: Oxford University Press, 2003.

14. RELIGION AND THE ENVIRONMENT

LYNN ROSS-BRYANT

The "environment" has always played an important and varied role in religions in the United States: from the wilderness against which the Puritans struggled to its veneration by John Muir and the preservation movement; from outdoor camp meetings and the Chautauqua movement to National Park campfires and nature walks; from the current "greening" of some American Jewish and Christian institutions to the nature religion of neo-pagans and radical environmentalists. The study of these widespread and elusive phenomena may not fully constitute a field, but the extensive work in this area actively engages many of the current trends in the study of American religions, including especially the theme of communalist visions and that of the sacralization of secular politics, both outlined in the introduction to this volume.

The rather recent interest in studying religion in its cultural and societal contexts has led to a focus on particularized—and necessarily fragmented—studies, rather than "grand narratives" that purport to tell the whole story. The theme of religion and the environment fits well into this approach, both in calling attention to the environment, an element of the story that contextualizes in a particular way, and in lacking a grand narrative itself. The recent interest in "implicit religion" is also well served by this topic, because it requires ways of studying forms of "religion" or "spirituality" that lie outside institutions. The topic also invites studies of how institutional religions cross over boundaries to work together and with secular institutions in the society.

This chapter organizes the story of religion and the environment in the study of religions in the United States around two foci, which often overlap and which build on the current trend in the study of religion of acknowledging the importance of "place"—an element largely ignored by "word"-oriented religions—and scholars. Thomas Tweed, for example, in his introduction to a collection of essays titled *Retelling U.S. Religious History* (1997) (and his more recent *Crossing and Dwelling: A Theory of Religion* [2006]) suggests the importance of an awareness of geographical and social settings in shaping both what the scholar sees and how the religious actors interact with their environments. The second half of his book stresses "Contact and Exchange at Geographical Sites." In *The Transformation of Virginia, 1740–1790* (1982), an earlier version of this approach, Rhys Isaac grounds his narrative of the religious and political transformation of Virginia in the particularities of the environment. Wanting to study religion amid the dynamics of daily life, he sees physical setting as a crucial element in understanding embodied religion.

Building on this understanding of the importance of place, in the first section of this chapter I will look at studies emphasizing the "Americanness" of the environment and the role that "nature" has played in Americans' cultural and religious identity. This approach puts religious studies scholars in dialogue with literary scholars, cultural geographers, and students in American studies. In the second section, I will look at studies that result from religions responding to the environmental movement, which generally yields a more global perspective and puts religious studies scholars in dialogue with scientists, environmental historians, and political scientists. In both cases, anthropological and sociological methods are useful. The second topic requires us to look at how the lines between scholarship and advocacy should or should not be drawn, since most scholars working in the area of environmentalism and religion want—as we all do—to discuss solutions to our "environmental crisis."

RELIGION AND AMERICAN LAND

The importance of the natural world in shaping American religion and culture has been a rich field of study since Perry Miller revitalized the study of the Puritans in the 1950s by focusing on the "Wilderness" the Puritans encountered in the "New World" and how it shaped their theology. This was an alternative to Frederick Jackson Turner's "Frontier Thesis," which Miller considered to be geographic determinism. As part of the myth and symbol school, Miller responded by emphasizing the way the *idea* of the wilderness shaped Puritan thought. This took him a step away from the daily lives of the people in their physical environment, but still offered insights into the development of religion in the environment of the northeastern colonies. Henry Nash Smith's *Virgin Land: The American West as Symbol and Myth* (1950) and Leo Marx's *The Machine in the Garden: Technology and the Pastoral Ideal in America* (1964) contributed to this theme, extending it west, and Sidney Mead's *The Lively Experiment: The Shaping of Christianity in America* (1963) connected the space of the American continent to its political and religious development.

A recent comprehensive study of the importance of American environment in shaping religions in the United States is Catherine Albanese's *Nature Religion in America: From the Algonkian Indians to the New Age*, which asserts the centrality of nature in American religious history, whether as pointing to a disembodied transcendental reality or as providing the rootedness for American identity. It is the tension between this idealism and materialism that links the various movements she looks at, using Native Americans as a model for nature religion—which she suggests may have affected the colonists with whom they came in contact—and then moving through American religious history from the Puritans to contemporary alternative spiritualities. Her readings of Revolutionary times (for example, wearing homespun cloth not only to boycott British products, but also to connect to the land) and the nineteenth-century food and health-care connections with religion and nature are especially intriguing. In looking at contemporary spiritualities, she places the study of American religion in a larger context, acknowledging the increasing influence of Asian religious practices.

The Transcendentalists occupy a central focus in Albanese's reading of American nature religion. Other writers have also explored the long-lasting effect of their connection of nature and spirit on religious thought and practice in the United States. This manifests in the "greening" of late-nineteenth- and early-twentieth-century institutional and popular religion, as seen in hymns, novels, church camps, scouting, and Chautauqua assemblies. All these combine the emphasis on spirit in nature with the sacrality of American nature. Although these developments have been studied as part of American religious history, little has been done with the focus on religion and the environment. Another legacy of the "nature writing" of Emerson and Thoreau that brought together nature and spirit is the lively development of this genre in the past twenty-five years, including, for example, the works of Annie Dillard, Gary Snyder, Barry Lopez, and Terry Tempest Williams. Studies of these writers from the angle of their religious vision have explored the literature in its complex interactions of environment, people, and the sacred.

Discussion of American place and religion invites the application of religious studies resources on "sacred space" and the examination of what spaces Americans consider sacred. It also invites placing the environment centrally in the ongoing debate about "Civil Religion and National Identity" (discussed at length in Manis, chap. 3, this volume). David Chidester and Edward Linenthal's edited volume

American Sacred Space problematizes the "mystification" of space and provides useful tools for analyzing how sacred space is created and contested within a particular social framework; essays in this book include Robert Michaelsen's "Dirt in the Court Room: Indian Land Claims and American Property Rights"; Bron Taylor's "Resacralizing Earth: Pagan Environmentalism and the Restoration of Turtle Island"; and Chidester's "'A Big Wind Blew Up During the Night': America as Sacred Space in South Africa," which probes the global implications of the American view of land.

Adrian Ivakhiv's *Claiming Sacred Ground: Pilgrims and Politics at Glastonbury and Sedona* also positions itself globally, pairing an American and a British sacred site, and explores a narrative—variously identified as "New Age," "earth spirituality," or "neo-paganism"—that looks to earth locations as sites of sacred power for the salvation of both earth and humans. Not eager to demystify, he uses his study of the many religious groups in Sedona, Arizona, as an attempt to develop a model, borrowing a phenomenological approach from anthropology and cultural geography, for studying how such places become sacred to a community and for articulating their "practices of place" in a way that takes into account the community's experiences of sacred place. Meanwhile, *Place and Belonging in America* (2002), by David Jacobson, addresses the "interplay of geographies—moral, social, and physical" in American religious history, utilizing insights from cultural geographers on sense of place and emphasizing the political dimension. He explores physical place and identity in the early republic; discusses the development of national parks and monuments to mediate a unified nation after the Civil War; and brings the theme up to the present, asking the very timely question of how a sense of place—and the connection of the citizenry with American land—has been affected by immigration since 1965.

In "Sacred Sites: Nature and Nation in the U.S. National Parks," Lynn Ross-Bryant also looks at how the national parks became both sacred sites of the nation, perpetually reenacting the New World wilderness, and the sites of inevitable conflicts as the values of a nation that venerated both industrial "progress" and "pristine nature" met and clashed. This wilderness motif is also an inheritance from the Transcendentalists, Thoreau especially, via John Muir, who brought together with spirit and nature the political activism that has characterized the wilderness movement. Cultural geographer Linda Graber studies this dimension of American religious-political culture in *Wilderness as Sacred Space* (1976). She asserts that the only way to understand the way Americans talk about wilderness and make policy decisions related to it is to see the way it functions for them as sacred space. She relies on Yi-Fu Tuan's idea of "geopiety," as evinced in *Topophilia: A Study of Environmental Perception, Attitudes, and Values* (1974). Cultural geographers have provided religious studies scholars useful models for talking about the human experience of place. With this last motif, we see the coming together of American sacred space and environmentalism, which is our next topic.

THE GREENING OF RELIGION

The area of greatest growth in the field of American religion and the environment has been the practice and study of institutions and movements that marry their spiritual connections to the land with awareness of environmental destruction. For many, the impetus for this movement among both religious practitioners and scholars was Lynn White Jr.'s essay, "The Historical Roots of Our Ecologic Crisis." White finds the source of our environmental problems in the dominant teachings of Christianity concerning the relationship of humans to the natural world. Because Western science and technology grew out of the Christian mind-set, they too are infected. He does not reject religion in general or Christianity in particular, but looks to Saint Francis of Assisi, for example, as a model for a less destructive Christianity (acknowledging the positive contribution of Zen Buddhism, but seeing it as bound to an Asian worldview). He firmly asserts that science by itself cannot solve our problems because our religious views shape how we do science. This piece has been remembered as a condemnation of religion, which it is not, by both Christians and Jews (who were also implicated by White's references to the story of Creation) and by the secular environmental movement. Protestants, Catholics, and Jews have all developed extensive environmental programs and very often begin by offering an alternative version to White's.

Scholars also often begin their studies of religion and environmentalism with White's essay, but they take his assertion that religion shapes how we do science and either try to test that idea or use it as the foundation for studying relationships between science, nature, and religion. Scholars in the sciences or social sciences beginning with environmental issues often agree with White and see the necessity of including religion in their studies. The assertion, shared by many, that the joint efforts of religious groups and scholars of religious studies and environmental studies are needed to save the environment (and by some to save the spiritual life of Americans) has shaped the way this aspect of religion and the environment has been studied.

People who study how religions deal with environmental issues probably are looking for answers themselves—as well as wanting their academic work to have influence in the larger world. Nonetheless, it raises interesting questions about what the scholarly role is. It is well accepted that no scholars are "objective" in their work—we all speak from some standpoint, even as we try to work with the material we are studying in the way that will generate the fullest understanding. The question of how much advocacy should be part of our job as scholars is highly contested among the researchers involved in this area.

Two substantial scholarly projects that have addressed this issue as well as at least some aspects of the vast array of connections between religion and nature are the Harvard Center for the Study of World Religions' project "World Religions and Ecology," led by Mary Evelyn Tucker and John Grim (conferences held from 1996 to 1998, and nine resulting publications that appeared from 1997 to 2003), and the two-volume *Encyclopedia of Religion and Nature*, edited by Bron Taylor. Because these projects reflect the "global" nature of environmental concerns, one must search for specific studies of American religion, but together they include entries or essays by many of the people working in this field and are thus rich resources for the study of American religions and the environment. Both also intentionally reflect on the scholar-advocate dimension of this topic.

As background to the Harvard project, we should be aware of the "Earth Charter" document. Drafted at the Earth Summit in Rio de Janeiro in 1992, and endorsed by the United Nations in 2000, it involved the active participation of numerous scholars of religion. In 1996, not long after this process began, Harvard initiated its "World Religions and Ecology" project. Over 600 scholars, religious leaders, and environmental activists came together; the distinction among specialties was not always clear, as many participants fell into more than one category. The decision to include participants from within the religious traditions, including environmental activists, indicated a commitment to a participatory understanding of scholarship. In the series foreword, Tucker and Grim identify the work of the conference as reexamining world religions "in light of the current environmental crisis." Their premise, which they said they share with environmental ethicist J. Baird Callicott, is that "the religions of the world may be instrumental" in helping to solve the crisis. They acknowledge the potential danger of exploiting religious communities, as well as the spotty record of religions in regard to environmental issues. Nonetheless, they assert in a volume outside the series (*Worldviews and Ecology: Religion, Philosophy and the Environment*) that one must look to the wisdom of various religious traditions because, just as biodiversity makes for a healthy ecosystem, diversity is needed in religious thought about the environment.

The project and the volumes are, then, "engaged scholarship" and, for the purposes of this essay's subject, somewhat mixed. Because of the strong emphasis on global issues, the subject of American environment and religion is frequently bypassed.. For example, in the 768-page volume *Christianity and Ecology: Seeking the Well-Being of Earth and Humans* (2000), edited by Dieter T. Hessel and Rosemary Radford Ruether—the goal of which is to "recast Christian beliefs and ethics in terms of their combined ecological and social significance"—the emphasis is on the constructive rather than the analytic side. There is no specific work on American Christianity. Although "eco-justice" is part of the aim, it is only in the final section, on praxis, that "on the ground" studies are found where we get to some particulars of American activities—including one by Larry Rasmussen on organizing in North American communities and one on the National Religious Partnership for the Environment (NRPE), a U.S. ecumenical group that formed after the Rio conference. The volume's strength is that it contains essays by mostly mainline Christian theologians and ethicists who are leaders in the area of Christianity and ecology.

Many of the other volumes in the series are significant in bringing together leading scholars in a tradition, but they are often people who have not had previous interest or background in the topic of the environment. For example, *Buddhism and Ecology* (1998), edited by S. K. Pathak, also includes essays by scholars (and practitioners) who have worked on ecology and Buddhism, as well as a useful section on American Buddhism. *Judaism and Ecology: Created World and Revealed Word* (2003), edited by Hava Tirosh-Samuelson, has an informative essay on the very active Jewish contingent of the NRPE, the Coalition on the Environment and Jewish Life (COEJL), by its executive director, Mark Jacobs. Most of the other essays bring in leading scholars in various aspects of Judaic studies, who have no previous work in religion and environment. This is true with many of the traditions. This does not mean that the essays do not offer "wisdom" from the traditions in relation to environmentalism, for they do. Perhaps even more importantly, the conferences undoubtedly got many scholars not only thinking about these issues for the first time, but also examining their own environmental ethics.

The *Encyclopedia of Religion and Nature*, edited by Bron Taylor, is an ambitious two-volume work that addresses the subject globally, but provides much rich material on religion and nature in the United States, even if in an abbreviated form. The encyclopedia reflects the "practitioner" dimension of the subject by including articles labeled as such, as well as "engaged" scholarly work through essays marked "scholarly perspectives" (though some articles not marked in this way also include advocacy positions). Bron Taylor's essay, "Religious Studies and Environmental Concern," traces the establishment of the field in the American Academy of Religion, noting that many involved feel ethically compelled to do this scholarship. He acknowledges that some in the academy criticize them for "missionizing," highlighting again the issues of scholarship and advocacy. He criticizes the academy itself for focusing on the major traditions of the world and their mainline forms, thus excluding many who are more actively engaged in the concerns of the conference. He also attacks their "idea" orientation, neglecting "on the ground" religion. The encyclopedia fills in these gaps, focusing on Asian and indigenous religions, alternative religions of various forms, and "implicit" religion. Although some attention is given to mainstream religion, it is not center stage.

A smaller project, the *Oxford Handbook of Religion and Ecology*, edited by Roger Gottlieb, combines some of each of the other two, including in its part I the various traditions studied at Harvard, various connections of religion with outside approaches in part II, and religious environmental activism in part III. Together these projects present the issues to be addressed and the extensive amount of material that is there to be studied. Outlets for this research include journals that grew out of the Harvard conference and the encyclopedia project: *Worldviews: Religion, Culture, Environment* and *Journal for the Study of Religion, Nature, and Culture.*

When we turn to journal articles and books, we find several useful analyses of religion's entry into environmental issues. Robert Fowler's *The Greening of Protestant Thought* studies the development of Protestant environmentalism from 1970 (the first Earth Day) to 1990. Fowler contextualizes various forms of Protestant thought on the environment, with attention to differences and similarities among conservative and liberal Christians. His analysis also includes a useful distinction between those theologies holding a "steady state" vision of nature and those emphasizing nature as process.

Other works have explored similar themes, including sociologist of religion Laurel Kearns's study of Christian ecological activism, "Noah's Ark Goes to Washington: A Profile of Evangelical Environmentalism." She makes clear—as Fowler does—both the reality of Christian environmentalism and its presence among conservative as well as liberal Christians. Kearns identifies three models of Christian ecological activism: Christian stewardship, based in the Bible; eco-justice, in dialogue with liberation theology; and Creation spirituality, with a focus on cosmologies. We might want to add eco-feminism and process theology (which Fowler includes). Although there is overlap, the categories are useful for showing the range of approaches within Christian theology.

Using these categories, we can catch a glimpse of the richness of this body of material. The Bible-oriented group would include evangelical environmentalism—for example, Calvin DeWitt and his Au Sable Institute. Eco-justice—an alignment of environmental concerns with social justice issues among many mainline theologians—is seen, for example, in Sallie McFague's *Body of God: An Ecological Theology* (1993), which also shares the concerns of Creation and process theology in weaving a scientific understanding into Christian theology. Thomas Berry and Matthew Fox share Creation theology approaches, and Jay McDaniel is one of many who work Whiteheadian process thought into their Christian theology. Rosemary Radford Ruether's *Gaia and God: An Ecofeminist Theology of Earth Healing* (1992) identifies with Creation spirituality, eco-feminism, and eco-justice; and the book reads like a response to Lynn White as she reexamines classical Western culture to unveil its legacy of destruction in order to move to what is healing in it.

Among the eco-justice literature is *"To Love the Wind and the Rain": African Americans and Environmental History*, edited by Dianne Glave and Mark Stoll, which grew out of the 1991 People of Color Environmental Leadership Summit. Rejecting many of the approaches mentioned earlier, they affirm an environmentalism that is "woven into an overall framework of social, racial, and economic justice." Similarly, another people-of-color group, this one not Christian, came together at the North American Native Workshop for Environmental Justice to affirm both eco-justice and preservation of sacred lands. The publication from this conference, *Defending Mother Earth: Native American Perspectives on Environmental Justice*, edited by Jace Weaver, significantly extends *American Indian*

Environments: Ecological Issues in Native American History (1980), edited by Christopher Vecsey and Robert Venables. A final group that we might put under eco-justice concerns animal rights or animal liberation, a topic that appears here and there throughout most of the literature. Three examples are Christian theologian Jay McDaniel's *Of God and Pelicans: A Theology of Reverence for Life* (1989); essays by eco-feminist writers in *Ecofeminism and the Sacred* (1993), edited by Carol Adams; and *Environmental Ethics, Ecological Theology, and Natural Selection: Suffering and Responsibility*, edited by Lisa H. Sideris, in which alternative "constructions" of animals other than humans are considered.

Some studies have been done of these various contributions in religious thought, but most of the work, even by religious studies scholars, has been constructive rather than analytic. Further explorations are needed in terms of both the ways environmental issues are shifting Christian theology and the resources it may be offering to the environmental movement. Mark Stoll's *Protestantism, Capitalism, and Nature in America* offers an excellent exploration of how Calvinist Protestant doctrine bears on nature and how Protestants have acted on nature in history. Although it is not a surprise that industrial capitalism, with its consequences for the environment, has been influenced by this religious thought, Stoll makes a good case that the environmental movement has also been shaped by the Protestant influence.

Also needed are more studies that examine what this religious thought looks like "on the ground"—how religious people are acting out the relation between religion and the environment. A step in this direction is represented by the abundant sociological studies done in the 1990s that proved or disproved Lynn White's thesis by looking at how people from different Protestant denominations did or did not reflect their religion in their environmental opinions (see, for example, Andrew Greeley's "Religion and Attitudes Toward the Environment"). What may prove to be a more useful approach to studying the environmental understanding and activity of religious practitioners is Sarah McFarland Taylor's *Green Sisters: A Spiritual Ecology*, a feminist ethnographic and historical study of groups of Catholic nuns who have shaped their communities around living in relation to the earth. McFarland successfully argues that the communities combine traditionalism and innovation in a spirituality that encompasses their care for and interactions with the environment.

ECUMENICAL GREENING

Another "on the ground" expression of religion and environmentalism is the ecumenism that is attached to this movement—across faith traditions, within faith traditions, and between religion and science. If Lynn White's essay was an impetus for religious leaders' and scholars' involvement in environmental issues, the spark for the joint endeavors of many groups seems to be the "Open Letter" from Carl Sagan and other leading scientists to religious leaders, appealing to them to recognize that environmental issues involve religious as well as scientific dimensions and to make religious people aware of the role they ought to play (*New York Times*, January 20, 1990). Religious leaders from most major Protestant groups (including African American National Baptists and the Southern Baptist Convention), Roman Catholic, Greek Orthodox, all the major forms of Judaism, and an Onondaga tribal leader responded with a "Summit on Environment" in 1991 and affirmed the importance of both defense of the poor (eco-justice) and care for the earth (sustainable future). Out of this meeting grew the National Religious Partnership for the Environment (NRPE), which broke into four groups for more local work: the National Council of Churches (NCC), the U.S. Conference of Catholic Bishops (USCCB), the Coalition on the Environment and Jewish Life (COEJL), and the Evangelical Environmental Network (EEN). From here, the ideas went to local congregations, with the intent of putting ideas into action. One study of this project is Mark A. Shibley and Jonathan L. Wiggins's "The Greening of Mainline American Religion: A Sociological Analysis of the Environmental Ethics of the National Religious Partnership for the Environment," which employs historical and qualitative analyses to explore how ethics affect institutional culture and are used to justify actions. They have some interest in comparing the four groups, but their intention is not to examine the results of the interactions among them.

The importance of this ecumenical move is also seen in joint publications by members of different faiths. *The Greening of Faith: God, the Environment, and the Good Life*, edited by John E. Carroll, Paul Brockelman, and Mary Westfall, begins with the assertion that the environmental crisis requires a paradigm shift that can come only through religion and that this is the spiritual issue of our time. The compilation includes essays on Judaism, evangelical Christianity, ecumenical Protestantism, and Catholicism, as well as "different voices"—Buddhist, American Indian, eco-feminist, and cosmological. Another volume, edited by R. J. Berry, *The Care of Creation: Focusing Concern and Action*, is ecumenical in another sense, bringing together evangelicals with differing views on the "Evangelical Declaration on Care of Creation," a statement put out to represent the Evangelical Environmental Network (although some evangelicals, like Calvin Beisner, criticize the document). There are also collections like Steven Rockefeller and John Elder's *Spirit and Nature: Why the Environment Is a Religious Issue* (1992), which calls itself an "interfaith dialogue" and includes Christianity as only one of a number of faiths. This quite remarkable coming together of religious leaders around the issue of the environment may well be the central ecumenical phenomenon of our time—and to date it has received little study.

Another area of "ecumenism," as indicated by the scientists' "Open Letter," is the conversation between religion and science and the attention paid by each to

the other. Most of the various forms of eco-theology, including evangelical, actively engage science and its role in the development of their theology. For some, like
evangelical Calvin DeWitt, the emphasis is on the need to acquire the scientific
foundation before asking the relevant theological questions. For others with interest in Creation theology or process thought (such as Sallie McFague and Thomas
Berry), the goal is a seamless weaving of science and religion. Those with a focus
on eco-justice, such as Larry Rasmussen, might use science as a necessary tool to
actualize economic and environmental justice.

From the scientists' side, the statement of the "Open Letter" is affirmed and
scientists assert the necessity of dialogue with religion (see, for example, forest
biologist Lawrence Hamilton's preface to his collection *Ethics, Religion, and Biodiversity* [1993]). The dialogue is also apparent in Stephen Kellert and Timothy
Farnham's *The Good in Nature and Humanity: Connecting Science, Religion, and
Spirituality with the Natural World* (2002), which grew out of a conference sponsored by the Yale School of Forestry and Environmental Studies, Yale Divinity
School, Wilderness Society, and NRPE.

Willett Kempton, James Boster, and Jennifer Hartley's cognitive anthropological study, *Environmental Values in American Culture* (1995), argues for a
holistic view of environmental thinking that includes the belief systems and
values that provide a foundation for attitudes toward the environment. Of particular interest is their identification of the disjunction between what scientists think they are saying and how it is received by laypeople and how this is
related to the cultural models—the constructions—of nature out of which they
are operating. Another example related to the construction of nature that may
indicate a new direction for the study of religion and the environment is David
Lodge and Christopher Hamlin's *Religion and the New Ecology: Environmental Responsibility in a World in Flux*. It brings historians of religion, scientists,
philosophers, and theologians together to consider a model of nature as "flux"
rather than equilibrium.

In a related ecumenical manner, issues of environment and religion have
led scholars in a variety of fields to address concerns of the study of religion.
Joe Bowersax, a political scientist, asserts in "Greening the Divine: Religion, the
Environment, and Politics in 21st Century North America" that studies of environmentalism have neglected the contribution of Christian environmentalists,
and he goes on to analyze a broad range of writers who have been mentioned
here. Interestingly—and contrarily—he criticizes Christians for "accommodating" religion to science. Instead of sounding like secular environmentalists,
they should be making truth claims based not on science, but on their religion.
Environmental historian Thomas Dunlap's *Faith in Nature: Environmentalism
as Religious Quest* offers an interesting variation on this theme as he analyzes
environmentalism as a "secular faith" and imagines a new way of understanding
religion that could build on science to ask the ultimate questions science cannot

ask. In his exploration of U.S. culture, religion, and science, he includes not only Christian thought, but also deep ecology, eco-feminism, and nature writers. Sociologists John Bartkowski and Scott Swearingen look at this phenomenon "on the ground" in "God Meets Gaia in Austin, Texas: A Case Study of Environmentalism as Implicit Religion," their study of the "sacralization of a prized natural resource in Austin," which revealed the implicitly religious character of grassroots environmentalism—a phenomenon that has been largely ignored in research on environmentalism.

ALTERNATIVE RELIGIONS AND THE ENVIRONMENT

The new forms of religion that emerged in the 1960s frequently include a sense of connection with the earth or the sacredness of nature, both of which easily link with the environmental movement's outcry against the destruction of the environment. "New Age" religions frequently have an earth-related component, often through incorporating elements from Asian or Native American religions; Wicca and other neo-pagan groups are "nature religions" by definition; and some radical environmental groups, like Earth First!, consider their protection of the earth to be a sacred duty.

Jon Bloch's study "Alternative Spirituality and Environmentalism" shifts the sociological study of religion and environment away from Christian denominations, using in-depth interviews to demonstrate that spiritual beliefs and their relation to environmentalism can be studied outside religious bodies—an underexplored area at that time and in that field. Bron Taylor's two-part "Earth and Nature-Based Spirituality," which takes this idea and the groups studied much further, argues that although many of these groups might reject the label of religion, they share characteristics of religious movements. He shows the diverse practices and contestations that occur among them, but also argues for their continuities. He also addresses the appropriation of Native American traditions as an issue in many of these groups. Taylor's primary ethnographic work has focused on Earth First!; his "Resacralizing Earth" presents this group as part of a larger movement of radical environmentalism growing out of John Muir's preservationism, deep ecology's ecosophy, and various Asian and pantheistic traditions. In *Beneath the Surface: Critical Essays in the Philosophy of Deep Ecology* (2000), Taylor offers a critique of deep ecology and Michael E. Zimmerman looks at political issues of an "earth-based religiosity." Because "deep ecology" is such a difficult set of ideas or persons to pin down, Taylor's method of studying particular groups and seeing their beliefs in a lived setting seems most useful.

There are many studies of neo-paganism, although not all of them pay much attention to the "nature" side of this nature religion. Margot Adler's early collection of interviews with neo-pagans, *Drawing Down the Moon: Witches, Druids, Goddess-Worshippers, and Other Pagans in America Today* (1979), provides an early glimpse of this field. She assumed an ecological concern in her questions, but found something of a split between eco-activists and those "nature visionaries" who revered the earth meditatively. Sabina Magliocco's ethnographic *Witching Culture: Folklore and Neo-Paganism in America* (2004) includes discussions of the cosmology of her informants, along with their understanding of the relation of humans to nature and their commitment to helping the earth recover. Sarah Pike, in *Earthly Bodies, Magical Selves: Contemporary Pagans and the Search for Community*, not only considers the relation to environmentalism of the community she is observing, but through her ethnographic study also explores their ritual activities as acted out in space. Her model suggests that the way to understand an earth-based religion is to see its enactments in relation to the earth.

I have not given a comprehensive account of either the religious practitioners or the scholars who study them in this chapter. My hope has been to trace the outlines of an emerging, controversial, and lively area of study and to point out some of the many expressions of religion and the environment that are ripe for analysis. In general, this area provides an excellent opportunity to study religion as it is actively involved in the fray of actual events that matter in the world of America and its environment.

REFERENCES

Albanese, Catherine. *Nature Religion in America: From the Algonkian Indians to the New Age*. Chicago: University of Chicago Press, 1990.

Barnhill, David Landis, and Roger S. Gottlieb, eds. *Deep Ecology and World Religions: New Essays on Sacred Grounds*. Albany: State University of New York Press, 2001.

Bartkowski, John P., and W. Scott Swearingen. "God Meets Gaia in Austin, Texas: A Case Study of Environmentalism as Implicit Religion." *Review of Religious Research* 38, no. 4 (1997): 308–327.

Berry, R. J., ed. *The Care of Creation: Focusing Concern and Action*. Leicester, Eng.: InterVarsity Press, 2000.

Bloch, Jon P. "Alternative Spirituality and Environmentalism." *Review of Religious Research* 40, no. 1 (1998): 55–74.

Bowersox, Joe. "Greening the Divine: Religion, the Environment, and Politics in 21st Century North America." In *Religion, Politics, and American Identity: New Directions, New Controversies*, edited by David S. Gutterman and Andrew R. Murphy, 199–220. Lanham, Md.: Lexington Books. 2006.

Carroll, John E., Paul Brockelman, and Mary Westfall, eds. *The Greening of Faith: God, the Environment, and the Good Life.* Hanover, N.H.: University Press of New England, 1997.

Center for the Study of World Religions, Harvard Divinity School. World Religions and Ecology. http://www.hds.harvard.edu/cswr/resources/print/catalog.html#rwe.

Chidester, David, and Edward T. Linenthal, eds. *American Sacred Space.* Bloomington: Indiana University Press, 1995.

Dunlap, Thomas R. *Faith in Nature: Environmentalism as Religious Quest.* Seattle: University of Washington Press, 2004.

Fowler, Robert Booth. *The Greening of Protestant Thought.* Chapel Hill: University of North Carolina Press, 1995.

Gatta, John. *Making Nature Sacred: Literature, Religion, and Environment in America from the Puritans to the Present.* New York: Oxford University Press, 2004.

Glave, Dianne D., and Mark Stoll, eds. *"To Love the Wind and the Rain": African Americans and Environmental History.* Pittsburgh: University of Pittsburgh Press, 2006.

Gottlieb, Roger S., ed. *The Oxford Handbook of Religion and Ecology.* Oxford: Oxford University Press, 2006.

Graber, Linda H. *Wilderness as Sacred Space.* Seattle: Association of American Geographers, 1976.

Greeley, Andrew. "Religion and Attitudes Toward the Environment." *Journal for the Scientific Study of Religion* 32, no. 1 (1993): 19–38.

Farmer, Jared. *On Zion's Mount: Mormons, Indians, and the American Landscape.* Cambridge, Mass.: Harvard University Press, 2009.

Ivakhiv, Adrian J. *Claiming Sacred Ground: Pilgrims and Politics at Glastonbury and Sedona.* Bloomington: Indiana University Press, 2001.

Katz, Eric, Andrew Light, and David Rothenberg, eds. *Beneath the Surface: Critical Essays in the Philosophy of Deep Ecology.* Cambridge, Mass.: MIT Press, 2000.

Kearns, Laurel. "Noah's Ark Goes to Washington: A Profile of Evangelical Environmentalism." *Social Compass* 44, no. 3 (1997): 349–366.

Lodge, David M., and Christopher Hamlin, eds. *Religion and the New Ecology: Environmental Responsibility in a World in Flux.* Notre Dame, Ind.: University of Notre Dame Press, 2006.

Pike, Sarah M. *Earthly Bodies, Magical Selves: Contemporary Pagans and the Search for Community.* Berkeley: University of California Press, 2001.

Ross-Bryant, Lynn. "Sacred Sites: Nature and Nation in the U.S. National Parks." *Religion and American Culture* 15, no. 1 (2005): 31–62.

Shibley, Mark A., and Jonathan L. Wiggins. "The Greening of Mainline American Religion: A Sociological Analysis of the Environmental Ethics of the National Religious Partnership for the Environment." *Social Compass* 44, no. 3 (1997): 333–348.

Sideris, Lisa. *Environmental Ethics, Ecological Theology, and Natural Selection: Suffering and Responsibility.* New York: Columbia University Press, 2003.

Stoll, Mark. *Protestantism, Capitalism, and Nature in America.* Albuquerque: University of New Mexico Press, 1997.

Taylor, Bron. "Earth and Nature-Based Spirituality," parts 1 and 2. *Religion* 31, no. 2 (2001): 175–193, and 31, no. 3 (2001): 225–245.

——, ed. *Encyclopedia of Religion and Nature*. 2 vols. London: Continuum, 2005.

Taylor, Sarah McFarland. *Green Sisters: A Spiritual Ecology*. Cambridge, Mass.: Harvard University Press, 2007.

Tucker, Mary Evelyn, and John A. Grim, eds. *Worldviews and Ecology: Religion, Philosophy, and the Environment*. Maryknoll, N.Y.: Orbis Books, 1994.

Weaver, Jace, ed. *Defending Mother Earth: Native American Perspectives on Environmental Justice*. Maryknoll, N.Y.: Orbis Books, 1996.

White, Lynn. "The Historical Roots of Our Ecologic Crisis." *Science* 155 (1967): 1203–1207.

15. RELIGION AND POPULAR CULTURE

PHILIP GOFF

In recent decades, as American religious historians have turned away from doctrine and belief systems as the heart of the story of religion in America, the study of religion's relationship to popular culture has increased. The purpose of this chapter is to delineate how various schools of thought direct their inquiries at popular culture and how, in recent years, those who study religion in America have seized on those models to help us better understand the marrow of American religious life.

POPULAR CULTURE

The study of popular culture is a rather recent phenomenon that has been accompanied by some significant debates about definition, scope, and method. Its earliest roots might be seen in the literary critical assessments of British scholar Frank Raymond Leavis, who argued in the 1930s for a highly trained, discriminating elite within universities that could preserve the cultural continuity of British literature and life. Set against a "culture of the masses," this defense of what came to be called "high culture" set the tone for much of the discussion of what would eventually be known as "popular culture." Because of its negative connotations from these early conversations, popular culture continued without a basic definition, thereby adding to its expansive meaning once people began to study it seriously.

For much of the twentieth century, popular culture was understood to be anything between high culture and folk culture. While nearly all the terms are debatable, specialists generally regarded high culture as unique, difficult to create, and highly individual. The creations of elite culture aspire to break the boundaries of tradition, challenge common beliefs, and validate the experience of the individual. Its formation is an aesthetic act; that is, it seeks truth and beauty. Because of this, creations of high culture are sui generis self-justifying; its design or message confronts our worldviews and challenges the way we perceive things.

Folk culture, on the contrary, produces handiwork that is "communal" and "anticipated." That is, the creator and audience belong to the same social group, and the creator employs the daily experiences of that group. Whether the subject is music, art, or stories, one might describe the creations of folk culture as participating in a culture of continuity rather than a highly individual challenge to tradition. However, similar to high culture, folk culture audiences are limited to the group in which the creation is made. Neither has extensive influence outside their intrinsic social groups.

Between these two poles exists a vast arena for study: popular culture. Unlike high culture, it is not unique or difficult. Purveyors of popular culture must appeal to the masses inside the margins and employ methods and even messages (at least the apparent ones) that are common and familiar. Unlike folk culture, popular culture cannot be overly personal and tradition-based. While it may relate to everyday experiences, it cannot be exclusively established on them. In other words, while its medium or message may be familiar, popular culture will not limit itself to implicit appeals to tradition in order to draw and keep an audience; rather, popular culture is willing to look beyond what has worked in the past even if it employs tropes that appear recognizable and comfortable. Finally, as its name connotes, "popular" culture cannot too blatantly appeal to special or sectarian interests. High and folk cultures exist within small circles (perhaps even classes) of society; but popular culture must appeal broadly across a spectrum of differences, including regions, races, genders, and religious or political persuasions.

This is why for many scholars, popular culture often assumes the presence of mass media. Even further, while there were at least theoretically forms of mass communication as far back as the sixteenth century with the printing press, and printed texts grew in availability over the next four centuries, many scholars presume that we cannot speak of popular culture until the creation of radio, television, and motion pictures in the twentieth century. This assumption can be limiting, of course, as we try to understand the role of popular culture in any aspect of American life over the centuries. Still, many of the methods formed by scholars of popular culture to study the phenomenon during the twentieth century have proved useful to those who seek to understand it in America's earlier days.

Generally, there are three ways scholars approach the study of popular culture: textual analysis, audience analysis, and production analysis. Textual analysis consists of investigations into both the content of popular culture (arrived at through surveys, such as how many minorities appear in television commercials) and the interpretations of the texts. Often semiotics comes into play here, as mass media attempts to communicate to popular culture through various popular signifiers. Among others, scholars study closely how rhetoric is employed and ideologies are transferred through texts, including such forms of mass media as election-day sermons of the eighteenth century, political speeches of the nineteenth, corporate advertising on radio and sitcom television programs of the twentieth, or political speeches from any period in history.

Other scholars approach popular culture through audience analysis. Again, much of this work presumes mass media's presence and therefore is focused on the twentieth century or current events. In the case of studies centered on current snapshots of popular culture, scholars can employ surveys and opinion polls to measure the reactions of voters, consumers, or fan bases. Such studies help us understand the existence and role of subcultures within the broader popular culture. For instance, by breaking out responses to a large survey, scholars can distinguish among the hopes, fears, and habits of subcultures based on age, gender, ethnicity, economic class, or region. Some researchers, however, leave behind the panorama of surveys for micro-studies tightly focused on one group in popular culture. Through ethnographic participant observation, scholars can learn about and write about the worldviews, behaviors, and habits of subcultures in a manner that teaches us how similar sizable subcultures understand the world and behave in it. In other words, by studying the microcosms of subcultures, ethnographers reveal how aspects of popular culture are translated into the lives of individuals and communities.

Perhaps no aspect of the study of popular culture depends so much on the existence of mass media as production analysis does. Whether the focus is on how mass media culture reflects the values of the producers of that culture or on how constraints in the production processes shape the content of popular culture (for instance, how television forces the role of the visual to the fore), production analysis assumes, perhaps even emphasizes, a media-driven homogenization of popular culture. At least in regard to mass media, production analysis supplements textual analysis and audience analysis by placing popular culture in its larger context of capitalist, profit-driven mass production.

From its beginning, then, the topic of popular culture has been discussed and later studied from various angles. Its amorphous meaning, the result of its earliest usage, has been both its boon and its bane. Because it is a pliable term, scholars (and journalists) have molded it effectively to fit their purposes—which makes it both a popular and a mistreated topic of inquiry.

TYPOLOGIES OF RELIGION AND POPULAR CULTURE

Among the most influential recent studies of the relationship between religion and popular culture is the collection of essays found in Bruce David Forbes and Jeffrey H. Mahan's *Religion and Popular Culture in America*. The book explores the multiple ways these two components interact and influence each other. These essays generally approach the topic through textual analysis and audience analysis, but include some discussion about the authors of and the cultural meaning of texts. Most important, Forbes and Mahan offer a helpful typology for understanding the relationship between religion and popular culture. This section will look at all the essays in that volume.

The first category addressed in the volume, "religion in popular culture," denotes how religion situates itself into its larger context through constant negotiation. Trendy films based on religious themes might be the most obvious example of this. Some of them are explicitly religious, such as *The Ten Commandments*" and *Little Buddha*. In others, the religious themes might be implicit but touch "cosmic chords" in their audiences. The *Star Wars* series, with its Eastern religious premises, is a good example, alongside *E.T.*, with its popular healing character from outer space. And, of course, there are many popular books, especially novels, in which religion and religious characters play a major role. Here Robert Thompson's "Consecrating Consumer Culture: Christmas Television Specials" and Terry Muck's "From American Dream to American Horizon: The Religious Dimension in Louis L'Amour and Cormac McCarthy" lead us into deeper understandings of how religion situates itself in popular culture through the media of television and popular fiction. Likewise, Mark Hulsether's essay "Like a Sermon: Popular Religion in Madonna Videos" relates how new forms of visual and musical media connote religious images and act as sermons in modern culture. Meanwhile, Jane Iwamura shows how, through film, the image of the Oriental monk "reflects a disillusionment with Western frameworks, and the hopes and fears attached with the alternative spiritualities of the East" ("The Oriental Monk in Western Culture," 37).

The negotiations taking place between religion and popular culture are truly two-way. Just as religion appears in popular culture, so popular culture infiltrates religion, as addressed in part II of the volume. Indeed, there are many and ubiquitous examples of this, especially among proselytizing forms of religion, which ironically tend to make appeals to popular culture in an attempt to save it from its evil ways. The recent phenomenon of "Christian rock" music is but the latest instance of this. A great deal of debate surrounded its birth in the 1970s, including charges by "traditionalists" that it introduced "the devil's music" into the sacred halls of the church. But evangelical Christianity's long flirtation with popular forms of music (setting doctrinal poems to tavern tunes to create new hymns) probably decided the winner in that debate long before its outcome was apparent. Today Christian rock musicians and "cross-over" artists win Grammy Awards right alongside the secular musicians—whose music sounds very much like that played by Christian artists. Along these lines, William Romanowski's "Evangelicals and Popular Music: The Contemporary Christian Music Industry" is particularly important. Examining whether evangelism is truly the goal of contemporary Christian music, he concludes that this genre is pitched less at the unconverted than at those already within the folds of the church, with the intention of confirming the identity of its already-Christian audience. Still, the effort of Christian rock to expand its influence has led it to be highly influenced by secular forms of consumer marketing and even the creation of celebrities.

Alongside this, Gregor Goethals indicates, in "The Electronic Golden Calf: Transforming Ritual and Icon," how ritual-driven televangelists have become. Heirs to the iconoclasm and ritual avoidance of the Protestant Reformation, they have nonetheless been influenced by the expectations of the visual medium through which they work and today stand as mass-mediated icons. In "The Cross at Willow Creek: Seeker Religion and the Contemporary Marketplace," Stewart Hoover, a leader in media studies, also observes closely the entertaining but nonetheless seemingly bland world of the megachurch, formed in a world of television and corporate culture meant to appeal to many and discourage none. By examining how the cross is used and not used by Willow Creek, he shows how religion adapts to its culture and admonishes scholars not to discount the depth of faith exhibited in this new type of congregation.

Not only does religion appear in popular culture, and vice versa, but there is reason to argue that, at times anyway, religion itself *is* popular culture, as scholars do in part III of Forbes and Mahan's volume. Those who study this aspect of the possible relationships between religion and popular culture avoid the traditional forms of religion and look instead at how some cultural activities mimic the purposes and social forms of religion. Employing such categories as myth (stories with meaning) and ritual, they argue that some secular activities act in religious ways by shaping the beliefs and values of culture. Here the work of Michael Jindra, in "It's About Faith in Our Future: *Star Trek* Fandom as Cultural Religion," on the rituals and beliefs of those dedicated to the *Star Trek* television series is revelatory. For "Trekkies," the program offers frameworks for understanding the cosmos that are analogous to religion's teaching about the nature and meaning of life. In "Losing Their Way to Salvation: Women, Weight Loss, and the Salvation Myth of Culture Lite," Michelle Lelwica looks at the religious language and rituals of dieting and eating disorders of young women. The "ideal body" is articulated in religious terms (observe the headline "Diet Winners and Sinners of the Year," for instance, in *People* magazine) and with religious zeal. Joseph Price, meanwhile, approaches that cultural phenomenon most popularly associated with this category: sports. To his mind, the rituals and symbols of sports fans—and especially the passionate highs and lows they experience during games—operate like a form of religion, as discussed in "An American Apotheosis: Sports as Popular Religion."

The most important question in all this, according to David Chidester, is what really constitutes religion. Employing various definitions, he approaches baseball, Coca Cola, and rock 'n' roll. "They evoke familiar metaphors—the religious institution of the church, the religious desires attached to the fetish, and the religious exchanges surrounding the sacred gift—that resonate with other discourses, practices, experiences, and social formations that we are prepared to include within the orbit of religion," he concludes. "Why do they not count as religion?" ("Church of Baseball, the Fetish of Coca-Cola, and the Potlatch of Rock 'n' Roll," 235).

Finally, religion and popular culture are analyzed as existing in dialogue with each other. In some ways, this is the "catchall" grouping for topics that do not fit easily into the previous categories that Forbes and Mahan put forward. But it is really more important than that and can encompass a number of issues: religious people can listen carefully to the voices of popular culture and be challenged by them; others may condemn the influence of popular culture; some secularists may view religion as a partner in certain causes. The point is, these are public dialogues between people and the cultures they live in. "They interpenetrate one another, and many of the participants in this dialogue are themselves involved both in a religious community and in popular culture," claim Forbes and Mahan. "For many, however, religion provides an interpretive lens through which culture may be critiqued, and popular culture raises realities and themes that cast religion in a different light." For instance, Robert Jewett's discussion of one of Clint Eastwood's movies in "The Disguise of Vengeance in *Pale Rider*" shows a Christian biblical studies scholar finding new insights in Paul's writings on vengeance in the book of Romans after watching and thinking through this film. Comparing the appeal to vengeance in the film with Romans 12, Jewett plays the interlocutor between Scripture and popular culture and finds both enriched through the experience. In "Rap Music and Its Message: On Interpreting the Contact Between Religion and Popular Culture," Anthony Pinn, meanwhile, runs against the grain of most religious–popular cultural interaction (which tends toward critics applying religious principles to analyze popular culture) by employing blues and rap music to evaluate African American religious explanations of evil and suffering. To his mind, these forms of popular music cast doubt on the efficacy of the theological explanations often used by the black church. Finally, in "Lost in Cyberspace? Gender, Difference, and the Internet 'Utopia,'" Meredith Underwood, a

Christian feminist, examines how women are presented on the Web, as well as how the Web might serve the genders in different ways.

POPULAR RELIGION AND RELIGIOUS CULTURE IN AMERICAN HISTORY

The typologies developed by scholars, as described earlier, are formed around relationships between religion and popular culture as they existed in the late twentieth century. That is, each of the studies just discussed assumes a certain type of relationship based on the development of mass media since the dawning of television and the golden age of motion pictures. But what about colonial America, or the watershed years of the nineteenth century during which so much of our national culture was formed? What about the so-called outsiders with powerfully identifiable subcultures? What sort of relationships have they had with popular culture? Here historians differ considerably.

Many historians studying Catholic and Jewish immigrants see the rise of popular culture coinciding with the waves of new citizens who arrived in the United States beginning in the mid-nineteenth century. R. Laurence Moore argued that the sort of urban entertainment that developed during this period was the creation of the ethnic working class. The work of Robert Orsi proves especially helpful in understanding how a theology of the streets developed in tandem with the struggles of ethnic, economic, and gender differences. In time, Catholics began to use tools of mass media—print culture, radio, television, and motion pictures—to insinuate themselves into the nooks and crannies of American culture. Later, such major motion picture makers as Leo McCarey and Martin Scorsese drew images from the religious world formed by the immigrant experience to give their films the texture of Catholics making their way in a new world. According to historian Una Cadegan, this was in line with a very purposeful attempt to protect a form of democracy in America that best advantaged the otherwise disadvantaged Catholics in a largely Protestant or secular culture.

Meanwhile, several scholars have noted the importance of the Jewish experience, among others, in shaping American popular culture. Works by Neal Gabler, Paul Buhle, and Harvey Pekar have documented the role of Jews in developing popular culture in the twentieth century. Everything from the Jewish experience in vaudeville to expressions of Jewish culture have been studied in attempts to understand this relationship without falling prey to the anti-Semitism that marked early forays into this topic. The powerful struggles between Jewish movie producers and Catholic censors in Hollywood indicated that the common view of a white Protestant–dominated culture was in severe need of revision. Books by Colleen

McDannell on Catholic films, Warren Rosenberg on Jewish comics, and Judith Weisenfeld on black cinema have brought a new appreciation to the ways those traditionally considered "outsiders" exerted a great deal of cultural agency, who often went beyond creating a space for their own subculture to actually shape broader American culture.

For those whose interests predate modern forms of technology, a powerful model for understanding religion's relationship to American culture can be found in Nathan Hatch's highly influential *The Democratization of American Christianity*. Tracing the development of a democratic form of Christianity in the early American republic, Hatch argues that "the democratization of Christianity, then, has less to do with the specifics of polity and governance and more with the incarnation of the church into popular culture" (9). Popular religious movements during this period expressed a "profoundly democratic spirit" by denying the distinction between clergy and laity, by accepting the spiritual impulses of the laity without subjecting them to traditional theological vetting, and by making Christianity a force for liberating the average person to think and act for himself rather than depending on a trained ministry. Those forms of Christianity that exhibited the optimistic spirit that animated Jeffersonian-Jacksonian politics in popular culture were destined to explode onto the scene on the Western stage, while those who clung to their traditional and authoritative forms of religiosity were doomed to failure.

Hatch's profoundly influential book inspired the next generation of historians to think about religion's relationship to American culture in much the same way. While print culture and stage-shaking sermons were the contemporary form of mass communication (and thus there are some similarities to the approaches of those scholars discussed earlier), the focus was clearly on the ways religion reflected, partook of, or rejected an antebellum popular culture deeply implicated by politics and economic structures. Hatch's work explores the relationship between popular proselytization, spiritual recruitment, and the market economy of religion, a major theme of this volume. Hatch's central insights about the popular origins and theological traditions of plain-folk evangelicalism are further discussed in this volume by Mark Noll (chap. 4) and Douglas Sweeney (chap. 5).

Here the perspective of Clifford Geertz is most useful. The cultural anthropologist with the greatest influence on American historians during the 1980s and 1990s, Geertz defined religion as (1) a system of symbols that acts to (2) establish powerful, pervasive, and long-lasting moods and motivations in men by (3) formulating conceptions of a general order of existence and (4) clothing these conceptions with such an aura of factuality that (5) the moods and motivations seem uniquely realistic (*Interpretation of Cultures*, 4). Religion, then, could be perceived as part of mental states—moods and motivations—that exhibited themselves alongside other cultural forms in symbolic ways. With this understanding, a generation of historians was able to move on to follow Hatch's lead.

But those influenced by Geertz and Hatch were more likely to write about the relationships between religion and popular culture in the years after 1800. Why? It proved difficult to discuss popular culture before the rise of cheap printed texts and the advances in transportation that allowed for the spread of ideas, or, better, the mental states that evidenced themselves as "popular culture." Without this evidence, what early American historians were left discussing was perhaps a cousin of American popular culture, one that also exhibited the DNA of precolonial Europe: "popular religion" and "religious culture."

Appearing at the same time as Hatch's work, David Hall's *Worlds of Wonder, Days of Judgment: Popular Religious Belief in Early New England* approached the religious world of early New England as "a history of the religion of the people, or popular religion" that would illuminate the ways that culture worked (3). "We may think of culture as both ordered and disordered," he asserted, "or, as I prefer to say, ambivalent. It has multiple dimensions: it presents us with choice even as it also limits or restrains the possibilities for meaning" (3–4). Passing by the traditional ways of understanding the Puritans—creeds, catechisms, formal theology—Hall delved into aspects of the popular religion itself, which often pitted the individual against the religious authorities. How did they understand their worlds and live their lives? In other words, what were the moods and motivations that determined the everyday lives of the people we generally typecast as Puritans? Mindful of the differences between the scholarly category of popular religion for premodern European scholars and his New World subject, in his book Hall underscored the role of the "folk," the geography of religion, the relationship between church and state, the appeal of radical religion as well as magic, and the importance of literacy.

In the end, Hall concludes that the fluidity of power in the social structure "limits the significance of 'high' and 'low,' 'elite' and 'popular,' as descriptive of how culture was related to society" (*Worlds of Wonder*, 245). Popular religion in early America has since come to be understood along the lines Hall proposed—as part of a culture shared among the various constituents. The term "popular culture" is generally avoided among studies of this earlier era in recognition of the absence of the types of mass media that are usually viewed as more uniformly shaping the broad culture in modern America. Still, there were at least two media available in early America: sermons and print, the latter a topic on which Hall spent considerable time. Harry S. Stout's *The New England Soul: Preaching and Religious Culture in Early New England*, also appearing in the late 1980s, provided a fresh reading of the importance of the spoken word each Sunday in helping to shape the mental world of the laity. Standing in stark distinction to the printed sermons (which were usually given on special occasions) that had garnered so much attention from scholars are the more than 10,000 spoken regular sermons used by Stout to get into the "religious culture" of New Englanders. Here, then, was another option for historians to follow: despite the lack of mass printing technology, which would not develop until the 1830s, spoken sermons provided a means to shape at least a subculture—the religious culture—of a region.

Armed with the three models provided by Hatch, Hall, and Stout, historians in the early 1990s were able to offer more nuanced studies of religion's relationship to popular culture. Two cases in point are the works of Frank Lambert and Candy Gunther Brown. In *Pedlar in Divinity: George Whitefield and the Transatlantic Revivals, 1737–1770*, Lambert showed how the evangelist George Whitefield employed the developing press in the colonies to advertise his campaigns and shape public opinion before he arrived in a region. Brown's *The Word in the World: Evangelical Writing, Publishing, and Reading in Modern America, 1789–1880* gives a longer view of evangelical publishing to indicate how important the literary world was in shaping this massive subculture's emphasis on purity and hopes of transforming America. Both of these studies employ aspects of popular culture, via Hatch, and of its close cousins, popular religion and religious culture. Scores of other books and articles followed in this vein.

Today we read across the centuries, from seventeenth-century New England to early-twenty-first century North America, and place the work of modern studies of religion and popular culture alongside the concerns of historians without a second thought. But there is a reason we can do this so easily: This postmodern world touted by scholars and some journalists is in fact a not-so-distant cousin of the premodern world of the early Puritans. The symbolic representations of religion in popular culture are quite similar in the two eras. While historians may generally avoid the term "popular culture" when describing early America, modern studies of religion in the United States freely employ the terms "popular religion" and "religious culture" (which tends to refer to a religious subculture). This blurring of the lines, whatever its reason, ironically honors the history of the term "popular culture." Meaning more than one thing, it appears to have a long life ahead of it.

REFERENCES

Albanese, Catherine. "Religion and American Popular Culture: An Introductory Essay." *Journal of the American Academy of Religion* 59, no. 4 (1996): 733–742.

Badaracco, Claire H, ed. *Quoting God: How Media Shape Ideas About Religion and Culture*. Waco, Tex.: Baylor University Press, 2005.

Bivins, Jason. *Religion of Fear: The Politics of Horror in Conservative Evangelicalism*. New York: Oxford University Press, 2009.

Brasher, Brenda. *Give Me That Online Religion*. New Brunswick, N.J.: Rutgers University Press, 2001.

Brown, Candy Gunther. *The Word in the World: Evangelical Writing, Publishing, and Reading in Modern America, 1789–1880*. Chapel Hill: University of North Carolina Press, 2004.

Buhle, Paul, and Harvey Pekar. "Introduction." In *Jews and American Popular Culture*, edited by Paul Buhle, ix–xiv. 3 vols. New York: Praeger, 2007.

Cadegan, Una. "Guardians of Democracy or Cultural Stormtroopers? American Catholics and the Control of Popular Media, 1934–1966." *Catholic Historical Review* 87, no. 2 (2001): 252–282.

Carey, James W. *Communication as Culture: Essays on Media and Society*. New York: Routledge, 1992.

Chandler, Daniel. *Semiotics: The Basics*. New York: Routledge, 2007.

Chidester, David. *Authentic Fakes: Religion and American Popular Culture*. Berkeley: University of California Press, 2005.

——. "The Church of Baseball, the Fetish of Coca-Cola, and the Potlatch of Rock 'n' Roll." In *Religion and Popular Culture in America*, edited by Bruce David Forbes and Jeffrey H. Mahan, 213–232. Berkeley: University of California Press, 2000.

Cullen, Jim. *Restless in the Promised Land: Catholics and the American Dream*. Franklin, Wis.: Sheed and Ward, 2001.

Detweiler, Craig, and Barry Taylor. *A Matrix of Meanings: Finding God in Pop Culture*. Grand Rapids, Mich.: Baker Academic, 2003.

de Vries, Hent, and Samuel Weber, eds. *Religion and Media*. Stanford, Calif.: Stanford University Press, 2001.

Fisher, James T. "Catholicism as American Popular Culture." In *American Catholics, American Culture: Tradition and Resistance*, edited by Margaret O'Brien Steinfels, 101–111. Franklin, Wis.: Sheed and Ward, 2004.

Forbes, Bruce David. "Introduction: Finding Religion in Unexpected Places." In *Religion and Popular Culture in America*, edited by Bruce David Forbes and Jeffry H. Mahan, 1–20. Berkeley: University of California Press, 2000.

Fuller, Robert C. *Spiritual but Not Religious: Understanding Unchurched America*. New York: Oxford University Press, 2001.

Geertz, Clifford. *The Interpretation of Cultures*. New York: Basic Books, 1973.

Goethals, Gregor. "The Electronic Golden Calf: Transforming Ritual and Icon." In *Religion and Popular Culture in America*, edited by Bruce David Forbes and Jeffry H. Mahan, 125–144. Berkeley: University of California Press, 2000.

Goff, Philip. "We Have Heard the Joyful Sound: Charles E. Fuller's Radio Broadcast and the Rise of Modern Evangelicalism." *Religion and American Culture* 9, no. 1 (1999): 67–95.

Greeley, Andrew. *God in Popular Culture*. Chicago: Thomas More Press, 1988.

Griffith, R. Marie. *Born Again Bodies: Flesh and Spirit in American Christianity*. Berkeley: University of California Press, 2004.

Hall, David. *Worlds of Wonder, Days of Judgment: Popular Religious Belief in Early New England*. Cambridge, Mass.: Harvard University Press, 1990.

Hangen, Tona. *Redeeming the Dial: Radio, Religion, and Popular Culture in America.* Chapel Hill: University of North Carolina Press, 2002.

Harvey, Paul. *Freedom's Coming: Religious Culture and the Shaping of the South from the Civil War Through the Civil Rights Era.* Chapel Hill: University of North Carolina Press, 2005.

Harvey, Paul, and Philip Goff, eds. "Popular Religion." In *The Columbia Documentary History of Religion in America Since 1945*, edited by Paul Harvey and Philip Goff, 319–372. New York: Columbia University Press, 2005.

Hatch, Nathan. *The Democratization of American Christianity.* New Haven, Conn.: Yale University Press, 1989.

Hoover, Stewart M. "The Cross at Willow Creek: Seeker Religion and the Contemporary Marketplace." In *Religion and Popular Culture in America*, edited by Bruce David Forbes and Jeffrey H. Mahan, 139–153. Berkeley: University of California Press, 2000.

——. *Religion in the Media Age.* London: Routledge, 2006.

Hoover, Stewart M., and Lynn Schofield Clark, eds. *Practicing Religion in the Age of the Media: Explorations in Media, Religion, and Culture.* New York: Columbia University Press, 2002.

Hoover, Stewart M., and Knut Lundby. *Rethinking Media, Religion, and Culture.* Thousand Oaks, Calif.: Sage, 1997.

Hulsether, Mark D. "Like a Sermon: Popular Religion in Madonna Videos." In *Religion and Popular Culture in America*, edited by Bruce David Forbes and Jeffrey H. Mahan, 77–100. Berkeley: University of California Press, 2000.

Inge, M. Thomas. *The Handbook of American Popular Culture.* 2nd ed. 3 vols. New York: Greenwood Press, 1989.

Iwamura, Jane Naomi. "The Oriental Monk in American Popular Culture." In *Religion and Popular Culture in America*, edited by Bruce David Forbes and Jeffrey H. Mahan, 25–43. Berkeley: University of California Press, 2000.

Jewett, Robert. "The Disguise of Vengeance in *Pale Rider*." In *Religion and Popular Culture in America*, edited by Bruce David Forbes and Jeffrey H. Mahan, 243–257. Berkeley: University of California Press, 2000.

Jindra, Michael. "It's About Faith in Our Future: *Star Trek* Fandom as Cultural Religion." In *Religion and Popular Culture in America*, edited by Bruce David Forbes and Jeffrey H. Mahan, 165–179. Berkeley: University of California Press, 2000.

Lambert, Frank. *Pedlar in Divinity: George Whitefield and the Transatlantic Revivals, 1737–1770.* Princeton, N.J.: Princeton University Press, 1994.

Lelwica, Michelle M. "Losing Their Way to Salvation: Women, Weight Loss, and the Salvation Myth of Culture Lite." In *Religion and Popular Culture in America*, edited by Bruce David Forbes and Jeffrey H. Mahan, 180–200. Berkeley: University of California Press, 2000.

Levine, Lawrence. *Highbrow/Lowbrow: The Emergence of Cultural Hierarchy in America.* Cambridge, Mass.: Harvard University Press, 1988.

Lippy, Charles. *Being Religious: A History of Popular Religiosity.* Westport, Conn.: Greenwood Press, 1994.

Mahan, Jeffrey H. "Conclusion: Establishing a Dialogue About Religion and Popular Culture." In *Religion and Popular Culture in America*, edited by Bruce David Forbes and Jeffrey H. Mahan, 292–300. Berkeley: University of California Press, 2000.

——. "Reflections on the Past and Future of the Study of Religion and Popular Culture." In *Between Sacred and Profane: Research Religion and Popular Culture*, edited by Gordon Lynch, 47–62. London: Tauris, 2007.

Marti, Gerardo. *Hollywood Faith: Holiness, Prosperity, and Ambition in a Los Angeles Church*. New Brunswick, N.J.: Rutgers University Press, 2008.

Mazur, Eric Michael, and Kate McCarthy. *God in the Details: American Religion in Popular Culture*. New York: Routledge, 2000.

McDannell, Colleen, ed. *Catholics in the Movies*. New York: Oxford University Press, 2008.

——. *Material Christianity: Religion and Popular Culture in America*. New Haven, Conn.: Yale University Press, 1995.

McLoud, Sean. *Divine Hierarchies: Class in American Religion and Religious Studies*. Chapel Hill: University of North Carolina Press, 2007.

Muck, Terry C. "From American Dream to American Horizon: The Religious Dimension in Louis L'Amour and Cormac McCarthy." In *Religion and Popular Culture in America*, edited by Bruce David Forbes and Jeffrey H. Mahan, 56–76. Berkeley: University of California Press, 2000.

Orsi, Robert. *The Madonna of 115th Street: Faith and Community in Italian Harlem*. New Haven, Conn.: Yale University Press, 1985.

——. *Thank You, Saint Jude: Women's Devotion to the Patron Saint of Lost Causes*. New Haven, Conn.: Yale University Press, 1998.

Ostwalt, Conrad. *Secular Steeples: Popular Culture and the Religious Imagination*. Harrisburg, Pa.: Trinity Press, 2003.

Pinn, Anthony, ed. *Noise and Spirit: The Religious and Spiritual Sensibilities of Rap Music*. New York: New York University Press, 1993.

——, ed. "Rap Music and Its Message: On Interpreting the Contact between Religion and Popular Culture." In *Religion and Popular Culture in America*, edited by Bruce David Forbes and Jeffrey H. Mahan, 258–275. Berkeley: University of California Press, 2000.

Poole, Scott. *Satan in America: The Devil We Know*. New York: Rowman & Littlefield, 2009.

Popular Culture: Resources for Critical Analysis. http://culturalpolitics.net/popular_culture/.

Price, Joseph L. "An American Apotheosis: Sports as Popular Religion." In *Religion and Popular Culture in America*, edited by Bruce David Forbes and Jeffrey H. Mahan, 201–218. Berkeley: University of California Press, 2000.

Romanowski, William D. "Evangelicals and Popular Music: The Contemporary Christian Music Industry." In *Religion and Popular Culture in America*, edited by Bruce David Forbes and Jeffrey H. Mahan, 105–124. Berkeley: University of California Press, 2000.

——. *Eyes Wide Open: Looking for God in Popular Culture*. Grand Rapids, Mich.: Brazos Press, 2007.

Rosenberg, Warren. "Coming Out of the Ethnic Closet: Jewishness in the Films of Barry Levinson." *Shofar: An Interdisciplinary Journal of Jewish Studies* 22, no. 1 (2003): 29–43.

Schmaltzbauer, John. "Popular Culture." In *The Blackwell Companion to Religion in America*, edited by Philip Goff, 254–275. Oxford: Blackwell-Wiley, 2010.

Schofield, Lynn Clark, ed. *Religion, Media, and the Marketplace*. New Brunswick, N.J.: Rutgers University Press, 2007.

Schultze, Quentin. *Televangelism and American Popular Culture: The Business of Popular Religion*. Grand Rapids, Mich.: Baker Books, 1991.

Stout, Harry S. *The New England Soul: Preaching and Religious Culture in Early New England*. New York: Oxford University Press, 1988.

Thompson, Robert J. "Consecrating Consumer Culture: Christmas Television Specials." In *Religion and Popular Culture in America*, edited by Bruce David Forbes and Jeffrey H. Mahan, 44–55. Berkeley: University of California Press, 2000.

Toulouse, Mark G. *God in Public: Four Ways American Christianity and Public Life Relate*. Louisville, Ky.: Westminster John Knox Press, 2006.

Underwood, Meredith. "Lost in Cyberspace? Gender, Difference, and the Internet 'Utopia.'" In *Religion and Popular Culture in America*, edited by Bruce David Forbes and Jeffrey H. Mahan, 276–291. Berkeley: University of California Press, 2000.

Wacker, Grant. *Heaven Below: Early Pentecostals and American Culture*. Cambridge, Mass.: Harvard University Press, 2001.

Weinstein, Simcha. *Up, Up, and Oy Vey! How Jewish History, Culture, and Values Shaped the Comic Book Superhero*. Baltimore: Leviathan, 2006.

Weisenfeld, Judith. *Hollywood Be Thy Name: African American Religion in American Film, 1929–1949*. Chapel Hill: University of North Carolina Press, 2007.

Williams, Peter. *Popular Religion in America: Symbolic Change and the Modernization Process in Historical Perspective*. Englewood Cliffs, N.J.: Prentice-Hall, 1980.

16. RELIGIOUS CONSERVATISM AND FUNDAMENTALISM

MARGARET BENDROTH

Fundamentalism is one of the most important and one of the most difficult topics in American religious history. Simply put, fundamentalists are "people of the Book"; that is, they uphold a divinely inspired Scripture as the final authority in every matter. Beyond that, the definition is considerably more complicated: scholars disagree over fundamentalism's basic nature, its origins, and its trajectory—even whether it can rightly be called conservative. It is best understood as a form of American popular religion with a deeply ambivalent stance toward twentieth-century modernity, a line of inquiry that promises to move an old and embattled subject area in many different new directions.

The narrative history of fundamentalism begins in the 1870s, with rising concern among mostly northern, white evangelical Protestants about the perceived secular drift of American society. For many, the presenting issue was new scholarship on the Bible, the so-called higher criticism, which appeared to undermine its authority. This methodology, which originated in German universities and filtered into American Protestant seminaries and pulpits after the Civil War, analyzed the biblical text as a historical document, not as a divinely inspired spiritual guide.

Worried Protestants searched for an adequate response. Ernest Sandeen's pioneering study, *The Roots of Fundamentalism: British and American Millenarianism, 1800–1930*, documents the rise of two key doctrines in the emerging "proto-fundamentalist" movement: the inerrancy of Scripture and dispensational premillennialism. His work suggests much about the high theological base of popular religious movements, one of the themes outlined in the introduction to this volume. Inerrancy was associated with a group of conservative scholars at Princeton Theological Seminary, most notably Archibald Alexander Hodge and Benjamin B. Warfield. The Princetonians argued that every word in the Bible was inspired by God; thus the original texts were perfect in every respect. Despite their high view of divine inspiration, Hodge, Warfield, and their followers were not biblical literalists who required blind obedience to the Bible's every word; like other Protestants they made common-sense distinctions between poetic and literal language. But they insisted that every text was equally inspired and equally authoritative.

Dispensationalism refers to a set of teachings introduced in the United States by Irish scholar and preacher John Nelson Darby, a founder of the Plymouth Brethren movement. Darby argued that all biblical prophecies, in both the Old and New Testaments, should be taken at face value; in his view, these passages were not scattered spiritual metaphors but fed into a single narrative of decline, laid out in seven discrete dispensations, or time periods. Although adherents disagreed about the precise timing of events in the last days, and generally refused to set a date for Christ's return, they agreed on a basic framework: the world would undergo a period of Tribulation, to be followed by a thousand years of unbroken peace, known as "the Millennium," and then stand for a final judgment. Dispensationalists also believed that the Bible gave a special role to the Jews and that their return to Israel would necessarily precede Christ's return.

Although the inherent pessimism of premillennial dispensationalism stood in vivid contrast to the dogged faith in progress that had long been typical of American evangelical Protestants, it worked well as a means of rousing the faithful. Because dispensationalists were convinced that Christ would not return until all the earth had heard the Christian message of salvation, they devoted enormous energy to foreign missions and evangelism. Revivalists like Dwight L. Moody and Billy Sunday also injected a note of premillennial urgency into their citywide evangelistic campaigns, urging deeper consecration to spiritual ideals and warning Christians not to place their faith in social reform. Moody famously pronounced the world a "wrecked vessel" heading for sure disaster. "God," he declared, "has given me a lifeboat, and said to me, 'Moody, save all you can.'" This phrase quickly entered the canon of American preaching, a classic example of American proselytization.

Until World War I, fundamentalism existed mainly as a loose network of cobelligerents. George Marsden's magisterial history of the movement, *Fundamentalism and American Culture: The Shaping of Twentieth-Century Evangelicalism, 1870–1925*, charts its gathering force in revival meetings and Bible schools, local evangelistic organizations and national groups like the Niagara Bible Conference. Fundamentalism also found a voice in the growing array of idiosyncratic periodicals, including Arno C. Gaebelein's scholarly *Our Hope*, devoted to the conversion of the Jews, and James Brooke's defiantly titled *The Truth; or, Testimony for Christ*.

Not all religious conservatives were fundamentalists, of course. A growing body of work on religion in the American South demonstrates that, at least before the 1960s, the movement had limited appeal below the Mason-Dixon Line, largely because the majority of Methodist and Baptist churches there felt relatively little threat from liberalism. Although many fundamentalist leaders were born and raised as southerners—including J. C. Massee, William Bell Riley, Mark Matthews, John R. Rice, and J. Frank Norris—in the early twentieth century the movement's strongest appeal was in the Northeast and upper Midwest. There fundamentalism's rhetoric of alienation resonated strongly with many immigrant groups, especially the confessionally oriented Dutch in the Christian Reformed Church and Germans in the Missouri Synod, and the pietistic Swedes in the Evangelical Free Church.

The fundamentalist ethos also crossed over into Holiness and Pentecostal groups, although the exact form of influence is a matter of debate. Although clearly distinct from fundamentalists in social location—members of Holiness and Pentecostal churches tended to be poorer and more racially diverse—they shared a bond of opposition to religious liberalism and to the moral drift of the dominant culture. The two camps also disagreed vehemently over the nature of conversion, with Holiness and Pentecostal groups holding out the possibility of moral perfection, or "entire sanctification," in the lifetime of an ordinary believer. Fundamentalist dispensationalists rejected this possibility, as well as the Pentecostal gift of tongues, which they believed was a spiritual experience intended only for the first-century church.

A recognizable fundamentalist movement took shape under the cultural strain of the World War I years. In 1920, Baptist editor Curtis Lee Laws coined the name "fundamentalist" to describe those Christians willing to "do battle royal" for "the faith once delivered." By then, conservatives in the northern Presbyterian church had already issued a list of five "fundamentals" deemed to be the core doctrines of orthodox Christianity:

- The inerrancy of scripture
- The virgin birth of Christ
- The "substitution theory" of the atonement, a particular understanding of Christ's death as a satisfaction for human sin
- The physical resurrection of Christ
- The authenticity of the miracles reported in the Bible.

The term was also associated with twelve scholarly volumes, published between 1910 and 1915, called simply *The Fundamentals*. Although their content was hardly incendiary, the books found a broad audience, thanks to California businessmen Lyman and Milton Stewart, who distributed some 3 million copies free of charge.

During the 1920s, fundamentalist militancy reached its height, with pitched battles for control of major denominations. The most intense efforts arose among northern Baptists and Presbyterians—Methodists and Episcopalians were generally shielded from the spreading controversy by their hierarchical polity and Congregationalists by their decentralized one. Among Baptists, the Fundamentalist Federation took aim at supposed modernist teaching in the denomination's seminaries and colleges. The Presbyterian dispute centered on control of funding for the foreign mission boards and the leadership of the Princeton Theological Seminary.

Opposition to the teaching of evolution also galvanized the emerging fundamentalist movement into a public crusade. The peak—and end—of this militant phase came with the Scopes trial, conducted in Dayton, Tennessee, in 1925. When a high-school teacher, John Scopes, used a textbook sympathetic to Darwinism, he was charged, brought to trial, and quickly made the center of a national controversy. The "great commoner," William Jennings Bryan, argued for the prosecution on behalf of the World Christian Fundamentals Association, and Clarence Darrow, enlisted by the American Civil Liberties Union, took up Scopes's defense, in a courtroom spectacle relayed across the country by a largely unsympathetic press. *Baltimore Sun* journalist H. L. Mencken took the lead in ridiculing the small-town southern culture of Dayton and the uncritical piety vividly illustrated by Bryan's disastrous defense of the literal truth of Genesis. Although Scopes was convicted and fined (though the penalty was later overturned on a technicality), fundamentalists lost an important public relations battle. In ensuing decades, the movement settled into the American popular imagination as basically rural, southern, and anti-intellectual.

The Scopes trial was only one of a series of bitter reversals fundamentalist forces endured after 1925. In 1929, Presbyterian conservatives, led by Princeton professor J. Gresham Machen, left to form a new school, Westminster Theological Seminary, in suburban Philadelphia. In 1936, they organized a new denomination, the Orthodox Presbyterian Church. Weakened by division, northern Baptist fundamentalists also suffered a series of staged departures, with the General Association of Regular Baptists formed in 1932 and the Conservative Baptist Association of America in 1947. Their agenda in disarray and their beliefs a laughingstock of American popular culture, fundamentalists disappeared from public sight, seemingly for good.

But the reports of their demise proved premature. As Joel Carpenter demonstrates in his account of the years after Scopes, *Revive Us Again: The Reawakening of American Fundamentalism*, many fundamentalist institutions thrived in the midcentury decades. Bible institutes continued to flourish, often maturing into colleges and seminaries; fundamentalist entrepreneurs also learned to adapt new technologies, especially the radio, to evangelistic purposes. During the 1930s and 1940s, Charles E. Fuller's *Old Fashioned Revival Hour* grew to attract an audience of some 15 to 20 million listeners, making it the largest prime-time radio broadcast in the country. After World War II, evangelistic organizations like Youth for Christ steadily increased the grassroots appeal of fundamentalist piety and brought a generation of charismatic evangelical preachers, most notably Billy Graham, into the popular limelight. During the 1950s, Graham's citywide campaigns enjoyed unprecedented success—and gave rise to complaints from old-line fundamentalists unhappy with their inclusive public strategy and upbeat platform technique.

The organization of the National Association of Evangelicals (NAE) in 1942 was an important benchmark in the history of fundamentalism. Rejecting the unyielding separatism of the American Council of Christian Churches, organized in 1941, and the liberal agenda of the Federal Council of Churches, the NAE attempted to unite a new coalition of theologically conservative denominations in direct engagement with secular culture. By virtue of its success, this so-called neo-evangelical revival ultimately sidelined its more conservative predecessors. Staunch separatists like those at Bob Jones University, whose founder imposed strict rules on student social life, and the members of the Bible Presbyterian Church, who had objected to liberalizing tendencies among the Orthodox Presbyterians, looked with scorn on the new generation's positive cultural agenda. But the general flow of members and influence was toward the neo-evangelical camp; in many ways, after the 1960s, "fundamentalism" is not a useful term for describing conservative evangelical Protestants, as it most properly refers to a relatively small faction within that much larger and theologically diverse religious movement.

Indeed, defining the phenomenon known as fundamentalism has been a tricky business. Because the label "fundamentalist" is so often used pejoratively, few people adopt it willingly; most historians recognize the need to use it with care. The most basic disagreements have been methodological. Some students of fundamentalism employ the term as an adjective, in reference to a particular mode of belief that transcends theological or historical divisions between different religious bodies. Thus a Hindu or a Buddhist, as well as an evangelical Protestant, might take on a "fundamentalist" orientation to their beliefs. Religious historians prefer to use the term as a noun describing a specific development within American evangelical Protestantism at the turn of the twentieth century. Although the two approaches are not mutually exclusive, they do point toward some of the ambiguities that complicate scholarly discussion, a difficulty amplified by widespread and inaccurate use of "fundamentalist" simply as a synonym for "conservative."

The Fundamentalism Project, led by the University of Chicago's Martin Marty and R. Scott Appleby, typifies the first, more synthetic approach. The project brought together a large network of scholars, representing a variety of disciplines, and sought to understand the movement in the broadest possible terms. Their analytical starting point was the surprising resurgence of religion in the late twentieth century and its connections to new forms of political radicalism. For many decades, social theorists had assumed that secularization was an inevitable reality and that religion, at least in its public institutional forms, would eventually disappear. Theorists conceded that although more privatized expressions of individual religiosity might survive, supernatural belief was basically incompatible with Western-style modernity. But by the early 1980s, the dramatic growth of religion, especially more dogmatic forms of Christianity and Islam, was changing the face of the developing world. The most explosive increase was occurring in places where, according to secularization theory, modern values would have made their greatest inroads, in cities and among the young.

The Fundamentalism Project analyzed this global revival within a postmodern intellectual framework, alert to the ways in which marginalized communities negotiate the demands of Enlightenment-style rationalism and the modern nation-state. The five volumes in the series sifted mountains of social data, connecting developments in Sri Lanka and Lebanon, Rio de Janeiro and Lynchburg, Virginia. The researchers eventually concluded that even culturally disparate forms of religious radicalism shared basic "family resemblances"—that is, an absolutist mind-set and a militant opposition to Western individualism. Concern for so-called traditional values, especially around the role of women and the sanctity of the family, was not just blind reaction to change, but a means of maintaining protective "enclave communities" where adherents could maintain an uncontested faith within a secular world. The general picture of fundamentalism was of a movement both reactive to change and supremely adaptive to it—in other words, an intrinsically modern phenomenon.

Historians have made fairly limited use of this paradigm. Like some critics of the Fundamentalism Project, they have viewed its ambitious scope with some reluctance, especially the use of a specifically American Protestant term to explain sectarian conflicts in other places around the world. But the more immediate reason historians have generally veered away from this broader theoretical position has been historiographical. Before Ernest Sandeen's *Roots of Fundamentalism* appeared in 1970, most historians attributed the movement to cultural dysfunction; it was at best a side narrative without much explanatory power. This prevailing scholarly view drew from Richard Hofstadter's thesis that "anti-intellectualism" lay behind what he labeled a "paranoid style" in American culture. Early works by Stewart Cole and Norman F. Furniss interpreted fundamentalism as a cultural phenomenon rather than a religious one, a desperate rearguard action by people who resented the explanatory power of science and the diversity of Gilded Age society. These accounts typically highlighted the dramatic confrontations of the evolution crusade and assumed that for all intents and purposes fundamentalism had vanished after the Scopes debacle.

During the 1970s, a new generation of historians led by Sandeen and Marsden began a lengthy and complex investigation into the origins of fundamentalism, convinced that the movement said something important about the larger story of religion in the United States. Their initial strategy was in part defensive, an attempt to convince their scholarly peers that fundamentalism was more than just a dying subspecies of nineteenth-century evangelical Protestantism. For the first time, Sandeen and Marsden presented it as a religious phenomenon worth taking seriously. As a consequence, histories of fundamentalism began to emphasize theological ideas more than the movement's well-known eccentricities and incivilities. The typical fundamentalist that emerged from this scholarship was a fairly undramatic figure: a bookish, spiritually earnest type of white evangelical Protestant, who had relatively little in common with the terrorists and radicals regularly featured in international headlines.

Both Sandeen and Marsden saw fundamentalists as theological innovators. They pointed out that dispensationalism and inerrancy were not "conservative" doctrines—in the sense of being meant to preserve a past doctrinal purity—but were genuinely new. Inerrancy, for example, was an intensification of a more general Protestant position: that the Bible is simply "infallible" in what it teaches. The contention that the Bible is free from all errors of historical, geographical, or mathematical fact served as a rallying point for fundamentalists, Presbyterian conservatives, and many other believers concerned about waning respect for the Bible's authority.

Defining fundamentalism as "militant antimodernism," Marsden added several more layers of complexity to Sandeen's two-tiered explanation. As the title of his book suggests, Marsden aimed to set the movement more firmly within its social context and to argue for its long-term historic significance. He traced fundamentalism's characteristic piety to the British Keswick Holiness movement and the paradoxical teaching that ordinary Christians might receive the Holy Spirit's "power for service" through metaphysical "death to self." He also highlighted the central role of Protestant revivalism, a recurring feature of American religion, but in the late nineteenth century a ready vehicle for the individualistic piety and incipient moralism that shaped fundamentalism's limited social agenda.

But most of all, Marsden reconstructed fundamentalism as a set of ideas drawn from major currents in Protestant thought, including common-sense rationalism and a Reformed Calvinist theory of religion and culture. To be sure, as historian Mark Noll argued in his passionate critique, *The Scandal of the Evangelical Mind*, fundamentalism's narrow pietism ultimately constricted any long-term intellectual inquiry—indeed, in some ways, Noll's work suggested that Hofstadter had been right on the mark. But the strength of Marsden's point—that fundamentalism has an internal logic and an intellectual lineage—recast scholarly understanding and set in motion a new wave of writing and research. Marsden's work highlighted the theological base of popular religious movements.

Marsden's book also raised a host of new analytic questions. He argued, for example, that the fundamentalist experience in the early twentieth century was key to understanding the behavior of modern evangelicals, especially what he described as their ambivalent stance toward American culture. (Marsden traced the connection between the two groups more fully in one of his other major works, *Redeeming Fundamentalism: Fuller Seminary and the New Evangelicalism.*) In his view, fundamentalists were never the group of outcasts they often portrayed themselves to be. Primarily Reformed both in their theological understanding and in their cultural orientation, twentieth-century fundamentalists believed themselves the true heirs of nineteenth-century Protestantism's cultural legacy. Their impulse toward separatism was therefore always mixed with yearning, a conflicting desire to be left alone, but not forgotten.

The argument that fundamentalism—and thereby the nineteenth-century evangelical Protestantism from which it was born—drew from primarily Calvinist roots raised a quick critical response from historians of the Wesleyan tradition, and those who studied its Holiness and Pentecostal offshoots. After all, by the end of the nineteenth century, Methodism had far outstripped all denominational competitors—if anything, the real bedrock of religion in the United States had been laid by John Wesley and his energetic followers. Historians of this tradition, including Timothy Smith and Donald Dayton, argued forcefully that Holiness and Pentecostal traditions deserved center stage, not Marsden's Calvinist Presbyterians and Baptists. Dayton's argument with Marsden was long-running, but partially summed up in his essay on Pentecostalism in *The Variety of American Evangelicalism*, edited by Dayton and Robert Johnston. There Dayton argued that all told, these socially marginal groups exercised far more influence on American evangelicalism than did fundamentalism, which he viewed as a discrete subspecies within the larger evangelical whole. Grant Wacker's *Heaven Below: Early Pentecostals and American Culture* draws an even more distinctive portrait of Pentecostalism, as a movement driven by its unique mixture of organizational pragmatism and full-out experiential supernaturalism.

Other scholars took issue with Marsden's narrative of declension. In *Revive Us Again: The Reawakening of American Fundamentalism*, Joel Carpenter argued that the militancy of the 1920s—for Marsden, the movement's most decisive decade—was really just a passing phase. Once that tumult had passed, fundamentalism reverted to its normative mode, as a form of popular religion dedicated to evangelism and revival. Citing the steady growth of fundamentalist institutions during the World War II era, Carpenter emphasized the movement's spiritual appeal to ordinary people, as a simple message that provided both a unifying cause and a useful angle of cultural critique. If Marsden had pressed the case for the theological base of popular religious movements, Carpenter emphasized the folk origins and popular spread of high theology.

This view of fundamentalism as a popular movement continued a line of argument suggested by Nathan Hatch in a concluding essay to his influential book *The Democratization of American Christianity* (1990). Hatch's study essentially reinterpreted the narrative of religion in the United States, placing the anti-elitist impulse of early-nineteenth-century Methodists, Disciples of Christ, and Christians at center stage; in his view, fundamentalism was a latter-day outgrowth of the same populist stream. Other close studies of fundamentalist institutions, most notably Virginia Brereton's *Training God's Army: The American Bible School, 1880–1940* (1990), also supported Carpenter's contention about the movement's grassroots appeal. Newer studies highlighting fundamentalists' eager embrace of modern technology, including Tona Hangen's *Redeeming the Dial: Radio, Religion, and Popular Culture in America*, also suggest that Marsden's depiction of fundamentalism as "antimodern"—or even somehow "conservative"—is far too narrow. If anything, fundamentalist were far more entrepreneurial and technically savvy than their mainline cousins, who were much slower to adopt their centrist message to the national airwaves.

More recently, debates about the social posture of American fundamentalism have been shaped by the infusion of gender theory. Sandeen, Marsden, and Carpenter focused on religious ideas and institutional leadership—in other words, those social locations where men have typically predominated. But outside of those spaces, fundamentalism takes on a different aspect. Early-twentieth-century fundamentalist spokesmen were notorious for their dislike of "flappers" and modern women, and, as Betty DeBerg first pointed out in her book *Ungodly Women: Gender and the First Wave of American Fundamentalism*, they often used antifeminist rhetoric to state their claim against worldliness and sin. The reinterpretation was striking and quickly inspired a new body of work about women's role. In his article "Women, Public Ministry, and American Fundamentalism, 1920–1950," Michael Hamilton took direct issue with DeBerg, following Carpenter's and Hatch's argument that, as a popular evangelistic movement, fundamentalism opened a far wider opportunity structure for women than did old-line liberal Protestant institutions. Margaret Bendroth's *Fundamentalism and Gender, 1875 to the Present* somewhat split the difference between the two approaches, arguing that although pragmatism often led fundamentalists to downplay gender differences, they also used gender rhetoric to rally the troops during times of cultural stress. The fundamentalists' theology of male hierarchies is clear; what is less clear is their response to women's role within their institutions.

All told, this line of inquiry conflicted with the emerging view of fundamentalism as a popular religious movement ruled by a pragmatic desire to spread the Christian gospel. But the debate is far from settled. A growing body of literature on gender and fundamentalism, now supplemented by a host of cross-cultural studies growing out of the Fundamentalism Project, is still missing close narrative work and critical analysis about women's experience within conservative institutions. A host of interesting questions about the meaning of fundamentalism for women—and for men—await further study.

The general dearth of studies about fundamentalism's rank and file suggests the most promising avenues for future work. In many ways, biographies are still the best sources for understanding its appeal to ordinary people. The

318 RELIGIOUS CONSERVATISM AND FUNDAMENTALISM

group portrait in C. Allyn Russell's *Voices of American Fundamentalism: Seven Biographical Studies*, now more than thirty years old, is essential to any exploration of the movement's history. Darryl Hart's biography of Presbyterian stalwart J. Gresham Machen (*Defending the Faith: J. Gresham Machen and the Crisis of Conservative Protestantism in Modern America* [2003]) offers a "thick description" of the convulsions of the 1920s and William Trollinger's study of Minnesota Baptist William Bell Riley (*God's Empire: William Bell Riley and Midwestern Fundamentalism*) adds a layer of regional analysis to the story of a notoriously rigid but compelling leader. Similarly Dale Soden's *The Reverend Mark Matthews: An Activist in the Progressive Era* covers the colorful exploits of Seattle's "pistol-packing parson" and demonstrates the crossover between fundamentalism and civic reform in the Pacific Northwest.

Attention to regional shades of difference in the national fundamentalist movement has also reopened some old questions about the movement's southern ties. Reacting to the stereotypes perpetuated by the Scopes trial, historians have tended to focus on its growth in the northeastern quarter of the country, in a geographical rectangle anchored by Boston, Philadelphia, St. Louis, and Minneapolis. But more nuanced understandings of northern-style conservatism's inroads into the Southern Baptist Convention, typified in studies by Barry Hankins, Nancy Ammerman, and Paul Harvey, have begun to modify that older narrative, especially with the recent emergence of self-declared "fundamentalists" at the center of denominational politics.

One more important perspective on fundamentalism's internal workings arises out of studies of individual congregations. Early on, Walter Ellis's dissertation, "Social and Religious Factors in the Fundamentalist–Modernist Schisms Among Baptists in North America, 1895–1934," analyzed the membership of the First Baptist Church in Minneapolis. But few other historians have followed this path. Sociologist Nancy Ammerman's *Bible Believers: Fundamentalists in the Modern World* is a classic study of a fundamentalist congregation in Connecticut. Margaret Bendroth's *Fundamentalists in the City: Conflict and Change in Boston's Churches, 1885–1950* (2005) analyzes membership data from two large downtown congregations. But, aside from several recent dissertations, the local picture of fundamentalism is woefully thin. Certainly close research on individual congregations could introduce a raft of interesting questions about worship and spirituality, and belief and behavior, but these avenues remain largely unexplored.

The tools of social history might also invigorate one of the most important and least understood areas of fundamentalism's twentieth-century narrative: its economic and social location. Most scholars have assumed the movement was anchored in the middle class, although others have just as easily alluded to its working-class or lower-middle-class roots. Were fundamentalists in any way "disinherited" by modern industrial capitalism, especially during the Great Depression? Or were they, like many other Americans, reasonably certain of their upward mobility? At present, fundamentalism lacks a social history, and a sustained and careful analysis of these important questions.

In many ways, the historiography of fundamentalism and of the other conservative religious groups it has touched is moving full circle. The first scholarly studies sought to understand it within the general framework of American culture. Hofstadter, Cole, and Furniss began with a master narrative built around political and economic themes, within which fundamentalism provided an instructive parable of social change gone awry. A subsequent generation of historians, led by Sandeen and Marsden, restored fundamentalism's religious identity. They emphasized the centrality of ideas that, they argued, were deeply rooted in a distinctly American theological tradition. Fundamentalism may have had its peculiarities, they admitted, but at bottom it was a system of belief with its own internal logic and rational line of defense. A succeeding wave of scholarship, intent on investigating fundamentalism's grassroots appeal, has been broadening understandings of its religious identity to include the experience of ordinary believers. From street level, the movement's boundaries are blurrier, and the theological taxonomies once useful to historians—differentiating strands of Holiness, Pentecostal, and other forms of conservative evangelical belief—begin to break down fairly quickly. In much of the emerging scholarship on fundamentalism, therefore, cultural and social markers take on new significance. All that remains is to reintegrate this broadly religious narrative of fundamentalism into other narrative strands of American history: economic, geographic, and social. But this time around historians have access to a new set of conceptual tools—from gender analysis to community studies to postmodern theories of culture—that promise new angles on a movement that, at least so far, has never been simple, predictable, or dull.

REFERENCES

Ammerman, Nancy. *Bible Believers: Fundamentalists in the Modern World*. New Brunswick, N.J.: Rutgers University Press, 1987.

Bendroth, Margaret Lamberts. *Fundamentalism and Gender, 1875 to the Present*. New Haven, Conn.: Yale University Press, 1993.

Carpenter, Joel. *Revive Us Again: The Reawakening of American Fundamentalism*. New York: Oxford University Press, 1997.

Dayton, Donald W., and Robert K. Johnston, eds. *The Variety of American Evangelicalism*. Downers Grove, Ill.: InterVarsity Press, 1991.

DeBerg, Betty. *Ungodly Women: Gender and the First Wave of American Fundamentalism*. Minneapolis: Fortress Press, 1990.

Ellis, Walter. "Social and Religious Factors in the Fundamentalist–Modernist Schisms Among Baptists in North America, 1895–1934." Ph.D. diss., University of Pittsburgh, 1974.

Hamilton, Michael. "Women, Public Ministry, and American Fundamentalism, 1920–1950." *Religion and American Culture* 3 (1993): 171–196.

Hangen, Tona. *Redeeming the Dial: Radio, Religion, and Popular Culture in America.* Chapel Hill: University of North Carolina Press, 2002.

Hankins, Barry. *God's Rascal: J. Frank Norris and the Beginnings of Southern Fundamentalism.* Lexington: University Press of Kentucky, 1996.

——. *Uneasy in Babylon: Southern Baptist Conservatives and American Culture.* Tuscaloosa: University of Alabama Press, 2002.

Harding, Susan. *The Book of Jerry Falwell: Fundamentalist Language and Politics.* Princeton, N.J.: Princeton University Press,

Hofstadter, Richard. *Anti-Intellectualism in American Life.* New York: Vintage Books, 1962.

Larson, Edward. *Summer for the Gods: The Scopes Trial and America's Continuing Debate over Science and Religion.* New York: Basic Books, 2006.

Marsden, George. *Fundamentalism and American Culture: The Shaping of Twentieth-Century American Evangelicalism, 1870–1925.* New York: Oxford University Press, 1980.

——. *Redeeming Fundamentalism: Fuller Seminary and the New Evangelicalism.* Grand Rapids, Mich.: Eerdmans, 1987.

Marty, Martin, and R. Scott Appleby, eds. *Fundamentalisms Comprehended.* The Fundamentalism Project, vol. 5. Chicago: University of Chicago Press, 1995.

Noll, Mark. *Between Faith and Criticism: Evangelicals, Scholarship, and the Bible in America.* New York: HarperCollins, 1986.

——. *The Scandal of the Evangelical Mind.* Grand Rapids, Mich.: Eerdmans, 1995.

Russell, C. Allyn. *Voices of American Fundamentalism: Seven Biographical Studies.* Philadelphia: Westminster Press, 1976.

Sandeen, Ernest. *The Roots of Fundamentalism: British and American Millenarianism, 1800–1930.* Chicago: University of Chicago Press, 1970.

Soden, Dale. *The Reverend Mark Matthews: An Activist in the Progressive Era.* Seattle: University of Washington Press, 2001.

Sutton, Matthew. *Aimee Semple McPherson and the Resurrection of Christian America.* Cambridge, Mass.: Harvard University Press, 2007.

Trollinger, William Vance. *God's Empire: William Bell Riley and Midwestern Fundamentalism.* Madison: University of Wisconsin Press, 1990.

Wacker, Grant. *Heaven Below: Early Pentecostals and American Culture.* Cambridge, Mass.: Harvard University Press, 2003.

Weber, Timothy. *Standing in the Shadow of the Second Coming: American Premillennialism, 1875–1982.* Chicago: University of Chicago Press, 1987.

17. CATHOLICISM IN AMERICA

LESLIE WOODCOCK TENTLER

Prior to 1830, Catholics were a negligible group in the American population: no more than 1 percent of the inhabitants counted in the census of 1790 and not much more than 2 percent in that of 1820. Anglo-American Catholics, living primarily in Maryland and Pennsylvania, were still the most numerous, although Irish and German numbers were growing steadily, while Catholics of African descent were a significant presence in parts of Maryland and Louisiana. French Catholics were concentrated in the vast Louisiana Territory, acquired by the United States in 1803, and—in much lesser numbers—in outposts along the upper Mississippi and around the Great Lakes, where pockets of Indian converts lived as well. But the French population was always small. The Spanish missions that formed a wilderness arc from present-day Texas to the Pacific were more impressive, at least in New Mexico and along the California coast, although these were mostly fated to disappear.

Beyond its Maryland epicenter, Catholicism in this period was weak institutionally. A great many Catholics, over half of whom lived south of what came to be known as the Mason-Dixon Line, seldom saw a priest. Catholics like these were frequently married before someone other than a priest, often enough to a non-Catholic, and faced the likelihood of dying without the last sacraments. Some eventually ceased to be Catholics as a result. Certain Catholic outposts in the rural South would prove to be as evanescent as the Spanish missions in New Mexico or the French efforts at Indian conversion on the Great Lakes frontier.

But from this era of small numbers and institutional fragility came strengths that would eventually define a distinctively American Catholicism: a tradition of lay volunteerism, a clergy shaped by the populist currents of missionary circuit riding, and an almost instinctive recognition—even where it was resisted—that Catholic identity could not be the property of any particular ethnic group. The *mestizo* culture that was so singular a product of Spain's New Mexico missions might stand as a metaphor for the American Catholic experience.

Change came quickly after 1830. By the time of the Civil War, Catholics— more and more concentrated in the North and increasingly in cities—constituted the nation's single largest denomination. Immigration fueled this remarkable growth, particularly from famine-stricken Ireland and Germany. It continued to do so into the 1920s, assisted by higher-than-average birthrates even among the native-born. Post–Civil War immigration came from a variety of locales, with the nations of southern and eastern Europe eventually displacing Ireland and Germany as principal immigrant sources. By 1900, the immigrant flood had produced a church of almost bewildering heterogeneity.

Making spiritual provision for this rapidly growing population placed tremendous burdens on the nation's bishops—predominantly of Irish origin, they numbered sixty-nine in 1886—and the priests and religious communities who served under their direction. Despite their relative poverty, those bishops presided over a remarkable story of institutional success, as churches proliferated and the numbers of clergy and women religious continued to grow. American Catholics by 1900 were distinguished by high rates of religious participation—higher, in many cases, than those in the immigrants' countries of origin—and active commitment to a school-building program probably without historical parallel. But Catholics were also contentious—deeply divided by language and ethnic loyalties. Even their episcopal leaders were divided among themselves, especially over issues pertaining to assimilation. To what extent could Catholics embrace American institutions and values? The question, which lay at the heart of the "Americanist" controversy of the 1890s, was given point throughout the period of heavy immigration by recurrent episodes of organized anti-Catholicism.

The end of unrestricted immigration in the 1920s ushered in a period of consolidation for American Catholics, which lasted until about 1965. Catholic religious practice was probably more fervent, and certainly more disciplined, in these decades than ever before or since; the construction of churches, schools, colleges, hospitals, and other social service institutions proceeded at a record pace; religious endogamy was the norm for Catholics in almost every part of the country. Anti-Catholicism ebbed dramatically after its last popular hurrah in 1928, resurfacing after World War II in much-weakened form as the genteel bigotry of a secular elite. Despite a growing middle class and even a small "aristocracy," Catholics as late as the 1940s were a preponderantly working-class population, social mobility for the most recent arrivals having been slowed by depression and war. But after

1945, Catholic upward mobility soared. No religious group benefited more from the G.I. Bill and postwar prosperity. By the mid-1950s, the Catholic population was marked by a new capacity for self-criticism and a new restiveness with regard to the institutional and psychic constraints that structured Catholic experience.

This altered mood among Catholics intersected in the early 1960s with both the presidency of John F. Kennedy and the reforms of the Second Vatican Council (1962–1965). The initial result was a kind of euphoria. To highly educated and committed Catholics, perhaps especially the young, the world then looked infinitely malleable. Catholic success in America suggested a country well equipped to solve its long-neglected problems of race and poverty. Conciliar reform of the liturgy, and especially the council's eventual endorsement of religious liberty, suggested a church well equipped to revivify and purify its enormously rich tradition. By 1965, however, the optimistic glow was dimming, even as the council was issuing its most consequential documents. In part, this reflected a souring political mood at home, particularly with regard to race. But it also reflected the council's failure to address the most pressing problem of the adult laity—the church's ban on all modes of "artificial" contraception. For probably a majority of Catholics, birth control ultimately required hard wrestling with the problem of religious authority and a painful transition to moral autonomy.

American Catholicism since the mid-1960s has been characterized by declining rates of religious participation, a weakened sense of identity, and an unprecedented degree of ideological polarization. Not that these years are all of a piece: the late 1960s and the early 1970s saw the most precipitous change. As many as 10 percent of priests resigned their ministries in these tumultuous years, as seminary enrollments plummeted; the population of women religious, without whom many Catholic schools were no longer viable, declined even more rapidly. The institutional cocoon that had nurtured so many urban Catholics simply ceased to exist: those Catholic institutions that survived the time of upheaval generally refashioned themselves in an ecumenical mode. Catholic rates of religious intermarriage, which leaped upward in the later 1960s, eventually reached levels comparable to those among American Jews, with similar effects on communal cohesion and identity. Weekly Mass attendance declined, albeit gradually, over the course of the 1960s and much more rapidly in the 1970s. By the mid-1970s, moreover, large numbers of American Catholics, once known for the regularity of their sacramental practice, had ceased to go to confession on even an annual basis.

Most of these trends continued in the 1980s and after, particularly with regard to religious observance and vocations. But the Catholic landscape since 1980 has changed in significant ways, at least in the United States. The long papacy of John Paul II provided many American Catholics with a strengthened sense of religious purpose and confessional identity. Catholic immigration—from Southeast Asia, Africa, and especially Hispano-America—reached a critical mass in the 1980s, revivifying parishes in cities and suburbs around the nation and inspiring in many

Catholics a new appreciation for their own immigrant pasts, intimately linked to the church. The diminished ranks of clergy and religious have been generously supplemented since the late 1970s by a veritable army of lay ministers, the great majority of them women. More lay ministers than priests now serve in the nation's parishes. But one could also argue that the period since 1980 will ultimately be defined by scandal—the sexual abuse of children and youth by priests and other church personnel. These widely publicized scandals, which first surfaced in the 1980s, have been devastating for Catholic morale. Speculations about the future shape of Catholicism in the United States must take this fact centrally into account.

Historical scholarship on American Catholicism tends, not surprisingly, to mirror the historical experience of Catholics in the United States. Until very recently, Catholic historiography constituted a remarkably isolated subfield of the historical profession, only distantly connected to debates in the scholarly mainstream. As late as the 1950s, most historians of American Catholicism—nearly always Catholics themselves—were trained in departments of church history and wrote for a Catholic audience. They had their own professional association—the American Catholic Historical Association (ACHA), founded in 1919—and their own journal, the *Catholic Historical Review*, where medievalists tended to take pride of place. Historians of Catholicism were not typically hostile to the larger profession; every founding member of the ACHA was also a member of the American Historical Association, and the two groups have long met annually in joint session. But— again, until quite recently—historians of American Catholicism have understood themselves as working to very different purposes from their secular colleagues.

In the earliest years of the twentieth century, most Catholic historical scholarship—and certainly that on the United States—was unabashedly apologetic. For historians of American Catholicism, this meant scholarly refutation of persistent anti-Catholic canards, principally those having to do with Catholicism's alleged incompatibility with American political values. Catholic historians scurried to find exemplary Catholic patriots in the American past. (Peter Guilday, the dean of American Catholic historians in the nineteenth century, contended that not a single Catholic in Revolutionary America had been a loyalist.) Numerous historians of American Catholicism as late as the 1940s were preoccupied with establishing the impact of Catholic thought on the American founders, as the title of James J. Walsh's *Education of the Founding Fathers: Scholasticism in the Colonial Colleges* (1935) rather artlessly indicates. Still others stressed the importance of Columbus and various French and Spanish explorers for the subsequent history of the United States. Much of this work was naïve; some was tendentious. The best, however, was thoroughly researched and, at least in retrospect, possessed of a certain sophistication. What historian today would deny the continued salience of the medieval heritage for so-called Enlightenment Europe or the multicultural origins of the American nation?

American Catholic history was characterized after 1945 by a new professional-ism and markedly less defensive tone. Emblematic is the work of John Tracy Ellis and Thomas T. McAvoy, C.S.C. That both men were priests is emblematic, too: Catholic intellectual life in the United States was clerically dominated as late as the 1950s, with upwardly mobile Catholics until then having generally opted for business, law, or politics. Both Ellis and McAvoy wrote in an assimilationist mode, reflecting the rapid Americanization of a newly prosperous Catholic popu-lation. American society, they argued, had much to offer its Catholic minority, despite a history of conflict between Catholics and other Americans. Ellis's two-volume biography of Cardinal James Gibbons (*Life of James Cardinal Gibbons: Archbishop of Baltimore, 1834–1921* [1952]) and McAvoy's work on the American-ist controversy (*The Great Crisis in American Catholic History, 1895–1900* [1957]) explored with judicious enthusiasm the rich possibilities of being both Catholic and American. McAvoy and Ellis were not Catholic apologists in the mode of their predecessors. Both were scrupulous researchers, fair-minded weighers of evi-dence, and frank critics of their tradition. Ellis, indeed, is best known today for his indictment of American Catholic intellectual life, which he characterized for a surprisingly receptive Catholic public in 1955 as scandalously underdeveloped. At the same time, both Ellis and McAvoy believed that Catholicism, with its absolute truth-claims, had much to offer a culture marooned in a rising tide of relativism.

Respected members of the historical profession, Ellis and McAvoy aspired to integrate American Catholic history into the broader national narrative. They cannot be said to have succeeded, if only because of an insufficient audience. (That Catholics constituted roughly 25 percent of the U.S. population by 1960 did not enhance their salience as historical actors for the vast majority of American historians.) For professional consolation, McAvoy and Ellis presumably looked chiefly to their students. Young Catholics flooded into graduate schools in the 1950s and 1960s, in eloquent testimony to their families' now-comfortable stand-ing in the middle and even upper-middle class. The brightest and most ambitious usually attended elite secular institutions, as no Catholic university yet possessed anything close to a first-rank scholarly reputation. Ellis's students at Catholic Uni-versity continued to be mostly priests and seminarians; McAvoy had his principal impact on smart undergraduates at Notre Dame, where he taught the likes of David O'Brien. The presence of young Catholics at universities like Yale and Har-vard, however, delighted men like Ellis and McAvoy, who had long lamented the insularity of what passed for Catholic intellectual life. Catholic scholars with Ivy League credentials, who could meet and even exceed the standards of their vari-ous academic disciplines, seemed at the time a vindication of both men's careers.

Young scholars of American Catholicism in the 1960s and 1970s focused almost exclusively on the laity. This in itself marked their work as distinctive, for their scholarly predecessors had been primarily interested in the episcopate. Their tone and interpretative biases were different, too. What interested young scholars was lay initiative: the propensity of the laity, in the context of American religious volunteerism, to assume leadership roles in the parish and develop a sense of ownership with regard to the church. The Catholic laity, as they emerged in this scholarship, looked remarkably Protestant: independent, mildly suspicious of clerical authority, assertive of their putative rights. Episodes of "trusteeism" in the nineteenth-century church, where parish trustees—usually elected—came into conflict with priests or bishops over issues of property ownership and parish management, were treated by young scholars with lively sympathy, as evidence of the democratizing effects of church-building in a pluralistic society. Their predecessors, when they addressed such conflicts at all, nearly always saw them as aberrant breaches of Catholic good order, the unhappy consequence of too few priests in a country given to populist excess.

Since historians of American Catholicism have until recently worked mainly on the period before 1920, the laity who are so central to this new Catholic history were primarily immigrants and their children. Young Catholic scholars made important contributions to the field of immigration history, itself in a state of energetic expansion by the 1970s; there had been an early tendency in that field to downplay or even ignore the role of religion in the immigrant experience. At the hands of scholars like Jay P. Dolan and Philip Gleason, Catholic immigrants emerged as parish-founders, church-builders, supporters of schools, hospitals, and orphan asylums—as people, in short, whose religious involvement both hastened assimilation and facilitated the creation of an ethnic communal identity. It was not difficult for Catholic scholars to see that this religiously rooted sense of peoplehood was dynamic and ultimately expansive: even in the nineteenth century, there were discernibly American parishes in the United States, where Catholics of varied ethnic backgrounds found a common identity in their religion and shared American experience. Being an "American Catholic"—which was not incompatible with sentimental ties to a largely imagined "Old Country"—meant enlarging the circle of fictive kinship beyond the boundaries that one's parents and grandparents had negotiated. Few experiences are more central to the American national story.

Young historians of American Catholicism in the 1960s and 1970s were deeply affected by the Second Vatican Council and the sea change in the American Church that seemed to flow from it. (As with previous generations, most of these historians were themselves Catholic.) The Catholic past they retrieved looked in many respects like the postconciliar Catholic present: creative, energetic, fractious, incipiently democratic, and optimistically open to the future. The American Catholic story, in other words, was as American as it was Catholic—a saga of liberation, midwived by American circumstances. Indeed, as David O'Brien has recently noted, the young Catholic historians of the 1960s and 1970s can be seen in retrospect as the last of the Catholic Americanists. Their patriotism was far more conflicted than that of their predecessors, given the war in Vietnam and the nation's imploding cities. But they still regarded Catholics as beneficiaries of the

American experiment and believed that their story could be told only in terms of a larger American narrative. Incapable by the 1970s of more than two cheers for the country of their birth, young historians of American Catholicism still felt a vestigial gratitude to it; they were just old enough to have witnessed the happy conclusion of the Euro-American Catholic liberation story. Their preoccupations were thus intensely national—no matter that the Catholic Church is an international institution—and primarily with those aspects of Catholic experience that linked Catholics to other Americans.

The "Americanist" impulse had waned by the late 1970s. Like historians of other self-defined minorities, historians of Catholicism since that time have focused mainly on Catholic difference—on the particulars of Catholic experience in the United States rather than the journey to full American citizenship. (Not that the first wave of "new" Catholic historians had much to say about assimilated Catholics, given their aversion to twentieth-century topics; mobility-as-liberation was simply the moral of the immigrant story.) This "internalist" approach has opened up the field to a variety of new subject matter, as a perusal of the journal *U.S. Catholic Historian*, founded in 1980, will readily demonstrate. But at the same time, it has tended to perpetuate the field's isolation. Historians who work on American Catholicism have arguably had more impact on educated Catholics than on their fellow American historians. They have not altered the dominant American historical narrative much more perceptibly than John Tracy Ellis was able to do, and for much the same reason. Not many historians are yet convinced that knowing something about Catholicism in the United States is essential to understanding the nation's culture and politics.

Let us now review in necessarily cursory fashion the many achievements of recent decades. Historians since the 1970s have produced significant studies of Catholic religious practice and "lived religion"—the quintessence of Catholic difference. They have explored distinctively Catholic understandings of freedom and sexuality, historically the stuff of political and social conflict in the United States, and examined the changing content and culture of Catholic education. Gender history has had an increasing, if belated, impact, with studies appearing of the female laity—their education, organizations, and religious practice—as well as women religious. Accounts of the Hispanic Catholic experience are starting to appear, raising provocative questions about parallels and discontinuities with earlier episodes of Catholic migration history. Even episcopal biography has made a minor comeback, as exemplified by biographies of cardinal archbishops in Chicago (Edward Kantowicz, *Corporation Sole: Cardinal Mundelein and Chicago Catholicism*), Boston (James O'Toole, *Militant and Triumphant: William Henry O'Connell and the Catholic Church in Boston, 1859–1944*), and Washington, D.C. (Morris MacGregor, *Steadfast in the Faith: The Life of Patrick Cardinal O'Boyle*).

Other achievements have been more limited in scope. The international dimension of Catholicism remains largely unexplored, partly because of the linguistic demands such research imposes. (Would that today's historians of American Catholicism were as adept at languages as earlier generations of priest-scholars.) Some interesting beginnings have been made here, however, as well as with the much less daunting problem of regional variations in the American Catholic experience. Priests remain an oddly underresearched population, particularly the diocesan clergy, notwithstanding Scott Appleby's pioneering essay "Present to the People of God," on the changing contours of clerical life between 1930 and 1980, and Michael Pasquier's *Fathers on the Frontier: French Missionaries and the Roman Catholic Priesthood in the United States, 1789–1870*. Priests of particular religious orders have fared a bit better, having found sympathetic historians in Christopher Kauffman (*Tradition and Transformation in Catholic Culture: The Priests of Saint Sulpice in the United States from 1791 to the Present*), Stephen Ochs (*Desegregating the Altar: The Josephites and the Struggle for Black Priests, 1871–1960*), and Terence McDonough (*Men Astutely Trained: A History of the Jesuits in the American Century*). Also worth noting is David O'Brien's *Isaac Hecker: An American Catholic*, a luminous biography of that quintessentially American Catholic.

Robert Orsi and Joseph Chinnici are the most influential authorities to date on the history of Catholic religious practice in the United States. Orsi's principal interest has been Catholic devotionalism—that variety of modalities by which Catholics, and especially female Catholics, have established intimate relations with the divine. Orsi has written detailed studies of devotion to Mary in Italian Harlem (*The Madonna of 115th Street: Faith and Community in Italian Harlem*) and women's devotion to St. Jude (*Thank You, St. Jude: Women's Devotion to the Patron Saint of Hopeless Causes*), whose American cult dates from as recently as 1929. Devotionalism, in Orsi's telling, is something that happens mostly outside the church—not just "church" in a physical sense but also in the sense of clerical authority. His subjects participate in a Catholicism of the streets—literally, in the case of the annual Marian procession in Harlem, and metaphorically, in the case of St. Jude. Theirs is a Catholicism created by lay imagination and responsive to lay needs. When the clergy appear, it is as agents of control and as enemies, in particular, of women's autonomy and psychic wholeness. Orsi's interpretations are never black and white; his conclusions are psychologically informed and invariably subtle. But he does represent, in his pervasive anti-institutionalism, an interpretive mode not uncommonly found among historians of American Catholicism, who are probably more divided by their visceral attitudes toward the church than by any allegiance to particular historiographic schools.

Joseph Chinnici, who as a Franciscan priest is very much "inside" the church, has focused mainly on elite modes of spirituality—on prayer styles and devotional literature popular among highly educated Catholics, including those in vowed religious life. Not surprisingly, Chinnici's subjects had more austere religious imaginations than Orsi's and were more at home in the institutional church. As educated men and women, they were not remotely "representative" of the American Catholic population, at least until very recently. But they have sometimes been good predictors of change in Catholic mentalities, as Chinnici's *Living Stones: The History and Structure of Catholic Spiritual Life in the United States* makes clear. Chinnici warns against viewing the Second Vatican Council as a watershed event—against viewing the changes of the 1960s as abruptly discontinuous with the past. Those changes, he concedes, did indeed constitute a "great rupture." But a "spirituality of participation" had in fact been gaining ground since the 1930s among educated Catholics, whose numbers grew exponentially after 1945. The same Catholics were thus primed—psychologically and in terms of their inherited religious categories—for a spirituality of worldly engagement and autonomous moral judgment.

Chinnici has most recently developed this argument in "The Catholic Community at Prayer, 1926–1976," an essay in an anthology edited by James M. O'Toole, *Habits of Devotion: Catholic Religious Practice in Twentieth-Century America*, which also examines such staples of twentieth-century Catholic practice as confession (O'Toole's "In the Court of Conscience: American Catholics and Confession, 1900-1975"), Eucharistic devotion (Margaret McGuinness's "Let Us Go to the Altar: American Catholics and the Eucharist, 1926–1976"), and Marian devotion (Paula Kane's "Marian Devotion Since 1940: Continuity or Casualty?"). James McCartin's *Prayers of the Faithful: The Shifting Spiritual Life of American Catholics* represents the work of a new generation of historians but fits neatly into Chinnici's paradigm. Particularly since the 1930s, McCartin finds growing evidence of increasingly individualistic modes of piety among the laity. Further analysis of the Second Vatican Council's impact on lay spirituality can be found in Timothy Kelly's *The Transformation of American Catholicism: The Pittsburgh Laity and the Second Vatican Council, 1950–1972*. Kelly deploys statistical evidence, unusual in studies of Catholic piety, to demonstrate a pronounced decline in standard forms of Catholic devotionalism some years prior to the council's first session. Kelly also examines the implementation in Pittsburgh of the council's liturgical reforms, a subject that is clearly ready for historical analysis but has as yet been little explored

The extent to which Catholics see the world differently from other Americans is a question of central importance to contemporary historians of American Catholicism, and one that John McGreevy and Philip Gleason have explored with particular subtlety. McGreevy has been principally concerned with Catholic understandings of freedom. His first book, *Parish Boundaries: The Catholic Experience of Race in the Urban North*, examines a painful divide within the Catholic population over race, specifically the legitimacy of the claim that race should have no bearing on where a person lives. Some Catholics, most of them educated and relatively affluent, championed open-housing legislation in the 1950s and 1960s and worked, usually without much success, to facilitate the peaceful integration of urban neighborhoods. Many others, not exclusively working class, so conflated "neighborhood" and "parish" that their immediate surroundings took on a kind of sacred aura. Encouraged by their priests to invest in home ownership, these Catholics were deeply invested in their neighborhoods, both economically and psychologically. (Their church was deeply invested too, given its vast urban network of churches, schools, rectories, and convents.) McGreevy does not deny an essential racism in this population: African Americans were not welcome in these neighborhoods even if they were Catholic. But he does insist that uninflected "white racism" is an inadequate explanation for racial conflict in the urban North. Catholics responded to African Americans and their claims to freedom in a manner conditioned by religious values. The neighborhood-as-sacred-space, in the eyes of many Catholics, trumped the rights of individuals to live wherever they pleased.

In *Catholicism and American Freedom: A History*, McGreevy has more recently considered Catholic ideas about freedom in a broad historical survey, ranging from Catholic views on slavery to those on abortion law. American Catholic intellectuals were deeply influenced by the Catholic revival in nineteenth-century Europe, which took place in the context of struggle against a militantly anti-clerical republicanism. American Catholics did not typically repudiate the republicanism that was their American inheritance. But they did insist that freedom meant the freedom to do what was right. It was not simply about individual choice, even when such choices did no demonstrable harm to other persons. American Catholic thinkers were also accepting of hierarchy in a way that their Protestant and secular counterparts were not and were more skeptical when it came to amelioration of the human condition. Such differences made for strained relations between Catholics and advocates of progressive reform, even when Catholics were part of various reform coalitions, as happened most spectacularly during the New Deal. McGreevy's important work illuminates American political dynamics in striking fashion, perhaps especially for the 1930s and after. Appropriately, it has received wide attention. His book might usefully be supplemented by Philip Gleason's masterful *Contending with Modernity: Catholic Higher Education in the Twentieth Century* and my *Catholics and Contraception: An American History*. These last-mentioned books are certainly in the "internalist" mode, seemingly more attuned to Catholic than secular debates. But they help to explain the contours of Catholic thinking on such currently salient issues as marriage, gender roles, sexuality, and the purposes of education, as well as the culture in which this thinking has evolved.

Women religious—"sisters," if you will—have probably had a greater impact on American Catholic life and culture than any other Catholic subpopulation. Their almost-free labor made possible the systems of Catholic schools that eventually characterized most of the nation's large and middle-size cities, at least outside the South. They staffed Catholic hospitals, orphanages, and other social-service institutions. Perhaps most important, they modeled a distinctively Catholic way of being, one that both reflected and shaped Catholicism's sometimes confusing assumptions about gender and individuality. Sisters were in the world but obviously not of it, simultaneously female and asexual, deferential to male authority yet living independently of the family, sentimental in their piety but not infrequently the best-educated women in the parish. (Sisters both fascinated and horrified non-Catholics, as nineteenth-century "convent narratives" so vividly indicate.) For all their importance, however, American women religious have only recently become subjects of historical analysis. Nor have they yet been integrated into the larger narrative of American women's history, despite their having offered for a very long time women's principal institutional alternative to family life and the broadest path to professional status for women of modest background. Today's gender historians are in this respect much like their feminist forebears, few of whom could see in convent life even the potential for liberation.

The new historical work on sisters has tended to focus on particular religious orders, for obvious archival reasons. No survey yet exists of sisters' American work in general, although Carol K. Coburn and Martha Smith tried in *Spirited Lives: How Nuns Shaped Catholic Culture and American Life, 1836–1920*, their history of the Sisters of St. Joseph of Carondelet, to limn the general outlines of sisters' experience and influence in the nineteenth-century United States, building on the earlier work of Mary Ewens, in *The Role of the Nun in Nineteenth-Century America*. One can also consult Patricia Byrne's fine essay "In the Parish but Not of It: Sisters," on change in the lives, work, and self-understanding of women religious from 1930 to 1980. Suellen Hoy's *Good Hearts: Catholic Sisters in Chicago's Past* examines several religious orders in that proud center of Catholic social activism. And Amy Koehlinger has produced *The New Nuns: Racial Justice and Religious Reform in the 1960s*, a lively study of sisters who gravitated to the "racial apostolate" in the 1960s and 1970s, in the context of which they typically redefined the meaning of vowed religious life.

Excellent studies also exist of sister-nurses in the Civil War (Mary Denis Maher, *To Bind Up Wounds: Catholic Nurses in the U.S. Civil War*), hospital nursing sisters in the nineteenth century (Sioban Nelson, *Say Little, Do Much: Nurses, Nuns, and Hospitals in the Nineteenth Century*), and the still-too-little appreciated impact that sister-run social welfare institutions had on the evolution of the American welfare state. On this last topic, see especially *The Poor Belong to Us: Catholic Charities and American Welfare*, by Dorothy Brown and Elizabeth McKeown, and Maureen Fitzgerald's *Habits of Compassion: Irish Catholic Nuns and the Origins of New York's Welfare System, 1830–1920*. Mary Oates's *The Catholic Philanthropic Tradition in America* merits mention, given the central role in Catholic philanthropy played by women religious. Even studies devoted to a single order can illuminate significant aspects of the American past. Such is the case with Diane Batts Morrow's *Persons of Color and Religious at the Same Time: The Oblate Sisters of Providence, 1828–1860*, which examines a small community of African-descended women in antebellum Baltimore. It is even truer of Emily Clark's work on the

Ursuline sisters of New Orleans, *Masterless Mistresses: The New Orleans Ursulines and the Development of a New World Society, 1727–1834*, whose ministry, despite their small numbers, had surprising effects on the city's politics of race and gender in the colonial and early national periods.

The energy evident in historical work on women religious is somewhat less so when it comes to studies of the female laity. This probably reflects the dominant role that women religious played in the Catholic community when it came to voluntary social work. Catholic lay women did eventually found settlement houses and otherwise organize for purposes of social amelioration, but later than Protestant women and in proportionately much smaller numbers. As members of a heavily working-class population, moreover, relatively few Catholic women until quite recently received the education necessary for distinction in the professions or the arts. Notwithstanding these daunting realities, Kathleen Sprows Cummings has recently uncovered an impressive record of activism by both lay and religious women in the Progressive Era, as discussed in *New Women of the Old Faith: Gender and Catholicism in the Progressive Era*, as has Deirdre Moloney, in *American Catholic Lay Groups and Transatlantic Social Reform*. Their books are nicely supplemented by Tracy Schier and Cynthia Russett's anthology, *Catholic Women's Colleges in America*, since the earliest of these colleges date from the same period. As for the symbol-rich gender system of American Catholicism, elaborated in the context of hierarchical anti-modernism, it holds out rich possibilities for research. Paula Kane has explored the subject with particular fruitfulness in *Separatism and Subculture: Boston Catholicism, 1900–1920*, as also in her work on Marian devotion.

Until very recently, little historical work has been done on the rapidly growing population of Hispanic Catholics in the United States. The need for such work is obvious, given that Hispanics now account for roughly 33 percent of the American Catholic population. Their arrival in large numbers is of recent vintage, however, and they remain concentrated in the Southwest, which is terra incognita for the great majority of American Catholic historians. (The geographic locus of the field has been the cities of the Northeast and, to a somewhat lesser extent, the upper Midwest.) Catholics of Mexican origin, by far the largest group of Spanish-speaking Catholics in the United States, have received most of the scholarly attention, particularly those in the long-established communities of Texas. Timothy Matovina's *Guadalupe and Her Faithful: Latino Catholics in San Antonio, from Colonial Origins to the Present* provides a case in point. Tracing the evolution of devotion to Our Lady of Guadalupe in San Antonio, Texas, from colonial times to the present, Matovina's study combines archival research with oral history, his own observations as a participant in the devotion, and theological reflection. His reconstruction of the past is hindered by a relative paucity of archival resources, a chronic problem for historians of Hispano-American Catholicism. But his book attests to the richness of the research possibilities. Matovina achieves a seamless "internationalism" in his study, as his subjects progressively reimagine a devotion born in colonial Mexico, of which San Antonio was originally part. Guadalupe's faithful, by means of the devotion, simultaneously affirm their cultural connection to a Mexico both real and imagined and an evolving sense of Mexican American peoplehood.

Scholarship on Hispanic American Catholicism, one hopes, will ultimately gravitate toward the comparative. How has the experience of Mexican American Catholics differed from that of Central Americans or of those from the Spanish-speaking Caribbean? A book by David Badillo, *Latinos and the New Immigrant Church*, which examines the religious experience of Mexican, Puerto Rican, and Cuban Catholics in the United States, points the way in this regard. Which groups are most apt to embrace charismatic styles of Catholic worship or, as is increasingly the case, various forms of Protestantism? (Among Hispanic Protestants, as with Hispanic Catholics, Pentecostal modes of worship are enormously popular.) How have these devotional preferences—something genuinely new to American Catholicism, at least in terms of degree—affected the larger Catholic population? One wonders especially about the Euro-American priests who in growing numbers since the 1950s have been drawn to Hispanic ministry. Their work has helped to provide the American priesthood, a profession in obvious trouble, with a badly needed measure of visibility and prestige. It has also built bridges in countless communities between Spanish-speaking immigrants and the Euro-American church—an evocative example of the numerous ways in which religion, perhaps paradoxically, helps a badly divided society hang together. Finally, historians of American Catholicism must compare the experience of Hispanic Catholics with that of earlier immigrant groups. This will not be easy, since relatively few American historians are genuinely multilingual and the project requires a thorough grounding in political and economic as well as religious history. But it is clearly important.

The international dimension of Catholicism is no less important. Historians of American Catholicism have mostly thought in national terms, partly because they share the parochialism so integral to our discipline and partly because the American Church was indeed shaped in major ways by the particulars of American society and culture. But there is no such thing in the Catholic tradition as a national church; all Catholics belong to a universal institution, whose temporal head resides in Rome. The so-called American Church has always possessed a strikingly international dimension, and not only because of an immigrant laity: until the end of the nineteenth century, many—in some dioceses, most—of its clergy and religious were born and trained abroad. (As for the present day, roughly 25 percent of Catholic seminarians were born outside the United States.) European struggles over church–state relations, theology, and modes of piety inevitably affected Catholics in the United States, albeit at times indirectly. Anti-Catholic zealots have made much of the church's "foreignness," which is probably another reason that American Catholic historians have shied away from the topic. But

Catholics are in fact different. As the late Peter D'Agostino once pointed out, Protestant denominations do not have secretaries of state.

D'Agostino's *Rome in America: Transnational Catholic Ideology from the Risorgimento to Fascism* is the most ambitious effort to date at situating the American Catholic Church in an international context. Based on copious research in Italian archives, the book examines the American history of the so-called Roman question from its inception in 1848 until 1940. At issue in this debate was the temporal power of the pope, definitively lost with Italian unification in 1870. Five successive popes refused to accept what now seems historically inevitable, posing from 1870 until 1929 as "prisoners of the Vatican" and urging the Catholic faithful to support their claims to the former Papal States. (Matters were finally resolved in 1929, by means of a concordat between Pius XI and Benito Mussolini.) According to D'Agostino, the "Roman question" played a dominant role in shaping both American Catholic consciousness and the image of Catholics held by American Protestants and Jews. American Catholicism, in his telling, was hardly American at all: militantly defensive, hostile to liberalism, oriented to an international realm of myths and symbols rather than American realities. The book is most successful in its discussion of the fascist era, during portions of which a compliant papacy aided the Italian government in manipulating Italian priests and lay leaders in the United States, the better to pursue fascist aims abroad. It is less successful, in my view, in demonstrating its principal thesis. (The ethnic messiness of American Catholicism is oddly missing in the book, as is the optimism required—and generated—by institution-building.) But D'Agostino was right to urge his colleagues to a more cosmopolitan scholarly agenda. He has set a standard for research that is likely to endure.

The international dimension of American Catholicism would seem to be the single most promising area for future research. One looks forward particularly to studies of the nineteenth-century European Catholic revival and its multiple effects on the United States, especially in the realm of devotionalism. The decades since 1945, only now coming into something like historical perspective, need work as well. What was the state of American Catholicism on the eve of the Second Vatican Council? To what extent did high rates of religious observance mask doubts about discipline and doctrine, perhaps especially with regard to eschatology? How were conciliar reforms explained and implemented in communities across the United States? And what about the seeming collapse of Catholic élan that set in shortly thereafter? Hispanic Catholics, as previously mentioned, remain an underresearched population. So do the female laity. And the rich symbol-system of Catholicism, coupled with its lush tradition of ritual practice, offers multiple opportunities for scholarly exploration, especially with regard to sexuality and the body.

The single most important task, however, is convincing our fellow historians that Catholics matter. Historians of American Catholicism have been focused for a very long time on what American realities meant for Catholicism. It is now time to turn the question around.

REFERENCES

Appleby, R. Scott. "Present to the People of God." In *Transforming Parish Ministry: The Changing Roles of Catholic Clergy, Laity, and Women Religious,* by Jay P. Dolan, R. Scott Appleby, Patricia Byrne, and Debra Campbell, 3–107. New York: Crossroad, 1986.

Badillo, David A. *Latinos and the New Immigrant Church.* Baltimore: Johns Hopkins University Press, 2006.

Brown, Dorothy M., and Elizabeth McKeown. *The Poor Belong to Us: Catholic Charities and American Welfare.* Cambridge, Mass.: Harvard University Press, 1997.

Byrne, Patricia. "In the Parish but Not of It: Sisters." In *Transforming Parish Ministry: The Changing Roles of Catholic Clergy, Laity, and Women Religious,* by Jay P. Dolan, R. Scott Appleby, Patricia Byrne, and Debra Campbell, 111–200. New York: Crossroad, 1986.

Carey, Patrick. *People, Priests, and Prelates: Ecclesiastical Democracy and the Tensions of Trusteeism.* Notre Dame, Ind.: University of Notre Dame Press, 1987.

Chinnici, Joseph P. *Living Stones: The History and Structure of Catholic Spiritual Life in the United States.* 2nd ed. Maryknoll, N.Y.: Orbis Books, 1996.

Clark, Emily. *Masterless Mistresses: The New Orleans Ursulines and the Development of a New World Society, 1727–1834.* Chapel Hill: University of North Carolina Press, 2007.

Coburn, Carol K., and Martha Smith. *Spirited Lives: How Nuns Shaped Catholic Culture and American Life, 1836–1920.* Chapel Hill: University of North Carolina Press, 1999.

Cumming, Kathleen Sprows. *New Women of the Old Faith: Gender and Catholicism in the Progressive Era.* Chapel Hill: University of North Carolina Press, 2009.

D'Agostino, Peter R. *Rome in America: Transnational Catholic Ideology from the Risorgimento to Fascism.* Chapel Hill: University of North Carolina Press, 2004.

Davis, Cyprian. *The History of Black Catholics in the United States.* New York: Crossroad, 1990.

Dolan, Jay P. *The American Catholic Experience: A History from Colonial Times to the Present.* Garden City, N.Y.: Doubleday, 1985.

Fisher, James Terence. *The Catholic Counter-Culture in the United States, 1933–1962.* Chapel Hill: University of North Carolina Press, 1989.

Fitzgerald, Maureen. *Habits of Compassion: Irish Catholic Nuns and the Origins of New York's Welfare System, 1830–1920.* Urbana: University of Illinois Press, 2001.

Fogarty, Gerald P. *The Vatican and the American Hierarchy from 1870 to 1965.* Stuttgart: Hiersemann, 1982.

Ewens, Mary. *The Role of the Nun in Nineteenth-Century America.* New York: Arno Press, 1978.

Gleason, Philip. *Contending with Modernity: Catholic Higher Education in the Twentieth Century.* New York: Oxford University Press, 1995.

Halsey, William. *The Survival of American Innocence: Catholicism in an Era of Disillusionment, 1920–1940.* Notre Dame, Ind.: University of Notre Dame Press, 1980.

Henhold, Mary J. *Catholic and Feminist: The Surprising History of the American Catholic Feminist Movement.* Chapel Hill: University of North Carolina Press, 2008.

Hoy, Suellen. *Good Hearts: Catholic Sisters in Chicago's Past*. Urbana: University of Illinois Press, 2007.

Kane, Paula M. *Separatism and Subculture: Boston Catholicism, 1900–1920*. Chapel Hill: University of North Carolina Press, 1994.

Kantowicz, Edward R. *Corporation Sole: Cardinal Mundelein and Chicago Catholicism*. Notre Dame, Ind.: University of Notre Dame Press, 1983.

Kauffman, Christopher J. *Tradition and Transformation in Catholic Culture: The Priests of Saint Sulpice in the United States from 1791 to the Present*. New York: Macmillan, 1988.

Kelly, Timothy. *The Transformation of American Catholicism: The Pittsburgh Laity and the Second Vatican Council, 1950–1972*. Notre Dame, Ind.: University of Notre Dame Press, 2009.

Koehlinger, Amy L. *The New Nuns: Racial Justice and Religious Reform in the 1960s*. Cambridge, Mass.: Harvard University Press, 2007.

MacGregor, Morris J. *Steadfast in the Faith: The Life of Patrick Cardinal O'Boyle*. Washington, D.C.: Catholic University of America Press, 2006.

Maher, Mary Denis. *To Bind Up Wounds: Catholic Nurses in the U.S. Civil War*. Baton Rouge: Louisiana State University Press, 1999.

Matovina, Timothy. *Guadalupe and Her Faithful: Latino Catholics in San Antonio, from Colonial Origins to the Present*. Baltimore: Johns Hopkins University Press, 2005.

McCartin, James P. *Prayers of the Faithful: The Shifting Spiritual Life of American Catholics*. Cambridge, Mass.: Harvard University Press, 2010.

McDonough, Peter. *Men Astutely Trained: A History of the Jesuits in the American Century*. New York: Free Press, 1992.

McGreevy, John T. *Catholicism and American Freedom: A History*. New York: Norton, 2003.

——. *Parish Boundaries: The Catholic Experience of Race in the Urban North*. Chicago: University of Chicago Press, 1996.

Moloney, Deirdre M. *American Catholic Lay Groups and Transatlantic Social Reform*. Chapel Hill: University of North Carolina Press, 2002.

Morrow, Diane Batts. *Persons of Color and Religious at the Same Time: The Oblate Sisters of Providence, 1828–1860*. Chapel Hill: University of North Carolina Press, 2002.

Nelson, Sioban. *Say Little, Do Much: Nurses, Nuns, and Hospitals in the Nineteenth Century*. Philadelphia: University of Pennsylvania Press, 2001.

Oates, Mary J. *The Catholic Philanthropic Tradition in America*. Bloomington: Indiana University Press, 1995.

O'Brien, David J. *Isaac Hecker: An American Catholic*. New York: Paulist Press, 1992.

Ochs, Stephen J. *Desegregating the Altar: The Josephites and the Struggle for Black Priests, 1871–1960*. Baton Rouge: Louisiana State University Press, 1990.

Orsi, Robert A. *The Madonna of 115th Street: Faith and Community in Italian Harlem*. New Haven, Conn.: Yale University Press, 1985.

——. *Thank You, St. Jude: Women's Devotion to the Patron Saint of Hopeless Causes*. New Haven, Conn.: Yale University Press, 1996.

O'Toole, James M. ed. *Habits of Devotion: Catholic Religious Practice in Twentieth-Century America*. Ithaca, N.Y.: Cornell University Press, 2004.

——. *Militant and Triumphant: William Henry O'Connell and the Catholic Church in Boston, 1859–1944*. Notre Dame, Ind.: University of Notre Dame Press, 1992.

Pasquier, Michael. *Fathers on the Frontier: French Missionaries and the Roman Catholic Priesthood in the United States, 1789–1870*. New York: Oxford University Press, 2010.

Schier, Tracy, and Cynthia Russett, eds. *Catholic Women's Colleges in America*. Baltimore: Johns Hopkins University Press, 2002.

Tentler, Leslie Woodcock. *Catholics and Contraception: An American History*. Ithaca, N.Y.: Cornell University Press, 2004.

Treviño, Roberto R. *The Church in the Barrio: Mexican American Ethno-Catholicism in Houston*. Chapel Hill: University of North Carolina Press, 2006.

18. AMERICAN JUDAISM

ALAN T. LEVENSON

American Jewry constitutes both a religion and an ethnicity—this is the principal distinguishing element in any analysis of American Judaism. An American Jew may not practice Judaic rituals, may not pray regularly, may even content himself or herself with entering a synagogue a couple of times a year and on life-cycle events, and still consider himself or herself a committed, rather than lapsed, Jew. Moreover, as long as this person either traveled to Israel; belonged to a Jewish social, political, or charitable organization; or showed some sign of identification, most American Jews would concur with this self-assessment.

Whether Christians or Muslims in America would apply the same standard (to themselves or to others) is not for me to say, but this clearly highlights a facet of American Jewry worth emphasizing. In the early twentieth century, American Jews imported and developed a variety of surrogate ideologies—Yiddishism, socialism, Unionism, and Zionism. These ideologies were intended to supplant religious Judaism; thus these secularist movements play a role analogous to that of fringe Christian movements. On a broader plane, many American Jews in the first half of the twentieth century found the comfort of ethnic neighborhoods, family circles, occupational environments, and the kitchens of wives and mothers the linchpin of their Jewish identity. Not accidentally, that period corresponded to the ethnic highpoint of Jewishness and the highest percentile of Jews in the overall American population. Judaism as practiced religion, therefore, has often been an ancillary element in an individual Jew's identity.

These comments serve to alert the reader that this chapter attempts to focus exclusively on Judaism as a religion: part of the picture of the Jewish experience in America is thereby excluded in the interests of space. Conceptually, the author is aware that this division requires ignoring important elements of popular and material culture. Jenna Weissman Joselit's *The Wonders of America: Reinventing Jewish Culture, 1880–1950* (1996) and Andrew Heinze's *Adapting to Abundance: Jewish Immigrants, Mass Consumption, and the Search for American Identity* (1990) deal precisely with the commodification of life-cycle events, holidays, and ritual items with distinctly religious valence. Similarly, Deborah Dash Moore's *GI Jews: How World War II Changed a Generation* (2006) offers a nuanced picture of the syncretism of Judaism and patriotism under duress. Even in peacetime, Beth Wenger has demonstrated in *History Lessons: The Creation of American Jewish Heritage*, the celebration of American holidays played a huge role in American Judaism.

Even historically, this twofold dimension of the American Jewish experience, religious and ethnic, cannot be neatly disentangled into distinct strands. The first Jews who arrived in New Amsterdam (later New York) in 1654 came because of religious intolerance. When the Portuguese retook Pernambuco (Recife) in Brazil from the Dutch, the Inquisition was sure to follow. Once the Jews were settled in New Amsterdam, against the wishes of the Dutch colonial governor, the first institutions they established were specifically religious ones: synagogues, schools, charitable societies, cemeteries, and ritual baths (*mikvaot*). Even in the period of mass immigration from eastern Europe, the informal social clubs and more formally organized *Landsmannschaften* established by the immigrants offered many services previously provided by the religio-centric communities (*kehillot*) of the Pale of Settlement (the area of permitted Jewish settlement established by Russian czars at the beginning of the nineteenth century, and abolished with the Russian Revolution of 1917). Even the social service dimension of these organizations—such as interest-free loans, primitive life and unemployment insurance, burial rights—were thinly veiled transplants of services offered by the traditional Jewish communities of eastern Europe.

The growth of American Jewry was modest for the first 150 years of its settlement. Although historians traditionally put the population of Jews at 2,500 at the time of the American Revolution, the number was probably smaller, and the majority of these families ultimately integrated (through intermarriage and conversion) into the general environment. Only Charleston, Philadelphia, and New York had more than 200 Jews in 1776. Although both Ashkenazic (central and western European) and Sephardic (originally from Iberia) Jews were found in colonial America, their low numbers enforced cooperation and a melding of customary differences. Most scholars would agree that the freedoms enshrined by the founding documents of this nation were a more important legacy to subsequent Jewries than the accomplishments of this small group. The American

Jewish population has been composed mainly of Ashkenazic Jews. In recent decades, a considerable number of Jews from Israel and the former Soviet Union, as well as small communities of Jews from Arab lands and Persia (Iran), have added to the ranks of American Jewry.

Religious, not ethnic, expression remained dominant throughout this period and the subsequent migration from central Europe (1820s–1860), and the consolidation of that immigration in the years following the Civil War. The Civil War was the first conflict in which a large number of Jewish men served in the ranks—about 7,000 for the Union and 3,000 for the Confederacy. In this second period of expansion, the synagogue-community of the colonial period gave way to a community of multiple synagogues, as historian Jonathan Sarna observed in *American Judaism: A History*. As noted, the mass migration from eastern Europe (1881–1921) introduced a rich variety of Jewish expressions, including some secular-tending viewpoints. Today, however, the pendulum seems to have swung back toward those Jews who practice Judaism—and that by no means includes all American Jews—seeking greater religiosity/spirituality than the preceding two or three generations. Nevertheless, fewer professing Jews than professing Christians attend religious services regularly. For a century, Jewish leaders have bemoaned the fact that less than 50 percent of the Jewish population belongs to a synagogue at any given moment. (The percentages over an entire lifetime would be higher, as many Jews affiliate during their children's upbringing and disaffiliate later.)

Scholars customarily divide American Judaism by era and by denomination (or movement, as most scholars of Judaism avoid the word "denomination" as an essentially Protestant concept without sufficient attention to the differences between Christian and Jewish self-definition). We have hinted at the first division and turn now to the second. American Judaism during the colonial period may be called lax traditionalism. In the absence of a trained clergy, traditional academies of study, and established cities, there was no way that American Jewry could replicate the patterns of European Jewish life. (The desire to reject religious authority would be increasingly pronounced in the second and third immigration waves.) Synagogues sprang up in Savannah, Georgia; Charleston, South Carolina; Philadelphia; Lancaster, Pennsylvania; New York; Newport, Rhode Island; and Montreal. Although the colonial-era Jews established some of the institutions of Europe, they lived highly individualistic lives, worked on the Sabbath, socialized with non-Jewish Americans, and led what would have passed for extremely secular lives in Europe. Some Jews strove to be more observant; some felt guilty that greater observance on a communal basis was impossible. Surveying colonial-era Jewry, the pioneering scholar of the subject, Jacob Rader Marcus, noted in "The American Colonial Jew: A Study in Acculturation" that there were almost as many Judaisms as there were individual Jews.

REFORM JUDAISM

The so-called German Jews came from central Europe; many were speakers of Judeo-German, a bridge language between German and Yiddish. Nevertheless, the moniker "German" fits because the intellectual leaders of this group were the products of German universities, published periodicals in German, and reflected the contemporary religious concern among German Jewry—the urge to adapt to modernity by means of reforming the divine service. While the term "German Jews" can stand, the question of what drove the pace, process, and substance of reform has been debated. Certainly the impact of the 1848 revolutions that rocked European regimes has been exaggerated. While families such as those of future justice Louis Brandeis were among the so-called '48ers, Cleveland had been settled by Bavarians several years earlier, and the first ordained rabbi to serve in America, Abraham Rice, left Bavaria for occupational advancement. Historians Naomi W. Cohen, in *Jews in Christian America: The Pursuit of Religious Equality*, and Michael M. Meyer, in *Response to Modernity: A History of the Reform Movement in Judaism*, have stressed the impact of university-educated rabbis and the Reform theological agenda in shaping American Reform. Leon Jick's *The Americanization of the Synagogue, 1820–1870* stressed that the reforms were laity-driven, the product of economic climbing and acculturation, and highly sensitive to local synagogue politics. For Jick, the move toward family pews, organ music, the policing of observance levels for clergy, and the adoption of new prayerbooks was piecemeal, "folk-driven," and inconsistent.

The motor of these changes is debatable; the end result is not. By the beginning of the great immigration from eastern Europe (1880s), Reform Judaism had a seminary (Hebrew Union College), a professional organization (Central Conference of American Rabbis), and a union of synagogues (Union of American Hebrew Congregations). Reform was thus the first organized movement of American Judaism, and its leaders considered it (incorrectly) the only viable path for the American Jewish future. (Note that these organizations employed terms such as "American" and "Union" rather than terms that highlighted a theological position.) The differences of opinion among Reform leaders loomed larger in their day than in retrospect. Radical Reformers (especially on the East Coast) had no problem with Sunday Sabbaths; wanted a liturgy almost entirely free of Hebrew, with no mention of revival of the dead; and insisted on a prayer book that reflected these beliefs. Rabbi David Einhorn—student of the radical reformer Samuel Holdheim, and a strident abolitionist who fled his Maryland pulpit (Har Sinai) before relocating to Philadelphia's Keneseth Israel—exemplifies this brand of Reform. Midwestern and southern Reform tended to be more moderate on theological and liturgical matters. The great hero of American Reform, Isaac Mayer Wise, represented this tendency; unlike Einhorn, who believed in the importance of German, Wise wanted Americanization. Wise's successor at the head of Hebrew Union College, Einhorn's son-in-law Kaufmann Kohler, represented something of a compromise between the two approaches.

Classical Reform, as it came to be known in America, persisted from the Pittsburgh Platform (1885) through the San Francisco Platform (1976). Under the pressure of historical events, especially the rise of Nazism in the 1930s, classical Reform tempered its strict "religion as confession" posture. The Columbus Platform (1937) marked a less thorough rejection of Jewish nationalism (that is, Zionism) than that expressed in Pittsburgh. The Columbus Platform also took a more guarded view of the superiority of modern scholarship over tradition, very pronounced in the Pittsburgh Platform, but a reembrace of ritual and spirituality has marked Reform only in the past quarter-century.

CONSERVATIVE JUDAISM

Moshe Davis's *The Emergence of Conservative Judaism: The Historical School in Nineteenth-Century America* argued that the movement known as positive-historic Judaism in Europe began in the United States in the 1870s and 1880s. Jonathan Sarna supports this evaluation in *American Judaism* by focusing on the Philadelphia and New York figures associated with a renewal of American Jewish energies. Sarna links this flourishing to the Second Great Awakening and to a recurrent feature of American Judaism: the ability of people on the periphery of American Jewish life to bring new energy to the enterprise.

Notwithstanding these observations, the reorganization of the Jewish Theological Seminary (JTS) under Solomon Schechter (1902) remains the canonical date for the birth of American Conservative Judaism. The Jewish Theological Seminary became a magnet for second-generation children of immigrants who championed traditional Judaism but were equally committed to Americanization. These new rabbis, including Mordecai Kaplan, a major figure in twentieth-century American Judaism, sermonized in English, presided over mixed-seating congregations, and sought to promote the synagogue as a vehicle for communal identity as well as religious worship (unlike the Reform movement). Jeff Gurock, in *American Jewish Orthodoxy in Historical Perspective*, and others have highlighted the closeness of Conservative and Orthodox personnel in these first few decades of the twentieth century in terms of membership and leadership (both congregants and rabbis flitted between the two movements). But Schechter's writings showed his ideological distance from Orthodoxy. Although JTS avoided teaching Torah (Pentateuch) in these years in order to avoid the sensitive question of Mosaic authorship, the rabbinic enactments that followed the Bible were acknowledged to be of purely human creation, open to historical study, and subject to change. American Conservative Judaism, as Neil Gilman's accessible study, *Conservative Judaism: The New Century*, shows, began with a deep commitment to modernity.

Jewish Theology Seminary—by virtue of its location (New York has been the largest Jewish settlement since the Revolution), its stellar faculty (including Solomon Schechter, Mordecai Kaplan, Abraham Joshua Heschel, Louis Ginzberg, Louis Finkelstein, and Gerson Cohen), and its hold over its rabbinic graduates—could claim to have been the most important center of Jewish learning at midtwentieth century. (No single place could make that claim now, in large measure because of the proliferation of Jewish studies departments at top-tier universities.) Unlike Reform, which placed synagogue autonomy on a pedestal, the faculty at JTS exerted great influence on the pulpit rabbis of Conservative Judaism, with problematic consequences. While second- and third-generation American Jews of eastern European descent felt more comfortable in the Conservative synagogues than in the Reform ones, their personal level of observance was not that different from that of the more fully acculturated German Jews. Thus Conservative Judaism, as Charles Liebman expressed it, suffered from schizophrenia. Its "elite" (rabbis, cantors, seminary teachers, and a small section of congregants) were as fully observant as their Orthodox counterparts, but a much larger rank and file routinely innovated "folk" compromises on such central matters as dietary laws (*kashrut*), Sabbath observance, and laws of family purity.

As World War II veterans returned home, made their careers, and started families, Conservative Judaism expanded rapidly. The 1950s and 1960s also saw the growth of the other two major denominations—probably a good indication that demographics, economics, and the overall fortunes of America will ever be the decisive influence on this country's Judaism. In *New York Jews and the Quest for Community: The Kehilla Experiment*, Arthur (Aryeh) Goren called this period the "Golden Era" of American Judaism, Liebman's analysis notwithstanding. In the past couple of decades, as Reform has reembraced many aspects of Jewish ritual life and modern Orthodoxy has proved to be a viable option for acculturated American Jews, the Conservative movement has struggled to define its place in the religious spectrum. After the 1980s decision to ordain female rabbis, a right-wing group within the movement split off; today, debate over whether to include the Matriarchs as well as the Patriarchs in a central prayer (the *Amidah*) once again threatens congregational secession. Similarly problematic for the Conservative movement is the issue of homosexuality. Whereas the Orthodox seminaries clearly will not ordain openly gay men, and whereas the Reform seminary (Hebrew Union College, now with branches in New York, Los Angeles, and Cincinnati) will ordain gay men and women, the Ritual Committee of the Conservative movement has struggled to express a clear position.

ORTHODOX JUDAISM

My describing American Orthodoxy last among the three major movements must seem counterintuitive to the reader who assumes that Judaism was always "Orthodox" until the modern era. But "traditional" is a far better term to describe Jewish practices until the nineteenth century for a number of reasons, including the absence of an ideological alternative, the presumption that all Jews shared the basic framework of observances (*halachah*), and the need to take a conscious position of "resistance" or "accommodation" to outside stimuli. Traditional Jews, even in the immigrant generation in America, found folk compromises with the majority culture relatively unproblematic; the increasingly committed Orthodox of recent decades have worked harder to define boundaries of acceptable practice and belief. While America saw representatives of tradition before the eastern European immigration (among others, Isaac Leeser of Philadelphia and Abraham Rice of Baltimore), it was only in the twentieth century that an American Orthodox Jewish movement took clear shape.

Jeff Gurock and Marc Lee Raphael have used the rubric "resistance and accommodation." In Raphael's *Judaism in America*, it is clear that while in the immigrant generation both models existed, by the time of World War II the accommodators seemed ascendant. Abraham Lesser, Leo Jung, and Joseph Soloveitchik, strictly Orthodox figures, possessed a broad mastery of modern culture and a positive attitude toward it. The establishment of a modern Orthodox yeshiva (RIETS) in 1915, and its development into a modern college (Yeshiva University) in 1928, signaled the emergence of a coherent third movement in the American Jewish landscape. The early leaders of Yeshiva University, Bernard Drachman and Bernard Revel, fall clearly into the ranks of the "accommodators."

There were resistors, too, but they remained largely without influence until after World War II. Then, many Orthodox survivors of the Nazi Holocaust came to America, sometimes as direct transplants. European *yeshivot* were resettled in Lakewood, New Jersey, and in Cleveland. In New York, Hasidic dynasts led the remnants of once-numerous communities in Kiryat Joel, Monsey, Crown Heights, and Borough Park. Within a generation, large-scale investment in day schools (both financial and personal) proved to be a strategic coup. Highly committed teachers, including many from Israel, influenced "modern Orthodox" students who went on to achieve success in the outside world. As a further consequence of early marriage ages, higher average birth rates, and superior social networks, Orthodoxy has become a vibrant element within American Jewry. For the first time since the onset of modernity, Orthodoxy appears to be gaining rather than losing strength. The hubris of Reform at the end of the nineteenth century regarding its role as representing the only viable American Jewish future is being replicated in many Orthodox circles today.

RECONSTRUCTIONIST JUDAISM

Reconstructionism, a fourth movement, appeared formally only in the 1960s, although its ideological formulator, Mordecai Kaplan, articulated the principles of the movement in the 1920s and, by 1934, had published *Judaism as a Civilization: Toward a Reconstruction of American-Jewish Life*, very likely the most influential work on Judaism in American history.

Kaplan's position can be summarized in his own formula: "Judaism is an evolving religious civilization." Judaism is defined by folkways, customs, concern for other Jews, a special land (Israel), communal processes, and values—a broader set of concerns than ordinarily encompassed by "religion." But this civilization has been deeply defined by religion: in Kaplan's view, the Jewish viewpoint toward sex, learning, family, and economic justice stems from books (for example, the Bible and rabbinic literature) and living traditions (for example, Jewish life-cycle events, dietary laws/habits) *marked* everywhere by their religious origins. Finally, Kaplan displays the positive-historic orientation of the JTS, where he taught for many decades. Judaism expresses fundamentals in time-bound idioms (for example, the God-Idea, observance of the Commandments) and occasionally sheds seeming fundamentals as hopelessly outworn (for example, hilltop shrine worship in ancient Israel, the idea of Jewish chosenness in democratic America). Since Judaism is an organic entity (read: civilization), such changes can always be adopted without rupturing the spiritual-emotional resonance of inherited forms, which Kaplan called *sacra*. Kaplan's new prayer book (1941) and new Passover Haggadah (1945) embodied this deeply pragmatic view of religion, and stirred up much controversy among the Orthodox and his faculty colleagues at JTS.

Reconstructionism, at its inception, was a second-generation phenomenon— the product of immigrants' children who could take Jewish "belonging" for granted, be extremely catholic about "believing," and could locate "behaving" as somewhere in between these poles of importance. In the 1960s and 1970s, when the movement created formal institutions, the Reconstructionist Rabbinical College and the Federation of Reconstructionist Congregations and Havurot easily assimilated America's countercultural emphasis on smallness, democracy, and group participation. Until today, the typical Reconstructionist congregation tends to be smaller than those of the other movements and expects its rabbis and cantors to be facilitators as well as spiritual leaders. The newness and smallness of Reconstructionism has also made it, on the whole, more open than "the big three" to the Eastern-style meditation, incorporation of kabbalistic kinesthetics, acceptance of gays and lesbians, and environmentalism.

Reconstructionism represents the last coherent movement to have emerged in American Judaism. A number of smaller postdenominational rabbinic academies also thrive, but to paint the story of American Judaism in the past couple of generations from an institutional perspective would be to miss much of the picture. Yet even what might be termed the "civil religion" of American Jews offers a more complicated view than a generation ago.

Beginning with Israel's miraculous victory in the Six-Day War of June 1967, nearly a generation of American Jews seemed united by a theology that combined pride in Israel and a determination to avoid an outbreak of anti-Semitism comparable to that which resulted in the Holocaust (or Shoah). As Jacob Neusner noted in *Stranger at Home*, only in the months leading up to Israel's "miraculous" victory did the Holocaust deeply penetrate Jewish American consciousness. From 1967 onward, a level of pro-Israel activism and a desire to educate Americans about the Holocaust have been motivators of extraordinary proportions. To take three examples of this activism: the erection of the American Museum of the Holocaust, just off the Mall in Washington, D.C.; the enormous success of the alliance of the American Israel Public Affairs Committee (AIPAC) with evangelical Christians; and, least problematically, the mobilization on behalf of Soviet Jewry in the 1970s. But the very success of the mainstreaming of Holocaust education and its universalizing has rendered the Holocaust less potent as a vehicle of Jewish identity, especially a the remaining survivors of that crime die off. Similarly, the image of Israel a beleaguered ally, once shared by all Jews, seems much more complicated to a generation that has watched two Palestinian uprisings on television.

American Judaism today resists simple characterization. Even an adequate description of the four organized movements of Judaism would fail to reflect the diversity of worship styles within each. Additionally, trends such as the push for gender equality, the growth of gay and lesbian congregations, the much larger presence of Jews-by-choice (that is, converts), various forms of religious syncretism, and the idiosyncratic identity-definition of Generations X and Y stymie simple explanation. The Jewish population of America is decreasing, but at over 5 million, it is still larger, as Jonathon Sarna notes, than many of the numerous religious denominations in the United States and larger than most of the famed cultures of the Jewish past. Never before has Jewry been so integrated into mainstream American life, and numerous trends in the religious landscape (for example, de-institutionalization, individualism, a consumer mentality in matters of observance and affiliation, charismatic leadership, electronic and Web-based virtual communities) have Jewish counterparts.

Although the greatest Jewish influence on the non-Jewish majority, by far, has been in the realm of secular and popular culture (for example, Tin Pan Alley, Broadway, Hollywood, the bagel), representatives of Judaism have at times spoken to non-Jewish Americans in influential ways. Rabbi Joshua Loth Leibman's *Peace of Mind* (1946) topped the *New York Times* best-seller list, as did Rabbi Harold Kushner's *Why Bad Things Happen to Good People* (1981). Chaim Potok's popular trio of coming-of-age novels—*The Chosen* (1967), *The Promise* (1969), and *My*

Name Is Asher Lev (1972)—delved deeply into matters of faith. Elie Wiesel's *Night* (1960) and *The Diary of a Young Girl* by Anne Frank (1947) have surely had more readers in English than in their original languages (Yiddish and German, respectively). Abraham Joshua Heschel's theological works moved a generation of liberal Protestant theologians, who were impressed by his burning religious commitment to civil rights.

The relationship of Judaism and Christianity has been complicated. Even in the United States, where the record of Jewish–Christian relations is far better than in Europe, Christian pressures on Jewry have not been absent. Since 1945, anti-Semitism has receded from American life, with the probable exception of segments of the Islamic American and African American communities. Ben Halpern's essay "America Is Different" (1954) observed that anti-Semitism has been a less violent and central factor in American history, and one might have expected the absence of this irritant to have ended departures from Judaism. However, even in an era of decreased discrimination, apostasy from Judaism has not stopped, only changed its idiom. The 1990 Council of Jewish Federation statistics place the number of born-Jews living as Christians at more than 200,000—an astonishing fact when the price exacted for being Jewish and the premium paid for being Christian is so low. Messianic Judaism represents part of this aggregate. These congregations have been created not by anti-Semitism, as with the despised "New Christians" following the Spanish Expulsion of 1492, but by voluntary self-segregation on the part of Jews who believe in the messiah-ship of Jesus but are proud of their Jewish descent.

Twenty-five years ago, nobody would have anticipated that non-Western religions would claim many Jewish advocates. Yet this has happened in the case of American Buddhism and Hinduism, which counts Bernard Glassman, Baba Ram Dass (né Richard Alpert), Jonathan Omer-Man, and others as leading spokespersons. For Western-born Buddhists, Jews have played a prominent role. Far from demanding the denial of Jewishness (or even Judaism), Eastern religions insist that the path to individual enlightenment include an acceptance of one's own background. Alongside formal Buddhist adherence, Eastern mysticism, pseudo-kabbalistic rituals, and meditation have won many adherents within the Jewish (and Gentile) world. The success of Rodger Kamenetz's *The Jew in the Lotus: A Poet's Rediscovery of Jewish Identity in Buddhist India* (1994) and *Stalking Elijah: Adventures with Today's Jewish Mystical Masters* (1997) may be offered as a case in point. Whatever one may think of JUBUs (Jewish-Buddhists) or messianic Jews, their emergence must be reckoned as a surprise story in modern American Judaism. And the funky, tattooed, pagan Jewishness captured in Lisa Schiffman's *Generation J* (1999) suggests that syncretism has not yet run its course.

American Jews had no ancient cities or long-established centers of learning, never lived in ghettos, and only sometimes had to fight for political equality. On first glance, American Jewry would seem a geographic unity when contrasted with

European Jewry. This impression would be erroneous: alongside generational factors, geography has also played a profound role in shaping American Judaism. Metropolitan New York, for instance, has been the home of at least half of the Jewish population since the great eastern European migration (1881–1921). New York City, by 1900, was the largest and densest Jewish settlement in the world, with a cultural, social, intellectual, and gastronomic richness unequaled elsewhere. The culture of New York and the culture of Jewishness have been popularly associated in the American mind; the comedian Lenny Bruce, with his routine "Jewish and Goyish," famously gibed that if you are from New York you are Jewish even if you are not, and that if you are from Iowa you are Gentile, even if you went to synagogue. While this humor traded on ethnic, not religious, differences, Bruce's routine pointed to stylistic differences in Judaism too. The Eastern Seaboard and Midwest remain "thicker" Jewishly, exhibiting higher rates of synagogue affiliation and lower rates of intermarriage. Southern Jewry kept a generally low profile in the 1960s—the lynching of Leo Frank in 1913 remained an unspoken topic in well-heeled circles. Contrariwise, the Southwest and Pacific Coast display a more informal atmosphere, manifested in everything from synagogue architecture to names and appearances of children. The old punchline to a hundred jokes, "Funny, you don't look Jewish," will be incomprehensible to America's next Jewish generation, which will be the product of an intermarriage rate of more than 50 percent. One might see this as the natural product of successful acculturation and the perception of Americans that one chooses one's identity—a concept foreign to traditional Judaism.

Feminism is arguably the single most creative force in American Judaism. Feminism advocates a set of propositions at odds with traditional Judaism. Feminists claim that gender roles in society are socially constructed, that Judaism has spoken for only one-half of its adherents, and that religious forms such as dogmatics (Christianity) or *halachah* (Judaism) constitute intrinsically male modes of discourse. Feminism has accomplished a revolution in Jewish life, beginning with that bastion of tradition: the synagogue. In the academy, Jewish feminists have helped make gender a powerful analytic tool. Such works as Sylvia Barack Fishman's *A Breath of Life: Feminism in the American Jewish Community*, Lynn Davidman and Shelly Tenenbaum's anthology *Feminist Perspectives on Jewish Studies*, Tamar Rudavsky's anthology *Gender and Judaism: The Transformation of Tradition* (1995), and Marc Raphael's anthology *Gendering the Jewish Past* (2002) represent the tip of an ever-growing iceberg.

By the mid-1990s, there were 254 ordained female rabbis in the United States; according to Yale University's Paula Hyman, that number has now passed 400. In Cleveland, for instance, three of the four large congregations (Temple-Tifereth Israel, Fairmount-Anshe Hesed, and Park Synagogue) have female rabbis, as do several of the smaller congregations. In counseling, pastoral, and educational roles, the impact of female rabbis is at least as great as in the pulpit. There are also more than 200 female cantors, who play a very important role in determining the liturgical style of the worship service, preparations for life-cycle events, and the overall tone of the temple/synagogue. The promotion of women to synagogue presidencies is a national trend. The glass ceiling may still exist in the business world, but not in the world of congregational leadership. The running of the synagogue, whether we refer to paid professionals, lay leaders, or volunteer organizations, has been transformed by the presence of women. The popularity of the bat mitzvah ceremony—instituted in 1922, but dormant until the 1970s—has created a generation of Jewish youth whose passage into adulthood is marked in gender-equal terms. In liberal Judaism, the counting of women in prayer quorums, the distribution of honors, and service participation have been fully equalized. Retrospectively, it seems quaint that in nineteenth-century America, liberal congregations debated the appropriateness of seating men and women together. A physical barrier between men and women, or a second-story women's gallery, is found today exclusively in Orthodox congregations.

The gender revolution in Judaism finds dramatic expression in synagogal changes, but occurs along a much broader front. First, Jewish education has been equalized, providing women for the first time in Jewish history with access to the sources of Judaism and training in the skills needed to employ those sources. Second, Jewish adult education has thrived in the past twenty-five years. Some of this flowering may be attributed to the success of American acculturation and the concomitant anxiety about Jewish survival; some may also be attributed to the desire of Jewish women and men to bring their Jewish learning on par with their general education. Whatever the motives, this adult-education boom has been unisex. In traditional Judaism, the adult male was universally more familiar with the elite texts of the tradition; even learned women generally had even more learned husbands and/or fathers. In contemporary Judaism, this is no longer the case. The Jewish mother or grandmother always played an enormous role in conveying Jewishness mimetically—this role has now been expanded to the intellectual appreciation of Judaism. Women's prayer and study groups have proliferated across this country, in both liberal and Orthodox circles. Many life-cycle events (for example, a welcoming ceremony for newborn girls paralleling the male circumcision, redemption of the daughter, traditionally reserved for boys, New Moon festivals) appropriate the practices of Jewish women in traditional society. The impact of feminism can be felt within Orthodoxy, too—outside the very small group of Ultra-Orthodox circles—accommodation, not resistance, is the dominant direction.

This chapter began with the caveat that Jewry and Judaism are distinguishable. The major fears of American Jewry—declining numbers, high intermarriage rates, "American vagabondism"—touch as much on the ethnic as on the religious coherence of the group. American Jewry is declining in numbers, relative and absolute. Yet there remain many signs of vibrancy, including the enrollment of over 200,000 children in day schools, a full 250,000 in supplemental schools, and many thousands in summer camps with varying Jewish content; the success of Jewish studies; and the popularity of programs such as "Birthright," which offer free trips to Israel. Despite an alarming tide of anti-Israel sentiment, anti-Semitism in the United States remains relatively marginal. American Judaism seems destined to remain what it has been since the colonial period: a prominent non-Christian religion, both admired and disdained, and destined to serve the needs of its adherents to balance the sincere desires for both full Americanism and group survival.

REFERENCES

Berman, Lila Corwin. *Speaking of Jews: Rabbis, Intellectuals, and the Creation of a Public Identity.* Berkeley: University of California Press, 2009.

Cohen, Naomi W. *Jews in Christian America: The Pursuit of Religious Equality.* New York: Oxford University Press, 1992.

Cohen, Steven M., and Arnold Eisen. *The Jew Within: Self, Family, and Community.* Bloomington: Indiana University Press, 2001.

Davidman, Lynn, and Shelley Tenenbaum, eds. *Feminist Perspectives on Jewish Studies.* New Haven, Conn.: Yale University Press, 1993.

Davis, Moshe. *The Emergence of Conservative Judaism: The Historical School in Nineteenth-Century America.* Philadelphia: Jewish Publication Society, 1963.

Diner, Hasia. *In the Almost Promised Land: American Blacks and Jews, 1915–1935.* Baltimore: Johns Hopkins University Press, 1995.

——. *A New Promised Land: A History of Jews in America.* New York: Oxford University Press, 2003.

Dinnerstein, Leonard. *Antisemitism in America.* New York: Oxford University Press, 1994.

Fishman, Sylvia Barack. *A Breath of Life: Feminism in the American Jewish Community.* New York: Free Press, 1993.

Freedman, Samuel. *Jew Versus Jew: The Struggle for the Soul of American Jewry.* New York: Simon and Schuster, 2000.

Gilman, Neil. *Conservative Judaism: The New Century.* West Orange, N.J.: Behrman House, 1993.

Goldman, Karla. *Beyond the Synagogue Gallery: Finding a Place for Women in American Judaism.* Cambridge, Mass.: Harvard University Press, 2000.

Goren, Arthur. *New York Jews and the Quest for Community: The Kehilla Experiment.* New York: Columbia University Press, 1970.

Grose, Peter. *Israel in the Mind of America.* New York: Knopf, 1983.

Gurock, Jeffrey S. *American Jewish Orthodoxy in Historical Perspective.* Hoboken, N.J.: KTAV, 1996.

Gurock, Jeffrey S., and Jacob J. Schachter, eds. *A Modern Heretic and a Traditional Community: Mordecai Kaplan, Orthodoxy, and American Judaism*. New York: Columbia University Press, 1997.

Heilman, Sam, and Steven Cohen. *Cosmopolitans and Parochials: Modern Orthodox Jews in America*. Chicago: University of Chicago Press, 1989.

Hertzberg, Arthur. *The Jews in America: Four Centuries of an Uneasy Encounter*. New York: Simon and Schuster, 1989.

Howe, Irving. *The World of Our Fathers: The Journey of the East European Jews to America and the Life They Found and Made*. New York: Harcourt Brace Jovanovich, 1976.

Jick, Leon. *The Americanization of the Synagogue, 1820–1870*. Hanover, N.H.: University Press of New England, 1976.

Kaplan, Dana. *Contemporary American Judaism: Transformation and Renewal*. New York: Columbia University Press, 2009.

Marcus, Jacob R. "The American Colonial Jew: A Study in Acculturation." In *The American Jewish Experience*, ed. Jonathan Sarna, 6–17. New York: Holmes and Meier, 1997.

Meyer, Michael. *Response to Modernity: A History of the Reform Movement in Judaism*. New York: Oxford University Press, 1988.

Neusner, Jacob. *Stranger at Home*. Chicago: University of Chicago Press, 1981.

Raphael, Marc Lee. *Judaism in America*. New York: Columbia University Press, 2003.

——. *Profiles in American Judaism*. San Francisco: Harper & Row, 1984.

Sarna, Jonathan. *American Judaism: A History*. New Haven, Conn.: Yale University Press, 2004.

——, ed. *The Jewish American Experience*. 2nd ed. New York: Holmes and Meier, 1997.

Soloveitchik, Haym. "Reconciliation and Rupture." *Tradition: A Journal of Orthodox Thought* 28, no. 4 (1994): 64–131.

Staub, Jacob, and Rebecca Alpert. *Exploring Judaism: A Reconstructionist Approach*. Wyncote, Pa.: Reconstructionist Press, 1985.

Weiser, Michael R. *A Brotherhood of Memory: Jewish Landsmanshaftn in the New World*. New York: Basic Books, 1985.

Wenger, Beth. *History Lessons: The Creation of American Jewish Heritage*. Princeton, N.J.: Princeton University Press, 2010.

Wertheimer, Jack. *A People Divided: Judaism in Contemporary America*. New York: Basic Books, 1993.

——, ed. *The Uses of Tradition: Jewish Continuity in the Modern Era*. Cambridge, Mass.: Harvard University Press, 1992.

Whitfield, Stephen. *In Search of American Jewish Culture*. Hanover, N.H.: University Press of New England, 1999.

Woocher, Jonathan. *Sacred Survival: The Civil Religion of American Jews*. Bloomington: Indiana University Press, 1986.

19. THE CHURCH OF JESUS CHRIST OF LATTER-DAY SAINTS ("MORMONS")

D. MICHAEL QUINN

Headquartered in Salt Lake City, Utah, the Church of Jesus Christ of Latter-day Saints (LDS) has a worldwide membership of more than 14 million, with two-thirds of these adherents outside the United States. It likewise received international media attention in 2008 as the proudly avowed faith of a "conservative Republican" candidate for the U.S. presidency. This merging of ecclesiastical growth with political prominence began to characterize North America's homegrown religion within a few years of its formal inception on April 6, 1830, in western New York State. That amalgam resulted from the faith's insistence that there is no real distinction between the secular and the religious, "for all things are spiritual" to God.

This church dates its spiritual inception first to the original Christian era in Palestine and second to a "divine restoration" that began in 1820 at the village of Manchester, New York, next to the larger village of Palmyra. In between was a "Great Apostasy"—during which the Gnostic, Catholic, Orthodox, reformist, and Protestant versions of Christianity erred in doctrine and liturgy because they had lost the authority of the original church as established by Jesus and his twelve apostles.

Despite its own exclusionary assertions of authority, truth, and liturgy, Mormon/LDS theology regards those religious "others" as having equal claim to "salvation." Thus, like all non-Christians throughout human existence, the devout believers in "apostate Christianity" are guaranteed salvation (that is, resurrection) by the intercession of Jesus Christ; this "atonement" does not require the individual to accept Jesus as personal savior. Mormon/LDS theology, however, reserves the special status of "exaltation in the presence of God" for those who acknowledge the "grace of Christ" and "continue faithful" by their own attitudes and behavior after receiving special ordinances, beginning with baptism. If not administered during one's mortal existence, these ordinances can be performed for the individual "by proxy" by the living and be accepted by each person after death. Such unusual mixes of exclusivity/inclusiveness and grace-works are examples of what has emerged from Mormon/LDS claims of continued revelation to a series of "living prophets of God" on earth in modern times. This claim alone separates Mormonism from traditional Christianity.

The first of these prophets was Joseph Smith Jr. (1805–1844). Born in Sharon, Vermont, he moved with his family to Palmyra in western New York in late 1816, when the village was in the midst of an interdenominational "revival" that continued through 1817. This and subsequent religious "awakenings" in their neighborhood heightened the tensions between his father, Joseph Sr., who believed in Universalist views of unrestricted salvation for all, and his mother, Lucy Mack Smith, who was inclined toward Presbyterian views of "election to grace" for the few, with damnation to a "hell" of unending suffering for humanity's unbelievers, lukewarm Christians, well-intentioned "backsliders," and the world's willfully wicked people.

In June 1818, Palmyra had a Methodist revival (without participation by other denominations) in an adjacent forest, the first such camp meeting since the Smith family's arrival. Young Joseph was twelve at the time, and he later said that this was his age upon first becoming interested in religion and Bible reading, a spiritual awakening he credited the Methodists for initiating. The neighborhood's next revival, also a Methodist camp meeting, occurred in the late spring of 1820. According to an official account written a decade later, it was this spring when Joseph Smith had his "First Vision," in which he saw God and Jesus standing side by side in a grove of trees. Obtaining forgiveness of his adolescent sins, he reputedly received divine instruction at this time to join none of the existing churches.

He claimed that three and a half years later, on the night of September 21/22, 1823, he was visited three times by an angel (later identified as Moroni), who commissioned him to find and "translate" (from "Reformed Egyptian") some ancient records, which were inscribed on plates of gold. This ultimately resulted in the unschooled young man's dictating to a scribe during a six-week period in 1829 a manuscript more than 500 printed pages in length when published as *The Book of Mormon* in Palmyra in March 1830. Proclaiming itself to be the revealed text of overlapping scriptures written by ancient Israelites and Christian believers living on the American continent more than 1,400 years earlier, it introduced readers to "Nephites" and "Lamanites," who recorded their violence-filled religious history from when they left Jerusalem around 600 b.c.e. until their extinction during internecine wars around 400 c.e. Condensed by the last surviving Nephite prophet (named Mormon), the text also backtracked to a brief account of the "Jaredites," who had arrived in the New World almost two millennia earlier from the Tower of Babel, having had only one contact with the Nephite-Lamanite peoples.

Within two weeks, the publication of this book by a farmer-prophet—one of many examples of the theme of the folk origins of high theology discussed in the introduction to this volume—led to the organization of a new church. Since the "First Vision," the angelic visits, and the "Hill Cumorah" (from which Smith said he dug up the gold plates) were all in Manchester, it competed in religious significance with the town of Fayette, New York, where he had "translated" the new scripture "by the gift and power of God." Because most of his followers then lived in or near Fayette, the new church's organizational meeting occurred there on April 6, 1830.

Regarding the book as a crudely written competitor to the Holy Bible, disbelievers immediately referred to the upstart publication as the "Mormon Bible" and gave to its believers the epithet of "Mormonites," later shortened to "Mormons." As with the term "Christians," used by pagans to insult the ancient world's believers, these followers of a modern charismatic eventually transformed this term of mockery into self-description.

Complicating this religious chronology was the fact that Joseph Jr. himself, as well as his father and mother, had been participating in various forms of traditional folk magic and the occult from the time of their arrival in Palmyra until he began the "translation." According to neighbors (including early believers like *Book of Mormon* "witness" Martin Harris and Smith's future bodyguard, Orrin Porter Rockwell), this included dream-divination, palmistry, and treasure-seeking with divining rods (rhabdomancy) or with "peep-stones"/"seer-stones" (scrying).

Labeling young Joseph as a "Glass looker" in early 1826 (when he was still a legal minor), court documents portrayed his trial as a "disorderly person" for using stone-divination in the commercial enterprise of treasure-digging. It was a misdemeanor for which the minor would have been at most fined, not imprisoned, but the court's scribe wrote that Joseph Jr. was simply allowed to leave the county, a judicial banishment common to rural courts in this era. Three years later, he used one of his treasure-digging seer-stones, a "brownish" one, to translate ancient American scriptures from an unknown language into the biblical English of the King James Version (KJV) in 1829.

Documentary and artifactual evidence of these events also begin in 1829. A relative's surviving letter that year emphasized Joseph Sr.'s wooden divining rod, which is itself not preserved. This period's surviving artifacts (handed from father to son within one branch of the Smith family for 150 years) include a dagger (inscribed according to instructions in Francis Barrett's *The Magus* [1801]) for drawing "magic circles," used in treasure-digging, and parchments ("lamens") inscribed with symbols of ritual magic and astrology identical to those published in a dozen printings of Ebenezer Sibly's *New and Complete Illustration of the*

Occult Sciences before 1826. The family of Joseph Jr.'s widow preserved one seer-stone and a Jupiter talisman, inscribed according to illustrations in Barrett's occult handbook. Photos of all of these have been published. Smith's other seer-stones were inherited by his scribe's widow and various relatives before being stored for a hundred years as "sacred relics" inside a walk-in vault at the LDS Church's headquarters in Utah. Although described in print, those artifacts have not been photographed.

Smith's early experience with folk magic was only one of the controversies swirling around Mormonism during its formative years. For traditional Christians, its most obvious heresy was the claim of an "open canon"—that the Bible is insufficient as a guide and must be supplemented by added scriptures. In addition to *The Book of Mormon*, Smith's revelations were collected during his lifetime as *The Doctrine and Covenants* and more of his "inspired" writings were published after his death as *The Pearl of Great Price*. Along with the KJV Bible, these three modern books constitute the canonized "Standard Works" of the LDS Church.

Among their official doctrines, the most offensive to traditional Christians is the Mormon claim that the Trinity involves three separate divinities—the unembodied Holy Ghost, plus the eternal God and the resurrected Christ, who are two separate "personages," each with "a body of flesh and bones, as tangible as man's." Equally controversial, Smith's published revelations also restructured Christian concepts of afterlife. "Hell" becomes only a temporary condition of suffering, after which all humans (even the most wicked on earth) will be resurrected with bodies of flesh and bone. As opposed to a unitary "heaven," the Last Judgment will assign nearly all to one of three eternal "kingdoms," or "degrees of glory" (Celestial, Terrestrial, Telestial). Even in the lowest, the "Telestial Kingdom," murderers will have eternal happiness and a portion of God's presence. The traditionally Christian concept of hell was restricted by Smith's revelations to a very few whose sin is "unpardonable" because it was against God personally, not simply contrary to divine commandments or even the most heinous act against humans. These "sons of perdition" are the only ones who never repent, and thus never receive divine forgiveness.

Because of his status as God's first prophet on earth in modern times, every pronouncement of Joseph Smith Jr. continued to have doctrinal significance to all generations of Mormons. That included his uncanonized, but frequently published, sermon that God was once a human being, that humans can become gods in every sense that their "Heavenly Father" is, and that God is literally the biological father of each individual spirit of all humans, who lived before birth in a "preexistence" with God and a "Heavenly Mother." By this LDS construct, Jesus Christ was the spiritual brother of all humans before becoming their savior.

This was the beginning of Mormonism's emphasis on "the Eternal Family." As eventually defined, this meant eternal linkages in two directions. First, as husband and wife (or wives) on earth who are "sealed for time and eternity" in marriage and linked eternally by that sealing to each of their children and his or her respective spouse, throughout all their descendants. Second, from each husband and wife, as sealed to each of their ancestors and his or her respective spouse-ancestor back to Adam and Eve, and then to God, "the Father of all." The Mormon temple's rite of "the endowment" symbolically portrays this progression of individuals and married couples from premortal existence, through mortality, with instructions for the means to return to God's presence in the Celestial Kingdom.

Despite technically having the designation of "prophets, seers, and revelators," successive presidents of the LDS Church have not had equivalent status doctrinally. Their sermons and official pronouncements are revered during their lifetimes, but a subsequent president can (and often has) modified or reversed the statements and policies of prophets other than the founder. The most recent example was the June 1978 pronouncement that ended Brigham Young's policy of prohibiting priesthood to all persons of black African ancestry since 1847. This returned the Utah church's practices to those of the founding prophet, who authorized the ordination of non-slave African Americans in the late 1830s and early 1840s. Smith preached publicly that social opportunities were all that separated poor blacks from white elites, whereas Young insisted that blacks were racially inferior. Mormons practiced a racialized religion while they preached a universal god, another way they exemplify one of the major themes of religion in American history.

Likewise, while Joseph Smith publicly advocated the peaceful, financially compensated abolition of slavery during the last year of his life, Brigham Young (as Utah Territory's first governor) instructed a compliant legislature to legalize the slavery of African Americans in 1852, while legally prohibiting the enslavement of Mexicans and Native Americans. As a result, pioneer Utah Mormons bought and sold African Americans, whom they also paid as "tithing" to LDS headquarters, but adopted Mexican and Indian children when offered for sale or barter by rival tribes. While the first practice demonstrated Young's new policy of promoting the dominant racism of his times, the latter reflected a *Book of Mormon* doctrine akin to early American society's attitudes toward "the Noble Savage." Indians and *mestizo* Mexicans were divinely blessed "Lamanites," whose lapsed cultures and religious lives should be "redeemed" by white Latter-day Saints. In the mid-twentieth century, this led to the LDS "Placement Program," by which tens of thousands of parents on reservations were persuaded to allow their children to be "placed" in homes of middle-class, white Mormons for each school year, returning only during summer vacation from their public schools. During the same time period, intensive proselytizing throughout Latin America led to Spanish being the most commonly spoken language by Mormonism's millions in the twenty-first century, with English remaining its official lingua franca.

Publicized earliest and most frequently during Joseph Smith's lifetime were Mormon theocratic prerogatives, starting with a written revelation of 1833. Giving the LDS president divine authorization to nullify civil laws, ignore elected leaders, and form private armies, this revelation provided doctrinal justification for Smith's leading a ragtag military expedition ("Zion's Camp") from the church's seven-year headquarters at Kirtland, Ohio, to Missouri in 1834; solemnizing civil marriages without legal license in Ohio in 1835; forming an unchartered "wild-cat" bank in Kirtland in 1837 before fleeing the state to avoid prosecution after its collapse; and serving as "commander in chief" of a highly organized army at the months-old headquarters of Far West, Missouri, in 1838 when his troops took up arms against state militias. After Smith escaped from a Missouri jail in 1839 while awaiting trial for treason, he returned to his thousands of American followers who were gathering at the new headquarters in Nauvoo, Illinois.

Because bloc-voting Mormons could change the balance of political power in a state equally divided by two major parties, Illinois politicians initially gave Smith everything he asked, first by conferring on Nauvoo a "city charter" that allowed it to be nearly autonomous. The governor appointed the LDS president as "Lieutenant General of the Nauvoo Legion" from 1840 to 1844, during which it grew to be the nation's largest militia, second in size only to the U.S. Army. During those years, he served simultaneously as vice mayor (then mayor) of Nauvoo, chief judge of its municipal court, and exclusive agent for all its land transactions. Beginning in December 1843, he campaigned as independent candidate for the U.S. presidency, and then secretly organized in March 1844 a theocratic "Council of Fifty" that privately ordained him "king over Israel on earth" and commissioned "ambassadors" from the city-state of Nauvoo to England, France, the Republic of Texas, and even Washington, D.C. Smith continued campaigning as a presidential candidate until he was murdered by a mob in June 1844 while in jail. He was awaiting trial on charges of treason against Illinois and the Constitution of the United States for ordering the destruction of Nauvoo's anti-Mormon newspaper after it promised to expose his secret practices, including kingship.

Harassed by mobs in Illinois in 1844 and 1845, Mormons began leaving Nauvoo en masse in February 1846, crossing the Mississippi River to the Great Plains, and making their way to the Great Salt Lake Valley, where Brigham Young established church headquarters anew in July 1847. He led a majority of the church's membership in this modern "Exodus of Israel," the rest choosing to follow seven other routes for filling the founding prophet's absence, a confusing set of possibilities that he himself had created. Rather than resolving this succession crisis in 1844, Mormons at Nauvoo had chosen the stability of continuity when they publicly "sustained" Young to continue leading the church as senior member and president of "The Quorum of the Twelve Apostles" organized by Smith a decade earlier. Mormon historians designate the period from 1844 to 1847 as the church's "apostolic interregnum" following the prophet's martyrdom. In December 1847, the pioneers publicly sustained Young's decision to replicate what the founder had done by forming a "First Presidency," himself as church-president with two counselors.

In what he called the State of Deseret (after a *Book of Mormon* word for "honeybee"), Brigham Young expanded the church-theocracy that Smith had inaugurated. Even though the federal government had named the territory Utah after the Ute Indians, U.S. presidents temporarily acquiesced to Mormon theocracy. Young served as federally appointed governor from 1850 to 1857, and the highest LDS leaders ("general authorities") composed one-third of the Mormon legislature, which voted unanimously on all but one item of legislation until the American Civil War and retained general authorities as Utah legislators until the 1880s.

Even after Young was removed from office during the "Utah War" of 1857/1858, when President James Buchanan sent a regiment of troops to suppress what he supposed to be a "Mormon rebellion," the LDS president continued to decide who would be elected to territorial, county, and local offices. Territorial Utah was a "democratic" theocracy in which the rank and file voted for candidates selected in advance by ruling elders whom the believing electorate trusted. Dissenting votes were minimal, less than 5 percent every election until Young's death in 1877. Pioneer Utah's electorate included women, among the nation's first to receive the legal right to vote, just as those Mormons were almost the only American women in the mid- to late nineteenth century with legal rights to sign contracts, obtain divorces for "incompatibility," own property independently, run businesses by themselves, and be physicians or lawyers. America had seen nothing like the nineteenth-century ministerial theocracy of the Mormon hierarchy.

The federal government was able to dismantle Mormon theocracy (and nearly destroy the LDS Church) by attacking the other practice that Brigham Young had publicly institutionalized in Utah—Joseph Smith's secret practice of marrying multiple wives. As early as his dictating *The Book of Mormon*'s text in 1829, Smith had asserted the possibility for a divine restoration of polygamy. After some indirect statements on this matter to a few in 1831 and 1832, he secretly married his seventeen-year-old housekeeper in 1833 in a ceremony performed by her uncle, whom Smith advanced to the position of general-authority "Seventy" two years later. Because of problems this caused when rumors of their relationship surfaced in Kirtland in the years 1835 to 1837, Smith held off on marrying other women. Aside from one possible marriage in Missouri before his arrest at the end of that state's religious "Civil War" in 1838, he waited until the 1840s to make more proposals in Illinois. During the three years before his death, he married at least thirty-two more women, with some research indicating a dozen beyond that. Most were in their twenties and thirties, a few were in their forties and fifties, and others were teenagers (one age fourteen) who married him by permission of their believing parents. Ten of his secret wives already had husbands with whom they were living. Before Smith's death, a couple of children were born to polygamous wives he had "sealed" to other men, and one of his polyandrous wives gave birth to a child she confided was Smith's. These were difficult realities that his legal wife and some associates wanted to simply deny and forget.

Instead, Brigham Young insisted on continuing the practice, because he and several other apostles had received new wives from the prophet, who taught them that polygamy was an "eternal principle" on which the progress of the church depended. Young's determination to continue this cohabitation and performance of plural marriages caused a permanent split with the prophet's widow, Emma. Her surviving sons and like-minded followers eventually established in Independence, Missouri, their "Reorganized Church," which repudiated polygamy, the name Mormons, and anything distinctive to Utah Mormonism. Ultimately, this Protestant-like fellowship adopted the name Community of Christ on the eve of the twenty-first century.

After authorizing the secret performance of new polygamy for eight years (during which it was consistently denied), Young permitted its public announcement in 1852 as "Celestial Marriage." Mormons of the time equated that term with plural marriage, rather than with the "eternal sealing" of monogamous couples. For nearly forty years, polygamous Celestial Marriage visibly and stridently remained part of Mormon society in the Far West. This led to the federal government's increasingly punitive efforts to end the practice. Aimed at the Mormons, the Morrill Act of 1862 outlawed "bigamy" in all U.S. territories. However, federal courts in territorial Utah had difficulty obtaining proof of the actual ceremony of polygamy, leaving this law poorly enforced. After the Supreme Court ruled in 1879 that the Morrill Act was *not* an unconstitutional infringement on religious freedom (as detailed further in Ravitch, chap. 7, this volume), Mormon leaders publicly vowed to continue performing and living in plural marriages anyway. As a result, the Edmunds Act of 1882 sidestepped the difficulty of proving the polygamous ceremony—by specifying imprisonment for those convicted of "unlawful cohabitation." As a result, a thousand Mormon men went to penitentiaries in Utah and surrounding territories during the next ten years, while thousands more went into hiding (the "Mormon Underground") to escape arrest.

The Edmunds Act also denied all male polygamists the rights of voting, holding public office, and serving on juries. In 1882, the same year as the act was passed, the Department of State instructed its diplomatic officers to cease aiding Mormon missionaries who were arrested for proselytizing in foreign countries. The Edmunds-Tucker Act of 1887 disfranchised all women of Utah (reducing Mormon voting strength by half), disincorporated the LDS Church, declared all its assets as forfeit to the federal government, and provided the administrative means to confiscate those assets. In 1889 federal judges began to refuse naturalization to Utah's immigrants who admitted believing in polygamy, and officials began to deport from Ellis Island new immigrants who admitted to belief in polygamy. In February and May 1890, the Supreme Court decided against the Mormons twice, first by declaring the confiscation act of 1887 as constitutional and second by ruling that it was constitutional to deny all rights of citizenship to native-born Americans who were members of the LDS Church. In response to the latter, both houses of Congress began to prepare legislation during the summer to disfranchise Mormons everywhere.

The final step in the successful campaign to force compliance was the decision in August 1890 to confiscate the church's most sacred structures, the temples. The federal government stopped exempting them from confiscation because their rites of "endowment" and "sealing" were not open to the public.

As a result, LDS president Wilford Woodruff decided to surrender a religious practice to federal authority, in order to prevent the destruction of the church as an institution. In September 1890, he issued a "Manifesto" urging all Latter-day Saints to "refrain from contracting any marriage forbidden by the law of the land." As privately required by President Benjamin Harrison, this document was ratified by the church's next "general conference" (Salt Lake City's semi-annual meeting that votes to sustain the church's leaders and policies). The next year, the First Presidency disavowed theocracy in a published statement.

Those actions allowed the re-incorporation of the LDS Church, return of its confiscated assets, admission of Utah into the union as a state (after forty-six years of failed attempts), and acceptance of Mormons as loyal citizens. The last seemed assured when the First Presidency advised LDS men to serve in the Spanish-American War of 1898. Giving up polygamy's literal practice was—as it had always been—the only nonnegotiable requirement by the federal government.

As their opponents had predicted for decades, surrendering polygamy slowly transformed radical Mormons into mainstream Americans. For example, the Mormon Tabernacle Choir started making inroads against traditional prejudices just months before the beginning of the Great Depression. In July 1929, the NBC network launched national radio broadcasts of the group's Sunday morning hymn-singing. It was the start of a cultural conversion through radio, record albums, far-flung concerts, and eventually televised broadcasts. This reached a crescendo sixty years later, when President George H. W. Bush called it "the nation's choir" as they sang for his inauguration.

Ironically, the First Presidency's opposition to the New Deal's programs after 1933 began gaining the LDS Church the kind of widespread respect among Americans that it had never before experienced. Responding to President Franklin D. Roosevelt's "socialistic" remedies for the national depression, LDS president Heber J. Grant and his counselor J. Reuben Clark Jr. (former undersecretary of state and U.S. ambassador) launched the church's own Welfare Program in 1936. Admired nationally for its self-help approach to economic distress, this program eventually provided disaster relief to non-Mormons throughout the world.

Although young Mormon men had served for two years or more as full-time missionaries (at their own expense) outside the United States since the 1830s, proselytizing efforts grew substantially after the end of World War II in 1945. Between 1955 and 1958, LDS temples began to provide special ordinances in Switzerland, England, and New Zealand. Critical mass was achieved by the 1960s, when there was an explosion of convert-baptisms in Latin America, followed next by Oceania, Asia, and North America. High LDS birthrates continued the traditionally geometric growth in the "Mormon Culture Region" of the far western United States and in the western provinces of Canada. Young women and retired couples joined the ranks of missionaries (soon numbering in the tens of thousands annually), and total LDS membership doubled about every fifteen years.

In 1978, advertising in the *Reader's Digest* became an ultimate symbol of Mormonism's wealth and its acceptance into America's mainstream. The LDS Church paid the enormous fees required for eight-page inserts of religious ads in monthly issues. Its *Book of Mormon* insert reached 19.2 million subscribers in 1982. This reflected the degree to which Americans were seeing Mormons as prominent contributors to diverse fields in literature, politics, education, and sports.

Not coincidentally, the LDS Church started flexing its political power on the national level during those years. In the 1970s, for example, LDS headquarters used its military-style command system to conduct a grassroots political campaign in twenty states to defeat the proposed Equal Rights Amendment (ERA), which would ban all discrimination based on gender. Joining with organizations of evangelical Protestants, conservative Catholics, and Orthodox Jews in anti-ERA propaganda of "family values," this sometimes-covert campaign helped to defeat the proposed amendment in 1982. A decade later, with the same religious allies, LDS headquarters publicly spearheaded a political campaign against the legalization of same-sex marriages and in opposition to gay rights legislation at the national, state, county, and local levels.

That process of assimilation has been almost equally remarkable throughout the rest of the world, where denial of visas, then surveillance, imprisonment, and expulsion had once been common for LDS missionaries. Nearly 200 of the religion's most sacred structures, temples, are now scattered throughout every inhabited continent and in many island nations. The most dramatic example was the dedication in 1985 of an LDS temple in Freiberg, approved by East Germany's Communist regime, which was officially atheist. Another example involves the quick and relatively high rates of baptism in sub-Saharan Africa after the LDS Church began allowing the ordination of all races. Non-LDS sociologist Rodney Stark has conducted computer analysis indicating that Mormons worldwide will number some 265 million by the year 2080.

In January 2008, Mormon president Gordon B. Hinckley died. On the one hand, he represented both the weaknesses and the strengths of gerontocracy typical of the LDS Church's highest leadership since the late nineteenth century. On the other, he was the most politically astute and media-savvy leader of Mormonism since the death of J. Reuben Clark in 1961. During his nearly thirteen years of officially being church president, Hinckley remained physically vigorous, and did so until just a few days before his death at age ninety-seven. He was the most-traveled counselor-president in LDS history, presiding over the planning of more than a hundred temples throughout the world.

He became an apostle when the church was on the verge of a cash-flow crisis, but oversaw its financial growth to the point that it could pay all the building and operating costs for local congregations and partially subsidize 50,000 full-time missionaries annually. As counselor and president, he openly participated in the national campaigns against gay rights and same-sex marriage. Media-savvy to the last, he enjoyed holding unscripted news conferences, plus having disarming chats on-camera with hard-boiled interviewers like Mike Wallace of 60 *Minutes*. Serving in the First Presidency while the church nearly tripled its 1981 membership of 4.9 million, Hinckley concluded: "We are part of an incomparable miracle!"

His successor, Thomas S. Monson, was sustained as LDS president on April 5, 2008. Active as an executive in church-owned enterprises since the 1950s, he had received an MBA degree from Brigham Young University and entered the Quorum of the Twelve Apostles in 1963 at age thirty-six. The LDS "miracle" of increased numbers and real powers has also involved various tensions, which scholars have incompletely analyzed for contemporary Mormonism. More attention must be given to issues involving institutional pressures against American intellectuals, academics, and feminists—both in and away from the church's Brigham Young University—as the hierarchy's response to centrifugal tendencies of massive growth. Correspondingly, more analysis of sociology and social anthropology is needed in comparing the varieties of Mormon life and thought as typified by the "headquarters culture" of Salt Lake City versus Utah at large; the "Mormon Culture Region" of the far western states other than Utah versus Mormonism in other regions of the United States; and each of its major population centers in Latin America and Oceania (in particular), as well as Mormon social dynamics in Europe, Asia, and Africa. Despite its hierarchical structure and tendencies toward homogeneity and group-think, the image of monolithic Mormonism is overstated. Moreover, in view of the actual influence of the LDS Church on Utah politics and its increasingly frequent intrusions into the regional and national political spheres of the United States, political scientists in various countries might have fertile fields of analysis for Mormon political behavior thousands of miles from any border of the United States.

REFERENCES

Alexander, Thomas G. *Mormonism in Transition: A History of the Latter-day Saints, 1890–1930.* Urbana: University of Illinois Press, 1986.

Arrington, Leonard J. *Great Basin Kingdom: An Economic History of the Latter-day Saints, 1830–1900.* Cambridge, Mass.: Harvard University Press, 1958.

Beecher, Maureen Ursenbach, and Lavina Fielding Anderson. *Sisters in Spirit: Mormon Women in Historical and Cultural Perspectives.* Urbana: University of Illinois Press, 1987.

Bloom, Harold. *The American Religion: The Emergence of the Post-Christian Nation.* New York: Simon and Schuster, 1992.

Bradley, Martha S. *Pedestals and Podiums: Utah, Women, Religious Authority, and Equal Rights.* Salt Lake City: Signature Books, 2005.

Bringhurst, Newell G. *Saints, Slaves, and Blacks: The Changing Place of Black People Within Mormonism.* Westport, Conn.: Greenwood Press, 1981.

Brooke, John L. *The Refiner's Fire: The Making of Mormon Cosmology, 1644–1844.* New York: Cambridge University Press, 1996.

Bushman, Claudia. *Contemporary Mormonism: Latter-day Saints in Modern America.* Westport, Conn.: Praeger, 2006.

Bushman, Richard Lyman. *Joseph Smith: Rough Stone Rolling.* New York: Knopf, 2005.

Butler, Jon. *Awash in a Sea of Faith: Christianizing the American People.* Cambridge, Mass.: Harvard University Press, 1990.

Church of Jesus Christ of Latter-day Saints. *2011 Church Almanac.* Salt Lake City: Deseret News, 2010.

Compton, Todd M. *In Sacred Loneliness: The Plural Wives of Joseph Smith.* Salt Lake City: Signature Books, 1997.

Conkin, Paul K. *American Originals: Homemade Varieties of Christianity.* Chapel Hill: University of North Carolina Press, 1997.

Davies, Douglas J. *An Introduction to Mormonism.* Cambridge: Cambridge University Press, 2003.

Daynes, Kathryn M. *More Wives Than One: Transformation of the Mormon Marriage System, 1840–1910.* Urbana: University of Illinois Press, 2001.

Flake, Kathleen. *The Politics of American Religious Identity: The Seating of Senator Reed Smoot, Mormon Apostle.* Chapel Hill: University of North Carolina Press, 2004.

Givens, Terryl L. *People of Paradox: A History of Mormon Culture.* New York: Oxford University Press, 2007.

Gordon, Sarah Barringer. *The Mormon Question: Polygamy and Constitutional Conflict in Nineteenth-Century America.* Chapel Hill: University of North Carolina Press, 2002.

Hardy, B. Carmon. *Solemn Covenant: The Mormon Polygamous Passage.* Urbana: University of Illinois Press, 1992.

Hatch, Nathan O. *The Democratization of American Christianity.* New Haven, Conn.: Yale University Press, 1989.

Jessee, Dean C., Mark Ashurst-McGee, and Richard L. Jensen. *The Joseph Smith Papers: Journals.* Vol. 1, 1832–1839. Salt Lake City: Church Historian's Press/Church History Department of the Church of Jesus Christ of Latter-day Saints, 2008.

Ludlow, Daniel H. *Encyclopedia of Mormonism: The History, Scripture, Doctrine, and Procedure of the Church of Jesus Christ of Latter-day Saints.* 5 vols. New York: Macmillan, 1992.

Lyman, Edward Leo. *Political Deliverance: The Mormon Quest for Utah Statehood.* Urbana: University of Illinois Press, 1994.

Mauss, Armand L. *The Angel and the Beehive: The Mormon Struggle with Assimilation.* Urbana: University of Illinois Press, 1994.

Mazur, Eric Michael. *The Americanization of Religious Minorities: Confronting the Constitutional Order.* Baltimore: Johns Hopkins University Press, 1999.

Ostling, Richard, and Joan K. Ostling. *Mormon America: The Power and the Promise.* San Francisco: HarperCollins, 1999.

Quinn, D. Michael. *Early Mormonism and the Magic World View.* Salt Lake City: Signature Books, 1998.

———. *The Mormon Hierarchy.* Vol. 1, *Origins of Power.* Salt Lake City: Signature Books, 1994.

———. *The Mormon Hierarchy.* Vol. 2, *Extensions of Power.* Salt Lake City: Signature Books, 1997.

Shipps, Jan. *Mormonism: The Story of a New Religious Tradition.* Urbana: University of Illinois Press, 1985.

20. ISLAM IN AMERICA

JANE SMITH

The Muslim community in the United States is undergoing significant and serious changes. With its unique blend of immigrant, African American, and other American-born Muslims, it is becoming increasingly heterogeneous even as efforts are under way to stress commonality over individuality. Muslim institutions are proliferating, Islamic education is taking new forms, various individuals and groups are vying for positions of leadership, and young people are often choosing paths of greater religiosity than their parents at the same time that the label on their religion seems to read "made in America." The history of the Muslim faith in America exemplifies many of the principles associated with the ninth theme discussed in the introduction to this volume: immigration, the globalization of American religious communities, and ethnic insularity and self-definitions.

September 11, 2001—a defining moment in American history—has left its irreparable mark on American Muslims as anti-Islamic prejudice in American society continues to rise, Muslim civil rights are challenged, and relations between Sunnis and Shi'ites reflect the sectarian divisions of the Middle East. Even as Muslims are trying to persuade the citizens of the United States that Islam is peace-loving, open, and viable in its newly adopted home, Americans today—although relieved that several potential new attacks by Muslim terrorists have been intercepted—continue to express rising anxiety and suspicion about Islam and about the increasing presence of Muslims in public life. Muslims in the West in general vehemently disavow any relationship between true Islam and terrorism and are struggling to be good citizens of the United States, although they often are afraid to be too visible.

Reports on the number of Muslims in America vary greatly, depending on the claimant. Four to 6 million is a reasonable estimate, with more than eighty countries represented in the mix. Once American Muslims were easily classified as either immigrants or African Americans. With the rise of second, third, and fourth generations of Muslims born in America, however, new forms of identification are needed. The simplest may be "foreign-born" and "American-born" (the latter also including white, Latino/a and other converts); the students, temporary workers, diplomats, and others who never intend to make America their home are also included in this tally. Approximately one-third of the community is African American, members of Sunni Islam or one of many sectarian movements. Most of the major cities of the United States have Muslim populations, with the largest concentrations located in New York, Chicago, Los Angeles, Houston, and Detroit.

EARLY HISTORY

A significant body of literature is now growing, especially among African American scholars, that argues that Muslims have been present on American soil far longer than earlier supposed. Some slight evidence has been collected to suggest both a pre-Columbian presence and early West African explorations in the Caribbean. Spanish Muslim sailors may well have served as guides for Spanish and Portuguese discoverers. With the expulsion of Muslims from Spain in 1492 by monarchs Ferdinand and Isabella, some may have fled Europe and made their way to the Americas. Even if this is true, there is no record that they were able to maintain their Islamic identity.

The first significant entry of Muslims onto the American continent took place with the African slave trade from the seventeenth to the nineteenth century. Perhaps as much as one-fifth of the Africans brought as slaves were Muslims. Fragments of records, including a few narratives and a Qur'an apparently copied from memory, indicate that in the beginning some slaves attempted to practice their religion, including those who were probably forced to convert to Christianity. Michael Gomez's encyclopedic work *Black Crescent: The Experience and Legacy of African Muslims in the Americas* traces the extent of Islamic influence among Africans in the New World; the story is complex and, because of the paucity of sources, difficult to track, but the Islamic influence on slaves is certainly greater than what scholars had thought previously, even in cases where slaves practiced Islam without fully being aware of its sources (such as bowing down eastward to pray or avoiding pork, as some slave-era sources relate). There is evidence that in 1758 in Haiti and 1835 in Brazil there were some Muslim revolts—an indication of the presence of Islam in the America several centuries ago. For the most part, however, Islam arrived on American shores with the first immigrants from the Middle East in the late nineteenth century. The apparent disappearance of earlier African Muslims in America was reversed in the twentieth century with the growth of African American Islam and the increase in immigration from continental Africa.

MUSLIM IMMIGRATION TO AMERICA

The earliest Muslim immigrants arrived between 1875 and 1912 from the rural areas of Greater Syria in the Ottoman Empire, what today is Lebanon, Syria, Jordan, the Palestinian Authority, and Israel. Muslims in this group were far outnumbered by their Christian compatriots. Mainly unskilled and uneducated, they were economically motivated single men who worked as migrants and merchants, factory and mine workers, or peddlers. Some were fleeing conscription into the Turkish army. Many never realized their dreams either of earning a fortune in the new land or of returning home, but stayed to settle in the eastern United States, the Midwest, and along the Pacific coast.

A second and larger group of Muslim immigrants came after World War I and the demise of the Ottoman Empire. The end of that war ushered in the period of Western colonial rule in the Middle East under the mandate system created to "govern" Arab lands. Significant numbers of Muslims decided to move to the West, now for political as well as economic reasons. Many joined relatives who had arrived earlier. Immigration during this period, however, was soon curtailed by the institution of the "national origins quota system." During the 1930s, the movement of Muslims to America slowed drastically, being largely limited to relatives of those already resident.

Between the mid-1940s and the mid-1960s, a third period of immigration saw Muslims arriving from countries other than the Middle East, including eastern Europe and the Soviet Union, and then the Indian subcontinent after the 1947 partition of India and the creation of Pakistan. While many of the earlier immigrants had moved to rural as well as urban areas of America, now they settled almost exclusively in major cities. Most were urbanized and better educated than their predecessors. Some came hoping to escape political oppression, including Palestinians after the creation of the state of Israel, Egyptians whose land had been taken after Abdel Nasser's nationalization, and Iraqis escaping after the revolution of 1948.

The most recent wave of Muslim immigration occurred after 1965, with the passing of President Lyndon Johnson's bill repealing the system of quotas by national origin. Preference now was given to relatives of those already living in the United States or to people with occupational skills needed in the American labor market. More Muslims started coming from Asia as well as the Middle East, often for educational or professional advancement. This movements continues, although the past four decades have also seen slowly growing numbers of less well educated, often illiterate, workers from areas such as Yemen and Palestine, and Shi'ites from Lebanon. Over the past several decades, political turmoil in their home countries has been a primary motive for many of the Muslims choosing to come to the United States. Refugees have arrived in significant numbers as a result of such troubles as the Six-Day War between Israelis and Arabs in 1967; the civil war in Lebanon and the recent Israeli invasion of that country; civil war and famine affecting Afghans, Somalis, Sudanese, and others; ethnic cleansing in the former Yugoslavia; and the Gulf War and Operation Iraqi Freedom, which caused Kurds, Palestinians, and Iraqis to flee. The Iranian Revolution and ascent to power of Imam Khomeini in 1979, followed by nearly a decade of war between Iran and Iraq, brought a large number of Iranians to the West. It is estimated that around 1 million Iranians live in the United States today.

While Pakistanis, Indians, and Bangladeshis were a minor part of Muslim immigration for most of the twentieth century, in the past several decades their ranks have grown significantly and today they probably number over 1 million. In general, South Asian Muslims have been well educated, Westernized, and fluent in English. Pakistani and Indian Muslims, many of whom are skilled professionals such as doctors and engineers, have played an important role in the development of Muslim groups in the United States and in lay leadership of mosque communities. Today increasing numbers of Muslims are arriving from countries such as Indonesia and Malaysia. Many of these immigrants are also highly trained and often assume positions of leadership in American Islam.

SHI'ITE MUSLIMS

Shi'ites make up about one-fifth of the Muslim population of the United States, which is predominantly Sunni. Shi'ites are concentrated in New York, Detroit, Washington, D.C., Los Angeles, and Chicago, as well as several major cities in Canada, with some seventy mosques and Islamic centers. Little attention was paid to the Shi'ite community in America until recently, partly because Muslims wanted to play down sectarian divisions in Islam and partly because only a relatively small number of Shi'ites emigrated to America before the 1979 revolution in Iran and the Iran-Iraq war. As a result of these events, the number of Shi'ites in

America has swelled. More have come since the Lebanese civil war and the Israeli invasions of Lebanon in 1982 and 2006, as well as the recent invasion of coalition forces in Iraq. California and Michigan have become major areas of settlement for Shi'ites.

Most of the Shi'ites in America are members of the Ithna 'Ashari (Twelver) branch of Islam, who believe that the twelfth Imam disappeared in the tenth century and will return at the end of time to establish justice in the world. In the meantime, Twelvers acknowledge the authority of their religious scholars (*ayatollahs*) in Iran, Iraq, and Lebanon, although one of the issues currently concerning the American community is the extent to which Shi'ism in this country can be defined in distinction from such allegiances. Substantial numbers of Iranian Twelver Shi'is who have settled in areas of Texas and southern California hope that eventually Prince Reza Pahlavi, son of the late shah, will be restored to power in Iran.

The other main Shi'ite group in America is the Isma'ilis (Seveners), under the leadership of Prince Karim Aga Khan. More than 80,000 Isma'ilis live in Canada, especially in Vancouver and Toronto, and small communities are located throughout the United States, particularly in New York and California. There are also small number of 'Alawi Shi'ites from Syria, Lebanon, and Turkey, and Zaydiyah from Yemen, in various parts of the United States.

AFRICAN AMERICAN ISLAM

As immigrant Muslims started to become visible in the early twentieth century, some American blacks, only recently freed from slavery, began to adopt forms of Islam in their effort to find an identity and a place in American society—another example of two of the major themes in this volume: the theological base of popular religious movements, and the history of racialized religion and the desire for a universal god. The charismatic Noble Drew Ali (Timothy Drew), for example, preached that the true religion for "Asiatics" (blacks) is not the white man's Christianity, but Islam. Drew founded the Moorish American Science Temple in 1913, in Newark, New Jersey, claiming to have discovered a *Koran* that was, in fact, completely different from the Holy Qur'an of Islam. The movement spread to such major areas as Detroit and Philadelphia, eventually weakening after Drew Ali died. Small pockets of Moorish Americans can be found today in more than seventy cities of America.

It was not until the rise of the Nation of Islam (NOI) that Americans really began to take notice of Islam as an American religion. The beginnings of the Nation are still obscure. In Detroit, Michigan, in 1929 W. D. Fard began to preach that the true identify of American blacks was Islam. Like Drew Ali, he argued that blacks have been separated from their Eastern homeland, describing what came to be known as "The Lost-Found Nation of Islam in the Wilderness of North America," or simply the Nation of Islam. Fard's message was particularly persuasive to a preacher named Elijah Muhammad, born Elijah Poole, who soon became the movement's leader, or "Messenger of God." Elijah worked to help the community build up its self-respect, ethical integrity, and economic independence from whites.

While the Nation of Islam performed a real service to American blacks, it is questionable as an Islamic movement. Some of its doctrines are clearly antithetical to orthodox Islam, such as Elijah assuming the title of Messenger, a role reserved for the Prophet Muhammad. Against the egalitarianism of Islam, Elijah taught that the problem for blacks lies in the fact that the white man is the really the devil. Blacks can succeed only by separating themselves from their longtime oppressors, which requires ethical responsibility, moral uprightness, and hard work. This twin message of identification of the cause of their suffering and the means of alleviating it appealed to many members of the black community.

Nation of Islam temples were established in many urban areas, with the headquarters moving permanently to Chicago. In its time of greatest popularity, the NOI attracted a number of prominent African American leaders. By the 1960s, however, problems began to plague the community. Elijah and his most articulate spokesman, Malcolm X, who had converted to Islam in prison and became a deeply committed member of the Nation, had a serious falling out. That, along with his experience of the universal nature of Islam while on pilgrimage to Mecca, brought Malcolm to break with the Nation. Malcolm was assassinated at a religious rally in 1965, a crime for which two Nation of Islam members were later convicted.

When Elijah Muhammad died, the fortunes of the Nation of Islam changed significantly. His son Wallace, well trained in classical Sunni Islam, assumed leadership under the Islamic name Warith Deen Mohammed. He began to lead the community away from the separatist teachings of his father and closer to the egalitarian understanding of Sunni Islam, insisting that the former focus had been essential to the recovery of the black community in America at the time, a necessary transitional step in their movement from a slave mentality toward accepting true Islam. Warith Deen Mohammed immediately began to lead the movement through a number of name changes. From Nation of Islam, it became the American Bilalian Community (after the first black convert to Islam), then the World Community of Islam in the West (1976) and the American Muslim Mission (1980). Later it was called the Muslim American Society, the Ministry of W. Deen Mohammed, and then the American Society of Muslims. In 1985. the community was urged to integrate into mainstream Sunni immigrant Islam, where it remains. Warith Deen Mohammed's broadcasts are heard every weekend on more than thirty radio stations across the country.

At the death of Elijah Muhammad, some of the members of the NOI elected to remain with Minister Louis Farrakhan, who is still the titular head of the Nation although he is in waning health. The NOI has remained dedicated to the establishment of a strong black economic system in which members can be independent of the dominant white structures. Nation of Islam members are well known for their efforts to combat drugs and drug-related crime in local communities. The main headquarters of the Nation is still in Chicago, although several other groups claim to be the authentic Nation of Islam under different leaders in Baltimore, Detroit, and Atlanta. Although small in number, the Nation still has a strong appeal to some blacks, especially those incarcerated in large urban prisons.

African American and immigrant Muslims for the most part have maintained separate communities in the United States, although there are increasing efforts at cooperation. Significant issues remain to be resolved between the various communities that make up the body of American Islam. Some African Americans believe that they are more diligent than their immigrant brothers and sisters in observing the strict codes of diet, dress, and other forms of practice. Immigrants often tend to think that as lifelong Muslims they have a better understanding of Islam than do those who recently have converted. Some immigrant groups are still not clear about the distinction between African American Sunnis and the Nation of Islam. Roughly one-third of the Muslims in continental America are African Americans who have decided to join either mainstream Islam or one of the sectarian movements—such as Dar al-Islam, the Five Percenters, and the Ahmadiyya—that are directly or loosely identified with Islamic doctrines.

OTHER CONVERTS TO ISLAM

Leaders in the Islamic community estimate that there are between 50,000 and 100,000 white converts to Islam in the United States. Most of them are women, sometimes having married Muslim men and adopting the faith themselves and sometimes converting because they feel that Islam holds more advantages for women than other religions. A number of Americans who have found themselves at odds either with their own religious tradition or with the prevailing norms of American culture have looked to Islam to provide alternatives. Most recently, an increasing number of Latino/Latina men and women have been adopting Islam, often because they see similarities between traditional Muslim cultures and their own heritage and values. Proportionally, however, converts other than African Americans remain small in number.

Some Americans have been attracted to Islam because Sufi groups offer a more mystical, and sometimes musical, way to approach God. Although many Sufi groups have not been recognized by immigrant Sunni Muslims as legitimate, they are coming to be acknowledged as belonging to the complex fabric of Muslim life in the United States. The resurgence of interest among young Americans in religions of the East, most prevalent in the 1960s, contributed to the popularity of these Sufi movements. Today interest in Sufism is increasing among the college-age children of immigrants as they search for a moderate Islam in the post–September 11 atmosphere in the United States. White Sufi converts—such as Hamza Yusuf of the Zaytuna Institute in Hayward, California—attract young seekers who at times take a year or two off from their academic studies to immerse themselves in Islamic knowledge.

THE COMPLEX FACE OF AMERICAN ISLAM

The largest communities of immigrant Muslims in America today are from South Asia, the Arab world, Iran, sub-Saharan Africa, East Asia, and the former Soviet Union. For the most part, and increasingly, they are highly educated, successful professionals who are leaders in the development of a transnational, transethnic American Islam. In contrast to those Muslims are the growing numbers of refugees from Africa, the Middle East, and the former Soviet Union, and the many African American Muslims who still have not been able to share fully in the American dream.

Among the first Muslim communities in the United States were those in the Midwest. In the earliest years of the twentieth century, Muslims organized for prayers in North Dakota, Iowa, and Indiana. Many came directly from the Middle East to Dearborn, Michigan, to work at the Ford Motor Company plant. Together with Arab Christians, Muslims in Michigan (both Sunnis and Shi'ites) form the largest Arab-American settlement in the country. The shipyards in Quincy, Massachusetts, have provided jobs to Muslim immigrants since the late nineteenth century. Islam has been present and visible in New York City for over a century. Home to a rich variety of ethnic groups, its Muslim population has included a broad spectrum of nationalities from virtually every country in the world, and mosque-building activity has flourished there.

By the early twentieth century, Chicago is said by some to have had more Muslims in residence than any other American city. Chicago Muslims, immigrant and African American and other, now form one of the most heterogeneous Islamic communities in the country. They are active in promoting their faith, providing a range of services to the Islamic community, and interacting with one another as well as with non-Muslims. Similarly, Muslims in Los Angeles and San Francisco have flourished. They represent most areas of the Muslim world, most notably

Iranians and representatives of a number of African countries. The Islamic Center of Southern California is one of the largest Muslim entities in the United States, known for its publications and community leadership.

In the earlier part of the twentieth century, many Muslims, as has been true of other immigrant communities, found that the "American melting pot" did not actually work to include them. For many years, the response of American Muslims was to attempt to hide their religious and ethnic identities, to change their names to make them sound more American, and to refrain from participating in practices or adopting dress that would make them appear "different" from the average citizen. Gradually, as the Muslim community became larger, more diversified, better educated, and more articulate about its own self-understanding, attempts to blend into American society have given way to more sophisticated discussions about the importance of living in America, but still retaining a sense of one's own religious culture.

MUSLIM IDEOLOGIES AND INSTITUTIONS IN AMERICA

By the middle part of the twentieth century and the end of Western control over most Islamic states, Muslims originally from the Middle East tended to subscribe to the ideologies of Arab socialism or nationalism. Muslim in name, they usually were more secular than religious in orientation. Since the Six-Day War of 1967 and the general rise of a more conservative Islam in the Middle East and other parts of the world, Muslim immigrants have begun to reflect the growing Islamic consciousness that has developed, largely as a result of American foreign policy, in many Muslim nations. More recently, particularly since the beginning of Operation Iraqi Freedom, far greater numbers of immigrants from the Arab world, Southeast Asia, and Africa profess themselves to be Islamically committed. Rarely extremists, they are interested in living as responsible Muslims in the American context, although they may differ sharply with American foreign policies. The majority are well-educated professionals who often belong to and contribute to solid religious communities in the United States.

Most American Muslims today are grateful for the freedom of religious thought and practice made possible because the United States is founded on principles of secularism, and some are building a case for a new kind of American Islam that can flourish in such an environment. On the whole, the freedoms allowed by the Constitution have worked well for American Muslims. Yet some still perceive secularism itself to be an anti-religious ideology. As such, it is the antithesis of all that Islam stands for, and therefore may sometimes be seen by those who are committed to an Islamist philosophy as the enemy against which the walls of American Islam must be fortified.

In fact, however, while it can be argued that American Muslims have become more religiously observant since September 11, 2001, it is still true that many think of themselves as secular by definition. One of the great difficulties that Muslims have faced since the terrorist attacks is the public assumption that the only two alternatives for being Muslim in America are moderation (according to the U.S. government's definition) or extremism. Like members of all religious traditions in America, Muslims locate themselves at many points on a scale from "not religious at all" (secular, "un-mosqued") to "very religious" (observant). Secular American Muslims who have played prominent roles in education, business, politics, medicine, science, social and philanthropic organizations, and many other aspects of public life may never be recognized by other Americans as being associated in any way with Islam.

Most Muslims who come to America from overseas, or whose families were immigrants in the twentieth century, choose to live in this country not only for its economic and educational advantages but because they value the freedom of its citizens to speak publicly without worrying about recrimination. Today, however, many fear that they are unable to exercise that very freedom because of American public and governmental backlash. Muslims worry that such realities as the USA Patriot Act, profiling in airports and other public places, and freezing of the assets of Muslim charities are resulting in a loss of Muslim civil liberties.

The proliferation of Muslim organizations in America—religious, political, professional, and cultural—has both helped structure Muslim life and contributed to the complex issue of leadership. The Muslim Student Association (MSA) in the United States and Canada was founded in 1963 by a small group of students to provide services to the many thousands of Muslim students from overseas enrolled on American campuses, many of whom have returned to play major leadership roles in national and international Islamic movements. Increasingly active today, the MSA regularly sponsors Friday prayers and other events and services for Muslim students on college campuses. The organization is international in perspective and advocates an Islam that transcends all linguistic, ethnic, and racial distinctions.

The single largest Muslim organization is the Islamic Society of North America (ISNA), which grew out of the MSA and today coordinates a large number of mosque communities. Somewhat smaller and more sociopolitically conservative is the Islamic Circle of North America (ICNA), known for its adherence to the spirit and law of Islam. For many Muslims, however, these "religious" voices are less authoritative than others advocating for Muslim civil rights. Groups such as the American Muslim Council, a nonprofit sociopolitical organization working to develop increased political power for Muslims, and KARAMAH: Muslim Women Lawyers for Human Rights are speaking with increasingly authoritative voices in the emerging conversation about Islam in America. Islamic organizations are proliferating, representing the different social, political, ethnic, and professional interests of their members.

Also rapidly changing is the public face of Muslim worship in the United States. The earliest immigrants to continental America often were single, young, and not well informed about Islamic practices or doctrines. Busy with their economic pursuits and often seeing their stay in America as only temporary, they did not attempt to locate religious communities or identify structures for worship. Gradually, however, small groups gathered for prayer, often led by someone in the community who was not educated in the essentials of the faith. A number of communities began to consider the importance of establishing a mosque in their area, and soon new structures were built as Muslims started to develop organizations and institutions. Finding or erecting buildings to serve as mosques or Islamic centers began in the 1920s and 1930s; by 1952, more than twenty mosques formed the Federation of Islamic Associations (FIA) in the United States and Canada.

The number of Islamic institutions in the United States has now risen to more than 2,500, of which nearly 1,500 are mosques and Islamic centers. Many mosques are converted houses or office buildings, but new purpose-built structures are going up rapidly. Both the construction of mosques and the creation of Islamic organizations have been aided in the past several decades by support coming from oil-rich Gulf countries. The process of mosque-building, however, is not without its problems. Financing is often difficult, and communities must decide if they want a "foreign" or an American-looking building. Many neighborhoods are not eager to have a mosque erected in their midst, particularly if it involves a public call to prayer. Especially since September 11, Muslims have adopted a more public face of Islam, and increasingly are looking for appropriate physical and institutional structures through which they can practice their faith.

ISSUES AND CONCERNS FOR THE AMERICAN MUSLIM COMMUNITY

The question of leadership—religious, political, communal—is a major concern to Muslims, particularly since September 11. The American public, suddenly aware of the presence of Islam in the United States and wanting to know more about the religion, has wondered who speaks for Islam. Muslims from religious, professional, and academic perspectives have all risen to public prominence as they have attempted to distance Islam from terrorism and to participate in the effort to present an honest, realistic, and contemporary interpretation of the faith. Muslims worry about the lack of well-trained religious leadership, specifically imams, who know both the Islamic sciences and American culture. They hope to develop Islamic seminaries and institutions of religious education in this country and to expand the important area of training chaplains for ministry in prisons, universities, hospitals, police forces, and other institutions. In many mosques, the imam plays an important role in the ritual and spiritual life of the community, but cedes organizational leadership to its professional and well-educated lay members.

Leadership is no longer the province only of males. Many American Muslim women are beginning to challenge the dominance of male leadership. Women have long played important roles in the development of mosques in America and are increasingly visible as members of its boards of directors and in other leadership positions. Many women's organizations, both local and national, are assuming the roles of interpreters of Islam legally, socially, and religiously. Muslim women are prominent in American intellectual life and are taking their place on the faculties of major colleges and universities. However, not all Muslims approve of this emerging female presence in positions of authority, and it is clear that questions about appropriate public roles for women will continue to be high on the agenda of American Islam. The theme outlined in the introduction—male hierarchies and the feminization of American religion—applies as much to American Islam as it does to other religious traditions.

Both women and men are taking advantage of the new opportunities for communication provided by the Internet, as well as other technological means of communication. While many American Muslims still listen with great seriousness to the opinions of internationally known scholars and sheikhs, many are also beginning to incorporate the opinions of "everyday Muslims" who share their interpretations and understandings in chatrooms, on Web sites, and in other public accessible technological ways.

The question of religious education is a major one for many in the Muslim community. Islamic schools, while growing in number, are not available for most children and cannot always claim to compete academically with good public or private secular institutions. Muslim young people attending public schools (still the great majority) often find themselves isolated from their classmates, particularly if they wear forms of Islamic dress. Practicing Muslim students need to ask for accommodation to do ablutions and pray or to have time for religious holidays, requests that are not always granted. Many Muslim parents fear that when their children make non-Muslim friends in school they may lose touch with the ethics of their own faith and be tempted by the socialization of American youth culture.

Observant Muslims struggle to come to terms with how to honor Islamic restrictions in financial transactions. The average Muslim income is higher than the American average per se, although Muslims have seen a significant drop since September 11. Since making interest on one's money is forbidden by Islamic law, they are reluctant to deposit their money in banks that give interest, as they are to take out mortgages, buy on time, or take capital gains on investments. Muslims have devised creative ways to pay for their homes and businesses, called "*hahal* [acceptable] financing," including the opening of Islamic banks in several American cities. With the closure by the government of some charitable Muslim agencies overseas suspected of having terrorist connections, Muslims must rethink their religiously required *zakat* contributions to charity. Muslims may be expected to pledge money to mosques, a concept unknown in the Islamic world but increasingly requested in America as mosques are coming to function more like churches and synagogues. Organizations such as the North American Islamic Trust are being developed to help observant Muslims better understand the options and obligations for use of their money.

Extremely important to American Muslims is the complicated set of relationships they maintain with Muslim cultures, movements, and religious entities abroad. The 1970s and 1980s saw serious efforts on the part of Gulf countries such as Saudi Arabia to finance minority Muslim communities in various parts of the world. Some American Muslims benefited greatly from these efforts as the recipients of trained religious leadership and of money to build new mosques and centers. That funding has lessened, and at the same time American Muslims are struggling to decide whether they want it anyway, insofar as it may entail expectations of certain ideological commitments.

One of the issues of deepest concern to Muslims has been the persistent and heightening instances of prejudice in North America against Islam, Arabs, and Muslims. Muslims are concerned about the distorted and inaccurate picture of Islam presented by the media and the biased treatment of Muslims in textbooks, news coverage, and entertainment programming. The events of September 11 and the backlash they set in motion have resulted in increased levels of discrimination and hate crimes. Muslims have been jolted out of any complacency that they might have felt about being considered full and accepted members of American society. The negative press has made it necessary to organize to meet the increasing demands to persistently and constantly prove their patriotism. Every time violence in the name of Islam is committed anywhere in the world, American Muslims pay a price in terms of discrimination, despite their efforts to explain the essentially peaceful nature of Islam.

More women then ever before in America are choosing to wear some form of Islamic dress, from a simple headscarf to an enveloping robe. Americans generally find it very difficult to understand why anyone would want to dress in what seems to be such a restrictive fashion and hard to believe that it really represents a woman's choice. Muslim women wearing Islamic dress encounter discrimination in public and in the workplace. Some school systems do not allow female teachers to wear even headscarves, and women face discrimination in hiring, promotion, and retention in many kinds of businesses. Young women on college campuses find that they are more comfortable with Muslim than non-Muslim friends and often adopt the scarf as a show of solidarity and belonging.

On the whole, Muslims have found the United States to be a place where they can prosper, can live Islamic lives to the degree they are comfortable with, and, by taking care about their choices, can raise their children in the manner that they feel is appropriate. The question remains, however, whether the democratic and pluralistic principles espoused by the West will really allow for a non–Judeo-Christian religion with a distinctive culture and alternative values to flourish in its midst. Muslims are posing a challenge to America's vision of itself and its publicly professed values. They are demanding that America live up to its values of pluralism and freedom of speech and religion and make room for its Muslim citizens, allowing them to be Muslim and to define their own religion. The answer, ironically, may lie not in the actions of Muslims in America themselves but of their co-religionists in other parts of an increasingly turbulent world that is growing short on patience with the United States.

STUDIES ON AMERICAN ISLAM

Until fairly recently, most of the studies on Islam in the United States focused on particular cities, areas, or communities. Generally, these were presented in an anthropological framework. In the past decade, a number of attempts have been made to consider the phenomenon of Islam in the United States as a totality, reflecting a maturity in American studies as well as an acknowledgment of the establishment of Islam as a legitimate claimant to the status of an American religion. A number of these studies venture comparisons of Islam in America with that in Europe, paying special attention to the phenomenon of so-called Islamophobia, and particularly to the reasons why it appears less likely that American Muslims will succumb to extremism than may be true of their European counterparts.

Scholars of Islam in America are now relying on a much wider range of disciplines for information and material than was true only a few years ago. In addition to history, anthropology, and sociology, information is being drawn from the arts, literature, socioeconomics, education, political theory, and many more disciplines. Studies are being done not only about adults and their circumstances, but also about youth and the new ways—for instance, through dress, music, and religious study—in which they are finding their identity as Muslim Americans. For the first time in recent years, Muslim and non-Muslim scholars are building on the work of each other, and the resulting scholarship is richer for it. The bibliography for this chapter gives a short listing of some of the major recent works that readers will want to consult.

The most serious tension in the study of American Islam today is between those who see the Islamic religion and culture as a threat to their country's way of life and those who proceed from the assumption that Islam is an established and respectable American religion. This tension has resulted in acrimony and mutual accusation, and is accentuated whenever an international terrorist event suggesting the complicity of Islamist forces takes place.

Many areas of study still need serious attention as the American Muslim community is challenged to address new circumstances. Among these are the various forms of African American Islam, the demise of old forms of Islamic leadership and the creation of new forms, the question of Islam as an ethnicity as well as a religion, the new forms of religiosity being developed by Muslim youth, responses to the need for religious education for both youth and adults, and the challenge posed by the Internet to all of these, and many other, issues. Literature on Islam in the United States is growing to the point where it is now quite abundant, and it is clear that a rich new field of religious study has come into its own.

REFERENCES

Athar, Shahid. *Reflections of an American Muslim.* Chicago: KAZI, 1994.
Barlas, Asma. *Islam, Muslims and the U.S.: Essays on Religion and Politics.* New Delhi: Global Media, 2004.
Bukhari, Zahid H., Sulayman S. Nyang, Mumtaz Ahmed, and John L. Esposito, eds. *Muslims' Place in the American Public Square: Hope, Fears, and Aspirations.* Walnut Creek, Calif.: AltaMira Press, 2004.
Cesari, Jocelyne. *When Islam and Democracy Meet: Muslims in Europe and the United States.* New York: Palgrave, 2004.
Clegg, Claude Andrew. An Original Man: The Life and Times of Elijah Muhammad. New York: St. Martin's Press, 1997.
Dannin, Robert. *Black Pilgrimage to Islam.* New York: Oxford University Press, 2002.
Gomez, Michael. *Black Crescent: The Experience and Legacy of African Muslims in the Americas.* Cambridge: Cambridge University Press, 2005.
——. *Exchanging Their Country Marks: The Transformation of African Identities in the Colonial and Antebellum South.* Chapel Hill: University of North Carolina Press, 1998.
Haddad, Yvonne Yazbeck. *The Muslims of America.* New York: Oxford University Press, 1991.
Haddad, Yvonne Yazbeck, and John L. Esposito. *Muslims on the Americanization Path?* New York: Oxford University Press, 2000.
Haddad, Yvonne Yazbeck, Jane I. Smith, and Kathleen M. Moore. *Muslim Women in America: The Challenge of Islamic Identity Today.* New York: Oxford University Press, 2006.
Hasan, Asma Gull. *Why I Am a Muslim: An American Odyssey.* London: HarperCollins, 2004.

Jackson, Sherman A. *Islam and the Blackamerican: Looking Toward the Third Resurrection*. New York: Oxford University Press, 2005.

Kahera, Akel Ismail. *Deconstructing the American Mosque: Space, Gender, and Aesthetics*. Austin: University of Texas Press, 2002.

Leonard, Karen Isaksen. *Muslims in the United States: The State of Research*. New York: Russell Sage Foundation, 2003.

Lin, Phylis Lan, ed. *Islam in America: Images and Challenges*. Indianapolis: University of Indianapolis Press, 1998.

Marr, Timothy. *The Cultural Roots of American Islamicism*. Cambridge: Cambridge University Press, 2006.

McCloud, Aminah Beverly. *Transnational Muslims in American Society*. Gainesville: University Press of Florida, 2006.

Metcalf, Barbara Daly. *Making Muslim Space in North America and Europe*. Berkeley: University of California Press, 1996.

Moore, Kathleen M. *Al-Mughtaribun: American Law and the Transformation of Muslim Life in the United States*. Albany: State University of New York Press, 1995.

Poston, Larry A., and Carl F. Ellis Jr. *The Changing Face of Islam in America: Understanding and Reaching Your Muslim Neighbor*. Camp Hill, Pa.: Horizon Books, 2000.

Schmidt, Garbi. *Islam in Urban America: Sunni Muslims in Chicago*. Philadelphia: Temple University Press, 2004.

Smith, Jane I. *Islam in America*. Rev. ed. New York: Columbia University Press, 2007.

——. *Muslims, Christians, and the Challenge of Interfaith Dialogue*. New York: Oxford University Press, 2007.

Turner, Richard Brent. *Islam in the African American Experience*. Bloomington: Indiana University Press, 1997.

abolitionism An antebellum American radical reform movement, heavily influenced by the perfectionist tendencies within American evangelicalism, demanding an immediate and uncompensated end to slavery. Led by figures such as William Lloyd Garrison, abolitionism was at its height from 1831 to 1861.

African Methodist Episcopal Church (AME) First independent black denomination in the United States, formed by Richard Allen and other black Philadelphians originally in the late 1780s, the AME Church was officially incorporated as a denomination in 1816, and soon became one of the most influential expressions of black Christianity in the United States.

Allen, Richard (1760–1831) Born a slave, Allen achieved his freedom in Pennsylvania and helped to establish the African Methodist Episcopal Church in Philadelphia.

American Board of Commissioners for Foreign Missions (ABCFM) Founded in 1812 by graduates of Williams College, the ABCFM was the first Protestant foreign missionary agency established on American soil, and served as the centralized missionary agency for American Presbyterians and Congregationalists. A product of the evangelical enthusiasm of the Second Great Awakening, it sponsored missionaries who served in countries all over the world, including placing the first American missionaries in China in the late 1820s, as well as among American Indian tribes. One of its earliest secretaries, Jeremiah Evarts, was an eloquent critic of Indian removal from the Southeast. Rufus Anderson, general secretary from the 1830s to the 1860s, did much to regularize and systematize the foreign missionary efforts of American denominations.

American Indian Religious Freedom Act (AIRFA; 1978)   Passed originally as a sort of symbolic statement, the AIRFA was intended to express the federal government's willingness to work with Indian tribal leaders to protect the free exercise of religion by Native Americans, especially in cases where a particular practice might conflict with federal law (such as the gathering of eagle feathers). Congress amended the law in 1994, after the *Smith v.* Oregon peyote case made it clear that the Supreme Court was willing to uphold restrictions on some religious activities of Native groups, such as the use of peyote.

American Missionary Association (AMA)   Founded in 1846, the AMA served as a Congregationalist abolitionist and philanthropic group. It is best known for its missionary work in the South after the Civil War, where it established a large number of black schools, colleges, and universities, including Howard University in Washington, D.C., and Fisk University in Nashville. The AMA published the magazine *American Missionary* from 1846 to 1934.

American Tract Society   Founded in New York in 1825 during the Second Great Awakening, the American Tract Society was one of a number of evangelical organizations that blanketed the United States with tens of millions of pieces of Christian literature, temperance tracts, and social reform pamphlets through the antebellum era. The organization, now based in Texas, remains active today.

Anglican   Member of the Church of England, a hybrid faith of Protestant beliefs and Roman Catholic worship style.

antinomianism   The belief that the gospel frees humans from any obligation to rely on or obey religious authorities or law handed from above. In America, antinomianism is often associated with Anne Hutchinson in Puritan New England, with the Quakers (because of their rejection of appointed ministers and their reliance on the "inner light"), and with utopian and communal groups of the nineteenth and twentieth centuries.

Apess, William (1798–1839)   First known Native American author of full-length texts, Apess (also spelled Apes), of mixed Indian (Pequot) and white ancestry, grew up in early nineteenth-century New England. Author of the autobiography *A Son of the Forest*, Apess was a minister in the Methodist Protestant Church and author of a classic condemnation of white American treatment of Native American people, *Eulogy on King Philip*, published originally in 1836.

Arminianism   A Protestant belief system that highlighted human free will. Developed by seventeenth-century Dutch theologian Jacobus Arminius, an ardent foe of Calvinism, the belief was popularized during the nineteenth-century revivals by preachers who taught that humans could play some positive role in their own salvation.

Assemblies of God   Founded in 1914, the Assemblies of God now stands as the largest (predominantly) white Pentecostal organization in the United States. Headquartered in Springfield, Missouri, the Assemblies began as a merger of a number of different Holiness-Pentecostal groups that had emerged in the early twentieth century. The Assemblies provided a regular denominational order and doctrine for this assemblage of smaller groups. Today the Assemblies of God supports a sizable denominational apparatus and overseas missionary effort, and recently became known as the home church of John Ashcroft, President George W. Bush's first appointee as attorney general.

Baptist   A religious movement, later a variety of denominations, originating in seventeenth-century England, emphasizing the necessity of baptism by total water immersion and total autonomy of each congregation. Coming to America in the seventeenth century, Baptists spread quickly in both North and South, and grew to be one of the major evangelical traditions of the United States.

Barton, Bruce (1886–1967)   An advertising executive whose biography of Jesus, *The Man Nobody Knows*, famously portrayed Jesus as a manly, successful businessman who had created the greatest corporate organization the world had ever seen.

Beecher, Henry Ward (1813–1887)   Son of Lyman Beecher, one of the best-known Calvinist ministers of the early nineteenth century, and brother to Harriet Beecher Stowe (author of *Uncle Tom's Cabin*), Beecher made his name as a socially liberal, theologically adaptable, and oratorically gifted minister of the Plymouth Congregational Church in Brooklyn, New York, where he began preaching in 1847. Beecher was an abolitionist and supported anti-slavery forces in Kansas, where rifles used by free soil settlers came to be known as "Beecher Bibles." In the 1870s, Beecher became involved in one of the most sensational sex scandals of the nineteenth century, when he was accused of adultery with a friend's wife (Elizabeth Tilton) and of hypocrisy by Elizabeth Woodhull, a flamboyant advocate of "free love" and the first woman to attempt to run for president in the United States.

Black Elk (1863–1950)   A Lakota holy man, Black Elk survived the Battle of the Little Big Horn in 1876 as well as the Wounded Knee massacre of 1890, toured with Buffalo Bill's Wild West show in Europe, and later adopted Catholicism alongside his Native American religious traditions. In 1932 his personal reflections, *Black Elk Speaks*, drew widespread attention, and the book remains popular to this day. Black Elk spoke of the power of Catholic Christianity as well as the force of *Wakan Tanka*, the Lakota concept signifying a divine force within the universe.

Black Muslims   African American version of Islam, originated in America by Noble Drew Ali and given prominence by Elijah Muhammad and his protégé, Malcolm X, in the 1960s. Black Muslims preach black self-determination and opposition to white Christianity.

black theology   Intellectual movement that saw God as identified with African Americans (and, by implication, with all poor and oppressed people). Dating from the nineteenth century and Henry McNeal Turner but blossoming in the 1960s and 1970s with such writers as James Cone, black theology served as a critique of the white supremacist assumptions of American Christianity. (See Blum, chap. 10, this volume.)

Blackwell, Antoinette (1825–1921)   A native of New York, Blackwell converted to Christianity and the Congregational Church during the Second Great Awakening. Later she attended Oberlin College, where, over the objection of many faculty and students, she studied theology. In 1852 she was ordained by a Congregational congregation, making her the first woman to be ordained by a regularly constituted Protestant church. Blackwell continued her active work in abolitionism in the women's suffrage movement, and in the 1880s pursued ordination into the Unitarian ministry.

Blanshard, Paul (1892–1980)   Trained as a Congregationalist minister, Blanshard became an editor for the *Nation* magazine and a critic of organized religion, especially Catholicism. His book *American Freedom and Catholic Power*, published in 1949, drew a correspondence between the Vatican and the Kremlin, thus portraying Catholicism as a threat to American republican liberties.

Bradford, William (1590–1657)   An English-born Separatist Puritan who was a leader and governor of the Plymouth Colony, signer of the Mayflower Compact (which defined the goals of that colony), and author of a set of journals (now published as *Of Plymouth Plantation*) that documented the life of the Pilgrims from their landing at Plymouth to the mid-1640s.

Brainerd, David (1718–1747)   A graduate of Yale College, friend of Jonathan Edwards, and early missionary to Native Americans in Stockbridge, Massachusetts, and among the Delaware Indians in Pennsylvania. Brainerd's life was memorialized by Edwards and others as a heroic symbol of Christian sacrifice and service during the early years of the First Great Awakening.

Branch Davidians   A sect of the Davidian Seventh-Day Adventists. In 1993, eighty-two of its members, including leader David Koresh, died after a standoff with the Federal Bureau of Investigation and other governmental entities in central Texas.

Brook Farm   Established as a Transcendentalist utopian experiment in West Roxbury, Massachusetts (just south of Boston), in 1841, and lasting until 1847, Brook Farm was a short-lived but highly influential experiment in communal socialism, agriculture, and free thought that drew the attention and participation of well-known literary figures such as Henry David Thoreau and Ralph Waldo Emerson. Nathaniel Hawthorne, a founding member of Brook Farm, later portrayed and satirized the experiment in his novel *Blithedale Romance*.

Brown, John (1800–1859)   Born in Connecticut and largely unsuccessful in a series of business ventures through his life, Brown gained notoriety for his actions in slaughtering pro-slavery settlers in Kansas during the "Bleeding Kansas" era of the 1850s, and most especially for his failed attempt to organize an uprising of slaves at Harper's Ferry, Virginia, in 1859. Captured at Harper's Ferry and brought to trial before his execution, Brown famously delivered a soliloquy before the court giving an idealistic religious justification for his actions, and shortly before his death wrote the following: "I, John Brown, am now quite certain that the crimes of this guilty land will never be purged away but with blood."

Brownson, Orestes (1803–1876)   Brownson's remarkable intellectual career in New England through the first half of the nineteenth century gave him a key role in the founding of the Transcendentalism movement, a religious move from Presbyterianism to Unitarianism, and association with social and intellectual radicals and utopian communities during the 1830s. In 1844, Brownson famously converted to Catholicism, and remained a preeminent Catholic intellectual, one largely attracted to conservative ideas of social order, from his conversion to his death. Brownson's career traces the rise of as well as the disillusionment with utopian radicalism in antebellum New England.

Bryan, William Jennings (1860–1925)   Populist orator and perennial presidential candidate, Bryan was a progressive in politics later best known for his defense of biblical creationism at the 1925 Scopes Trial in Tennessee, at which he served as a caricature of fundamentalism.

Buckley, William, Jr. (1925–2008)   One of the foremost American conservative thinkers of the twentieth century, Buckley first made his name with his book *God and Man* *at Yale*, a conservative Catholic's stinging critique of the secularism of the nation's elite universities. Later Buckley founded the magazine *National Review*, which has served as an organ of political conservatism, and has produced numerous articles and books that, in erudite language, espouse the virtues of Catholic teachings and critique secular liberalism.

Burroughs, Nannie (1879–1961)   As a black Baptist woman's leader, Burroughs organized the Women's Auxiliary to the National Baptist Convention in 1901, and later founded the National Training School for Women and Girls in Washington, D.C., the first educational institution in the country wholly owned and run by African American women. Burroughs provided a powerful, religiously progressive voice for upwardly mobile African American religious women through much of the twentieth century.

Bushnell, Horace (1802–1876)   A long-time pastor of a Congregational church in Hartford, Connecticut, and a prolifically published theologian, Bushnell influenced a generation of New Englanders gradually away from Puritan Calvinism into ideas of religious intuition and emotion befitting the Romantic movement of the nineteenth century. His book *Christian Nurture* advised parents in the ways of raising godly children through persuasion and empathy.

Cabeza de Vaca, Álvar Núñez (ca. 1490–ca. 1557)   An early Spanish explorer who gained fame from his eight-year adventure wandering through uncharted regions of the New World following a shipwreck in Florida that destroyed most of his original expedition. Cabeza de Vaca's account of his journeys from Florida to the Pacific from 1528 to 1536 introduced many European readers for the first time to the variety of Native American groups living in North America, and to many of their religious practices.

Calvinism   The theological system founded by John Calvin, a major leader of Reformation thought, which emphasizes the absolute sovereignty of God and the totality of human depravity. Election by God, not human action, decided one's eternal fate.

Campbell, Will (b. 1924)   An unorthodox white Southern Baptist minister, writer, and raconteur known for his work in the civil rights movement and for his memoir *Brother to a Dragonfly*. A self-described "bootleg Baptist preacher," Campbell represented an alternative Southern vision influenced by the neo-orthodoxy of Reinhold Niebuhr as well as by the folk traditions of the region.

Cantwell v. Connecticut (1940)   A seminal religious freedom case that resurrected Jefferson's notion of the wall of separation between church and state. The case involved the right of Jehovah's Witnesses to proselytize without an official license in a heavily Catholic area of New Haven, Connecticut. The Court overturned their arrest and conviction for disturbing the peace, and "incorporated" the Free Exercise Clause of the First Amendment into a national protection for the free exercise of religion against restrictions placed on that by the state.

Carroll, John (1735–1815)   A native of Maryland, Carroll served as the first bishop and archbishop of the Catholic Church in the United States. He was the founder of Georgetown University, and oversaw the building of the Basilica of the National Shrine of the Assumption of the Blessed Virgin Mary in Baltimore.

Catholic Worker Movement   A radical Catholic organization based in New York City and founded in the early 1930s by Dorothy Day (1897–1980) and Peter Maurin. The movement emphasizes liberation theology, nonviolence, justice, and radical economics based on a communal vision of sharing.

charismatic   A twentieth-century movement based on the belief that ordinary believers can receive the "gifts" of the Holy Spirit, particularly speaking in tongues. The term is sometimes used to distinguish those outside the historical Pentecostal churches—such as Charismatic Catholics—from those who historically have been Pentecostals.

Chavez, Cesar (1927–1993)   Son of Mexican immigrants whose Catholic mysticism and social justice consciousness propelled him to leadership in the United Farm Workers Union, which advocated on behalf of the Mexican and Central American migrant farm workers who picked crops throughout California and the American West.

Christian Century   Founded originally in Iowa in the 1880s under a different name, the *Christian Century* magazine took its present name and form in Chicago, where it is still published today as an organ of mainline, ecumenical Protestantism. It is generally seen as supportive of the center and left of Protestantism, while its competitor magazine, *Christianity Today* (founded in 1956), espouses views more in line with traditional conservative evangelicalism.

Christian Coalition   An interdenominational and interreligious political advocacy group founded originally in 1989 by television minister and religious broadcaster Pat Robertson following his unsuccessful run for the presidency the previous year, and also associated with Ralph Reed, a young Christian politico who effectively mobilized conservative Protestants, Catholics, Jews, Mormons, and others into support for candidates who supported "Judeo-Christian values" (as defined by conservative political viewpoints). The Christian Coalition has served as an arm of the "religious right" through its use of churches and direct mailing techniques to energize supporters into action on specific political issues, including opposition to abortion and to gay rights.

Christian Identity Movement   A small, loose-knit affiliation of churches, preachers, and believers who generally believe in a theology that white Europeans are descended from the ten captive tribes of Israel in the Old Testament and are, therefore, God's chosen people, commanded not to intermix with other races or religions. Originally a set of doctrines known as "British Israelism," Christian Identity's murky origins include a variety of far-right and fascist thinkers in the mid-twentieth century. More recently, the group has been associated with small white supremacist communities in Idaho and the Ozarks, where believers engage in survivalist training and await the end times, and sometimes come into conflict with the Federal Bureau of Investigation and other authorities.

Christian Science   A movement founded by Mary Baker Eddy. The core ideas are found in Eddy's central work, *Science and Health with Key to the Scriptures*, first published in 1875. Monistic in nature, this system of metaphysics teaches that physical matter is illusory and unreal. All that is real is Spirit, and salvation/healing lies in the realization of this truth. Disease, sin, and death are illusory and will vanish on the complete assimilation of this truth by the believer. (See Stein, chap. 13, this volume.)

Church of God (Cleveland, Tennessee)   A Holiness-Pentecostal denomination founded by Ambrose Jessup Tomlinson in the early twentieth century. The church was centered originally in the highlands of Tennessee and North Carolina, and later grew into a regional organization attracting plain-folk whites. In the 1920s and later again in the 1940s, the denomination split over the financial dealings of its founder, Tomlinson, and also over issues of who was to be his successor.

Church of God in Christ   Headquartered in Memphis, Tennessee, the Church of God in Christ stands as the largest organization of black Pentecostals in the United States. The denomination was founded by Charles Harrison Mason and Charles Price Jones, early black Holiness-Pentecostal figures who eventually split over the issue of whether tongues speech represented true evidence of the "complete sanctification" of the soul. Jones's smaller group (Church of God, Holiness) remained in Mississippi, while Mason, after being converted to the doctrine of tongues speech at the Azusa Street revivals in 1906, took his Church of God in Christ to Memphis. The church is internationally famous for its vibrant musical traditions, producing rhythm and blues and soul stars such as Al Green and Sam Cooke.

Church of Jesus Christ of Latter-day Saints   A church founded by Joseph Smith Jr. in 1830. Commonly known as Mormonism, this faith began with a new set of scriptures (*The Book of Mormon*) meant to complete the stories in the Old and New Testaments. Members of the early church were forced to move on several occasions. After Smith's murder in 1844, the majority followed Brigham Young to Utah, where the church continues to flourish. (See Quinn, chap. 19, this volume.)

Church Women United   Originally called United Council of Church Women, this group formed in 1941 from the alliance and merger of numerous women's groups in various denominations. During the 1960s, the group, then called United Church Women, took on issues of race and civil rights, supporting younger women in the Student Nonviolent Coordinating Committee and organizing northern women to travel South to support civil rights activities.

civil religion   The interplay between sacred and secular notions of the state, placing religious significance in the nation itself and its leaders. (See Manis, chap. 3, this volume.)

Comstock, Anthony (1844–1915)   A native of Connecticut and a Civil War veteran, Comstock was the founder of the New York Society for the Suppression of Vice and the author of what became known as the Comstock Laws, which forbade the distribution of "obscene, lewd, or lascivious" materials through the mail. This included not only pornographic scenes but also any material related to sex at all, including information on birth control. Later, Margaret Sanger emerged as a national advocate for birth control and the foremost opponent of the Comstock Laws.

Cone, James Hal (b. 1938)   A professor at Union Theological Seminary in New York City and author of numerous works, including *Black Theology and Black Liberation* and *The Spirituals and the Blues*, which pioneered the modern intellectual movement of Black Theology.

Congregationalist (or **Congregationalism**)   A denomination that emerged from the original Puritans of seventeenth-century New England, emphasizing the autonomy of local churches and a mild form of Calvinist conversionist theology. Congregationalism became something like the established church of New England in the eighteenth and early nineteenth centuries. Later it provided the basis for important liberal splinter groups, including the Unitarians and the Universalists.

conjuring (or **conjuration**)   An African American folk tradition with roots in African practices, invoking the supernatural powers of items such as roots and herbs in healing, harming, and counterharming individuals. Widespread in the slave community, conjuring lived on into the twentieth century and entered the broader streams of American folk culture.

Conwell, Russell (1843–1925)   A Philadelphia Baptist minister best known for being the founder and first president of Temple University and for his famous self-help sermon, "Acres of Diamonds," which he preached over six thousand times across the country during the Gilded Age. In it, Conwell suggested that every Christian could and should be wealthy, for "acres of diamonds" were there all around for the industrious.

Coughlin, Charles (1891–1979)   Dubbed the "radio priest," the Michigan-based Father Coughlin's radio broadcasts during the Depression drew tens of millions of listeners to his populist and increasingly anti-Semitic version of a Christian response to the trials of the Great Depression. Originally a supporter of Franklin Delano Roosevelt's New Deal, Coughlin later turned against the president, and used the newspaper of his organization, the National Union for Social Justice, to espouse his suspicions of the country's banking system and of New Deal administrators.

covenant   Usually referring to a kind of contract or promise between two parties, the term was employed by American Calvinists—most prominently the Puritans—to describe a theological system of agreements between humans and God. The Puritans and other types of Calvinists after them taught that people entered into a number of agreements with God related to their own devotion and God's reciprocal blessings. See also **Puritans**.

Crummell, Alexander (1819–1898)   Black Episcopalian minister and founder of the Negro Academy, Crummell served as a missionary to Liberia for about twenty years and was an advocate of bringing civilization and Christianization to Africans. Crummell received a memorable appreciation in W. E. B. Du Bois's *Souls of Black Folk*.

Cushing, Frank (1857–1900)   A pioneering ethnologist of Native Americans, Cushing was appointed by John Wesley Powell in 1879 to write reports for the newly created Bureau of American Ethnology series on Native American life and culture in the American West. Enraptured by the Zuni Indians in New Mexico and Arizona, Cushing became a participant-observer in the life of the Zunis, being inducted into their secret societies and taking their side in disputes with the Navajos. Cushing was one of the first to practice ethnocultural forms of anthropological practice, and he represented as well a romantic vision of Indian life as an antidote to fears about the stresses and costs of American civilization.

Dabney, Robert Lewis (1820–1898)   A Presbyterian minister in the South and vigorous proponent of the Confederate cause in the Civil War. A conservative theologically and socially, Dabney supported slavery and secession, and later segregation and post–Civil War racism. Dabney is remembered and honored today by some Presbyterians for his fierce defense of old school Presbyterianism.

Dalai Lama   Tibetan religious leader, considered the fourteenth manifestation of the Buddhist Bodhisattva of Compassion. The current Dalai Lama, Tenzin Gyatso (b. 1935), fled into exile from China in 1959 and has since served as a spokesman for repressed and exiled Tibetans and is internationally known as an ecumenical spokesman for peace and religious freedom.

Daly, Mary (b. 1928)   A pioneering feminist theologian. Daly's well-known book *Beyond God the Father* hoped to tear theology from "its function of legitimating patriarchy." Daly's subsequent work *Gyn/Ecology* explained that she could no longer use words such as "God," "since there was no way to remove masculine imagery from them." Daly's work has provided a theoretical and theological context for women who seek to explore a spirituality not defined by church fathers.

Darwinism (or **evolution**)   The scientific explanation for the origins and development of species through natural selection, proposed originally by Charles Darwin in *On the Origin of Species* (1859). Darwin's theory of evolution was challenged from the time of its inception by creationism and other forms of religious thought that insist on divine presence and design in all forms of life on earth.

Dass, Ram (b. 1931)   Born Richard Alpert, Ram Dass is best known for his book and philosophy *Be Here Now*. In this work, he traces his transformation from a high-achieving Harvard psychology professor to a guru for the counterculture, achieved after extensive travels through India and encounters with holy men and psychedelic drugs that allowed him to access internal mystical experiences and be present "in the moment." Today, Dass runs a spiritual institute based near Santa Fe, New Mexico.

Davies, Samuel (1723–1761)   A New Light Presbyterian minister in Virginia, Davies was a devoted advocate of spreading the Great Awakening in his home state, where he was known to be continuing his itinerant preaching in spite of suffering from tuberculosis. Later he became the fourth president of Princeton before his untimely death.

Dawes Act (1887)   By this act, Congress gave up the fiction that Indian tribes were independent powers, abolished the treaty system, and recognized Indians as wards of the state. Indian reservation lands formerly held by tribal groups were to be "allotted" to individual Indian families, with the remainder being sold to help fund Indian boarding schools. The result was a massive land loss for Native Americans, as well as widespread fraud through oil leasing and other provisions that defrauded individual Indian families of their land allotments. The provisions of the Dawes Act were later repealed by the "Indian New Deal" of 1934.

Deism   A radical form of Unitarian belief that flourished in the Age of Reason. Deism postulated a rational deity that created the world and then left it to run according to natural laws. By denying divine intervention in the form of miracles, Deism focused on the present world and the laws governing it. Through recognizing and employing these natural laws in human affairs, most Deists thought, stable governments and societies could be created. This religious philosophy was most associated with American Enlightenment thinkers (including Thomas Jefferson and Benjamin Franklin) of the late eighteenth century.

Deloria, Vine, Jr. (1933–2005)   Author of more than twenty books and a longtime professor, Deloria was a pioneer in Native American religious studies and an outspoken advocate for indigenous rights. His best-known works include *Custer Died for Your Sins* and *God Is Red*. In both, he critiqued Western religious and theological traditions and contrasted them with a Native American emphasis on space and geography as opposed to linear time.

denomination   A voluntary religious grouping that became the predominant form of religious organization in American history. Denominations (literally, "named, called" in Latin) include groups such as the Southern Baptist Convention, the Assemblies of God, and the Methodist Episcopal Church.

Disciples of Christ   A denomination founded in the early nineteenth century by Alexander Campbell and Barton Stone, emphasizing the doctrine of "no creed but the Bible." It was part of the "Restorationist" movement of the era, which called for a return to the purity of the "primitive" church and the elimination of the excesses and "poperies" of modern denominations.

dispensational premillennialism   Doctrine of the end times originating in the later nineteenth century, most closely associated with conservative and fundamentalist evangelicals. Emphasizes the seven periods (or "dispensations") into which God had divided the world's history and the climactic battle of Armageddon, which would precede the final establishment of God's kingdom in heaven and the ascension of the saints.

Dorsey, Thomas (1899–1993)   Often called the "father of gospel music," Dorsey began his musical career as a blues and jazz musician first in Georgia, where he was known as "Barrelhouse Tom," and later in Chicago, where he was the piano player for the blueswoman Ma Rainey. Following the death of his wife in the early 1930s, Dorsey turned his immense musical talent to the service of what soon became known as "gospel blues"—now usually called "black gospel"—a synthesis of the emotion and "blue note" of black secular song with religious lyrics that speak of a deeply personal relationship with Jesus. Dorsey founded the National Convention of Choirs and Choruses, which became a primary vehicle for spreading the black gospel sound. Dorsey also authored numerous hymns and songs, including his best-known work "Take My Hand, Precious Lord," a tune sung at the funeral of Martin Luther King Jr.

Douglass, Frederick (1818–1895)   Escaped slave and famous orator, abolitionist, editor, and presidential advisor in the nineteenth century. Douglass's autobiography, updated through several editions, become one of the classics of American literature. Douglass was a severe and biting critic of pro-slavery religion and, after the Civil War, of the deficiencies of the black church.

Dow, Lorenzo (1777–1834)   A Connecticut-born Methodist minister best known for being one of the most famously boisterous, emotional, and charismatic of the itinerating ministers during the Second Great Awakening of the early nineteenth century. Dow traveled widely and ceaselessly to proclaim the gospel, usually to open-air crowds who responded enthusiastically to this new style of evangelical stumping.

Du Bois, W. E. B. (1868–1963)   One of the greatest American intellectuals of the twentieth century, Du Bois is best known for his 1903 classic *Souls of Black Folk*, which memorably portrayed the "double consciousness" of African Americans and poignantly invoked the "sorrow songs" (spirituals) as epigraphs for chapters that explored the spiritual meaning of African American culture. (See Blum, chap. 10, this volume.)

Dwight, Timothy (1752–1817)   An American Congregationalist minister and theologian who served as the eighth president of Yale University from 1795 to 1817. Dwight was identified with the "New Divinity," a product of the Great Awakening. The "neo-Edwardseans," including Dwight, emphasized the necessity of an identifiable conversion experience. Politically, Dwight was a conservative who opposed disestablishment of the Congregationalist Church in Connecticut and was active in the Federalist Party, where he opposed the influence of French revolutionary ideas in America.

Dyer, Mary (1611?–1660) English-born Quaker and ally of Anne Hutchinson who, in 1660, was executed on the Boston Common for her public espousal of Quaker beliefs and for defying Massachusetts laws banning Quakers from the colony.

Eddy, Mary Baker (1821–1910) Teacher, author, and founder of the Church of Christ, Scientist, and the newspaper the *Christian Science Monitor*. New England born and bred, Eddy's theological insights included the idea that ill health was a product of sinful thinking and not a physical reality.

Edwards, Jonathan (1703–1758) Often called America's greatest theologian, Edwards was a minister and theologian from Connecticut who was a key figure in the First Great Awakening. Edwards's many works of theology, including "Sinners in the Hands of an Angry God," married eighteenth-century ideas of knowledge acquired through the senses to the Calvinist and conversionist theology of the colonial Great Awakening.

Eliot, John (1604–1690) Born in England, Eliot migrated to Boston in 1631 as part of the first great wave of Puritan settlers in New England. Eliot served as a minister in the region but was best known for being the "Apostle to the Indians," an advocate of Christian evangelization of Natives in New England. Eliot set up a series of Praying Towns for Christianized Indians, and in 1663 published the first Bible produced in North America, in the language of the Massachusett Indians. (See Fisher, chap. 1, this volume.)

Emerson, Ralph Waldo (1803–1882) Great American writer who rejected a ministerial career in the Congregationalist and Unitarian churches of New England and led the Transcendentalist movement of the mid-nineteenth century. Although often seen (and oversimplified as) the prophet of "self-reliance," Emerson was a complex and profound thinker whose works formed a central part of what literary historians refer to as the "American Renaissance."

Engel v. Vitale (1962) Supreme Court case that declared unconstitutional the practice of group prayer in schools. The case originated in a New York school district that began its school day with this prayer: "Almighty God, we acknowledge our dependence upon Thee, and we beg Thy blessings upon us, our parents, our teachers, and our country. Amen." The Court, by a 6–1 margin, decided that even if the group prayer was voluntary, it still violated the Establishment Clause of the First Amendment because it served as a governmental establishment of religion.

Enlightenment Eighteenth-century intellectual movement through the Western world that most commonly valued the role of man's reason and intellect over religion and superstition as the principles that should organize social and intellectual life, beginning with the scientific and philosophical issues of the Renaissance and broadening the range of concern, giving it a freer, more secular tone. The core of Enlightenment thought was the question: How do we know things to be true? The leading thinkers argued that human reason, combined with materials obtained through empirical observation, was the path to reliable knowledge.

establishment A system of public financing for religion that characterized colonial America and was modeled on the national church system of Europe. A religious tax was levied on citizens for the support of the official religion of the colony—for example, the local Congregational Church in Massachusetts, or the Church of England in

Virginia. Most states disestablished religion at the time of the American Revolution (Massachusetts and Connecticut were the exceptions), and the First Amendment to the Constitution banned the national government from establishing a religion for the American people. (See Ravitch, chap. 7, this volume.)

evangelicalism   A religious movement reflecting the surge of spiritual life after the Great Awakening. The movement has been interpreted as a revolt against rationalism and the notion that the Christian life involved only observing the outward formalities of religion. Emphasizing religious experience, particularly one's conversion or "new birth," evangelicalism came to dominate Protestant culture in the nineteenth century. (See Sweeney, chap. 5, this volume.)

Everson v. Board of Education (1947)   A seminal Supreme Court case in "incorporating" the Establishment Clause of the First Amendment ("Congress shall make no law respecting the establishment of religion, or prohibiting the free exercise thereof"). In a 5–4 decision defending the right of New Jersey to use tax monies to bus parochial school students, Supreme Court Justice Hugo Black laid down the foundation for what would become Supreme Court doctrine for the establishment clause: "The 'establishment of religion' clause of the First Amendment means at least this: Neither a state nor the Federal Government can set up a church. Neither can pass laws which aid one religion, aid all religions or prefer one religion over another. Neither can force nor influence a person to go to or to remain away from church against his will or force him to profess a belief or disbelief in any religion. No person can be punished for entertaining or professing religious beliefs or disbeliefs, for church attendance or non-attendance. No tax in any amount, large or small, can be levied to support any religious activities or institutions, whatever they may be called, or whatever form they may adopt to teach or practice religion. Neither a state nor the Federal Government can, openly or secretly, participate in the affairs of any religious organizations or groups and vice versa. In the words of Jefferson, the clause against establishment of religion by law was intended to erect 'a wall of separation between Church and State.'"

Falwell, Jerry (1934–2007)   Son of an abusive alcoholic father, Falwell became one of the best-known Baptist preachers of the twentieth century. As minister at Thomas Road Baptist Church in Lynchburg, Virginia, Falwell built a national audience through his *Old-Time Gospel Hour*, and, later, his key role as a founder of the Moral Majority, an organization devoted to pursuing conservative Christian values in the political world. Because of his work with the Moral Majority and his founding of Liberty College, Falwell is often seen as a "father" of the "religious right."

Fellowship of Southern Churchmen   An informal network of southern religious liberals and radicals founded originally by a Presbyterian preacher-activist, Howard Kester, and carried forward until the early 1960s mostly by white ministers and professionals concerned with issues of racial and economic justice. The group's periodical, *Prophetic Religion*, provided a rare outlet for southern religious liberals to articulate their sentiments. During the late 1940s and early 1950s, the North Carolina Presbyterian minister Charles Jones led the group into civil rights activism.

feminist theology   Originating in the nineteenth century (especially with Elizabeth Cady Stanton's Woman's Bible), feminist theology reached its apex in the later twentieth century, as female religious thinkers began entering and teaching in seminaries and recasting religious thought to account for the historic sexism of many religious traditions and to incorporate notions of women's equality into sacred texts, hymns, sermons, and theological treatises.

Finney, Charles (1792–1875)   The "father of modern revivalism," Finney was born in Connecticut and raised in New York. Trained as a lawyer, he began a highly successful career as an evangelist after his conversion to Protestant evangelicalism in 1821. He refused formal theological training but still managed to be licensed by the local presbytery. Finney was known for his legal style of preaching, literally "arguing" people into a decision to convert. A strong advocate of social reform, he trained a generation of like-minded college students while president of Oberlin College in Ohio.

First Amendment   Adopted as part of the Bill of Rights in 1791, the First Amendment to the Constitution prohibits the federal government from establishing a religion or denying the free exercise of religion. In the 1940s this amendment was extended by the Supreme Court to state and local governments via the Fourteenth Amendment. (See Ravitch, chap. 7, this volume.)

Focus on the Family   A conservative parachurch evangelical organization founded originally in California in 1977, Focus on the Family currently is headquartered in Colorado Springs, Colorado, where it employs over 1,300 people. Founded by James Dobson, originally a child psychologist known for a book on child rearing, *Dare to Discipline*, Focus on the Family oversees myriad activities devoted to advocating for and preserving the "traditional" nuclear family, including pressing for child-friendly laws, combating gay and lesbian rights, and preaching Christian "family values" to a large radio audience that tuned in to Dobson's daily broadcasts. Focus on the Family has worked closely with conservative presidential administrations to articulate the political voice of the "religious right," and has drawn criticism for its close relationship with Republican politicians at the state and national levels.

Fourteenth Amendment   A constitutional amendment, added in 1868, that guarantees the protection of due process of law to all U.S. citizens. This amendment allowed the Supreme Court during the twentieth century to apply other individual rights and government restrictions once reserved for the federal level to all levels of government, including the individual right to free exercise of religion.

Freemasonry   Teachings and rituals of a secret society founded on a complex mixture of Renaissance occultism, Enlightenment rationalism, and eventually a claim to wisdom of the stonemasons who had built Solomon's Temple. It served as a means to create bonds among men of professional classes. Many evangelicals decried its secret practices in the early to mid-nineteenth century, even founding political parties expressly committed to ending Freemasonry.

free thought   A movement largely tied to Deism in the late eighteenth and early nineteenth centuries that rejected traditional institutional Christianity for a religion based on Enlightenment reason. Thomas Paine and Ethan Allen published two of the more famous free thought documents, arguing against the illogical claims of Christianity and for a religion founded on empiricism and reason.

Fuller, Charles (1887–1968)   One of the most popular "radio evangelists" of the mid-twentieth century, Fuller, a Baptist minister in Los Angeles, broadcast his show, *The Old Fashioned Revival Hour*, for more than thirty years to over 650 radio stations nationwide. Fuller also founded Fuller Theological Seminary in southern California, which serves today as a large interdenominational theological seminary generally espousing mainstream evangelical thought.

Fuller, Margaret (1810–1850) A New England Unitarian and Transcendentalist, Fuller was one of the most influential intellectual women of the antebellum era. From 1840 to 1842, Fuller worked with Ralph Waldo Emerson in editing the *Dial*, a landmark publication in the early years of what literary critics call the "American Renaissance," and a few years later served as the first female correspondent for a major American newspaper, Horace Greeley's *New York Tribune*. Fuller's work *Woman in the Nineteenth Century*, published in 1845, was a landmark in the history of American feminism.

fundamentalism Militantly anti-modernist, conservative Protestant evangelical thought, arising in the early twentieth century with the publication of *The Fundamentals* in 1914. Emphasizes a strict literalist interpretation of the Bible and a rejection of many forms of "modern" thought, especially Darwinism. (See Benderoth, chap. 16, this volume.)

Garvey, Marcus (1887–1940) A mass orator in Harlem in the 1920s who advocated black separatism and was the leader of the United Negro Improvement Association. A Jamaican by birth, Garvey was an early advocate for some of the themes that later would emerge in black theology.

Ghost Dance A pan–Native American movement that emerged during the late nineteenth century. The moving spirit was the prophet Wovoka, whose vision showed the followers of the Ghost Dance being resurrected after the earth opened up and swallowed all of humanity and the restoration of the departed ancestors of the Native Americans. In 1890, a large body of Ghost Dancers among the Lakotas of South Dakota were slaughtered by a contingent of the U.S. Army.

Gladden, Washington (1836–1918) A leading Congregational minister and one of the founding writers of what became known as the "Social Gospel" movement, Gladden was a long-time pastor of the First Congregational Church in Columbus, Ohio, where he served for thirty-two years. Gladden was active in local politics, making his name as a progressive critic of political corruption, and also served as president of the American Missionary Association, where he expressed opposition to the imposition of racial segregation during the rise of Jim Crow. Gladden wrote more than forty books, in which he espoused his views of applying the themes of Christianity to the social problems of modernizing America.

Goddess religion A late-twentieth-century movement that claims to recover beliefs and practices of ancient times, before the advent of patriarchal religions. The publications and rites of this movement, which is often tied to "neo-pagan" practices, emphasize feminine myths and symbols found in pre-Christian Europe and Native American, Hindu, and Mesoamerican traditions.

Grace, Bishop Charles M. ("Sweet Daddy"; 1881–1960) A Caribbean-born African American minister best known for being the founder of the United House of Prayer for All People, which made its name during the Depression for large services in which scores of hungry people were fed, and in which "Sweet Daddy" Grace encouraged exuberant emotional expression of religiosity.

Graham, William (Billy; b. 1918)　Revivalist and preacher, Graham got his start working for Youth for Christ. Following World War II, he led massive revivals in the United States and throughout the world. A friend of prominent Republican politicians, Graham also racially desegregated his revivals in the late 1950s, but later was burned by his close personal relationship with President Richard Nixon just before and during the Watergate crisis.

Great Awakening　A massive revival that occurred along the entire English-speaking Atlantic seaboard in the late 1730s and 1740s. Emphasizing the personal, intense religious experience of emotional conversion as playing a central role in the process of salvation, the revival helped to create the American evangelical tradition. Leading proponents included Jonathan Edwards, George Whitefield, and Gilbert Tennent.

Grimké, Sarah and Angelina (1792–1873 and 1802–1879)　Born in Charleston, South Carolina, to a large family of slaveholders, the Grimké sisters became two of the best-known female abolitionists, suffragists, and feminist radicals of the nineteenth century. In the 1820s, Sarah took her father for medical care to Philadelphia. She converted to Quakerism, and her sister, who married the abolitionist Theodore Weld, soon followed. In 1836, Angelina published *An Appeal to the Christian Women of the South*, a pamphlet that argued that slavery corrupted the white family by inviting forced miscegenation; in 1839, the sisters followed with *American Slavery as It Is: Testimony of a Thousand Witnesses*, which compiled newspaper stories documenting the horrors of slavery.

harmonial religions　Those forms of belief and personal practice in which spiritual, physical, and sometimes even economic health are understood to flow from a person's relationship to the cosmos. These traditions frequently have unusual features, such as charismatic founders, complicated institutional structures, secret doctrines, or elaborate rituals. Harmonial religions cut across traditional lines of religious division by emphasizing different patterns of belief and practice that tend to be highly individualistic.

Hedgeman, Anna Arnold (1899–1990)　An African American Methodist woman who, after a childhood in the rural Midwest, had a long career of activism in church organizations through the YMCA, United Church Women, and various civil rights groups. Hedgeman was also one of the founding members of the National Organization for Women in 1966, and served on the Commission on Religion and Race for the National Council of Churches.

Henry, Carl F. H. (1913–2003)　American theologian who defended the tenets of traditional evangelicalism against the assaults of modernism. Henry was one of the founders of the National Association of Evangelicals and was the first editor in chief of *Christianity Today*, a magazine that defended evangelical ideas against the more liberal or modernist notions propounded in publications such as *Christian Century*. Henry upheld evangelicalism while also rejecting separatist fundamentalism, leading evangelicals into a more open engagement with modern culture.

Heschel, Rabbi Abraham Joshua (1907–1972)　A professor at the Jewish Theological Seminary of America, a center for Conservative Judaism, Heschel became nationally known for his prophetic statements in sympathy with civil rights activists in the 1960s, and later for Soviet Jews unable to escape an oppressive communist regime. Heschel remains one of the most significant and influential Jewish theologians of modern American history, known for deep spiritual exploration of Jewish texts and for applying those texts to the dilemmas of modern life.

Higginson, Thomas Wentworth (1823–1911)   A New England–born author, intellectual, and activist who championed writers such as Emily Dickinson through his influential essays in the *Atlantic* and other publications. Among religious historians, Higginson is best known as a Unitarian minister who led a contingent of black troops during the Civil War, and later published his account of that experience in his classic work *Army Life in a Black Regiment*. Higginson was among the first to write seriously about the spirituals as folk music whose music and lyrics told of the religious strivings of black Americans.

higher criticism   A scholarly, critical analysis of biblical texts in order to learn their origins and the intention of the authors. This pursuit treats scripture as any other historical source—to be read as a document of its time and region. Beginning in the nineteenth century, it led to a division among Christians as they argued whether its academic approach to what had been understood as an inspired document was appropriate. These divisions eventuated in the fundamentalist movement, a reaction to attempts to read the Bible as a human rather than a divine text.

Hodge, Charles (1797–1898)   A Presbyterian minister and theologian who founded the *Princeton Review* (a high-toned theological periodical) and later became the head of Princeton Theological Seminary, a center for classical Reformed Calvinist intellectual life in America. Hodge's intellectual and theological influence was wide and deep in shaping Presbyterian thought through the nineteenth century. He was famous for saying that Princeton never originated a new idea, by which he somewhat wryly defended Princeton's role as a stalwart advocate for the Westminster Confession style of Presbyterianism and Calvinism in America.

Holiness tradition   Body of theological thought and practice originating from Methodism in the mid-eighteenth century, and popularized in America by Phoebe Palmer, a New York Methodist woman, in the mid-nineteenth century, and later by the Holiness and Pentecostal denominations of the twentieth century. Holiness traditions emphasize the purification of the soul and quest for sanctification that defines the Christian believer's pilgrimage following conversion.

Howe, Julia Ward (1819–1910)   An abolitionist and author, member of the Unitarian Church and suffragist, most noted for composing the lyrics to "Battle Hymn of the Republic," which was set to its familiar tune and published first in the *Atlantic Monthly* in 1862.

Hubbard, L. Ron (1911–1986)   Author of the book *Dianetics* and founder of the Church of Scientology, Hubbard remains a controversial figure, considered by Scientologists to be a guru and by many others to be a charlatan and creator of a church that serves as a money-making empire.

Hutchinson, Anne (1591–1643)   English-born woman who, after her migration to Puritan New England, fell into conflict with Puritan authorities for her leadership of Bible study classes in her home. Seeming to challenge the authority of the Puritan leadership, and to advocate heterodox doctrines, she was banished from the Massachusetts Bay Colony in 1638, and in 1643 was killed by Indian enemies of the

Puritans. She and Mary Dyer stand as symbols of religious freedom in Puritan New England.

Jackson, Jesse (b. 1941) Black Baptist minister and long-time civil rights activist known for his work with Martin Luther King Jr. in the 1960s, and later for founding the "Rainbow Coalition" and running for president in 1984 and 1988.

Jackson, Mahalia (1911–1972) A native of New Orleans, Louisiana, and migrant to Chicago during the 1920s, Jackson went on to become what most consider as the greatest vocal stylist in the genre of black gospel music. Her recordings of classic tunes such as "How I Got Over" and "Precious Lord" defined the sound, which originated with the work of Thomas Dorsey.

Jakes, T. D. (Thomas Dexter; b. 1957) A well-known contemporary minister, from a Pentecostal "Oneness" tradition, who pastors the Potter's House, a huge interdenominational megachurch in Dallas, Texas. Jakes is known for huge annual revivals called "MegaFest," and for a novel and annual conferences called "Woman, Thou Art Loosed." Jakes is one of a number of celebrity televangelists who arose from specific religious traditions but now represent a more general prosperity theology appealing to members of megachurches.

Jehovah's Witnesses A religious denomination founded by Charles Taze Russell in 1872, an enduring movement in the millennialist tradition. It was based on the belief that Jesus had inaugurated a "Millennial Dawn" with his return in the "upper air" in 1874 and an expectation of the millennial consummation of the worldly order in 1914. Jehovah's Witnesses proclaimed that Satan's three great allies were false teachings in the "churches," tyrannies of human government, and the oppressions of business. They are well known for their door-to-door evangelism, their key role in Supreme Court cases extending the bounds of religious freedom (especially in *Cantwell v. Connecticut* [1942]), and their publication the *Watchtower*.

Jesuit Relations Published from the early 1630s until the 1670s, *Jesuit Relations* represented the annual reports of missionaries from the Society of Jesus back to their sponsors in France. The *Relations* chronicled the heroic endeavors of French Jesuit missionaries in New France, concentrated around the Great Lakes region of the New World and later into the Mississippi Valley, and devoted extended attention to the social, cultural, and religious customs of the various Indian tribes—the Hurons, the Iroquois, the Montagnais, and others—among whom the Jesuits missionized. The accounts also related the stories of the martyrdom of several of the missionaries, as well as the famous story of Kateri Tekakwitha, the first Native American to be nominated for sainthood.

Jones, Charles Colcock (1804–1863) As a Presbyterian minister and educator and a large slaveholder in Liberty County, Georgia, Jones organized a large-scale effort to conduct missions among the slaves, believing this to be the best way to civilize and Christianize African American slaves as well as to temper the worst excesses of the practices of slavery. Jones's work has been documented memorably in the Pulitzer Prize–winning study of Erskine Clarke, *Dwelling Place: A Plantation Epic* (2005).

Judaism The ancient faith of the Jewish people, practiced in the United States in Reformed, Orthodox, and Conservative forms. Reform Judaism was led initially by Isaac Mayer Wise. Deeply influenced by the work of Moses Mendelssohn and the upwardly mobile status of Jews in Germany, nineteenth-century Reform Jews in America emphasized contemporary decorum in worship as opposed to conducting services in Hebrew. Reform Judaism used models found in contemporary Protestant practice; families were seated together, and organs and choirs were used. It also discontinued the wearing of the yarmulke and prayer shawl. The Reform Jews are defined as a progressive religion and not inextricably bound by the ancient biblical ideas. The Orthodox movement was dedicated to a traditional emphasis on the Torah and Talmud. Orthodox Jews are generally united by the precept that Jewish law remains binding on Jews. Conservative Judaism provides a middle ground between the Orthodox and Reform sections. (See Levenson, chap. 18, this volume.)

kachinas (or **katsinas**)   Symbolic objects representing naturally divine or spiritual forces in the world, often represented as doll-like objects that manifest themselves in the ceremonies of Hopi and Puebloan peoples of the American Southwest. To the Spanish who first encountered them, kachinas represented Indian "superstition" and "shamanism" that was to be overcome through the power of Christian symbols. Today, "kachina dances" at the pueblos of New Mexico and Arizona attract crowds of tourists seeking to experience some representation of traditional Native cultural customs.

King, Martin Luther, Jr. (1929–1968)   African American civil rights leader and Baptist minister, born originally in Atlanta. Leader of the Montgomery bus boycott of the mid-1950s and subsequently the organizer of the Southern Christian Leadership Conference, King won the Nobel Peace Prize in the 1960s for his efforts in the black civil rights movement.

kiva   The underground, cylindrical sacred spaces of Puebloan peoples of the Southwest, where religious ceremonies and initiation rites historically took place. Kivas were generally open only to male members of the tribe, and were considered the home of openings in the earth (*sipapu*) by which the forces of other worlds entered human life, and through which natural life first made its way to earth.

Ku Klux Klan   The first Ku Klux Klan was a sort of paramilitary wing of white Democrats in the Reconstruction-era South; it sought a restoration of political power and white supremacy. The second Klan reached its height in the 1920s, when millions of white Protestants joined a group avowedly in defense of "100% Americanism" and focused on the dangers posed by immigrants, Catholics, and Jews. The Klan was revived a third time during the civil rights movement, again in defense of white supremacy in the South against the black struggles for civil rights.

Lee, Jarena (b. 1783)   African Methodist Episcopal church exhorter who unsuccessfully petitioned to become an ordained minister. In 1836, Lee published her autobiography detailing her preaching in New Jersey. This was one of the first works published by an African American woman in the United States.

liberation theology   Body of thought that emphasizes God's "preferential option" for the poor and neglected of the Third World and of America. It is most often associated with Latin American and African theologians of the twentieth century, who sought to resist colonialism, economic exploitation, and oppression.

Lutheran   Denomination that emerged first in Germany, later spreading worldwide, from the work of Martin Luther in the early Protestant Reformation. Highly structured denomination with closely followed worship rituals that are closer to Catholicism than many other Protestant groups. In America, strongest in the Midwest and other areas settled by German immigrants.

Machen, J. Gresham (1881–1937) A conservative Presbyterian theologian and founder of Westminister Theological Seminary and of the Orthodox Presbyterian Church, Machen was best known for revolting against modernist theology at Princeton, where he taught from 1915 until 1929, and upholding what he saw as purer Presbyterian/Calvinist doctrines.

Madonna of 115th Street The name given to Our Lady of Mount Carmel, the image of the Virgin treasured by Italian Americans in a manner similar to the Virgin of Guadalupe among Latino Catholics. Our Lady of Mount Carmel first made her way into America in 1881, where she presided over an Italian-American Catholic church erected on 115th Street in East Harlem, New York. Soon, the Madonna became the focus of a large street festival held every year in mid-July that culminated in extreme acts of unction that parishioners paid to the image of Our Lady of Mount Carmel. Italian American women controlled much of the devotions enacted for the Virgin, who was considered to be emblematic of and soothing to the struggles and suffering of Italian working-class immigrants in a poor and grimy section of New York City. Robert Orsi's book interpreting the festival of the Madonna of 115th Street is considered a classic in the field of American religious studies.

Malcolm X (1925–1965) Born Malcolm Little, Malcolm X converted to a version of Black Islam while in prison after a youth of petty crime. In the 1960s, Malcolm became internationally known as a fiery speaker, critic of the integrationist thrust of the civil rights movement, and proselytizer for the Honorable Elijah Muhammad and Islam as the true religion of the black man. Shortly before his assassination in 1965, Malcolm visited the Middle East and converted to a more orthodox brand of Islam, alienating him from many of his allies in the Black Muslim movement.

manifest destiny A cultural complex articulated by a political phrase—coined originally by Democratic columnist John O'Sullivan in 1845, who supported the annexation of Texas—that suggested that God had given divine imprimatur to the inevitable expansion of Anglo-Saxon Protestants across the North American continent.

Martínez, Antonio José (1793–1867) A well-known priest, educator, politician, and community leader among Hispanics in New Mexico, Martínez was accused of fomenting the "Taos Revolt" following the Mexican-American War, in which New Mexicans revolted against the newly instituted American rule. Following the accession of New Mexico by the United States, Martínez fought a protracted conflict with Archbishop Jean Baptist Lamy, appointed to supervise Catholics in the region and determined to modernize Latino Catholic customs and mandate tithing among New Mexican parishioners. Martínez defended Latino Catholics in the region and was eventually excommunicated by Lamy. Martínez was later fictionally portrayed by a character in Willa Cather's *Death Comes to the Archbishop*.

Mather, Cotton (1663–1728) The son of the well-known Puritan minister Increase Mather, and named after his grandfather John Cotton, Mather was an enormously influential theologian, social commentator, and scientist during the third generation of Puritanism. Author of *Magnalia Christi Americana* (1702), Mather continued the Puritan vision of interpreting the American experiment within an Old Testament framework of a "chosen people" and their travails and triumphs. Mather was also known for being a critic of the use of "spectral evidence" during the Salem witch trials (1692), for his experiments with plant hybridization, and for his advocacy of smallpox inoculation following an outbreak of smallpox in Boston in the early 1720s.

McPherson, Aimee Semple (1890–1944)   An evangelist, preacher, and founder of the International Church of the Foursquare Gospel in Los Angeles, McPherson was one of the first ministers to harness the power of the radio for publicity.

megachurch   A nickname for large (over 2,000 members) churches, sometimes denominationally affiliated but often not, run by "star" pastors who generally operate relatively independently and in an entrepreneurial spirit. Megachurches are often known for contemporary service styles featuring "praise music" projected onto big screens, with family-friendly programming featuring activities for all age groups, and with an emphasis on generic evangelical doctrines over any denominationally specific preaching.

Men and Religion Forward Movement   A huge interdenominational set of gatherings for men in 1911 and 1912, sponsored by Protestant leaders of the day, which advocated a "muscular Christianity," decried the "feminization of religion," implored men to exert their power in churches, and generally affiliated with a mild form of Social Gospel theology. In some ways, the movement was a precursor to the Promise Keepers gatherings of the 1980s and 1990s, although the latter tended to be more associated with a conservative theology.

Merton, Thomas (1915–1968)   A European-born Trappist monk whose numerous works of theology, philosophy, mysticism, and activism (including *The Seven Storey Mountain*) have proved influential landmarks of Catholic monastic thought in the twentieth century. Merton's concepts of pursuing social justice through nonviolence and through personal purity, as well as his ventures in interreligious dialogue, brought his works and ideas to a wide audience.

Methodists   Founded by Charles and John Wesley in the 1740s as a reform movement within the Anglican Church, Methodists later went on to become the dominant American denomination of the nineteenth century because of their emphasis on free will and divine grace and their successful system of itinerating preachers combined with a close church organization overseen by bishops and an elaborate structural hierarchy.

millennium   Literally, "a thousand years"; metaphorically, the final end time, usually seen by Christians as the time of the final establishment of God's Kingdom and the end of earthly time.

Miller, William (1782–1849)   Miller inspired a number of millennialist movements in the nineteenth century, including the Seventh-Day Adventists and the Jehovah's Witnesses, through his careful biblical study leading to a prediction that the Second Coming of Jesus would occur sometime in 1843 or 1844. When the years passed without such an event, those who remained after the "Great Disappointment" worked in a number of Christian groups that focused on the imminence and chronological details of Christ's coming. Over time, these groups became part of the larger scene of American Protestantism.

Monk, Maria (1816–1839)   A troubled Canadian-born woman who, in 1836, published (under her own name, but likely ghostwritten by anti-Catholic propagandists) *Awful*

Disclosures of Maria Monk; or, The Hidden Secrets of a Nun's Life in a Convent Exposed. The sensational and wholly fictitious "memoir" told a story of nuns raped by priests who then strangulated the resulting infants from these illicit unions. Although widely denounced at the time, the tale fed into widespread anti-Catholic prejudice that led to such incidents as the attack on a Ursuline Catholic convent in Charlestown, Massachusetts, in 1834, and later to the formation of the nativist and anti-Catholic American Party (popularly known as the Know-Nothing Party).

Moody, Dwight (1837–1899)   Famous Chicago-based mass evangelist of the later nineteenth century and founder of the Moody Bible Institute in Chicago. Moody created many of the techniques and forms of what we now consider mass Protestant evangelism, along with a body of music composed and led by his musical director, Ira Bliss, that came to be called "gospel music."

Moon, Charlotte Diggs ("Lottie"; 1840–1912)   A well-bred native of Virginia and devout Southern Baptist, Moon served as a missionary in China for the Southern Baptist Foreign Mission Board from 1873 to 1912. Her long tenure inspired what became the annual Lottie Moon foreign missions offering, which finances about half of the huge Southern Baptist missionary effort worldwide.

Moravians   A product of religious movements in fifteenth-century Bohemia, the shorthand "Moravians" refers to the Unitas Fratrum, or the Unity Brethren. Renewed through the work of Nicholas Zinzendorf in the eighteenth century, the Moravians came to North America in 1742, where their most successful settlements were in Pennsylvania (where the church found its home and center in Bethlehem and Nazareth) and around Winston-Salem, North Carolina. The Moravians conducted extensive missionary work among Indians and African American slaves, and in the South drew a substantial body of African American followers. The Moravians were known for "love feasts," in which the body and blood of Christ were shared with all in the community, and for their enthusiastic hymn singing.

Muhammad, Elijah (1897–1975)   Disciple of W. D. Fard and a founder of the Nation of Islam. In Detroit in the 1930s and 1940s, he built the Nation of Islam into a powerful black self-help organization.

Muir, John (1838–1914)   A founder of modern environmentalism and of the Sierra Club. Muir's writing portrayed the natural environment in purist, quasi-religious terms. He opposed the ideas of "conservation" as depicted by governmental representatives such as Gifford Pinchot, who sought to balance land use versus land preservation.

Murray, John Courtney (1904–1967)   A Catholic theologian best known for reconciling traditional church doctrine with American ideas of religious pluralism and religious freedom, Murray played a key role in many of the modernizing ideas that came out of Vatican II. He wrote the seminal text *Dignitatis Humanae Personae*, which became the official Catholic statement on religious liberty and on church–state relations.

National Baptist Convention (NBC)   Established in 1895, the National Baptist Convention is the largest organization of African American Baptists in the country. It emerged originally as a merger of three different African American Baptist organizations that had arisen after the Civil War. In 1915, the NBC split over the issue of who controlled its publishing house, which was the largest black-owned publishing firm in the country. In the 1960s, the NBC split again when Martin Luther King Jr.

and other progressive ministers objected to the relatively conservative stance of the dominant NBC leadership; the breakaway faction formed the Progressive National Baptist Convention.

National Council of Churches (NCC)   A transdenominational Protestant agency that addresses social concerns. Begun in 1950, the NCC succeeded the Federal Council of Churches (begun in 1908) as the leading Protestant voice in the cultural arena for the middle third of the twentieth century. Its members include the mainline Protestant denominations, the Eastern Orthodox churches, most of the African American Baptist and Methodist denominations, and a number of smaller groups.

Nation of Islam   The official organization of Black Muslims, made most famous by Malcolm X. (See Blum, chap. 10, and Smith, chap. 20, this volume.)

Native American Church   Formally incorporated in 1918, the Native American Church is best known for its sacrament of peyote use as a central part of its religious ritual. While the religious use of peyote dates back hundreds of years, the Native American Church synthesizes Christian beliefs and doctrines with peyote rituals. One member of the church became involved in the Supreme Court case *Smith v. Oregon*, in which the Court defended laws banning the use of peyote as an illicit drug, against the objections of advocates of religious freedom who insisted that peyote use as part of a religious ceremony was protected by the First Amendment. (See O'Brien, chap. 2, this volume.)

natural theology   A term used in the eighteenth and nineteenth centuries to specify the knowledge of God that comes through nature rather than through scripture or revelation. Most Christians during that period believed that God is revealed through both nature and scripture, the latter being a more precise revelation that taught the way of salvation. Natural theology was especially popular among Deists, who claimed that since nature evidenced the being and attributes of God, no further revelation was necessary.

Neolin   Delaware Indian prophet. Neolin's visions in the 1750s, involving a rejection of European ways and a return to Indian customs, inspired Indians in the Ohio Valley, including Pontiac, who led a large-scale rebellion in the 1760s. Neolin's visions were resurrected by other prophets and warriors, including Tecumseh, in the early nineteenth century. Neolin was part of what some scholars have called the "Indian Great Awakening" in the mid-eighteenth century.

neo-paganism   Contemporary expression of what its believers see as ancient traditions and rituals that pay homage to the natural and feminine forces (including the Goddess, hence the term "Goddess religion") that govern earth and spiritual life, those forces that were worshiped in the ancient pagan traditions. Neo-paganism is sometimes associated with witchcraft or with "New Age" religions.

New Age   A movement, more than a formal religion, that tends to have no agreed-on holy text, central organization, or membership, focusing more on private practices in seeking spiritual meaning. Usually these practices incorporate a number of non-traditional means, including channeling, astrology, healing crystals, tarot cards and palmistry, meditation, near-death experiences, reincarnation, ecological mysticism, radical feminism, acupuncture, and yoga.

New Lights   Revivalist wing of the Congregational Church during the Great Awakening of the mid-eighteenth century.

New Thought   A philosophical/religious movement developed in the mid- to late nineteenth century through the work of Phineas Parkhurst Quimby. Drawing from an intellectual heritage of Transcendentalist thought, New Thought emphasized that "the kingdom of heaven is within," and thus humans, through concrete acts of affirmation, may experience the immediate presence of a divine spirit that envelops the universe. New Thought, in its various branches, appealed to a variety of Gilded Age and Progressive Era intellectual explorers and thinkers who were seeking alternatives to received religious traditions.

Niebuhr, Reinhold (1892–1971)   Considered one of America's greatest theologians of the twentieth century, Niebuhr was a Lutheran parish minister from Detroit and later professor at Union Theological Seminary in New York. Niebuhr articulated a body of theology emphasizing the reality of human sin and evil and the necessity of state power to restrain that evil, part of what is often called neo-orthodox theology. Niebuhr's thought was a response to and critique of the more positive Social Gospel theology of the earlier twentieth century.

Noyes, John Humphrey (1811–1886)   A Vermont-born and Yale-trained minister who, in the mid-1840s, founded the utopian commune of the Oneida Community, where Noyes and his followers followed the founder's striving for perfectionism through a system of complex marriage, male continence to manage reproduction, and communal living.

Occom, Samson (1723–1792)   A member of the Mohegan tribe in Connecticut, this Native American Presbyterian minister was instrumental in the First Great Awakening and the founding of Dartmouth College. Occom left some of the earliest writings of an Indian evangelical, and was a critic as well of white evangelical racism and mistreatment of Native peoples.

Olcott, Henry Steele (1832–1907)   Sometimes called "America's first white Buddhist," Olcott was one of the founders of the Theosophical Society with Helena Blavatsky in the mid-1870s, and worked to impart ideas of Eastern religious traditions, especially Buddhism, to a wider American audience. Olcott lived in Sri Lanka for long periods, where he established schools and is revered today. See also Theosophy.

Osborn, Sarah (1722–1796)   A native of Rhode Island, Osborne kept up a series of devotional writings for more than thirty years during the eighteenth-century period of evangelical awakening, which historians now see as evidence of the widespread influence of the Lockean sensory ideas of the Enlightenment on evangelical experience in eighteenth-century America.

PADRES   Founded in the 1970s, PADRES is an acronym for Padres Asociados para Derechos Religiosos, Educativos, y Sociales (Priests Associated for Religious, Educational, and Social Rights). PADRES was a group of Mexican-American priests who sought to advance Latino ecclesiastical rights within a largely Irish American–dominated American Catholic Church. PADRES succeeded in winning the confirmation of the first Latino Catholic bishop in the United States.

Palmer, Phoebe (1807–1874)   A New York–born Methodist woman whose ideas about Christian perfection and the "entire sanctification" and holiness of the individual, taught to others in home classes and later through an itinerant ministry, crystallized the ideas that later burgeoned into the Holiness tradition.

Parham, Charles (1873–1929)   A key figure in the development of Pentecostalism, Parham's teaching at a Bible school in Topeka, Kansas, in the early twentieth century became one of the roots of the doctrine of speaking in tongues as evidence of the movement of the Holy Spirit in the soul.

Parker, Theodore (1810–1860)   A Unitarian minister, Transcendentalist, and abolitionist whose sermons and writings in Boston defined the nature of New England theological liberalism and social radicalism in the mid-nineteenth century. Parker rejected the authenticity of the miracles of the Bible and advocated conscious rejection of the Fugitive Slave Law of 1850. His congregation in Boston, which included William Lloyd Garrison, Julia Ward Howe, and other well-known New England abolitionists, served as a bellwether of American social reform. Parker's famous dictum—The arc of the moral universe is long, but it bends towards justice—was later paraphrased by Martin Luther King Jr. in his "Letter from a Birmingham Jail."

parochial schools   Private schools formed by Catholics in response to anti-Catholic prejudice in public schools.

Peale, Norman Vincent (1898–1993)   A Protestant minister who wielded wide influence in twentieth-century American culture through his book *The Power of Positive Thinking*, his editorship of the interdenominational evangelical magazine *Guideposts*, and his radio program *The Art of Living*, broadcast for more than fifty years.

Penn, William (1644–1718)   An English Quaker who prevailed on King Charles II to give him a large land grant to settle debts with his family. This colony was called Pennsylvania—"Penn's woods." Penn and his followers did not restrict this land to Quakers, but wanted it open for all.

Pentecostalism   Twentieth-century theological and denominational movement emphasizing the "third work" of the Holy Spirit, as evidenced by speaking in tongues, as the final culmination of the Christian journey. It is currently a huge worldwide movement incorporating many variety of "charismatic" Christians who embrace bodily expressions of the Holy Spirit. (See Sweeney, chap. 5, this volume.)

Phelps, Elizabeth Stuart (1844–1911)   A New England author, Phelps wrote several novels about heaven that were influential in altering Victorian ideas of the afterlife.

postmillennialism   The belief that the thousand-year kingdom described in the book of Revelation would occur only after the Second Coming of Jesus, and that the obligation of believers therefore was to perfect this world in preparation for that Second Coming.

premillennialism   The belief that the Second Coming of Jesus would come before the millennium, with a subsequent rapture of believers and a period of tribulation on earth before the final establishment of Christ's kingdom.

Presbyterian   Historic "mainstream" denomination that took root in America in the eighteenth century and became one of the major evangelical groups of American history. Usually associated with orthodox Calvinist theology, a strong emphasis on the Protestant work ethic and educational attainment, and a form of church government run by local presbyters and regional synods.

Primitive Baptists   Those Baptists who reject "society" or "denominational" forms of organization, hold to a strict Calvinist view of the sovereignty of God, and oppose the use of "means," such as missionaries, to spread the word of God. Primitive Baptists emerged in the antebellum era, are predominantly concentrated in the upland South, and often practice distinctive forms of a capella singing, best known today as the basis for Ralph Stanley's vocal bluegrass stylings.

Protestant General name given to Christian groups that emerged from Martin Luther's "protest" against the Catholic Church in the early sixteenth century. Most Protestants emphasize the creed of the "priesthood of the believer" and direct access of the believer to God, without the requirement of the intervention of priests or saints.

Protestant Ethic Term coined by the sociologist Max Weber to describe the historic propensity in Protestant countries for hard work and the accumulation of wealth, all done for the greater glory of God; later secularized into the term "work ethic."

Puritans Originally a movement of devout Englishmen and -women who sought to "purify" the Anglican Church, to excise its remaining vestiges of Catholicism; later the dominant group of English believers who settled New England in the seventeenth century and founded many of the key institutions of the colonial era in the North.

Quakers Radical religious movement originating in seventeenth- and eighteenth-century England that emphasized a rejection of all forms of authority (including ministers and organized churches) in favor of lay-led spirituality. Quakers taught the value of silence in listening for the "inner light" that would bring one to spiritual truth. In America, the Quakers under William Penn founded the colony of Pennsylvania.

Redstick Revolt A Native American millennialist military action against Anglo-American land encroachments in "Creek" (or more properly called Muskogee) land in the Southeast, the Redstick Revolt represented a carryover of traditions of Indian millennialism from the various forms of "spirited resistance," including Neolin's vision and Pontiac's rebellion, from the mid-eighteenth century. Andrew Jackson's forces defeated the Natives at what Anglos called the Battle of Horseshoe Bend, opening up large tracts of land in present-day Alabama to white settlers.

Reformed A term used to refer to the theological system and the membership of a variety of denominational traditions from the Calvinist branch of Protestantism.

Restorationism (or **Restoration Movement**) Originally termed in the nineteenth century the "Campbell-Stone movement," Restorationism historically has sought to "restore" a purer form of Christianity, devoid of man-made creeds and doctrines, and has operated under the principle "No creed but the Bible." The Restoration Movement resulted in denominations such as the Disciples of Christ and the Churches of Christ, originally the same group but splitting in the early twentieth century over issues of church organization. Restorationists are also sometimes called "primitivists," after their desire to restore the pure and "primitive" Christian church.

Reynolds v. Uniited States (1879) A Supreme Court decision that declared that religious duty was not necessarily a defense for conduct that was otherwise illegal. The case involved a Mormon convicted of polygamy, in spite of the fact that the defendant considered polygamy to be a religious duty within the context of his Mormon beliefs. The case held wide significance in defining the boundaries of the "free exercise" of religion guaranteed by the First Amendment.

ring shout A West African religious tradition, often followed by slaves in the American South, wherein members would rotate counterclockwise while singing, chanting, and dancing.

Roberts, Oral (1918–2009)   A Pentecostal evangelist who arose from poor rural roots in Oklahoma to be one of the best-known ministers and faith healers in America and founder of Oral Roberts University in Tulsa.

Robinson, V. Eugene (b. 1947)   Robinson was the first gay man to be ordained as a bishop in the General Convention of the Episcopal Church. Robinson's nomination and acceptance as a bishop ignited a worldwide controversy within Episcopal congregations, leading many American Episcopalian churches to withdraw from the General Convention and join Anglican communions elsewhere that stood against gay ordination and condemned homosexual conduct as unbiblical.

Rowlandson, Mary (1635/37–1711)   A woman in Puritan New England who was captured by attacking Indians during King Philip's War of 1676, dragged into captivity, and later ransomed back home. Rowlandson's account of her captivity, *A Narrative of the Captivity and Restoration of Mrs. Mary Rowlandson*, became a classic in the genre of Indian captivity narratives, which enthralled New Englanders during the eighteenth century.

Rush, Benjamin (1745–1813)   A Philadelphia Presbyterian, delegate to the Constitutional Convention of 1789, and medical doctor and educator whose views against slavery and capital punishment and for advanced medical treatments for physical and psychiatric illnesses were widely influential in the early republic.

Ryan, John (1869–1945)   Thought of as the leading figure of the Catholic Social Gospel, Father John Ryan served for twenty-five years as the director of the social action department of the National Catholic Welfare Council. Ryan wrote the *Bishop's Statement of Social Reconstruction* (1919), which became a seminal document of Catholic progressive liberalism, and advocated many of the ideas that later became social policy during the New Deal, including the minimum wage and collective bargaining rights for unionized workers. For his close association with Franklin Delano Roosevelt, he was given the nickname the "Right Reverend New Dealer."

Sabbatarian   One who observes Saturday as the Sabbath Day. Among the Sabbatarians are Jews and a number of small Protestant groups such as the Seventh-Day Adventists.

Salem witch trials (1692)   An outbreak of religious intolerance, fueled by community factionalism between different parts of Salem Village and Salem Town as well as by gendered and patriarchal notions of who should hold property (men) and who was most likely to be affected by penetrations by the devil (women), the witchcraft trials in Salem, Massachusetts, resulted in the executions of 20 people, and the imprisonment of more than 150 others. Eventually, Puritan authorities put the trials to an end when it became clear that the episode threatened to create a colony-wide hysteria and threaten the basis of Puritan rule.

Sallman, Warner (1892–1968)   A Chicago-based painter internationally known for his painting *Head of Christ* (1941), the most reproduced artistic image of the twentieth century.

sanctification   Nineteenth-century doctrinal development originating in Methodism and emphasizing the dwelling of the Holy Spirit within an individual believer's soul, resulting in the complete cleansing of all sin and a higher state of spiritual life.

Sankey, Ira (1840–1908)   Dwight Moody's musical sidekick during the great Moody revivals of the last quarter of the nineteenth century. Sankey composed more than 1,200 hymns, known at the time as "Sankeys" and later as "gospel hymns," that updated and set Protestant lyrics to catchy tunes that drew the affection of millions.

Scopes Trial (1925)   A media event in which the perennial presidential contender and Protestant spokesman William Jennings Bryan defended a Tennessee law prohibiting the teaching of evolution and the nationally known lawyer Clarence Darrow defended the schoolteacher (John T. Scopes), who had deliberately violated the law as a test case. Although Bryan's side won the case, Darrow's cross-examination compelled Bryan to admit inconsistencies and problems in the biblical account of creation, and it made fundamentalism an object of national ridicule.

Scottish commonsense philosophy   A school of thought that emerged from the Scottish Enlightenment of the mid-eighteenth century that took as its starting point the argument that all humans possess an innate sense (common sense) that complements the physical senses and can help to acquire knowledge and make judgments. It ran contrary to the skeptical arguments of other philosophies by democratically advocating for a "common" sense shared by all people that uses inductive rather than deductive reasoning and that helps to establish morality common to all people.

Serra, Junípero (1713–1784)   Founder of the California missions, the Spanish-born Father Serra arrived in California in 1769, and worked to establish a system of missions to help convert and Christianize the California Indians. The missions eventually stretched from San Diego in southern California to Sonoma in northern California, and took more than 30,000 Indians into their environs. The independent Mexican state eventually secularized the missions, closed them in the 1830s, and distributed mission lands to the Californians.

Seventh-Day Adventists   A product of millenarian movements in the mid-nineteenth century, the Seventh-Day Adventists were incorporated as a church body in 1863, and today look to Ellen G. White as their founding inspiration. Adventists are known for practicing the Sabbath from Friday sunset to Saturday sunset, the seventh day of the week, and for holding to strict health doctrines that forbid the use of tobacco, alcohol, and other substances. Because of their millenarian background dating from the ideas of William Miller in the 1840s, the Adventists also hold to a strong theology forecasting a time of tribulation and trouble prior to the coming of Jesus to usher in the end times.

Shakers   One of the longest-lived utopian communal societies in American history. Officially called the United Society of Believers in Christ's Second Appearance, they came into being through the life and work of "Mother" Ann Lee, who they believed was the Second Coming of Christ. Among other beliefs, they taught that since they now lived in the millennium, there was no need for marriage and sex. Shakers became known for craftsmanship in furniture. They combined the Protestant work ethic and "plain style" of the Puritans with the celibate life of medieval monasticism and the enthusiastic religious expressions of utopian groups. (See Stein, chap. 13, this volume.)

shaman   A Native American religious specialist who functions, among other things, as a healer of the sick. Shamans, who are considered to hold knowledge of the tradition, also have the ability to engage in trance voyages in the supernatural realm.

shape-note singing   A style of hymnology in which notations are symbolized not by their position on the musical staff but by their "shape." Sometimes called "fasola" singing because of its use of the "do-re-mi-fa-so-la" scale and teaching method, shape-note singing was widespread in the United States in the early antebellum era. Later, as most churches modernized hymnbooks, updated musical education, and purchased musical instruments, the style became associated with the rural South, where it thrives today in various shape-note-singing conventions.

Sheldon, Charles (1857–1946)   Congregationalist minister, Christian Socialist, Social Gospel writer, and author of the novel *In His Steps*. The famous question he posed in the novel—"What Would Jesus Do?"—inspired a generation of social gospelers and Christian socialists who sought to reform the gross inequities in American society.

Shuttlesworth, Fred (b. 1922)   A native of Alabama and minister in Birmingham during the great civil rights crusades of the early 1960s, Shuttlesworth was a close associate of Martin Luther King Jr. and other ministers in the Southern Christian Leadership Conference. During the 1950s, Shuttlesworth had established the Alabama Christian Movement for Human Rights in response to the state of Alabama outlawing the NAACP, and endured a series of beatings, arrests, and harassments for his efforts to secure civil rights for African Americans.

Smith, Joseph (1805–1844)   New York farmer and religious seeker who claimed to have discovered some tablets in the late 1820s that, when translated, became *The Book of Mormon*. He was the leader of the new sect of the Church of Jesus Christ of Latter-day Saints until his execution by anti-Mormon vigilantes in 1844. (See Quinn, chap. 19, this volume).

Smith, Lucy   A native of Georgia, Elder Lucy Smith migrated to Chicago in 1910 and, in 1916, founded the All Nations Pentecostal Church on the south side of the city. This predominantly female, African American church served the tens of thousands of black migrants who flowed into Chicago as part of the first "Great Migration" of African Americans out of the South. Smith was (after Aimee Semple McPherson) one of the first women to host a religious radio broadcast, and, during the Depression, Smith was known for feeding large numbers of destitute Chicagoans. Smith represented the power of independent female ministers in early Pentecostalism.

Social Gospel   Theological and social movement dating from the late nineteenth and early twentieth centuries emphasizing the role of individual believers and churches in reforming and perfecting this world in preparation for the final coming of God's Kingdom. The Social Gospel was a key part of the progressive movement from the 1890s to the 1920s and served as a political avenue of expression for many liberal religious thinkers and activists.

Society for the Propagation of the Gospel in Foreign Parts (SPG)   An Anglican missionary organization formed in 1701 with the intent of missionizing in the British colonies. In North America, the SPG became known for its earnest but mostly ineffectual efforts to evangelize among Native Americans and slaves.

Sojourners   A magazine and social movement founded in 1971 by Jim Wallis and continuing today. Wallis and *Sojourners* seek to marry evangelical Christianity to a concern for issues of social justice, including poverty and racism. *Sojourners* is usually seen as a flagship publication of the evangelical left.

Southern Baptist Convention (SBC)   Formed in 1845 as a regionally southern branch of Baptists in America, in the twentieth century the SBC became the largest Protestant denomination in the United States, numbering more than 18 million members at its height. It is generally seen as the major conservative evangelical denomination of the South, but with a strong nationwide presence. Its flagship seminary in Louisville is the largest Protestant theological seminary in North America.

Southern Christian Leadership Conference (SCLC)   Formed out of the Montgomery bus boycott of 1955/1956, the SCLC became internationally known for its leaders, including Martin Luther King Jr. and Ralph Abernathy, and its instrumental role in organizing a movement of nonviolent civil disobedience in southern cities such as Birmingham during the American civil rights movement.

speaking in tongues. See **Pentecostalism**.

Speer, Robert Elliot (1867–1947)   A Presbyterian minister and graduate of Princeton best known for being one of the foremost proponents of the foreign missions movement (especially in China) in the first half of the twentieth century, under the slogan "The evangelization of the world in this generation."

Spiritualism   A movement that arose in the nineteenth century that claimed it to be possible to have contact with the dead through a variety of means, including séances and "spirit boxes." Its chief publicist was Andrew Jackson Davis, whose books helped popularize the movement in Victorian America.

spirituals   Black folk religious songs, of uncertain or collective authorship, originating during the period of the rise of evangelicalism among African American slaves, including classics such as "Steal Away to Jesus," "Swing Low, Sweet Chariot," and "Roll, Jordan, Roll." Discovered, notated, and published by whites mostly during and after the Civil War, the spirituals were later both condemned as "cornfield ditties" by some critics and exalted as "sorrow songs" that best captured the religious feeling of the race. Black choirs after the Civil War raised funds for black colleges through their internationally famous performances of the songs, and during the civil rights era authors of "freedom songs" set the tunes of the spirituals to new lyrics emphasizing black freedom in this world.

Strong, Josiah (1847–1916)   Protestant clergyman widely influential in the early years of the Social Gospel movement. Strong was also, notably, the author of *Our Country: Its Possible Future and Its Present Crisis*, which warned of the numerous dangers (ranging from immigration to "Popery" to the urban working poor to Mormonism) imperiling the American republic, and urged Anglo-Saxon Protestants to exert their influence to civilize and Christianize the benighted classes of people then populating American cities.

Student Nonviolent Coordinating Committee (SNCC)   Formed originally at a meeting of youth volunteers for the Southern Christian Leadership Conference in 1960, SNCC soon became one of the best-known and most fearless of civil rights organizations in the early 1960s, particularly through its participation in the "Freedom Rides" of 1961. SNCC also organized "Freedom Summer" in 1964, which brought hundreds of northern volunteers to Mississippi to assist in voter registration. SNCC'S initial emphasis on Christian love, justice, and nonviolence gradually gave way to a more pronounced tilt toward Black Power, before the group disbanded in the later 1960s.

Sunday, Billy (1863–1935)   American evangelist who reached his greatest audience around the time of World War I. A former professional baseball player, Sunday became a full-time itinerant preacher and was a colorful orator and advocate of Prohibition.

Suzuki, Daisetz Teitaro (1870–1966)   Suzuki was born in Japan and trained in a Japanese monastery. In 1897 he traveled to the United States for the first time, and later produced numerous influential works on Buddhist thought and founded an English-language journal about Buddhism. Through much of the twentieth century, Suzuki's works on Zen and Buddhism reached a wide audience in the United States, and he became a teacher and guru for many seeking religious insight outside of Western traditions. In the 1950s, he founded the Cambridge Buddhist Association in Massachusetts, and became the best-known teacher of Japanese religious traditions in the United States.

Swami Vivekananda (1863–1902)   A native of Bengal, India, Swami Vivekananda's lectures on Eastern religion, yoga, and Vedanta at the World's Parliament of Religions in 1893 are generally seen as the first major and widely followed introduction of Eastern religious thought into the American mainstream.

Tekakwitha, Kateri (1656–1680)   Born of a Catholic Algonquian mother and a Mohawk father, Tekakwitha's short life was affected by smallpox, which nearly blinded her. Converted by a Jesuit father, she became one of a small number of Indian women who practiced extreme acts of unction. Feeling compelled to flee her home, Tekakwitha settled in the Christian Indian reserve of Sault-Sainte-Marie during the last years of her life. Immediately following her death, her life was chronicled in a hagiography, and in the nineteenth century she was nominated for sainthood. Today, Native American Catholics still press her case for canonization.

televangelism   A term that arose in the late twentieth century to describe the ubiquitous presence of television ministries. Most of the ministers are evangelical in leanings and help to popularize that style of ministry through their programs.

Tharpe, Sister Rosetta (1915–1973)   A native of Arkansas and member of the Pentecostal Church of God in Christ, Tharpe became nationally known for bringing her swinging, guitar-playing style of gospel music not only to churches, but also to concert halls and nightclubs. After her appearance in the famous "From Spirituals to Swing" concert in 1938, which featured the history of black American music presented to a largely white audience, Sister Rosetta made a number of recordings, including tunes such as "This Train," which set gospel lyrics to innovative blues-influenced guitar licks. Tharpe's style influenced a future generation of both white and black performers, and brought the gospel sound to secular audiences.

theosophy *or* **Blavatsky, Helena** (1831–1891)   Part of the "New Thought" traditions of the late nineteenth century, generally considered to be among the most important influences of the contemporary New Age movement. Originally coming from the writings of a Russian immigrant named Helena Blavatsky, and her close ally and associate Henry Steel Olcott, theosophy emphasizes the higher wisdom of the ancients, who exist in an ethereal realm, and the means humans may use to access that ancient wisdom.

Thoreau, Henry David (1817–1862)   A New England representative of Transcendentalism whose thoughts on civil disobedience to the unjust laws of a state (in particular, the Fugitive Slave Law), on life in the natural world, and on accessing the divine spirit within were vastly influential both in his own generation and to later activists who employed civil disobedience in energizing social movements against injustice.

Thornwell, James Henry (1812–1862)   South Carolina native and prominent Presbyterian minister in Charleston who was instrumental in the formation of the Presbyterian Church of the Confederate States of America. Thornwell was also known for his sermon "The Christian Doctrine of Slavery" (1850), which enunciated a defense of slavery not on racial grounds, which he rejected, but on the basis of a defense of a conservative social order against the threats of infidelity (heresy) and anarchism that southern conservatives perceived as encircling the orthodox Christian South.

Thurman, Howard (1900–1981)   Trained as a black Baptist minister at Morehouse College (later to be Martin Luther King Jr.'s alma mater), Thurman went on to become an active member of the Fellowship of Reconciliation, an early interracial civil rights group, and the founder of the Church for the Fellowship of All Peoples, based in San Francisco. Thurman traveled extensively abroad, where his contacts with international peace figures such as Mahatma Gandhi deeply influenced the civil rights generation of the 1950s and 1960s, as did Thurman's authorship of the seminal text *Jesus for the Disinherited*.

Tikkun   A politically progressive Jewish periodical founded by Rabbi Michael Lerner of San Francisco, *Tikkun* carries forward the tradition of Jewish political advocacy on the center and left of the political spectrum.

Tituba   A teenage girl in Puritan New England, of either black or Native American ancestry (or both), who served in the household of Samuel Parris. In 1692, Tituba was accused of bewitching other girls in the Parris household, and these accusations soon exploded into what became the Salem witch trials.

Transcendentalism   A literary, philosophical, and religious movement that emerged in the 1830s, centered in Massachusetts but with far-reaching influences, with emphasis on the continuity between the divine, the human, and the natural. Its major proponents were Ralph Waldo Emerson, Henry David Thoreau, and Walt Whitman.

Transcendental Meditation (TM)   A set of meditation techniques, based on chanting mantras to achieve a state of "restful alertness," originated first in 1957 and popularized in America and worldwide by Maharishi Mahesh Yogi. "TM" soon became trademarked and marketed as a user-friendly introduction to Eastern meditation techniques.

Truth, Sojourner (1797–1883)   Born in New York as a slave named Isabella Baumfree, Sojourner Truth took on her new name in 1843, when she felt called by the spirit to engage in itinerant preaching and abolitionist work. Truth spoke to hundreds of audiences in the 1840s and 1850s, and became famous for a speech (perhaps apocryphal) defending the womanhood of African American females by reciting the depth of her work and suffering and then exclaiming, "Arn't I a woman?" and on another occasion lifting her blouse to reveal her breast to a heckling audience member who challenged that she was a man in disguise. Truth worked to free fugitive slaves and recruit black men for the army during the Civil War, and after the war endeavored to secure land grants on which freedpeople could settle families. Truth remains today an inspirational figure of African American abolitionism.

Turner, Henry McNeal (1834–1915)   Freeborn African American minister originally from South Carolina. Turner served as a bishop in the African Methodist Episcopal

Church. After a political career that included serving repressed African American constituents in the Georgia legislature during Reconstruction, Turner later became known as a progenitor of Black Theology and an advocate for emigration to Africa as the only respite from a hopelessly racist America.

Turner, Nat (1800–1831)   Born in Southampton County, Virginia, Turner was a slave rebel, Baptist preacher, and messianic thinker whose visions in the late 1820s inspired one of the largest slave rebellions in American history. Turner's revolt resulted in the deaths of more than fifty-seven whites and more than fifty of Turner's associates during the rebellion itself, as well as more than a hundred other innocent African Americans in the county who were murdered in the ensuing crackdown. The lawyer Thomas Ruffin Gray interviewed Turner after the rebellion and Turner's capture; the resulting volume, the *Confessions of Nat Turner*, remains one of the most seminal (if controversial and untrustworthy) documents from the slave era.

Union Theological Seminary   Established originally in New York City by Presbyterians in 1836, Union Seminary in the late nineteenth century became a landmark institution of theological liberalism and modernism, and one of the most important theological institutions in the United States. Union's faculty has included Harry Emerson Fosdick (long-time minister of the Riverside Church, near Union Theological Seminary on the Upper West Side of New York City), Reinhold Niebuhr (a key figure in neo-orthodox theology), Paul Tillich (a well-known modernist theologian of the mid-twentieth century), and James Cone (father of Black Theology).

Unitarianism/Universalism   A Christian movement that denies the Trinitarian nature of God, arguing instead that God exists as only one person. This idea emerged first in Transylvania and then in England in the seventeenth century and traces its religious roots to Reformation-era "free spirits" such as Servetus and Socinus. The movement gained ground in New England Congregational churches in the late eighteenth and early nineteenth centuries.

United Church of Christ (UCC)   A mainline Protestant denomination formed in 1957 from the union of the Evangelical and Reformed Church with the Congregational Christian Churches. The UCC, generally perceived as being in the moderate or liberal wing of American Protestantism, carries on the congregational traditions arising from American Puritanism as well as the socially activist side of Social Gospel–style Protestantism. It numbers some 1.2 million members.

United Methodist Church   Denomination formed in 1968 from a merger of the United Methodist Church and the Evangelical Church of the Brethren. This merger had been preceded in 1939 by the reuniting of the northern and southern branches of the Methodist Episcopal Church along with the Methodist Protestant Church.

utopian communities   Idealistic communities in the early and mid-nineteenth century that lacked sectarian aspirations or were anti-religious. One of the most famous was New Harmony, founded by Robert Owen, and Brook Farm, which served as a gathering place for New England intellectuals. (See Stein, chap. 13, this volume.)

Vatican II (or **Second Vatican Council**)   The most important modern church council, which met from 1963 to 1965. Called by Pope John XXIII, it addressed more issues than had been addressed since the Council of Trent (1564) in the effort of the Roman Catholic Church to come to terms with the modern world. The council redefined the Church's character through a much greater emphasis on the role of the laity and an updating of the church's rituals. Some saw this loosening of the Catholic Church's traditions as a result of the growing influence of its American membership.

Virginia Statute for Religious Freedom   Written by Thomas Jefferson in 1779 after the disestablishment of the Church of England in Virginia, the statute was not fully adopted by the state until 1786. The document argues for the freedom of conscience in religious matters. It helped to influence the drafting of the religion clauses of the First Amendment. (See Ravitch, chap. 7, this volume.)

Virgin of Guadalupe   Originally appearing as an apparition to a native Mexican Indian on a hill overlooking Mexico City in 1531, the Virgin of Guadalupe, or the "Empress of the Americas," has served in North America as a profound symbol of Mexican American Catholic identity. As the patron saint of Latino Catholics, *la Virgen* embodies the struggles and sufferings of the people, best symbolized by Cesar Chavez's effective use of the symbol during his farm workers' crusades of the 1960s and 1970s.

Walker, David J. (1785–1830)   Born a free person of color in North Carolina, Walker is best known for his stinging condemnation of slavery and call for a violent rebellion against it, *Appeal to the Coloured Citizens of the World*, published in 1829 and circulated widely throughout the country. In this work, Walker effectively employed religious rhetoric to condemn the slaveholding South. Walker mysteriously died in Boston in 1830, but the slave rebellion led by Nat Turner in 1831 was considered, by many fearful white southerners, to be inspired by Walker's *Appeal*.

wall of separation   A phrase in a letter by Thomas Jefferson to the Baptists of Danbury, Connecticut, describing his understanding of the role the First Amendment plays in the new federal government in regard to religion. This argument for separate spheres, secular government, and religion without government interference, as well as Jefferson's phrase, was picked up by the Supreme Court in the mid-twentieth century.

Warren, Rick (b. 1954)   A California-born pastor of the large Saddleback Church in Orange County, California, a prototypical "megachurch" despite Warren's Southern Baptist affiliations. Warren is best known for his huge-selling book *The Purpose-Driven Life*, which extends advice to both religious and secular followers about imparting a sense of purpose and mission into individual lives.

Watts, Alan (1915–1973)   English-born Episcopalian priest who popularized Eastern thought and Zen in the 1950s and 1960s through his very successful public lectures. Watts was a friend and mentor to many beatniks and originators of the counterculture, and wrote extensively of his experiments with psychedelic drugs, which he originally saw as one means to accessing mystical experiences.

Weninger, Francis X. (1805–1888)   A native of Austria and trained in the Jesuit tradition, Weninger came to America as a Catholic missionary in the 1840s, where he became known as a Catholic priest capable of preaching in the American revival tradition, appealing to the masses through charismatic exhortations that compelled listeners to search their souls, repent of their sins, and make religious commitments.

Wesley, Charles (1707–1788)   English Methodist preacher and hymn writer. Wesley's songs defined first Methodism, and later mainline Protestantism, throughout the nineteenth and much of the twentieth century.

Wesley, John (1703–1791)   English evangelical preacher in the Church of England and founder of Methodism. Wesley's organization greatly influenced religion in America through its theology and evangelical style.

Wheaton College   A flagship private interdenominational evangelical institution of higher learning originally founded in 1860, now located just west of Chicago. Sometimes called the "evangelical Harvard," Wheaton is home to the Institute for the Study of American evangelicals as well as the Billy Graham Center.

White, Ellen G. (1827–1915)   A religious visionary of the nineteenth century, White was one of the founders of the Seventh-Day Adventist Church. During the Second Great Awakening and through the nineteenth century, White claimed to have received a series of visions involving not only the coming of the end times but also divine instructions as to taking care of the body as the temple of the holy spirit. White advocated, among other health reforms, a vegetarian diet, and established a health center in Battle Creek, Michigan, to promote her notions of spiritual living.

Whitefield, George (1714–1770)   The "Grand Itinerant" of the First Great Awakening, Whitefield was a young Anglican preacher who turned the revivals into a transatlantic event. Known for his simple but powerful oratory, he became the spokesperson for the evangelical movement first in his well-attended meetings and later in his published journals and sermons.

Wilkinson, Jemima (1752–1819)   Born to a Quaker family in Rhode Island, Wilkinson was known as a charismatic but eccentric religious leader during the early republic. Following a brush with death when twenty years of age, Wilkinson declared that she now embodied the spirit of God. Renaming herself the "Universal Publick Friend," she preached a gospel of total sexual abstinence and gender equality to a small group of followers. She was one of the earliest female itinerant preachers in the United States.

Willard, Frances (1839–1898)   Willard is best known as the long-time leader of the Woman's Christian Temperance Union and a committed suffragist who itinerated tirelessly on behalf of both causes.

Williams, Roger (1604–1683/84)   Early Puritan dissenter exiled from Massachusetts for rejecting the authority of the Congregational Church. Williams was the founder of Rhode Island, a theorist of religious liberty, the father of the Baptist Church in America, and a translator of Indian languages.

Winthrop, John (1588–1649)   Leader of an early English Puritan migration to New England in the early 1630s, best known for his speech describing the Puritan experiment in the New World as establishing a "city set upon a hill," a shining light for all the world to see.

Wise, Rabbi Isaac Mayer (1819–1900)   An emigrant from Russia to Cincinnati, Wise made his name as an advocate for Jewish theological education in the United States, resulting in his founding of Hebrew Union College in 1875. Wise also advocated reform of Jewish tradition to meet the realities of daily life in America; his congregation, for instance, was the first to institute family pews in the synagogue.

Woman's Bible   Published originally in 1895, the Woman's Bible was a product of the free-thinking mind and feminist temperament of women's suffrage pioneer Elizabeth Cady Stanton, who reshaped the Bible and interpreted its passages so as to defend women's rights. Stanton's Woman's Bible may be paralleled with Thomas Jefferson's Bible, which he produced in the late eighteenth century in an effort to excise the ancient texts of myths and stories and leave behind the residue of timeless truth.

Woman's Christian Temperance Union (WCTU)   Founded in 1874, a reform organization dedicated to the abolition of alcohol. Headed by Frances Willard in the late nineteenth century, the WCTU became the single largest women's organization in American history to that time, and one of the most powerful reform organizations of the Progressive Era.

Women's Aglow   Now called Aglow International, Women's Aglow began in Seattle in 1967 as an informal meeting of women from various denominational traditions committed to deepening their evangelical experience and sense of mission and developing a stronger sense of fellowship with other churchwomen. Today it counts thousands of chapters around the globe, and has been the subject of a careful academic study by scholar R. Marie Griffith.

Woolman, John (1720–1772)   A Quaker idealist who traveled the American colonies urging Quakers to dissociate themselves from slavery. Woolman was instrumental in persuading the Quakers as a body to renounce slavery, and is often seen as the first American abolitionist.

Worcester, Samuel (1798–1859)   A minister and Congregationalist missionary with the American Board of Commissioners for Foreign Missions whose life became intimately involved with the fate of the Cherokees in the Southeast. Worcester's friendship with Elias Boudinot (originally named Buck Oowatie) led him to a lifetime of missionary work among the Cherokees in Tennessee and Georgia, including an instrumental role in the establishment of the *Cherokee Phoenix* newspaper and defending the rights of Cherokee sovereignty in the seminal Supreme Court case *Worcester v. Georgia*. In the latter case, Chief Justice John Marshall declared the Cherokees to be a "domestic dependent nation" with rights of sovereignty, but President Andrew Jackson, seeking Cherokee removal from the Southeast, famously retorted, "Justice Marshall has made his law. Now let him enforce it."

World's Parliament of Religions   Worldwide meeting of religious leaders held at the World Columbian Exposition in Chicago in 1893. It is often seen as one of the first major forums for representatives of Eastern religions, especially Hinduism and Buddhism, to make their case before a broad American public.

Young, Brigham (1801–1877)   An early follower of Joseph Smith in the Latter-day Saints movement. After Smith's death, Young was appointed successor and presided over the movement of the Mormons to Utah and their subsequent growth. (See Quinn, chap. 19, this volume).

Young Men's Christian Association (YMCA) and **Young Women's Christian Association** (YWCA)   Founded in mid-nineteenth century England, the YMCA and YWCA soon spread worldwide and were part of Social Gospel and reform movements designed to address the needs of urbanizing and industrializing countries and the perceived disorder and irreligion that might afflict a generation of young people moving from farms to cities. In the early twentieth century, the YMCA and YWCA leadership became some of the most important advocates for the Social Gospel movement.

Zen Buddhism   School of Buddhism popularized by Shunryu Suzuki and the West Coast Beat poets of the 1950s, most often associated with the use of paradoxical koans (such as "What is the sound of one hand clapping?") to communicate ineffable spiritual truths.

Zionism   Late-nineteenth-century movement in Jewish thought, led by Theodor Herzl, that emphasized a revitalization of the Jewish faith. Eventually, it became attached to support for the state of Israel, established in 1948, as the spiritual and temporal home for Jews worldwide.

BIBLIOGRAPHY

GENERAL WORKS

Ahlstrom, Sydney E. *A Religious History of the American People*. New Haven, Conn.: Yale University Press, 2004.

Albanese, Catherine L. *America: Religions and Religion*. Belmont, Calif.: Wadsworth, 2006.

Baker, James T. *Religion in America: Primary Sources in U.S. History*. 2 vols. Belmont, Calif.: Wadsworth, 2006.

Bedell, George C., Leo Sandon Jr., and Charles T. Wellborn. *Religion in America*. New York: Macmillan, 1982.

Butler, Jon, Grant Wacker, and Randall Balmer. *Religion in American Life: A Short History*. New York: Oxford University Press, 2007.

Eck, Diana L. *A New Religious America: How a "Christian Country" Has Become the World's Most Religiously Diverse Nation*. New York: HarperCollins, 2002.

Fox, Richard Wightman. *Jesus in America: Personal Savior, Cultural Hero, National Obsession*. San Francisco: HarperOne, 2005.

Gaustad, Edwin S., and Leigh Schmidt. *The Religious History of America: The Heart of the American Story from Colonial Times to Today*. New York: HarperOne, 2004.

Goff, Philip, ed. *The Blackwell Companion to Religion in America*. Malden, Mass.: Wiley-Blackwell, 2010.

Goff, Philip, and Paul Harvey, eds. *Themes in Religion and American Culture*. Chapel Hill: University of North Carolina Press, 2004.

Hemeyer, Julia Corbett. *Religion in America*. 6th ed. Upper Saddle River, N.J.: Prentice Hall, 2009.

Hudson, Winthrop S., and John Corrigan. *Religion in America*. 7th ed. Upper Saddle River, N.J.: Prentice Hall, 2003.

Marsden, George M. *Religion and American Culture*. Belmont, Calif.: Wadsworth, 2000.

Marty, Martin E. *Pilgrims in Their Own Land: Five Hundred Years of Religion in America*. Boston: Little, Brown, 1984.

Prothero, Stephen. *American Jesus: How the Son of God Became a National Icon*. New York: Farrar, Straus and Giroux, 2003.

Stein, Stephen, ed. *The Cambridge History of Religions in America*. Cambridge: Cambridge University Press, forthcoming.

Stephens, Randall J., ed. *Recent Themes in American Religious History: Historians in Conversation*. Columbia: University of South Carolina Press, 2009.

Williams, Peter W. *America's Religions: From Their Origins to the Twenty-First Century*. Urbana: University of Illinois Press, 2001.

GENERAL PRIMARY AND SECONDARY SOURCE READERS

Allitt, Patrick, and Thomas Paterson, eds. *Major Problems in American Religious History*. New York: Houghton Mifflin, 1999.

Butler, Jon, and Harry S. Stout, eds. *Religion in American History: A Reader*. New York: Oxford University Press, 1998.

Gaustad, Edwin S., and Mark A. Noll, eds. *A Documentary History of Religion in America to 1877*. Grand Rapids, Mich.: Eerdmans, 2003.

Griffith, R. Marie, ed. *American Religions: A Documentary History*. New York: Oxford University Press, 2007.

Hackett, David G., ed. *Religion and American Culture: A Reader*. New York: Routledge, 2003.

Harper, Keith, ed. *American Denominational History: Perspectives on the Past, Prospects for the Future*. Tuscaloosa: University of Alabama Press, 2008.

Harvey, Paul, and Philip Goff, eds. *The Columbia Documentary History of Religion in America Since 1945*. New York: Columbia University Press, 2005.

Mathisen, Robert R., ed. *Critical Issues in American Religious History: A Reader*. Waco, Tex.: Baylor University Press, 2006.

McDannell, Colleen, ed. *Religions of the United States in Practice*. 2 vols. Princeton, N.J.: Princeton University Press, 2001.

Porterfield, Amanda, ed. *American Religious History*. Malden, Mass.: Blackwell, 2002.

Porterfield, Amanda, and John Corrigan, eds. *Religion in American History*. Malden, Mass.: Wiley-Blackwell, 2010.

Williams, Peter W., ed. *Perspectives on American Religion and Culture*. Malden, Mass.: Blackwell, 1999.

ATLASES AND GENERAL REFERENCE WORKS

Bowden, Henry Warner. *Dictionary of American Religious Biography*. Westport, Conn.: Greenwood Press, 1993.

Carroll, Brett E. *The Routledge Historical Atlas of Religion in America*. New York: Routledge, 2000.

Gaustad, Edwin Scott, Philip L. Barlow, and Richard W. Dishno. *New Historical Atlas of Religion in America*. New York: Oxford University Press, 2001.

Lindner, Eileen W. *Yearbook of American and Canadian Churches, 2008*. Nashville, Tenn.: Abingdon Press, 2008.

Lippy, Charles H., and Peter W. Williams, eds. *Encyclopedia of the American Religious Experience: Studies of Traditions and Movements*. New York: Scribner, 1988.

Mead, Frank S., Samuel S. Hill, and Craig D. Atwood. *Handbook of Denominations in the United States*. Nashville, Tenn.: Abingdon Press, 2005.

Melton, J. Gordon. *Encyclopedia of American Religions*. Detroit: Gale Cengage, 2002.

——. *Religious Leaders of America: A Biographical Guide to Founders and Leaders of Religious Bodies, Churches, and Spiritual Groups in North America*. Detroit: Gale, 1999.

Newman, William M. *Atlas of American Religion: The Denominational Era, 1776–1990*. Walnut Creek, Calif.: AltaMira Press, 2000.

Queen, Edward L., Stephen R. Prothero, and Gardiner H. Shattuck Jr., eds. *Encyclopedia of American Religious History*. 2 vols. New York: Facts on File, 2001.

Shriver, George H., and Bill J. Leonard. *Encyclopedia of Religious Controversies in the United States*. Westport, Conn.: Greenwood Press, 1997.

Williams, Peter, and Charles Lippy, eds. *Encyclopedia of Religion in America*. Washington, D.C.: CQ Press, 2010.

FILMOGRAPHY

DOCUMENTARIES

Acting on Faith: Women's New Religious Activism in America. DVD. Directed by Rachel Antell. Cambridge, Mass.: Pluralism Project at Harvard University, 2005.

America's New Religious Landscape. DVD. Director not listed. Princeton, N.J.: Films for the Humanities and Sciences, 2003.

Apocalypse. VHS. Directed by William Cran and Ben Loeterman. Alexandria, Va.: PBS Home Video, 1999.

Awake My Soul: The Story of the Sacred Harp. DVD. Directed by Matt Hinton and Erica Hinton. Atlanta: Awake Productions, 2006.

Becoming the Buddha in L.A. VHS. Directed by Michael Camerini. Boston: WGBH, 1993.

Beyond Theology. DVD. Directed by Dave Kendall. Topeka, Kans.: KTWU/Channel 11, 2007.

Born in the USA: Muslim Americans. DVD. Directed by Ahmed Soliman. Sterling, Va.: Astrolabe Pictures, 2003.

Briars in the Cotton Patch: The Story of Koinonia Farm. DVD. Directed by Faith Fuller. Americus, Ga.: Cotton Patch Productions, 2003.

Buddhism Comes to America. VHS. Directed by Elda Hartley. Cos Cob, Conn.: Hartley Film Foundation, 1990.

Buddhism in Anchorage. VHS. Directed by Lisa Kemmerer. Anchorage: Lisa Kemmerer, 1997.

Chase the Devil: Religious Music of the Southern Appalachians. DVD. Directed by Delta Hicks. Newton, N.J.: Shanachie, 2003.

Delta Jews. DVD. Directed by Mike DeWitt. New York: Mike Dewitt Productions, 1998.

Devil's Playground. DVD. Directed by Lucy Walker. New York: Stick Figure Productions, 2002.

Faith and Doubt at Ground Zero. DVD. Directed by Helen Whitney. New York: PBS DVD Video, 2002.

Family Fundamentals. DVD. Directed by Arthur E. Dong. New York: Docurama, 2004.

For the Bible Tells Me So. DVD. Directed by Daniel Karslake. Brooklyn, N.Y.: First Run/Icarus Films, 2007.

Friends of God: A Road Trip with Alexandra Pelosi. DVD. Directed by Alexandra Pelosi. New York: HBO Films, 2007.

Frisbee: The Life and Death of a Hippie Preacher. DVD. Directed by David Di Sabatino. San Francisco: KQED and Jester Media, 2006.

From Shtetl to Swing: A Musical Odyssey. DVD. Directed by Fabienne Rousso-Lenoir. Los Angeles: Seventh Art Releasing, 2005.

The Gates of Heaven. DVD. Directed by Errol Morris. Northcote, Australia: Umbrella Entertainment, 1978.

God in America. DVD. Directed by David Belton, Greg Barker, and Sarah Colt. Boston: WGBH, Frontline, American Experience, 2010.

Godless in America. DVD. Directed by Leslie Woodhead. Sydney: SBS, 2007.

God's Architects. DVD. Directed by Zach Godshall. N.p.: Zach Godshall, 2009.

God's Will. Directed by Michael Letcher. Tuscaloosa: University of Alabama Center for Public Television and Radio, 2000.

The Hajj: One American's Pilgrimage to Mecca. VHS. Orland Park, Ill.: MPI Home Video, 1997.

Half the Kingdom. DVD. Directed by Francine Zuckerman. Waltham, Mass.: National Film Board of Canada, National Center for Jewish Film, 1990.

Hell House. DVD. Directed by George Ratliff. Brooklyn, N.Y.: Plexifilm, 2001.

A History of Christianity: The First Three Thousand Years. DVD. Directed by Diarmaid MacCulloch. London: BBC Worldwide, 2010.

Holy Ghost People. VHS. Directed by Peter Adair. Del Mar, Calif.: CRM/McGraw-Hill Films, 1968.

In Good Conscience: Sister Jeannine Gramick's Journey of Faith. DVD. Directed by Barbara Rick. New York: Out of the Blue Films, 2006.

In the Beginning: The Creationist Controversy. VHS. Directed by Jack Ginay. Alexandria, Va.: PBS Video, 1995.

Jesus Camp. DVD. Directed by Heidi Ewing and Rachel Grady. Los Angeles: Magnolia Home Entertainment, 2006.

The Jesus Experience: Christianity Around the World. DVD. Directed by Silvia Gambardella. Chicago: Questar, 2002.

The Jewish Americans. DVD. Directed by David Grubin. Hollywood, Calif.: PBS Home Video, 2008.

Jonestown: The Life and Death of People's Temple. DVD. Directed by Stanley Nelson. Alexandria, Va.: PBS Home Video, 2007.

Knocking. DVD. Directed by Joel P. Engardio and Tom Shepard. Harriman, N.Y.: New Day Films, 2006.

The Late Great Planet Earth. DVD. Directed by Robert Amram and Rolf Forsberg. 1979; Los Angeles: Trinity Home Entertainment, 2004.

Let the Church Say Amen. DVD. Directed by David Petersen. New York: Film Movement, 2004.

A Life Apart: Hasidism in America. DVD. Directed by Menachem Daum and Oren Rudavsky. New York: First Run/Icarus Films, 1997.

Mahalia Jackson: The Power and the Glory. DVD. Directed by Jeff Scheftel. Santa Monica, Calif.: Xenon Pictures, 2002.

Methodist Camp Meetings. VHS. Directed by Schuyler Sackett. Thousand Oaks, Calif.: Goldhil Video, 1998.

Mine Eyes Have Seen the Glory. VHS. Directed by Julian Norridge. Worcester, Pa.: Gateway Films/Vision Video, 1992.

Miss Navajo. DVD. Directed by Billy Luther. San Francisco: Independent Television Service, 2007.

Monkey Trial. DVD. Directed by Christine Lesiak. Alexandria, Va.: WGBH Educational Foundation and Nebraskans for Public Television, 2004.

The Mormons. DVD. Directed by Helen Whitney. Arlington, Va.: PBS Home Video, 2007.

The Muslim Americans. DVD. Director not listed. Washington, D.C.: WETA, 2007.

The Peyote Road. VHS. Directed by Fidel Moreno, Gary Rhine, and Phil Cousineau. San Francisco: Kifaru Productions, 1992.

Pioneer Spirit: Sectarianism and Utopianism in the Nineteenth Century. VHS. Directed by Eugene Williams. Olathe, Kans.: RMI Media Productions, 1993.

Powerhouse for God. VHS. Directed by Barry Dornfeld. Watertown, Mass.: Documentary Educational Resources, 1989.

The Puritan Awakening. VHS. Directed by Eugene Williams. New York: Insight Media, 1994.

Puritan New England. VHS. Directed by Schuyler Sackett. Thousand Oaks, Calif.: Goldhil Video, 1998.

Rebels in the Pulpit. DVD. Directed by Wendy Reed Bruce. Tuscaloosa: University of Alabama Center for Public Television and Radio, 2002.

Religions of the World: African and African-American Religions. DVD. Directed by Coley Coleman. Wynnewood, Pa.: Schlessinger Media, 1998.

Religions of the World: Native American Spirituality. DVD. Directed by Peter Randall Lippman. Wynnewood, Pa.: Schlessinger Media, 1998.

Religions of the World: Protestant Christianity. DVD. Directed by Elizabeth Coker. Wynnewood, Pa.: Schlessinger Media, 1998.

Religulous. DVD. Directed by Larry Charles. Santa Monica, Calif.: Lionsgate, 2009.

Sacred Steel: The Steel Guitar Tradition of the House of God Churches. DVD. Directed by Robert L. Stone. El Cerrito, Calif.: Arhoolie Foundation, 2001.

Saturday Night, Sunday Morning: The Travels of Gatemouth Moore. VHS. Directed by Louis Guida. San Francisco: California Newsreel, 1992.

Say Amen, Somebody. DVD. Directed by George T Nierenberg. New York: Ryko Filmworks, 2007.

Searching for the Wrong-Eyed Jesus. DVD. Directed by Andrew Douglas. Chicago: Home Vision Entertainment, 2006.

The Shakers. DVD. Directed by Ken Burns. Alexandria, Va.: PBS Home Video, 2004.

Shalom Y'all: The Documentary Film. DVD. Directed by Brian Bain. New Orleans: Shalom Y'all, 2002.

Sister Aimee. DVD. Directed by Linda Garmon. Boston: Carousel Films, 2007.

Sister Helen. DVD. Directed by Rebecca Cammisa and Rob Fruchtman. Burlington, Vt.: Docurama, 2003.

Soul Searching. DVD. Directed by Timothy Eaton. CITY: Revelation Studios, 2007.

Telegrams from the Dead. VHS. Directed by Matthew Collins. Boston: WGBH, 1994.

This Far by Faith: African-American Spiritual Journeys. DVD. Directed by W. Noland Walker. Boston: WGBH, 2003.

Trouble the Water. DVD. Directed by Kimberly Rivers Roberts. New York: Zeitgeist Films, 2009.

Waiting for Armageddon. DVD. Directed by Kate Davis. New York: First Run Features, 2010.

The Way West. Episode 4, *Ghost Dance, 1877–1893*. DVD. Directed by Ric Burns. Boston: WGBH and Shanachie Entertainment, 1995.

We Shall Not Be Moved. DVD. Directed by Bernie Hargis. Worcester, Pa.: Gateway Films, 2001.

With God on Our Side: George W. Bush and the Rise of the Religious Right in America. DVD. Directed by Calvin Skaggs and David Van Taylor. New York: First Run/Icarus Films, 2004.

With God on Our Side: The Rise of the Religious Right in America. VHS. Directed by Calvin Skaggs and David Van Taylor. Alexandria, Va.: PBS Home Video, 1996.

FEATURE FILMS

Agnes of God. DVD. Directed by Norman Jewison. Culver City, Calif.: Columbia TriStar Home Entertainment, 1985.

Angels in America. DVD. Directed by Mike Nichols. New York: HBO Films, 2003.

The Apostle. DVD. Directed by Robert Duvall. West Hollywood, Calif.: Butchers Run Films, 1997.

Avalon. DVD. Directed by Barry Levinson. Culver City, Calif.: Columbia TriStar Home Video, 1990.

Black Robe. DVD. Directed by Bruce Beresford. Santa Monica, Calif.: MGM Home Entertainment, 1991.

Book of Eli. DVD. Directed by Albert Hughes and Allen Hughes. Burbank, Calif.: Warner Home Video, 2010.

Bury My Heart at Wounded Knee. DVD. Directed by Yves Simoneau. New York: HBO Films, 2007.

Cabeza de Vaca. DVD. Directed by Nicolas Echevarria. Los Angeles: New Concorde, 1991.

Conversion. DVD. Directed by Nanobah Becker. New York: Nanobah Becker, 2006.

The Crucible. DVD. Directed by Nicholas Hytner. Moore Park, Australia: Twentieth Century Fox Home Entertainment, 1996.

Dances with Wolves. DVD. Directed by Kevin Costner. Santa Monica, Calif.: MGM Home Entertainment, 1990.

Dead Man Walking. DVD. Directed by Tim Robbins. Santa Monica, Calif.: MGM Home Entertainment, 1995.

Doubt. DVD. Directed by John Patrick Shanley. Burbank, Calif.: Buena Vista Home Entertainment, 2009.

Elmer Gantry. DVD. Directed by Richard Brooks. Beverly Hills, Calif.: Twentieth Century Fox Home Entertainment, 1960.

The Exorcist. DVD. Directed by William Friedkin. Burbank, Calif.: Warner Home Video, 1973.

God's Army. DVD. Directed by Richard Dutcher. Valencia, Calif.: Tapeworm Video, 2000.

Going My Way. DVD. Directed by Leo McCarey. Universal City, Calif.: Universal Studios Home Entertainment, 1944.

Hallelujah. VHS. Directed by King Vidor. Culver City, Calif.: MGM/UA Home Video, 1929.

Hazel's People. VHS. Directed by Charles Davis. Worcester, Pa.: Vision Video, 1973.

Henry Poole Is Here. Directed by Mark Pellington. Burbank, Calif.: Anchor Bay Entertainment, 2008.

Household Saints. VHS. Directed by Nancy Savoca. Burbank, Calif.: Columbia TriStar Home Video, 1993.

Inherit the Wind. DVD. Directed by Stanley Kramer. Culver City, Calif.: MGM/UA Home Video, 1956.

Jesus of Montreal. DVD. Directed by Denys Arcand. Port Washington, N.Y.: Koch Vision, 1989.

Keeping the Faith. DVD. Directed by Edward Norton. Burbank, Calif.: Buena Vista Home Entertainment, 2000.

Kingdom Come. DVD. Directed by Doug McHenry. Beverly Hills, Calif.: Twentieth Century Fox Home Entertainment, 2001.

Leap of Faith. DVD. Directed by Richard Pearce. Hollywood, Calif.: Paramount Pictures, 1992.

Left Behind: The Movie. DVD. Directed by Victor Sarin. Culver City, Calif.: Sony Pictures Home Entertainment, 2000.

Lilies of the Field. DVD. Directed by Ralph Nelson. Santa Monica, Calif.: MGM Home Entertainment, 1963.

Little Buddha. VHS. Directed by Bernardo Bertolucci. Burbank, Calif.: Miramax Home Entertainment, 1993.

Marjoe. DVD. Directed by Sarah Kernochan and Howard Smith. New York: New Video Group, 1972.

Minority Report. DVD. Directed by Steven Spielberg. Universal City, Calif.: DreamWorks Home Entertainment, 2002.

The Miracle Woman. VHS. Directed by Frank Capra. Burbank, Calif.: Columbia TriStar Home Video, 1931.

The Mission. DVD. Directed by Roland Joffé. Burbank, Calif.: Warner Home Video, 1986.

Mississippi Masala. DVD. Directed by Mira Nair. Santa Monica, Calif.: MGM Home Entertainment, 1991.

Northfork. DVD. Directed by Michael Polish. Hollywood, Calif.: Paramount, 2003.

Oh God! DVD. Directed by Carl Reiner. Burbank, Calif.: Warner Brothers, 1977.

The Omega Code. DVD. Directed by Robert Marcarelli. New York: GoodTimes Entertainment, 1999.

The Only Good Indian. DVD. Directed by Kevin Willmott. N.p.: TLC Productions, 2009.

The Rapture. DVD. Directed by Michael Tolkin. Burbank, Calif.: New Line Home Entertainment, 1991.

Rosemary's Baby. DVD. Directed by Roman Polanski. Hollywood, Calif.: Paramount Pictures, 1968.

The Scarlet Letter. DVD. Directed by Roland Joffé. Burbank, Calif.: Hollywood Pictures Home Entertainment, 1995.

A Serious Man. DVD. Directed by Joel Coen and Ethan Coen. Universal City, Calif.: Universal, 2010.

Star Wars. DVD. Directed by George Lucas. Beverly Hills, Calif.: Twentieth Century Fox Entertainment, 1977.

There Will Be Blood. DVD. Directed by Paul Thomas Anderson. Hollywood, Calif.: Paramount Home Entertainment, 2008.

A Thief in the Night. Directed by Donald W. Thompson. 1972; Des Moines, Iowa: Russ Doughten Films, 2006.

The Trouble with Angels. DVD. Directed by Ida Lupino. Burbank, Calif.: Columbia Pictures, 1966.

We're No Angels. DVD. Directed by Neil Jordan. Hollywood, Calif.: Paramount, 1989.

Wise Blood. VHS. Directed by John Huston. Universal City, Calif.: MCA Home Video, 1979.

The Word. VHS. Directed by Richard Lang. Troy, Mich.: Anchor Bay Entertainment, 1978.

DISCOGRAPHY

AMERICAN ORIGINALS (MORMON, CHRISTIAN SCIENCE, SPIRITUALIST)

Hilton, L. M. *Mormon Folk Songs*. CD. Washington, D.C.: Smithsonian Folkways, 1952.

Mack, Susan, and Ellen Hanna. *His Tender Love and Watchful Care*. CD. St. Louis: Solo Committee, 2006.

Mormon Tabernacle Choir. *Come, Come, Ye Saints*. CD. Salt Lake City: BWE Classics, 1997.

——. *The Essential Mormon Tabernacle Choir*. CD. New York: Sony BMG Music Entertainment, 2006.

——. *Faith of Our Fathers*. CD. New York: Sony Music Entertainment, 1993.

Solo Committee. *Sweet Sacred Solos*. CD. St. Louis: Solo Committee, 2003.

Wong Gee, Carla, and Toynette Wong Johnson. *On Wings of Harps*. CD. Lily Dale, N.Y.: National Spiritualist Association of Churches.

BAHÁ'Í, BUDDHIST, AND HINDU

Bahá'í Gospel Singers. *We Have Come to Sing Praises*. CD. Hendersonville, Tenn.: Global Music, 1993.

Cheb i Sabbah. *Shri Durga*. CD. San Francisco: Six Degrees Records, 1999.

Chinese Cultural Theater Group. *Chinese Instrumental Music*. CD. Washington, D.C.: Smithsonian Folkways, 1998.

Gayatri Mantra. CD. Newark, Del.: Biswas, 2000.

Hwang Kao, Jason, and Edge. *Stories Before Within*. CD. St. Paul, Minn.: Innova, 2007.

Jhaveri, Sweta. *Anahita*. CD. Berkeley: Intuition Music and Media, 1998.

Kanyakumari: Three Vesper Hymns. CD. Albany, N.Y.: Albany Records, 2004.

Krishna Das. *Breath of the Heart*. CD. New York: Karuna/Razor and Tie, 2001.

Sacred Songs LIVE from the Baha'i House of Worship for the North American Continent, Wilmette, Illinois. CD. Wilmette, Ill.: Baha'i House of Worship, 2007.

Sam-Ang Sam and Ensemble. *Silent Temples, Songful Hearts: Traditional Music of Cambodia*. CD. Danbury, Conn.: World Music Press, 1991.

Shankar, Ravi. *At the Monterey International Pop Festival*. CD. Albany, N.Y.: One Way Records, 1967.

Taiko Drum Ensemble. *Soh Daiko*. CD. New York: Lyrichord, 1991.

Tan Dun and the BBC Scottish Symphony Orchestra. *On Taoism*. CD. Elbigenalp, Austria: Koch Schwann, 1993.

CHRISTIAN

Catholic and Orthodox

Bahaman Songs, French Ballads and Dance Tunes, Spanish Religious Songs and Game Songs. LP. Washington, D.C.: Library of Congress, Division of Music, Recording Laboratory, 1942.

Baron, Ludovic, and the Manhattanville Glee Club. *Gregorian Chant: Musically Speaking*. CD. Washington, D.C.: Smithsonian Folkways, 2003.

Chant Traditions of the Orthodox Christian Church. CD. Crestwood, N.Y.: St. Vladimir's Seminary Press, 2005.

Dark and Light in Spanish New Mexico. CD. New York: New World Records, 1978.

Early American Psalmody: The Bay Psalm Book–Cambridge, 1640; Mission Music in California: Music of the Southwest. CD. Washington, D.C.: Smithsonian Folkways, 1965.

Gonzáles, Facundo. *Facundo Gonzáles: New Mexican Violinista*. CD. Washington, D.C.: Smithsonian Folkways, 1979.

The Holy Office of Orthros. CD. Northridge, Calif.: Narthex Press, 2000.

Krémer, Gérard. *Misas y Fiestas Mexicanas*. CD. Paris: Arion, 1994.

Latin High Mass for Nostalgic Catholics. CD. Schiller Park, Ill.: World Library, 1969.

O Hierarch Nicholas: St. Nicholas Vespers. CD. Detroit, Mich.: Greek Orthodox Diocese of Detroit, 2002.

Sanchez, Joe, Delio Villareal, and Ray Casias. Cassette tape. *Matachines: Social and Religious Music of Northern New Mexico*. Albuquerque, N.M.: Ubik Sound, 1990.

Society of Catholic Medical Missionaries. *Joy Is Like the Rain*. LP. N.p.: Avante Garde, 1970.

Spanish and Mexican Folk Music of New Mexico. CD. Washington, D.C.: Smithsonian Folkways, 1952.

Traditional Christmas Hymns of the Syrian Orthodox Church of Antioch. CD. Teaneck, N.J.: Archdiocese of the Syrian Orthodox Church for the Eastern United States, 1998.

Protestant

An American Idyll: American Songs from 1800–1860. CD. Buffalo, N.Y.: Fleur de Son Classics, 1997.

Anthology of American Folk Music. Disc 4. CD. Washington, D.C.: Smithsonian Folkways/Sony Music Special Products, 1997.

Barker, Sister R. Mildred. *Early Shaker Spirituals*. CD. Cambridge, Mass.: Rounder Records, 1996.

Beck, Charles D., and Church of Christ (Holiness). *Urban Holiness Service*. CD. Washington, D.C.: Folkways, 1957.

Best of Blue Grass: Preachin', Prayin', and Singin'. CD. New York: Polygram Records, 1996.

Blackwood Brothers. *1953*. Vol. 1. CD. Rome, Ga.: Bibletone, 1990.

Campbell Brothers. *Can You Feel It?* CD. Philadelphia: Ropeadope, 2005.

Carter Family. *Can the Circle Be Unbroken? Country Music's First Family*. CD. Toronto: Sony, 2000.

——. *In the Shadow of Clinch Mountain*. 12 CDs. Hambergen, Germany: Bear Family Records, 2000.

Cat-Iron. *Cat-Iron Sings Blues and Hymns*. CD. Washington, D.C.: Smithsonian Folkways, 1958.

Dixie Hummingbirds. *Move On Up a Little Higher*. CD. Orlando, Fla.: Frank Music, 2000.

Dorsey, Thomas Andrew. *Precious Lord: The Great Gospel Songs of Thomas A. Dorsey*. CD. New York: Columbia Records/Legacy, 1994.

Dranes, Arizona. *Arizona Dranes Complete Recorded Works in Chronological Order, 1926–1929*. CD. Vienna, Austria: Document Records, 1993.

Eastern Mennonite University Chamber Singers. *Singing: Treasures from Mennonite Worship*. CD. Newton, Kans.: Herald Press, 2001.

Fisk Jubilee Singers. *Fisk Jubilee Singers*. CD. Washington, D.C.: Smithsonian Folkways, 1955.

Five Blind Boys of Mississippi. *The Great Lost Blind Boys Album*. CD. Narberth, Pa.: Collectables Records, 2001.

Goodbye, Babylon. CD. Atlanta: Dust-to-Digital, 2003.

The Gospel Tradition: The Roots and the Branches. Vol. 1. CD. New York: Columbia Records, 1991.

Harmonies Workshop. *Amish Music Variety: Hymns to Harmonica*. CD. Leola, Pa.: Harmonies Workshop, 1997.

An Introduction to Gospel Song. CD. Washington, D.C.: Smithsonian Folkways, 1962.

Jackson, Mahalia. *18 Greatest.* CD. Plattsburgh, N.Y.: Direct Source Special Products, 2006.

Lost Music of Early America: Music of the Moravians. CD. Cleveland: Telarc, 1998.

Louvin Brothers. *Satan Is Real.* CD. Nashville, Tenn.: Capitol Nashville, 1996.

Make a Joyful Noise: Mainstreams and Backwaters of American Psalmody, 1770–1840. CD. New York: New World Records, 1978.

McIntosh County Shouters. *Slave Shout Songs from the Coast of Georgia.* CD. Washington, D.C.: Smithsonian Folkways, 1984.

Music of the Shakers. CD. Washington, D.C.: Smithsonian Folkways, 1976.

Negro Spirituals, 1909–1948. CD. Vincennes, France: Frémeaux & Associés, 1999.

Old Harp Singers of Eastern Tennessee. *Old Harp Singing.* CD. Washington, D.C.: Smithsonian Folkways, 1951.

Old Sturbridge Singers. *New England Harmony: A Collection of Early American Choral Music.* CD. Washington, D.C.: Smithsonian Folkways, 1964.

Religious Recordings from Black New Orleans, 1924–1931. LP. New Orleans: 504 Records, 1989.

The Rock Revival. Vol. 1, *Feeling the Spirit.* CD. Malibu, Calif.: Sonrise Music, 1991.

The Rock Revival. Vol. 2, *Remembering the Future.* CD. Malibu, Calif.: Sonrise Music, 1991.

The Rock Revival. Vol. 3, *Jesus People Music Festival.* CD. Malibu, Calif.: Sonrise Music, 1994.

Sacred Steel: Traditional Sacred African-American Steel Guitar Music in Florida. CD. El Cerrito, Calif.: Arhoolie, 1997.

Sellers, John. *Brother John Sellers Sings Baptist Shouts and Gospel Songs.* CD. Washington, D.C.: Smithsonian Folkways, 1958.

Sing for Freedom: The Story of the Civil Rights Movement Through Its Songs. CD. Washington, D.C.: Smithsonian Folkways, 1990.

Songs of the Old Regular Baptists. CD. Washington, D.C.: Smithsonian Folkways, 1997.

St. Olaf College Choir. *Home, Harvest, and Healing: A Sing for Joy Hymn Festival.* CD. Northfield, Minn.: St. Olaf Records, 2004.

Tharpe, Sister Rosetta. *Precious Memories.* CD. Jackson, Miss.: Malaco Music Group, 1997.

Through the Church Year with the Best in Lutheran Hymns. CD. New York: American Lutheran Publicity Bureau, 1961.

Voices of the Civil Rights Movement: Black American Freedom Songs, 1960–1966. CD. Washington, D.C.: Smithsonian Folkways, 1997.

White, Josh. *Josh White, Complete Recorded Works.* Vol. 2, *1933–1935.* CD. Vienna, Austria: Document Records, 1993.

White Gospel. CD. Narberth, Pa.: Collectables Records, 1990.

White Spirituals from the Sacred Harp: The Alabama Sacred Harp Convention. CD. New York: New World Records, 1977.

Wiregrass Sacred Harp Singers. *Desire for Piety: Songs from the B. F. White Sacred Harp.* CD. New York: New World Records, 1997.

MUSLIM

Black Music of Two Worlds. CD. Washington, D.C.: Smithsonian Folkways, 1977

Chicago Classical Oriental Ensemble/Hicham Chami. *The Songs of Sheikh Sayyed Darweesh: Soul of a People*. CD. Chicago: Xauen Music, 2006.

Hakmoun, Hassan, with Adam Rudolph. *Gift of the Gnawa*. CD. Chicago: Flying Fish, 1991.

Love and Compassion Hob Wa Haneen: Celebrating the Arab American National Museum. CD. Dearborn, Mich.: Arab American National Museum, 2005.

The Music of Arab Americans: A Retrospective Collection. CD. Cambridge, Mass.: Rounder Records, 1997.

Sulaiman, Amir. *Like a Thief in the Night*. CD. Laguna Beach, Calif.: Uprising Records, 2007.

JEWISH

Bikel, Theodore. *Theodore Bikel's Treasury of Yiddish Theatre and Folk Songs*. CD. Burbank, Calif.: Elektra and Rhino Hand Made, 2003.

Brandwein, Naftule. *The King of the Klezmer Clarinet*. CD. Cambridge, Mass.: Rounder Records, 1997.

Folk Masters: Great Performances, Recorded Live at the Barns of Wolf Trap. CD. Washington, D.C.: Smithsonian Folkways, 1993.

Kanefsky, Joseph. *Friday Night Service*. LP. New York: Folkways, 1962.

Klezmer Conservatory Band. *Old World Beat*. CD. Cambridge, Mass.: Rounder Records, 1992.

Klezmer Music, 1910–1942. CD. New York: Global Village, 1996.

Klezmer Plus! Old Time Yiddish Dance Music Featuring Sid Beckerman and Howie Leess. CD. Chicago: Flying Fish, 1991.

Koussevitzky, David. *Cantorials*. CD. Washington, D.C.: Smithsonian Folkways, 1951.

Olf, Mark. *Hebrew Folk Songs*. LP. New York: Folkways, 1957.

NATIVE AMERICAN

An Anthology of North American Indian and Eskimo Music. 3 Vols. CD. Washington, D.C.: Smithsonian Folkways, 1973.

Beautiful Beyond: Christian Songs in Native Languages. CD. Washington, D.C.: Smithsonian Folkways, 2004

A Cry from the Earth: Music of the North American Indians. CD. New York: Folkways, 1979.

Hawaiian Drum Dance Chants: Sounds of Power in Time. CD. Washington, D.C.: Smithsonian Folkways, 1989.

Healing Songs of the American Indians. LP. New York: Folkways, 1965.

Navajo Songs from Canyon de Chelly. CD. New York: New World Records, 1990.

Songs of the Mormons and Songs of the West. CD. Cambridge, Mass.: Rounder Records, 2002.

RELIGIOUS-THEMED JAZZ, CLASSICAL, EXPERIMENTAL, AND NEW AGE

Behrman, David. *On the Other Ocean/Figure in a Clearing.* CD. New York: Lovely Music, 1978.

Bernstein, Leonard, and various artists. *Leonard Bernstein's Mass.* CD. New York: CBS Masterworks, 1971.

Coltrane, John. *A Love Supreme.* CD. Los Angeles: Impulse! Records, 2003.

Ellington, Duke, Brock Peters, and Herman McCoy Choir. *Concert of Sacred Music.* CD. Paris: RCA, 1966.

Harbison, John, and various artists. *The Flight into Egypt and Other Works.* CD. New York: New World Records, 1990.

Lauridsen, Morten, and various artists. *O Magnum Mysterium and Other Choral Cycles.* CD. Holzgerlingen, Germany: Hänssler Classic, 2006.

OHM: The Early Gurus of Electronic Music, 1948–1980. CD. Roslyn, N.Y.: Ellipsis Arts, 2000.

Sun Ra. *Angels and Demons at Play/The Nubians of Plutonia.* CD. Conshohocken, Pa.: Evidence Music, 1993.

The Twenty-Five-Year Retrospective Concert of the Music of John Cage. CD. Mainz, Germany: Wergo, 1994.

Vollenweider, Andreas. *Caverna Magica.* CD. New York: CBS, 1983.

Williams, Mary Lou. *Mary Lou's Mass.* CD. Washington, D.C.: Smithsonian Folkways, 1975.

VODOU AND SANTERIA

Marassa. *Santeria! Musica de Raiz.* CD. Miami: Piátano Records, 2001.

Rhythms of Rapture: Sacred Musics of Haitian Vodou. CD. Washington, D.C.: Smithsonian Folkways, 1995.

Sacred Rhythms of Cuban Santería. CD. Washington, D.C.: Smithsonian Folkways, 1995.

SELECTED ONLINE AMERICAN RELIGIOUS

HISTORY RESOURCES

E-MAIL LISTS AND BLOGS

H-AmRel (History of American Religion). www.h-net.org/~amrel
H-Buddhism (Buddhist Scholars Information Network). www.h-net.org/~buddhism
H-Catholic (History and Culture of Catholicism). www.h-net.org/~catholic
H-Pentecostalism. www.h-net.org/~pentcost
H-Southern-Religion (in association with the *Journal of Southern Religion*). www.h-net
    .org/~southrel
Immanent Frame: Secularism, Religion and the Public Sphere. http://blogs.ssrc.org/tif
Religion Dispatches. http://religiondispatches.org
Religion in American History Blog. http://usreligion.blogspot.com
Religion in the American West. Relwest.blogspot.com
Religion News Blog. www.religionnewsblog.com

GENERAL ACADEMIC RESOURCES

American Women's History: A Research Guide–Religion. http://frank.mtsu.edu/~kmiddlet
    /history/women/wh-rel.html
Andover-Harvard Theological Library: Resource Guides. www.hds.harvard.edu/library
    /research/guides

Early American Literature to 1700 (Perspectives in American Literature). www.csustan
.edu/english/reuben/pal/chap1/chap1.html

Religion Collections in Libraries and Archives (Library of Congress): A Guide to Resources in Maryland, Virginia, and the District of Columbia. www.loc.gov/rr/main/religion

LIBRARIES AND ARCHIVES

American Jewish Historical Society. www.ajhs.org

Arab American National Museum Library. www.arabamericanmuseum.org/Library-
Resources.id.37.htm

Archives of the Evangelical Lutheran Church in America. www.elca.org/Who-We-Are
/History/ELCA-Archives.aspx

Associated Archives at St. Mary's Seminary and University. www.stmarys.edu/archives

Church of the Nazarene Archives. www.nazarene.org/ministries/administration/archives
/display.aspx

Concordia Historical Institute, Department of History and Archives of the Lutheran
Church–Missouri Synod. lutheranhistory.org

Congregational Library (Congregational Christian Historical Society). www.14beacon.org

Dixon Pentecostal Research Center, Church of God (Cleveland, Tennessee). www
.cogheritage.org

Episcopal Church Archives. www.episcopalarchives.org

Family Search, Church of Jesus Christ of Latter-day Saints. www.familysearch.org/Eng
/default.asp

Flower Pentecostal Heritage Center, Assemblies of God. http://ifphc.org/index.cfm
?fuseaction=home.main

General Commission on Archives and History for the United Methodist Church. http://
www.gcah.org/site/c.ghKJI0PHI0E/b.2858857/k.BF4D/Home.htm

Islam in America Collection, DePaul University. www.lib.depaul.edu/Collections
/IslamAmerica.aspx

Jacob Rader Marcus Center of the American Jewish Archives. www.americanjewisharchives
.org

New England Province of the Society of Jesus (Jesuits) Archives. http://academics.holycross
.edu//library-archives/jesuit

Online Swedenborgian Library. http://www.swedenborgdigitallibrary.org/

Presbyterian Historical Society. www.history.pcusa.org

Southern Baptist Historical Library and Archives. www.sbhla.org

University of Notre Dame Archives, Catholic. http://archives.nd.edu

MUSIC

Archives of African American Music and Culture. www.indiana.edu/~aaamc

Hispano Music and Culture of the Northern Rio Grande: The Juan B. Rael Collection (American Memory) (Library of Congress). http://memory.loc.gov/ammem/rghtml /rghome.html

Music for the Nation: American Sheet Music, 1870–1885 (American Memory) (Library of Congress). http://memory.loc.gov/ammem/smhtml/smhome.html

"Now What a Time": Blues, Gospel, and the Fort Valley Music Festivals, 1938–1943 (American Memory) (Library of Congress). http://memory.loc.gov/ammem/ftvhtml /ftvhome.html

Southern Mosaic: John and Ruby Lomax 1939 Southern States Recording Trip (American Memory) (Library of Congress). http://memory.loc.gov/ammem/lohtml/lohome .html

ONLINE JOURNALS

American Religious Experience. http://are.as.wvu.edu

Common-Place. www.common-place.org

Electronic Journal of the Material History of American Religion Project. www.materialreligion .org/journal.html

Journal of Religion and Film. www.unomaha.edu/jrf

Journal of Southern Religion. http://jsr.fsu.edu

North Star: A Journal for African American Religious History. http://northstarjournal.org /index2.html

PRIMARY SOURCE MATERIAL

African American Odyssey (Library of Congress). http://memory.loc.gov/ammem/aaohtml /exhibit/aointro.html

American Life Histories: Manuscripts from the Federal Writers Project, 1936–1940 (American Memories) (Library of Congress). http://memory.loc.gov/wpaintro/ wpahome.html

Documenting the American South, University of North Carolina University Library. http://docsouth.unc.edu/index.html

Early Virginia Religious Petitions (American Memory) (Library of Congress). http:// memory.loc.gov/ammem/collections/petitions

First-Person Narratives of the American South, 1860–1920 (American Memory) (Library of Congress). http://memory.loc.gov/ammem/award97/ncuhtml/fpnashome .html

International Mission Photography Archive, University of Southern California. http:// digarc.usc.edu/impa/controller/index.htm

In the Beginning Was the Word: The Russian Church and Native Alaskan Cultures (Library of Congress). www.loc.gov/exhibits/russian/russcho.html

Making of America Digital Library. http://quod.lib.umich.edu/m/moagrp/index.html

National Humanities Center's Divining America: Links to Online Resources. http://nationalhumanitiescenter.org/tserve/nineteen/nlinksaarcwgm.htm

Religion and the Founding of the American Republic (Library of Congress). www.loc.gov/exhibits/religion

PROFESSIONAL, ORGANIZATIONS, CENTERS, AND ONLINE PROJECTS

American Academy of Religion. www.aarweb.org

American Society of Church History. www.churchhistory.org

Beliefnet. www.beliefnet.com

Boisi Center for Religion and American Public Life, Boston College. www.bc.edu/centers/boisi

Buddhist Studies at U.C. Berkeley. http://buddhiststudies.berkeley.edu

Center for the Study of Religion, Princeton University. www.princeton.edu/~csrelig

Center for the Study of Religion, UCLA. www.humnet.ucla.edu/humnet/religion/home.html

Center for the Study of Religion and American Culture, Indiana University–Purdue University Indianapolis. www.iupui.edu/~raac

Center for the Study of Religion and Culture, Vanderbilt University. www.vanderbilt.edu/csrc/overview.html

Center for the Study of World Religions, Harvard Divinity School. www.hds.harvard.edu/cswr

Cushwa Center for the Study of American Catholicism, University of Notre Dame. www.nd.edu/~cushwa/

French and Spanish Missions in North America. www.ecai.org/na-missions

Institute for the Study of American Evangelicals, Wheaton College. www.wheaton.edu/isae

Leonard E. Greenberg Center for the Study of Religion in Public Life, Trinity College. www.trincoll.edu/Academics/AcademicResources/values/greenbergcenter/default.htm

Material History of Religion Project. www.materialreligion.org

Mormon History Association. www.mhahome.org

Religion and American Culture Caucus of the American Studies Association. www.theasa.net/caucus_religion

Religious Movements Homepage at the University of Virginia. http://web.archive.org/web/20060907005952/http://etext.lib.virginia.edu/relmove/

Society for Pentecostal Studies. www.sps-usa.org

Spirituality in Higher Education: A National Study of College Students' Search for Meaning and Purpose, UCLA. www.spirituality.ucla.edu

Wesleyan Theological Society. http://wesley.nnu.edu/wts

RELIGION AND FILM

Gordon Matties's Religion and Film Bibliography. www.cmu.ca/faculty/gmatties
/Religion%20and%20Film%20Bibliography.htm
Journal of Religion and Film. www.unomaha.edu/jrf
Judith Weisenfeld's Selected Filmography of American Films at the Material History of
American Religion Project. www.materialreligion.org/journal/filmography.html
Religion and Myth in the Movies: A Bibliography of Books and Articles in the U.C.
Berkeley Libraries. www.lib.berkeley.edu/MRC/religionbib.html

RELIGION IN THE NEWS

Beliefnet: News and Blogs. www.beliefnet.com/index/index_400.html
Christian Science Monitor: Religion and Ethics. www.csmonitor.com/living/religionEthics
.html
Journal of Southern Religion: Southern Religion in the News. http://jsr.fsu.edu/news.htm
National Public Radio: Religion. www.npr.org/templates/topics/topic.php?topicId=1016
Religion and Ethics Newsweekly. www.pbs.org/wnet/religionandethics/index_flash.html
Religion News from the Pew Forum on Religion and Public Life. http://pewforum.org
/news/
Religion News Service. www.religionnews.com/index.html
Washington Post: Religion. www.washingtonpost.com/wp-dyn/content/religion

STATISTICS AND MAPS

American Ethnic Geography: Map Gallery of Religion in the U.S. www.valpo.edu
/geomet/geo/courses/geo200/religion.html
The American Religion Data Archive. www.thearda.com/index.asp
Glenmary Research Center. www.glenmary.org/grc/default.htm
The Pew Forum on Religion and Public Life: Research, News, Discussion. http://
pewforum.org
The Pew Forum on Religion and Public Life: U.S. Religious Landscape Survey. http://
religions.pewforum.org/maps

TEACHING AMERICAN RELIGIOUS HISTORY

Center for the Study of Religion and American Culture: Young Scholars in American
Religion Syllabi (1991–2006). www.iupui.edu/~raac/youngscholars/ysp20052006.html

Indiana Humanities Council: Teaching the Role of Religion in American History. www
.indianahumanities.org/HTG/htgRE.htm

The National Humanities Center's Divining America: Religion and the National Culture. http://nationalhumanitiescenter.org/tserve/divam.htm

Teacher Resources for PBS's Frontline Documentaries on Religion. www.pbs.org/wgbh
/pages/frontline/teach/categories.html#rel

The Wabash Center for Teaching and Learning Theology and Religion. www.wabashcenter
.wabash.edu/home/default.aspx

TELEVISION AND RADIO PROGRAMS

Being. http://being.publicradio.org/

God in America. www.pbs.org/godinamerica/

Religion and Ethics Newsweekly. www.pbs.org/wnet/religionandethics/index_flash.html

Religious Broadcasting Site at the University of Virginia. http://etext.lib.virginia.edu
/relbroad/home.html

CONTRIBUTORS

Paul Harvey is professor of history at the University of Colorado, Colorado Springs, and the author of *Freedom's Coming: Religious Cultures and the Shaping of the South from the Civil War Through the Civil Rights Era*. Along with Randall Stephens, he runs the blog *Religion in American History* (http://usreligion.blogspot.com).

Edward J. Blum is professor of history at San Diego State University and the author of *W. E. B. Du Bois: American Prophet* and the co-author, with Paul Harvey, of *Jesus in Red, White, and Black: The Son of God and the Saga of Race in American History*.

Randall Stephens is professor of history at Eastern Nazarene College and the author of *The Fire Spreads: Holiness and Pentecostalism in the American South* and *The Anointed: America's Evangelical Truth in a Secular Age*.

Margaret "Peggy" Bendroth is executive director of the Congregational Library in Boston and the author of *Fundamentalism and Gender, 1875 to the Present*.

Jason C. Bivins is professor of religion at North Carolina State University and the author of *Religion of Fear: The Politics of Horror in Conservative Evangelicalism*.

Ira R. Chernus is professor of religious studies at the University of Colorado, Boulder, and the author of *Apocalypse Management: Eisenhower and the Discourse of National Insecurity*.

Linford D. Fisher is professor of history at Brown University and the author of *The Indian Great Awakening: Religion and the Shaping of Native Cultures in Early America*.

Philip Goff is director of the Center for the Study of Religion and American Culture at Indiana University–Purdue University, Indianapolis, and the co-editor (with Paul Harvey) of *Themes in Religion and American Culture*.

Alan T. Levenson is Schusterman Professor of Jewish Intellectual and Religious History at the University of Oklahoma and the author of *Modern Jewish Thinkers: An Introduction.*

Andrew M. Manis is professor of history at Macon State University and the author of *A Fire You Can't Put Out: The Civil Rights Life of Birmingham Reverend Fred Shuttlesworth.*

Mark Noll is Francis A. McAnaney Professor of History at the University of Notre Dame and the author of *America's God: From Jonathan Edwards to Abraham Lincoln.*

Suzanne Crawford O'Brien is professor of religion and culture at Pacific Lutheran University and the author of *Religion and Healing in Native America: Pathways of Renewal.*

Anthony Michael Petro is a postdoctoral fellow in religion at New York University and the author of "After the Wrath of God: AIDS, Sexuality, and American Religion."

D. Michael Quinn is an independent scholar and the author of *Early Mormonism and the Magic World View.*

Frank S. Ravitch is professor of law at Michigan State University and the author of *Masters of Illusion: The Supreme Court and the Religion Clauses.*

Lynn Ross-Bryant is professor emerita in the Department of Religious Studies at the University of Colorado, Boulder, and the author of *Nature and Nation: Pilgrimage and U.S. National Parks.*

Jane Smith is senior lecturer in divinity at Harvard Divinity School and the author of *Islam in America.*

Stephen J. Stein is Chancellor's Professor Emeritus in the Department of Religious Studies at Indiana University and the author of *Communities of Dissent: A History of Alternative Religions in America.*

Douglas A. Sweeney is professor of church history and the history of Christian thought and the director of the Carl F. H. Henry Center for Theological Understanding at Trinity Evangelical Divinity School and the author of *The American Evangelical Story: A History of the Movement.*

Leslie Woodcock Tentler is professor of history at the Catholic University of America and the author of *Catholics and Contraception: An American History.*

Roberto R. Treviño is professor of history at the University of Texas, Arlington, and the author of *The Church in the Barrio: Mexican American Ethno-Catholicism in Houston.*

Timothy Tseng is president of the Institute for the Study of Asian American Christianity and the author of *Unbinding Their Souls: Chinese Protestant Women in Twentieth-Century America.*

INDEX

Abbot, Lyman, 114

Abernathy, Ralph, 13

Abington School District v. Schempp (1963), 161

abolitionist movements, 17, 175. *See also* slaves and slavery

Abortion and the Politics of Motherhood (Luker), 18

Abzug, Robert H., 144

Acoma Pueblo Indians, 24

"Acres of Diamonds" (sermon, Conwell), 21

Adams, Carol, 288

Adams, John, 38, 155

Adapting to Abundance (Heinze), 339

Adler, Margo, 291–292

Afghanistan, Muslim immigration from, 368

African American Exodus, An (Dvorak), 221–222

African American Jeremiad, The (Howard-Pitney), 94

African American religions: anti-Semitism in, 347; burial rituals of, 217; Catholicism and, 330; in colonial America, 4; early black churches of, 214–216; emancipation, post-emancipation, and, 221–225; evangelical Protestantism and, 10–11, 40–41, 46, 134, 215, 218–219, 226, 272; Great Depression and, 226; Great Migration and, 214, 215, 225–226; homosexuality and, 205; Islam and, 226–227, 366–367, 369–371; manipulation of Christian traditions and ideas and, 12, 219–221; in Mormon Church, 356; Old/New World syncretism and, 218–219; research recommendations for, 228, 233; "ring shout" and 217; women in, 191, 223–225. *See also* segregation; slaves and slavery; *specific religions*

African American Religious History (Sernett), 216, 225

African American Religious Thought (West and Glaude), 216

African American Women and Christian Activism (Weisenfield), 200

African Methodist Episcopal Church, 94, 215, 217, 272

African Methodist Episcopal Zion Church, 215, 272

African Muslims in Antebellum America (Austin), 227

Africans, enslaved. *See* slaves and slavery

Africans, free, 59–60, 64, 65, 203–204

"After the Wrath of God" (Petro), 206

Ahlstrom, Sidney E., 238

Aimee Semple McPherson and the Resurrection of Christian America (Sutton), 199

Albanese, Catherine, 91, 169, 173, 282

alcohol, as acculturation tool, 74

Algonquian Indians, 3, 57

Ali, Noble Drew, 227

alien land laws, 256

Allen, Richard, 110, 220

alternative religious movements: from American Revolution to World War II, 269–273; in colonial America, 267–269; contemporary classification of, 277–278; environment and, 291–292; terminology of, 266–267; from World War II to present, 273–276. *See also specific movements*